LIST OF THE OFFICERS OF
THE BENGAL ARMY

Printed and bound in Great Britain by Antony Rowe Ltd, Eastbourne

LIST OF THE OFFICERS
OF THE BENGAL ARMY

1758–1834

*Alphabetically Arranged and Annotated
with Biographical and Genealogical
Notices by*

MAJOR V. C. P. HODSON
INDIAN ARMY (RETIRED LIST)
AUTHOR OF 'HISTORICAL RECORDS OF THE VICEROY'S BODY-GUARD'

O - R

O

OAKE, Henry (1777-1818). Captain, 29th N.I. *b.* 18 Dec. 1777. Cadet 1798. Arrived in India 26 Mar. 1800. Ensign 5 Sept. 1799. Lieut. 28 Oct. 1799. Capt. 17 Oct. 1805. *d.* Barrackpore 20 Aug. 1818.

bapt. Christchurch, Hants, 21 Sept. 1780. Son of John Oake. Cousin of John Day, of Milverton, Somerset, atty., and of Catherine Oake, of Ringwood, Hants.

Services : Posted Lieut. to 2nd Bengal Eur. Regt. 15 Apr. 1801. Transfd. to Marine Regt. (became 20th N.I.) in 1803. At P.W.I. 1804-6. Fur. 6 Sept. 1806 till 3 Oct. 1810. Capture of Java 1811 ; Capt. 1/20th N.I. At Malacca 1814-15. Transfd. to newly-raised 1/29th N.I. in 1815. Siege and capture of Hathras ; Capt. 1/29th N.I.

Refs. : Will dated camp before Hathras, 22 Feb. 1817 ; codicil dated Barrackpore, 26 July 1818 ; proved 24 Aug. 1818.

OAKE, John (1779-1801). Cornet, 2nd N.C. *bapt.* Ringwood, Hants, 7 Nov. 1779. Cadet 1798. Arrived in India 26 Mar. 1800. Cornet 16 June 1800. *d.* Cawnpore 24 May 1801.

Son of Henry Oake and Fanny his wife. (*Probably* cousin of Henry Oake, *q.v.*)

Services : Posted Cornet to 2nd N.C. in 1800. No record of active service.

OAKES, John (1789-1824). Captain, 4th N.I. *b.* Itteringham, Norfolk, 13 Dec. 1789. Cadet 1804. Arrived in India 2 June 1806. Ensign 22 Oct. 1805. Lieut. 26 Mar. 1806. Capt. 1 Sept. 1822. *d.* Benares 31 Jan. 1824.

bapt. ptely. 25 Dec. 1789. Son of John Oakes and Hannah his wife. *m.* Dinapore 28 May 1811, Miss Eliza Frances Mullins. (*See also* Thomas Alexander Hepworth.)

Services : Barasat C.C. Posted to 2/4th N.I. in 1806. (? Operations in Bundelkhand 1809 ; Rajaoli ; Ajaigarh ; Lieut. 1/4th N.I.) Intr. & Qmr. 1/4th N.I. 4 May 1815 till 1821.

OATLEY, James (1809-1839). Lieutenant, 39th N.I. *b.* Albrighton, Salop, 1 May 1809. Cadet 1828. Arrived in India 4 May 1829. Ensign (8 Jan. 1829) 14 Sept. 1829. Lieut. 27 Sept. 1837. *d.* Agra 1 July 1839.

bapt. Albrighton 18 Sept. 1811. Youngest son of Thomas Oatley, of Albrighton Hall, and Caroline his wife. Brother of Harriet, Ann Belinda, and Frances, all of whom were *bapt.* 18 Sept. 1811.
Services: Posted Ensign to 39th N.I. Sept. 1829. Suspended by G.C.M. from rank, pay and allowances 16 Sept. 1837 till 30 July 1838; do. for 6 mos. Jan. 1839. No record of active service.
Refs.: A.J. N.S. xxviii. 291; xxix. 265. M.I. at Agra.

O'BEIRNE, Thomas Ormsby (1810-1839). Captain, 25th N.I. *b.* 1810. Cadet 1826. Arrived in India 17 May 1827. Ensign 18 Jan. 1827. Lieut. 22 June 1833. Capt. 15 May 1837. *d.* Cawnpore 24 Nov. 1839.
bapt. Barnchurch, co. Kilkenny, 2 Aug. 1813, " aged near 3 yrs." Son of Lewis Francis O'Beirne and Rebecca his wife. Brother of James O'Beirne, R.N., and of Jane, 1st wife of Major Armine Simcoe Henry Mountain (*D.N.B.*).
Services: Ensign d.d. 46th N.I. 28 May 1827; posted to 25th N.I. 19 June 1827, and served throughout with that Regt. No record of active service.
Refs.: Will dated camp nr. Jhansi, 3 Dec. 1838; proved 31 Dec. 1839.

O'BRIEN, Charles (1807-1857). Bt. Colonel, 3rd N.I. *bapt.* Drumcliff, co. Clare, 13 Feb. 1807. Cadet 1825. Arrived in India 20 Mar. 1826. Ensign 25 Oct. 1825. Lieut. 21 Dec. 1827. Capt. 18 Apr. 1841. Major 10 Sept. 1844. Bt. Lt. Col. 20 June 1854. Bt. Col. 3 Oct. 1857.[1] *d.* Fatehpur, U.P., 21 Oct. 1857: committed suicide.
Son of Matthew O'Brien, M.D., of Ennis, co. Clare, and Eliza Ellen Macmahon his wife. *m.* Simla 23 June 1838, Eliza, eldest dau. of Gavin Young, *q.v.* (She died Nelson, N.Z., 24 June 1874.) T.C.D.; Pensioner 7 July 1823, aged 16.
Services: Posted Ensign to 1st N.I. in 1826. Offg. Intr. & Qmr. 10th N.I. 28 Feb. 1831; do. 1st N.I. 30 Sept. 1831. Exchanged to 3rd N.I. 18 June 1832. Adjt. Nassiri Bn. 21 June 1832 till 30 Apr. 1841; actg. 2nd in comd. do. 2 June 1841; permanent do. 13 July 1841; Comdt. do. 7 Oct. 1848 till Aug. 1855. Rejoined 3rd N.I. at Saugor for a short time during 1842. First Sikh War; Aliwal; Sobraon (s.w.); comdg. Nassiri Bn. at Sobraon (Medal with clasp). Comdt. 2nd Regt. Sikh Inf. 1 Sept. 1855; do. 6th Oudh Irreg. Inf. 26 Dec. 1856, and was comdg. this Regt. when it mutinied at

Fyzabad. Ordered to proceed to Allahabad in June 1857 and assume comd. of that station on the departure of Bdr.-Gen. Neill. Ordered back to Fatehpur 17 Oct.
Refs.: *Memoir of James Young . . . of Aberdeen* (1894 edn.), p. 41. *Alumni Dub.* Will dated 25 Feb. 1851; proved 1 Mar. 1858. M.I. at Fatehpur.
¹ *Note*: Promoted Bt. Col. posthumously on 17 May 1859, with effect from 3 Oct. 1857.

O'BRIEN, Lucius Robert (1775-1825). Lieut. Colonel Comdt., C.B., 4th L.C. *b.* London 2 May 1775. Cadet 1794. Arrived in India 30 Oct. 1795. Cornet 25 Nov. 1795. Lieut. 1 Nov. 1798. Capt. 11 Mar. 1805. Major 27 Feb. 1812. Lt. Col. 26 Feb. 1820. Lt. Col. Comdt. 7 Oct. 1824. *d.* Sultanpur, Benares, 10 July 1825, of cholera.
bapt. St. George's, Hanover Sq., London, 11 June 1775. 2nd son of Sir Lucius O'Brien, 3rd Bart., and Anne his wife, dau. of Robert French, of Monivae, M.P. co. Galway. *m.* St. George's, Dublin, 6 Jan. 1824, Julia, 7th dau. of William Humphreys, of Gardiner's Row, Dublin. Father of William O'Brien (*see* Appendix A).
Services: Apptd. Cadet 6 May 1795; sailed for India in the *Woodcot* 18 June 1795. Posted Cornet to 2nd N.C. in 1796. Adjt. 3rd N.C. 1798-1800; transfd. as Qmr. to newly-raised 5th N.C. 29 May 1800. Capt. Lt. 5th N.C. 4 Aug. 1801. Fur. s.c̣. 1803-5. Transfd. to newly-raised 8th N.C. Mar. 1805. Raised and comdd. in Java, 1811-14, a Corps of Java Light Cav., with H.A. attached. Nepal War 1814-15; Major comdg. 8th N.C. Comdg. at Sultanpur, Benares, 2 Jan. 1815 till 1817. Third Mahratta War; in charge of Guide and Intelligence Dept. under Bdr.-Gen. Hardyman 1817; Jubbulpore 19 Dec. 1817; Mandala 1818; Major comdg. 8th N.C. Posted Lt. Col. to 8th L.C. in 1820. Fur. 1822 till 5 Apr. 1825. Transfd. to 6th L.C. May 1824; as Lt. Col. Comdt. to 4th L.C. Oct. 1824. C.B. 23 July 1823.
Refs.: Burke's *Peerage*, 1923, p. 1229, *s.n.* Baron of Inchiquin. *E.I.M.C.* ii. 362-4. Will dated 20 Aug. 1810; codicil dated Sultanpur, 10 July 1825; proved 23 July 1825. M.I. Sultanpur.

O'BRIEN, Stephen (1787-1809). Lieutenant, 22nd N.I. *b.* Barking, Middlesex, 14 July 1787. Cadet 1803. Arrived in India 2 Dec. 1804. Ensign 7 Nov. 1804. Lieut. 7 Nov. 1804. *d.* 29 Aug. 1809: kld. in action at the assault of Bhawani.
Younger son of Stephen O'Brien, Capt. R.N., and Mary his wife,

2nd dau. of —— French, of Shooter's Hill, Kent. Brother of Martin O'Brien, H.M. 78th Regt., and of Sophia, wife of Henry Owen, of Worksop, Notts., solicitor. Stepson of —— Clements, of 18 Hollies St., Cavendish Sq., London.

Services : Posted Lieut. to 1/22nd N.I. in 1805. Settlement of Hariana 1809; capture of Bhawani (kld.); Lieut. 1/22nd N.I.

Refs. : N. & Q. 7S. xi. 309. Will dated Rewari, 11 July 1809; proved 11 Apr. 1810.

O'BYRN, John. (*See* **BYRN, John.**)

OCHTERLONY, Sir David, first baronet (1758-1825). Major General, G.C.B., Colonel 55th N.I. *b.* Boston, Mass., 12 Feb. 1758. Cadet 1777. Ensign 7 Feb. 1778. Lieut. 17 Sept. 1778. Capt. 19 Jan. 1796. Major 4 Mar. 1800. Lt. Col. 18 Mar. 1803. Col. 1 Jan. 1812. Maj. Gen. 4 June 1814. *d. unm.* Meerut 14 July 1825.

1st Bart.; *cr.* 1816. Obtained a second patent, 8 Dec. 1823, re-creating him, with remainder to Charles Metcalfe Ochterlony, of Delhi, 2nd Bart. Eldest son of David Ochterlony, of Boston, New England (who was son of Alexander Ochterlony, laird of Pitforthy), and Katherine his wife, 2nd dau. of Andrew Tyler, of Boston. Stepson of Sir Isaac Heard, Garter King of Arms (*D.N.B.*), and kinsman of Alexander Legertwood, *q.v.* His dau. *m.* Henry Fisher Salter, *q.v.*

Services : See *D.N.B.* Apptd. Cadet 21 Mar. 1777; sailed for India in the *Lord North* 15 July 1777. Posted Ensign to 31st N.I. 1778. Lieut. 1/1st Bengal Eur. Regt. in Oct. 1779. Second Mysore War 1781-5; Cuddalore 25 June 1783 (w. and taken prisoner; released July 1783); Lieut. & Qmr. 24th (late 31st) N.I., with Col. Pearse's detachment. D.J.A.G. at Dinapore 1785-1801. Qmr. 5th Bengal Eur. Bn. *c.* 1787-94. Transfd. as Capt. to 1/12th N.I. 1796; as Major to 2/12th N.I. May 1800. Operations in Jumna Doab 1803; Sasni; Bijaigarh; Major 2/12th N.I. Comdt. Bijaigarh fort 1803. Second Mahratta War; D.A.G. of Lake's army; Koil; Aligarh; battle of Delhi; apptd. tempy. Resdt. at Delhi Sept. 1803; defence of Delhi 7-16 Oct. 1804. Permanent Resdt. at Delhi Oct. 1804 till Jan. 1806. Comdt. Allahabad fort 5 June 1806 till 1808. Comdd. a mixed force on Sikh frontier 1808-14. Nepal War 1814-15; Nalagarh; Malaun; Maj. Gen. comdg. 1st Div. Nepal War 1816; Makwanpur; comdg. the main force. Pindari War 1817-18; comdg. Rewari force. Resdt. in Rajputana 17 Mar. 1818; do. Delhi and Jaipur Dec. 1818;

THE BENGAL ARMY, 1758-1834 413

do. Malwa and Rajputana in addition 3 Dec. 1821. Resigned Apr.
1825. G.C.B. 10 Dec. 1816.
Refs.: Burke's *Peerage*, 1923, p. 1700, *s.n.* Ochterlony, Bart.,
of Ochterlony, co. Forfar. *D.N.B. D.I.B. E.I.M.C.* i. 379-87;
iii. 464-7. *Ency. Brit.* (11th edn.) xix. 990. *G.M.* 1826, i. 275.
Will dated 14 Nov. 1824; proved 2 Sept. 1825. The Ochterlony
column on the Calcutta *maidan* erected to his memory. Portrait,
A. W. Devis—H. Meyer; pub. Boydell, 1816.
Note: The best sketch of Ochterlony's career is that by Major
F. G. Cardew, O.B.E., pub. in the *Journal* of the Soc. for Army
Hist. Research, Vol. x, No. 39 (Jan. 1931), pp. 40-63.

OCTANDER, Nicholas M. (*See* **ARCTANDER.**)

ODELL, John Cornwall (1784-1833). Major, 41st N.I. *b.*
Ballingarry, co. Limerick, 22 Mar. 1784. Cadet 1804. Arrived
in India 21 June 1806. Ensign 8 Sept. 1805. Lieut. 9 Sept.
1805. Capt. 20 Mar. 1821. Major 2 Aug. 1828. *d.* Cork 18 June
1833.
bapt. Ballingarry 25 Mar. 1784. Son of Rev. William Butler
Odell, of Limerick. Brother of Constance, and of Major Robert
Deane Odell, 25th Madras N.I. Brother-in-law of David Fitzgerald,
of Limerick.
Services: Present as a Cadet at capture of C.G.H. in Jan. 1806,
under Sir David Baird. Posted Lieut. to 1/21st N.I. in 1806.
Leave s.c. 6 mos. to sea 21 May 1811; fur. s.c. 17 Mar. 1812 till
7 Oct. 1815. Transfd. to 41st N.I. (late 1/21st) May 1824. First
Burma War; Arakan 1825; Capt. 1st Gren. Bn. Tempy. comdg.
Chittagong Provl. Bn. 14 May 1825 till 3 Jan. 1826. With Left
Wing 41st N.I. protecting Muttra Cantt. during siege of Bhurtpore.
Leave s.c. 12 mos. to Cape and Mauritius 20 Oct. 1827. d.d. 37th
N.I. 26 Nov. 1831 till 26 Sept. 1832. Leave s.c. 1 yr. to Simla
6 Jan. 1832. Fur. s.c. 15 Jan. 1833 till death.
Refs.: *A.J.* N.S. xi. 279. Will dated Simla 26 May 1832;
proved 23 May 1834.
Note: His name sometimes appears in *A.L.* as O'Dell.

ODELL, William (*d.* 1794). Lieutenant, 13th Bn. Sepoys.
Country Cadet 1780. Cornet 11 May 1780. Lieut. 25 May 1781.
d. 26 Oct. 1794; kld. in action at the battle of Bitaurah.
Services: First Mahratta War; capture of Lahar fort 20 Apr.
1780; Vol. with a Bn. in Popham's detachment; afterwards
Cornet 1st Cav., with Goddard's force. Lieut. 13th Bn. Sepoys

in July 1787. Third Mysore War ; battle of Arikera ; operations before Savandrug ; Seringapatam ; Lieut. 13th Bn. Second Rohilla War ; battle of Bitaurah (kld.) ; Lieut. 13th Bn.

Refs.: Stubbs, i. 59. M.I. in St. John's churchyard, Calcutta.

O'DONEL, Hugh (1785-1837). Lieut. Colonel, 13th N.I. *b.* Newport, co. Mayo, 2 July 1785. Cadet 1803. Arrived in India 29 Apr. 1805. Ensign 7 Apr. 1805. Lieut. 14 Apr. 1805. Capt. 15 Aug. 1820. Major 1 Apr. 1830. Lt. Col. 13 Aug. 1835. *d.* Nasirabad, Rajputana, 27 Sept. 1837.

bapt. 8 July 1785. Son of Francis O'Donel, of Fahey Lodge, Kilcommon, co. Mayo, and Catherine his wife. *m.* Dinajpur, Bengal, 1 Dec. 1826, Miss Jane Finch.[1] (She died 8 Feb. 1892, aged 85.)

Services : Posted Lieut. to 7th N.I. in 1806. With Ramgarh Bn. 1811-13 ; comdd. the unsuccessful attack on Nowagarh 27 Feb. 1812, when his conduct was reported as having been " highly creditable." Adjt. 2/7th N.I. 25 June 1813 till 27 Sept. 1820. Third Mahratta War 1817-19. Transfd. to 13th N.I. (late 1/7th) May 1824. Actg. Bde. Major to Assam force 8 Aug. 1826. d.d. 49th N.I. 14 Aug. 1832 till Oct. 1833. Posted Lt. Col. to 13th N.I. 30 Jan. 1836.

Refs.: A.J. N.S. xxv. 37. M.I. Nasirabad.

[1] *Note :* Probably dau. of Henry Finch and grand-dau. of Sir Gabriel Martindell, *qq.v.*

O'DONNELL, Edmund Sexton[1] **Pery** (1762/63-1785). Lieutenant, Infantry. *b.* in Ireland 1762/63. Cadet 1780. Ensign 1780. Lieut. 31 July 1781. *d.* 23 Dec. 1785 : kld. by dacoits.

Son of John O'Donnell, of Limerick, Trough, Mt. O'Donnell and Ing, co. Clare, and Deborah his wife, dau. of William Anderson, of Garrinecanty, co. Tipperary. Brother of Henry Anderson O'Donnell, *q.v.*

Services : Apptd. Cadet 11 Apr. 1780 ; sailed for India in the *Earl of Dartmouth* 3 June 1780, aged 17. Granted leave s.c. to sea 23 Nov. 1783 ; fur. for 1 yr. 27 Sept. 1785:

Refs. : Burke's *Landed Gentry,* 15th edn., p. 2653, *s.n.* O'Donnell, of The Red House.

[1] *Note :* Sometimes spelt Sexten.

O'DONNELL, Henry Anderson (1758-1840). Lieut. Colonel, C.B. 13th N.I. *b.* in Ireland 1758. Cadet 1780. Admitted 8 May 1781. Ensign 1780. Lieut. 22 June 1781. Capt. 1 Nov. 1798. Major 21 Sept. 1804. Lt. Col. 8 Sept. 1809. Retired

4 June 1817. *d.* at his residence, George St., Limerick, 26 Dec. 1840, aged 81.

Of Limerick and Trough, co. Clare. 2nd son of John O'Donnell and Deborah his wife. *m.* 1st, 1793, "Domina Jan, a Persian Princess." (She died 1804.) *m.* 2nd, Calcutta 2 Jan. 1808, Maria, widow of John Brownrigg.

Services: Apptd. Cadet 11 Apr. 1780; sailed for India in the *Earl of Dartmouth* 3 June 1780, aged 19. Arrived at Madras Jan. 1781 and served there in a Corps of Cadets; volunteered to serve at sieges of Negapatam Oct.-Nov. 1781, and Trincomali Jan. 1782 (w. in head at assault of fort Osnaburg 11 Jan.). First Mahratta War; with Goddard's detachment. Transfd. from 1st Eur. Bn. to 7th Bn. Sepoys 5 Feb. 1790. Third Mysore War; Seringapatam; Lieut. 7th Bn. Operations in Jumna Doab 1803; Sasni; Bijaigarh; Capt. 12th N.I. Second Mahratta War; Agra; Laswari; Monson's retreat; capture of Deig; Bhurtpore (w. in rt. hip during 1st assault on 9 Jan. 1805); Major 12th N.I. Operations in Oudh 1807-8; Akbarpur; Pathar-serai; Major comdg. the force; Badri; Gurha; Major 2/12th N.I. Posted Lt. Col. to 2/4th N.I. in 1809. Fur. 13 Dec. 1814 till retirement. Transfd. to 1/13th N.I. in 1815. C.B. 4 June 1815.

Refs.: Burke's *Landed Gentry*, 15th edn., p. 2653, *s.n.* O'Donnell, of The Red House. *E.I.M.C.* i. 51-5. *G.M.* 1841, i. 221.

O'DONNELLY (or O'DONNELLAN), Sutton. *(See* **DONNELLY, Sutton.)**

OGILBY, Alexander Beaufort (1804-1834). Lieutenant, 27th N.I. *b.* Kingston-on-Thames 3 Dec. 1804. Cadet 1824. Arrived in India 15 May 1825. Ensign 14 Nov. 1824. Lieut. 30 Dec. 1825. *d.* Hansi 22 May 1834.

bapt. Portsmouth 26 May 1806. Eldest son of Lt.-Col. Sir David Ogilby, Kt., 9th Madras N.I., and Mary his 2nd wife, of Roxburgh, Mass. Ed. Charterhouse Sept. 1817-Jan. 1819.

Services: Posted Ensign to 27th N.I. and served throughout with that Regt.; actg. Intr. & Qmr. 10 Sept. 1833. No record of active service.

Refs.: Burke's *Landed Gentry of Ireland*, p. 530, *s.n.* Ogilby, of Ardnagle, co. Londonderry. *Charterhouse School List.*

OGILVIE, Alexander (*d.* 1768). Lieutenant, Infantry. Cadet (?) Ensign 5 Nov. 1766. Lieut. 1767. *d.* in India 12 Feb. 1768.
Services: N.F.P.

OGILVIE, William (*d.* 1783). Captain. Infantry. Cadet 1769. Ensign 20 Sept. 1769. Lieut. 26 June 1771. Capt. 7 Sept. 1779. Dismissed at Madras 1781. *d.* Basra, Irak, 9 May 1783, while on his way home overland.

Eldest son of William Ogilvie, of Banff, merchant, and Helen his wife. Glasgow Univ.; matric. 1763.

Services: Lieut. in H.M.S.[1] Sailed for India as a Cadet in the *Neptune* 3 Jan. 1769. First Rohilla War; battle of St. George; Lieut. 10th Bn. Sepoys. 1st Bengal Eur. Regt. in Sept. 1777; Capt. 2/3rd Eur. Regt. in Oct. 1779. Second Mysore War 1781; with Col. Pearse's detachment. Given sick leave to Masulipatam in June 1781, and rejoined the army at Nellore on 30th of that month. Col. Pearse, writing to the C.-in-C. in June 1781, expresses a wish that Ogilvie may be ordered to return to Bengal, and hopes that he will never be permitted to return to the force under his comd. Sentenced to dismissal by C.M. at Chittoor, Madras, 19 Oct. 1781.

Refs.: *S.M.* 1783, p. 447. Will dated 4 Oct. 1777; proved 5 Apr. 1784.

[1] *Note*: One of this name was Ensign 32nd Ft. 25 Sept. 1757; Lieut. do. 11 Jan. 1760.

OGILVY, David (1807-1876). Bt. Captain. 15th N.I. *b.* Ainley, co. Forfar, 22 Sept. 1807. Cadet 1824. Arrived in India 6 May 1825. Ensign 8 Jan. 1825. Lieut. 20 Dec. 1826. Bt. Capt. 8 Jan. 1840. Retired 24 May 1841. *d.s.p.* Inverquharity, Hobart Town, Tasmania, 8 Oct. 1876.

5th son of Sir William Ogilvy, 8th Bart., Rear Adm. R.N., and Sarah his wife, dau. of James Morley, Bo. C.S., and sometime of Kempshott Park, Hants. Cousin-german of Mark Napier Ogilvy, *q.v. m.* Cawnpore 17 Mar. 1835, Caroline Helena, eldest dau. of Lt.-Col. Samuel George Carter, 17th Foot. (*See also* Robert Raikes Kinleside.) (She died 7 Jan. 1911, aged 92.)

Services: Ensign d.d. 68th N.I. 23 May 1825; posted to 9th N.I. in 1825; transfd. to 15th N.I. in 1826. Fur. s.c. 12 Jan. 1828 till 18 Nov. 1830. Intr. & Qmr. 15th N.I. 30 May 1835; Adjt. do. 21 Oct. 1835 till 7 Jan. 1841. Leave s.c. 2 yrs. to Tasmania 10 Apr. 1837. Retired on h.p. and settled in Tasmania. No record of active service.

Refs.: Burke's *Peerage*, 1923, p. 1702, *s.n.* Ogilvy, Bart., of Inverquharity, co. Forfar.

OGILVY, Hon. Donald (1788-1863). Lieutenant. 16th N.I. Subsequently Colonel Forfarshire Mil. *bapt.* Kirriemuir, co.

Forfar, 10 May 1788. Cadet 1805. Arrived in India 13 Dec. 1806. Ensign 3 Dec. 1806. Lieut. 26 Dec. 1809. Resigned 13 Nov. 1813. *d.* 30 Dec. 1863.
Of Clova, co. Forfar, J.P. and D.L. 3rd son of Walter Ogilvy, by courtesy 5th Earl of Airlie, and Jane his 2nd wife, dau. of John Ogilvy, of Murkle. Younger brother of David, 6th Earl. *m.* Feb. 1815, Maria, 4th dau. of James Morley, of Kempshott Park, and aunt of David Ogilvy, *q.v.* (She died 9 Apr. 1843.)
Services: Barasat C.C. Posted Ensign to 16th N.I. in 1807. Operations in Bundelkhand against Gopal Singh 1809-11 ; Lieut. 16th N.I. (? Reduction of Kalinjar 1812 ; Lieut. 2/16th N.I.) Col. Forfarshire Mil. 28 Feb. 1828. M.P. for Forfarshire 3 Oct. 1831 till Jan. 1832.
Refs.: Burke's *Peerage*, 1923, p. 87, *s.n.* Airlie, E.

OGILVY, Mark Napier (1807-1835). Lieutenant, 2nd L.C. *b.* Dacca 5 Oct. 1807. Cadet 1825. Arrived in India 10 Aug. 1826. Cornet 4 Dec. 1825. Lieut. 4 Dec. 1827. *d.* Nimach 4 Sept. 1835.
bapt. Dacca 19 June 1809. Son of Alexander Ogilvy, Surg. at Dacca, and Marcia Anne his wife, dau. of Maj.-Gen. Hon. Mark Napier and sister of John George Napier, *q.v.*
Services: Posted Cornet to 2nd L.C. Fur. s.c. 13 Apr. 1830 till 18 Oct. 1832. Demonstration against Jodhpur 1834 ; Lieut. 2nd L.C.
Refs.: Burke's *Peerage*, 1923, p. 1701, *s.n.* Ogilvy, Bart., of Inverquharity, co. Forfar. *A.J.* N.S. xix. 206. M.I. Nimach.

OGLE, Robert (*d.* 1823). Lieut. Colonel. 14th N.I. Cadet 1769. Admitted 12 Apr. 1769. Ensign 21 Sept. 1769. Lieut. 15 Mar. 1773. Capt. 12 Jan. 1781. Major 1 Mar. 1794. Lt. Col. 25 Apr. 1797. Retired 24 Oct. 1798. *d.* Dijon, France, 24 Jan. 1823.
m. Frances Maria. (She died 4 Sept. 1849, aged 78.)
Services: Lieut. 30th Bn. Sepoys in 1777. Capt. comdg. one of the two Bns. of 23rd N.I. (late 30th Bn.) in 1781 ; 6th Bengal Eur. Bn. in July 1787 ; comdg. 30th Bn. Sepoys in 1792 ; comdg. at Baragaon in Nov. 1794. Fur. 27 Mar. 1797 till retirement.
Refs.: *G.M.* 1823, i. 383.

O'HALLORAN, John Nicholas (1810-1886). Lieutenant. 19th N.I. *b.* in India 26 Dec. 1810. Cadet 1827. Arrived in India 11 Dec. 1828. Ensign (12 June 1828) 3 June 1829. Lieut.

24 Sept. 1834. Retired 18 June 1835. *d.s.p.* at his residence, Courtenay Villa, Leamington, 30 Nov. 1886.

8th and youngest son of Sir Joseph O'Halloran, *q.v.*, and Frances his wife. *m.* Edinburgh 4 Oct. 1834, Elizabeth, youngest dau. of James Pringle, *q.v.* (She died 6 July 1889.) Addiscombe Cadet 1826-8.

Services : Ensign d.d. 24th N.I. 14 Jan. 1829; posted Ensign to 19th N.I. ; d.d. 2nd N.I. 17 Oct. 1831 ; actg. Adjt. 4th Local Horse 10 Oct. 1831 ; d.d. 63rd N.I. 7 Jan. 1832. Fur. s.c. 18 Dec. 1832 till retirement. Retired on h.p. as Ensign, viz. 3/- *p.d.* No record of active service.

Refs. : Burke's *Colonial Gentry,* i. 82, *s.n.* O'Halloran. *A.J.* N.S. xv. 180. *The Times,* 7 Dec. 1886.

O'HALLORAN, Sir Joseph (1763-1843). Major General, G.C.B., Kt., Colonel 30th N.I. *b.* Limerick 13 Aug. 1763. Country Cadet 1781. Admitted 1 Aug. 1781. Ensign 9 May 1782. Lieut. 6 Jan. 1785. Capt. 1 Jan. 1796. Major 1 Aug. 1810. Lt. Col. 4 June 1814. Col. 5 June 1829. Maj. Gen. 10 Jan. 1837. *d.* 42 Connaught Sq., London, 3 Nov. 1843, from the effects of a fractured thigh-bone, incurred in a street accident.

3rd and youngest son of Sylvester O'Halloran, of Limerick, surgeon, and Mary O'Casey his wife. *m.* Calcutta Dec. 1790, Frances, dau. of Col. Nicholas Bayly, of Redhill, Surrey, and niece of Henry, Earl of Uxbridge. (She died Calcutta 23 Jan. 1835.) Father of John Nicholas O'Halloran, *q.v.*, Ann Helen, wife of George Cuninghame, *q.v.*, Maria Nugent, wife of Thomas Vallencey Lysaght, *q.v.*, and Jane Baillie, wife of Sir George Moyle Sherer, *q.v.*

Services : See *D.N.B.* Midshipman in the *Swallow* East Indiaman 22 Feb. 1781. Lieut. 6th Eur. Bn. in 1787 ; apptd. Adjt. 4th Eur. Bn. 15 Dec. 1787 ; do. 4th Bn. Sepoys 1793. Family Paymr. 3rd Eur. Bn. 7 Mar. 1794. Adjt. & Qmr. at Midnapore June 1796 till Oct. 1802 ; Lieut. 1st N.I. in 1798. Transfd. from 1/15th to 1/18th N.I. 29 May 1800 ; Capt. Lt. do. 5 Jan. 1801. Second Mahratta War ; operations in Bundelkhand 1803-6 ; Kapsa ; defeat of Rajah Ram Singh ; Jaitpur 1804 ; Capt. 1/18th N.I. Operations in Bundelkhand 1809 ; Rajaoli ; Ajaigarh ; Capt. comdg. 1/18th N.I. Nepal War 1814 ; Tirhut ; Lt. Col. 1/18th N.I. Nepal War 1816 ; Harriharpur ; Lt. Col. comdg. 1/18th N.I., in 1st Bde. Centre Column. Cuttack insurrection 1816-17 ; Lt. Col. comdg. 1/18th N.I. Transfd. to 1/20th N.I. Aug. 1818 ; comdg. troops in P.W.I. ; Lt. Col. Comdt. 25th N.I. (late 1/20th)

May 1824. Bdr. on District Staff 13 Jan. 1825; to comd. at
Barrackpore 27 May 1825. Apptd. to Gen. Staff of Army as Bdr.
24 Dec. 1828; posted to Saugor Div. 12 Feb. 1829. Posted Col.
to 25th N.I. June 1829. Transfd. to Cawnpore Div. 25 Nov. 1830;
to Dinapore 24 Nov. 1831. Transfd. to 30th N.I. 29 July 1832.
Tour on Staff expired 24 Dec. 1833. Fur. s.c. 6 Jan. 1834 till death.
C.B. 21 Dec. 1816; K.C.B. 10 Mar. 1837; G.C.B. 12 Feb. 1840.
Kt. 18 Feb. 1835.

Refs.: Burke's *Colonial Gentry,* i. 82, *s.n.* O'Halloran. *D.N.B.*
D.I.B. E.I.M.C. ii. 468-72. *Hickey,* iv. 21. *S.M.* 1791, p. 306.
G.M. 1844, i. 92. *The Times,* 4 Nov. 1843.

O'HANLON, Edward Francis (1803-1824). Lieutenant, Artillery. (529) *b.* Newry, co. Down, 25 Jan. 1803. Cadet 1821.
2nd Lieut. 10 May 1822. Lieut. 29 Oct. 1824. *d.* 15 Dec. 1824 :
kld. in action at Kokein, nr. Rangoon.

Son of Patrick O'Hanlon, of Dublin and Newry, barr.-at-law,[1]
by his wife, dau. of Thomas Smyth, of Fencehouse, co. Chester
(? Fence Houses, co. Durham). Brother of Pringle O'Hanlon, *q.v.*
Addiscombe Cadet 1820-2.

Services: First Burma War 1824; Kokein (kld.); 2nd Lieut.
4th Coy. 5th Bn., with Sir A. Campbell's force.

Refs.: O'Hart's *Irish Pedigrees,* 3rd edn., p. 363.

[1] *Note:* He resided in Calcutta from Jan. 1826 till his death
on 20 Dec. 1850, aged 85, and was for some time police mgte.
at Alipore, Calcutta. He describes himself in his Will as, ' Commonly called The O'Hanlon, by Inheritance Standard Bearer of
Ireland.'

O'HANLON, Pringle (1800-1887). Lieut. Colonel. 1st L.C.
b. Newry, co. Down, 2 July 1800. Cadet 1819. Admitted
12 Sept. 1820. Cornet 24 May 1820. Lieut. 1 May 1824. Capt.
7 July 1833. Bt. Major 3 Apr. 1846. Retired 31 Jan. 1852.
Hon. Lt. Col. 28 Nov. 1854. *d.* 15 Nevern Sq., Earl's Court,
London, 23 May 1887.

Son of Patrick O'Hanlon, of Dublin and Newry, barr.-at-law.
Brother of Edward Francis O'Hanlon, *q.v. m.* Bright, co. Down,
26 Mar. 1827, Louisa Alexander, youngest dau. of E. S. Ruthven,
of Oakley Park, co. Down. (She died 19 May 1886.)

Services: Posted Cornet to 1st L.C. in 1820. Fur. s.c. 4 Nov.
1825 till 9 Oct. 1830. d.d. 9th L.C. 13 Mar. 1832. Suspended by
G.C.M. from rank and pay Nov. 1834 till 1 Dec. 1835. d.d. 9th
L.C. 4 Jan. 1836. Fur. p.a. 27 Jan. 1837 till 15 Jan. 1842. First

Afghan War 1842 ; reoccupation of Kabul ; Capt. 1st L.C., with Gen. Pollock's force (Medal). Bde. Major at Ludhiana 13 Sept. 1844. First Sikh War ; Mudki ; Ferozshahr ; Sobraon ; Capt. 1st L.C., Bde. Major (Medal with 2 clasps). Bde. Major at Mhow 1846 ; do. Ludhiana 1848 ; Barrackpore Feb. 1850 ; Ambala 27 Sept. 1850 ; Barrackpore Feb. 1852. Leave s.c. 1 yr. to Simla 1 Oct. 1850.

Refs.: O'Hart's *Irish Pedigrees*, 3rd edn., p. 363. *A.J.* N.S. xvi. 263-5 ; xix. 291-2 ; xx. 99-101. *The Times*, 25 May 1887.

O'HARA, Alexander (1765-1793). Lieutenant, 5th Bn. Bengal Vols. b. in Ireland 1765. Cadet 1781. Arrived in India July 1783. Ensign 22 May 1781. Lieut. 4 Sept. 1782. d. Tamluk, Midnapore, Bengal, 6 Oct. 1793, aged 27.

Services : Lieut. 8th Bn. Sepoys in July 1787. Third Mysore War ; Lieut. Bengal Vols.

Refs. : M.I. in Tamluk town, Midnapore.

O'HARA, Brabazon Rawdon (1787-1814). Lieutenant, 6th N.I. A.D.C. to Sir Robert Rollo Gillespie. b. St. Thomas's, Dublin, 10 Jan. 1787. Cadet 1804. Arrived in India 1 Oct. 1805. Ensign 9 July 1805. Lieut. 10 July 1805. d. 31 Oct. 1814 : kld. in action at the assault of Kalanga.

Son of Oliver O'Hara, of the family of O'Hara of the Route and Crebilly, and Honoria his wife, elder dau. of Bryan MacManus, of Mount Davys, co. Antrim.

Services : Ensign Antrim Mil. Posted Lieut. to 6th N.I. in 1806 ; Adjt. 1/6th N.I. 26 Sept. 1807 till death. Nepal War 1814 ; A.D.C. to Sir R. Gillespie, and kld. at his side.

Refs. : Burke's *Landed Gentry of Ireland*, p. 609, *s.n.* Rowan, of Mount Davys.

*O'HARA, Charles (*d.* 1760). Factor and Asst. Engineer. Arrived in India 15 July 1750. d. Calcutta 11 Sept. 1760.

Services : Apptd. in England, 1749, Asst. to Benjamin Robins, Chief Engr. at Madras, to rank as Writer ; sailed for Fort St. David in the *Grantham*. Asst. to Lieut. John Brohier, Engr. at Fort St. David, Aug. 1751 ; transfd. to Bengal with Col. Caroline Frederick Scott Aug. 1753. A Factor at Calcutta in 1756 ; employed as one of the two Engrs. during the siege and was apptd. a Lieut. of the Train, or Art. Coy. Escaped to Fulta 19 June, " privately withdrew out of the back gate, deserted the factory and embarked on board the shipping." Sub-Treasurer at Calcutta

1 Aug. 1757 till 20 Sept. 1759 ; Member of Council at Patna 13 Aug. 1759. Apptd. Capt. in the Mil. Feb. 1759.

Refs.: Hill, *passim.* Will dated 18 Nov. 1759 ;˙ proved 1760. *Note:* Said to have been 22 yrs. of age in 1756.

O'HARA, Charles (1800-1874). Major. 4th L.C. *b.* Ardrahan. co. Galway, Oct. 1800. Cadet 1820. Arrived in India 17 Nov, 1821. Cornet 19 June 1821. Lieut. 1 May 1824. Capt. 26 Mar. 1838. Retired 1 Mar. 1843. Hon. Major 28 Nov. 1854. *d.* Raheen, Gort, co. Galway, 19 Nov. 1874.

Son of Robert O'Hara, of Raheen, and Frances his wife, dau. of Walter Taylor, of Castle Taylor. Uncle (? cousin-german) of William Maxwell (1814-1882), *q.v.* *m.* Dublin Feb. 1845, Charlotte, 7th and youngest dau. of Anthony Gildea, of Clooncormack and Port Royal, D.L. (She died 17 Dec. 1881.) T.C.D. ; Pensioner 12 Oct. 1818.

Services: Posted Cornet to 4th L.C. Siege and capture of Bhurtpore ; Lieut. 4th L.C. (India medal). Adjt. 6th Local Horse 14 Mar. 1827. Actg. 2nd in comd. 2nd Nassiri Bn. 13 Dec. 1827. Second in comd. 2nd Local Horse 29 Feb. 1828 ; Comdt. do. 3 Sept. 1839 till 12 Sept. 1842.

Refs.: Burke's *Landed Gentry of Ireland,* p. 534, *s.n.* O'Hara, of Lenaboy, co. Galway ; p. 685, *s.n.* Shawe-Taylor, of Castle Taylor, co. Galway ; p. 266, *s.n.* Gildea, of Clooncormack, co. Mayo. *Alumni Dub.* *The Times,* 1 Dec. 1874.

OLDFIELD, Charles James (1800-1878). Lieut. Colonel. 4th N.I. *b.* Kishunnagar, B. & O., 13 Aug. 1800. Cadet 1819. Admitted 30 May 1820. Ensign 10 Jan. 1820. Lieut. 11 July 1823. Capt. 21 Jan. 1838. Major 22 Aug. 1847. Retired 7 July 1848. Hon. Lt. Col. 28 Nov. 1854. *d.* Bourne, Lincs., 3 Aug. 1878.

bapt. Kishunnagar 28 Aug. 1800. 2nd son of Christopher Oldfield, of Lendal, Yorks., B.C.S., second judge of the court of appeal at Murshidabad, and Mary Johanna his wife, dau. of George Morris, of Spiddal, and sister of Edmond Morris, *q.v.* Brother of Christopher Edward Thomas Oldfield, *q.v.*, and cousin-german of Thomas Wilson Oldfield, *q.v.* Stepson of Thomas Macan (*d.* 1848), *q.v.* *m.* 5 June 1855, Isabel, dau. of —— Stinton. (She died 29 Oct. 1861, aged 36.) (? *m.* 2nd, Sarah Anne, who died 5 July 1876, aged 29.) Ed. Rugby ; admitted 11 Aug. 1810.

Services: Posted Ensign to 2/3rd N.I. Transfd. as Lieut. to 1st N.I. in 1823 ; to 4th N.I. (late 2/1st) May 1824. Attached to

Champaran L.I. 29 Nov. 1823. First Burma War; Assam 1824-5; Lieut. Champaran L.I. (India medal). Actg. Adjt. Champaran L.I. 25 Aug. 1826; do. Left Wing 4th N.I. 4 Aug. 1827 and 8 Jan. 1829; actg. Intr. & Qmr. 4th N.I. 2 Oct. 1829. Fur. p.a. 24 Jan. 1831 till 11 Sept. 1834. Actg. Bde. Major in Rohilkhand and Kumaon 22 Apr. till 7 Oct. 1841. A.D.C. to C.-in-C. 26 Jan. till 1 Oct. 1842. Comdt. 2nd Regt. Oudh Local Inf. Oct. 1842 till 14 July 1843. Fur. 1848.

Refs.: Burke's *Family Records*, p. 448, *s.n.* Oldfield. *Rugby School Register. The Times*, 6 Aug. 1878.

OLDFIELD, Christopher Edward Thomas (1804-1850). Bt. Lieut. Colonel, C.B., 5th L.C. *b*. Murshidabad, Bengal, 17 Nov. 1804. Cadet 1820. Arrived in India 25 May 1821. Cornet 13 Jan. 1821. Lieut. 13 May 1825. Capt. 14 Dec. 1835. Major 21 Aug. 1849. Bt. Lt. Col. 30 Apr. 1844. *d. unm.* Nakodar, Punjab, 16 Apr. 1850.

bapt. Berhampore 4 July 1805. 3rd son of Christopher Oldfield, B.C.S., and Mary Johanna his wife. Brother of Frederick Bevan Rocke Oldfield, *q.v.*

Services: Cornet d.d. 8th L.C. June 1821. Posted to 5th L.C. July 1821. Offg. Intr. & Qmr. 5th L.C. 13 July 1825; permanent do. 25 Aug. 1826 till 2 Oct. 1827. Fur. p.a. 5 Jan. 1833 till 16 Dec. 1835. First Afghan War 1840-2; operations against Ghilzais 1841; Kurutu 5 Aug. 1841; comdd. rear guard on march from Khurd Kabul to Tazin Oct. 1841 (*Lond. Gaz.* 11 Feb. 1842); Tazin; Jagdalak; defence of Jalalabad (ib. 7 & 10 June, 8 Aug. 1842) (Medal); Mamu Khel; Bt. Major 5th L.C. (Medal). Apptd. Hon. A.D.C. to G.G. 1 Apr. 1842. Apptd. Comdt. 8th Irreg. Cav. 4 Apr. 1842. Comdd. 4th Irreg. Cav. Dec. 1842 till Feb. 1845. Gwalior campaign; Maharajpur (ib. 8 Mar. 1844); Major comdg. 4th Irreg. Cav. (Bronze star). Hon. A.D.C. to G.G. 23 July 1844. Fur. s.c. 10 Feb. 1845 till 1 Nov. 1849, when he rejoined 5th L.C. C.B. 4 Oct. 1842.

Refs.: Burke's *Family Records*, p. 448, *s.n.* Oldfield. *De Rhé-Philipe. I.M.* 4 June 1850, p. 326. *G.M.* 1850, ii. 109. Will dated 27 July 1835; proved 7 June 1850. M.I. at Nakodar and in York Minster.

OLDFIELD, Frederick Bevan Rocke (1807-1834). Captain, 25th N.I. *b.* Berhampore 22 Sept. 1807. Cadet 1823. Arrived in India 12 June 1824. Ensign (?) Lieut. 1 Oct. 1824. Capt. 17 Jan. 1834. *d. unm.* Agra 23 Aug. 1834.

bapt. Calcutta 5 May 1808. 4th and youngest son of Christopher Oldfield, B.C.S., and Mary Johanna his wife. Brother of Charles James Oldfield, *q.v.* Ed. Harrow 1819/20 till 1823.
Services : Posted Ensign to 40th N.I. First Burma War ; Chittagong 1824-5 ; Lieut. 40th N.I. Transfd. to 25th N.I. 2 Mar. 1827. S.A.C.G. 13 June 1828 ; D.A.C.G. 2 cl. 29 Nov. 1833.
Refs. : Burke's *Family Records,* p. 448, *s.n.* Oldfield. *Harrow School Register. A.J.* N.S. xvi. 195. Will dated Agra, 27 Mar. 1834 ; proved 14 Feb. 1835. M.I. in Agra Cantt. cemetery.

OLDFIELD, John Rawdon (1812-1883). Colonel. Engineers.
b. Fort George, Inverness, 31 Jan. 1812. Cadet 1827. Arrived in India 12 Dec. 1828. 2nd Lieut. 15 June 1827. Lieut. 28 Sept. 1827. Capt. 1 Jan. 1843. Major 21 Aug. 1854. Lt. Col. 10 Mar. 1857. Retired 20 Sept. 1857. Hon. Col. 23 Oct. 1857. *d.* Dorchester 22 Nov. 1883.
bapt. Westbourne, Sussex, 18 Jan. 1816. Eldest son of Gen. John Oldfield, K.H., Col. Comdt. R.E. (*D.N.B.*), and Mary his 1st wife, dau. of Christopher Arden, of Dorchester. *m.* Dorchester 26 May 1846, his cousin Jane, dau. of Christopher Arden, of Dorchester. (She died Ticehurst 7 Feb. 1873.) Addiscombe Cadet 1826-7.
Services : d.d. S. & M. at Aligarh 14 Jan. 1829. Actg. Asst. Engr. 13th (Rajputana) Div. P.W.D. 10 Mar. 1835 ; permanent do. 19 July 1836. Bde. Major Engr. Dept. of force assembled for service in Marwar 6 Sept. till 14 Oct. 1839, when the force was broken up. Executive Engr. at Darjeeling 21 Oct. 1839. Fur. p.a. 29 Feb. 1840 till 7 Oct. 1842. Field Engr. with force in Bundelkhand 7 Apr. 1843. Fur. s.c. 16 Feb. 1844 till 1846. P.W.D. Agra Div. 26 Dec. 1846 till Apr. 1850. Second Sikh War ; operations in Jullundur Doab ; action of heights of Dalla ; Field Engr. (Medal). Executive Engr. Peshawar 19 Apr. 1850. Principal of Thomason Coll. of Civil Engineering at Roorkee 28 Feb. 1852 till retirement. Fur. s.c. 12 Feb. 1856 till retirement.
Refs. : Burke's *Landed Gentry,* 4th edn., p. 1116, *s.n.* Oldfield, of Oldfield Lawn, Sussex. *The Times,* 27 Nov. 1883.

OLDFIELD, Thomas Wilson (1812-1872). Colonel. 74th N.I.
b. Fulford, Yorks., 1 June 1812. Cadet 1831. Arrived in India 18 July 1832. Ensign (8 Dec. 1831) 10 Dec. 1833. Lieut. 15 Dec. 1835. Capt. 22 Dec. 1844. Major 1 Feb. 1849. Lt. Col. 11 Nov. 1854. Retired 20 Feb. 1856. Hon. Col. 20 Feb. 1856. *d.* York 26 Jan. 1872.

Of Potterne, Devizes. *bapt.* Fulford 2 June 1812. 2nd son of William Oldfield, of York, wine merchant, and Ann Tamer his wife, dau. of Thomas Wilson, alderman of York. His sisters *m.* Richard Cautley and Joseph Alexander Weller, *qq.v.* Cousin-german of Charles James Oldfield, *q.v.* Addiscombe Cadet 5 Feb. 1830 till 8 Dec. 1831.

Services : Ensign d.d. 44th N.I. 4 Sept. 1832 ; posted to 74th N.I. Dec. 1833. Adjt. 74th N.I. 16 Dec. 1836 till 9 Apr. 1840. Adjt. Inf., Sindhia's Contingent, 9 July 1840 ; Adjt. Cav. do. 30 Oct. 1841 till Mar. 1844. Fur. s.c. 17 Mar. 1844 till 1846. Offg. Bde. Major 2 Feb. 1848. Posted Lt. Col. to 74th N.I. Jan. 1855. No record of active service.

Refs. : Burke's *Family Records*, p. 448, *s.n.* Oldfield. *The Times*, 29 Jan. 1872.

OLDHAM, Daniel (*d.* 1769). Ensign, Infantry. Cadet 1767. Ensign 15 Sept. 1767. *d.* 1769.

Services : Sailed for India in the *Lord Holland* 16 Dec. 1766.

OLDHAM, James Oldham (1804-1884). Lieutenant. 60th N.I. Subsequently incumbent of St. Luke's, Edgbaston, Birmingham. *b.* Calcutta 3 Nov. 1804. Cadet 1820. Arrived in India May 1821. Ensign 16 Jan. 1821. Lieut. 11 July 1823. Resigned 18 June 1834. *d.* Jersey 18 Apr. 1884.

Eldest son of James Oldham Oldham, B.C.S., 4th judge of the provl. court of appeal at Bareilly (afterwards of Bellamour Hall, Staffs., which he purchased from Lady Blount in 1824), and Elizabeth Jane his wife, dau. of Hercules Skinner, *q.v.* Grandson of James Oldham Oldham, of Missenden Abbey, Bucks., sheriff of Bucks. 1802, and nephew of William Henry Cooper, *q.v. m.* 1st, 19 Mar. 1833, Maria, youngest dau. of Robert Haig, of Roebuck and Dodderbank, co. Dublin, and grand-dau. of Sir William Wolseley, of Wolseley, Staffs., 6th Bart. (She died 5 Dec. 1863.) *m.* 2nd, 1864, Henrietta L. Trimble. (She died 1916.)

Addiscombe Cadet 1819. T.C.D. ; Fellow Commoner 1 July 1836 ; B.A. 1839 ; M.A. 1842.

Services : Posted Ensign to 1/2nd N.I. in 1821 ; d.d. 2/15th N.I. 15 Jan. 1822 ; transfd. to 2/15th N.I. 5 Mar. 1822 ; as Lieut. to 2/31st N.I. July 1823 ; to 62nd N.I. (late 2/31st) May 1824 ; exchanged to 60th N.I. 21 Aug. 1824 ; d.d. 6th N.I. 27 Dec. 1824. Siege and capture of Bhurtpore ; Lieut. 60th N.I., A.D.C. to Lord Combermere, C.-in-C. (India medal). Adjt. Bareilly Provl. Bn. 25 Feb. 1826 ; do. Bhagulpur Hill Rangers 13 June 1827 till 1 Sept.

THE BENGAL ARMY, 1758-1834

1831. Fur. p.a. 31 Jan. 1832 till 28 Jan. 1835, when he resigned with effect from 18 June 1834. Took holy orders. Incumbent of St. Luke's, Birmingham.
Refs.: Foster's *Families of Royal Descent,* i. 347. Family information. *Alumni Dub. The Times,* 25 Apr. 1884.

OLIPHANT, George (1793-1826). Captain, 22nd N.I. *b.* St. Margaret's, Westminster, 17 May 1793. Cadet 1807. Arrived in India 1 Feb. 1809. Ensign 7 Feb. 1809. Lieut. 16 Dec. 1814. Capt. 24 Dec. 1825. *d.* at sea 9 Oct. 1826, on board the *Snipe,* on his passage to N.S.W.
Son of Campbell Oliphant, of Cockspur St., London, later of Swaffham, and Mary his wife. Brother of Henry Oliphant, *q.v.*
Services: Barasat C.C. Posted Ensign to 2nd N.I. Reduction of Kalinjar 1812 ; Ensign 2/2nd N.I. Operations in Baghelkhand 1813 ; Entauri ; Ensign 2/2nd N.I. Transfd. to 22nd N.I. (late 2/2nd) May 1824. Leave s.c. 12 mos. to N.S.W. 15 June 1826.

OLIPHANT, Henry (1797-1823). Lieutenant, 8th N.I. *b.* London 1 Dec. 1797. Cadet 1818. Ensign (?) Lieut. 10 June 1820. *d.* Hansi 2 Nov. 1823.
bapt. Cockspur St., London, 28 Dec. 1797. Son of Campbell Oliphant and Mary his wife. Brother of George Oliphant, *q.v.*
Services: Ensign d.d. 9th N.I. 1819. Posted Lieut. to 2/8th N.I. in 1820. Fur. s.c. 30 Sept. 1820 till 1822. No record of active service.
Refs.: A.J. xvii. 561.

OLIPHANT, James (1780-1804). Lieutenant, 11th N.I. *b.* Largo, co. Fife, 29 July 1780. Cadet 1798. Arrived in India 22 Dec. 1799. Ensign 5 Oct. 1799. Lieut. 28 Oct. 1799. *d. unm.* Gohad (? Gwalior), C.I., 16 Sept. 1804.
bapt. Largo 1 Aug. 1780. Eldest son of Rev. Spence Oliphant, minister of Largo 1777-1821, and Fotheringham his wife, dau. of James Duddingston, of St. Fort. Ed. St. Andrews Univ.
Services: Posted Lieut. to 2/11th N.I. 15 Apr. 1801. Second Mahratta War ; Bundelkhand 1803 ; Kapsa ; Kalpi ; capture of Gwalior Feb. 1804 ; Lieut. 2/11th N.I.
Refs.: Scott's *Fasti,* v. 219. *S.M.* 1805, p. 805. Will dated Gwalior 9 June 1804 ; proved 1 Feb. 1805.

OLIPHANT, William (1792-1828). Captain, Artillery. (420) *b.* Forgandenny, co. Perth, 9 Aug. 1792. Cadet 1809. Arrived in India 2 Aug. 1810. Fireworker 3 Aug. 1810. Lieut. 25 Sept. 1817. Capt. 1 May 1824. *d. unm.* Calcutta 27 Aug. 1828.

2nd son of Ebenezer Oliphant, VII of Condie, and Mary his wife, 3rd dau. of Sir William Stirling, Bart., of Ardoch. Woolwich Cadet; nominated to R.M.A. 17 June 1807.

Services: Third Mahratta War; (? Taragarh); Lieut. 5th Coy. 1st Bn. Foot Art. Asst. Sec. Mily. Board, Ord. Dept., 10 June 1825 till death. Siege and capture of Bhurtpore; Capt. 3rd Coy. 4th Bn.

Refs.: Burke's *Landed Gentry*, 13th edn., p. 1337, *s.n.* Oliphant, of Condie, co. Perth. *A.J.* xxvii. 249. Will dated 21 Aug. 1828; proved 1 Sept. 1828. M.I. in S. Park St. cemetery, Calcutta.

OLIVER, Archibald (1784-1841). Major. 23rd N.I. *b.* Weens, Hobkirk, co. Roxburgh, 7 May 1784. Cadet 1800. Arrived in India 14 Oct. 1801. Ensign 19 Oct. 1801. Lieut. 30 Sept. 1803. Capt. 19 Jan. 1816. Major 1 May 1824. Retired 29 Apr. 1826. *d.* 10 Nov. 1841.

Of Bush or Overton Bush. *bapt.* Hobkirk 15 May 1784. 2nd son of William Oliver, of Dinlabyre, sheriff-depute of co. Roxburgh, and Jane his wife, 3rd dau. of John Rutherfurd, of Edgerston, advocate. Brother of Elizabeth, mother of William Oliver Young, and of Violet, wife of David Thomas Richardson, *qq.v. m.* Calcutta 16 May 1812, Ann, dau. of John Anderson (*d.* 1812), *q.v.* (*See also* Browne Roberts and William Henville Wood.) (She died Trinity, nr. Edinburgh, 4 Feb. 1859.)

Services: Barasat C.C. Ensign d.d. 1st Eur. Regt. in 1802; posted Ensign to 4th N.I. in 1803. Second Mahratta War; Agra (w. 10 Oct. 1803); Ensign 4th N.I. (? d.d. 1/14th). With Farrukhabad Provl. Bn. 1804-6. Professor and Adjt. Barasat C.C. 1807 till 1 Sept. 1811, when it was closed down. Asst. Mily. Auditor Gen. 1811; Dy. Paymr. at Benares 1 Jan. 1813 till 1824. Capt. 2/4th N.I.; transfd. as Major to 23rd N.I. (late 2/4th) May 1824. Fur. 1824 till retirement.

Refs.: Burke's *Landed Gentry*, 13th edn., p. 1539, *s.n.* Rutherfurd, of Edgerston, co. Roxburgh. *Annals of a Border Club*, by Tancred, p. 344. Portrait by Sir J. W. Gordon at Edgerston.

OLIVER, Edward. Cornet. Cavalry. Country Cadet 1779. Cornet 7 Sept. 1779. Struck off 12 Feb. 1781.

Services: Apptd. Cadet for Cav. 19 Aug. 1779; struck off, never having joined his Corps.

OLIVER, James (1795-1843). Captain, 73rd N.I. *b.* Corstorphine, Midlothian, 4 Aug. 1795. Cadet 1811. Arrived in India Oct. 1812. Ensign 25 Sept. 1814. Lieut. 5 Dec. 1815. Capt. 21 May 1829. *d.* Delhi 30 June 1843.

bapt. Corstorphine 15 Aug. 1795. 2nd son of Rev. James Oliver, minister of Corstorphine 1792-1814, and Elizabeth Hamilton his wife, natural dau. of Douglas, Duke of Hamilton. Ed. Edinburgh High School.

Services : Cadet d.d. 2/21st N.I. 1812 ; d.d. Rangpur Local Bn. Dec. 1813 till Sept. 1814. Transfd. to 1/9th N.I. Sept. 1814. Promoted Ensign in Nov. 1814 with effect from 25 Sept. 1814, and posted to 1/23rd N.I. ; transfd. to 1/1st N.I. 25 Apr. 1815. Third Mahratta War ; Jawad ; Lieut. 1/1st N.I., with Left Div. Adjt. 1/1st N.I. 16 Oct. 1823 till July 1825. Transfd. to 2nd N.I. (late 1/1st) May 1824 ; to newly-raised 5th Extra Regt. (became 73rd N.I.) July 1825. Adjt. 73rd N.I. 12 July 1825 till 21 July 1829.

Refs. : Scott's *Fasti*, i. 8. *De Rhé-Philipe. I.M.* 10 Oct. 1843, p. 145. M.I. in Rajpura cemetery, Delhi.

OLIVER, John (1791-1844). Lieut. Colonel, 55th N.I. *b.* Bury St. Edmunds 26 July 1791. Cadet 1805. Arrived in India 14 Apr. 1807. Ensign 13 Apr. 1807. Lieut. 14 Feb. 1810. Capt. 7 Nov. 1822. Major 27 Aug. 1833. Lt. Col. 9 July 1840. *d.* Mussoorie 18 Sept. 1844.

3rd son of Laver Oliver, of Bury St. Edmunds, upholsterer, alderman 1801, and Susannah his wife, dau. of Powle Peppere, of Edmaston, farmer and maltster. *m.* Calcutta 29 July 1820, Eliza Maria, 3rd dau. of Jacques Grand-Jean de Fouchy, of Chandernagore. (*See also* Henry Hodgson.) (She died Cheltenham 23 Feb. 1871, aged 74.) His daus. *m.* Robert Campbell (1800-1889), George Moore (1789-1848), and A. G. F. J. Younghusband, *qq.v.*

Services : Posted Ensign to 11th N.I. in 1808. Reduction of Kalinjar 1812 ; Lieut. 11th N.I. Siege and capture of Hathras 1817 ; Lieut. 2/11th N.I. Third Mahratta War 1817-19 ; Lieut. 2/11th N.I. Adjt. 2/11th N.I. 1818 till 7 Nov. 1821. Offg. Sub-Asst. in Stud Dept. 23 Sept. 1823 ; permanent do. 31 July 1824 ; posted to Hissar Stud 18 Feb. 1825 ; removed from Stud Dept. 13 May 1829. Transfd. to 17th N.I. (late 2/11th) May 1824. Posted Lt. Col. to 22nd N.I. 3 Oct. 1840, and joined 24 Nov. 1840. Transfd. to 10th N.I. and joined 19 Nov. 1841 ; to 55th N.I. 15 Nov. 1843.

Refs. : Family information.. Burke's *Royal Families*, Ped. lxii. *I.M.* 6 Nov. 1844, p. 594. M.I. Landour.

OLIVER, Laver (1740-1813). Ensign. Infantry. *b.* 10 Dec. 1740. Cadet 1771. Ensign 1771. Resigned 27 Nov. 1771. *d.* Brill, Bucks., 10 Dec. 1813.

Of Kimpston, Marelands, Hants, and of Brill House, Bucks., which he rented. 2nd son of Laver Oliver, of Blackfriars, baker, and Elizabeth Wilson his wife. *m.* 21 Oct. 1785, Mary,[1] 6th dau. of John Shakespear, alderman of London, and sister of Colin Shakespear, *q.v.* (She died Leamington 1 Aug. 1845, aged 82.)

Services: Sailed for India in the *Rochford* 2 Apr. 1771. After resigning the Service he remained for some years in India, returning later to England with a fortune. He held for some time the appt. of Accountant and Auditor Gen. at the Court of Oudh; apptd. Paymr. to New Bde. at Fatehgarh 7 Aug. 1777; do. at Lucknow 29 Feb. 1780 till 31 May 1781.

Refs.: Pedigree of Shakespear of London, and of Brookwood, Hants, by Sir Thomas Phillipps, Bart., in the Bodleian. *G.M.* 1813, ii. 700. *S.M.* 1814, p. 638. M.I. in All Saints, Brill.

[1] *Note:* She and her baby were painted by Romney.

OLIVER, Thomas (1789-1872). General. Colonel 37th N.I. *b.* St. Osyth, Essex, 17 Nov. 1789. Cadet 1804. Arrived in India 25 Mar. 1806. Ensign 17 Mar. 1805. Lieut. 18 May 1805. Capt. 16 Nov. 1818. Major 18 July 1827. Lt. Col. 3 July 1832. Col. 13 Mar. 1844. Maj. Gen. 20 June 1854. Lt. Gen. 4 May 1858. Gen. 19 June 1866. *d.* 43 Duke St., Grosvenor Sq., London, 22 Apr. 1872.

Son of Samuel Oliver and Susan his wife. Marlow Cadet.

Services: Posted Lieut. to 6th N.I. in 1806. Nepal War 1814-15; Lieut. 2/6th N.I., in 1st Div. (India medal). Survey Dept. 1819-29. Asst. Surveyor of Sirmoor 2 Oct. 1819; to superintend revenue survey in Delhi territory 22 Aug. 1822. Transfd. to 3rd N.I. (late 1/6th) May 1824. Posted Lt. Col. to 3rd N.I. 9 July 1833. (? Shekhawat expedn. 1834; Lt. Col. 3rd N.I.) Fur. s.c. 28 Jan 1835 till 20 Dec. 1838. Transfd. to 12th N.I. 24 Mar. 1838, and assumed comd. 20 Jan. 1839. To comd. force at Bettiah on Nepal frontier 4 Nov. 1840. Tempy. Bdr. 2 cl. 28 Nov. 1840. Transfd. to 30th N.I. 2 Feb. 1843; to 65th N.I. 20 Jan. 1844. Fur. p.a. 14 Dec. 1843 till death. Posted Col. to 23rd N.I. 6 May 1844; to 37th N.I. 20 June 1844.

Refs.: Boase. *The Times*, 1 May 1872.

OLIVER, Thomas Samuel (1784-1841). Lieut. Colonel, 5th N.I. *b.* London 9 Sept. 1784. Cadet 1803. Arrived in India 1 Dec.

THE BENGAL ARMY, 1758-1834   429

1804. Ensign 16 Oct. 1804. Lieut. 16 Oct. 1804. Capt. 21 Oct. 1818. Major 16 May 1829. Lt. Col. 18 June 1834. *d*. 23 Nov. 1841 : kld. in action on the Bemaru heights, nr. Kabul.

bapt. St. Mary's, Whitechapel, 9 Oct. 1784. Only son of Samuel Oliver, of Antigua and of Prescot St., Bath, comdr. of the *Ceres* West Indiaman, and Jane his wife. *m.* Cawnpore 21 Dec. 1810, Frances Matilda, dau. of Frederick Marsden, *q.v.* (She *re-m.* Sir Hugh Massy Wheeler, *q.v.*)

Services : Posted Lieut. to 9th N.I. in 1805. Operations against Dhundia Khan 1807 ; Komona ; Ganauri ; Lieut. 1/9th N.I. Actg. Adjt. 5 Coys. 1/9th N.I. 20 Feb. 1809. Settlement of Hariana 1809 ;, Bhawani ; Lieut. 1/9th N.I. Operations in Oudh 1809-10 ; Pragpur ; Lieut. 1/9th N.I. With 3rd Vol. Bn. 1813-16 ; proceeded to Java Mar. 1813. Transfd. as Capt. to 2/9th N.I. With 1st Ceylon Vol. Bn. 10 Oct. 1818 till Mar. 1820. Operations in Oudh 1822 ; Bardgaon ; Capt. 2/9th N.I. Transfd. to 21st N.I. (late 2/9th) May 1824. Siege and capture of Bhurtpore ; Capt. 21st N.I. Posted Col. to 21st N.I. 24 Dec. 1834 ; transfd. to 39th N.I. 24 July 1835 ; to 8th N.I. 17 Dec. 1836 ; to 5th N.I. 25 Feb. 1840. First Afghan War 1840-1 ; left Kabul 27 Sept. 1841 in comd. of a force to punish rebels in Zurmat valley ; Kabul insurrection ; 2nd sortie from Kabul against village of Bemaru 23 Nov. (kld.) ; Lt. Col. comdg. 5th N.I.

Refs. : Caribbeana, iv. 71. Will dated Kabul 22 Sept. 1841 ; proved 11 Feb. 1842. M.I. in St. Peter's, Fort William, Bengal.

OLPHERTS, Edward (1788-1805). Cadet, Infantry. *bapt.* Armagh 29 Mar. 1788. Cadet 1803. Never arrived in India. *d. unm.* at sea 27 Jan. 1805, on board the *Harriet*, on the voyage to India.

3rd and youngest son of Richard Olpherts (who added the final 's' to his name) and Barbara his 2nd wife, 2nd dau. of William Blacker, of Carrick Blacker, co. Armagh. Cousin-german of George Blacker and Edward Dunkin, *qq.v.*

Refs. : Burke's *Landed Gentry of Ireland*, p. 537, *s.n.* Olphert, of Ballyconnell, co. Donegal.

OMMANNEY, Cornthwaite (1785-1833). Lieutenant. 23rd N.I. Subsequently Capt. 24th Light Dgns. *b.* London 26 Sept. 1785. Cadet 1803. Arrived in India 2 Sept. 1804. Ensign 2 Sept. 1804. Lieut. 21 Sept. 1804. Resigned 4 Jan. 1810. *d.* Chichester 14 Sept. 1833.

bapt. St. John the Evangelist, Westminster, 20 Oct. 1785. Son of Cornthwaite Ommanney, Rear Adm. R.N., and Martha his wife, dau. of Francis W. Manaton. Brother of Sir John Ackworth Ommanney, K.C.B., Adm. R.N. (*D.N.B.*), and uncle of Edward Lacon Ommanney, *q.v.*

Services: Posted Lieut. to 23rd N.I. in 1805; A.D.C. to Sir George Hilaro Barlow, Bart., actg. G.G., 1806. Operations against Dhundia Khan 1807; Lieut. 1/23rd N.I. Lieut. 1st Royal Dgns. (13 Aug. 1812) 17 Apr. 1815. Battle of Waterloo (s.w.). Capt. 24th Light Dgns. 24 Dec. 1818; h.p. same day.

Refs.: *Misc. Gen. et Her.* 4S. i. 61. *G.M.* 1833, ii. 555. *A.J.N.S.* xiii. 67.

OMMANNEY, Edward Lacon (1810-1896). Major Géneral. Engineers. *b.* Gt. Yarmouth 2 Oct. 1810. Cadet 1828. Arrived in India 2 Oct. 1829. 2nd Lieut. 13 Dec. 1827. Lieut. 22 Jan. 1834. Capt. 5 Apr. 1844. Major 15 Apr. 1856. Lt. Col. 1 Oct. 1857. Col. 18 Feb. 1861. Retired 1 Sept. 1863. Hon. Maj. Gen. 1 Sept. 1863. *d.* 111 Warwick Rd., London, 3 Nov. 1896.

bapt. Gt. Yarmouth 22 Oct. 1810. Son of Edward Symonds Ommanney, of Yarmouth, merchant, and Henrietta Maria his wife, eldest dau. of Sir Edmund Lacon, 1st Bart. Nephew of Cornthwaite Ommanney, *q.v.*, and of Sir Francis Molyneaux Ommanney, sometime M.P. for Barnstaple. *m.* Dacca 2 Oct. 1832, Elizabeth, 2nd dau. of John Woodhouse Martin, Asst. Surg. H.M.S. (*See also* John Welchman.) (She died 3 Mar. 1895, aged 79.) Addiscombe Cadet 1826-7.

Services: Employed in surveying Burdwan to Bihar 11 Dec. 1829, and remained in Survey Dept. till 1 May 1837. Executive Engr. Ramgarh Div. 23 Oct. 1837. Fur. p.a. 22 Feb. 1840 till 8 Apr. 1842. Offg. Executive Engr. 10th (Agra) Div. 15 Apr. 1842; Executive Engr. 3rd (Dinapore) Div. 28 Sept. 1842 till May 1854. Offg. Civil Architect and Garr. Engr. at Ft. Wm. 17 Oct. 1851; offg. Suptg. Engr. Lower Provinces 15 Oct. 1852; permanent do. 3 May 1854; do. 2nd Circle 27 Oct. 1854 till 1859. Offg. Chief Engr. Punjab 14 Apr. 1857 and 1860.

Refs.: Burke's *Peerage*, 1923, p. 1319, *s.n.* Lacon, Bart. *The Times*, 4 Nov. 1896.

*ONGE, Francis. Ensign. 1st Bengal Eur. Regt. Cadet 1764. Ensign (5 Mar. 1765) 16 Aug. 1765. Dismissed and ordered to be sent home Jan. 1767.

Services: Sailed for India in the *Lord Anson* 29 May 1764. Posted to 1st Bengal Eur. Regt. 13 Aug. 1765. Was serving in

1st Bde. at Monghyr in Oct. 1766 ; dismissed for signing an Address on behalf of Sir Robert Fletcher, *q.v.*, after the latter had been cashiered.

Refs. : *B.M. Add. MS.* 6050, p. 67. Proc. of Select Committee, 6 Jan. 1767.

Note : His name appears as John Onge in G.O. of 13 Dec. 1765 ; the surname also appears in I.O. records as Ong and Oonge. The Will of Francis Onge, Blackhorse Lane, co. Dublin, proved P.C. Dublin, 1801.

ONSLOW, Sir Matthew Richard, fourth baronet (1810-1876). Major. 4th L.C. *b.* London 12 Sept. 1810. Cadet 1826. Arrived in India 24 May 1827. Cornet 19 Nov. 1826. Lieut. 15 Nov. 1837. Capt. 8 May 1849. Retired 1 Jan. 1851. Hon. Major 28 Nov. 1854. *d.* at his seat, Hengar House, nr. Bodmin, 3 Aug. 1876.

4th Bart. ; *s.* 20 Nov. 1870. 2nd son of Sir Henry Onslow, 2nd Bart., Capt. R.A., and Caroline his wife, dau. of John Bond, of Mitcham, Surrey. *m.* 1st, Karnal 1 May 1837, Eliza Antonia, 2nd dau. of Newton Wallace, *q.v.* (*See also* William Wynne Apperley.) (She died 15 June 1854, aged 37.) *m.* 2nd, Kingston Langley, Wilts., 6 Dec. 1855, Mary, dau. of J. Salter. (She died 1892.)

Services : Cornet d.d. 9th L.C. 2 June 1827 ; posted Cornet to 4th L.C. 19 June 1827. Leave s.c. to Hills 2 Feb. 1834 till 2 Feb. 1835. Adjt. 4th L.C. 12 Mar. 1835 till 7 Feb. 1840. Fur. s.c. 12 Jan. 1840 till 15 Nov. 1842. (? Gwalior campaign ; Maharajpur ; Lieut. 4th L.C.—Bronze star.) Asst. Supt. Remount Depot at Karnal 20 Nov. 1845 till retirement.

Refs. : Burke's *Peerage*, 1923, p. 1711, *s.n.* Onslow, Bart., of Hengar House, Cornwall. *Boase. I.L.N.* 26 Aug. 1876, p. 208. *The Times,* 8 Aug. 1876.

ORANGE, John Edward (1805-1871). Ensign. 26th N.I. Subsequently Col. h.p. 34th Regt., Staff Ofr. of Pensioners at Halifax. *b.* Stafford 16 June 1805. Cadet 1824. Arrived in India 8 May 1825. Ensign 9 Jan. 1825. Resigned 10 Mar. 1826. *d.* Halifax, Yorks., 24 Feb. 1871.

bapt. St. Mary's, Stafford, 20 July 1805. Son of William Nesbitt Orange, of Caen, Capt. 38th Regt., afterwards Lt. Col. 67th Regt., and Eliza his wife, dau. of W. B. Phillipson, of Peterborough. (*Probably* related to Joseph Nesbitt, *q.v.*)

Services : Ensign d.d. 28th N.I. 23 May 1825 ; posted Ensign to 26th N.I. in 1825. First Burma War; Arakan 1825; Ensign 26th N.I. (India medal). Ensign H.M. 13th Ft. 29 June 1825; Lieut. do. 25 Oct. 1827. Lieut. 81st Ft. 20 Nov. 1828; Capt. 27 Dec. 1833 till 1844. Bt. Major 9 Nov. 1846; Bt. Lt. Col. 20 June 1854; Bt. Col. 13 Dec. 1858; h.p. of Capt. 34th Ft., unattached, 30 July 1844 till death. Staff Ofr. of Pensioners 13 Feb. 1844 till 1871.

ORCHARD, formerly JEFFERY, Joseph (1790-1847). Bt. Colonel, C.B., 1st Eur. Bengal Fus. *b.* Trinity, Newfoundland, 7 Aug. 1790. Cadet 1804. Arrived in India 11 July 1806. Ensign 1 Aug. 1806. Lieut. 3 Mar. 1808. Capt. 1 Jan. 1824. Major 15 Dec. 1830. Lt. Col. 27 July 1836. Bt. Col. 9 Nov. 1846. *d.* Sabathu 19 Feb. 1847, from injuries sustained when thrown from his horse on parade some months earlier.

Formerly Joseph White Jeffery: name changed to Joseph Orchard (*Lond. Gaz.* 13 June 1807, p. 819; M.C. 27 Sept. 1810). Late of Poole. (*Probably* son of Joseph White Orchard, who died at Poole 12 Oct. 1834, aged 81, for many yrs. an alderman of that borough.) Nephew of John Jeffery. *m.* 1st, Dinapore 23 May 1819, Sarah, 2nd dau. of Francis Kirchoffer, of Dublin, and sister of Thomas Kirchoffer, *q.v. m.* 2nd, St. John's, Calcutta, 2 June 1824, Maria Esperança Douglas, niece of John Lewis Stuart, *q.v.* (She died Agra 24 June 1856.) His dau. *m.* Christopher Hasell, *q.v.*

Services : Barasat C.C. till Mar. 1808. Posted Ensign to Bengal Eur. Regt. 1 Feb. 1807. Served in Amboyna and E. Archipelago Nov. 1810 till end of 1816. Third Mahratta War; Lieut. Eur. Flank Bn., in Centre Div. Siege and capture of Bhurtpore; Capt. 1st Bengal Eur. Bn. Fur. s.c. Mar. 1834 till 2 Jan. 1837. Posted Lt. Col. to Left Wing, Eur. Regt. Nov. 1836; transfd. to 31st N.I. Jan. 1837; to Bengal Eur. Regt. 10 Oct. 1838. First Afghan War 1838-40; capture of Ghazni (w.) (Medal); occupation of Kabul; attack on Pashut, comdg. the force; operations in Waziri valley 1840; Kajja; Lt. Col. Bengal Eur. Regt. Comdd. a Bde. of Army of Reserve (for Afghanistan) Nov. 1842 till Jan. 1843. First Sikh War; Sobraon (Medal). Apptd. to comd. 4th Bde. 14 Feb. 1846. C.B. 20 July 1838. Durani 3 cl. 15 Feb. 1842.

Refs.: De Rhé-Philipe. *G.M.* 1847, ii. 658. Will dated camp Ferozepore, 9 Feb. 1846; proved 7 May 1847. M.I. at Sabathu; name on 1st Eur. Bengal Fus. M.I. in Winchester cathedral.

ORIEL, William Churchee [1] (1792-1854). Major. 32nd N.I. *bapt.* Esher 27 Dec. 1792. Cadet 1807. Arrived in India 15 Oct.

THE BENGAL ARMY, 1758-1834

1808. Ensign 5 Nov. 1808. Lieut. 14 Nov. 1813. Capt. 1 May 1824. Major 23 Feb. 1835. Invalided 19 Sept. 1836. Retired 3 Sept. 1839. d. Marlborough Pl., St. John's Wood, London, 7 Sept. 1854, aged 61.

Son of Thomas Oriel and Mary his wife.

Services: Barasat C.C. for 8 mos. Posted Ensign to 16th N.I. in 1809. Operations in Bundelkhand 1809-11. (? Reduction of Kalinjar 1812; Ensign 2/16th N.I.) Lieut. 2/16th N.I. Intr. & Qmr. 7th Gren. Bn. 1816. Transfd. to 32nd N.I. (late 2/16th) May 1824. First Burma War; Arakan 1825; Capt. 2nd L.I. Bn. (India medal). Actg. Intr. & Qmr. 2nd L.I. Bn. 12 Oct. 1825. Fur. s.c. 3 Mar. 1832 till 5 Mar. 1836, and 3 Mar. 1837 till 2 Dec. 1840, when he was placed on the retired list with effect from 3 Sept. 1839.

Refs.: *G.M.* 1854, ii. 445. *I.M.* 19 Sept. 1854, p. 531.

¹ *Note:* His second christian name is variously given as Churchee, Churcher, and Churchey.

ORME, Alexander (1757/58-1837). Major. 22nd N.I. *b.* Scotland 1757/58. Cadet 1780. Ensign 1780. Lieut. 21 July 1781. Capt. 31 July 1799. Major 30 June 1804. Retired 5 June 1805. d. Fitzroy Sq., London, 28 Dec. 1837.

(*Perhaps* son of David Orme, writer in Edinburgh, and Margaret Guthrie his wife.) Brother of Cosmo Orme, of the firm of Longman, Orme & Co., publishers (now Messrs. Longmans, Green & Co.). *m.* Berhampore 14 Mar. 1789, Hannah Mary, 3rd dau. of John Fortnom, *q.v.* (*See also* Samuel Cox.) (She died London 19 Jan. 1857, aged 84.)

Services: Sailed for India in the *York* 12 Feb. 1780, aged 22. Bde. Major 1782-1802. Apptd. Bde. Major 1st Bde. 18 Apr. 1782; at Berhampore 1784-6; apptd. to 1st Bde. 12 June 1786; at Berhampore 1788-9; at Chunar in 1790; at Fatehgarh in July 1798. Capt. 2/3rd N.I. Transfd. to newly-raised 19th N.I. 29 May 1800. Fur. 19 Jan. 1803 till retirement. Transfd. as Major to newly-raised 22nd N.I. in 1804.

Refs.: *G.M.* 1838, i. 217; 1859, ii. 312.

ORME, David (*d.* 1797). Lieutenant, Infantry. Cadet 1783. Admitted 5 Nov. 1783. Ensign 3 Mar. 1785. Lieut. 7 Apr. 1793. d. Cawnpore 18 Nov. 1797.

Services: Apptd. Cadet 18 Dec. 1782; sailed for India in the *Duke of Kingston* 11 Mar. 1783. Posted to 5th Bengal Eur. Bn. 15 Feb. 1790; transfd. from 3rd do. to 2nd do. 22 Oct. 1792.

ORMSBY, William Carleton (1805-1875). Lieut. Colonel. 3rd Bengal Eur. Regt. *b.* Muncaster, Cumberland, 5 July 1805. Cadet 1821. Arrived in India 13 May 1822. Ensign 20 Dec. 1821. Lieut. 12 Jan. 1825. Capt. 20 Jan. 1835. Major 15 Nov. 1853. Bt. Lt. Col. 20 June 1854. Retired 1 Sept. 1855. *d. unm.* Plymouth 11 June 1875.

bapt. Muncaster 21 July 1805. 3rd son of Henry Michael Ormsby, 7th Regt., and Mary Theresa his wife, 2nd dau. of John Howard Kyan, and sister of Thomas Sutton Kyan, *q.v.*

Services : Posted Ensign to 32nd N.I. ; transfd. to 63rd N.I. (late 1/32nd) May 1824. First Burma War ; Arakan 1825 (India medal). Siege and capture of Bhurtpore ; Lieut. 63rd N.I. (clasp to India medal). Fur. s.c. 1 Apr. 1829 till 18 July 1832. Operations in the Panch Mahals against the Naickras in 1838. Fur. p.a. 20 Feb. 1840 till 28 Oct. 1842. First Sikh War ; Ferozshahr ; Sobraon (s.w.) ; Capt. 63rd N.I. (Medal with clasp). Fur. p.a. Feb. 1853 till retirement. Posted to newly-raised 3rd Bengal Eur. Regt. 15 Nov. 1853.

Refs. : Misc. Gen. et Her., 2S. ii. 222.

ORR, Alexander (1788-1825). Captain, 39th N.I. *b.* Paisley 22 Mar. 1788. Cadet 1806. Arrived in India 21 July 1807. Ensign 15 Aug. 1807. Lieut. 22 Feb. 1811. Capt. 1 May 1824. *d.* in Scotland 30 Oct. 1825.

bapt. Paisley 23 Mar. 1788. Son of John Orr, manufacturer, and Annabella Renfrew his wife.

Services : Barasat C.C. Posted Ensign to 19th N.I. in 1808. Nepal War 1814-15 ; Lieut. 1/19th N.I., in 1st Div. Third Mahratta War ; Chanda ; Lieut. 1/19th N.I. Fur. 1823 till death. Transfd. to 39th N.I. (late 2/19th) May 1824.

ORR, Edward Marjoribanks (1802-1861). Captain. 58th N.I. *b.* Edinburgh 4 Mar. 1802. Cadet 1819. Admitted 14 June 1820. Ensign 2 Dec. 1819. Lieut. 6 Nov. 1822. Capt. 26 Dec. 1830. Retired 15 Apr. 1840. *d.* 19 July 1861.

Son of John Orr, of Braehead, and of York Pl., Edinburgh, S.S.C., and Janet his wife, dau. of John Dunsmure and sister of Alexander (Conway) Dunsmure, *q.v. m.* Lohoo Ghat, U.P., 2 Oct. 1832, Lucy Maria, youngest dau. of Thomas Courtayne, of Woodpark, co. Kerry. Ed. Edin. High School.

Services : Posted Ensign to 1/29th N.I. ; transfd. to 58th N.I. (late 2/29th) May 1824. First Burma War ; Assam 1824 ; Lieut. 1/29th N.I. (India medal). Intr. & Qmr. 58th N.I. 12 July 1825.

Siege and capture of Bhurtpore ; Lieut. 58th N.I. (clasp to India medal). Adjt. Benares Provl. Bn. 6 Feb. 1826 till 28 Dec. 1827. Fur. s.c. 21 Nov. 1827 till 19 July 1830 ; p.a. 12 Nov. 1837 till retirement.

ORROK,[1] **John** (1782-1823). Captain. 17th N.I. *bapt.* West Church, Aberdeen, 26 Nov. 1782. Cadet 1798. Arrived in India 25 Nov. 1799. Ensign 22 Sept. 1799. Lieut. 28 Oct. 1799. Capt. 15 Feb. 1808. Retired 8 Jan. 1820. *d.* suddenly Aberdeen 6 Oct. 1823, from a ruptured blood-vessel in the head.

Of Orrok, co. Aberdeen. 2nd son of John Orrok, Capt. E.I.C.N.S. (who purchased the estate of Colpnaw in psh. of Belhelvie and changed its name to Orrok), and Sarah his wife, eldest dau. of Bailie John Dingwall, of Rannieston, co. Aberdeen, and sister of Agnes, mother of John Thomson (1801-1840), *q.v. m.* 2 Aug. 1823, Mary, dau. of James Cockburn, of Lime St. Sq., London. (She died 1 Jan. 1861.) Aberdeen Univ. ; matric. 1794.

Services : Posted Lieut. to 2/17th N.I. 15 Apr. 1801. Operations in Jumna Doab 1803 ; Lieut. 2/17th N.I. Second Mahratta War ; Lieut. 2/17th N.I. Capt. Lt. 17th N.I. 8 Jan. 1808. Fur. 1811-14. Nepal War 1814-15 ; Capt. 1/17th N.I., in 2nd Div. Transfd. to 2/17th N.I. Fur. 1817 till retirement.

Refs. : *Misc. Gen. et Her.* 4S. v. 4-5. *Letters of John Orrok,* p. 212. *Scottish N. & Q.* 3S. viii. 144. *G.M.* 1823, ii. 646. *S.M.* 1823, ii. 767. M.I. inside gable of Old Church, Belhelvie.

[1] *Note :* The name frequently appears as Orrock.

OSBORN, Henry Roche (1798-1849). Lieut. Colonel, 13th N.I. *b.* 26 Jan. 1798. Cadet 1818. Arrived in India Oct. 1819. Ensign (?) Lieut. 1 Jan. 1821. Capt. 18 May 1833. Major 13 Jan. 1842. Lt. Col. 18 July 1848. *d.* Ferozepore 10 Mar. 1849.

bapt. Swanage 29 June 1798. Son of William Osborn, Lieut. R.N., and Elizabeth his wife. *m.* Agra (? Koil) 10 Aug. 1830, Charlotte, 3rd dau. of Major Robert Durie, 11th Light Dgns. (*See also* William Beckett (1798-1844).) (She died Midhurst 22 Sept. 1894, aged 85.) Father of Lt.-Col. Robert Durie Osborn (*D.N.B.*).

Services : d.d. Bengal Eur. Regt. Nov 1819 ; do. 1/25th N.I. May 1820. Posted to 1/27th N.I. Jan. 1821. d.d. 1st Nassiri Bn. 8 Jan. till Nov. 1822, and Mar.-Oct. 1823. Transfd. to 54th N.I. (late 2/27th) May 1824. Actg. Adjt. 54th N.I. Sept. 1824. Supy. S.A.C.G. Sept. 1825. Siege and capture of Bhurtpore ; Supy. S.A.C.G. S.A.C.G. 27 Mar. 1826 ; D.A.C.G. 2 cl. 26 Aug.

1831; 1 cl. 10 July 1834; A.C.G. 2 cl. 14 Aug. 1837 till 20 Dec. 1842. Apptd. A.C.G., 1st Inf. Div., Army of the Indus, 13 Sept. 1838, but left in Jan. 1839 owing to ill health. Leave s.c. Cape and Tasmania 9 Feb. 1841 till 30 Dec. 1842. Comdd. 54th N.I. 31 Mar. 1843 till May 1846. First Sikh War; Ferozshahr; Major comdg. 54th N.I. (Medal). Fur. s.c. May 1846 till 9 Nov. 1848. Posted Lt. Col. to 12th N.I. Aug. 1848; to 61st N.I. 10 Oct. 1848; to 18th N.I. 24 Oct. 1848; to 13th N.I. (then on service) 19 Nov. 1848. Apptd. to comd. post of Ramnagar 10 Jan. 1849. His death occurred whilst he was on his way to Mussoorie on sick leave.

Refs.: De Rhé-Philipe. Will dated 18 Sept. 1848; proved 3 Mar. 1849. M.I. in Civil cemetery, Ferozepore.

OSBORN, Thomas Hoadley (or Hadley) (*d.* 1789). Ensign. Infantry. Cadet 1783. Ensign 14 Jan. 1785. Struck off 1789. *d.* Chinsura, Bengal, 21 Feb. 1789.

Services: Lieut. Staffs. Mil. 21 Mar. 1780. Apptd. Cadet 8 Apr. 1783; sailed for India in the *Berrington* 2 Feb. 1784. Granted fur. on h.p. 2 Oct. 1786. Transfd. to H.M.S. Ensign 76th Ft. 1 Nov. 1788.

*OSBORNE, John (*d.* 1821). Major. Comdt. of Nawab-Wazir of Oudh's L.I. Bn. Country Cadet 1766. Ensign May 1766. Lieut. 2 Sept. 1767. Capt. (?) Major (in 1779). Resigned before July 1787. *d.* Melchet Park 9 Jan. 1821.

Of Melchet Park, Wilts. (now Melchet Court, Hants), which he purchased from John Lockhart in 1791-2, where he erected in 1800 a Hindu temple, designed by Thomas Daniell, R.A., dedicated to his patron Warren Hastings. *m.* 2 June 1785, Margaret, 2nd dau. of Gen. James Whorwood Adeane, M.P. for Cambs., and sister of the mother of George John Law, *q.v.* (She survived him.)

Services: Came out in a private capacity. Was a junior officer in the 1st Bde. at Monghyr in Oct. 1766; dismissed and ordered home in Jan. 1767 for having signed an Address in favour of Sir Robert Fletcher, *q.v.*, after the latter had been cashiered. Reinstated 1767. Tried by C.M. in 1770 for "unmannerly, unmilitary and disrespectful behaviour" to Lt.-Col. James Morgan, *q.v.*, and suspended from the Service for one month. Osborne thereupon called out Col. Morgan and shot him in the hip-bone, after which he left Dinapore without leave and went to Patna, and ultimately to Calcutta, whence he was sent back to Patna under escort. For these irregularities committed during his suspension he was again tried by C.M. (May-Sept. 1771) and sentenced to dismissal. Appealed to C.D. in Dec. 1772 against his dismissal; requests to be restored to his rank 26 Feb. 1776. Appears to have been allowed to enter the Nawab's service c. 1778; arrived Lucknow c. July 1778 and was given comd. of the Nawab's L.I. Bn. He held this comd., latterly as Major, until the corps was disbanded in 1780. Sailed for England from Calcutta Dec. 1780; returned to India in the *Berrington*, which sailed 2 Feb. 1784. Acted as host to Warren Hastings at Melchet Park in Oct. 1811.

Refs.: Burke's *Landed Gentry*, 13th edn., p. 7, *s.n.* Adeane, of Babraham, Cambs. *B.: P.P.* No. 80, pp. 71-8. Lawson's *Life of Warren Hastings*, pp. 248-9. *Macpherson*, pp. 56, 67, 69, 75. *N. & Q.* cliv. 190. *Eur. Mag.* xliii. pp. 448-9. *Bath Chron.* 11 Jan. 1821. Admon. 15 Feb. 1821: another grant was taken out in 1854.

O'SHEA, Andrew (1787-1817). Captain, 8th N.I. *b.* Cork 21 Mar. 1787. Cadet 1803. Arrived in India 2 Dec. 1804. Ensign 7 Oct. 1804. Lieut. 8 Oct. 1804. Dismissed by G.C.M. 12 July 1807. Restored 27 Jan. 1809. Capt. 31 Oct. 1816. *d.* Mirzapur, U.P., 18 Nov. 1817.

2nd son of Andrew O'Shea, of Baker St., Portman Sq., London, and Clara (or Clarissa) his wife, dau. of Thomas Trant.

Services: Posted Lieut. to 8th N.I. in 1805. Operations against Apparbal Singh 1806; storm of Badekh; Lieut. 2/8th N.I. Capture of Mauritius 1810; Lieut. 2nd Vol. Bn. Nepal War 1816; Lieut. 2/8th N.I., in 4th Bde. Centre Column.

Refs.: G.M. 1818, i. 639. M.I. Mirzapur.

OSWALD, John (*d.* 1761). Captain, Infantry. Lieut. 16 Oct. 1757. Capt. 9 Dec. 1758. *d.* 1761.

Services: Ensign on Madras Est. Served in Bengal under Clive 1757; battle of Plassey; Ensign in Capt. G. F. Gaupp's Coy. of Madras Inf. Transfd. to Bengal Est. 1757.

OTTLEY, George O'Bryen (1810-1880). Lieut. Colonel. 5th Bengal Eur. Inf. *b.* I. of Antigua 21 Sept. 1810. Cadet 1826. Arrived in India 5 Oct. 1827. Ensign (20 May 1827) 3 Jan. 1828. Lieut. 1 Apr. 1829. Capt. 28 Feb. 1850. Major 29 July 1857. Retired 31 Mar. 1859. Hon. Lt. Col. 31 Mar. 1859. *d.* 225 Cornwall Rd., London, 1 Oct. 1880.

Of Alban Tower, S. Norwood. Eldest son of George Weatherill Ottley, of Antigua, planter, and member of council for that I., and Jane his wife, dau. of Boyce Ledwell, of Antigua. Cousin-german of Richard Horsford, *q.v. m.* Chunar 31 Jan. 1843, Mary

Arabella Burges, 6th and youngest dau. of William Lamb, *q.v.* (*See also* William Barr.) (She died London 7 Jan. 1895, aged 70.)

Services: Posted Ensign to 6th N.I. 3 Jan. 1828; actg. Intr. & Qmr. 73rd N.I. 24 Dec. 1836; do. 40th N.I. 27 Mar. 1837. Fur. s.c. 11 May 1838 till 18 July 1841. Actg. Intr. & Qmr. 69th N.I. 17 Sept. 1841; rejoined his Regt. Jan. 1842. First Afghan War 1842; with Gen. Pollock's force; offg. S.A.C.G. at Jalalabad 8 Sept. 1842 (Medal). Offg. Intr. & Qmr. 1st L.C. 31 Jan. 1843. Actg. S.S.O. at Muttra 5 May 1843. Asst. to Resdt. in Nepal, and comd. his escort, 28 Sept. 1844 till 1845. Fur. s.c. 27 Jan. 1847 till Nov. 1849. Sub-Asst. in Stud Dept. at Ghazipur 15 July 1853; Asst. 2 cl. at Ghazipur 2 June 1854 till 1857. Fur. s.c. Aug. 1857 till retirement.

Refs.: Burke's *Landed Gentry*, 4th edn., p. 1136, *s.n.* Ottley, of the West Indies. *The Times*, 4 Oct. 1880. Oliver's *Hist. of Antigua*, ii. 372.

OTTO, William (1788-1817). Lieutenant, 11th N.I. *b.* Dalkeith 20 July 1788. Cadet 1803. Arrived in India 2 Dec. 1804. Ensign 6 Oct. 1804. Lieut. 6 Oct. 1804. *d.* 19 Jan. 1817.

bapt. Dalkeith 14 Aug. 1788. Son of William Otto, merchant, and Christian Briggs his wife.

Services: Posted Lieut. to 11th N.I. in 1805. Reduction of Kalinjar 1812; Lieut. 1/11th N.I.

OUSELEY, John Ralph (1801-1850). Lieut. Colonel, 57th N.I. *b.* London 12 May 1801. Cadet 1817. Admitted 15 Aug. 1818. Ensign 14 Mar. 1818. Lieut. 1 Aug. 1818. Capt. 2 Oct. 1829. Major 2 Dec. 1836. Lt. Col. 5 Feb. 1843. *d.* Dinapore 17 Feb. 1850.

2nd son of Sir William Ouseley, Kt., of Crickhowell, the Oriental scholar and traveller (*D.N.B.*), and Julia Frances his wife, dau. of Lt.-Col. John Irving. Brother of Richard Ouseley, *q.v.*, and nephew of Joseph Walker Jasper Ouseley, *q.v.* His sisters *m.* Sir John Fowler Bradford, *q.v.*, and John Augustus Scott, *q.v.* *m.* 1839, " Elizabeth Sophia, dau. of a high caste Brahmin." (She died 9 Mar. 1868.) Ed. Harrow; admitted 1816, left the same year.

Services: Posted Lieut. to 1/30th N.I. in 1818. Junior Asst. to A.G.G., Saugor & Narbada territories, 7 May 1823 till 1834. Transfd. to 60th N.I. (late 2/30th) May 1824. Placed at disposal of C.-in-C. during employment of his Regt. at Bhurtpore. Siege and capture of Bhurtpore; Lieut. 60th N.I. P.A. Hoshangabad

1834 ; offg. A.G.G., S.W. frontier, 6 Feb. 1839 ; permanent do. 27 June 1839 till Nov. 1849, when he was removed from his appt. and ordered to join his Regt., 57th N.I. Posted Lt. Col. to 42nd N.I. 18 May 1843 ; transfd. to 45th N.I. 1 Dec. 1843 ; to 11th N.I. 9 Aug. 1844 ; to 67th N.I. 1846 ; to 57th N.I. 1849.

Refs.: Foster's *Baronetage*, p. 477, *s.n.* Ouseley, Bart. *Harrow School Register. I.M.* 22 Mar. 1850, p. 160 ; 18 Apr. 1850, p. 225.

OUSELEY, Joseph Walker Jasper (1800-1889). Colonel. 40th N.I. *b.* 21 June 1800. Cadet 1818. Ensign (?) Lieut. 1 Jan. 1821. Capt. 8 Apr. 1827. Major 30 Nov. 1840. Lt. Col. 11 Mar. 1847. Retired 17 Sept. 1846. Hon. Col. 28 Nov. 1854. *d.* 10 Inverness Terr., London, 29 Oct. 1889.

bapt. Limerick 29 June 1800. 3rd son of Major Ralph Ouseley and Mary his 2nd wife, dau. of —— Collins. Half-brother of Sir William Ouseley, Kt. (*D.N.B.*), and of Sir Gore Ouseley, 1st Bart. (*D.N.B.*). *m.* Ghazipur 31 Dec. 1822, Elizabeth, dau. of Rev. William Palmer, Bengal chaplain, and sister of Henry Palmer, *q.v.* (*See also* Sir Francis Wheler, Bart.) (She died Calcutta 18 June 1842.)

Services : Ensign d.d. Bengal Eur. Regt. 1819 ; posted to 1/14th N.I. in 1820. Mily. student at Coll. of Ft. Wm. 1820-2 ; passed honour examination in Persian and Arabic. Intr. & Qmr. 1/14th N.I. 1822-3. Transfd. to 28th N.I. (late 1/14th) May 1824. Examiner at Coll. of Ft. Wm. 1823-32 ; apptd. Professor of Persian and Arabic 17 Mar. 1825 ; Sec. and librarian to the Coll. 7 Apr. 1832 till 1838. Supt. Mysore Princes 11 July 1838, and Persian Translator under Govt. till 1 June 1844. Fur. 17 Mar. 1844 till retirement. Posted as Lt. Col. to 40th N.I. in 1847, but shortly after retired with effect from 17 Sept. 1846. Professor of Persian and Arabic at Haileybury 1844-59 ; Examiner in Oriental languages to Civil Service Commission 1862-83 ; one of the Council of King's Coll., London.

Refs. : Foster's *Baronetage*, p. 477, *s.n.* Ouseley, Bart. *D.I.B.* Boase. *The Times*, 31 Oct. 1889, p. 5 ; 9 Nov. 1889, p. 6.

OUSELEY, Richard (1809-1868). Lieut. Colonel. 50th N.I. *b.* 29 June 1809. Cadet 1825. Arrived in India 18 Mar. 1826. Ensign 28 Sept. 1825. Lieut. 10 Jan. 1829. Capt. 9 May 1848. Bt. Major 11 Nov. 1851. Removed from the Service 3 Mar. 1853.[1] *d.s.p.* 9 Aug. 1868.

bapt. Crickhowell, co. Brecon, 26 July 1809. 3rd son of Sir William Ouseley, Kt., and Julia Frances his wife. Brother of

John Ralph Ouseley, *q.v.*, and of Sir William Gore Ouseley, K.C.B. (*D.N.B.*). m. 29 June 1836, Frances Sarah Place, dau. of William Walter Jones, of Gurrey, co. Carmarthen. (She *re-m.* 9 Apr. 1870, Sir Atwell King Lake, Bart.)

Services: Posted Ensign to 50th N.I. Asst. to Comr. in Chota Nagpur Nov. 1832; Senior Asst. to A.G.G., S.W. frontier, 9 Dec. 1833. Fur. s.c. 19 Aug. 1834 till 18 Sept. 1838. Offg. Asst. to A.G.G., S.W. frontier, 4 Mar. till 1 June 1840; Junior Asst. to Comr. in Chota Nagpur 12 Aug. 1840; Principal Asst. to A.G.G., S.W. frontier, 22 Jan. 1844; rejoined 50th N.I. 4 Oct. 1848. Fur. s.c. 30 Jan. 1849 till 20 Dec. 1851. Suspended 11 Dec. 1852. No record of active service.

Refs.: Foster's *Baronetage*, p. 477. *I.M.* 17 July 1852, p. 417; 17 May 1853, p. 256.

[1] *Note:* Without prejudice to his retiring pension. More than 10 yrs. later he was placed on the retired list as Lt. Col.

OWEN, Arthur (1782-1824). Major, 26th N.I. *bapt.* St. Bridget's, Dublin, 26 Sept. 1782. Cadet 1798. Arrived in India 26 Mar. 1800. Ensign 1 Jan. 1800. Lieut. 29 May 1800. Capt. 7 Aug. 1814. Major 1 May 1824. *d.* Calcutta 11 Oct. 1824.

Son of Rev. Hugh Owen and Mary his wife. *m.* a dau. of Andrew Wilson Hearsey, *q.v.*, sister of Hyder Young Hearsey (Appendix A) and half-sister of Sir John Bennet Hearsey, *q.v.* (*See also* James Oram Clarkson.)

Services: Posted Lieut. to 1/13th N.I. 15 Apr. 1801. Second Mahratta War; Bundelkhand 1803-6; Kapsa; Kalpi; defeat of Rajah Ram Singh; capture of Jaitpur; Lieut. 1/13th N.I. Adjt. 2/13th N.I. 28 Aug. 1809 till 27 Oct. 1814. Pindari War; Asirgarh 1819; Capt. 2/13th N.I. First Burma War; Chittagong 1824; Capt. 2/13th N.I. Transfd. as Major to 26th N.I. (late 1/13th) May 1824.

Refs.: Will dated Chittagong Sept. 1824; proved 4 Dec. 1824.

OWEN, John (1757/58-1827). Lieut. Colonel. 6th N.I. *b.* 1757/58. Cadet 1779. Admitted 12 Feb. 1780. Ensign 13 June 1779. Lieut. 7 Feb. 1781. Capt. 30 Oct. 1797. Major 30 Sept. 1803. Lt. Col. 19 Feb. 1806. Retired 29 Nov. 1809. *d.* London 27 Mar. 1827.

A native of Herts. Uncle of John Owen, *q.v.*

Services: Apptd. Cadet 28 Oct. 1778; sailed for India in the *Atlas* 7 Mar. 1778, aged 21. Adjt. 9th Bn. Sepoys in Mar. 1786

THE BENGAL ARMY, 1758-1834 441

and in 1795 ; Capt. 3rd N.I. in 1798. Fur. 20 Jan. 1799 till 13 Aug. 1804. Major 3rd N.I. Comdg. at Chittagong in 1805 ; posted Lt. Col. to 2nd N.I. in 1806. Fur. 17 Feb. 1808 till retirement. Transfd. to 6th N.I. in 1809.

OWEN, John (1782-1823). Major, Invalid Est. 28th N.I. *bapt.* St. Mary's, Reed, Herts., 2 Aug. 1782. Cadet 1796. Arrived in India 9 Nov. 1798. Ensign 17 Oct. 1797. Lieut. 10 Sept. 1798. Capt. 23 Feb. 1807. Major 1 Aug. 1818. Invalided 10 Nov. 1821. *d.* Cawnpore 5 Dec. 1823.
Son of William Owen and Mary his wife. Brother of Thomas Owen, *q.v.*
Services: Posted Lieut. to 8th N.I. 1798. Operations in Jumna Doab 1803 ; Sasni ; Bijaigarh ; Kachaura ; Lieut. 8th N.I. Capt. Lt. 8th N.I. 25 Dec. 1804. Second Mahratta War ; Capt. Lt. 8th N.I. Fur. 1810-12. Transfd. to newly-raised 2/28th N.I. in 1815. Third Mahratta War ; Dhamoni ; Bt. Major 2/28th N.I.

OWEN, John Ord (1806-1847). Lieutenant. 5th N.I. *b.* London 26 Oct. 1806. Cadet 1824. Ensign 13 Apr. 1825. Lieut. 2 Feb. 1827. Resigned 4 Jan. 1828. *d.* nr. Dublin 12 Apr. 1847.
bapt. Fulham 29 Dec. 1806. 3rd and youngest son of Rev. John Owen, of Fulham, and Charlotte his wife. Ed. Charterhouse Jan. 1820-Dec. 1823 ; Cambridge Univ. Magdalen Hall, Oxon. ; matric. 26 June 1828.
Services: Posted Ensign to 5th N.I. No record of active service.
Refs.: Charterhouse School List. Alumni Oxon. G.M. 1847, i. 670.

OWEN, Thomas (1788-1820). Captain, 16th N.I. *b.* Hormead, Herts., 10 Oct. 1788. Cadet 1803. Arrived in India 14 Aug. 1804. Ensign 23 Aug. 1804. Lieut. 21 Sept. 1804. Capt. 1 Aug. 1818. *d.* Kishenganj, B. & O., 12 Aug. 1820.
Son of William Owen and Mary his wife. Brother of William Owen, *q.v.*, of Mrs. Holmes, and of the Misses R. and S. Owen.
Services: Posted Lieut. to 16th N.I. Operations in Bundelkhand 1807 ; Chamir ; Sehlehuganj ; Lieut. 1/16th N.I. Operations in Bundelkhand against Gopal Singh 1810-11 ; Lieut. 1/16th N.I. Actg. Adjt. 1/16th N.I. in 1812.
Refs.: Will dated Chittagong 22 May 1818 ; codicil dated Kishenganj 6 Aug. 1820 ; proved 11 Oct. 1820.

*OWEN, Thomas Colby (1727/28-1765/66). Cadet. Infantry. Afterwards Lieutenant Madras Est. *b.* Twickenham, Middlesex, 1727/28. Cadet 1759. Transfd. to Madras Est. 1759. *d.* in India before 1 Apr. 1766.

Services: Apptd. Cadet for Bengal Mar. 1759; sailed for India in the *Prince Henry* in 1759, aged 31. Ensign (Madras) 26 Oct. 1759; Lieut. 31 Dec. 1762. Assault of Madura 26 June 1764 (w.); Lieut. Madras Inf.

Refs.: Will dated 27 Nov. 1764; proved (Madras) 14 Oct. 1766.

OWEN, William (1784-1804). Lieutenant, 2nd N.I. *bapt.* Reed, Herts., 3 Oct. 1784. Cadet 1799. Arrived in India 7 Jan. 1801. Ensign 13 Oct. 1800. Lieut. 13 July 1803. *d.* Sikandra 24 Aug. 1804: kld. in action on the banks of the Banas R. during Monson's retreat.[1]

Son of William Owen and Mary his wife. Brother of John Owen, *q.v.*, and nephew of John Owen, *q.v.*

Services: Posted Lieut. to 1/2nd N.I. 17 Apr. 1801. Operations in Jumna Doab 1803; Sasni; Bijaigarh; Kachaura; Lieut. 2nd N.I. Second Mahratta War; battle of Delhi; Agra; Monson's retreat (kld.); Lieut. 2/2nd N.I.

Refs.: Pester, p. 192.

[1] *Note:* (? Taken prisoner by Holkar at Hinglaisgarh fort 16 July 1804, and subsequently murdered by him at the Bundi Pass, Rajputana.)

P

PADMAN, Selby (*d.* 1772). Captain. Bengal Eur. Regt. Subsequently Fort Marlbro' C.S. Lieut. (from H.M.S.) 5 Aug. 1765. Capt. 15 Sept. 1767. Resigned 21 Dec. 1767. *d.* Fort Marlbro', Sumatra, 20 Apr. 1772.

Son of Selby Padman, of Hampstead. Brother of Jenner and Margaret Padman.

Services: Ensign H.M. 84th Ft. 26 June 1762; Lieut. do. 20 Jan. 1764; h.p. do. 25 Dec. 1764 till death. Apptd. in England 28 Dec. 1764, Lieut. on the Bengal Est.; sailed in the *Grenville* 4 Mar. 1765. Lieut. in 3rd Bde. in May 1766, when he resigned his Commission during the "Batta mutiny"; restored soon afterwards. Apptd. in England 31 Jan. 1770, Factor on Fort Marlbro' Est.

Refs.: Will dated Fort Marlbro', 18 Apr. 1772; proved 19 May 1773.

PAGE, Gore (1803-1820). Ensign, Infantry. *b.* Bredwardine, co. Hereford, 29 July 1803. Cadet 1818. Ensign 16 Aug. 1819. *d.* nr. Allahabad 27 Sept. 1820: drowned whilst bathing from his budgerow.

bapt. Bredwardine 18 Aug. 1803. Youngest son (of 20 children) of John Page and Charlotte Ann his wife. Brother of Henry Edwin Page, *q.v.*

Services: Ensign d.d. Bengal Eur. Regt. 1819.

Refs.: *A.J.* xi. 511.

PAGE, Gregory (1789-1819). Bt. Captain, 7th N.I. *b.* London 10 Apr. 1789. Cadet 1804. Arrived in India 21 June 1806. Ensign 10 Oct. 1805. Lieut. 26 Nov. 1805. Bt. Capt. 1 Jan. 1819. *d.* at the Cape 14 June 1819.

bapt. St. Bartholomew, Exchange, London, 9 May 1789. Son of John Page and Mary his wife. Marlow Cadet.

Services: Posted Lieut. to 7th N.I. in 1807. Reduction of Kalinjar 1812; Lieut. 1/7th N.I. Nepal War 1814-15; Lieut. 1/7th N.I., in 2nd Div. (? Third Mahratta War; Lieut. 1/7th N.I.)

Refs.: *G.M.* 1819, ii. 377. *S.M.* 1819, ii. 487.

PAGE, Henry Edwin (1788-1829). Captain, Invalid Est. 15th N.I. *b.* Gloucester 27 Oct. 1788. Cadet 1803. Arrived in India 30 Aug. 1804. Ensign 20 Aug. 1804. Lieut. 21 Sept.

1804. Capt. 2 Jan. 1815. Invalided 1 Oct. 1815. d. Monghyr 31 Aug. 1829.

Son of John Page, of Wick, nr. Worcester. Brother of Gore Page, q.v. m. Calcutta 3 July 1812, Jane, dau. of Thomas Morgan (1760/61-1814), q.v. (See also Nathaniel Barrett Bromley.) (She died Calcutta 12 July 1847, aged 55.)

Services: Posted Lieut. to 2/15th N.I. in 1805; actg. Adjt. do. in 1809. Leave s.c. to Penang 1810-11. First Nepal War 1814-15; Capt. 2/15th N.I., in 4th Div. Fort Adjt. at Monghyr 10 Oct. 1816 till death. Leave s.c. to Cape Dec. 1816 till Dec. 1818; do. to Mauritius 1827-8.

Refs.: *Memoirs and Remains of Capt. H. E. Page*, by Andrew Leslie, Calcutta, 1830. Will dated 26 Aug. 1820; proved 22 Oct. 1829. M.I. at Monghyr.

PAGE, John (1803-1822). Lieutenant, 2nd L.C. b. Bennington, Herts., 12 July 1803. Cadet 1819. Cornet 10 Jan. 1820. Lieut. 3 Apr. 1822. d. Kaitha, U.P., 14 Sept. 1822.

bapt. Bennington 11 Sept. 1803. Son of William Page, Bo.C.S.; sometime member of council at Bombay, and Betty his 2nd wife, widow of William Freeman, Bo.C.S. Ed. Charterhouse Jan 1812-May 1819.

Services: Posted Cornet to 2nd L.C. No record of active service.
Refs.: *Charterhouse School List.* M.I. Kaitha.

PALEY, William (1811-1848). Captain, Artillery. (636) bapt. Witney, Oxon., 13 Nov. 1811. Cadet 1829. Arrived in India 30 May 1830. 2nd Lieut. (11 Dec. 1829) 30 May 1830. Lieut. 31 Dec. 1838. Capt. 1 Dec. 1847. d. Saugor 6 Feb. 1848.

Son of Rev. James Paley, vicar of Laycock, Wilts., and Alice his wife. Grandson of Archdeacon William Paley (*D.N.B.*). Addiscombe Cadet 1827-30.

Services: Apptd. Actg. 2nd Lieut. (having been over 2 yrs. in India) 2 July 1832. Actg. Adjt. Art. at Nimach 12 Jan. 1836; actg. Adjt. & Qmr. Nimach Div. Art. 12 Aug. 1838. Fur. s.c. 2 Mar. 1839 till 10 Feb. 1842. Comdt. of Art., Malwa Contingent, 2 Dec. 1842 till 29 Aug. 1845. No record of active service.

Refs.: Burke's *Landed Gentry*, 13th edn., p. 1359, s.n. Paley, formerly of Langcliffe and Ampton, Yorks. *Bath Chron.* 13 Apr. 1848. *I.M.* 4 Apr. 1848, p. 202. M.I. Saugor.

PALIN, Robert William (1809-1839). Lieutenant. 5th N.I. b. Serore, nr. Poona, 2 Dec. 1809. Cadet 1825. Arrived in

THE BENGAL ARMY, 1758-1834   445

India 21 Sept. 1826. Ensign 2 Mar. 1826. Lieut. 4 Jan. 1828. Resigned (? pensioned) 12 Mar. 1834. d. Calcutta 8 June 1839.

Son of Capt. Thomas Palin, 10th Bo. N.I. (who was son of Thomas Palin, of Painswick, clothier), and Elizabeth his wife. Cousin-german of Henry Weaver, q.v. Ed. Christ's Hospital.

Services : Posted Ensign to 5th N.I. 25 Sept. 1826. No record of active service.

Refs. : Atlas, 31 Aug. 1839.

PALK, Walter (1788-1812). Lieutenant, 6th N.I. b. at sea off the Cape 19 Apr. 1788. Cadet 1804. Arrived in India 25 Mar. 1806. Ensign 14 Mar. 1806. Lieut. 2 Feb. 1807. d. Delhi 9 July 1812.

Son of Thomas Palk, M.C.S., and Catherine his wife, dau. of Thomas Pelling, merchant, of the firm of Pelling & de Fries, Madras. Gt. nephew of Sir Robert Palk, 1st Bart., Govr. of Madras, and kinsman of Charles Welland, q.v. Cousin-german of Thomas Samuel Gibson (Appendix C).

Services : Barasat C.C. Posted to 1/6th N.I. in 1807. No record of active service.

PALLMER, Hampson Beckford (1781-?). Captain, 1st N.I. b. London 12 Feb. 1781. Cadet 1799. Arrived in India 8 Jan. 1801. Ensign 10 Aug. 1800. Lieut. 2 Oct. 1800. Capt. 7 Mar. 1813. Struck off 14 July 1812.

bapt. Marylebone 13 Mar. 1781. Son of Hampson Pallmer and Ismeney (? Ismay) Bruce his wife. Brother of John William Pallmer, q.v.

Services : Posted Lieut. to 1/1st N.I. 17 Apr. 1801. Operations in Bundelkhand 1804-6 ; Lieut. 1/1st N.I. Fur. 22 Jan. 1810 till struck off in 1817 with effect from 14 July 1812. Capt. Lt. 1st N.I. 25 Aug. 1811.

PALLMER, John William (1785-1816). Capt. Lieutenant, 22nd N.I. b. London 27 July 1785. Cadet 1800. Arrived in India 14 Oct. 1801. Ensign 5 Nov. 1801. Lieut. 30 Sept. 1803. Capt. Lt. 1 Sept. 1815. d. Calcutta 23 May 1816.

bapt. St. Margaret's, Westminster, 3 Sept. 1785. Son of Hampson Pallmer and Ismeney (or Ismay) his wife. Brother of Hampson Beckford Pallmer, q.v.

Services : Ensign d.d. 15th N.I. in 1802 ; posted to 16th N.I. ; transfd. to newly-raised 22nd N.I. 22 Dec. 1803. Adjt. & Qmr.

22nd N.I. 14 Feb. 1807 till July 1814 ; Intr. & Qmr. 2/22nd N.I.
1 July 1814 till 30 Oct. 1815. Nepal War 1816 ; Capt. 2/22nd
N.I., in 3rd Bde. Centre Column.

PALMER, Charles (1730/31-1764). Captain. Infantry. Subsequently Captain Bombay Est. *b.* 1730/31. Capt. (from Bo. Est.) 14 June 1757. Resigned 23 Oct. 1759. *d.v.p.* Sumatra 1764, aged 33.

Eldest son of Sir Charles Palmer, 5th Bart., of Dorney Court, and Anne his wife, dau. of Richard Harcourt. Cousin-german of Anna, maternal grandmother of C. G. Landon, *q.v. m.* 1st, 1757, Anna Martha, younger dau. of Rev. Gervas Bellamy, senior chaplain at Calcutta. (She died Calcutta 25 Sept. 1758, aged 18.) *m.* 2nd, Sarah, dau. of Thomas Clack, of Wallingford, and sister of Frances, Viscountess Courtenay. Father of Sir Charles Harcourt Palmer, 6th and last Bart.

Services : Ensign 2nd Regt. of Ft. Gds. Arrived in Bengal Mar. 1757 as a Lieut. with the Bombay detachment and served under Clive ; transfd. to Bengal Est. 1757. Battle of Plassey, having previously voted at the council of war against coming to immediate action. Was one of eleven signatories to the Memorial, dated Calcutta, 28 Aug. 1758, protesting against supercession by John Gowen, *q.v.* Resigned for fur. s.c. 23 Oct. 1759, and returned to England ; readmitted to Bo. Est. as Capt. 16 Apr. 1760.

Refs. : Burke's *Extinct Barts.* p. 602. *Orme MSS.—India*, xiii. p. 3639. *Broome,* p. 139. *Hill,* iii. 53. Will dated Nattal, Sumatra, 25 July 1764 ; proved (Bombay) 27 Sept. 1764.

PALMER, Charles Henry (1782-1803). Lieutenant, Artillery. (303) *b.* at the Cape July 1782. Cadet 1797. Arrived in India 26 June 1801. Fireworker (?) Lieut. 14 Feb. 1802. *d.* P.W.I. 30 July 1803, of a bilious fever.

Woolwich Cadet ; nominated for R.M.A. 29 Aug. 1798 ; obtained his certificate 5 Dec. 1800.

Services : Sailed for India in the *Active* in 1801. Expedn. to Macao 1801 till Nov. 1802 ; Lieut. 4th Coy. 1st Bn. Art.

Refs. : Stubbs, i. 199. *A.A.R.* vi. 177.

PALMER, Francis Charles [1] (1792-1862). Captain, Pension Est. 9th L.C. *b.* Calcutta 3 Apr. 1792. Cadet 1807. Arrived in India 14 Sept. 1808. Cornet 19 Sept. 1808. Lieut. 5 Nov. 1818. Capt. (9 Apr. 1823) 13 May 1825. Pensioned 28 Dec. 1827. *d.* Calcutta 19 Nov. 1862.[2]

bapt. Calcutta 8 June 1792. Eldest son of John Palmer, of the firm of Palmer & Co., Calcutta, "Prince of British merchants" and "The friend of the poor," and Mary Sarah Hampton his wife. Grandson of William Palmer (1740-1816), *q.v.* His sister *m.* Llewellyn Conroy, *q.v.* *m.* Calcutta 8 Feb. 1832, Miss Anne Elizabeth Burrows. Ed. Eton; in Remove in 1805. Haileybury, 1807.
Services: Barasat C.C. Posted to 3rd N.C. in 1809. Transfd. to 8th N.C. 18 June 1816. Offg. D.A.Q.M.G. with Bdr.-Gen. F. Hardyman's Div. in 1817. Third Mahratta War; Nagpur; Cornet 8th N.C. (India medal). D.A.Q.M.G. 3 cl. 1818; 2 cl. 1819-24. Transfd. as Capt. to newly-raised 9th L.C. 13 May 1825. Siege and capture of Bhurtpore; Capt. 9th L.C. (clasp to India medal).
Refs.: Eton School Lists.
[1] *Note:* Francis only (incorrectly) in official documents.
[2] *Note:* Bur. 20 Nov. as John Francis Palmer. The entry in the bur. register was corrected by affidavit in 1891.

PALMER, George (1801-?). Lieutenant, 21st N.I. *b.* London 23 Nov. 1801. Cadet 1817. Ensign (?) Lieut. 9 Sept. 1818. Cashiered by G.C.M. 18 Feb. 1826.
bapt. St. Bene't's, Gracechurch, London, 21 Dec. 1801. Son of Rev. William Palmer, Chaplain Bengal Est., and Elizabeth his wife, dau. of Rev. George Gaskin, D.D., rector of St. Bene't's. Brother of Henry Palmer, *q.v.*
Services: Posted Lieut. to 2/9th N.I. in 1819. Transfd. to 21st N.I. (late 2/9th) May 1824. (? Siege and capture of Bhurtpore; Lieut. 21st N.I.)

PALMER, George (1810-1831). Ensign, 27th N.I. *b.* London 16 Dec. 1810. Cadet 1827. Arrived in India 23 Oct. 1828. Ensign 10 May 1828. *d.* Gadarwara, C.P., 27 Nov. 1831.
bapt. St. Pancras 17 Jan. 1811. Only son of Thomas Palmer, of Russell Pl., Fitzroy Sq., London, and Isabella his wife.
Services: Ensign d.d. 33rd N.I. 20 Nov. 1828; posted to 27th N.I. 4 Mar. 1829. No record of active service.
Refs.: A.J. N.S. viii. 10. G.M. 1832, i. 648 'M.I. at Narsingh pur.

PALMER, Hamey Charles (*d.* 1811). Major General. Colonel, 12th N.I. Cadet 1772. Admitted Mar. 1772. Ensign 4 Jan. 1773. Lieut. 30 Mar. 1777. Capt. 26 Mar. 1781. Major 3 Oct.

1796. Lt. Col. 29 Apr. 1799. Col. 5 Nov. 1803. Maj. Gen. 25 July 1810. *d.* Barrackpore 24 Aug. 1811.

Only son of Hamey Palmer and Mary his wife, *née* Hall. Brother of Julia Maria Palmer, and 2nd cousin of Sir Ralph Verney, 2nd Earl Verney (*D.N.B.*). *m.* 1st, Calcutta 19 Nov. 1784, Elizabeth Macevoy. (She died Calcutta 30 June 1786.) *m.* 2nd, Cawnpore 28 June 1802, Susannah Sarah Coates. Lincoln's Inn; admitted 31 Oct. 1772.

Services: Returned to England as a Cadet 1773; sailed for India 1774. Supy. Capt., unposted, in July 1787; 2nd Eur. Bn. in Dec. 1788. Resigned in order to go home on fur. 25 Nov. 1789; re-admitted 20 Feb. 1795. Major 2nd Bengal Eur. Regt. in 1798; transfd. as Lt. Col. from 2/13th to 1/12th N.I. 25 Oct. 1799; posted Col. to 12th N.I. in 1803. (? Second Mahratta War. ? Operations in Oudh 1808; Col. 12th N.I.)

Refs.: *Genealogists' Mag.* Vol. ii. No. 3 (Sept. 1926), p. 69. Will dated Chittagong, 19 Jan. 1806; proved 20 Sept. 1811.

*PALMER, Henry (1807-1892). General. 48th N.I. *b.* White Waltham, Berks., 11 June 1807. Cadet 1825. Admitted 21 Aug. 1826. Ensign (13 Feb. 1826) 18 Aug. 1826. Lieut. 27 June 1835. Capt. 16 Oct. 1840. Major 5 June 1853. Lt. Col. 4 Oct. 1857. Bt. Col. 29 July 1857. Maj. Gen. 7 Feb. 1866. Lt. Gen. 28 Mar. 1874. Gen. 1 Oct. 1877. Retired 25 June 1881. *d.* Mussoorie, U.P., 23 Aug. 1892.

bapt. St. Bene't, Gracechurch St., London, 11 Apr. 1816. Son of Rev. William Palmer, Chaplain Bengal Est., and Elizabeth his wife. Brother of William Palmer (1804-1832), *q.v.*, and of Elizabeth, wife of Joseph Walker Jasper Ouseley, *q.v. m.* Calcutta 7 Aug. 1832, Susannah Elizabeth, widow of William Counsell, *q.v.* (She died Allahabad 9 Jan. 1856.)

Services: Was already in India when apptd. Cadet. Ensign d.d. 33rd N.I. 30 Aug. 1826; posted to 48th N.I. 26 Sept. 1826. Operations against the Bhils 1827-8. Wahabi rising 1831. Intr. & Qmr. 48th N.I. 17 Dec. 1832 till 6 Jan. 1841. Actg. Bde. Major 1st Bde., Army of Indus, 9 Dec. 1838; in Comst. Dept. in Afghanistan 9 Feb. till July 1839. First Afghan War 1838-40; action in Bolan Pass 20 Mar. 1839 (s.w.—matchlock ball through left thigh); capture of Ghazni (Medal). Dy. Postmr. to troops in Afghanistan 18 Mar. 1840; Persian Intr. to Maj.-Gen. Sir Willoughby Cotton, comdg. in Afghanistan, 12 Apr. 1840. Granted 12 mos. pay for wound. Actg. Comdt. 4th Inf. Levy 29 Sept. 1842. First Sikh War; Mudki; Ferozshahr (horse shot); Capt. comdg.

48th N.I.; Aliwal; Bde. Major 1st Bde. (Medal with 2 clasps). Expedn. against Kot Kangra Apr. 1846; Bde. Major to Bdr. Wheeler's force. Second Sikh War; Rangar Nagal; Dalla; Bde. Major to Bdr. Wheeler's force in Jullundur Doab (Medal). Mutiny campaign 1857-8; was comdg. 48th N.I. at Lucknow when the majority of that Regt. mutinied 30 May 1857; defence of Lucknow Residency; comdd. a detachment of all arms sent from Cawnpore against rebels in 1858 (Medal with clasp). Formed at Cawnpore in 1857 the "Regt. of Lucknow" (*Bailey Guard Paltan* —now 10th Bn. 7th Rajput Regt.) from the faithful remains of 13th, 48th and 71st N.I. Comdt. Regt. of Lucknow 13 Jan. 1859 till 21 Oct. 1861. Transfd. to Staff Corps 12 Sept. 1866.

Refs.: Boase. *The Times,* 23 Aug. 1892. M.I. Mussoorie.

PALMER, John Horseman. Ensign. 1st Bengal Eur. Regt. Country Cadet 1782. Ensign 1783. Dismissed by C.M. 31 May 1784.[1]

Services: Sailed for India as a private in the *Chapman* 13 Mar. 1781. Apptd. Cadet 15 Mar. 1782. Posted to 2nd Eur. Regt. 28 Feb. 1783; transfd. to 1st Eur. Regt.

[1] *Note:* For conduct unbecoming an ofr. and gentleman.

PALMER, formerly BUDWORTH, Joseph (1756-1815). Fireworker (? Lieut.). Artillery. (244) Miscellaneous writer. *b.* 1756. Cadet 1783. Fireworker 2 Jan. 1785. (? Lieut. 24 Nov. 1790). Resigned 26 Mar. 1791. *d.* Eastbourne 4 Sept. 1815, of apoplexy, aged 59.

Son of Joseph Budworth, originally of Coventry, afterwards master of the Bull's Head tavern, Manchester, and Frances Chapman his wife. Nephew of Rev. William Budworth, master of Brewood School, Staffs. (*D.N.B.*). *m.* St. James's, Westminster, 28 Mar. 1787, Elizabeth, sister of Roger Palmer, of Rush, nr. Dublin, and of Palmerstown, co. Mayo. (She was burnt to death at Ham Common 31 May 1832, aged 76, owing to her clothes catching fire from a candle.) Took his wife's surname of Palmer. (*Lond. Gaz.* 21 Mar. 1812.) Ed. Manchester Grammar School; admitted 10 Jan. 1769.

Services: See *D.N.B.* Ensign newly-raised 72nd Regt., or Royal Manchester Vols., 16 Dec. 1777; Lieut. do. 17 Apr. 1778. Siege of Gibraltar 1782-3 (s.w.); Lieut. 72nd Regt. Returned home with his Regt. in 1783, and accepted a Cadetship in Bengal Art. 2 Dec. 1783. Pensioned on Lord Clive's fund 19 Oct. 1791. Volunteered as Capt. in N. Hants Mil. during the war occasioned by the French

Revolution. Miscellaneous writer, especially to *G.M.* under the pseudonym of " Rambler." F.S.A. 4 June 1795.

Refs.: D.N.B. Burke's *Peerage, s.n.* Palmer, Bart., of Castle Lackin. *Manchester School Register,* i. 148 ; iii. 341. *G.M.* 1815, ii. 285, 388. *M.I.* W. Molesey, Surrey.

PALMER, Nicholas Power (1808-1842). Bt. Captain, 54th N.I. *b.* 11 Nov. 1808. Cadet 1825. Arrived in India 7 July 1826. Ensign 15 Mar. 1826. Lieut. 24 Feb. 1835. Bt. Capt. 15 Mar. 1841. *d.* nr. Kabul 13 Jan. 1842 : kld. in action during the retreat.

bapt. in the Palace at Waterford 20 Mar. 1809. 2nd son of George Palmer, Capt. 15th Foot, and Frances his wife, only dau. of Nicholas Power Trench (brother of 1st Earl of Clancarty), and cousin-german of Hon. Luke Henry Trench, *q.v.* *m.* Ballinasloe, co. Galway, 4 July 1839, Rebecca Carter, dau. of Charles Barrett, of Dungarvan, co. Waterford. (She *re-m.* 13 July 1847, Rev. M. Crofton, curate of Dungarvan.) Father of Gen. Sir Arthur Power Palmer, G.C.B. (*D.N.B.*).

Services : Ensign d.d. 39th N.I. 2 Aug. 1826 ; posted to 54th N.I. 26 Sept. 1826. Fur. s.c. 15 Mar. 1836 till 20 Jan. 1840. First Afghan War 1840-2 ; outbreak at Kabul ; retreat from Kabul (kld.) ; Bt. Capt. 54th N.I.

Refs. : Burke's *Colonial Gentry,* i. 48, *s.n.* Palmer, of Brisbane and S. Kennedy, Queensland, Aust. *A.J.* N.S. xxix. 341. M.I. Afghan Memorial Church, Bombay.

PALMER, Samuel (1762-1814). Colonel, 11th N.I. *b.* I. of St. Kitts, W.I., Sept. 1762. Cadet 1779. Ensign 12 Feb. 1780. Lieut. 21 Feb. 1781. Capt. 30 Oct. 1797. Major 13 July 1803. Lt. Col. 21 Sept. 1804. Col. 4 June 1813. *d.* Calcutta 5 Mar. 1814, aged 51 yrs. 6 mos.

Eldest son of William Palmer (1740-1816), *q.v.* Brother of William George Palmer, *q.v.* *m.* Khairan, a Mohamedan.

Services : Sailed for India in the *Fox* 7 Mar. 1779, aged 17. Lieut. 25th Bn. Sepoys in July 1787 and in 1790 ; comdg. the escort to his father at Sindhia's court in 1792. Capt. and Major 11th N.I. Second Mahratta War 1803-5 ; Bundelkhand 1803 ; Kapsa ; Kalpi ; Gwalior ; Lt. Col. 2/11th N.I. Operations against Rana of Gohad 1806 ; capture of Gohad ; Lt. Col. 2/11th N.I. Posted Col. to 11th N.I. in 1813. Comdg. at Aligarh 1813-14.

Refs. : *Cal. Gaz.* 10 Mar. 1814. M.I. in N. Park St. cemetery, Calcutta.

THE BENGAL ARMY, 1758-1834   451

PALMER, Thomas (1787-1854). Colonel, 72nd N.I. Comdg. Cawnpore Div. *b.* London 29 Jan. 1787. Cadet 1803. Admitted 24 Jan. 1805. Ensign 12 Sept. 1803. Lieut. 28 Oct. 1804. Capt. 11 Jan. 1818. Major 30 Sept. 1827. Lt. Col. 1 Oct. 1832. Col. 16 Apr. 1844. *d.* Mussoorie 15 Apr. 1854.

Son of William Palmer, of Brampton House, Hunts., Commissioner R.N. Brother of Rev. William Palmer, and cousin of Thomas William Palmer, sometime mayor of Hull.

Services : Posted Lieut. to 19th N.I. in 1805. Adjt. 2/19th N.I. 29 Jan. 1807 till 21 Oct. 1815. Expedn. to Mauritius 1810 ; Lieut. 2nd Vol. Bn. Nepal War 1814-15 ; Lieut. 2/19th N.I. (India medal). Capt. Lt. 2/19th N.I. 14 July 1815. Third Mahratta War ; Capt. 2/19th N.I. A.D.C. to Maj.-Gen. Sir John Arnold, *q.v.*, 8 Mar. 1823 till 1827. Transfd. to 39th N.I. (late 2/19th) May 1824. Major 39th N.I. Posted Lt. Col. to 39th N.I. 9 July 1833 ; to 21st N.I. 24 July 1835 ; to 27th N.I. 10 Nov. 1840. First Afghan War 1839-42 ; Nazian Valley ; defence of Ghazni ; Lt. Col. comdg. 27th N.I. (Medal). Comdd. the garr. of Ghazni during the siege Nov. 1841 till Mar. 1842 ; surrendered 6 Mar. ; taken prisoner ; released 21 Sept. 1842.[1] Transfd. to 15th N.I. 14 Feb. 1843 ; to 72nd N.I. 3 Apr. 1843. To comd. troops in Kaithal 12 May 1843. Posted Col. to 72nd N.I. 6 June 1844. Bdr. comdg. Ferozepore 13 June 1846 ; do. Delhi 1846. Posted to Divl. Staff of Army with rank of Bdr. Gen. and posted to Sirhind Div. 9 Apr. 1852. Comdd. Cawnpore Div. July 1852 till death.

Refs.: Boase. G.M. 1855, i. 438. *I.M.* 31 May 1854, p. 291. Will dated 3 Feb. 1853 ; proved 10 July 1854. M.I. Mussoorie.

[1] *Note :* For surrendering Ghazni he was afterwards tried by G.C.M. and acquitted. During his captivity he was tortured with tent peg and rope to force him to disclose buried treasure.

PALMER, Vaughan Lloyd (1794-1828 ?). Bt. Captain, Pension Est. 50th N.I. *bapt.* Bicton, Devon, 19 Mar. 1794. Cadet 1808. Arrived in India 27 Oct. 1809. Ensign 13 Mar. 1810. Lieut. 22 July 1814. Bt. Capt. 24 Apr. 1824. Pensioned 18 Nov. 1824. (*d.* 1828 ?) [1]

Son of William Vaughan Palmer, Capt. 26th Light Dgns., and Emily Warren his wife, eldest dau. of Rev. John Glubb, rector of Bicton. *m.* Chandernagore 4 Aug. 1825, Miss Catherine Perrin (? Piron) Imbert.

Services : Barasat C.C. Posted Ensign to 25th N.I. in 1810. With 6th Vol. Bn. in 1814. Siege and capture of Hathras 1817 ; Lieut. 1/25th N.I. Third Mahratta War ; Lieut. 1/25th

N.I. Transfd. to 2/25th N.I. ; to 50th N.I. (late 2/25th) May 1824.
  Refs. : Vivian's *Visitations of Cornwall*, p. 582, *s.n.* Glubb.
  [1] *Note* : His name is omitted from *E.I.R.* of 5 May 1829.

PALMER, William (1740-1816). Lieut. General. Colonel 4th N.I. *b.* 1740. Cadet 1766. Admitted 14 June 1767. Ensign 4 Aug. 1767. Lieut. 27 Sept. 1769. Capt. 12 May 1777. Major 29 July 1781. Lt. Col. 1 Mar. 1794. Col. 1 Nov. 1798. Maj. Gen. 1 Jan. 1805. Lt. Gen. 4 June 1813. *d.* Berhampore 20 May 1816.

  m. 1st, St. George and St. Peter, Basseterre, St. Kitts, either Sarah Hazell in 1761, or Sarah Melhado in 1762. Father of Samuel and William George Palmer, and grandfather of Francis Charles Palmer, *qq.v. m.* 2nd, Bibi Faiz Bakhsh, Sahiba (" Faizun-nissa "), Begum of Oudh. (She died Hyderabad 1828.) Father of William Palmer, known as " King " Palmer, founder and head of the Hyderabad firm of Palmer & Co., and of Mary, wife of James Arrow, *q.v.*

  Services : Ensign H.M. 70th Ft. 22 Mar. 1762, and served in the W.I. (" the Grenadoes ") with that Regt. ; left the Regt. as Ensign 25 Jan. 1765. Sailed as a Cadet in the *Calcutta* 31 Dec. 1766. Joined 3rd N.I. Aug. 1767. First Rohilla War 1774 ; Lieut. in 1st Bde. A.D.C. to Warren Hastings in 1774, and Mily. Sec. for some yrs. between 1776 and 1785. Comdt. G.G.B.G. 6 Apr. 1778 till (?) 1782. Was present at Benares with Hastings during the outbreak that occurred there in Aug. 1781. Resdt. at Lucknow 1782 ; at Sindhia's court 1797 till Mar. 1798 ; at Poona 1798 till 1801. To comd. 7th Bn. Sepoys 31 May 1786. Col. 17th N.I. in 1798 ; 4th N.I. 1804 till death. Comdg. at Monghyr 1804 ; do. Berhampore 1805-11.

  Refs. : *E.I.M.C.* ii. 451-2. *V.B.G.* List of *Mily. Secs. to Govrs. Gen. and Viceroys. D.I.B.* Portrait of himself and his Begum, by Zoffany. Will proved 6 July 1816.

PALMER, William (1804-1832). Lieutenant, 39th N.I. *b.* White Waltham, Berks., 16 Sept. 1804. Cadet 1820. Admitted 31 May 1821. Ensign 13 Jan. 1821. Lieut. 11 July 1823. *d.* at sea 10 Sept. 1832, on board the *Ferguson*.[1]

  bapt. White Waltham 29 Sept. 1804. Son of Rev. William Palmer and Elizabeth Gaskin his wife. Brother of George Palmer (*b.* 1801) and of the wife of Sir Francis Wheler, Bart., *qq.v.*

  Services : Posted Ensign to 2/9th N.I. ; transfd. as Lieut. to

19th N.I. July 1823 ; to 39th N.I. (late 2/19th) May 1824. Adjt.
39th N.I. 10 Oct. 1825 till 2 May 1829. Actg. D.J.A.G. Cawnpore
Div. 25 Jan. 1826, and 26 Oct. 1827. Apptd. D.J.A.G. on the Est.
11 Feb. 1829 and posted to Cawnpore ; removed from his appt.
23 Oct. 1830. Fur. s.c. 30 July (? 9 Sept.) 1832.
¹ *Note :* His death was so sudden and unexpected that an inquest was held.

*PALMER, William George (1763-1814). Major, 25th N.I. *b.*
I. of St. Kitts, W.I., 9 Jan. 1763. Cadet 1781. Admitted 22 Mar.
1783. Ensign 1781. Lieut. 14 Nov. 1782. Capt. 22 Aug. 1801.
Major 15 Aug. 1809. *d.* Calcutta 6 Apr. 1814.
bapt. St. George and St. Peter, Basseterre, 2 Feb. 1763. Eldest son of William Palmer (1740-1816), *q.v.,* and Sarah his 1st wife. Brother of Samuel Palmer, *q.v. m.* (before 1793) ?
Services : Apptd. Cadet for Madras 29 Dec. 1780 ; sailed for India in the *Asia* 13 Mar. 1781. Transfd. to Bengal Est. 22 Mar. 1783. Lieut. 2nd Bengal Eur. Bn. in July 1787 and in Dec. 1788 ; 25th Bn. Sepoys in 1790 ; with escort to his father at Sindhia's court in 1792. Capt. Bengal Eur. Regt. and Comdt. Ramgarh Bn. in 1803. Transfd. to newly-raised 25th N.I. in 1804. Dy. Paymr. at Dinapore 1805 ; do. Fatehgarh 1808-10. Major 2/25th N.I. Promoted Bt. Lt. Col. 4 June 1814, after his death.
Refs. : Cal. *Gaz.* 7 Apr. 1814. M.I. in N. Park St. cemetery, Calcutta.

PANTON, Patrick (1786-1813). Lieutenant, 12th N.I. *b.*
Kelso 25 Dec. 1786. Cadet 1807. Arrived in India 19 Aug.
1808. Ensign 19 Sept. 1808. Lieut. 18 Oct. 1811. *d.* Calcutta
26 Jan. 1813.
bapt. Kelso Jan. 1787. Son of Patrick Panton, of Edenbank, Kelso, writer, and Janet Panton his wife and cousin. Brother of William Panton, of Edenbank, Physician Gen. Bengal.
Services : Barasat C.C. Posted Ensign to 12th N.I. in 1809. No record of active service. Lieut. 1/12th N.I.
Refs. : Burke's *Colonial Gentry,* ii. 476, *s.n.* Panton. M.I. in S. Park St. cemetery, Calcutta.

PARDOE, James Kinnersley (1791-1812). Ensign, 14th N.I.
bapt. Burford, Oxon., 13 Oct. 1791. Cadet 1807. Arrived in India 16 Nov. 1808. Ensign 23 Nov. 1808. *d.* Calcutta 5 Aug. 1812.
Son of George Pardoe, of Cleeton and Nash Court, Salop, and

Ellen his wife, eldest dau. of Richard Dansey Dansey, of Easton Court, co. Hereford. Stepson of Rev. Thomas Rocke, of Tenbury.

Services : Barasat C.C. Posted Ensign to 14th N.I. in 1809. No record of active service.

Refs. : Burke's *Landed Gentry*, 13th edn., p. 1363, *s.n.* Pardoe, late of Nash Court, Salop.

*PARISOD, Solomon (1724/25-?). Cadet. Infantry. *b.* Lausanne 1724/25. Cadet 1757.

Services : Apptd. Cadet 1757 ; sailed for India in the *Hardwicke* in 1757, aged 32. N.F.P. Out of the Service before 1760.

PARK, Alexander (1755-1779). Ensign, Infantry. *b.* Kingston, Jamaica, 25 Mar. 1755. Country Cadet 1778. Ensign 14 May 1779. *d. unm.* Madras 28 Dec. 1779.

Eldest son of James Park, surgeon in Jamaica, later in practice at Newington, Surrey, and Elizabeth his wife, dau. of Donald Maclean, V of Torloisk. Brother of Sir James Alexander Park, Kt., justice of the common pleas (*D.N.B.*).

Services : Served for some yrs. in a Corps of Light Horse in Jamaica. Went out to Bengal in 1777 as overseer of a sugar works. Apptd. Cadet 11 Aug. 1778. Leave s.c. to Madras 16 Aug. 1779.

Refs. : *Griffith of Garn and Plasnewydd*, ed. T. A. Glenn (London, privately printed 1934). *Clan Maclean*, p. 352.

PARK, Archibald (1804-1867). Lieut. Colonel. 29th N.I. *b.* Selkirk 16 Dec. 1804. Cadet 1823. Arrived in India 3 May 1824. Ensign 9 Jan. 1824. Lieut. 13 May 1825. Capt. 5 Sept. 1841. Bt. Major 11 Nov. 1851. Retired 3 July 1854. Hon. Lt. Col. 16 Mar. 1855. *d.* Stone, Kent, 19 Apr. 1867.

bapt. Selkirk 15 Jan. 1805. 3rd and youngest son of Mungo Park, of Foulshiels, co. Selkirk, the African explorer (*D.N.B.*), and Alison his wife, eldest dau. of Thomas Anderson, of Selkirk, surgeon. *m.* (before 1847) Rachel Anne, niece of James Auchmuty (1775-1864), *q.v.* (She died 7 Nov. 1861.) Ed. Edin. Univ.

Services : Posted Ensign to 29th N.I. and served throughout with that Regt. ; Adjt. do. 13 Aug. 1832 till 31 Oct. 1841. Fur. s.c. 17 Jan. 1843 till 1846. Second Sikh War ; operations in Jullundur Doab ; action at Amb ; Capt. comdg. H.Q. and 5 Coys. 29th N.I. under Major David Simpson, *q.v.* (Medal). Fur. p.a. 3 Jan. 1852 till retirement.

Refs. : *G.M.* 1867, i. 823. *The Times*, 22 Apr. 1867.

THE BENGAL ARMY, 1758-1834 455

PARKE, Alexander. Captain. Infantry. Cadet 1770. Ensign 2 Apr. 1771. Lieut. 15 July 1776. Capt. 11 Feb. 1781. Resigned 18 Dec. 1783.
Of Lochore, co. Fife. *m.* Kinross House 20 Sept. 1784, Mary, dau. of John Graham, of Kernock, and of Nicholson St., Edinburgh, merchant, and sister of Thomas Graham, M.P. Kinross, and formerly Member of the Supreme Council in Bengal.
Services : Sec. to Col. Goddard, comdg. New Bde. at Fatehgarh, in Sept. 1777 ; to act as Persian Intr. at Fatehgarh 6 Oct. 1780 ; Sec. and Persian Intr. to Grainger Muir, *q.v.*, 28 Apr. till June 1781. First Mahratta War ; Sec. and Intr. to O.C. Bengal force. Afterwards Col. of the Loyal M'Leod Fenc.
Refs. : *S.M.* 1784, p. 503.

PARKE, John Charles Bliss (1788-1853). Lieut. Colonel. 34th N.I. *bapt.* Stoke Damerel, Devon, 8 Oct. 1788. Cadet 1803. Arrived in India 27 Sept. 1804. Ensign 25 Sept. 1804. Lieut. 25 Sept. 1804. Capt. 1 Jan. 1819. Major 2 June 1826. Lt. Col. 27 May 1830. Retired 1 Dec. 1832. *d.* Portarlington, Queen's Co., 18 Feb. 1853, aged 64.
Son of Andrew Parke, Major 8th Foot, and Eliza his wife.
Services : Posted Lieut. to 25th N.I. in 1805. Capture of Gohad 1806 ; Lieut. 25th N.I. Expedn. against Mauritius 1810 ; Lieut. 1st Vol. Bn. Actg. Adjt. 5 Coys. 1/25th N.I. May 1813. Fur. p.a. 22 Dec. 1814 till 28 Dec. 1817. Third Mahratta War ; Lieut. 2/25th N.I. Retransfd. as Capt. to 1/25th N.I. Apptd. Bde. Major on the Est. 5 June 1820 ; D.A.A.G. 28 Jan. 1825 ; at Cawnpore 22 Feb. 1825 till 30 Aug. 1826. Transfd. to 49th N.I. (late 1/25th) May 1824. Dy. Postmaster at Cawnpore July 1824 till Oct. 1826. Major 49th N.I. Posted Lt. Col. to 34th N.I. 16 Dec. 1830. Fur. p.a. 26 Feb. 1831 till retirement. Retired on a pension of £1 *p.d.*
Refs. : *I.M.* 16 Apr. 1853, p. 211.

PARKER, Charles (1783-1837). Colonel, Artillery. (316) *b.* Salford 28 Nov. 1783. Cadet 1800. Arrived in India 4 Feb. 1802. Lieut. 8 Apr. 1802. Capt. Lt. 10 July 1805. Capt. 12 July 1811. Major 8 Nov. 1818. Lt. Col. 1 May 1824. Col. 31 May 1833. *d.* Simla 28 Apr. 1837.
bapt. Salford 14 Dec. 1783. Son of Robert Parker and Lucy his wife. Father of Charles Parker, Lieut. in the Nizam's service, and of Lucy, wife of George Short, *q.v.* (? Woolwich Cadet.)
Services : Posted to 4th Coy. 3rd Bn. Art. 2 June 1802. Second

Mahratta War; Orissa and Cuttack 1803; Lieut. 6th Coy. 1st Bn. (d.d. from 4th Coy. 3rd Bn.), with force under Col. Harcourt. Transfd. to 7th Coy. 1st Bn. 22 Sept. 1806. Adjt. 1st Bn. Jan. 1807 till Oct. 1809. Adjt. & Qmr. 2nd Bn. Oct. 1809 till Jan. 1812. Comdd. Art. at Bencoolen Jan. 1812 till 1814. Comy. Ord. at Agra 8 June 1816 till Mar. 1819. To comd. Art. at Karnal Mar. 1819; do. Malwa Div. Art. Nov. 1819 till Sept. 1821. To charge of 4th (Golandaz) Bn. 22 Sept. 1821. To comd. Cawnpore Div. Art. 23 Dec. 1823. Posted as Lt. Col. to 4th Bn. Aug. 1824. Siege and capture of Bhurtpore; Lt. Col. comdg. Field Art. of 2nd Div. Comdd. 6th (late 4th) Golandaz Bn. till Feb. 1829. Transfd. to 5th Bn. 8 Apr. 1831. Leave to Tasmania and N.S.W. 16 Feb. 1831 till Jan. 1833. Posted Col. to 5th Bn. 25 Nov. 1833. Bdr. 2 cl. and comd. Art. at Ajmer for service in Rajputana 18 Nov. 1834. Shekhawat expedn. 1834; Bdr. comdg. Art. of the force. Leave s.c. to Simla Feb. 1836 till death. Died of fever contracted during a shooting trip.

Refs.: *De Rhé-Philipe.* *A.J.* N.S. xxiv. 98. Will dated Calcutta 16 Apr. 1831; proved 16 May 1837. M.I. outside R.C. cemetery, Simla.

PARKER, Francis Lee (1785-1804). Lieutenant, 4th N.I. *b.* Lancaster 28 May 1785. Cadet 1800. Admitted 11 Feb. 1802. Ensign 15 Dec. 1801. Lieut. 19 May 1803. *d.* Midnapore 8 Dec. 1804, of fever.

Only son of Richard Parker, of Burlington St., Bath, and Mary his wife. Brother of Mary, Margaret and Hannah.

Services: Ensign 16th N.I. Transfd. as Lieut. to 4th N.I. in 1803. (? Second Mahratta War; Aligarh; Lieut. 4th N.I.)

Refs.: *G.M.* 1805, ii. 877. Will dated Midnapore, 8 Dec. 1804; proved 9 Feb. 1805.

PARKER, Sir George, third baronet (1813-1857). Bt. Major, 74th N.I. Cantt. Mgte. at Cawnpore. *b.* London 3 Feb. 1813. Cadet 1832. Arrived in India 3 July 1833. Ensign (14 June 1832) 24 Sept. 1835. Lieut. 30 Jan. 1837. Capt. 3 Oct. 1845. Bt. Major 6 Dec. 1856. *d.* Cawnpore 8 June 1857, of sunstroke.

3rd Bart., of Harburn. *s.* 24 Mar. 1848. 2nd son of Sir William George Parker, 2nd Bart., Vice Adm. of the White, and Elizabeth his wife, dau. of James Charles Still, of E. Knoyle, Wilts. Brother of William James Parker, *q.v. m.* 1st, Dinapore, 24 Jan. 1838, Eliza Cecilia, dau. of Dr. John Marshall, Physician Gen. Bengal. (*See also* Ambrose Cardew.) (She died Calcutta 5 Aug. 1843.)

THE BENGAL ARMY, 1758-1834 457

m. 2nd, Meerut 10 Dec. 1846, Gertrude, youngest dau. of Lt.-Col. Charles Augustus Elderton, Madras Est., and grand-dau. of Lt.-Gen. Elisha Trapaud, Madras Engrs. (She died Meerut 12 May 1850, aged 26.) Addiscombe Cadet 17 Sept. 1830 till 14 June 1832.

Services: See *D.N.B.* d.d. Bengal Eur. Regt. 3 Aug. 1833 till Feb. 1834. Posted Ensign to 18th N.I. 11 Feb. 1834; transfd. to 74th N.I. 24 Sept. 1835. Jodhpur demonstration 1839-40; Lieut. 74th N.I. Second-in-comd. 1st and 2nd Bns. Bundelkhand Mily. Police 30 Sept. 1843 till Jan. 1846. Tempy. Comdt. Ambala Police Bn. Jan.-Sept. 1846. Comdt. Meerut Police Bn. Sept. 1846 till May 1847. Joint Cantt. Mgte. at Meerut 30 June 1847 till Feb. 1852. Fur. s.c. 21 Feb. 1852 till Jan. 1855. Cantt. Joint Mgte. at Cawnpore 5 May 1856 till death.

Refs.: Burke's *Peerage*, 1923, p. 1737, *s.n.* Parker, Bart., of Harburn (extinct). *D.N.B. D.I.B. De Rhé-Philipe. Boase. G.M.* 1857, ii. 467. Will dated Cawnpore, 4 June 1857; admon. 17 Jan. 1859. *M.I.* in St. James's, Delhi.

PARKER, George Henry (*d.* 1790). Lieutenant, 4th Bengal Eur. Bn. Cadet 1782. Arrived in India Aug. 1783. Ensign 15 Apr. 1783. Lieut. 15 Mar. 1790. *d.* Calcutta 25 Apr. 1790.

Services: Apptd. Cadet 26 Feb. 1782; sailed for India in the *Winterton* 11 Sept. 1782. Supy. Ensign, unposted, in July 1787. Posted to 4th Eur. Bn. 5 Feb. 1790.

Refs.: Will dated 8 Apr. 1790; proved 29 Apr. 1790.

PARKER,[1] James (*d.* 1783). Cadet, Infantry. Cadet 1783. *bur.* Calcutta 7 Nov. 1783.

Services: Apptd. Cadet 15 Nov. 1782; sailed for India in the *Atlas* 11 Mar. 1783; arrived in India 22 Oct. 1783.

[1] *Note:* His name appears as Pasker in the burial register.

PARKER, Jeremiah (1762/63-1785). Lieutenant, Infantry. *b.* Essex 1762/63. Cadet 1780. Ensign 1780. Lieut. 27 June 1781. *bur.* Calcutta 2 Dec. 1785.

Services: Sailed for India in the *Bellmont* 3 Apr. 1780, aged 17. N.F.P.

PARKER, John Neville (1740/41-1781). Bt. Colonel, Infantry. *b.* 1740/41. Capt. 27 July 1764. Dismissed 1766. Restored to the Service 1771. Lt. Col. 3 Oct. 1769. Bt. Col. 15 May 1780. *d.* 23 Apr. 1781: kld. in action at the Bhor Ghaut, aged 40. 3rd son of Harding Parker, of Passage West, co. Cork, high sheriff 1727, mayor 1740, and Catherine his wife, dau. of John Neville, of Furnace, co. Kildare. Uncle of Norcott Neville D'Esterre and St. Leger Hayward Gillman, *qq.v.* *m.* " a Begum." Father of William Neville Parker, *q.v.*

Services : Ensign newly-raised 2/12th Ft. 31 Aug. 1756 ; Lieut. 65th Ft. (late 2/12th) 29 Sept. 1757. Raised in England a Coy. of 100 men for E.I. Co. and was apptd. Capt. on the Bengal Est. 2 Mar. 1764 ; sailed for India in the *Lord Anson* 29 May 1764. Posted to 2nd Bengal Eur. Regt. 5 Aug. 1765. Dismissed by the Govr. in Council and sent home owing to participation in the " Batta mutiny " in 1766. Returned to India as a Capt. in the *Britannia* in 1771 ; restored to his full rank as Lt. Col. by C.D. 23 Dec. 1774. Comdg. at Dinapore in Oct. 1775. Operations in the Doab against Mahbub Khan 1776 ; battle of Korah ; Lt. Col. comdg. the force. Lt. Col. comdg. 1/3rd Bengal Eur. Regt. in Oct. 1779. First Mahratta War 1778-81 ; with a detachment under Lt.-Col. Matthew Leslie, *q.v.* ; later under Col. Thomas Goddard, *q.v.* ; siege of Ahmedabad Feb. 1780 (w. 11 Feb.) ; forcing of Bhor Ghaut Feb. 1781 ; retreat down the Bhor Ghaut in Apr. (" kld. while meditating a desperate atk. on the enemy's guns ") ; Bt. Col. comdg. rear guard. Renowned as an extremely gallant officer.

Refs. : Burke's *Landed Gentry of Ireland*, p. 551, *s.n.* Parker, of Passage West, co. Cork. *India Gazette*, 9 June 1781. *Cal. Gaz.* 8 Dec. 1791. Will dated 22 Apr. 1781 ; proved 2 July 1781.

PARKER, John Stephens (1791-1818). Ensign, 28th N.I. *bapt.* Scarborough 27 Aug. 1791. Cadet 1811. Ensign 22 July 1814. *d. unm.* in camp 24 Mar. 1818.

Son of Thomas John Parker, of The Cresc., Bath, and of Chesterfield, Jamaica, W.I. merchant, and Rachel Stephens his wife. Brother of Henry Parker, Cornet 8th Light Dgns.

Services : Posted Ensign to 1/28th N.I. in 1814. Third Mahratta War ; Ensign 1/28th N.I., with Reserve of Grand Army.

Refs. : Will dated 23 Mar. 1818 ; proved 15 Aug. 1818.

PARKER, Neville Anbury (1808-1853). Major, 58th N.I. *b.* at sea 22 Nov. 1808. Cadet 1825. Arrived in India 6 May, 1826. Ensign 18 Jan. 1826. Lieut. 8 June 1827. Capt. 8 Jan. 1842. Major 16 July 1849. *d.* Landour, U.P., 19 Oct. 1853.

bapt. Camberwell 24 Nov. 1809. Only son of William Neville Parker, *q.v.*, and Henrietta his wife. *m.* Agra 9 Dec. 1829, Susannah, dau. of Andrew Fraser (*d.* 1812), *q.v.*

Services : Posted Ensign to 58th N.I. 26 Sept. 1826. Adjt.

58th N.I. 13 Mar. 1834 till 3 Mar. 1838. Fur. p.a. 6 Feb. 1838 till 9 Sept. 1840. Intr. & Qmr. 58th N.I. 27 Nov. 1840 till 1 Apr. 1842. Offg. 2nd in comd. Assam L.I. 30 June 1841 ; permanent do. 1 Apr. 1842 till 14 Mar. 1843. Gwalior campaign ; Paniar (*London Gaz.* 8 Mar. 1844) ; Capt. 58th N.I. (Bronze star). Comdt. 4th Inf., Gwalior Contingent, 13 Jan. 1844 till Nov. 1849.
Refs.: *G.M.* 1854, i. 439. Will dated Hoshiarpur, 31 Dec. 1851 ; proved 16 Jan. 1854. M.I. Landour.

PARKER, Richard (1809-?). Ensign. 2nd N.I. bapt. Monk Fryston, Yorks., 20 Jan. 1809. Cadet 1827. Arrived in India 10 Jan. 1829. Ensign 10 July 1828. Resigned 24 Dec. 1833.
Son of John Toulson Parker, of Burton Salmon, Yorks., and Esther (? Hester) Arthur his wife, dau. of John Arthur Worsop, of Howden, Yorks.
Services : Ensign d.d. 55th N.I. 11 Feb. 1829. Posted to 48th N.I. 3 June 1829. Fur. s.c. 21 June 1831 till resignation. Transfd. to 2nd N.I. 2 Aug. 1832. No record of active service.
Refs. : Burke's *Landed Gentry*, 13th edn., p. 1365, *s.n.* Parker, of Browsholme, Yorks.

PARKER, William (*d.* 1769). Ensign, Infantry. Cadet 1769, Ensign 25 Feb. 1769. *d.* in India 1769.
Services : N.F.P.

PARKER, William (1804-1831). Lieutenant, 6th L.C. *b.* Kilmarnock, co. Ayr, 11 Jan. 1804. Cadet 1819. Admitted 14 June 1820. Cornet 2 Feb. 1820. Lieut. 30 Nov. 1822. *d.* Cawnpore 10 Apr. 1831, of smallpox.
bapt. Kilmarnock 8 Feb. 1804. 10th child of William Parker, of Assloss, merchant in Kilmarnock, and Agnes his wife, dau. of William Paterson, of Kilmarnock, and aunt of William Paterson (1791-1819), *q.v.*
Services : Posted Cornet to 6th L.C. Adjt. Rohilla Horse 14 June 1822 till 13 Nov. 1823. Actg. Adjt. newly-raised 2nd Extra Cav. 19 Sept. 1825. Siege and capture of Bhurtpore ; Lieut. 6th L.C. Actg. Adjt. 6th L.C. 28 Sept. 1827 and 17 Nov. 1830.
Refs. : *A.J.* N.S. vi. 138.

PARKER, William James (1811-1843). Bt. Captain, 1st Bengal Eur. L.I. *b.* 25 Sept. 1811. Cadet 1827. Arrived in India 23 Sept. 1828. Ensign 23 May 1828. Lieut. 8 Sept. 1835. Bt. Capt. 23 May 1843. *d.v.p.* Simla 4 Nov. 1843.

bapt. E. Knoyle, Wilts., 24 Oct. 1811. Eldest son of Sir William
George Parker, 2nd Bart., of Harburn, and Elizabeth his wife.
Brother of Sir George Parker, Bart., q.v. m. 1st, Dinapore 17 Feb.
1834, Phoebe, dau. of Dr. John Marshall, Physician Gen. Bengal.
(See also Ambrose Cardew.) (She died Agra 30 June 1836, aged
25.) m. 2nd, Serampore 29 July 1841, Margaret Ellen, eldest dau.
of William Greaves. (She died Tunbridge Wells 24 Nov. 1910,
aged 87.)

Services: Ensign d.d. 51st N.I. 5 Nov. 1828; do. 24th N.I.
16 Feb. 1829. Posted to 1st Bengal Eur. Regt. 4 Mar. 1829.
First Afghan War 1838-40; capture of Ghazni (Medal); Kabul;
operations in Waziri valley; capture of Kajja fort 19 Aug. 1840
(s.w.); Lieut. Bengal Eur. Regt. (Lond. Gaz. 9 Jan. 1841). Granted
12 mos. pay as wound gratuity. With Army of Reserve (for
Afghanistan) Oct. 1842 till Jan. 1843; Lieut. 1st Bengal Eur. L.I.
Leave s.c. to Simla 25 Apr. 1843 till death.

Refs.: Burke's Peerage, 1923, p. 1737, s.n. Parker, Bart., of
Harburn (extinct 17 Nov. 1903). De Rhé-Philipe. A.J. N.S. xxv.
175-6. M.I. in cart road cemetery, Simla.

PARKER, William Neville (1774-1853). Captain. Artillery.
(293) b. in India 4 Mar. 1774. Cadet 1790. Admitted 13 July
1791. Fireworker 6 Jan. 1792. Lieut. 21 Apr. 1800. Capt. Lt.
26 July 1804. Capt. 17 Sept. 1807. Retired 10 June 1808. d.
6 Kensington Pl., Bath, 18 May 1853.

bapt. St. Helena 9 Dec. 1778. Son of John Neville Parker, q.v.
Nephew of William Parker, Comdr. of the Albion, East Indiaman,
and cousin-german of Henry Martin D'Esterre, q.v. m. Henrietta.
(She died Camberwell Mar. 1811.) Father of Neville Anbury
Parker, q.v.

Services: Apptd. Cadet 14 Dec. 1790; sailed for India in the
Albion 23 Jan. 1791. To Madras in Aug. 1793 for siege of Pondicherry; Lieut. F. 1st Coy. 2nd Bn. Operations in Jumna Doab
1803; Sasni. Fur. 28 Feb. 1805 till 10 Oct. 1807. Resigned in
June 1808; subsequently placed on retired list from same date.
H.E.I.C. Recruiting Ofr. in Cork district 1811; do. Liverpool 1812;
do. Bath 1814-16.

Refs.: Bath Chron. 26 May 1853. G.M. 1853, ii. 99.

PARKER, Windsor (1802-1892). Captain. 10th L.C. Subsequently Lt. Col. W. Suffolk Mil. b. Isleworth, Middlesex,
3 Jan. 1802. Cadet 1820. Admitted 11 June 1821. Cornet
24 Nov. 1820. Lieut. 1 May 1824. Capt. 30 July 1829. Retired

10 July 1838. *d.* at his residence, Clopton Hall, Bury St. Edmunds, 29 Jan. 1892.

Of Clopton Hall, Suffolk, J.P. and D.L., high sheriff 1854, M.P. for W. Suffolk, 1859-80. Eldest son of William Parker, of the Castle, Ramsgate, late of Hardwicke Court, Gloucs., and Anne his wife, dau. of William Windsor. *m.* Mhow 19 Apr. 1830, Elizabeth Mary, dau. of Alexander Duncan (1780-1859), *q.v.* (*See also* Sir William Erskine Baker, K.C.B.) (She died Wilby Rectory, Suffolk, 30 Mar. 1883, aged 76.)

Services : Posted Cornet to 6th L.C. ; Intr. & Qmr. do. 25 Apr. 1825 ; transfd. to newly-raised 2nd Extra Cav. (became 10th L.C.) 17 June 1825. Siege and capture of Bhurtpore ; Lieut. 10th L.C. (India medal). A.D.C. to Maj.-Gen. G. H. Pine, *q.v.*, 20 Dec. 1826. Extra A.D.C. on personal staff of Lord Combermere, the C.-in-C., 22 Oct. 1827 ; actg. Persian Intr. at H.Q. 12 May 1828 ; to comd. Cav. of C.-in-C.'s escort on tour 18 Sept. 1828. Additional Bde. Major on the Est., for Mhow, 24 Jan. 1829 ; attached to Malwa F.F. 3 Feb. 1829. Leave s.c. to Hills 25 Jan. 1834 till 15 Nov. 1835. Bde. Major in Oudh 2 Sept. 1835. Fur. s.c. 27 Feb. 1836 till retirement on pension of 7/- *p.d.* Major 1st W. Suffolk Mil. 9 Oct. 1852 ; retired as Lt. Col. 19 May 1869.

Refs. : Burke's *Landed Gentry*, 13th edn., p. 1366, *s.n.* Parker, of Clopton Hall, Suffolk. *Boase. Walford. The Times,* 2 Feb. 1892.

PARKINSON, James. Lieutenant. Infantry. Cadet 1781. Never arrived in India. Ensign 2 June 1781. Lieut. 15 Sept. 1782. Struck off 1788.

Services : Was abroad when apptd. Cadet on 27 Mar. 1781.

PARLBY, James Templer (*c.* 1762-1826). Lt. Colonel Comdt. Engineers. *b. c.* 1762. Cadet 1781. Admitted 18 Nov. 1782. Ensign 1781. Lieut. 3 Sept. 1781. Capt. 15 Apr. 1806. Major 4 Oct. 1808. Lt. Col. 4 June 1814. Lt. Col. Comdt. 30 May 1824. *d.* Berhampore 1 Dec. 1826, aged 64.

Elder son of Thomas Parlby, of Stone Hall, Devon, and Lydia Martin his wife. Related to Samuel Parlby, *q.v.*, and cousin of Charles Templer, *q.v.*, and of George Templer, *q.v. m.* Calcutta 2 July 1795, Miss Louisa Munt, of Moidapore, nr. Murshidabad. (*See also* George Moore (1789-1848).) (She died Stonehouse, Plymouth, 24 Aug. 1808.)

Services : Capt. Lt. Engrs. 8 Jan. 1796. At Murshidabad 1804-6 ; at Bencoolen 1809-12. Supt. of embankments, Kasim Bazar R., 1814-19 ; in charge of embankments and palace bldgs. at Murshidabad 1819 till death.

Refs.: Burke's *Landed Gentry*, 11th edn., p. 1290, *s.n.* Parlby, of Manadon, Devon. *A.J.* xxiii. 857. M.I. at Berhampore.

PARLBY, Samuel (1789-1878). Lieut. Colonel. Artillery. (358) *bapt.* Boxted, Essex, 9 May 1789. Cadet 1804. Arrived in India 21 June 1806. Lieut. 28 Mar. 1806. Capt. Lt. 8 June 1816. Capt. 1 Sept. 1818. Major 26 Sept. 1830. Retired 3 Mar. 1831. Hon. Lt. Col. 28 Nov. 1854. *d.* Bishopston, Bristol, 21 Mar. 1878, aged 89.

Son of Rev. Samuel Parlby, curate of Stoke-by-Nayland, " where he took young gentlemen to qualify them for the University," afterwards rector of Wickham Market, Suffolk, and Ann Cooke, his wife. Related to James Templer Parlby, *q.v. m.* 1st, Boxted 23 Sept. 1817, Anne, dau. of Rev. Dr. Thomas Redman Hooker, of Rottingdean. *m.* 2nd, Cape Town 29 Aug. 1831, Hester, only dau. of Capt. Hungerford Vowe, late R.M. (She died at his estate, Kleine R. Valley, S.A., 19 Sept. 1835, aged 27.) *m.* 3rd, Rondebosch, S.A., 19 Dec. 1837, Miss Marian Emma Mathew. (She died 2 May 1871.) Woolwich Cadet; nominated for R.M.A. 7 Dec. 1803; obtained his certificate 27 June 1805.

Services: Served as Cadet at capture of C.G.H. Jan. 1806. Operations against Dhundia Khan 1807; Komona, from 28 Oct.; Ganauri; Lieut. d.d. 2nd Coy. 2nd Bn., from 4th Coy. 2nd Bn. 3rd Troop H.A. 4 Oct. 1809 till 1816. Adjt. & Qmr. H.A. in Java 1815. Leave s.c. 8 mos. to Malacca and Java 15 Mar. 1816; fur. s.c. 12 Aug. 1816 till 12 May 1818. Supt. of the Model Est. 1819; in charge of Tangent Scale Est. 6 Mar. 1820 till 7 June 1824. Engaged in the experimental manufacture of rockets at Dum-Dum from 18 Dec. 1823; Agent for gunpowder at Allahabad 28 May 1824 till 12 June 1829; tempy. charge of Allahabad mag. 24 Feb. 1829. Leave p.a. to Mauritius 1 Feb. till 10 Aug. 1830; fur. p.a. 21 Oct. 1830 till retirement. Retired on pension of 16/- *p.d.* After retirement submitted proposals for the establishment of a private gunpowder manufactory in Bengal, which were negatived by Govt. Edited "The Brit. Indian Mily. Repository," 3 vols., Calcutta, 1822-7.

Refs.: E.I.C.'s Arsenals & Manufactories, by Bdr.-Gen. H. A. Young, C.I.E., C.B.E. (Oxford, 1937). *G.M.* 1817, ii. 362. *A.J.* N.S. vi. 196. *The Times*, 27 Mar. 1878.

PARR, Thomas (1779-1804). Lieutenant, 2nd N.I. *b.* London 15 Apr. 1779. Cadet 1795. Arrived in India 4 Mar. 1797. Ensign 29 Oct. 1796. Lieut. 30 Oct. 1797. *d.* Sikandra 24 Aug.

THE BENGAL ARMY, 1758-1834

1804: kld. in action on the Banas R. during Monson's retreat.
bapt. St. James's, Westminster, 17 Apr. 1779. 2nd son of William Parr, of Hampstead Heath, and Mary Ann his wife, *née* Paschaud.
Services : Lieut. 2nd N.I. in 1798. Operations in Jumna Doab 1803 ; Sasni ; Bijaigarh ; Kachaura ; Lieut. 2/2nd N.I. Second Mahratta War ; battle of Delhi ; Hinglaisgarh ; Monson's retreat (kld.) ; Lieut. 2/2nd N.I.
Refs. : *Pester,* p. 55. *G.M.* 1805, i. 281.

PARROTT, Richard Leveridge (*d.* 1772). Lieutenant, Engineers. Country Cadet 1768. Ensign 5 Jan. 1769. Lieut. 8 Nov. 1769. *d.* Monghyr 4 Sept. 1772.
Son of —— Parrott and Mary his wife.
Services : Sailed for India as 4th Mate of the *Admiral Watson* Indiaman 23 Nov. 1767. " Distinguished himself on active service." Carried out a large-scale survey of Budge-Budge and the Hooghly R.

PARRY or PERRY, Ambrose (*d.* 1763). Captain, Bengal Eur. Regt. Cadet (?) Ensign 7 June 1757. Lieut. 30 Apr. 1759. Capt. 1761. *d.* 25 June 1763 : kld. in action at the assault of Patna.
(*N.B.*—One Ambrose Perry *m.* Bristol 6 Aug. 1740, Mary Mason.)
Services : N.F.P.
Refs. : *Broome,* p. 365. *Firminger,* p. 71. *Innes,* p. 169.

PARRY, Edward (1760/61-1800). Captain, 12th N.I. *b.* 1760/61. Cadet 1782. Admitted 15 Nov. 1782. Ensign 12 Feb. 1783. Lieut. 3 Feb. 1790. Capt. 7 Jan. 1796. *d.* Allahabad 27 Oct. 1800.
A native of Salop. *m.* Calcutta 14 May 1788, Philadelphia, dau. of William Bondfield (or Bonfield), of Calcutta, auctioneer.
Services : Sailed for India in the *Worcester* 6 Feb. 1782, aged 21. Posted to 3rd Bengal Eur. Regt. 28 Feb. 1783. Ensign 5th Eur. Bn. in July and Dec. 1787 ; posted Lieut. to do. 5 Feb. 1790 ; to 9th Bn. Sepoys 9 Sept. 1791 ; from 5th to 2nd Eur. Bn. 18 Aug. 1794 ; to 2nd Eur. Regt. June 1796.

PARRY, Richard. Lieutenant, Infantry. Cadet (?) Ensign 1 May 1759. Lieut. 18 Sept. 1761. *d.* Barrackpore (?)
Services : Out of the Service before Feb. 1767. N.F.P.
Note : There is possibly some confusion between this man and the following.

PARRY, Richard (d. 1763). Lieutenant, Artillery. (22) Cadet 1761. Fireworker 25 Oct. 1761. Lieut. 1763. d. unm. 5th, 6th or 11th Oct. 1763: massacred at or near Patna by order of Nawab Mir Muhammad Kasim. (See note to Hugh Mackay.) Formerly of the psh. of St. Saviour, Southwark, Surrey. Nephew of Stephen Parry.
Services: Assault of Patna city 25 June 1763 (w.).
Refs.: Broome, p. 365. Firminger, p. 71. Stubbs, i. 25. Will (P.C.C.); Admon. 9 June 1766.

PARRY, Richard (d. 1787). Lieutenant, 5th Bn. Sepoys. Country Cadet 1781. Ensign 20 Aug. 1781. Lieut. 5 June 1783. d. Calcutta 24 Aug. 1787.
Services: Asst. Comy. Gen. June-Nov. 1785.
Refs.: G.M. 1788, i. 366.

PARRY, Richard (1760/61-1794). Lieutenant, Infantry. b. 1760/61. Country Cadet 1782. Ensign 8 May 1783. Lieut. 2 June 1790. d. Chunar 10 Oct. 1794, aged 33.
Services: Apptd. Vol. by Sir Eyre Coote 9 Apr. 1782, and served as such with the Bengal detachment during Second Mysore War. Posted to 1st Bengal Eur. Regt. 28 Feb. 1783. Was an unposted Ensign in July 1787. Posted to 3rd Eur. Bn. 5 Feb. 1790; transfd. from 1st do. to 6th do. 27 Oct. 1792; to 35th Bn. Sepoys; to 5th Bn. Sepoys 16 Apr. 1793.
Refs.: M.I. Chunar (Shamspur) old cemetery, erected by his old schoolfellow Elliot Voyle, q.v.

PARSONS, James Duckett (1786-1868). Lieut. General, C.B. Colonel 50th N.I. b. Dublin Dec. 1786. Cadet 1805. Arrived in India 13 Dec. 1806. Ensign (24 May 1806) 19 Dec. 1806. Lieut. 13 Aug. 1812. Capt. 1 May 1824. Major 22 Apr. 1836. Lt. Col. 7 July 1842. Col. 31 Mar. 1853. Maj. Gen. 28 Nov. 1854. Lt. Gen. 18 Mar. 1863. d. Almora, U.P., 9 Nov. 1868.
bapt. St. Michan's, Dublin, 18 Jan. 1787. Younger son of William Parsons, of Lisburn St., Dublin, and Sarah his wife, dau. of William Barrett, of Castle Blake, co. Tipperary. Uncle of Georgina Rebecca, wife of Alexander William Hawkins, q.v., and nephew of Quintin Dick and of Richard Duckett, of Whitestown, co. Waterford. m. 1st, Fatehgarh 18 Dec. 1822, Maria, 7th dau. of Roger Swetenham (formerly Comberbach), and sister of Edmund Swetenham, q.v. (See also Adoniah Smith.) (She died Cawnpore 3 Aug. 1838.) m. 2nd, Mhow 12 Feb. 1848, Ellen Jacob, widow, dau. of Henry

Dawson, of Drummartyn Castle, co. Dublin, barr.-at-law. (She died 29 Aug. 1885.)
Services : Barasat C.C. Posted Ensign to 25th N.I. in 1807. Capture of Mauritius 1810; Ensign 1st Vol. Bn. Nepal War 1814-15 ; Lieut. 2/25th N.I., in 4th Div. Nepal War 1816 ; Lieut. 2/25th N.I., in 3rd Bde. Centre Column (India medal). Adjt. 2/25th N.I. 1 July 1814 till 4 Dec. 1822. Third Mahratta War. On service in Rajputana 1820. Supy. S.A.C.G. 30 Nov. 1822 ; S.A.C.G. 12 Dec. 1823. Transfd. to 50th N.I. (late 2/25th) May 1824. Supervisor of Hissar Stud 19 Sept. 1825 till 12 Apr. 1837. D.A.C.G. 2 cl. 1 May 1826 ; 1 cl. 3 Oct. 1828 ; A.C.G. 2 cl. 26 Aug. 1831 ; 1 cl. 29 Nov. 1833 ; D.C.G. 12 Apr. 1837 till 24 Dec. 1847. First Afghan War 1839 ; Ghazni (w.) ; D.C.G. (Medal) (*Lond. Gaz.* 30 Oct. 1839). Posted Lt. Col. to 18th N.I. 1843. Gwalior campaign ; Paniar (*Lond. Gaz.* 8 Mar. 1844) ; D.C.G. (Bronze star). Apptd. to 1st circle of supervision, Comst. Dept., 28 May 1844. First Sikh War ; Mudki ; Ferozshahr ; Sobraon ; D.C.G. (Medal with 2 clasps). Transfd. to 66th N.I. 1846. Bdr. comdg. Gwalior Contingent 5 Jan. 1848 till June 1853. Transfd. from 50th to 68th N.I. 6 Nov. 1851 ; to 48th N.I. 9 Apr. 1852. Posted Col. to 57th N.I. June 1853 ; to 50th N.I. Jan. 1854. Bdr. 2 cl. comdg. Rohilkhand district 29 July 1853 till Mar. 1856 ; afterwards Comdt. at Bareilly. Served 62 yrs. in the East without ever going home. C.B. 3 Apr. 1843. Durani 2 cl. 26 Mar. 1841.[1]

Refs.: Burke's *Landed Gentry*, 3rd edn., p. 479, *s.n.* Greene, of Kilmanahan Castle. *Greene* (portrait). *Boase.*

[1] *Note :* The letter D (signifying *Durani*) annexed to his name in the *A.L.* omitted at his request (*Cons.* 26 Jan. 1842).

PASCHOUD, Charles Frederick (1770-1812). Captain, 3rd N.I.
b. château de Daillens, canton Vaud, Switzerland, 5 Aug. 1770. Cadet 1790. Admitted 14 Sept. 1791. Ensign 25 Dec. 1792. Lieut. 5 Oct. 1794. Capt. 21 Sept. 1804. *d. unm.* Delhi 1 Sept. 1812.

bapt. Daillens 2 Sept. 1770. Younger son of Jean François Paschoud, seigneur de Daillens, *q.v.*, and Barbille Marguerite his wife. Brother of John Francis Paschoud, *q.v.* Godson of the Baron de Puellnitz et de Montriohor. Naturalized 14 Apr. 1808. Ed. Colmar école militaire 1784-7.

Services : Apptd. Cadet 19 Jan. 1791 ; sailed for India in the *Lord Hawkesby* 30 Mar. 1791. Transfd. from Art. to 1st Eur. Bn. 10 Sept. 1792 ; to 2nd do. 9 Oct. 1793. Second Rohilla War ; battle of Bitaurah ; Lieut. 2nd Eur. Bn. Lieut. 2/3rd N.I. in

1796 and in June 1798. Fur. 7 Mar. 1803 till 15 Sept. 1808. Capt. 2/3rd N.I.

Refs.: Paschoud: *Rameau des Seigneurs de Daillens*, by Dr. Emile Piguet, in *Recueil de Généalogies Vaudoises*, tome ii, fasc. 3. Will dated on board *Lord Nelson*, 10 Mar. 1803; proved 22 Oct. 1812.

*PASCHOUD, Jean François (1725-1783). Captain. Artillery.
b. Gantenaz, Switzerland, 1725. 2nd Lieut. (Madras) Art. 21 July 1755. Lieut. May 1756. Capt. Lt. (? 1757). Capt. (? June or 3 Oct. 1757). Resigned Dec. 1758. *d.* Daillens 28 Jan. 1783, of an apoplectic stroke.

bapt. Lutry, canton Vaud, 7 Jan. 1725. Only son of Moïse Paschoud and Anthoinaz his wife, dau. of Jean Gamaliel Cornut. *m.* in England 1760,[1] Barbille Marguerite, eldest dau. of Pierre Abram de Treytorrens. (She died Daillens 1823.) Father of Charles Frederick and John Francis Paschoud, *qq.v.*

Services: Sailed for Madras with the Swiss Coy. of Art. in the *Mountford* in 1753. Accompanied Clive to Bengal in Oct. 1756. Battle of Kasipur 5 Feb. 1757; capture of Chandernagore (bruised by the fall of a house); battle of Plassey, having voted at the council of war against immediate action; Capt. Art.[2] Apptd. to tempy. charge of Art. Coy. 3 Oct. 1757. On his return to Switzerland he resided at Daillens, the estate and seigneurie of which he had purchased from Col. Sigismond Weiss in 1760, and at Gantenaz.

Refs.: Dr. E. Piguet (*ut supra*). *Dict. biog. des Genevois et des Vaudois*, par A. de Montet. *Dict. hist., géog. et statistique du canton de Vaud*, par E. Mottaz, i. 597, *s.v.* Daillens. Memoir, par "F.P.," in the *Revue hist. vaudois*, 1898, p. 151. Leslie, No. 21.

[1] *Note*: Marriage resolemnized at Frauenkappelen 29 June 1762.

[2] *Note*: There is considerable doubt as to whether he or William Jennings, *q.v.*, was actually in comd. of the Art. at the battle of Plassey. As the question is of some historical interest it may be as well to quote the authorities on both sides. In a " List of the Troops in Bengal on 26 June 1757 " (*Orme MSS.*), three days after the battle, he is shown as Capt. (no date), and Jennings as Capt. Lt. (25 May 1757). Further, de Montet (op. cit.) states, "Dans une seconde bataille livrée à Plassey le 23 juin 1757, Paschoud, auquel on avait confié le commandement de l'artillerie, détermina par l'habilité de ses manœuvres et la précision de son tir la défaite complete du soubah, . . ." Also, in the original record of the council of war, now in the Powis MSS. (cited in *Forrest's*

Clive, p. 443), Passhaud (*sic*) comes before Jennings. On the other hand, it appears that Jennings, then a Lieut., was in comd. of the detachment of Madras Art. when it sailed from Madras for Bengal in Oct. 1756 ; and *Broome* (p. 139), in his list of those who voted at the council of war on 21 June, gives : " Capt. William Jennings, comdg. the Art. ; Capt. Lt. Francis Parshaw."

PASCHOUD, John Francis (1762-1814). Lieut. Colonel, Invalid Est. Artillery. (234) *b.* Binzen, Baden, 13 Feb. 1762. Cadet 1782. Admitted 3 Feb. 1783. Fireworker 16 Aug. 1782. Lieut. 14 Sept. 1790. Capt. Lt. 8 Jan. 1796. Capt. 15 Nov. 1802. Major 13 May 1807. Lt. Col. 11 Dec. 1810. Invalided 1 Mar. 1812. *d. unm.* Chunar 17 Jan. 1814.

Elder son of Jean François Paschoud, *q.v.*, and Barbille Marguerite his wife. Brother of Charles Frederick Paschoud, *q.v.* Ed. Stuttgart Mily. Acad.

Services : Sailed for India 11 Sept. 1782. Fireworker 2nd Bn. Art. in July 1787. Second Mahratta War ; siege of Deig (? w. in rt. arm) ; Capt. 1st Coy. 1st Bn., d.d. from 7th Coy. 1st Bn. Art. Comdt. at Bencoolen 1807-8.

Refs. : Dr. E. Piguet (*ut supra*). Will dated 17 Aug. 1806 ; admon. 10 June 1814. M.I. at Chunar.

PASMORE, William (1789-1837). Major, 19th N.I. *bapt.* Helston, Cornwall, 11 Aug. 1789. Cadet 1805. Arrived in India 19 Aug. 1806. Ensign 7 Sept. 1806. Lieut. 15 May 1810. Capt. 1 May 1824. Major 8 Oct. 1836. *d.* Madras 28 May 1837 : drowned in the surf when coming ashore from the *Clairmont*.[1]

Eldest son of William Pasmore, of Helston, and Gertrude his wife. *m.* (? Bridget, who died Calcutta 17 Mar. 1843, aged 44.) Ed. Blundell's 19 Aug. till 15 Dec. 1803.

Services : Barasat C.C. Posted Ensign to 3rd N.I. in 1807. (? Operations in Bundelkhand 1809 ; Rajaoli ; Ajaigarh ; Ensign 1/3rd N.I.) Capture of Java 1811 ; Lieut. L.I. Vol. Bn. Left Java July 1812. Adjt. & Qmr. 3rd N.I. 1812-14. Adjt. 1/3rd N.I. 1 July 1814 till 17 June 1824. Transfd. to 19th N.I. (late 2/3rd) May 1824. First Burma War ; Arakan 1825 ; Capt. 1st Gren. Bn. D.A.A.G. on Est. 27 Mar. 1829 ; posted to Presdy. 11 Apr. 1829 ; 2nd A.A.G. of the Army 5 Dec. 1829 ; 1st do. 16 Feb. 1831 ; D.A.G. of the Army (with official rank of Major) 28 Jan. 1832 till 7 Aug. 1834. Apptd. to comd. Persian troops disciplined by British officers 19 Jan. 1833. Granted local and tempy. rank of Col. whilst so employed 9 July 1833. (? Local Lt. Col. 1 Mar.

1834.) Sailed for Bushire from Bombay 20 Nov. 1833 ; comd. of regular Persian army conferred on him by Prince Regent Aug. 1834 ; left Persia on arrival of Sir Henry Bethune 8 Sept. 1836 ; arrived Bombay 27 Mar. 1837. Order of Lion and Sun, 2 cl., conferred on him by H.M. Mohd. Shah Oct. 1835 ; 1 cl. May 1837.

Refs.: *Blundell's School Register.* *G.M.* 1837, ii. 659. *A.J.* N.S. xxiv. 74, 103, 159.

[1] *Note :* Two other lives were lost on this occasion, and on the previous day a similar mishap caused the death of four persons.

*PATCH, Charles (1797-1818). Lieutenant, Artillery. (461)
b. Topsham, Devon, 30 Dec. 1797. Cadet 1814. Fireworker 14 Aug. 1817. Lieut. 1 Sept. 1818. *d.* in camp at Betul, C.P., 2 Nov. 1818.

bapt. Topsham 27 June 1798. Eldest son of James Patch, of Topsham, and Mary Elizabeth his wife, *née* Cox, of W.I. His sister *m.* Paul Wynch Willis, *q.v.* Addiscombe Cadet 1812-14.

Services : Third Mahratta War ; Dhamoni ; Mandala ; Lieut. 7th Coy. 1st Bn. ; d.d. 6th Coy. 3rd Bn. ; transfd. in June 1818 to 5th Coy. 2nd Bn.

Refs. : *Bath Chron.* 20 May 1819. M.I. Betul bazar and in St. Margaret's church, Topsham.

PATCH, Henry (1800-1858). Major, Invalid Est. 73rd N.I.
b. Dinapore 24 May 1800. Cadet 1816. Admitted 31 Mar. 1818. Ensign (?) Lieut. 1 Aug. 1818. Capt. 6 Aug. 1834. Major 29 May 1844. Invalided 4 Apr. 1845. *d.* Stoke, Devonport, 8 May 1858.

bapt. Dinapore 2 May 1804. Son of John Patch, Surg. Bengal, and Frances Catherine his wife, dau. of Henry Revell, B.C.S. Nephew of John Raithby Revell, *q.v.* His maternal aunt *m.* William Bedell, *q.v.* *m.* Azimgarh 21 Sept. 1826, Charlotte, only dau. of Robert Davies, *q.v.*, and widow of John Sturmer, of Nizamabad. (She died Clifton 2 Feb. 1878, aged 78.) Addiscombe Cadet 1816-17.

Services : Posted Lieut. to 1/5th N.I. in 1818. Transfd. to 11th N.I. (late 1/5th) May 1824 ; to 5th Extra Regt. (became 73rd N.I.) May 1825. Actg. Adjt. Gorakhpur L.I. 19 Sept. 1826 ; do. Left Wing 5th Extra Regt. 14 Apr. 1827. Fur. s.c. 1 Feb. 1838 till 22 Sept. 1841, 1845-6, 16 Feb. till 28 Dec. 1850, and 26 Feb. 1856 till death. No record of active service.

Refs. : Burke's *Visitation of Seats and Arms*, 1S. i. 69. *A.J.* xxiii. 529. *G.M.* 1858, i. 686. *The Times*, 13 May 1858.

PATER, John (d. 1764). Ensign, Infantry. Cadet (?) Ensign (?) bur. Calcutta 24 July 1764.
Services: N.F.P.

PATER,[1] John (1750/51-1817). Lieutenant. Cavalry. Afterwards Lt. Gen. Madras Cav. Cornet 21 Aug. 1779. Lieut. 10 Apr. 1781. Resigned 1 Aug. 1785. d. unm. Madras 18 Oct. 1817, aged 66.

Of Bossington, Hants. Brother of Adm. Charles Dudley Pater, R.N., and of Mrs. Charlotte Martin, of St. Anthony's, Cornwall.

Services: Was a Lieut. of Cav. in the Nawab of Arcot's service in Sept. 1779, when he was apptd. Cornet on the Bengal Est. Cornet 2nd Cav. in Sept. 1780. Granted leave p.a. to Madras 11 Sept. 1780. Second Mysore War 1781-5; Cuddalore; Capt. comdg. 1st Regt. Nawab's Cav.; " acted as a Cav. Ofr. during the whole of the Carnatic War by Sir Eyre Coote's permission." (Original Cons. 20 Mar. 1786, No. 20.) Resigned his Commission in Bengal Army at Madras and transfd. as Lieut. of Cav. to Madras Est. Capt. 22 Apr. 1784; Major 19 Nov. 1790; Lt. Col. 31 Dec. 1796; Col. 1 Jan. 1798; Maj. Gen. 1 Jan. 1805; Lt. Gen. 4 June 1813. Comdd. N. Div. of Madras Army 1809-13. Retired on Off-reckoning fund 13 Sept. 1813.

Refs.: Wilson, ii. G.M. 1818, ii. 91. Will dated 18 Sept. 1817; proved (Madras) 11 Nov. 1817. M.I. St. Mary's cemetery, Madras.

[1] Note: The name sometimes appears as Patter.

PATERSON, Francis Stuart (1816-1860). Major, 54th N.I. b. Kenton, Devon, 20 Nov. 1816. Cadet 1834. Arrived in India 21 July 1835. Ensign (12 Dec. 1834) 5 Feb. 1835. Lieut. 10 Sept. 1838. Capt. 13 Jan. 1842. Major 6 June 1858. d. Delhi 26 May 1860, of smallpox.

Elder son of William Paterson, Capt. R.N., C.B., of St. John's, Newfoundland, and Sarah his wife, dau. of S. Bisset. Nephew of James Paterson (1784-1850), q.v. m. Karnal 10 Aug. 1840, Jane Maria, widow of —— Cunninghame. (She died London 24 May 1897, aged 74.) Addiscombe Cadet 1 Feb. 1833 till 12 Dec. 1834.

Services: Ensign d.d. 66th N.I. 8 Aug. 1835. Posted to 55th N.I. 24 Sept. 1835. Transfd. to 54th N.I. 27 Nov. 1835. First Afghan War 1842; operations in Khyber Pass in Jan.; forcing of Khyber in Apr.; advance on Jalalabad; Capt. 54th N.I., d.d. 30th N.I., in Col. Wild's Bde. (Medal). First Sikh War; Ferozshahr; Capt. 54th N.I. (Medal). Was at Delhi in comd.

of a detachment at the Kashmir Gate when the 54th N.I. mutinied on 11 May 1857, but succeeded in escaping to Karnal, thence to Meerut.

Refs.: Burke's *Landed Gentry*, 13th edn., p. 1377, *s.n.* Paterson, of Castle Huntly, co. Perth. *De Rhé-Philipe. G.M.* 1860, ii. 322. *The Times*, 20 July 1860. M.I. in Kashmir Gate cemetery, Delhi.

PATERSON, James (1784-1850). Captain. 4th N.C. *b.* Longforgan, co. Perth, 25 June 1784. Cadet 1798. Arrived in India 12 Jan. 1801. Cornet 24 June 1800. Lieut. 11 Mar. 1805. Capt. 1 Jan. 1819. Retired 13 May 1819. *d.* 10 Jan. 1850.

bapt. Longforgan 11 July 1784. 6th son of George Paterson, M.D., of Castle Huntly, Longforgan, J.P. co. Perth, and Hon. Anne Gray his wife, youngest dau. of John, 12th Lord Gray, of Kinfauns. Uncle of Francis Stuart Paterson, *q.v. m.* 3 Sept. 1821, Davie, only dau. of David Erskine.

Services: Operations in Jumna Doab 1803; Sasni; Bijaigarh; Kachaura; Cornet 4th N.C. Second Mahratta War; Aligarh; Laswari; Cornet 4th N.C. (India medal). Fur. 30 Nov. 1805 till 17 Sept. 1808. Adjt. 4th N.C. 25 Aug. 1811 till 28 Feb. 1817. Fur. 22 Dec. 1816 till retirement.

Refs.: Burke's *Landed Gentry*, 13th edn., p. 1377, *s.n.* Paterson, of Castle Huntly, co. Perth.

PATERSON, James (*d.* 1810). Lieutenant, 14th N.I. Cadet 1799. Arrived in India 22 Dec. 1799. Ensign 4 Jan. 1800. Lieut. 29 May 1800. *d.* Midnapore 10 Apr. 1810.

Services: Fur. 4 Apr. 1801. Posted Lieut. to 1/14th N.I. 15 Apr. 1801. (? Second Mahratta War; battle of Delhi; Agra; Gwalior; Monson's retreat; Lieut. 1/14th N.I.)

PATERSON, James (1790-1862). Lieutenant. 18th N.I. *b.* Montrose 30 June 1790. Cadet 1811. Ensign 6 Mar. 1814. Lieut. 6 Oct. 1816. Resigned 22 Apr. 1823. *d.* Boulogne-sur-Mer 6 May 1862.

Son of David Paterson, M.D., and Helen Ballingall his wife. *m.* Calcutta 10 Dec. 1816, Miss Louisa Dawes. (? *See also* Thomas Gilbert Alder.) Ed. Edinburgh.

Services: Posted Ensign to 1/18th N.I. in 1814. Nepal War 1816; Ensign 1/18th N.I., in 1st Bde., Rt. Column. Insurrection in Cuttack Apr. 1816; Ensign 1/18th N.I. Third Mahratta War; Jawad; Lieut. 1/18th N.I. Fur. 1 yr. 24 Nov. 1820 till resignation.

Refs.: The Times, 13 May 1862.

THE BENGAL ARMY, 1758-1834   471

PATERSON, John (1783-1850). Captain. 1st N.I. b. Glentaggart, Douglas, co. Lanark, 13 Feb. 1783. Cadet 1804. Arrived in India 10 Sept. 1805. Ensign 19 Oct. 1805. Lieut. 22 Feb. 1806. Capt. 1 Jan. 1819. Retired 7 Nov. 1821. d. 10 Jan. 1850.

2nd son of James Paterson, in Glentaggart, and Agnes his wife, sister of George Ranken, of Whitehill, Sorn. Brother of James Paterson, of Carmacoup. m. 1st, Catherine. (She died 1819.) m. 2nd, Edinburgh 19 Feb. 1829, Ann, 2nd dau. of W. Howison, of Edinburgh, writer.

Services : Posted Lieut. to 1st N.I. in 1806. Fur. 2 Dec. 1808 till 1811. Third Mahratta War ; Rampur ; Jawad ; Lieut. 1/1st N.I., in Left Div. Intr. & Qmr. 1/1st N.I. 1818. Fur. 1819 till retirement. Capt. 1/1st N.I.

Refs. : Paterson's Hist. of Ayr and Wigton.

PATERSON, Thomas (d. 1791). Lieutenant, Infantry. Country Cadet 1782. Ensign 1 May 1783. Lieut. 1 May 1790. d. Calcutta 5 Feb. 1791.

Services : Posted Ensign to 3rd Bengal Eur. Regt. 28 Feb. 1783 ; unposted Ensign in July 1787 ; posted to 4th Eur. Bn. 5 Feb. 1790.

PATERSON, William (1751-1836). Lieutenant. 2nd Bn. Sepoys. b. Plaister, Ireland, 24 Mar. 1751. Cadet 1776. Ensign 15 Mar. 1777. Lieut. 12 Aug. 1778. Struck off 1793. d. Mason Lodge, co. Donegal, 24 Jan. 1836.

Of Mason Lodge, or Munfad, Taughboyne, and Tullybogley, co. Donegal. Son of Andrew Paterson, of Mason Lodge, and jure uxoris of Tullybogley, and Dorothea his wife, dau. of Rev. Matthew Leslie, rector of Kilmacrenan. Nephew of Matthew Leslie, q.v. m. Mar. 1789, Margaret, 4th dau. of William Babington, of Marble Hill, co. Donegal. (She died 7 Jan. 1845, aged 77.) His dau. was step-mother of Bristow Marshall, q.v.

Services : Apptd. Cadet 13 Dec. 1775 ; sailed for India in the Nassau 9 Jan. 1776. Apptd. A.D.C. to his uncle, comdg. Tempy. Bde. at Fatehgarh, 7 Aug. 1777. First Mahratta War ; served under his uncle with the Bengal detachment to Bombay. Fur. on h.p. 7 Feb. 1787 till struck off.

Refs. : Burke's Family Records, p. 460, s.n. Paterson. Burke's Landed Gentry, 15th edn., p. 71, s.n. Babington, of Pinnacle Hill.

PATERSON, William (1791-1819). Lieutenant, 30th N.I. b. Braehead, Kilmarnock, 24 May 1791. Cadet 1807. Arrived in

India 19 Aug. 1808. Ensign 28 Aug. 1808. Lieut. 16 Oct. 1810. d. Saugor 20 May 1819.

Of Kaimshill. Eldest son of William Paterson, of Kaimshill, writer in Kilmarnock. Brother of Martin Thomas Paterson, of Dublin, merchant, Margaret, and Elizabeth, wife of William Yule, q.v. Nephew of Henry Vansittart White, q.v., cousin-german of William Parker (1804-1831), q.v., and brother-in-law of John Hamilton. m. Calcutta 11 Sept. 1816, Charlotte Frances Nisbet, sister of James Temple Smoult, q.v. (She died 27 May 1819, aged 29.)

Services: Barasat C.C. Posted Ensign to 16th N.I. in 1810. Operations in Bundelkhand 1810-11; Lieut. 16th N.I. Transfd. to newly-raised 2/30th N.I. in 1815; Intr. & Qmr. do. 4 May 1815. Apptd. D.A.Q.M.G. 2 cl. 1 Jan. 1817. Third Mahratta War; D.A.Q.M.G. 2 cl., with Rt. Div. of Grand Army. District Bk.Mr. at Saugor 1818 till death.

Refs.: *S.M.* 1820, i. 94. Will dated Agra 28 Oct. 1817; proved 2 July 1819. M.I. at Saugor.

PATMAN, Samuel (1778-1805). Lieutenant, 18th N.I. *bapt.* St. Stephen's, Coleman St., London, 19 Mar. 1778. Cadet 1798. Arrived in India 6 Nov. 1799. Ensign 2 Dec. 1799. Lieut. 29 May 1800. d. 15 Mar. 1805.

Son of Samuel Patman and Mary his wife.

Services: Posted Lieut. to 1/18th N.I. 15 Apr. 1801. Second Mahratta War; Bundelkhand 1803; Narnaul; Kanun; defeat of Rajah Ram Singh July 1804; capture of Jaitpur; Lieut. 1/18th N.I.

Refs.: Intestate; admon. granted 9 Apr. 1805.

PATON, Charles (1791-1830). Lieutenant. 23rd N.I. Subsequently Supt. of Province of Arakan. b. 15 Nov. 1791. Cadet 1809. Arrived in India 9 Oct. 1810. Ensign 5 Apr. 1812. Lieut. 16 Dec. 1814. Resigned 15 June 1823. d. at sea 1830, on board the *Providence*, on his passage to the Cape.

bapt. Kingston-on-Hull 11 Dec. 1791. 3rd and youngest son of William Paton, dockman, and Elizabeth Wilson his wife, of Grimsby. Cousin-german of James George Brown Paton, q.v. m. 1st, ——. m. 2nd (before 1821), his 1st cousin Christian Henderson. (She died 21 Aug. 1827.) His dau. m. William Martin (1807-1888), q.v.

Services: Barasat C.C. Cadet d.d. 9th N.I. in 1811. Posted Ensign to 23rd N.I. in 1812. Adjt. 7th Gren. Bn. at Meerut 1815-16. Supt. construction of civil bldgs. at Saharanpur 1817-18; Asst. to Supt. of civil and mily. bldgs. in Lower Provinces 1819

THE BENGAL ARMY, 1758-1834 473

till resignation. Was Junior Comr. in Arakan in 1828 ; Supt. and Comr. of Province of Arakan in 1830.
Refs. : Burke's *Landed Gentry*, 8th edn., p. 2255, *s.n.* Wood, of Woolley Moor, Yorks. *A.J.* xxvi. 486 ; N.S. iii. 120. Will dated Calcutta 19 Apr. 1830 ; proved 19 Oct. 1830.

PATON, David (1780-1805). Lieutenant, Infantry. Unposted. *b.* Old Machar, Aberdeen, 1 July 1780. Cadet 1800. Never arrived in India. Ensign 24 Oct. 1801. Lieut. 30 Sept. 1803. *d.* at sea 1805, off the Cape on his passage to India.
bapt. Old Machar 11 July 1780. Son of Capt. John Paton, of Ferrachie and Grandhome, co. Aberdeen, and Mary his wife, dau. of William Lance.
Refs. : Burke's *Landed Gentry*, 10th edn., p. 1232, *s.n.* Paton, of Grandhome, co. Aberdeen.

PATON, James (1798-1847). Captain. Artillery. (466) *b.* 13 Sept. 1798. Cadet 1815. Admitted 1 Sept. 1816. Fireworker 14 Aug. 1817. Lieut. 1 Sept. 1818. Capt. 17 May 1833. Retired 1 Sept. 1840. *d.s.p.* Orchard Hill, Bideford, Devon, 29 Dec. 1847.
bapt. Lasswade 23 Sept. 1798. 2nd son of Rev. John Paton, minister of Lasswade, King's Almoner, and Margaret his wife, dau. of —— Main. *m.* (after 1838) Fanny Wilson, 2nd dau. of Surg. Henry Atkinson, Madras Est., and widow of James Corbett Taylor, M.C.S. (She died Lausanne 17 May 1880, aged 63.) Addiscombe Cadet 1813-16.
Services : Served with Rocket Troop H.A. 1820-6. Dy. Comy. Ord. 7 Aug. 1824 till 7 Mar. 1828. First Burma War 1824-6 ; capture of Panhlaing 19 Feb. 1825 (*Lond. Gaz.* 25 Oct. 1825) ; Donabyu 7 Mar. 1825 ; action of 5 Dec. 1825 ; Lieut. Rocket Troop, with Bdr. Cotton's column of Sir A. Campbell's force. Posted as Dy. Comy. Ord. to Saugor mag. in 1826 ; to Ft. Wm. arsenal 1 Mar. 1826. Junior Asst. to A.G.G., Saugor & Narbada territories, 8 Feb. 1828 ; 1st Asst. to Resdt. at Lucknow 25 June 1830 till retirement. Several times officiated for short periods as Resdt. Operations against *Thags*. Mutiny in Lucknow palace on death of the King 8 July 1837, when he was knocked down by the mob and beaten with the butts of muskets. Retired on pension of a Major.
Refs. : Burke's *Landed Gentry*, 13th edn., p. 1378, *s.n.* Paton, of Crailing, Jedburgh. *A.J.* N.S. xxiv. 246, 283. *G.M.* 1848, i. 217. Scott's *Fasti*, i. 330.

PATON, James George Brown (1809-1838). Lieutenant, 47th N.I. b. Rathen, co. Aberdeen, 24 Dec. 1809. Cadet 1826. Arrived in India 13 Oct. 1827. Ensign 8 May 1827. Lieut. 28 Feb. 1832. d. Angoora, nr. Kotah, Rajputana, 18 Apr. 1838: accidentally shot with his own gun in mounting his camel.[1]

bapt. Rathen 22 Jan. 1810. 2nd son of Peter Paton, of Brick Lodge, Fraserburgh, merchant, and Agnes his 1st wife, dau. of John Brown, of Buchan. Brother of John Paton and nephew of John Paton, *qq.v.* Marischal Coll., Aberdeen.

Services: Posted Ensign to 69th N.I. 3 Jan. 1828; transfd. to 47th N.I. 1828. d.d. Magh Sebundy Corps 8 Feb. till Sept. 1830. Disturbances in Cuttack Oct. 1832; Lieut. 47th N.I. Actg. Intr. & Qmr. 47th N.I. 21 Aug. 1832, and 3 Jan. 1838.

Refs.: Burke's *Landed Gentry*, 8th edn., p. 2255, *s.n.* Wood, of Woolley Moor, Yorks. *A.J.* N.S. xxvi. 244. M.I. Agra Cantt. cemetery and at Kotah.

[1] *Note:* He was proceeding from Agra on leave to visit his brother at Nimach. The charge shattered the left side and head and caused instant death. His body was sent to Kotah for burial.

PATON, John (1763-1824). Lieut. Colonel Comdt., 26th N.I. b. 18 Aug. 1763. Cadet 1783. Admitted 22 Oct. 1783. Ensign 10 Feb. 1785. Lieut. 15 Dec. 1791. Capt. 21 Sept. 1804. Major 30 Aug. 1809. Lt. Col. 16 Dec. 1814. Lt. Col. Comdt. 1 Mar. 1824. d. Calcutta 15 Feb. 1824.

5th son of William Paton and Christian his wife, dau. of Robert Scott, of Lumbs, in Buchan. Uncle of John Paton and cousin of James Perry, *qq.v.* *m.* Cawnpore 21 Apr. 1794, Mary, dau. of John Forbes (*d.* 1808), *q.v.* (*See also* William Henry Royle and Bernard Ryan.) (She died Calcutta 22 Sept. 1822, aged 45.) Father of John Forbes Paton and Susan Emily, wife of Sir Robert Henry Cunliffe, Bart., *qq.v.*

Services: Apptd. Cadet 4 Dec. 1782; sailed for India in the *Pigot* 11 Mar. 1783. Unposted Ensign in July 1787; posted to 5th Bengal Eur. Bn. 5 Feb. 1790. Third Mysore War 1791-2; Lieut. Bengal Vols. Lieut. 5th N.I. in June 1798. Adjt. 1/17th N.I. 29 May 1800. Actg. D.A.G. at Cawnpore in 1800. Capt. Lt. 5th N.I. 30 Sept. 1803. Bde. Major at Fatehgarh 1804-6; D.A.G. 1806; Q.M.G. of Bengal Army 18 Feb. 1808 till 1820. Major 2/5th N.I. Posted Lt. Col. to 1/4th N.I. in 1815. Transfd. to 1/14th N.I. in 1816; to 9th N.I. in 1818; to 2/26th N.I. in 1819. M.M.B. Comy. Gen. Nov. 1820 till 27 Nov. 1823. Hon. A.D.C. to G.G. Promoted in England before news of his death was received.

Refs.: Burke's *Landed Gentry*, 8th edn., p. 2255, *s.n.* Wood, of Woolley Moor, Yorks. *S.M.* 1824, ii. 255. Will dated 12 Sept. 1823 ; proved 25 Feb. 1824. M.I. in S. Park St. cemetery, Calcutta.

PATON, John (1803-1842). Bt. Major, 58th N.I. D.Q.M.G. of the Army. *bapt.* Strichen 11 Apr. 1803. Cadet 1818. Admitted 30 Oct. 1819. Ensign 10 June 1819. Lieut. 23 Aug. 1822. Capt. 16 July 1828. Bt. Major 23 Nov. 1841. *d.* 8 Jan. 1842 : kld. in action in the Khurd Kabul Pass during the retreat from Kabul.

Eldest son of Peter Paton, merchant in Fraserburgh, and Agnes his 1st wife. Brother of James George Brown Paton, *q.v.*, and cousin-german of Charles Paton, *q.v.*

Services : Ensign d.d. 18th N.I. 1820 ; posted Ensign to 2/29th N.I. ; Intr. & Qmr. do. 4 Nov. 1822. D.A.Q.M.G. 3 cl. 27 Nov. 1823. Transfd. to 58th N.I. (late 2/29th) May 1824. First Burma War ; Arakan 1825 ; in Q.M.G. Dept., with force under Bdr.-Gen. Morrison (*Lond. Gaz.* 1 Oct. 1825). Leave s.c. to Calcutta Dec. 1825 till Aug. 1826. D.A.Q.M.G. 2 cl. 8 Feb. 1828 ; brought on strength of Q.M.G. Dept. 8 June 1832 ; D.A.Q.M.G. 1 cl. 19 Dec. 1833. Shekhawat expedn. Sept. 1834 till Feb. 1835 ; D.A.Q.M.G. A.Q.M.G. of the Army 24 Apr. 1838 ; posted to 1st Div., Army of Indus, 9 Nov. 1838. First Afghan War 1838-42 ; capture of Ghazni 1839 (Medal) ; leave to India in 1841 ; Nazian Valley ; with Sale's force from Kabul to Gandamak Oct. 1841 ; Khurd Kabul Pass 12 Oct. Apptd. D.Q.M.G. of the Army (with official rank of Major) 5 Nov. 1841. Outbreak at Kabul ; action nr. Kabul 13 Nov. 1841 (s.w.—left arm amputated) ; retreat from Kabul (kld.) ; D.Q.M.G. Durani, 3 cl., 22 Oct. 1841.

Refs. : Burke's *Landed Gentry*, 8th edn., p. 2255, *s.n.* Wood, of Woolley Moor, Yorks. M.I. Afghan Memorial Church, Bombay.

PATON, John Forbes (1796/97-1827). Captain, Engineers. *b.* 1796/97. Cadet 1812. Ensign 6 May 1815. Lieut. 1 Sept. 1818. Capt. 10 May 1823. *d.* at sea 7 Feb. 1827, on board the *Palmyra*, aged 30.

Eldest son of John Paton, *q.v.*, and Mary his wife. Cousingerman of Charles Paton, *q.v. m.* Calcutta 22 Apr. 1820, Emily, 5th and youngest dau. of Hugh Stafford, *q.v.* (*See also* James Caulfeild.) Ed. Edin. High School. Addiscombe Cadet 1811-12.

Services : Nepal War 1814-15 ; Cadet, Asst. Surveyor with Gen. Marley's Div. Nov. 1814 till June 1815. Asst. Surveyor in Garhwal

—Sirmoor survey 1815 till Nov. 1816. Adjt. to a detachment of Engrs. in the field, Asst. Field Engr. Centre Div. of Grand Army, and Asst. to Lieut. William Morton, *q.v.*, at Bareilly in 1817. Third Mahratta War; Adjt. Engrs. Executive Ofr. in Kumaon 1819; do. Agra 1820-1; do. Aligarh 1822. Bk.Mr. 8th Div. 1823; do. Meerut Div. 1824. Offg. Supt. of public bldgs., S.W. frontier, 1826. Fur. s.c. 20 Oct. 1826 till death.

Refs.: Burke's *Landed Gentry*, 8th edn., p. 2255, *s.n.* Wood, of Woolley Moor, Yorks. *A.J.* xxiii. 889.

PATON, William. (*See* **PATTON, William.**)

PATRICKSON, William Gould (*d.* 1842). Lieut. Colonel. 20th N.I. Cadet 1797. Arrived in India 20 Sept. 1799. Ensign 3 Oct. 1798. Lieut. 1 Nov. 1798. Capt. 25 Jan. 1808. Major 19 July 1821. Lt. Col. 22 Oct. 1824. Retired 22 Apr. 1827. *d.* Burlington St., London, 21 Aug. 1842.

Was over 19 and under 22 yrs. of age on 23 Mar. 1799. Formerly of Dublin. (? Son of John Patrickson.) (? T.C.D.; Pensioner 7 Oct. 1793, aged 15; B.A. 1798.)

Services: Lieut. 5th N.I. Fur. 24 Dec. 1802 till 11 Sept. 1805. Capt. Lt. 5th N.I. Mar. 1807. Reduction of Kalinjar 1812; Capt. 2/5th N.I. D.J.A.G. 2nd and 3rd Divs. of Field Army 23 June 1814. (? Nepal War 1814-15; D.J.A.G.) Cantt. Staff Ofr. and Qmr. at Nagpur in 1817. 2nd A.A.G. of the Army 21 Oct. 1817. Third Mahratta War; 2nd A.A.G., with Centre Div. of Grand Army. A.A.G. of the Army 1819-21; D.A.G. 1822. Transfd. as Major to 1/5th N.I.; to 11th N.I. (late 1/5th) May 1824. Posted Lt. Col. to 31st N.I.; to 35th N.I.; to 22nd N.I. 18 Feb. 1825; to 20th N.I. 1826. Fur. 1825 till retirement.

Refs.: *G.M.* 1842, ii. 440. (? *Alumni Dub.*, *s.n.* William Patrickson.)

PATTENSON, Charles (1805-1868). Colonel, 4th N.I. *b.* Calcutta 22 Aug. 1805. Cadet 1825. Arrived in India 30 June 1826. Ensign 4 Dec. 1825. Lieut. 8 Oct. 1839. Capt. 22 Aug. 1847. Major 26 Apr. 1858. Lt. Col. (25 Oct. 1859) 1 Jan. 1862. Col. 18 Mar. 1863. *d.* Agra 9 May 1868.

bapt. Calcutta 24 Sept. 1805. Eldest son of Charles Pattenson, B.C.S., Supt. of the Sulkea salt *golahs* [1] (who was son of T. Pattenson, of Melmerby Hall, Cumberland), and Eliza his wife, dau. of S. Harris, of Comilla, Bengal. Brother of Thomas Francis Pattenson, *q.v.*, and of the wife of Sir James Tennant, *q.v. m.* Gorakhpur 28 Apr.

THE BENGAL ARMY, 1758-1834

1840, Mrs. Frances Courage. Magdalen Hall, Oxon.; matric. 17 July 1823, aged 17.
Services: Posted Ensign to 24th N.I. in 1826; transfd. to 4th N.I. 28 Sept. 1827; to 2nd N.I. 27 Aug. 1831; to 4th N.I. 18 Feb. 1832. Second Sikh War; Capt. 4th N.I., with Bdr. Wheeler's force in Jullundur Doab (Medal). Operations against the Aka Khel Afridis Mar. 1855 (s.w. 27 Mar.); Bt. Major comdg. 4 Coys. 4th N.I., with force under Lt.-Col. John Craigie-Halkett, *q.v.* Was comdg. Left Wing 4th N.I. at Kangra on the outbreak of the Mutiny. This Wing was disarmed 16 May 1857 and marched to Hoshiarpur, where it mutinied 5 May 1858, when he was still in comd. On disbandment of 4th N.I. in 1861, he did general duty at Delhi and Agra till death.
Refs.: Alumni Oxon.
[1] *Note:* Hind. *golā*—a store-house for grain or salt.

PATTENSON, Thomas (? *d.* 1811). Ensign. Infantry. Cadet 1770. Ensign 3 Apr. 1771. Resigned 24 Mar. 1775.
N.B.—The following is conjectural only: (? Of Melmerby Hall, Cumberland; high sheriff 1793. Only son of Rev. Lancelot Pattenson, rector of Melmerby, and Margaret his wife, 5th dau. of Charles Orfeur, of High Close.
m. 1769, Barbara, 4th dau. of John Grainger, of Bromfield. Grandfather of Charles Pattenson, *q.v.* Oriel Coll., Oxon.; matric. 14 Dec. 1764, aged 17. *d.* Melmerby Hall Dec. 1811.)
Services: N.F.P.
Refs.: (? Jefferson's *Hist. of Cumberland*, p. 302. *G.M.* 1811, ii. 662.)

PATTENSON, Thomas Francis (1811-1842). Lieutenant, 2nd N.I. *bapt.* Charmouth, Dorset, 9 Nov. 1811. Cadet 1827. Arrived in India 21 Nov. 1828. Ensign 18 June 1829. Lieut. 7 Mar. 1837. *d.* Kandahar 26 Mar. 1842, from the effects of wounds received 26 Dec. 1841.
Son of Charles Pattenson, Senior Merchant B.C.S., and Elizabeth his wife. Brother of Charles Pattenson, *q.v.*, and of the wife of Richard Horsford, *q.v.*
Services: Ensign d.d. 59th N.I. 14 Jan. 1829. Posted to 4th N.I. 3 June 1829; transfd. to 2nd N.I. 4 Nov. 1834. Intr. & Qmr. 2nd N.I. 9 Feb. 1837 till death. Actg. Staff Ofr. to convoy proceeding to Afghanistan under Lt.-Col. Newton Wallace, *q.v.*, 8 Feb. 1840. First Afghan War 1840-2; placed at tempy. disposal of P.A. Kandahar from 30 May 1840; Bde. Qmr. to detachment under

Sale 21 July 1840; operations against Duranis 1841; action at Landi-nawa 3 Jan. (w.), with detachment 2nd N.I. under Capt. H. W. Farrington, q.v.; action on banks of Helmand R., nr. Girishk, 3 July 1841, as A.P.A. with force under Capt. John Woodburn, q.v.[1]; mutiny of "Jan-baz" Horse nr. Kandahar 26 Dec. 1841 (s.w.); Lieut. 2nd N.I.

Refs.: M.I. Afghan Memorial Church, Bombay.

[1] *Note:* Whilst walking over the field towards morning after the engagement, he was severely stabbed in the right side by one of the wounded enemy.

PATTER, John. (*See* **PATER, John.**)

PATTERSON, James (*d.* 1780). Lieutenant, Infantry. Cadet 1769. Ensign 8 Dec. 1769. Lieut. 3 Apr. 1773. *d.* Benares Oct. 1780.

Services: Was Ensign in the Select Picket in Apr. 1772. Sec. to Lt.-Col. John Upton, q.v., on his Mission to Poona 1775-6, and returned to Calcutta shortly after the signing of the treaty in Mar. 1776. Capture of Gwalior Aug. 1780.

PATTERSON, John (*d.* 1797). Captain, Infantry. Country Cadet 1778. Admitted 9 Mar. 1778. Ensign 1778. Lieut. 23 Aug. 1779. Capt. 24 July 1796. *d.* Barrackpore 13 July 1797.

Services: Lieut. 2/1st Bengal Eur. Regt. in Oct. 1779. First Mahratta War; Baggage Mr. to Bengal force under Grainger Muir, q.v. Was Qmr. to the Fatehgarh detachment in Mar. 1786. Fur. 14 Feb. 1787 till after 1790. Sugar contractor 1796-7, having been engaged in the cultivation of sugar cane in the Saran district of Bengal since his return from fur.

PATTLE, Henry John (1782-1803). Lieutenant, 1st N.C. *b.* London 5 Apr. 1782. Cadet 1797. Arrived in India 2 Mar. 1799. Cornet 11 July 1799. Lieut. 16 June 1800. *d. unm.* Bijaigarh, in the Jumna Doab, 13 Feb. 1803: kld. by a wall falling on him during a hurricane.[1]

bapt. 11 June 1782. Son of Thomas Pattle, B.C.S., and Sarah Hasleby [2] his wife. Brother of William Pattle, q.v. (? and cousin-german of Charlotte, wife of Charles Marsack, q.v.). Ed. Charterhouse; admitted Apr. 1795.

Services: Operations in Jumna Doab 1803; Sasni; siege of Bijaigarh; Lieut. 1st N.C.

Refs.: Pester, p. 57. *I.M.* 4 Apr. 1848, p. 216. *N. & Q.* 11S. xi. 68, 115.

¹ *Note :* " We had a tremendous hurricane this afternoon [13 Feb. 1803] . . . Poor Pattle, of the Cavalry, with his groom, took shelter under a wall, which unfortunately was blown down upon them, and they were both killed with their horses on the spot." (*Pester.*)

² *Note :* Ann Hasleby *m.* Richard Becher, and was mother of the wife of Charles Marsack, *q.v.*

PATTLE, William (1783-1865). General, C.B. Colonel 19th Hussars. *b.* London 28 July 1783. Cadet 1798. Arrived in India 9 Dec. 1800. Cornet (9 Dec. 1800) 19 Mar. 1801. Lieut. 11 Mar. 1805. Capt. 8 June 1816. Major 26 June 1826. Lt. Col. 27 Apr. 1833. Col. 5 Jan. 1844. Maj. Gen. 20 June 1854. Lt. Gen. 18 July 1856. Gen. 9 Oct. 1863. *d.* Dawlish 9 Feb. 1865.

bapt. Marylebone 21 Aug. 1783. Son of Thomas Pattle, B.C.S., and Sarah his wife. Brother of Henry John Pattle, *q.v. m.* 1st, Wynberg, S.A., 28 June 1838, Isabella Clara, 6th and youngest dau. of Rev. Holt Okes, D.D. (She died 4 Nov. 1858, aged 44.) *m.* 2nd, Hove 12 Aug. 1859, Jane Anne, dau. of Rev. Robert Parkinson Brooke, Chaplain Bengal Est., and widow of Capt. Theodore Hickson, 80th Foot.

Services : Transfd. from Inf. to Cav. 1 Apr. 1801. Posted Cornet to 1st N.C. Operations in Jumna Doab 1803 ; Sasni ; Bijaigarh ; Kachaura ; Cornet 1st N.C. Second Mahratta War ; Koil ; Aligarh ; Delhi ; Agra ; Laswari ; capture of Deig ; Bhurtpore ; Lieut. 1st N.C. (India medal). Adjt. 1st N.C. 1806 till Jan. 1810. Operations in Bundelkhand against Gopal Singh 1810 ; Bichaund ; Lieut. 1st N.C. Fur. p.a. 9 Mar. 1811 till 26 Aug. 1815. Third Mahratta War 1817-19 ; Capt. 1st N.C. Leave s.c. 12 mos. to Cape 22 Jan. 1827 ; do. 18 mos. 15 Aug. 1834 ; do. 14 Feb. 1837 till 7 Nov. 1838. Bdr. 2 cl. comdg. 1st Cav. Bde., Army of Reserve (for Afghanistan), 6 June till 13 Oct. 1842. To comd. troops at Sukkur 24 Nov. 1842. Campaign in Sind 1843 ; Miani ; Hyderabad (*Lond. Gaz.* 9 May 1843) ; Lt. Col. comdg. the Cav., 2nd in comd. to Sir Charles Napier (Medal). Fur. s.c. 1845-8. Bdr. 2 cl. and posted to Barrackpore 4 Nov. 1850. Fur. s.c. 27 July 1851 till death. Lt. Col. 8th, 3rd, 4th, 10th, 9th, 1st, 5th L.C. Col. 4th L.C. 1849-58 ; 3rd Eur. L.C. 1858-62 ; H.M. 19th Hrs. 30 Sept. 1862 till death. C.B. 4 July 1843. A.D.C. to Queen Victoria.

Refs. : *The XIXth & their Times*, by Col. John Biddulph, pp. 226-7. Boase. *I.M.* 7 May 1844, p. 388. *The Times*, 18 Feb. 1865.

PATTON, David (*d*. 1771). Cadet, Infantry. Cadet 1771. *d*. Calcutta 29 Aug. 1771.
Services : N.F.P.

PATTON, David (*d*. 1778). Ensign, Infantry. Country Cadet 1773. Ensign 15 Aug. 1776. *d*. Calcutta 20 May 1778.
Son of Philip Patton, collector of customs at Kirkcaldy, co. Fife. Brother of Robert Patton (1743-1812), *q.v.*
Services : Apptd. a Vol. (*c*. June 1773), but not to draw pay till he is apptd. a Cadet. First Rohilla War ; battle of St. George ; Cadet in the Select Picket.
Refs.: Macpherson, p. 137.

*PATTON, Henry Robert (1760/61-1800). Bt. Captain, 17th N.I. *b*. 1760/61. Cadet 1781. Ensign 1781. Lieut. 13 Nov. 1782. Bt. Capt. 7 Jan. 1796. *d*. Bhagulpur, B. & O., 13 Nov. 1800, aged 39.
Brother of William, Charles, John, and Mary Ann Patton.
Services : Exchanged as Cadet from Madras to Bengal Est. Jan. 1783. Lieut. 5th Bengal Eur. Bn. in July 1787 ; 3rd do. in Dec. 1788. Third Mysore War 1791-2 ; Lieut. Bengal Vols. Lieut. 3rd Eur. Regt. in 1796 ; 17th N.I. in 1798.
Refs. : *Philippart MS*. *A.A.R.* iii. 105. Will dated 16 Mar. 1800 ; proved 2 Dec. 1800. M.I. at Bhagulpur.

PATTON, John Wogan (1794-1833). Captain, 37th N.I. *b*. 7 Nov. 1794. Cadet 1810. Admitted 22 Oct. 1811. Ensign 29 July 1813. Lieut. 20 Apr. 1818. Capt. 10 Dec. 1831. *d*. Burdwan, Bengal, 18 Sept. 1833, of fever contracted when surveying *bunds*.[1]
bapt. Kirkcaldy 19 Nov. 1794. Son of Robert Patton, *q.v.*, and Constantia his wife. Brother of Robert Patton, *q.v. m*. Mainpuri, U.P., 6 June 1816, Jane Mary, elder dau. of Brooke Chambers, of Rock Hill, co. Donegal, J.P., high sheriff of Donegal 1798. (*See also* Mossom Boyd.) (She died Weston-super-Mare 27 Oct. 1884, aged 90.)
Services : Entered R.N. and served as a Midshipman in the Walcheren expedn. 1809. Cadet d.d. 5th N.I. 1811-13 ; posted Ensign to 25th N.I. 1813. Nepal War 1814-15 ; skirmish at

Pirazee 19 Feb. 1815 ; Ensign 2/25th N.I., in 4th Div. Transfd. to newly-raised 1/29th N.I. in 1815 ; as Lieut. to 2/18th N.I. in 1818 ; to 36th N.I. (late 1/18th) May 1824 ; to 37th N.I. 31 Mar. 1825. Comdt. newly-raised Dromedary Corps 26 July 1815 till 1 Aug. 1819. Third Mahratta War ; storm and capture of Jawad 19 Jan. 1818 (s.w. in left wrist by sabre cut) ; Ensign comdg. Dromedary Corps (*Lond. Gaz.* 25 Feb. 1819). Granted wound pension for permanent injury. Apptd. Bk.Mr. Agra Div. 3 June 1819 ; do. Ghazipur district 1 Aug. 1819 ; do. 1st (Dum-Dum) Div. (title changed later to Executive Ofr.) 30 Dec. 1822 till Oct. 1832. Leave s.c. 18 mos. to N.S.W. 4 Oct. 1830. Offg. Supt. P.W.D. in Cuttack 1 Oct. 1832.

Refs.: Burke's *Landed Gentry*, 4th edn., p. 229, *s.n.* Chambers, of Fox Hall, co. Donegal. *The Hearseys*, pp. 206-7. *A.J.* N.S. xiii. 205. Will dated Barrackpore 24 June 1832 ; proved 15 Oct. 1833. M.I. at Burdwan.

¹ *Note*: Hind. *band*—an artificial embankment or dam.

PATTON, Robert (1743-1812). Captain. Infantry. Subsequently Colonel and Govr. of St. Helena. *b.* 1743. Country Cadet 1766. Ensign 21 May 1766. Lieut. 18 June 1767. Capt. 4 July 1771. Resigned 2 Mar. 1776. Col. 1776. *d.* Wallington, Hants, 14 Jan. 1812.

3rd son of Philip Patton, collector of customs at Kirkcaldy, co. Fife, and Agnes Loch his wife. Brother of David Patton (*d.* 1778), *q.v.*, and of Philip Patton, Adm. R.N. (*D.N.B.*). *m.* Calcutta 31 July 1772, Constantia Adriana Sally, one of the 17 children of Rev. Robert Mapletoft, chaplain at Ft. Wm., Bengal. (She died 31 Dec. 1811.) Father of John Wogan Patton, Robert Patton, Anne, wife of James Henry Brooke, Selina, wife of James Lumsdaine, and of the mothers of Frederick Torrens and Lumsdaine Walker, *qq.v.*

Services: See *D.N.B.* Apptd. locally in India an Asst. Surgeon 2 Feb. 1764 ; transfd. as a Cadet from medical est. in 1766. Sec. to Bdr.-Gen. Richard Smith, *q.v.*, 1767-9 ; Comdt. of the troop of Eur. Cav. known as " The Governor's Troop of Body Guards," 1769/70 till it was disbanded in 1772. Mily. Sec. to John Cartier, Govr. of Ft. Wm., 1770-2 ; A.D.C. to Warren Hastings, newly apptd. Govr. of Bengal, 13 Apr. 1772 ; afterwards Mily. Sec. to Hastings, who became Govr. Gen. from Oct. 1774. Was gazetted Col. on resigning his Commission. Govr. of St. Helena Mar. 1802 till July 1807, when he retired owing to ill health and returned to England. A presentation of plate was made to him by the inhabitants of St. Helena on his retirement. Author of two treatises upon "The Monarchy and Republic of Rome," 1797, and upon "Principles of Asiatic Monarchies," London, 1801.

Refs.: Family information. *D.N.B. V.B.G.* Col. Crawford's *Roll of I.M.S.,* No. B. 94. *List of Mily. Secs. to the Govrs. Gen. and Viceroys. G.M.* 1812, i. 93. Portrait in *St. Helena, 1502-1938,* by Philip Gosse (Cassell, 1938).

PATTON, Robert (1775-1837). Major General, C.B. Colonel, 62nd N.I. *b.* 1775. Cadet 1791. Admitted 7 Oct. 1791. Ensign 1792. Lieut. 7 Oct. 1794. Capt. 21 Sept. 1804. Major 16 Dec. 1814. Lt. Col. 3 May 1819. Lt. Col. Comdt. 1 May 1824. Col. 5 June 1829. Maj. Gen. 10 Jan. 1837. *d. unm.* at his residence in Bath 11 Nov. 1837.

Eldest son of Robert Patton, *q.v.,* and Constantia his wife. Brother of John Wogan Patton, *q.v.*

Services: Posted Lieut. to 1st Eur. Bn. 19 Nov. 1794. Adjt. 2/5th N.I. 22 Apr. 1799 till 1804. Reduction of Kalinjar 1812; Capt. 2/5th N.I. Comdd., as Major 2/5th N.I., a detachment which on 23 Apr. 1815 completely defeated a force under the Gurkha chief Hastee Dhull (*Lond. Gaz.* 16 Nov. 1815). Third Mahratta War; Major 2/5th N.I. Posted Lt. Col. to 2/5th N.I. in 1819; comdg. at Karnal 1821; posted Lt. Col. Comdt. to 20th N.I. (late 2/5th) May 1824; transfd. to 18th N.I. 12 Feb. 1825. Siege and capture of Bhurtpore; Lt. Col. 18th N.I., Bdr. comdg. 5th Inf. Bde. (w. 18 Jan. 1826 by explosion of our mine—ib. 12 June 1826). To comd. troops at Bhurtpore with rank of Bdr. Gen. 19 Feb. 1826. Transfd. to 15th N.I. 18 Jan. 1828; to 9th N.I. 26 May 1828. Bdr. on the Staff, and comdd. troops in Oudh 26 May 1828 till 11 Feb. 1835. Fur. s.c. 4 Apr. 1835 till death. Col. 9th N.I. June 1829; 62nd N.I. 1 July 1837. C.B. 8 Dec. 1815.

Refs.: Bath Chron. 23 Nov. 1837. *A.J.* N.S. xxv. 63. *G.M.* 1838, i. 109. Will dated Lucknow 20 Jan. 1835; proved 12 Oct. 1838.

PATTON, William (*d.* 1779). Captain, Infantry. Cadet 1764. Ensign 8 Mar. 1765. Lieut. 17 Dec. 1766. Capt. 16 Oct. 1769. *d.* Midnapore 11 Nov. 1779.

Services: Sailed for India in the *Success* 17 May 1764. Posted Ensign to 1st Bengal Eur. Regt. 13 Aug. 1765. Was one of the signatories in Oct. 1766 to an Address in favour of Sir Robert Fletcher, *q.v.,* for which he was dismissed and sent home in Jan. 1767; restored to the Service by C.D. in England, after a reprimand,

9 Dec. 1768 ; returned to India in the *Anson* 22 Mar. 1769. Apptd. to comd. 18th Bn. Sepoys 2 July 1777.
Refs.: Broome, p. lxxii. *Proc. of Select Committee*, 6 Jan. 1767.

PAUL, Henry (1795-1829). Lieutenant, 66th N.I. *b.* 30 Dec. 1795. Cadet 1813. Ensign 16 Dec. 1814. Lieut. 6 Oct. 1817. *d.* at sea 22 Sept. 1829.

bapt. ptely. 31 Jan.; publicly Cheddon Fitzpaine, Somerset, 6 Dec. 1796. 4th son of Henry Paul, " gentleman farmer," and Susannah his wife, dau. of Matthew Coombs. Brother of Matthew Coombs Paul and of the wife of John Fryer Goad, *qq.v.*
Services: Posted Ensign to 1/5th N.I.; transfd. to 2/8th N.I. 19 Dec. 1816. Third Mahratta War; Lieut. 2/8th N.I. Transfd. to newly-raised 33rd N.I. July 1823 ; to 66th N.I. (late 2/33rd) May 1824. Leave s.c. 8 mos. to Mauritius 9 Dec. 1828 till death.
Refs.: Family information.

PAUL (formerly McPHAIL), Lachlan [1] (1755/56-1781). Ensign, Infantry. *b.* in Scotland 1755/56. Cadet 1781. Ensign 25 Apr. 1781. *d.* Calcutta 17 Dec. 1781.

m. Mary Drummond, only dau. of Duncan Murray or MacGregor, XXI of MacGregor. Father of John Alexander Paul MacGregor, *q.v.*
Services: Apptd. Cadet 11 Jan. 1781, aged 25 ; sailed for India in the *Chapman* 13 Mar. 1781.

[1] *Note:* His first name is variously given as Lachlan, Lachlin, Lauchlin, and Laughlin.

PAUL, Matthew Coombs (1790-1865). Lieut. General. Colonel 29th N.I. *bapt.* Cheddon Fitzpaine 20 Jan. 1790. Cadet 1804. Arrived in India 16 May 1806. Ensign 23 Nov. 1805. Lieut. 23 Feb. 1807. Capt. 9 Oct. 1818. Major 11 Apr. 1828. Lt. Col. 15 Sept. 1833. Col. 2 Feb. 1845. Maj. Gen. 20 June 1854. Lt. Gen. 17 May 1859. *d.* 43 Harewood Sq., London, 7 Jan. 1865, aged 74.

3rd son of Henry Paul and Susannah his wife. Brother of Thomas Henry Paul, *q.v.* (Said to have *m.* an Indian lady.)
Services: Served as Cadet at capture of the Cape by Sir David Baird in Jan. 1806. Barasat C.C. 14 mos. Posted Lieut. to 8th N.I. in 1807. Capture of Mauritius 1810 ; Lieut. 2nd Vol. Bn. Nepal War 1814-15 ; Lieut. 1/8th N.I., in 4th Div. Nepal War 1816 ; Lieut. 1/8th N.I., in 2nd Bde. Left Column (India medal). Leave s.c. 6 mos. to sea 14 Feb. 1817. Third Mahratta War ;

Mandala; Capt. 2/8th N.I. With 1st Ceylon Vol. Bn. 1818-19. Transfd. to 9th N.I. (late 1/8th) May 1824. First Burma War; Arakan 1825 ; Capt. 1st Gren. Bn. (clasp to India medal). Major 9th N.I. Posted Lt. Col. to 9th N.I. 8 Feb. 1834. Bdr. 2 cl. comdg. 2nd Bde. 1st Div., Army of Reserve (for Afghanistan), 6 June 1842 till 10 Jan. 1843. Fur. s.c. 22 Feb. 1844 till death. Posted Col. to 29th N.I. 17 Apr. 1845.

Refs.: Family information. *Boase. The Times,* 11 Jan. 1865.

PAUL, Thomas Henry (1785-1866). General. Colonel 20th N.I. *b.* Cheddon Fitzpaine 26 July 1785. Cadet 1800. Arrived in India 4 Sept. 1801. Ensign 4 Sept. 1801. Lieut. 30 Sept. 1803. Capt. 16 Dec. 1814. Major 7 Nov. 1824. Lt. Col. 30 July 1828. Col. 9 July 1840. Maj. Gen. 23 Nov. 1841. Lt. Gen. 11 Nov. 1851. Gen. 22 Nov. 1862. *d.* Melcombe Pl., Dorset Sq., London, 11 June 1866.

bapt. Cheddon Fitzpaine 28 Mar. 1786. 2nd son of Henry Paul and Susannah his wife. Brother of Henry Paul, *q.v.* Ed. Blundell's 29 Jan. 1799 till 25 Mar. 1801.

Services: Ensign d.d. 5th N.I. in 1802 ; posted to 5th N.I. in 1803. Adjt. 1/5th N.I. Mar. 1805 till 1 Oct. 1806. Adjt. 5th L.I. Bn. 1808-10. Capture of Java 1811 (w.) ; Lieut. L.I. Bn. (Medal). Apptd. Adjt. of Prince Prangwedona's Legion 13 Feb. 1812. Capture of Jokyakarta June 1812. Left Java July 1812. Adjt. 1/5th N.I. 2 July 1811 till 4 May 1815. Capt. 1/5th N.I. (? Operations in Baghelkhand 1813 ; Entauri ; Capt. 1/5th N.I.) Transfd. to 20th N.I. (late 2/5th) May 1824. d.d. 2nd Gren. Bn. till 12 Feb. 1825. Posted as Lt. Col. to 20th N.I. 7 Nov. 1828. Shekhawat expedn. 1834. Bdr. 2 cl. and posted to 5th Inf. Bde., Army of Indus, 24 Oct. 1838. Bdr. 2 cl. at Ferozepore 27 Nov. 1840. Fur. p.a. 28 Feb. 1842 till death. Col. 20th N.I. July 1840 till death.

Refs.: Family information. *Blundell's School Register. Boase. The Times,* 14 June 1866.

Note: His son by an Indian lady was murdered during the Mutiny, and a dau. *d.* London in 1913, aged 103.

PAXTON, George Augustus (1806-1825). Cornet, 6th L.C. *b.* co. Carmarthen 29 Sept. 1806. Cadet 1823. Cornet 1 May 1824. *d.s.p.* nr. Ghazipur 15 Mar. 1825 : drowned in the Ganges by the capsizing of a boat.

6th and youngest son of Sir William Paxton, Kt., of Paxton, Cockerell, Traill & Co., Piccadilly, and of Middleton Hall, co.

THE BENGAL ARMY, 1758-1834

Carmarthen, high sheriff 1790, M.P. for Carmarthen, and Anne his wife, dau. of Thomas Dawney, of Aylesbury. His sister *m.* Arthur Goodall Wavell, *q.v.*
Services : Posted Cornet to 6th L.C. No record of active service.
Refs. : Burke's *Landed Gentry*, 5th edn., p. 1062, *s.n.* Paxton, of Cholderton, Wilts. *G.M.* 1825, ii. 382. Will dated 28 Oct. 1824 ; proved 17 May 1825.

PAYNE, George (1786-1806). Lieutenant, Artillery. (331) *b.* Shenley, Herts., 8 Nov. 1786. Cadet 1803. Arrived in India 14 Aug. 1804. Fireworker 20 Aug. 1804. *d.* Cawnpore 25 Oct. 1806, of wounds received in action at the storm of Badekh on 21 Oct.
bapt. 9 Dec. 1786. 4th surviving son of Edward Payne, of Warren St., Fitzroy Sq., London, and Maria his wife, *née* Houghton. Woolwich Cadet 12 Feb. 1802 till 26 Jan. 1804.
Services : Sailed for India in the *Lady Jane Dundas* in 1804. Operations against Apparbal Singh ; storm of Badekh 21 Oct. 1806 (s.w.) ; Lieut. 1st Coy. 3rd Bn. Art., comdg. two field guns with the detachment.
Refs. : Stubbs, iii. 538 *n.* *G.M.* 1807, i. 376.

PAYNE, James William (*d.* 1784). Lieutenant, Infantry. Cadet 1778. Ensign 23 Apr. 1778. Lieut. 4 Jan. 1781. *d.* Calcutta 21 Dec. 1784.
Services : First Mahratta War 1778-81 ; with Bombay detachment. Ensign 1/1st Bengal Eur. Regt. in Oct. 1779. Resigned at Bombay 7 Dec. 1781 ; withdrew his resignation 16 Sept. 1783.

PAYNE, William (1801-1876). Lieut. Colonel. 30th N.I. *bapt.* Barkham, Berks., 26 Nov. 1801. Cadet 1818. Admitted 4 Sept. 1819. Ensign 17 Apr. 1819. Lieut. 16 Dec. 1821. Capt. 30 Dec. 1828. Bt. Major 23 Nov. 1841. Retired 1 Feb. 1844. Hon. Lt. Col. 28 Nov. 1854. *d.* Laburnum cottage, Rownhams, nr. Southampton, 5 July 1876, aged 75.
Son of William Payne, of Tunbridge Wells, Capt. h.p. 8th Foot. *m.* Ghazipur 19 Jan. 1831, Sarah Rebecca, dau. of Michael Joseph Le Marchand, of Ghazipur, indigo planter, and grand dau. of Thomas Wharton, *q.v.*
Services : Ensign d.d. Bengal Eur. Regt. 1819 ; posted Ensign to 1/15th N.I. Intr. & Qmr. 2/15th N.I. 16 Oct. 1823 ; Adjt. do. 15 Nov. 1823. Transfd. to 30th N.I. (late 1/15th) May 1824 ; Adjt. do. 17 June 1824 till 24 June 1829. Comdd. 30th N.I.

20 Dec. 1838 till 20 Mar. 1839, and Aug.-Oct. 1840. First Afghan War 1842 ; action at entrance of Khyber 24 Jan., under Lt.-Col. Tulloch ; with rear column of Bdr. Wild's force on march from Landi Khana to Ali Masjid in Nov. ; Bt. Major 30th N.I. (Medal).
Refs.: The Times, 10 July 1876.

PAYNE, William Robert (1785-?). Cadet. Infantry. *b.* Stoke Damerel, Devon, 20 Nov. 1785. Cadet 1802. (? Never arrived in India.) Resigned (?).

bapt. Stoke Damerel 10 Jan. 1786. Son of William Payne and Jane his wife.

Services : N.F.P.

PEACH, Charles (1777-1837). Lieut. Colonel. 5th Extra Regt. *b.* 5 Feb. 1777. Cadet 1797. Admitted 10 Dec. 1798. Ensign 28 Sept. 1798. Lieut. 1 Nov. 1798. Capt. 8 Sept. 1809. Major 11 July 1823. Lt. Col. 15 Dec. 1824. Retired 13 Apr. 1827. *d.s.p.* Shipston-on-Stour, Worcs., 21 Oct. 1837.

Of Idlicote House, co. Warwick. *bapt.* Allhallows, Bread St., London, 2 Mar. 1777. 4th and youngest son of Samuel Peach, of Dunkirk House, Gloucs., and Christiana his wife, only dau. of Howard Cox, of Bristol and Virginia.

Services : Lieut. 13th N.I. ; transfd. to newly-raised 21st N.I. in 1804. Second Mahratta War 1804-5 ; Lieut. 21st N.I. Capt. Lt. 21st N.I. 2 Feb. 1809 ; Capt. 2/21st N.I. Comdt. Patna Provl. Bn. 8 Mar. 1811 till 1819 ; do. Burdwan Provl. Bn. 1819-24. Transfd. to 41st N.I. (late 1/21st) May 1824 ; posted Lt. Col. to 16th N.I. Jan. 1825. Fur. 1825 till retirement. Transfd. to 7th N.I. in 1826 ; to 5th Extra Regt. 7 July 1826.

Refs. : Burke's *Landed Gentry*, 7th edn., p. 1432, *s.n.* Keighley-Peach, of Idlicote House, co. Warwick. *Misc. Gen. et Her.*, ii. 308. *Bath Chron.* 30 Oct. 1837. Will dated 4 Dec. 1834 ; proved 8 Dec. 1837.

PEACH, Henry Edmund (1786-1833). Major, 16th N.I. Dy. Comy. Gen. *b.* Cheam, Surrey, 16 June 1786. Cadet 1804. Arrived in India 10 Sept. 1805. Ensign 4 Nov. 1805. Lieut. 3 July 1806. Capt. 11 July 1823. Major 13 Sept. 1829. *d.* Cawnpore 3 May 1833.

bapt. Cheam 7 July 1786. Son of Rev. Henry Peach, rector of Cheam, and Jane his wife, dau. of Rev. James Sanxay, rector of Sutton. Brother of Mrs. Henrietta Matilda Comber and of Mary, wife of Gen. Sir Charles Grene Ellicombe, K.C.B., R.E. (*D.N.B.*).

THE BENGAL ARMY, 1758-1834

Services : Posted Lieut. to 2/10th N.I. in 1806. (? On service in Bundelkhand 1808-9 ; Lieut. 2/10th N.I.) S.A.C.G. 11 July 1812 ; A.C.G. 19 Jan. 1816 ; do. 1 cl. 2 Oct. 1819 ; D.C.G. 14 Sept. 1831. With Rewah F.F. Sept. 1813. Nepal War. Attached to Light Bn., Nagpur Subsdy. Force, 1818. Leave s.c. to sea 3 Apr. 1819 till Feb. 1822. Supervisor to Hissar Est. 27 Nov. 1823. Fur. s.c. 23 Feb. 1826 till 23 Apr. 1830.

Refs. : *A.J.* N.S. xii. 191. *G.M.* 1833, ii. 478. Will dated 21 Apr. 1833 ; proved 8 June 1833. M.I. at Cawnpore.

PEACH, Joseph (*d.* 1770). Colonel, Infantry. Comdg. 1st Bde. Major 1 May 1764. Lt. Col. 4 May 1765. Col. 24 Jan. 1767. *d.* Monghyr 29 July 1770.

Brother of Henry Peach, of Writenham (?), Middlesex, and of Elizabeth, wife of Thomas Sadler, of Hardingstone, Northants. *m.* Calcutta 30 Jan. 1770, Apphia, 2nd dau. of Broome Witts, of Chipping Norton. (She *re-m.* 22 June 1772, Sir Thomas Lyttelton, 6th Bart., 2nd Lord Lyttelton, and died 9 Apr. 1840.)

Services : Lieut. H.M. 47th Ft. 28 June 1755. Apptd. in England 1 May 1764, a Field Ofr. on the Bengal Est. ; sailed in the *Prince of Wales* 16 May 1764. Lt. Col. comdg. 2nd Eur. Regt. in 2nd Bde. at Allahabad in 1765. First Mysore War 1767-70 ; arrived in Madras with a detachment from Bengal in Jan. 1768 ; operations against Narayan Deo in May 1768 ; Col. 1st Bengal Eur. Regt., and comdg. the Bengal detachment after the death of Col. William Smith, *q.v.*

Refs. : Burke's *Peerage*, 1923, p. 545, *s.n.* Cobham, V. *Wilson*, i. 254-5. *Macpherson*, p. 42. Will dated 24 Feb. 1770 ; proved 4 Dec. 1770.

PEACH, Onslow. (*See* **PECHÉ, Onslow.**)

PEACOCK, Francis William (*d.* 1795). Lieutenant, Infantry. Country Cadet 1781. Ensign 1 Oct. 1781. Lieut. 2 July 1783. *d.* in hospital at Calcutta ; *bur.* Ft. Wm. 30 Oct. 1795.

(*Probably* son of Francis Peacock, free merchant, and sometime Agent for the Coy. for the purchase of naval stores, and Sabina his wife, *née* Eyles. *Probably* uncle of Francis Walter, *q.v.*)

Services : Apptd. Vol. by Sir Eyre Coote 14 June 1781, and served as such with Bengal detachment during Second Mysore War. Lieut. 5th Bengal Eur. Bn. in July 1787 and in 1790 ; 27th Bn. Sepoys in Dec. 1792.

Refs. : Intestate ; admon. granted to his friend Robert Bowie, *q.v.*, 25 Apr. 1797.

PEACOCKE, Sir Joseph Francis, third baronet (1805-1877). Lieutenant. 5th N.I. Subsequently Lieut. 24th Foot. *b.* Barntick, co. Clare, 1 July 1805. Cadet 1821. Ensign 9 Dec. 1820. Lieut. 1824. Resigned 25 Nov. 1824. *d.s.p.* 1877.

3rd Bart., of Barntick. *s.* 1 Nov. 1847. Only son of Lt.-Col. Sir Nathaniel Levett Peacocke, 2nd Bart., and Henrietta his wife, eldest dau. of Sir John Morris, Bart., of Clasemont, co. Glamorgan. Sandhurst Cadet.

Services: Posted Ensign to 9th N.I. in 1822. Transfd. to 2nd N.I. in 1823; to 5th N.I. (late 1/2nd) May 1824. Ensign H.M. 59th Ft. 12 Oct. 1823; Lieut. do. 24 Nov. 1825; Lieut. 24th Ft. 25 June 1830. Exchanged with Lieut. Griffiths, h.p. 52nd Ft., 4 Jan. 1833. Retired 1 Apr. 1833.

Refs.: Burke's *Peerage,* 1859, p. 784, *s.n.* Peacocke, Bart., of Barntick, co. Clare. Burke's *Landed Gentry,* 11th edn., p. 1303, *s.n.* Peacocke, of Efford Park, Hants. *Walford.*

PEAD, Benjamin (1804-?). Lieutenant. 4th L.C. *b.* Walthamstow 6 Dec. 1804. Cadet 1824. Arrived in India 21 May 1825. Cornet (?) Lieut. 13 May 1825. Resigned 29 Dec. 1826. (Was living in 1851 when the India medal was awarded.)

Son of Benjamin Pead, of Broad St., London, merchant, and Susannah his wife, *née* Green. *m.* (before 1825)?

Services: Ordered to join 5th L.C. 10 June 1825; posted Lieut. to 4th L.C. 1825. Siege and capture of Bhurtpore; Lieut. 4th L.C. (India medal).

PEAKE, Joseph (*d.* 1771). Captain, Infantry. Country Cadet 1765. Ensign 12 Aug. 1765. Lieut. 28 Dec. 1766. Capt. 16 May 1770. *d.* Ghireti, Bengal, July 1771.

Services: Apptd. Cadet 17 Feb. 1765. Apptd. Adjt. 2nd Eur. Regt. 16 Aug. 1765, and was still holding this appt. at Allahabad in May 1766, when he refused to join in the "Batta mutiny."

Refs.: *Broome,* p. 601.

PEAKE, William (*d.* 1769). Captain, Infantry. Capt. 7 Sept. 1768. *d.* Monghyr 29 Dec. 1769.

Services: Ensign H.M. 51st Ft. 3 Aug. 1758; Lieut. do. 10 May 1760; h.p. 51st Ft., on reduction, 1763 till death. Transfd. as Capt. to Bengal Army Sept. 1768 (M.C. 1 Sept. 1768).

*PEAL, John (*d.* 1780). Ensign, Infantry. Cadet (?) Ensign (?) *bur.* Calcutta 30 Dec. 1780.[1]

Services : N.F.P.

¹ *Note :* Perhaps identical with John Peele, *q.v.* Both names, however, appear in the burial register, on successive dates. This may be merely a copyist's error.

PEARCE, Charles (1790-1873). Major. 29th N.I. *b.* Minehead, Somerset, 12 Jan. 1790. Cadet 1805. Arrived in India 19 Sept. 1806. Ensign 23 Sept. 1806. Lieut. 1 July 1809. Capt. 1 May 1824. Retired 24 Apr. 1833. Hon. Major 28 Nov. 1854. *d.* at his residence, Portishead, Somerset, 21 Feb. 1873.

Son of Francis Pearce. *m.* Gorakhpur 15 July 1813, Miss Louisa Georgiana Farrington. (She died Rose-hill Villa, Portishead, 17 Feb. 1882, aged 89.)

Services : Barasat C.C. Posted Ensign to 14th N.I. in 1807 ; actg. Adjt. 5 Coys. 2/14th N.I. 2 Nov. 1812. Nepal War 1814-15 ; Lieut. 2/14th N.I., in 3rd Div. (India medal). Actg. Adjt. 2/14th N.I. 1817-18 ; Intr. & Qmr. do. 2 Dec. 1820 ; Adjt. do. 24 Feb. 1821 till 17 June 1824 ; transfd. to 29th N.I. (late 2/14th) May 1824. Fur. s.c. 17 Oct. 1824 till 6 Aug. 1827.

Refs. : *The Times,* 25 Feb. 1873.

PEARCE, Elias (1790-1818). Lieutenant, 5th N.I. *b.* 1790. Cadet 1805. Arrived in India 11 July 1806. Ensign 6 Aug. 1806. Lieut. 22 Feb. 1809. *d.* in England 18 Aug. 1818.

Services : Apptd. Cadet 15 Jan. 1806, aged 15. Barasat C.C. Posted Ensign to 5th N.I. in 1807. Operations against Gopal Singh in Bundelkhand 1810 ; Tirowa ; Lieut. 1/5th N.I. Operations in Baghelkhand 1813-14 ; Entauri ; Lieut. 1/5th N.I. Fur. 1817 till death.

PEARCE, Thomas (1762/63-1782). (*See* **THOMAS, Pearce.**)

PEARD, Thomas (1785-1808). Lieutenant, 20th N.I. *bapt.* Stoke-Gabriel, Devon, 16 Mar. 1785. Cadet 1804. Arrived in India 6 Apr. 1806. Ensign 29 Mar. 1806. Lieut. 4 Apr. 1807. *d.* Bencoolen 10 Aug. 1808.

Son of Oliver Peard, of Wattan Court, later of Clifton, Somerset, and Catherine his wife. Stepson of John Greatrix Smyth, of Cheltenham. Ed. Blundell's ; admitted 16 Apr. 1793, aged 8 ; left 21 Dec. 1790.

Services : Barasat C.C. Posted Lieut. to 20th N.I. in 1807. No record of active service.

Refs. : *Blundell's School Register.* Will dated Fort Marlbro', 3 June 1808 ; proved 3 Oct. 1809.

PEARSE, Thomas (*d.* 1767). Lieutenant, Infantry. Cadet (?)
Ensign (?) Lieut. 30 May 1767. *d.* 1767.
Services : N.F.P.
Note : Perhaps identical with Thomas Peirce, *q.v.*

PEARSE, Thomas Deane (1741/42-1789). Colonel. Comdt.,
Bengal Art. (30) *b.* 1741/42. Major 2 Sept. 1768. Lt. Col.
30 Oct. 1769. Col. 12 Jan. 1779. *d.* on the river nr. Serampore,
Bengal, 15 June 1789, aged 47.[1]
Son of Thomas Pearse, Capt. R.N., and Martha his wife, only
dau. of George Purvis, of Darsham, Suffolk, Capt. R.N. 1st cousin
once removed of George Thomas Purvis, *q.v.* *m.* Panna Purree,
an Indian lady. (She died 1820.)
Services : See *D.N.B.* Fireworker (R.A.) 8 June 1757 ; 2nd
Lieut. 24 Oct. 1761 ; 1st Lieut. 3 Feb. 1766. Served at St. Malo
and Cherbourg in 1758 ; at Martinique and Guadaloupe in 1759 ;
Belleisle 1761 ; Havannah 1762. Transfd. as Major to Bengal
Art. (M.C. 1 Sept. 1768). Arrived in India 24 Aug. 1768. Second
Mysore War 1781-5 ; comdd. the force of 5 Regts. N.I. which
marched from Bengal to the aid of Madras Presdy., and served
under Sir Eyre Coote 1781-3 ; returned to Bengal May 1782 ;
rejoined army at Madras 5 Dec. 1782 ; siege of Cuddalore June
1783 (w.). Col. 1st Bn. Art., and Second in Comd. of Bengal Army
in July 1787. Received in Jan. 1785 a sword of honour from E.I.
Co. for his services in the Carnatic. Intimate friend of Warren
Hastings and acted as his second in his duel with Philip Francis
on 17 Aug. 1780.
Refs. : Burke's *Landed Gentry*, 2nd edn., p. 1085, *s.n.* Purvis, of
Darsham, Suffolk. *D.N.B.* *E.I.M.C.* ii. 247-50. *D.I.B.* *Kane's
List*, No. 303, and p. 168. Portrait in R.A. Mess at Woolwich.
Will dated Nellore 13 July 1781 ; proved 17 June 1789.
[1] *Note :* *D.N.B.* gives date of birth as " *c.* 1738."

*****PEARSON, Francis Hamilton** (*d.* 1800). Captain, Engineers.
Ensign (Bencoolen Est.) 17 Dec. 1781. Lieut. (do.) 16 June
1784. Capt. (Bengal) 7 Jan. 1796. *d.* Bencoolen 28 Nov. 1800.
His daus. *m.* John Fleming Hyde and Frederick George Lister,
qq.v.
Services : Ensign Surrey Mil. 24 June 1780. Transfd. to Bengal
Engrs. from Bencoolen Est. *c.* 1792, to rank between George Fleming
and William Golding, *qq.v.* Was Engr. at Fort Marlbro' Dec. 1796
till death.
Refs. : Intestate ; admon. 27 Nov. 1801.

THE BENGAL ARMY, 1758-1834

Note: His name would appear to have been confused with that of Francis William Peacock, *q.v.*, in more than one place.

PEARSON, Henry Edward (1809-1857). Major, 18th N.I. *b.* Stockton, Worcs., 28 July 1809. Cadet 1828. Arrived in India 5 May 1829. Ensign 8 Jan. 1829. Lieut. 26 June 1837. Capt. 12 Nov. 1848. Major 15 Jan. 1855. *d.* Rampati, nr. Bareilly, 6 June 1857 : kld. by villagers.

bapt. Stockton 27 Aug. 1809. 3rd son of Rev. Thomas Pearson, rector of Gt. Witley, Worcs., and Sarah his wife. *m.* Benares 10 Oct. 1838, Fanny, 2nd dau. of David Williamson, *q.v.* (*See also* Christopher George Fagan.) (She died 17 Nov. 1902.)

Services: Ensign d.d. 59th N.I. 10 June 1829. Posted to 18th N.I. 14 Sept. 1829. Fur. s.c. 30 Mar. 1832 till 21 Mar. 1835. Actg. Adjt. Jaunpur Depot 15 Dec. 1839. Adjt. 18th N.I. 23 Jan. 1841 till Nov. 1848. Second Sikh War; in garr. at Lahore; Capt. 18th N.I. (Medal). Was comdg. 18th N.I. at Bareilly when it mutinied 31 May 1857.[1]

Refs.: Burke's *Royal Families*, ped. lxii. Will dated Bareilly 18 Aug. 1856; proved 25 Nov. 1858.

[1] *Note:* " They (the sepoys) concealed the officers and allowed them to escape, but five were murdered in their flight by the villagers of Rampati." (Col. Gimlette's *Postscript to the Records of the Indian Mutiny.*)

PEARSON, James (1752/53-1826). Lieut. Colonel. 12th N.I. *b.* 1752/53. Cadet 1768. Arrived in India Aug. 1769. Ensign 20 Aug. 1769. Lieut. 31 Jan. 1773. Capt. 17 Jan. 1781. Major 1 Mar. 1794. Lt. Col. 26 Apr. 1797. Retired 19 Dec. 1798. *d.* Taunton 25 Jan. 1826, aged 73.

m. Calcutta 15 July 1791, Sarah, *née* Ware, widow of John Edmondson, *q.v.* (She died Taunton 1 Dec. 1839, aged 75.)

Services: Second Mysore War, with Col. T. D. Pearse's detachment 1781-5; Pollilur; Sholingarh; Vellore; Cuddalore; Capt. comdg. 2/25th N.I., and comdg. 25th Regt. from June 1781 in succession to Major John Wedderburn, *q.v.* Capt. comdg. 2nd Eur. Bn. in July 1787. Apptd. to comd. 20th Bn. Sepoys in 1788. Second Rohilla War; battle of Bitaurah; comdg. 20th N.I. Fur. 3 June 1797 till retirement.

Refs.: *E.I.M.C.* i. 75-6. *G.M.* 1826, i. 189. M.I. in St. Mary Magd., Taunton.

PEARSON, James (1787-1848). Major. 65th N.I. *b.* Polmont, co. Stirling, 24 Feb. 1787. Cadet 1803. Arrived in India 27 Jan.

1805. Ensign 28 Jan. 1805. Lieut. 29 Jan. 1805. Capt. 11 July 1823. Major 26 Feb. 1829. Retired 3 Jan. 1832. *d.* Edinburgh 1 May 1848.

bapt. 26 Feb. 1787. 3rd son of William Pearson, of Kippenross, co. Perth, and Jane his wife, eldest dau. of Sir James Campbell, of Aberuchill, 3rd Bart. *m.* 17 Dec. 1821, Agnes, youngest dau. of William Richardson, of Keithock.

Services : Posted Lieut. to 1/18th N.I. in 1806. Operations in Bundelkhand 1809; Rajaoli; Ajaigarh; Lieut. 1/18th N.I. Capture of Java; Cornelis 26 Aug. 1811 (w.); Lieut. L.I. Bn. (Medal). Capture of Palembang 1812; Lieut. Vol. Bn. Served with Vols. till 1813. Nepal War 1816; Lieut. 1/18th N.I., in 1st Bde. Rt. Column. Cuttack insurrection 1816-17; Khurda; Lieut. 1/18th N.I. Fur. p.a. 10 Dec. 1819 till 23 Sept. 1822. Transfd. as Capt. to newly-raised 33rd N.I. July 1823; to 65th N.I. (late 1/33rd) May 1824. Sailed for Penang on service in July 1825.

Refs. : Burke's *Colonial Gentry,* i. 398, *s.n.* Pearson, of Kilmany Park and Craigellachie, Victoria. *S.M.* 1822, i. 138. *I.N.* 1848, p. 386.

PEARSON, John (*d.* 1771). Lieut. Fireworker, Artillery. (105 Cadet (?) Fireworker 28 Feb. 1770. *d.* Calcutta 19 Oct. 1771.

Services : N.F.P.

PEARSON, Richard Sadleir (1759/60-1792). Lieutenant, 20th Bn. Sepoys. *b.* London 1759/60. Cadet 1778. Ensign 1778. Lieut. 28 Nov. 1778. *d.* Dinapore 9 Mar. 1792.

Services : Sailed for India in the *Osterley* 9 Feb. 1778, aged 18. Lieut. 25th Bn. Sepoys in July 1787.

Refs. : *G.M.* 1792, ii. 1153.

PEARSON, Thomas (1738/39-1781). Major. Infantry. *b.* 1738/39. Cadet 1761. Ensign 29 Apr. 1762. Lieut. 10 Sept. 1763. Capt. 20 Dec. 1764. Major 24 Feb. 1769. Resigned 12 Jan. 1770. *d.* Calcutta 5 Aug. 1781, aged 42.

Son of Mary Pearson, of Court Green, Dalton, Burton-in-Kendal, Westmorland. Brother of Agnes Stilwell. *m.* Calcutta 2 Dec. 1767, Sarah, dau. of James Irwin, Senr. Mercht. B.C.S., and sister of Eyles Irwin (*D.N.B.*). (She died Calcutta 9 Sept. 1768, aged 19.)

Services : Sailed for India in the *Norfolk* in 1761, aged 22. Campaign of 1764; Qmr. with the Army under Major Hector Munro. Apptd. Sec. to Bdr.-Gen. John Carnac, the C.-in-C., *q.v.,* 13 Feb. 1765. After resigning the Service he became Agent for

Mir Jafar Khan's gift to the Army, *i.e.*, Lord Clive's fund (*cf.* Part I. p. xxxi); returned to Bengal in 1776.
Refs.: *India Gazette*, 11 Aug. 1787. Will dated in England, 7 Apr. 1776; proved 18 Feb. 1783. M.I. in S. Park St. cemetery, Calcutta. His portrait appears in Benjamin West's picture of " Shah Alam, the Great Mogul, conveying the Grant of the Dewanny to Lord Clive, Aug. 1765," which hangs in the Finance Committee Room at I.O.

PEART, John (1786-1808). Ensign, 21st N.I. *bapt.* Tynemouth 2 Apr. 1786. Cadet 1805. Arrived in India 11 July 1806. Ensign 30 Aug. 1806. *d.* Cawnpore 5 Feb. 1808 : kld. by the accidental discharge of a fowling-piece.
Son of Isaac Peart, of N. Shields, Northumberland, mercer, and Eleanor his wife.
Services: Barasat C.C. Posted Ensign to 1/21st N.I. in 1807. No record of active service.

PECHÉ, James (1753/54-1797). Captain, Infantry. *b.* 1753/54. Cadet 1776. Ensign 30 Mar. 1777. Lieut. 24 Aug. 1778. Capt. 28 Nov. 1794. *d.* Dinapore 13 Feb. 1797.
A native of Surrey. *m.* (?).
Services: Sailed for India in the *Latham* 10 Apr. 1776, aged 22. Arrived in Bengal via Bombay in Sept. 1777, and was posted to 1st Bde. Lieut. 27th Bn. Sepoys in July 1786 and in Dec. 1790; Capt. 6th Eur. Bn. in Feb. 1796.
Refs.: Will dated 8 Dec. 1788; proved 19 June 1797.

PECHÉ, John (1774-?). Lieutenant, Infantry. Unposted. *b.* Surat, Bombay, *c.* Mar. 1774. Cadet 1794. Never arrived in India. Ensign 12 Oct. 1795. Lieut. 29 Jan. 1797. Struck off 1798. (? *d.* on the voyage out in 1795.[1])
Of Beech Hill, Surrey. Eldest son of Lt.-Gen. John Peché, Bombay Est., and Mary Bassett his 1st wife. (*Probably* nephew of James and Onslow Peché, *q.v.*)
Services: " Child " (*i.e.* Minor Cadet) on the Bo. Est. in 1782. Apptd. Cadet 25 Mar. 1795; sailed for India in the *Lord Thurlow* 24 May 1795.
[1] *Note:* His death is not recorded in the log of the *Lord Thurlow*.

PECHÉ, Onslow (1760/61-1788). Lieutenant, 1st Bn. Sepoys. *b.* Surrey 1760/61. Cadet 1779. Ensign 12 Feb. 1780. Lieut. 25 Mar. 1781. *d.* Chittagong 3 Nov. 1788.

Services: Apptd. Cadet 28 Oct. 1778; sailed for India in the *Prime* 16 June 1779, aged 18. Lieut. 1st Bn. Sepoys in July 1787.

PECKETT, James (1791-1848). Colonel, Engineers. *b.* London 27 Mar. 1791. Cadet 1807. Arrived in India 16 Nov. 1808. Fireworker (Art.) (396) 18 Nov. 1808. Ensign 18 Nov. 1808. Lieut. 1 July 1812. Capt. 1 Sept. 1818. Major 9 May 1829. Lt. Col. 10 July 1832. Lt. Col. Comdt. 31 Mar. 1840. Col. 13 Mar. 1844. *d.* Calcutta 5 Dec. 1848.

bapt. St. George's, Hanover Sq., London, 25 Apr. 1791. Son of James Peckett and Charlotte his wife. *m.* Merchiston House 23 Apr. 1823, Catherine Gordon, 2nd dau. of Robert Hepburne, of Clarkington, and sister of Cosmo Alexander Hepburne, *q.v.* (She died 4 Dec. 1862, aged 59.) Woolwich Cadet; nominated to R.M.A. 16 Oct. 1805.

Services: Transfd. from Art. to Engrs. 14 Nov. 1809. Asst. Surveyor in Cuttack 1811. Nepal War 1814-15; Asst. Field Engr. 4th Div. Suptg. construction of Patna-Gaya road. Third Mahratta War; Mandala (*Lond. Gaz.* 7 Dec. 1818); senior Engr. at storm of Satanwara June 1818; Field Engr. 3rd Div. Fur. p.a. 26 Jan. 1820 till 8 Oct. 1823. Bk.Mr. Burdwan Div. 7 June 1824 till 8 Jan. 1827. Fur. s.c. 21 Feb. 1828 till 24 Feb. 1834. Member of Clothing Board 1844-7. Passed over for post of Chief Engr. Fur. p.a. Oct. 1847 till Nov. 1848.

Refs.: *S.M.* 1823, i. 647. *G.M.* 1849, i. 335.

PECKHAM, Francis. Ensign. Infantry. Cadet 1783. Ensign 21 Mar. 1785. Never arrived in India. Struck off 1788. (? *d.* Kedgeree 1783.)

Services: Apptd. Cadet 20 Nov. 1782; should have sailed for India in the *Halsewell* 11 Mar. 1783.

PEEL, William (1801-1825). Lieutenant, 56th N.I. *b.* Wandsworth, London, 13 Aug. 1801. Cadet 1820. Arrived in India Sept. 1821. Ensign 5 May 1821. Lieut. 11 Sept. 1823. *d.s.p.* Arakan 22 Dec. 1825.

6th and youngest son of Joseph Peel, of Burton-on-Trent, Staffs., calico manufacturer, afterwards of Bowes, nr. London, and Ann his wife, dau. of Jonathan Haworth, of Harcroft, Lancs. Brother of Sir Lawrence Peel, P.C., C.J. of Bengal (*D.N.B.*), and nephew of Sir Robert Peel, 1st Bart.

Services: Posted Ensign to 2/6th N.I. in 1821. Transfd. to

THE BENGAL ARMY, 1758-1834 495

28th N.I. July 1823 ; to 56th N.I. (late 2/26th) May 1824. First Burma War ; Arakan 1825 ; Lieut. 56th N.I., d.d. 1st Gren. Bn.
Refs.: Burke's *Landed Gentry*, 13th edn., p. 1390, *s.n.* Peel, of Peele Fold, Lancs. Hunter's *Familiæ Min. Gent.* i. 215.

PEELE, John (*d.* 1780). Ensign, Infantry. Country Cadet 1779. Ensign 27 Sept. 1779. *bur.* Fort William 29 Dec. 1780.
Services: Apptd. Cadet 19 Aug. 1779. N.F.P. (*See* note to John Peal, *supra.*)

PEELE, Lowther (1753/54-1784). Lieutenant, Infantry. *b.* Cumberland 1753/54. Cadet 1781. Ensign 2 Apr. 1781. Lieut. 25 July 1782. *d.* Cawnpore 29 May 1784.
Services: Apptd. Cadet 27 Apr. 1781, aged 27. Sailed for India in the *Tartar* 26 June 1781, aged 27.

PEERS, James (1808-1829). Lieutenant, 49th N.I. *b.* Glenarm, co. Antrim, 25 Dec. 1808. Cadet 1824. Ensign 10 Feb. 1824. Lieut. 14 Oct. 1826. *d.* in Ireland 20 Apr. 1829.
Of Ballymena, co. Antrim. Son of —— Peers and Eliza his wife.
Services: Posted Ensign to 49th N.I. in 1825. Fur. s.c. 15 Aug. 1828 till death. No record of active service.

PEIRCE, Thomas (1746-1768). Lieutenant, Infantry. *bapt.* Calcutta 11 Jan. 1746. Cadet 1765. Ensign 4 Nov. 1765. Lieut. 28 Mar. 1767. *bur.* Calcutta 23 June 1768.[1]
Youngest child of Capt. Richard Peirce, of Calcutta, and Ann his wife, sister of William Shiers, of Bombay and of the Inner Temple.
Services: Posted to 2nd Bde. in 1766.
[1] *Note:* Incorrectly entered in the burial register as John Peirce. The name also appears as Pearce and Peiarce.

PELLY, Robert Parker (1790-1867). Lieutenant. 2nd N.I. *bapt.* Weston-sub-Edge, Worcs., 10 Jan. 1790. Cadet 1804. Arrived in India 10 Sept. 1805. Ensign 10 Oct. 1805. Lieut. 27 Nov. 1805. Retired 1 Dec. 1818. *d.* 11 June 1867.
4th son of Rev. John Pelly, rector of Weston-sub-Edge, and Eugenia his wife, dau. of —— Roberts, of Lisbon, merchant, and widow of Henry Creswick, of Morton, Gloucs. Cousin-german of Sir John Henry Pelly, 1st Bart., of Upton, Essex. *m.* (?).
Services: Posted Lieut. to 2nd N.I. in 1806. Reduction of Kalinjar 1812 ; Lieut. 2/2nd N.I. Operations in Baghelkhand 1813 ; Entauri ; Lieut. 2/2nd N.I. Fur. 1817 till retirement.

Refs.: Foster's *Baronetage*, p. 494, *s.n.* Pelly, Bart., of Upton, Essex.

PEMBERTON, George Richard (1789-1866). Lieut. General. Colonel 62nd N.I. *b.* London 11 July 1789. Cadet 1805. Arrived in India 13 Dec. 1806. Ensign (24 May 1806) 18 Oct. 1806. Lieut. 22 May 1809. Capt. 1 May 1824. Major 25 June 1832. Lt. Col. 13 Feb. 1839. Col. 19 Mar. 1849. Maj. Gen. 28 Nov. 1854. Lt. Gen. 6 Sept. 1862. *d.* at his residence, York House, Chertsey, 28 Apr. 1866.

bapt. Marylebone 5 Dec. 1789. Eldest son of Dr. Christopher Robert Pemberton, Physician Extraord. to George IV (*D.N.B.*), and Sarah his 1st wife. Cousin-german of the father of Thomas Francis Henry Pemberton, *q.v. m.* 1st (*c.* 1822), Maria Constantia Parker, 4th dau. of Rev. R. Barker Bell. (She died Nasirabad 18 May 1827, of cholera, aged 25.) *m.* 2nd, Langham church 26 Apr. 1831, Anne Martha Josephine Angelo, 7th dau. of A. A. M. Tremamondo, *q.v.*, and sister of John Angelo, *q.v.* (*See also* William Simonds and James Steel.) (She died 1897.)

Services : Barasat C.C. 15½ mos. Posted Ensign to 2nd N.I. in 1808. Capture of Java 1811 ; Cornelis ; Lieut. 3rd Vol. Bn. (Medal). Served with 3rd Vol. Bn. 1811-15. Transfd. to newly-raised 2/28th N.I. in 1815. Fur. s.c. Oct. 1817 till 16 Sept. 1819. Intr. & Qmr. 2/28th N.I. 19 Nov. 1821 till 22 June 1824. Transfd. to 56th N.I. (late 2/28th) May 1824. Actg. Bde. Major to W. Div. 24 Aug. 1825. A.D.C. to Bdr.-Gen. Alexander Knox, *q.v.*, comdg. Rajputana F.F., 7 Oct. 1825. Fur. p.a. 15 Jan. 1829 till 14 Nov. 1831. Comdd. 56th N.I. from Dec. 1835. Posted Lt. Col. to 56th N.I. 20 May 1839 ; to 67th N.I. 16 June 1840 ; to 62nd N.I. 3 Nov. 1844. Posted Col. to 62nd N.I. Mar. 1849. Fur. 1 Feb. 1850 till death.

Refs.: *Pemberton Pedigrees*, ed. by Rev. R. Pemberton (Bedford, 1923), chart xv, *s.n.* St. Albans family, Cambridge branch. *Boase. G.M.* 1827, ii. 573. *The Times*, 1 May 1866.

PEMBERTON, Robert Boileau (1798-1840). Captain, 44th N.I. *b.* W.I. 21 June 1798. Cadet 1817. Admitted 21 July 1818. Ensign (?) Lieut. 1 Aug. 1818. Capt. 21 July 1835. *d.* Berhampore 26 June 1840.

Eldest son of Rev. John Butler Pemberton, barr.-at-law, later rector of Trinity, Palmette Point, St. Kitts, and Harriet his wife (*née* Boileau), widow of Richard Price. *m.* Calcutta 7 Apr. 1832, Henrietta Peach, 2nd dau. of Duncan Macleod (1780-1856), *q.v.*

(She died London 10 July 1854, aged 43.) His dau. *m.* Sir George Udny Yule (*D.N.B.*).
Services : Posted Lieut. to 1/22nd N.I. Mily. student at Coll. of Ft. Wm. July 1820 till Dec. 1821. D.A.Q.M.G. 3 cl., under Surveyor Gen. of India, Jan. 1822. Transfd. to 44th N.I. (late 2/22nd) May 1824. Employed in survey and exploration work on N.E. frontier, Sylhet, Cachar, Manipur, Assam and Khasia till 1832. Saw active service in Manipur, having been chiefly instrumental in establishing the authority of Rajah Gambhir Singh in that country. Sent as a special Envoy to Bhutan Oct. 1837, on a salary of Rs. 2,000 *p.m.* A.G.G. Murshidabad 3 Jan. 1839 till death. Compiled a map of N.E. frontier of British India. Author of " Report on the E. frontier of British India," maps, 8vo, Calcutta, 1835.
Refs. : *Pemberton Pedigrees*, chart xiii, *s.n.* St. Albans family, W.I. branch. *Caribbeana*, i. 270. *D.I.B. I.N.* Vol. i. 106. Will dated Calcutta 27 June 1833 ; proved 28 July 1840. M.I. Berhampore.

PEMBERTON, Thomas Francis Henry (1809-1831). Ensign, 62nd N.I. *b.* Tottenham High Cross 12 Feb. 1809. Cadet 1826. Arrived in India 31 Oct. 1827. Ensign 25 May 1827. *d.* Karnal 15 Oct. 1831, of fever.
bapt. 9 Mar. 1809. Only son of Thomas Pemberton, of Tottenham (who was cousin-german of George Richard Pemberton, *q.v.*), and Susannah Elizabeth his wife.
Services : Ensign d.d. 40th N.I. Nov. 1827 ; posted to 67th N.I. 3 Jan. 1828 ; transfd. to 62nd N.I. 4 Nov. 1828. No record of active service.
Refs. : *Pemberton Pedigrees*, chart xiv, *s.n.* St. Albans family, Cambridge branch. *De Rhé-Philipe. A.J.* N.S. viii. 41.

PEMBLE, Charles (*c.* 1722-1770). Lieut. Colonel. Infantry. Subsequently C.-in-C. Bombay. *b. c.* 1722. Major 1764. Lt. Col. Feb. 1767. Retransfd. to Bombay Est. 1767. *d.* Bankot (Fort Victoria), Bombay, 11 May 1770, of dropsy.
m. Bombay 19 Jan. 1769, Louisa, widow of ―― Cooke and dau. of Samuel Hough, of Fetcham Park, Surrey. (She died Ryde Jan. 1814, aged 65.)
Services : Entered Bombay Army *c.* 1750. Lieut. Bo. Inf. 7 Feb. 1753 ; Capt. Lt. Bo. Art. 1 Mar. 1758 ; Capt. do. 10 Apr. 1758. Dir. of laboratory 1761. Comdt. Bo. Art. 1762-3. Embarked for Bengal 12 Oct. 1763, with Bombay troops under Major Hector

Munro, and arrived in May 1764. Served under Munro in comd. of 2 Coys. Inf. ; comdd. 2nd line at battle of Buxar (horse shot under him) ; Capt. Inf. (*London Gaz.* 18 June 1765). Major comdg. the force sent against Chunar fort in Dec. 1764. Retransfd. to Bo. Est. 1767. Bt. Major (Bo.) 1 Jan. 1765 ; Major 26 Mar. 1766. Apptd. 2nd in comd. of forces at Bombay in 1767 ; C.-in-C. Bombay 12 Feb. 1768 till death. Lt. Col. 12 Feb. 1768 ; Col. Jan. 1769.

Refs.: *Spring*, No. 33. *E.I.M.C.* ii. 87. *S.M.* 1771, p. 53. *M.M.* 1814, i. 79. Intest.; admon. 27 June 1770.

PEMBLE, Charles (1750/51-1775/76). Lieutenant. Engineers. *b.* 1750/51. Ensign 1770. Lieut. 29 Mar. 1771. Resigned 23 Nov. 1774. *d.* 1775/76.

Brother of James Pemble, *q.v.*, and of William and Margaret Pemble, of Greenwich.

Services: Lieut. F. Bo. Art. 2 Mar. 1768. Was on fur. from Bombay in Nov. 1769, and was probably transfd. to Bengal Est. about that date.

Refs.: *Spring*, No. 83. Will dated on board *British King*, at Bengal, on voyage home, 6 Dec. 1774 ; proved 20 Sept. 1776.

PEMBLE, James (*d.* 1772). Lieutenant, Infantry. Cadet 1767. Ensign 15 Sept. 1767. Lieut. 9 Apr. 1769. *d. unm.* Patna 30 Mar. 1772.

Brother of Charles Pemble (*d.* 1775/76), *q.v.*

Services: Held a Warrant as Cadet in R.A. ; apptd. Cadet 6 Mar. 1767.

Refs.: Will dated Patna 19 Mar. 1772 ; proved 28 May 1772.

PENGREE, George (1807-1875). Lieutenant, Invalid Est. 39th N.I. *b.* Loughor, co. Glamorgan, 1 Oct. 1807. Cadet 1827. Arrived in India 5 July 1828. Ensign 6 Mar. 1828. Lieut. 1 Oct. 1832. Invalided 13 Nov. 1837. *d.* at his residence, The Boundary, Simla, 9 Oct. 1875.

Son of George Pengree and Sarah his wife. *m.* Simla 29 Sept. 1841, Emily Sidney, only dau. of William Henry Hewitt, *q.v.* (She died Simla 28 Apr. 1851, aged 31.) Ed. Christ's Hospital.

Services: Ensign d.d. 46th N.I. 31 July 1828 ; posted to 39th N.I. 4 Nov. 1828 ; Adjt. do. 13 Dec. 1831 till 13 Nov. 1837. Leave s.c. to Simla 14 Mar. 1835 till 15 Feb. 1837. Supt. of roads in Simla and the neighbouring hills 15 Nov. 1842 till Oct. 1846. Apptd. Principal Comr. for Simla 9 Jan. 1857. He was for nearly 38 yrs. a permanent resident of Simla, where he owned much house property.

Refs.: *De Rhé-Philipe.* M.I. in cart road cemetery, Simla.

PENMAN, David (*d.* 1777). Captain, Engineers. Cadet 1767. Ensign 15 Sept. 1767. Lieut. 2 Apr. 1769. Capt. 26 Dec. 1772. *d.* Lakhipur, nr. Dacca 14 (or 17) Oct. 1777.
Son of Hugh Penman, of Edinburgh, goldsmith, and Catherine his wife, dau. of David Cleland. Brother of James Penman, of E. Florida, and of Rebecca, wife of Andrew Gairdner, of Edinburgh, merchant.
Services: Apptd. Engr. Cadet in England Nov. 1766; sailed for India (as a Cadet in the Train) in the *Lord Holland* 16 Dec. 1766. Lieut. and Dy. Civil Architect; Capt. and Sub-Dir. of Works at Ft. Wm. 21 Dec. 1772. (? First Rohilla War; battle of St. George.) Field Engr. with 2nd Bde. 1774-5; at Ft. Wm. in 1776; transfd. to Lakhipur 1777.
Refs.: *S.M.* 1778, p. 221. Will dated on board his budgerow at Barrelli, on his way to join the Army, 4 Sept. 1774; filed 14 Sept. 1778.

PENNEFATHER, Robert Perceval (1804-1874). Major. 3rd L.C. *b.* Newport, co. Tipperary, 8 July 1804. Cadet 1820. Admitted 19 July 1821. Cornet 4 Feb. 1821. Lieut. 1 May 1824. Capt. 1 Nov. 1838. Retired 1 Jan. 1846. Hon. Major 28 Nov. 1854. *d.* 14 Abbey Pl., St. John's Wood, London, 6 June 1874.
5th and youngest son of Rev. John Pennefather, D.D., rector of St. John's, Newport, and Elizabeth his wife, dau. of Major Perceval. *m.* 3 Nov. 1823, Elizabeth Anne Benson. (She died 28 Mar. 1887.)
Services: Posted Cornet to 3rd L.C. and served throughout with that Regt. Operations in Jodhpur 1823; capture of Lamba; Cornet 3rd L.C. Siege and capture of Bhurtpore; Lieut. 3rd L.C. (India medal). Actg. Adjt. 3rd L.C. 27 Oct. 1830; permanent do. 24 May 1831 till 9 Aug. 1834. Operations against the Kols 1832. First Afghan War 1838-9; capture of Ghazni; Capt. 3rd L.C. (Medal). With Army of Reserve (for Afghanistan) Oct. 1842 till Jan. 1843. Actg. Bde. Major at Ferozepore 30 Mar. 1843.
Refs.: Burke's *Landed Gentry of Ireland*, p. 554, *s.n.* Pennefather, of Rathsallagh, co. Wicklow. Ruvigny's *Plantagenet Roll of the Blood Royal*, Mortimer-Percy Vol., p. 357. *The Times*, 11 June 1874.

PENNINGTON, Edward (1749/50-1804). Colonel. Cavalry. *b.* 1749/50. Cadet 1772. Admitted 3 Oct. 1772. Ensign

12 July 1776. Lieut. 2 July 1778. Capt. 29 Oct. 1792. Major 1 Nov. 1798. Lt. Col. 23 June 1799. Col. 17 July 1801. Retired 4 Feb. 1802. *d.* Harmony Hall, nr. Millthorpe, Lancs., 28 Nov. 1804, aged 54.

Of Kendal. (*Probably* brother of James Pennington, *q.v.*, who bequeathed him one fourth part of his estate.) Resided as a youth in W.I. *m.* Bolton, Lancs., Nov. 1801, Miss Sparling.

Services : Ensign 2nd Bengal Eur. Regt. in Oct. 1777 ; transfd. to Cav. 5 Aug. 1778. Lieut. 11th Bn. Sepoys in July 1787 ; posted Capt. to 4th Eur. Bn. 22 Nov. 1792 ; Capt. 1st N.C. in Oct. 1798. Fur. 29 Dec. 1800 till retirement.

Refs. : *G.M.* 1804, ii. 1174.

PENNINGTON, Gervaise (1761/62-1835). Colonel, C.B., Artillery. (268) *b.* 1761/62. Cadet 1783. Admitted 21 Aug. 1783. Fireworker 12 May 1785. Lieut. 12 June 1793. Capt. Lt. 23 Feb. 1802. Capt. 21 Sept. 1804. Major 17 Feb. 1815. Lt. Col. 1 Sept. 1818. Lt. Col. Comdt. 1 May 1824. Col. 5 June 1829. *d.* Maltshanger House, nr. Basingstoke, 2 July 1835, aged 73.

Brother of Rev. Thomas Pennington, of Alford, Lincs., and uncle of Gervaise Pennington, *q.v. m.* at the Doune of Rothiemurcus 17 Dec. 1825, Jane, 2nd dau. of Sir John Peter Grant, Kt., of Rothiemurcus, C.J. of Calcutta (*D.N.B.*). (She *re-m.* James Gibson Craig, and died 1863, aged 63.)

Services : Came out as Inf. Cadet ; transfd. to Art. in 1785. On service to Madras June 1794 ; Lieut. 2nd Coy. 2nd Bn. Apptd. Dy. Paymr. to detachment of troops serving under Major Henry Hyndman, *q.v.*, 28 Apr. 1797. Fourth Mysore War 1799 ; Seringapatam ; Lieut. 3rd Coy. 1st Bn. A.D.C. to Maj.-Gen. George Deare, *q.v.*, 1801-2. Offg. Comy. Ord. at Chunar 1802-4. Second Mahratta War ; Bhurtpore (w. in 4th assault 21 Feb. 1805). Apptd. to comd. H.A. 1806 ; to comd. augmented corps of H.A. 4 Oct. 1809. Nepal War 1814-15 ; Kalanga ; Bt. Major 1st Troop, comdg. H.A. with 2nd Div. Siege and capture of Hathras 1817 ; Major comdg. H.A. Third Mahratta War ; Lt. Col. comdg. H.A. with Centre Div. Fur. p.a. 13 Dec. 1819 till 8 Oct. 1823 ; s.c. 11 Jan. 1825 till death. C.B. 3 May 1832.

Refs. : Burke's *Landed Gentry*, 5th edn., p. 1075, *s.n.* Pennington, of Thickthorne, co. Warwick. *Stubbs*, ii. 245-6. *E.I.M.C.* i. 158-62. *Memoirs of a Highland Lady*, ed. Lady Strachey, pp. 382, 393. *S.M.* 1826, i. 126. *G.M.* 1835, ii. 221. *A.J.* N.S. xvii. 279.

THE BENGAL ARMY, 1758-1834   501

PENNINGTON, Gervaise (1795-1835). Captain, Artillery. (454) *bapt.* Alford, co. Lincoln, 10 Nov. 1795. Cadet 1813. Admitted 5 Aug. 1814. Fireworker 4 Oct. 1816. Lieut. 1 Sept. 1818. Capt. 9 Oct. 1831. *d.* Meerut 13 Oct. 1835, aged 39.

One of the 19 children of Rev. Thomas Pennington, of Alford, rector of Bilsby, and Elizabeth his wife, dau. of C. Baggally, of Norton. Brother of William Pennington, of London, surgeon, and of Isabella, wife of John Dethick Crommelin, *q.v.*, and nephew of Gervaise Pennington, *q.v.* Addiscombe Cadet 1811-14.

Services: Posted to 1st Troop H.A. in 1815. Siege and capture of Hathras; Lieut. F. 1st Troop. Third Mahratta War; Lieut. 1st Troop. 3rd Troop 1819-20. Adjt. & Qmr. H.A. Bde. 22 Jan. 1820; do. 3rd Bde. H.A. 22 July 1825 till 7 Jan. 1832. Siege and capture of Bhurtpore; Adjt. 3rd Bde. Offg. A.A.G. Meerut Div. 21 May 1832. Transfd. to 3rd Troop 1st Bde. H.A. 24 Nov. 1834.

Refs.: Burke's *Landed Gentry*, 5th edn., p. 1075, *s.n.* Pennington, of Thickthorne, co. Warwick. *Bath Chron.* 11 Feb. 1836. *A.J.* N.S. xix. 206. Will dated 3 Apr. 1834; proved 23 Nov. 1835.

PENNINGTON, Henry (1761/62-1831). Lieutenant, Invalid Est. 1st Bengal Eur. Bn. *b.* 1761/62. Cadet 1778. Ensign 1778. Lieut. 1 Dec. 1778. Invalided 1 July 1792. *d.* Monghyr, B. & O., 21 Dec. 1831.

A native of Westmorland. (*Probably* brother of James Pennington, *q.v.*) Father of Henry Simpson Pennington (Appendix A). *m.* St. John's, Calcutta, 7 Sept. 1821, Miss Elfrida Cassandra Willoughby (*probably* dau. of Richard Willoughby, *q.v.*).

Services: Apptd. Cadet 25 Nov. 1778; sailed for India in the *Atlas* 7 Mar. 1779, aged 17. Lieut. 10th Bn. Sepoys in July 1787; transfd. to 1st Bengal Eur. Bn. 9 Sept. 1791.

Refs.: *A.J.* N.S. viii. 53. *M.I.* at Monghyr.

PENNINGTON, James (1760/61-1798). Captain, Infantry. *b.* 1760/61. Cadet 1778. Admitted 1778. Ensign 1778. Lieut. 24 Oct. 1778. Capt. 1 June 1796. *d.* Bencoolen 29 May 1798.

A native of Westmorland. (*Probably* brother of Edward Pennington, *q.v.*)

Services: Apptd. Cadet 6 May 1778, but was permitted to stay in England till the following year. Sailed for India in the *Atlas* 7 Mar. 1779, aged 18. Was Adjt. 17th Bn. Sepoys in Mar. 1786; Lieut. 10th Bn. in July 1787 and Dec. 1792. Served at Bencoolen Mar. 1796 till death.

Refs.: Will dated 5 Mar. 1796; proved 12 Nov. 1798.

PENNINGTON, Richard Charles (1810-1848). Captain, 11th N.I. b. London 15 Aug. 1810. Cadet 1828. Arrived in India 27 Aug. 1829. Ensign 5 June 1829. Lieut. 24 June 1839. Capt. 10 Nov. 1847. d. Bareilly 13 May 1848.

bapt. Marylebone 17 Sept. 1810. Son of Richard Pennington, of 6 Queen St., Brompton, and Esther Smith his wife. Nephew of Robert Rainey Pennington, of 18 Portman Sq., London.

Services : Ensign d.d. 61st N.I. Posted to 6th N.I. 23 Sept. 1830 ; transfd. to 11th N.I. 2 Aug. 1832. Fur. s.c. 16 Jan. 1839 till 17 Nov. 1841. (? Disturbances in Bundelkhand 1842 ; Lieut. 11th N.I.) Fur. s.c. 13 Dec. 1844 till 1847.

Refs. : I.M. 1 Aug. 1848, p. 465. G.M. 1848, ii. 334.

PENNY, Gabriel Richard (1783-1842). Major General. Colonel 11th N.I. Comdg. Dinapore Div. b. Calcutta Oct. 1783. Cadet 1798. Arrived in India 6 Sept. 1799. Ensign 1 Nov. 1799. Lieut. 17 Nov. 1799. Capt. 5 Mar. 1806. Major 25 Jan. 1815. Lt. Col. 12 Nov. 1820. Lt. Col. Comdt. 2 May 1824. Col. 5 June 1829. Maj. Gen. 28 June 1838. d. Calcutta 26 Aug. 1842.

2nd son of Robert Penny, of Calcutta, Capt. of a country vessel, afterwards of Weymouth, and Catherine Young his wife. Brother of Nicholas Penny, *q.v. m.* St. Michael's, Bath, 24 Jan. 1811, Elizabeth, only dau. of Sylvester Prior Bean, of Stoke-under-Ham, Somerset. His dau. *m.* John Edmonstone Landers, *q.v.*

Services : Posted Lieut. to 2/15th N.I. 15 Apr. 1801. Operations in Jumna Doab 1803 ; Sasni ; Bijaigarh ; Kachaura ; Lieut. 15th N.I. Second Mahratta War ; Aligarh ; Delhi ; Agra ; Laswari ; battle of Deig (w.) ; Bhurtpore ; Lieut. 15th N.I. Capt. Lt. 15th N.I. 2 Jan. 1806. Expedn. to Macao 1808-9 ; Capt. 15th N.I. Fur. p.a. 24 Oct. 1809 till 22 Oct. 1811. Nepal War 1814-15 ; Major 2/15th N.I., in 4th Div. Nepal War 1816 ; Major 15th N.I., in 4th Bde. Centre Column. Siege and capture of Hathras ; Major 2/15th N.I. Third Mahratta War ; Asirgarh ; Major 2/15th N.I. Posted Lt. Col. to 1/1st N.I. in 1820 ; Lt. Col. Comdt. to 33rd N.I. May 1824 ; to 11th N.I. 22 Dec. 1826. Leave s.c. to Cape 19 Apr. 1825 till 16 May 1827. To assume comd. of troops at Barrackpore 19 Nov. 1828 ; Bdr. to comd. Barrackpore 11 Feb. 1829. Fur. s.c. 7 Jan. till 13 Nov. 1838. Apptd. to Divl. Staff of Army 24 Dec. 1838. Comdd. Dinapore Div. 29 Dec. 1838 till death.

Refs. : E.I.M.C. i. 192. *Somerset & Dorset N. & Q.* xv. (1916), 61-2. G.M. 1843, i. 555. Will dated Dinapore 18 June 1842 ; proved 4 Nov. 1842. M.I. Circular road cemetery, Calcutta.

PENNY, Nicholas (1790-1858). Major General, C.B. Colonel 2nd Eur. Bengal Fus. Comdg. Meerut Div. *b.* Weymouth 12 Mar. 1790. Cadet 1806. Arrived in India 21 July 1807. Ensign (5 Feb. 1807) 16 Aug. 1807. Lieut. 19 Dec. 1812. Capt. 13 May 1825. Major 2 Feb. 1842. Lt. Col. 29 July 1848. Col. (7 June 1849) 15 Sept. 1854. Maj. Gen. 28 Nov. 1857. *d.* Kakrala, nr. Budaon, U.P., 30 Apr. 1858 : kld. at the head of his column in a skirmish with mutineers : *bur.* at Meerut.

bapt. Melcombe Regis, Dorset, 24 Nov. 1790. 4th son of Robert Penny, of Weymouth, and Catherine his wife. Brother of Gabriel Richard Penny, *q.v. m.* Dinapore 26 May 1830, Louisa Margaret, 3rd and youngest dau. of John Gerrard, *q.v.* (*See also* Sir Alexander Knox.) (She died 5 Oct. 1876.)

Services : See *D.N.B.* Barasat C.C. 12 mos. Posted Ensign to 1/14th N.I. July 1808. Adjt. 1/14th N.I. 9 Dec. 1814 till Sept. 1822. Nepal War 1814-15 ; Jitgarh ; Lieut. 1/14th N.I., in 3rd Div. (India medal). Third Mahratta War ; Mandala ; Garhakota ; Lieut. 1/14th N.I., in Left Div. Fur. s.c. 10 Jan. 1823 till 4 Oct. 1825. Transfd. to newly-raised 2/34th N.I. Sept. 1823 ; to 68th N.I. (late 2/34th) May 1824 ; to 1st Extra Regt. (became 69th N.I.) July 1825. Siege and capture of Bhurtpore ; D.A.Q.M.G. 2nd Div. (clasp to India medal). Bde. Major Agra & Muttra frontier 2 Oct. 1826 till 19 May 1828 ; D.A.A.G. Dinapore 19 May 1828 ; A.A.G. Presdy. Div. 9 July 1832 till June 1841. Comdd. Nassiri Bn. 2 June 1841 till 7 Oct. 1848. First Sikh War ; Aliwal, comdg. Nassiri Bn. ; Sobraon (w.) ; comdg. 2nd Inf. Bde. (Medal with clasp). Posted Lt. Col. to 69th N.I. 27 Sept. 1848. Second Sikh War ; Chilianwala, comdg. 6th Bde. in Reserve ; Gujerat, comdg. 3rd Bde. ; pursuit of Sikhs and Afghans to Peshawar, comdg. 2nd Bde. (Medal with 2 clasps). Transfd. to 70th N.I. Jan. 1849 ; to 2nd Bengal Eur. Regt. Mar. 1849 ; to 40th N.I. 12 Nov. 1850. Bdr. 2 cl. comdg. Rohilkhand district 15 July 1851 ; Ambala 1 Nov. 1851 ; Jullunder F.F. (became Sirhind Div.) 2 Feb. 1852 ; Sind Sagar district 22 Nov. 1853 ; Sialkot Bde. 19 Jan. 1854. Transfd. to 19th N.I. July 1852 ; to 61st N.I. Oct. 1852. Col. 12th N.I. May 1855. Comdg. Cawnpore Div. June 1855 till Aug. 1856. Apptd. as Maj. Gen. to Divl. Staff of Army and posted to Meerut 30 June 1857. To comd. Delhi F.F. in conjunction with that from Meerut 30 Sept. 1857 (Mutiny medal). Posted Col. to 65th N.I. Dec. 1857 ; to 2nd Eur. Bengal Fus. 22 Jan. 1858. C.B. 27 June 1846. A.D.C. to Queen Victoria 5 June 1849 till 20 June 1854.

Refs. : *D.N.B. D.I.B. De Rhé-Philipe. Boase. Somerset & Dorset N. & Q.* xv. 61-2. *G.M.* 1858, ii. 191. *I.M.* 1858, p. 509.

Will dated 17 June 1848; proved 5 Aug. 1858. M.I. St. James's, Delhi.

PENNYNG, Thomas (1733/34-1784). Major, Invalid Est. 26th Bn. Sepoys. *b.* London 1733/34. Cadet 1764. Ensign 27 Dec. 1764. Lieut. 5 Dec. 1766. Capt. 16 Nov. 1769. Major 10 Jan. 1781. Invalided 1778. *d.* Chunar 22 July 1784.

Services: Sailed for India in the *Duke of Albany* 4 Mar. 1764, aged 30. Actg. A.D.C. to Col. A. Champion, *q.v.*, 11 May 1771. Chaplain to 1st Bde. 21 Jan. 1774 till Aug. 1777; apptd. to comd. newly-raised 26th Bn. Sepoys Aug. 1777; to comd. Invalids at Chunar 20 June 1778.

Refs.: *Macpherson*, pp. 77, 177. Will dated 23 June 1783; proved 2 Nov. 1784. M.I. at Chunar.

PENRICE, George (1815-1848). Bt. Captain, Artillery. (661) *b.* Fritton, Suffolk, 7 June 1815. Cadet 1832. Arrived in India 16 June 1834. 2nd Lieut. 11 June 1833. Lieut. 23 Dec. 1840. Bt. Capt. 11 June 1848. *d.* Phillaur, Punjab, 30 June 1848.

Eldest son of Dr. George Penrice, of Gt. Yarmouth, formerly Asst. Surg. Bengal Est., and Ann his wife. Addiscombe Cadet 1 Aug. 1831 till 11 June 1833.

Services: Posted to 4th Coy. 1st Bn. Foot Art. 22 Dec. 1836; transfd. to 2nd Coy. 5th Bn. 14 June 1837; actg. Adjt. 3rd Bn. 16 Mar. till Aug. 1841; transfd. to 4th Coy. 7th Bn. Sept. 1842. Comdg. whole of Art. Depots of Army of Reserve (for Afghanistan) at Karnal Oct. 1842 till Jan. 1843. Tempy. comdg. No. 18 Light Field Battery 15 Jan. 1844 till Jan. 1845. Actg. Adjt. 9th Bn. Sept. 1846. Offg. Dy. Comy. Ord., in charge of Ludhiana and Phillaur mags., Mar. 1848 till death. No record of active service.

Refs.: *De Rhé-Philipe.* *G.M.* 1848, ii. 446. M.I. at Phillaur.

PENROSE, Charles Henry [1] (1794-1824). Lieutenant, 54th N.I. *b.* Chelsea 1 Apr. 1794. Cadet 1812. Ensign 1 Nov. 1814. Lieut. 30 Apr. 1815. *d.* Benares 29 July 1824.

bapt. St. Luke's, Chelsea, 10 Feb. 1813. Son of James Penrose and Eliza his wife. Grandson of James Penrose, of Hatfield, Herts., physician. *m.* London 22 Oct. 1821, Miss Barlow, of Brompton. (She *re-m.* Henry Hailes and died 12 Jan. 1861, aged 70.)

Services: Posted Ensign to 2/27th N.I. Leave to sea 1815. Transfd. to 1/27th N.I. (? Third Mahratta War; Madhurajpura; Lieut. 1/27th N.I.) Retransfd. to 2/27th N.I. Fur. 25 Nov. 1820 till 1822. Intr. & Qmr. 2/27th N.I. 17 June 1823 ; transfd. to 54th N.I. (late 2/27th) May 1824 ; Intr. & Qmr. do. June 1824 till death.

Refs. : Vivian's *Visitations of Cornwall*, p. 369, s.n. Penrose, of Manaccan. Will dated Hatfield, 21 Jan. 1822 ; proved 19 Oct. 1824. M.I. Benares.

[1] *Note :* He calls himself Charles Henry in his Will, but the second name is omitted in official records.

PENROSE, William Henry (1810-1896). Lieutenant. 30th N.I. b. Waterford 8 July 1810. Cadet 1826. Arrived in India 27 Oct. 1827. Ensign 17 June 1827. Lieut. 4 Oct. 1832. Resigned 28 Jan. 1833. d. 1896.

Of Low Park, Dedham, Essex, and Lehane, co. Cork. J.P. Essex and Suffolk. Only son of Samuel Penrose and Elizabeth his wife, dau. of Richard Sparrow, of Oaklands. Stepson of Sir Richard Keane, Bart. m. 1st, 16 July 1840, Hon. Georgiana Isabella, youngest dau. of John, 1st Lord Keane, G.C.B. (She died 14 Apr. 1854.) m. 2nd, 1856, Louise, dau. of John Hyde, of Castle Hyde, co. Cork. (She died 1857.) m. 3rd, 1858, Anne Agnes, eldest dau. of Charles Lillingstone, of The Chantry, Ipswich. (She died 13 May 1860.) m. 4th, 1863, Elizabeth Watherston, youngest dau. of Capt. Robert Tait, R.N., of Pirn, Midlothian, and grand-niece of Dalhousie Watherston, *q.v.*

Services : Posted Ensign to 63rd N.I. 20 Feb. 1828. Transfd. to 13th N.I. 21 Mar. 1828 ; to 30th N.I. 1 July 1828. Fur. u.p.a. 1 yr., without pay, 12 Dec. 1831 till resignation. No record of active service.

Refs. : Burke's *Landed Gentry of Ireland*, p. 555, s.n. Penrose, of Lehane, co. Cork.

PENSON, Thomas (1763/64-1835). Colonel, 50th N.I. b. 1763/64. Country Cadet 1782. Admitted 1 July 1783. Ensign 28 Mar. 1783. Lieut. 4 Mar. 1790. Capt. 13 July 1803. Major 16 Dec. 1814. Lt. Col. 9 Dec. 1818. Lt. Col. Comdt. 1 May 1824. Col. 5 June 1829. d. Cheltenham 27 June 1835, aged 71.

Services : Posted to 1st Bengal Eur. Bn. 5 Feb. 1790 ; 35th Bn. Sepoys in Dec. 1792 ; 10th N.I. in 1798 ; d.d. 5th N.I. 1800. Adjt. 2/10th N.I. in 1801. Fur. s.c. 23 Jan. 1802 till 15 Nov. 1804. Transfd. to newly-raised 27th N.I. in 1805. Operations against Dhundia Khan 1807 ; Komona ; Ganauri ; Capt. 27th N.I. Served in Bk. Dept. 1810-23. Apptd. Supt. of mily. bldgs. in the field 27 Jan. 1810. Offg. civil architect W. Provs. 23 Feb. till

4 Oct. 1816. Major 1/27th N.I. Leave s.c. to sea 27 Jan. 1818 till 25 Oct. 1819. Posted Lt. Col. to 19th N.I. 1819 ; to 24th N.I. 1820 ; to 19th N.I. 1821 ; to 2/16th N.I. 1821 ; to 10th N.I. 1822. Resigned office of Supt. public bldgs. W. Provs. 6 June 1823. Fur. s.c. 26 Jan. 1824 till death. Posted Lt. Col. Comdt. to 65th N.I. May 1824 ; to 5th Extra Regt. (became 73rd N.I.) May 1825. Col. 73rd N.I. June 1829 ; 50th N.I. 13 Jan. 1830.

Refs. : *G.M.* 1835, ii. 220.

PEPPER, Hampden Nicholson (1801-1855). Lieut. Colonel. Artillery. (527) *b.* Ballymackey, co. Tipperary, 11 Dec. 1801. Cadet 1821. Arrived in India 23 Mar. 1822. 2nd Lieut. 9 June 1821. Lieut. 29 Aug. 1824. Capt. 6 Dec. 1839. Major 1 Oct. 1849. Retired 1 July 1853. Hon. Lt. Col. 28 Nov. 1854. *d.* Kilkee, co. Clare, 30 Dec. 1855 : drowned.[1]

10th and youngest son of Simon Pepper, Capt. 14th Light Dgns., and Eleanor his wife, 2nd dau. of John Andrews, of Firmount, King's Co. Second cousin of Henry Stephen Pepper, *q.v.* *m.* 1847, Penelope Briggs, of Bandon. (She died Cawnpore 7 Sept. 1850.) Addiscombe Cadet 1819-21.

Services : Asst. to Supt. of roads in Saugor & Narbada territories 8 Mar. 1827 till Dec. 1828. Comdg. Art. at Saugor 20 Apr. 1838 till Jan. 1840. Disturbances in Bundelkhand 1841 ; storm and capture of Chirgaon. Fur. 10 Jan. 1845 till 22 Dec. 1847. Posted Major to 8th Bn. Foot Art. Nov. 1849 ; transfd. to 1st Bn. 8 Mar. 1853.

Refs. : Burke's *Landed Gentry of Ireland*, p. 556, *s.n.* Pepper, of Ballygarth Castle, co. Meath. *G.M.* 1856, i. 212.

[1] *Note :* He and his fiancée, Miss Smithwick, dau. of Peter Smithwick, of Shanbally, co. Tipperary, were visiting the Puffington table-rock to admire the effects of an Atlantic storm, when they were sucked in by the retreating waves, and both drowned.

PEPPER, Henry Stephen (1780-1828). Lieut. Colonel, C.B., 6th N.I. *b.* Ballygarth, co. Meath, 20 Sept. 1780. Cadet 1798. Arrived in India 3 Sept. 1799. Ensign 8 Nov. 1799. Lieut. 21 Apr. 1800. Capt. 30 June 1811. Major 12 Aug. 1820. Lt. Col. 1 May 1824. *d. unm.* Dublin, 4 Mar. 1828.

4th son of Thomas Pepper, M.P. for Kells 1761 and 1768, and Henrietta his wife, eldest dau. of Richard Moore, of Barne, co. Tipperary. Brother of Richard Pepper, *q.v.*, and 2nd cousin of Hampden Nicholson Pepper, *q.v.* T.C.D. ; Pensioner 6 Oct. 1794, aged 14.

THE BENGAL ARMY, 1758-1834

Services: Posted Lieut. to 1/3rd N.I. 15 Apr. 1801. Adjt. & Qmr. 3rd N.I. 13 Mar. 1803 till 1811. Capt. 2/3rd N.I. A.D.C. to Maj.-Gen. Samuel Watson, *q.v.*, comdg. Dinapore Div., 1811-13. Fur. 1813 till 20 Aug. 1815. Transfd. to 1/3rd N.I. in 1816. Posted Lt. Col. to 6th N.I. (late 1/3rd) May 1824. Siege and capture of Bhurtpore; Lt. Col. comdg. 6th N.I. Fur. p.a. 2 Feb. 1827 till death. C.B. 26 Dec. 1826.

Refs.: Burke's *Landed Gentry of Ireland*, p. 556, *s.n.* Pepper, of Ballygarth Castle, co. Meath. *Alumni Dub.* Will dated 5 Feb. 1827; proved 9 Sept. 1828.

PEPPER, Richard (1778-1871). Lieutenant. 8th N.C. Subsequently Major R. Meath Mil. *b.* 12 May 1778. Cadet 1797. Arrived in India 31 Oct. 1798. Cornet 1 Nov. 1798. Lieut. 29 May 1800. Struck off in 1814, with effect from 31 Mar. 1809. *d.* 27 Dec. 1871.

bapt. Ballygarth, co. Meath, 23 May 1778. 3rd son of Thomas Pepper and Henrietta his wife. Brother of Henry Stephen Pepper, *q.v. m.* Margaret, dau. of Rev. John Aldwell, of co. Tipperary.

Services: Cornet 1st N.C. Operations in Jumna Doab 1803; Sasni; Bijaigarh; Kachaura; Lieut. 1st N.C. Second Mahratta War; Aligarh; battle of Delhi; Laswari; Lieut. 1st N.C. (India medal). Transfd. to newly-raised 8th N.C. in 1805; Adjt. do. 1805-6. Fur. 19 Sept. 1806 till struck off. Major R. Meath Mil. 27 July 1808.

Refs.: Burke's *Landed Gentry of Ireland*, p. 556, *s.n.* Pepper, of Ballygarth Castle, co. Meath.

PEPPIN, William Wade (1787-1816). Lieutenant, 27th N.I. *bapt.* Clipston, Northants, 16 Apr. 1787. Cadet 1804. Arrived in India 13 May 1806. Ensign 11 Apr. 1806. Lieut. 19 Nov. 1807. *d.* Cape of Good Hope 28 Nov. 1816.

Son of William Peppin and Anne his wife. Brother of Matthew, John, and Mary Ann, and nephew of Edward Peppin, of Clipston.

Services: Barasat C.C. Posted to 27th N.I. in 1807. Operations against Dhundia Khan 1807; Komona; Ganauri; Lieut. 2/27th N.I. Operations in Oudh 1810; Lieut. 2/27th N.I. Leave to Cape 1815 till death.

Refs.: *A.J.* iv. 530. Will dated 25 Nov. 1815; proved 4 Mar. 1817.

PERCEVAL, George (1784-1805). Lieutenant, Artillery. (321) *b.* Kilmorgan, co. Sligo, 22 Sept. 1784. Cadet 1800. Arrived in India 27 Aug. 1803. Lieut. 1 Sept. 1803. *d*. 9 Jan. 1805 : kld. in action at the siege of Bhurtpore.

Brother of King Perceval, *q.v.*, and of Michael Perceval, Capt. R.M.

Services : Second Mahratta War ; siege of Deig ; Bhurtpore (kld.) ; Lieut. 3rd Coy. 2nd Bn. Art.

Refs. : Will dated 7 Jan. 1805 ; proved 16 Apr. 1805.

PERCEVAL, King (1785-1815). Lieutenant, Invalid Est. 20th N.I. *b*. Coolock, co. Dublin, July 1785. Cadet 1803. Arrived in India 21 Aug. 1804. Ensign 16 Aug. 1804. Lieut. 21 Sept. 1804. Invalided 4 Mar. 1815. *d*. Serampore, Bengal, 21 Aug. 1815.

Brother of George Perceval, *q.v.*

Services : Posted Lieut. to 1/20th N.I. Capture of Java 1811 ; Lieut. 1/20th N.I.

PERCEVAL or PERCIVAL, William (1786-?). Lieutenant. 26th N.I. *b*. Laracor, co. Meath, spring of 1786. Cadet 1806. Arrived in India 17 Mar. 1808. Ensign 17 Feb. 1808. Lieut. 4 Nov. 1811. Resigned in India 12 Dec. 1815.

Son of Robert Perceval (or Percival), of Knightsbrook, co. Meath. *m*. Calcutta 20 July 1811, Miss Elizabeth Wroughton (? sister of Henry Francis Wroughton, *q.v.*). (*See also* James Eckford.)

Services : Barasat C.C. Ensign d.d. 15th N.I. 1810 ; do. 10th N.I. 1811. Posted Lieut. to 1/26th N.I. in 1811. Served with Inf. Vols. in Java 1812-15.

PERCIVAL, Edward Gledstanes (1812-1831). 2nd Lieutenant,[1] Artillery. (628) *b*. Dublin 8 Nov. 1812. Cadet 1828. Arrived in India 15 Jan. 1830. 2nd Lieut. (12 June 1829). *d.s.p.* Ryde, I.W., 29 July 1831 ; *bur*. Binstead, nr. Ryde, 4 Aug.

bapt. 22 Nov. 1812. Elder son of Edward Cropper Percival, M.B., of Lambridge House, Bath, and Sophia his wife, dau. of George Gledstanes. Ed. Winchester ; K.S. 1823 ; left 12 June 1827. Addiscombe Cadet 1827-9.

Services : Fur. s.c. 26 Dec. 1830 till death. No record of active service.

Refs. : Howard & Crisp, ii. 70, *s.n.* Percival. *Kirby. G.M.* 1831, ii. 189.

[1] *Note :* Rank cancelled and reduced to Cadet (G.G.O. 31 May 1830) under instructions from C.D.

PERCY, John. (*See* **PIERCY.**)

THE BENGAL ARMY, 1758-1834 509

PEREIRA, Isaac (1788-1847). Lieut. Colonel, Artillery. (361)
b. Jamaica 9 Jan. 1788. Cadet 1804. Arrived in India 14 June 1806. Lieut. 30 Mar. 1806. Capt. Lt. 21 Apr. 1817. Capt. 1 Sept. 1818. Major 20 Aug. 1831. Lt. Col. 27 Jan. 1837. *d.* Dum-Dum 9 Aug. 1847.

Brother of Benjamin Pereira. *m.* 1st, Calcutta 13 Apr. 1810, Miss Caroline Ann Sophia Butler. (*See also* James Nicolson.) (She died 1 July 1845, aged 55.) His daus. *m.* Frederick Dayot Atkinson, *q.v.*, George Alexander Barbor, *q.v.*, and William Veysie, *q.v. m.* 2nd, St. Mary's, Paddington, 4 Apr. 1846, Emily, dau. of Barrett Wadden, of Kingston, Surrey.

Services: Served as Cadet at capture of Cape in Jan. 1806. Capture of Mauritius 1810-11 ; actg. Adjt. to Royal and Bengal Art. Jan.-July 1811, when he returned to Bengal. Nepal War 1814-15 ; Lieut. 3rd Coy. 2nd Bn., with 4th Div. Siege and capture of Hathras ; Lieut. 3rd Coy. 2nd Bn. Third Mahratta War ; (? Taragarh) ; Madhurajpura ; Capt. 5th Coy. 1st Bn., comdg. two Mortar Batteries (*Lond. Gaz.* 8 July 1819). Apptd. to charge of Art. park, Bhurtpore force, with rank of Comy. Ord. 1 Dec. 1825. Siege and capture of Bhurtpore ; Capt. 4th Coy. 3rd Bn., Comy. Ord. Posted to 1st Bn. 28 Dec. 1831 ; to 3rd Bn. 29 Nov. 1833. To comd. Art. Div. at Nimach 24 Feb. 1836. Transfd. to 6th Bn. ; to 3rd Bn. 28 Oct. 1836. Comdd. Mewa Div. Art. 17 Apr. till 13 Nov. 1836 ; assumed comd. of Art. at Mhow 27 Nov. 1836. Transfd. to 1st Bn. 10 Feb. 1843 ; to 3rd Bn. 20 Nov. 1844. Comdg. Art. Div. Agra 11 Nov. 1843 ; do. detachment of Train of Army of Exercise 25 Dec. 1843. Fur. 1845-6. Transfd. to 2nd Bn.

Refs.: G.M. 1847, ii. 558. *I.M.* 5 Oct. 1847, p. 583. M.I. in old cemetery, Dum-Dum.

PERKINS, Christopher William (*d.* 1784). Ensign, Infantry. Country Cadet 1781. Ensign 2 July 1782. *bur.* Calcutta 5 Apr. 1784.
Services: Apptd. Cadet July 1781. N.F.P.

PERKINS, James (1782-?). Ensign. Infantry. *bapt.* St. James's, Bristol, 18 Oct. 1782. Cadet 1799. Arrived in India 9 Dec. 1800. Ensign (no rank assigned). Resigned 8 Jan. 1801. Son of Thomas Perkins and Charlotte his wife.
Services: N.F.P.

PERKINS, William Hill (1778-1849). Lieut. General. Colonel 47th N.I. *b.* 23 Aug. 1778. Cadet 1793. Arrived in India

17 Feb. 1795. Ensign 20 Sept. 1794. Lieut. 8 Jan. 1796. Capt.
21 Sept. 1804. Major 16 Dec. 1814. Lt. Col. 9 June 1819.
Col. 5 June 1829. Maj. Gen. 10 Jan. 1837. Lt. Gen. 4 Nov.
1846. *d.* Paris 8 Mar. 1849.

bapt. Deptford 16 Sept. 1778. Son of William Perkins, of Redhouse Wharf, and Ursula his wife. *m.* Ellen. (She died Saugor 24 Nov. 1823.)

Services: Lieut. 10th N.I. Transfd. as Capt. to newly-raised 1/27th N.I. in 1804. Operations against Dhundia Khan 1807; Komona (s.w.); Capt. 1/27th N.I. Fort Adjt. at Buxar 15 Sept. 1807 till 1815. Ordered to raise a body of recruits 14 Oct. 1814. Transfd. as Major to newly-raised 2/29th N.I. in 1815. Operations against the Bhattis of Hariana Sept.-Oct. 1818; Major 2/29th N.I. Fur. p.a. 4 Feb. 1819 till 19 Dec. 1822. Posted Lt. Col. to 15th N.I. 1819; to 2/12th N.I. 1819; to 1/27th N.I. 1822; as Lt. Col. Comdt. to newly-formed 2nd Bengal Eur. Regt. May 1824. Fur. p.a. 8 Mar. 1825 till death. Col. 2nd Bengal Eur. Regt. June 1829; Left Wing Eur. Regt. Jan. 1830; 18th N.I. 21 Dec. 1833; 47th N.I. 1843.

Refs.: *A.A.R.* x. 21.

PERREAU, Charles James Horton (1810-1847). Captain, 58th N.I. *b.* Fort Marlbro', Sumatra, 7 June 1810. Cadet 1826. Arrived in India 16 June 1827. Ensign 7 Feb. 1827. Lieut. 16 July 1828. Capt. 10 Aug. 1842. *d.* on board a boat nr. Nadia, Bengal, 10 Nov. 1847.

Son of Robert Samuel Perreau, Malay Translator and Asst. to the Resdt. in Sumatra, and Elizabeth his 2nd wife, widow of John Braham, Fort Marlbro' C.S., sometime Resdt. at Manna. *m.* St. Andrew's, Calcutta, 5 Sept. 1836, Isabella Anna, only dau. of John Robeson, *q.v.*

Services: Posted Ensign to 36th N.I. 19 June 1827; transfd. to 58th N.I. in 1827. Actg. Adjt. Left Wing 58th N.I. 19 Oct. 1829. To take charge of 7th Coy. Pioneers 12 Nov. 1831. Fur. s.c. 30 Dec. 1832 till 11 Dec. 1835. Adjt. 58th N.I. 3 Mar. 1838 till 11 Sept. 1842. Fur. s.c. 9 Jan. 1844 till 1845. No record of active service.

Refs.: *I.M.* 10 Jan. 1848, p. 6. *Hickey,* iv. 447.

PERRET, Henri Vincent Frederick (1788-1818). Lieutenant, 3rd N.C. *b.* Villeneuve, canton Vaud, Switzerland, 5 Aug. 1788. Cadet 1805. Arrived in India 11 July 1806. Cornet 11 July 1806. Lieut. 12 Nov. 1813. *d.* Samarang, Java, 28 Apr. 1818.

THE BENGAL ARMY, 1758-1834 511

bapt. Villeneuve 22 Aug. 1788. Son of François Perret, châtelain et bourgeois de Villeneuve, and Sophia Rosselet his wife. Godson of Frederick David Wild, Membre du Conseil Souverain de la ville de Berne. (*Probably* related to Charles Frederick Wild, *q.v.*) *m.* Calcutta 16 July 1812, Miss Eliza Hutchinson, eldest dau. of J. Hutchinson.
Services: Barasat C.C. Posted Cornet to 3rd N.C. in 1807. (? Operations against Lachman Dawa 1809 ; Rajaoli ; Ajaigarh ; Cornet 3rd N.C.) Served with Java L.C. 1812-15. Siege and capture of Hathras 1817 ; Lieut. 3rd N.C. Leave to Java 1817 till death.

PERRY, George (*d.* 1786). Ensign, Engineers. Ensign 15 May 1783. *d.* Hooghly, Calcutta, 12 Mar. 1786.
m. (before 1783) Maria.
Services: Was already in India when recommended by Bdr.-Gen. G. Stibbert, the Provl. C.-in-C., *q.v.*, for the appt. of Ensign and Practitioner Engr. An Asst. in Surveyor-Gen.'s Dept. in 1785.

PERRY, James (1777-1806). Captain, 15th N.I. *b.* London 24 Nov. 1777. Cadet 1796. Admitted 13 Mar. 1798. Ensign 6 Oct. 1797. Lieut. 10 Sept. 1798. Capt. 1 Nov. 1805. *d.* Chunar 1 Jan. 1806.
bapt. St. Anne's, Westminster, 18 Dec. 1777. Son of James Perry and Helen his wife. Cousin of John Paton (1760/61-1824), *q.v.*
Services: Posted Lieut. to 16th N.I. in 1798. Operations in Jumna Doab 1803 ; Sasni ; Bijaigarh ; Kachaura ; Lieut. 1/15th N.I. Second Mahratta War ; Agra (w.) ; Laswari ; battle of Deig 13 Nov. 1804 (s.w.) ; Lieut. 1/15th N.I. Adjt. & Qmr. of Eur. Invalids at Chunar 1805 till death.
Refs.: *G.M.* 1806, ii. 676. Will dated 6 Nov. 1802 ; proved 24 Apr. 1806.

*PERRY, John (*d.* 1763). Ensign, Bengal Eur. Regt. Cadet (?) Ensign (?) *d.* 5th, 6th or 11th Oct. 1763 : massacred at or near Patna by order of Nawab Mir Muhammad Kasim. (*See* note to Hugh Mackay.)
Services: N.F.P.
Refs.: *Broome,* p. 365. *Innes,* p. 169. *Swinton of Kimmerghame Records,* p. 50.

PERRY, Richard. (*See* ***PARRY, Richard.**)

PESTER, John (1778-1856). Lieut. Colonel. 13th N.I. *b.* Odcombe, Somerset, 22 Dec. 1778. Cadet 1799. Arrived in

India 8 Dec. 1800. Ensign 5 Sept. 1800. Lieut. 17 July 1801. Capt. 29 Oct. 1812. Major 11 July 1823. Lt. Col. 16 Dec. 1824. Retired 6 Jan. 1826. *d.* Millbrook, nr. Southampton, 1 Aug. 1856.

bapt. Odcombe 8 Sept. 1779. Son of Emanuel Pester and Peggy his wife. *m.* Montacute, Somerset, Apr. 1811 Elizabeth, eldest dau. of Rev. William Phelips, of Montacute, and sister of Charles Henry Phelips, *q.v.* (She died Millbrook 6 Nov. 1859.)

Services : Posted Ensign to 1/2nd N.I. 17 Apr. 1801. Operations against refractory zemindars in Shikohabad district Aug. 1802. Operations in Jumna Doab 1803 ; Sasni ; Kachaura (w.) ; Lieut. 1/2nd N.I. Second Mahratta War ; Koil ; Aligarh ; battle of Delhi ; Agra ; Lieut. 1/2nd N.I. ; apptd. Bde. Major 4th Inf. Bde. 26 Oct. 1803 ; Gwalior ; Bde. Major 4th Bde. 1804 ; capture of Deig ; Bhurtpore (India medal). Fur. s.c. 2 Jan. 1806 till 1811. Capt. Lt. 2nd N.I. 14 June 1809. Bde. Major Benares 7 Aug. 1813 ; do. Dinapore Div. 1817. Transfd. to newly-raised 1/30th N.I. in 1815. D.A.Q.M.G., and in charge of Guide and Intelligence Dept., with Bdr.-Gen. W. Toone's Div. during third Mahratta War. Bde. Major and Dy. Postmr. at Cuttack 1821-2. Fur. 1823 till retirement. Transfd. to 59th N.I. (late 1/30th) May 1824. Posted Lt. Col. to 13th N.I. in 1825.

Refs. : Burke's *Landed Gentry*, 13th edn., p. 1405, *s.n.* Phelips, of Montacute, Somerset. *E.I.M.C.* iii. 381-4. *Farley's Bristol Journal,* 27 Apr. 1811. His journal for the years 1802-6, edited by his grand-nephew, was pub. London, 1913, under the title of " War and Sport in India, 1802-6." It has frequently been referred to in these pages.

PETER, Edward (1789-1818). Lieutenant, Invalid Est. 1st N.I. *b.* St. Merryn, Cornwall, 29 Mar. 1789. Cadet 1804. Arrived in India 21 June 1806. Ensign 22 Apr. 1805. Lieut. 23 Sept. 1805. Invalided 1 Dec. 1814. *d. unm.* Chunar 4 Aug. 1818.

4th son of Hoblyn Peter, of Porthcothan, and Elizabeth his wife, dau. of John Pomeroy.

Services : Posted Lieut. to 1st N.I. in 1806, and served throughout with that Regt.

Refs. : Burke's *Landed Gentry*, 12th edn., p. 951, *s.n.* Peter-Hoblyn, of Colquite, Cornwall. Vivian's *Visitations of Cornwall*, p. 607, *s.n.* Peter, of Harlyn. M.I. at Chunar.

GRANT-PETERKIN, Peter (1787-1878). Lieut. Colonel. 66th N.I. *b.* St. Thomas, Jamaica, 2 Oct. 1787. Cadet 1804. Arrived

in India 6 Apr. 1806. Ensign 6 Mar. 1806. Lieut. 1 Feb. 1807.
Capt. 1 May 1824. Major 4 Jan. 1832. Retired 8 May 1832.
Hon. Lt. Col. 28 Nov. 1854. *d.* Greeshop, Forres, 24 Nov. 1878.
Of Invererne, Forres, co. Moray. Son of George Grant and
Elizabeth McDermot his wife. *m.* Grange Hall, Forres, 13 Sept.
1836, Mary Anne, dau. of James Peterkin, of Grange. (She died
10 Dec. 1854.) Assumed, on his marriage, the surname of Peterkin
in addition to his own name of Grant.
Services : Lieut. Elgin Vols. Barasat C.C. Posted Lieut. to
4th N.I. Capture of Java 1811; Lieut. 4th Bengal Vol. Bn.
(Medal). Transfd. to newly-raised 2/28th N.I. in 1815. Third
Mahratta War; Dhamoni; Lieut. 2/28th N.I. Comdd. Delhi
Palace Gds. 22 Feb. 1823 till 1 Nov. 1831. Transfd. to newly-raised
33rd N.I. 11 July 1823; to 66th N.I. (late 2/33rd) May 1824.
Fur. p.a. 10 Jan. 1832 till retirement. The title " Tuhuwar-ood-
Dowlah,[1] Bahadur, Dilawar Jang " was conferred on him by
Muhammad Akbar Shah II, titular King of Delhi, in the 28th year
of his reign.
Refs. : Family information. *A.J.* N.S. xxi. 121. *The Times,*
27 Nov. 1878.
[1] *Note : i.e., Tahawwur-u'd-Daula,* or Intrepid (bulwark) of State.

PETRE, Philip William (1792-1846). Lieutenant. 26th N.I.
b. Bath 24 Jan. 1792. Cadet 1809. Admitted 2 Aug. 1810.
Ensign 6 Mar. 1812. Lieut. 1 Oct. 1816. Dismissed by G.C.M.
30 Oct. 1821. *d.* 22 Aug. 1846.
bapt. Corn St. Chapel, Bath, 24 Jan. 1792. 3rd son of Hon.
George Petre (who was younger son of Robert Edward, 9th Baron
Petre) and Maria his wife, dau. of Philip Howard, of Corby. *m.*
1833, Mrs. Maria Annoot.
Services : Barasat C.C. Cadet d.d. 2nd N.I. 1811; posted
Ensign to 26th N.I. in 1812. Third Mahratta War; Dhamoni;
Lieut. 1/26th N.I.
Refs. : Burke's *Peerage,* 1923, p. 1767, *s.n.* Petre, B.

PETRIE, John (1741/42-1826). Lieutenant. 1st Bengal Eur.
Regt. Afterwards Senior Merchant, B.C.S. *b.* 1741/42.
Country Cadet 1763. Ensign 26 Aug. 1763. Lieut. 16 Apr. 1764.
Resigned 15 May 1766. *d.* Calais, France, 5 Feb. 1826 aged 84.
Of Gatton Park, Surrey, and of Deans Court, Devon. M.P. for
Gatton borough 1796-1802; D.L. co. Surrey. Son of Rev. Robert
Petrie, of an old Perthshire family, minister of Canonbie 1734-64,
and Margaret his wife, only dau. of Andrew Waugh, of Selkirk.

Brother of William Petrie, M.C.S., actg. Govr. of Madras 1807. *m.* Calcutta 11 Nov. 1779, Miss Ann Keble, sister of John Petrie Keble, *q.v.* His dau. was mother of Gen. Reynell George Taylor (*D.N.B.*).

Services : Permitted to proceed to India as a free merchant 22 Sept. 1762. War with Mir Muhammad Kasim 1763. Campaign of 1764-5 under Major Hector Munro ; apptd. Qmr. 26 Jan. 1765. Apptd. A.D.C. to Major G. Stibbert, *q.v.*, 2 May 1765 ; posted to 1st Bengal Eur. Regt. 13 Aug. 1765. Resigned during the " Batta mutiny " and returned to England. Apptd. a Factor on the Bengal Est. 27 Nov. 1772 ; arrived in India 18 Aug. 1773. Junior Merchant 1778 ; Collector of Govt. Customs 1779 ; Naval Storekeeper 1780 ; Senior Merchant 1782 ; compiled " Standing Orders " 1783 ; out of the Service in 1788. Tried at Calcutta Qr. Sessions, 29 Nov. 1773, for killing Mr. Rochford in a duel, and was acquitted. Owned land in I. of Tobago, and sat as Deputy for it in the French Assembly. He was thus a member of both English and French Parliaments at the same time. Purchased Gatton Park, which afterwards passed into the possession of Sir Mark Wood, Bart., *q.v.*, for £110,000. Owing to heavy financial losses was obliged to retire to France in 1803, where he later became one of Napoleon's *détenus.*

Refs. : Reynell Taylor, by Gambier Parry, pp. 4-5. *N. & Q.* 10S. vi. 401. *Macpherson*, p. 163. *Cal. Gaz.* 31 Aug. 1786. *G.M.* 1826, i. 287. *B : P.P.* ix. 101. Scott's *Fasti*, ii. 229.

PETTINGAL, Edward (1790-1860). Major General. Colonel 12th N.I. *b.* Bath 14 May 1790. Cadet 1804. Arrived in India 13 May 1806. Ensign 15 Mar. 1806. Lieut. 1 Feb. 1807. Capt. 21 Oct. 1821. Major 25 July 1839. Lt. Col. 18 Mar. 1845. Col. 28 Feb. 1855. Maj. Gen. 4 Nov. 1856. *d.* 134 Regent St., London, 17 Nov. 1860.

bapt. St. James's, Bath, 28 Apr. 1797. Son of Hanbury Pettingal of Bath, silk mercer, and Winifred his wife. *m* (?)

Services : Present as Cadet at capture of Cape in Jan. 1806 under Sir David Baird ; volunteered for active service, but was considered too young to carry a musket. Barasat C.C. Posted Lieut. to 19th N.I. in 1807. Capture of Mauritius 1810 ; Lieut. 2nd Vol. Bn. Nepal War 1814-15 ; Kalanga ; Lieut. 2/19th N.I., in 1st Div. (India medal). Third Mahratta War ; Lieut. 2/19th N.I. Actg. Adjt. 2/19th N.I. 16 Oct. 1820. Transfd. to 39th N.I. (late 2/19th) May 1824. First Burma War ; Cachar 1824-5 ; Capt. 39th N.I. (clasp to India medal). Actg. Bde. Major at Muttra

THE BENGAL ARMY, 1758-1834   515

7 July 1832. Comdd. 5th Local Horse 1 Nov. 1832 till 1845, and was in addition for some yrs. in charge of Bhopawar Political Agency. Posted Lt. Col. to 39th N.I. 6 June 1845. Transfd. to 26th N.I. Fur. p.a. 20 June 1846 till 31 July 1850. Transfd. to 28th N.I. 31 July 1850; to 60th N.I. Mar. 1851; to 55th N.I. July 1852; to 12th N.I. Mar. 1854. Tempy. Bdr. 2 cl. May 1855; comdg. at Barrackpore 23 Nov. 1855 till June 1856. Posted Col. to 12th N.I. May 1855. Fur. p.a. 27 June 1856 till death.

Refs.: Boase. *The Times,* 22 Nov. 1860. *I.M.* 27 Nov. 1860, p. 888.

PETTIT, John (*d.* 1790). Lieutenant, Infantry. Cadet 1772. Ensign 3 July 1776. Lieut. 24 June 1778. *d.* Calcutta 26 Nov. 1790.

Services : Insane 1785 till death.

PEW, Peter Lawrie (1790-1851). Colonel, Artillery. (378) *b.* Urr, co. Kirkcudbright, 29 Mar. 1790. Cadet 1806. Arrived in India 21 July 1807. Fireworker 4 May 1807. Lieut. 15 May 1807. Capt. Lt. 14 July 1818. Capt. 1 Sept. 1818. Major 2 July 1835. Lt. Col. 31 Dec. 1839. Col. 16 June 1848. *d.* Singapore 2 Feb. 1851.

bapt. Urr 4 Apr. 1790. 3rd son of John William Pew, of Hillowtown, Kirkcudbright, and Margaret his wife, dau. of Alexander Lawrie, of Ernespie. Brother of Mary Watson, wife of James Drysdale, *q.v.,* and of Elizabeth, wife of Sir William Drysdale, of Pitteuchar, Kt. *m.* Dumfries 2 Aug. 1831, Harriet, only dau. of John Syme, of Ryedale. Woolwich Cadet 2 May 1804 till 6 Jan. 1807.

Services : Fur. s.c. 17 Dec. 1811 till 24 Oct. 1814. Third Mahratta War; Garhakota Oct. 1818; Lieut. 6th Coy. 2nd Bn. Actg. Adjt. & Qmr. to detachment of Art. under Major Robert Hetzler, *q.v.,* 7 Feb. 1818. Fur. s.c. 20 May 1820 till 14 Sept. 1822. Siege and capture of Bhurtpore; Capt. comdg. 2nd Coy. 3rd Bn. (Field Battery). On fur. in 1831. To tempy. charge of Delhi mag. 7 Nov. 1834. Posted to 4th Bn. 18 Nov. 1835. To comd. Nimach Div. Art. 11 Sept. 1837; 2nd Bn. 15 Nov. 1837. Comdd. experimental Camel Battery till 1 Aug. 1838. First Afghan War 1838-9; Quetta; Ghazni (*Lond. Gaz.* 30 Oct. 1839); Bt. Lt. Col. 4th Bn., comdg. Art. (Medal). Transfd. to 5th Bn. 24 July 1845. Leave s.c. 2 yrs. to N.S.W. Nov. 1849 till death. Edited the *Delhi Gazette* c. 1834-5, and was one of the founders of the *Benares Recorder* c. 1847-8. Chairman of the Ganges Steam Co.; Dir. of the Benares

Bank Sept. 1845 till Mar. 1849. This bank suspended payment in Aug. 1849, when he became bankrupt. " A great speculator—in 1845, he is said to have been worth £250,000." Durani 3 cl. 15 Aug. 1840.

Refs.: Burke's *Heraldic Illustrations* (1853), ii. plate lxxxv, *s.n.* Pew, of Scotland. Boase. *A.J.* N.S. xx. 188. *G.M.* 1851, i. 573. *I.M.* 5 Jan. 1850, p. 3 ; 2 Apr. 1851, p. 190. Will dated 1 Aug. 1846 ; admon. 28 Oct. 1851.

PEYTON, Abel (1759/60-1781). Lieutenant, Infantry. *b.* London 1759/60. Cadet 1780. Ensign 1780. Lieut. 14 June 1781. *d.* in India 1781.

Son of Abel Peyton, of W. Smithfield, and Hannah his wife, 2nd dau. of Rev. Samuel Shaw, of Mansfield.

Services: Apptd. Cadet 8 Dec. 1779 ; sailed for India in the *Neptune* 3 June 1780, aged 20 ; arrived in India Mar. 1781.

Refs.: Hunter's *Familiæ Minorum Gentium* (Harleian Soc. xxvii), i. 377. Intestate ; admon. 20 Dec. 1781.

PFEIFER, Charles Frederick John Jacob (1789-1806). Cadet, Cavalry. *b.* Arolsen, Fürstenthum of Waldeck, 29 May 1789. Cadet 1805. Never arrived in India. *d.* Dec. 1806, on his passage to India, in the wreck of the *Skelton Castle.* Struck off with effect from 5 Nov. 1806. (*See* note to David Allan.)

bapt. Arolsen 1 June 1789. Son of Charles Jeremias Frederick Pfeifer and Elizabeth his wife, *née* Brendli, of Zurich. His sponsors were, John Jacob Brendli, of Zurich, and Frederick Henry Pfeifer, goldsmith. Marlow Cadet.

PHAYRE, Sir Arthur Purves (1812-1885). Lieut. General, G.C.M.G., K.C.S.I., C.B. 4th Eur. Infantry. Govr. of Mauritius. *b.* Shrewsbury 7 May 1812. Cadet 1827. Arrived in India 3 Feb. 1829. Ensign 13 Aug. 1828. Lieut. 9 July 1838. Capt. 16 May 1849. Major 10 Jan. 1855. Lt. Col. 22 Jan. 1859. Col. 18 Feb. 1866. Maj. Gen. 9 Aug. 1870. Lt. Gen. 1 Oct. 1877. *d. unm.* Bray, nr. Dublin, 14 Dec. 1885 : found dead in his bed.

2nd son of Richard Phayre, of Claremont, Shrewsbury, and Maria his wife, dau. of James Leech Ridgeway, of 169 Piccadilly, London, publisher. Ed. Shrewsbury School 1819-26.

Services: See *D.N.B.* Ensign d.d. 30th N.I. 3 Mar. 1829 ; posted to 7th N.I. 3 June 1829. Served in the administration of Burma 1834-48. Rejoined 7th N.I. in Punjab 1848-9. Comr. of Arakan 20 Apr. 1849 ; do. province of Pegu 30 Dec. 1852 ; Envoy to Burmese Court July 1855. Posted to newly-raised 6th Eur. Inf. in 1858; transfd. to 4th Eur. Inf. 21 Oct. 1859. Transfd. to Staff Corps 18 Feb. 1861. Chief Comr. of newly-formed province of British Burma 31 Jan. 1862 till 16 Feb. 1867. Fur. s.c. 2 yrs. 16 Mar. 1867. Govr. of Mauritius 14 Nov. 1874 till 31 Dec. 1878. Author of " History of Burma," 1883. C.B. (Civil) 30 Mar. 1863; K.C.S.I. 24 May 1867; G.C.M.G. 12 Dec. 1877.

Refs.: Burke's *Landed Gentry*, 15th edn., p. 2660, *s.n.* Phayre, *formerly* of Grange. *D.N.B. D.I.B. Boase. Shrewsbury School Register. The Times*, 17 Dec. 1885. Portrait by Sir Thomas Jones in E.I.U.S. Club; statue by Thomas Nelson Maclean at Rangoon.

PHELIPS, Charles Henry (1799-1823). Lieutenant, 10th N.I.
b. Montacute, Somerset, 3 June 1799. Cadet 1817. Ensign (?) Lieut. 20 Oct. 1818. *d.* Berhampore 4 Aug. 1823.

6th son of Rev. William Phelips, of Montacute, vicar of Yeovil, and Anna Aletheia Elizabeth his wife, dau. of Rev. John Paget. His sister *m.* John Pester, *q.v. m.* Chunar 21 Nov. 1820, Harriet, dau. of William Bedell, *q.v.* (*See also* Archibald Dickson.) (She *re-m.* Philip Brewer, *q.v.*) Ed. Sherborne.

Services: Posted Supy. Lieut. to 2/10th N.I. in 1819; actg. Adjt. & Qmr. of Eur. Invalids at Chunar 1820-1; Adjt. Murshidabad Provl. Bn. at death. No record of active service.

Refs.: Burke's *Landed Gentry*, 13th edn., p. 1404, *s.n.* Phelips, of Montacute, co. Somerset. Will dated Berhampore 25 Apr. 1821; proved 4 Aug. 1823.

PHIBBS, John Kingston (1806-1879). Lieut. Colonel. 41st N.I.
b. E. Barnet 16 Oct. 1806. Cadet 1825. Arrived in India 24 Nov. 1825. Ensign 13 May 1825. Lieut. 2 Aug. 1828. Capt. 1 July 1846. Bt. Major 12 Nov. 1851. Lt. Col. 15 June 1855. Retired 26 Mar. 1855. *d.* Pelham House, 30 Sutherland Gdns., London, 25 Feb. 1879.

bapt. E. Barnet 13 Nov. 1806. Son of William Henry Phibbs, of Mortimer St., wine merchant, and Jane his wife. Brother of William Henry Phibbs, *q.v. m.* Christ Church, Marylebone, 23 July 1838, Eliza, 2nd dau. of Capt. Cuthbert Fetherstone Daly, R.N., C.B., and cousin-german of Frederick Daly, *q.v.*

Services: Posted Ensign to 41st N.I., and served throughout with that Regt. Fur. s.c. 17 Jan. 1836 till 19 Jan. 1839. First Sikh War; Ferozshahr; Sobraon; Bt. Capt. 41st N.I. (Medal with clasp). Fur. s.c. Jan. 1853 till 15 Jan. 1855.

Refs.: A.J. N.S. xxvii, 68. *The Times*, 27 Feb. 1879.

PHIBBS, William Henry (1803-1837). Lieutenant, Pension Est. 21st N.I. *b.* E. Barnet 31 May 1803. Cadet 1819. Admitted 14 June 1820. Ensign 10 Jan. 1820. Lieut. 11 July 1823. Pensioned 19 Mar. 1833. *d.* Chandernagore, Bengal, 2 Jan. 1837.
bapt. E. Barnet 25 June 1803. Son of William Henry Phibbs, wine merchant, and Jane his wife. Brother of John Kingston Phibbs, *q.v.* Addiscombe Cadet 1817-19.
Services: Posted Ensign to 2/1st N.I. Transfd. as Lieut. to 9th N.I. July 1823; to 21st N.I. (late 2/9th) May 1824. Siege and capture of Bhurtpore; Lieut. 21st N.I.

PHILIPPS, Henry (1785-1808). Lieutenant, 26th N.I. *b.* May 1785. Cadet 1803. Arrived in India 18 Mar. 1805. Ensign 20 Mar. 1805. Lieut. 21 Mar. 1805. *d.* Calcutta 8 Oct. 1808 : kld. in a duel by William Sheppard, *q.v.*, against whom a verdict of " Manslaughter " was returned.
bapt. Llangathen, co. Carmarthen, 22 May 1785, aged 3 weeks. Son of William Philipps and Sarah his wife. *m.* Partabgarh, U.P., 13 Oct. 1806, Eliza, dau. of Richard Henry, *q.v.* (*See also* Augustus Thomas Watson.) (She died 20 Feb. 1809, aged 20.)
Services: Posted Lieut. to 26th N.I. in 1806. Operations in Bundelkhand 1807; capture of Sehlehuganj; Lieut. 1/26th N.I.
Refs.: M.I. in N. Park St. cemetery, Calcutta.

PHILIPPS, Robert Howell (1788-1827). Captain, 49th N.I. *b.* Leeds 14 Feb. 1788. Cadet 1807. Arrived in India 16 Nov. 1808. Ensign 28 Nov. 1808. Lieut. 7 Apr. 1814. Capt. 10 Aug. 1824. *d.* Ramree, Burma, 17 Nov. 1827.
bapt. Leeds 29 Feb. 1808. Son of Samuel Philipps, of Leeds, and Mary his wife (who *re-m.* Joseph Vickers, of Leeds).
Services: Barasat C.C. Posted Ensign to 25th N.I. in 1809. Siege and capture of Hathras 1817; Lieut. 1/25th N.I. Transfd. to 49th N.I. (late 1/25th) May 1824. Intr. & Qmr. 49th N.I. June-Aug. 1824. First Burma War; Arakan 1825; Capt. 49th N.I., D.A.Q.M.G. Asst. to Comr. in Arakan 8 Sept. 1826 till death.
Refs.: A.J. xxv. 683.

PHILLIPPS, Robert Samuel (1792-1840). Captain. 67th N.I. *b.* Bodmin, Cornwall, 1 May 1792. Cadet 1807. Arrived in India 16 Nov. 1808. Ensign 2 Dec. 1808. Lieut. 16 Dec. 1814. Capt. 13 May 1825. Invalided 15 Feb. 1836. Retired 27 June 1838. *d.* Bodmin 20 June 1840.
bapt. publicly Bodmin 3 Feb. 1796. 5th son of Rev. Nicholas

Phillipps, rector and patron of Lanivet, Cornwall, and Dennis his wife, eldest dau. of William Flamank, of Boscarne. *m.* 7 July 1821, Elizabeth Jane, dau. of Major Shortt. (She died Bodmin 19 Feb. 1838, aged 38.)

Services : Barasat C.C. for 8½ mos. Posted Ensign to 26th N.I. in 1809. Lieut. 2/26th N.I. Transfd. to 1/26th N.I. in 1818. (? Third Mahratta War ; Dhamoni ; Lieut. 1/26th N.I.) Fur. p.a. 19 Jan. 1819 till 16 Jan. 1822. Retransfd. to 2/26th N.I. 31 Jan. 1822 ; Adjt. do. 17 May 1822. Transfd. to newly-raised 2/34th N.I. July 1823 ; Adjt. do. 1 Oct. 1823. Transfd. to 67th N.I. (late 1/34th) May 1824 ; Adjt. do. 17 June 1824 till 1 Aug. 1825. First Burma War ; Arakan 1825 ; Capt. 67th N.I. Fur. s.c. 23 Oct. 1828 till 23 Oct. 1831, and 3 Jan. 1837 till retirement. Retired on full pay, viz. 10/6 *p.d.*

Refs. : Vivian's *Visitations of Cornwall*, p. 163, *s.n.* Flamank, of Boscarne. *A.J.* N.S. xxvi. 59.

PHILLIPS, Sir Benjamin Travell (1804-1880). Major General, Kt. 4th L.C. Lieut. of the Yeomen of the Guard. *b.* psh. of St. Clement Danes, London, 10 Oct. 1804. Cadet 1820. Arrived in India May 1821. Cornet 16 Jan. 1821. Lieut. 1 May 1824. Capt. 26 Dec. 1832. Major 28 Sept. 1841. Lt. Col. 6 Aug. 1851. Retired 14 Nov. 1853. Bt. Col. 28 Nov. 1854. Col. 25 Mar. 1856. Maj. Gen. 25 Mar. 1856. *d.* Louvre Hotel, Paris, 10 May 1880.

bapt. St. Clement Danes 13 Dec. 1804. 2nd son of Stephen Howell Phillips, of 12 Norfolk St., Strand, London, solicitor, and of Harroldstone, co. Pembroke, and Mary his wife, dau. of John Tappen, of Forest Hill, Sydenham. *m.* St. Mary's, Bryanston Sq., London, 29 Aug. 1833, Marianne Henrietta Sophia, dau. of Major James Marrie, of Gt. Cumberland St., Hyde Pk., and of Brettenham Pk., Suffolk.[1] Ed. Merchant Taylors' Mar. 1813-Oct. 1818.

Services : Posted Cornet to 7th L.C. Operations against the Bhils 1822-3 ; Cornet 7th L.C. In 1824 made a forced march of upwards of 80 miles with a detachment of 7th L.C. to relief of Jaipur Residency. Adjt. 7th L.C. 29 May 1826 till 28 Jan. 1830. Leave s.c. Nov. 1827 till Jan. 1830 ; fur. s.c. 28 Jan. 1830 till 10 June 1834 ; s.o. to Cape 21 July 1835 till 17 June 1837. Tempy. comdg. 1st Irreg. Cav. 21 Dec. 1841. To raise and comd. Cav. Depot at Cawnpore 11 Feb. 1842. Fur. 1846 till 30 Jan. 1847. Second Sikh War ; Major 7th L.C., with Bdr. Wheeler's force in Jullunder and Bari Doabs (Medal). Posted Lt. Col. to 4th L.C. 18 Nov. 1851. Fur. s.c. 14 May 1851 till 1856, when he retired with effect from 14

Nov. 1853. Transfd. to 3rd L.C. Mar. 1855; to 5th L.C. Oct. 1855. Lieut. of the Yeomen of the Guard 23 July 1857 till Dec. 1861. Kt. 18 Feb. 1858.

Refs.: Robinson. Boase. *The Times*, 14 May 1880, p. 9 *f.* *A.J.* N.S. xii. 139.

[1] *Note:* (? *m.* 1st, Cape Town 23 Nov. 1831, Rosa Maria, eldest dau. of Charles Whitcombe, atty.-at-law.)

PHILLIPS, Francis (1752/53-1786). Ensign, 22nd Sepoys. *b.* Shropshire 1752/53. Cadet 1782. Ensign 22 Apr. 1783. *d.* Calcutta 30 Mar. 1786.[1]

Services: Apptd. Cadet for Bombay June 1780; sailed for India in the *Nassau* in Feb. 1782 as Cadet for Bengal, aged 29; detained 3 mos. at Bombay; arrived in Bengal 7 Mar. 1783. Ensign 22nd Sepoys in May 1785.

[1] *Note:* His christian name is given as John in the bur. register.

PHILLIPS, James Smith (*d.* 1785). Captain, Infantry. Cadet (?) Ensign 10 Dec. 1772. Lieut. 9 Mar. 1777. Capt. 10 Mar. 1781. *d.* in the Sundarbans, Bengal, 24 Mar. 1785.

Services: Lieut. 30th Bn. Sepoys in 1777; apptd. Adjt. do. 22 Mar. 1780. Apptd. from Eur. Inf. to comd. a Bn. of Sepoys 1 Nov. 1781.

PHILLIPS, John Cockerell (1813-1892). Lieut. Colonel. 3rd Bengal Eur. Inf. *b.* London 13 Sept. 1813. Cadet 1830. Arrived in India 21 Mar. 1831. Ensign 21 Mar. 1831. Lieut. 13 Mar. 1837. Capt. 1 Mar. 1851. Bt. Major 28 Nov. 1856. Lt. Col. 18 Feb. 1861. Retired 31 Dec. 1861. *d.* 14 Royal Cresc., Notting Hill, London, 10 Oct. 1892.

bapt. Marylebone 18 Sept. 1814. Son of John Cockerell Phillips and Jane his wife. *m.* Lahore 3 Oct. 1853, Mary Anne Catherine Eliza, dau. of Owen Henry Parry. (She died London 10 Jan. 1900.)

Services: Cadet d.d. 63rd N.I. 13 Apr. 1831; d.d. 72nd N.I. 7 Jan. 1832. Actg. Ensign 26 Mar. 1833. Posted Ensign to 60th N.I. 19 Oct. 1833. Offg. Adjt. 60th N.I. 6 Mar. 1840. First Afghan War 1842; action at entrance of Khyber Pass 24 Jan. 1842 (w.); various engagements leading to reoccupation of Kabul; Lieut. 50th N.I., with Gen. Pollock's force (Medal). Gratuity of 6 mos. pay for wound. Actg. Intr. & Qmr. 60th N.I. 9 Dec. 1843. Second in comd. 18th Irreg. Cav. (became 8th Bengal Cav.) 13 Feb. 1846 till Oct. 1858. Posted to newly-raised 3rd Bengal Eur. Inf. 15 Nov. 1853, and served with that Regt. Dec. 1853 till June 1854.

Comdt. newly-raised 1st Mahratta Horse 15 Oct. 1858 till it was disbanded in 1861.
Refs.: *The Times*, 12 Oct. 1892.

PHILLIPS, John Henry (1807-1839). Bt. Captain, 42nd N.I. *b*. London 13 Mar. 1807. Cadet 1823. Arrived in India 11 Oct. 1824. Ensign 17 June 1824. Lieut. 16 June 1826. Bt. Capt. 17 June 1839. *d*. Almora, U.P., 11 Dec. 1839.

bapt. St. George's, Hanover Sq., 7 Apr. 1807. Son of Henry Phillips, of Bond St., London, merchant, and Frances Mary his wife.

Services: Posted Ensign to 69th N.I. 31 Mar. 1825. d.d. 1st Gren. Bn. 11 Apr. 1825. First Burma War; Arakan 1825; Ensign 1st Gren. Bn. Transfd. to 16th N.I. in 1825; to 42nd N.I. in 1826. Actg. Adjt. of a Coy. of Pioneers 4 Feb. till 19 Oct. 1826. Fur. s.c. 12 Dec. 1828 till 5 Dec. 1831. Leave s.c. to Mussoorie 15 Mar. 1835 till 1 Mar. 1836. Asst. to A.G.G. Delhi 27 July 1835. Leave s.c. 24 Mar. 1836 till 1 Nov. 1837. Offg. Junior Asst. to Comr. of Kumaon 21 May 1839.

Refs.: *G.M.* 1840, i. 554. *The Times*, 14 Mar. 1840, p. 7. Will dated 1 Oct. 1838; proved 8 Apr. 1840.

PHILLIPS, Joseph Scott (1812-1884). Major. Artillery. (652) *b*. London 24 Sept. 1812. Cadet 1830. Arrived in India 29 Dec. 1831. 2nd Lieut. 9 June 1831. Lieut. 25 Mar. 1840. Capt. 10 Mar. 1849. Retired 24 Mar. 1855. Hon. Major 11 May 1855. *d*. Wimbledon, Surrey, 18 Dec. 1884.

Eldest son of Thomas Phillips, professor of painting in the Royal Academy (*D.N.B.*), and Elizabeth Fraser his wife, of Fairfield, Inverness. *m*. Milford, Hants, 30 Mar. 1843, Anne Maria, 2nd dau. of William Reynolds, of Milford House, and widow of Capt. Thomas Baillie-Hamilton, 1st Bombay L.C. (who was younger brother of Ker Baillie-Hamilton, *q.v.*). (She died 19 Feb. 1889, aged 74.) Addiscombe Cadet 1830-1.

Services: Posted to Foot Art. 11 Dec. 1835. In charge of revenue survey in Tippera district, Bengal, 30 Nov. 1836 till Feb. 1841. Fur. s.c. 18 Feb. 1841 till 15 Mar. 1844. Posted to 4th Troop 2nd Bde. H.A. 18 Nov. 1837; to 2nd Coy. 1st Bn. Foot Art. 21 Dec. 1838. Dy. Comy. Ord. at Sukkur 12 Nov. 1845; do. Ludhiana 1846. Comy. Ord. at Cawnpore 9 Feb. 1852 till retirement. No record of active service.

Refs.: Burke's *Peerage*, 1859, p. 471, *s.n.* Haddington, E. *A.J.* N.S. xl. 441. *The Times*, 20 Dec. 1884.

PHILLIPS, Owen (1789-1846). Bt. Lieut. Colonel. 56th N.I. *bapt.* St. Thomas's, Haverfordwest, 30 June 1789. Cadet 1808. Arrived in India 31 Oct. 1809. Ensign 8 July 1810. Lieut. 15 Sept. 1814. Capt. 29 June 1824. Major 4 Mar. 1845. Bt. Lt. Col. 30 Apr. 1844. Retired 4 July 1845. *d. co.* Pembroke 30 July 1846.

6th and youngest son of Dr. George Phillips, physician, and Eliza his wife, dau. of John Lort, of Prickeston. *m. co.* Pembroke 12 Apr. 1823, Charlotte Anne, dau. of Capt. Thomas Bowen, of Storehall, Haverfordwest. (She died Clifton 24 Jan. 1882.) His nieces *m.* Henry Foquett and George Tebbs, *qq.v.*

Services: Posted Ensign to 15th N.I. in 1810. With 3rd Vol. Bn. in 1812; transfd. to newly-raised 1/28th N.I. in 1815; with 4th Vol. Bn. 1815-16. Third Mahratta War; Dhamoni; Lieut. 1/28th N.I. Fur. p.a. 21 Sept. 1820 till 21 Oct. 1823. d.d. 2/10th N.I. 25 Nov. 1823. Intr. & Qmr. 1/28th N.I. 7 Feb. 1824; transfd. to 56th N.I. (late 2/28th) May 1824; Adjt. 56th N.I. 17 June 1824 till 10 Aug. 1825. Tempy. Comdt. 5th Local Horse 14 Jan. 1826. Actg. Executive Ofr. 13th Div., P.W.D., 16 July 1827. Leave u.p.a. 6 mos. to Hills 14 Apr. 1829, and 16 Apr. 1830. Comdt. 1st Depot Bn. at Benares 4 Mar. 1842 till broken up on 1 Mar. 1843. Gwalior campaign; Maharajpur (*Lond. Gaz.* 8 Mar. 1844); Bt. Major 56th N.I. (Bronze star). Fort Adjt. at Ft. Wm., and Supt. of Gentlemen Cadets, 8 Apr. 1844.

Refs.: Burke's *Landed Gentry*, 11th edn., p. 1332, *s.n.* Phillips, of Lawrenny Park, co. Pembroke; p. 1824, *s.n.* Willyams, of Carnaton, Cornwall. *Patrician*, ii. 95. *G.M.* 1823, i. 644. M.I. Holy Trinity Church, Tunbridge Wells.

PHILLIPS, Robert (1749/50-1838). General, Infantry. Senior officer in the Coy.'s service. *b.* 1749/50. Cadet 1771. Admitted 13 Aug. 1771. Ensign 16 Dec. 1772. Lieut. 15 Mar. 1777. Capt. 15 Mar. 1781. Major 27 July 1796. Lt. Col. 1 Nov. 1798. Col. 30 Sept. 1803. Maj. Gen. 25 July 1810. Lt. Gen. 4 June 1814. Gen. 10 Jan. 1837. *d.* Abbey Foregate, Shrewsbury, 4 Nov. 1838, aged 88.

Uncle of Richard Langslow, *q.v. m.* Buildwas, Salop, 17 June 1816, Miss Elizabeth Poole, of Shrewsbury.

Services: Transfd. from Bengal Eur. Regt. to Sepoy Corps Nov. 1781; Capt. 4th Bengal Eur. Bn. in July 1787. Lt. Col. comdg. 2/4th N.I. Col. 18th N.I. 1805; 5th N.I. 1813 till 1824, when he was placed on the Senior Officers List. Fur. 24 Dec. 1802 till death. "Distinguished himself in several actions in India."

THE BENGAL ARMY, 1758-1834

Refs.: Bristol Mirror, 9 Sept. 1816. *G.M.* 1838, ii. 669. *A.J.* N.S. xxvii. 340. *The Times,* 12 Feb. 1839.

PHILLOTT, Johnson (1810-1857). Bt. Major, 10th N.I. *bapt.* Bath 29 June 1810. Cadet 1827. Arrived in India 5 Oct. 1828. Ensign 11 May 1828. Lieut. 1 Jan. 1837. Capt. 1 Jan. 1851. Bt. Major 20 June 1854. *d.* 4 July 1857 : accidentally drowned in the Ganges at Singhee Rampore whilst escaping from Fatehgarh.

Eldest son of Johnson Phillott, of Bath, banker, and Mary Elizabeth his wife, eldest dau. of Robert Fuge, of Elford. *m.* Calcutta cathedral 21 Jan. 1841, Agnes Mary, dau. of Joseph Taylor (1790-1835), *q.v.* (*See also* William Edmund Maule Ramsay Hay.) (She *re-m.* Robert Henry Scott Campbell, B.C.S., and died his widow 4 Jan. 1895, aged 70.)

Services : Ensign d.d. 23rd N.I. 5 Nov. 1828 ; posted to 25th N.I. 4 Mar. 1829 ; transfd. to 10th N.I. 22 Apr. 1829. Rising in Cuttack July 1836 ; Ensign 10th N.I. Fur. s.c. 23 Mar. 1838 till 31 Dec. 1840. Dy. Paymr. to Army of Reserve (for Afghanistan) 21 Oct. 1842 till 22 Mar. 1843. Actg. Adjt. 10th N.I. 15 Oct. 1844 ; permanent do. 10 Mar. 1845 till 11 Mar. 1851. Second Burma War 1852-3 ; capture of Pegu ; Capt. 10th N.I. (Medal).

Refs.: *G.M.* 1857, ii. 566. M.I. All Sts. Memorial Church, Cawnpore.

PHILLOTT, William Joseph (1802-1839). Captain, Invalid Est. 34th N.I. *b.* Winscombe, Somerset, 26 Aug. 1802. Cadet 1818. Admitted 10 Feb. 1820. Ensign 16 Aug. 1819. Lieut. 29 Apr. 1822. Capt. 8 Mar. 1830. Invalided 17 Dec. 1832. *d.* Calcutta 22 May 1839.

Son of William Downes Phillott, of Winterhead Cottage, nr. Bristol, sometime Lieut. H.M. 20th Regt., and H.G. his wife, *née* Phillips. *m.* 1st, a dau. of Peter Mendes and step-dau. of Hon. William Hamilton, *q.v.* (She died Serampore 4 July 1835, aged 20.) *m.* 2nd, Calcutta 24 Apr. 1837, Elizabeth Ann, 2nd dau. of Melchior Portner, of Calcutta, merchant. (She *re-m.* Calcutta 3 Nov. 1858, W. Woollen.) Ed. Blundell's 15 Aug. 1816 till 29 June 1818.

Services : Posted Ensign to 2/17th N.I. ; transfd. to 35th N.I. (late 2/17th) May 1824 ; to 34th N.I. 31 Mar. 1825. Actg. Adjt. 34th N.I. 24 Oct. 1825, 8 Sept. 1826, 15 June 1827. Operations against the Kols in Chota Nagpur Feb. 1832 ; Capt. 34th N.I., under Lt.-Col. Herbert Bowen, *q.v.* Granted leave s.c. 12 mos. to sea 6 May 1839, but did not live to embark.

Refs.: *Blundell's School Register.* *A.J.* N.S. xxiv. 208.

PHILMORE,[1] **Abraham.** Cadet Infantry. Cadet. 1771. Resigned 12 Apr. 1773.

Services: 4th Mate, *Duke of Richmond* Indiaman; dismissed for neglect of duty 8 Jan. 1768. Sailed as a Cadet in the *Ponsborne* 15 Jan. 1771. Granted by the C.D. a pension of 10d. *p.d.* (Court Minutes, 27 Jan. 1774.)

[1] *Note:* His name also appears in contemporary records as Filmore.

PHIPPS, Pownoll (1780-1858). Colonel, K.C. 51st N.I. *b.* Watton Court, nr. Totnes, 9 Jan. 1780. Cadet 1798. Arrived in India 27 Mar. 1800. Ensign 28 Oct. 1799. Lieut. 28 Oct. 1799. Capt. 10 Oct. 1810. Major 23 Sept. 1821. Lt. Col. 1 May 1824. Retired 9 July 1825. Hon. Col. 28 Nov. 1854. *d.* Oaklands, nr. Clonmel, 5 Nov. 1858.

Of Oaklands, co. Tipperary. *bapt.* Stoke-Gabriel 7 Feb. 1780. 3rd son of Constantine Phipps, of St. Kitts, W.I., and Elizabeth his wife, youngest dau. of James Tierney, of Theobald's, Herts. Uncle of John Powell (1804-1881), *q.v.* *m.* 1st, Calcutta 10 Aug. 1802, Henrietta, dau. of Comte de Beaurepaire, an Ofr. in the Navy of Louis XVI. (She died Berhampore 3 Apr. 1812.) *m.* 2nd, Muttra 17 Apr. 1813, Sophia Matilda, only dau. of Gen. Benedict Arnold, and sister of Edward Shippen Arnold, *q.v.*[1] (She died Sunbury 10 June 1828.) *m.* 3rd, Bern 6 Nov. 1834, Anna Charlotte, younger dau. of Major Robert Smith, R.M. (She died 22 Jan. 1898, aged 89.)

Services: 1st N.I. Mar.-Oct. 1800. Expedn. to Egypt 1801-2; Lieut. Vol. Regt. (Peninsula medal). Posted Lieut. to 1/13th N.I. 15 Apr. 1801; to 2/13th N.I. July 1802; Adjt. do. 1804-9. Fort Adjt. & Bk.Mr. at Agra 29 July 1809 till Oct. 1816. Supt. of civil and mily. bldgs. in Lower Provinces 4 Oct. 1816 till 1822. Transfd. to 1/13th N.I. in 1817; as Major to 2/13th N.I.; as Lt. Col. to 51st N.I. May 1824. Fur. 10 Jan. 1823 till retirement. K.C. 1802.

Refs.: Family information. *Life of Col. Pownoll Phipps,* by Rev. P. W. Phipps, privately printed, London, 1894 (portrait). Burke's *Landed Gentry,* 7th edn., p. 44, *s.n.* Arnold, of Little Missenden Abbey, Bucks. *G.M.* 1858, ii. 652. *The Times,* 10 Nov. 1858. Will dated 7 July 1855; codicil dated 10 Jan. 1857; admon. 14 June 1859.

THE BENGAL ARMY, 1758-1834 525

[1] *Note:* She was granted, by sign manual, 19 June 1805, a pension of £100 *p.a.* in recognition of the services of her father.

PHIPPS, Thomas (1753/54-1794). Lieutenant. Infantry. *b.* London 1753/54. Cadet 1778. Ensign 1778. Lieut. 2 Oct. 1778. Resigned 15 Mar. 1791. *d.* Aldeburgh, Suffolk, 21 Nov. 1794.

Son of Thomas Phipps, of Leadenhall St., London. *m.* (? Sarah).
Services: Ensign H.M. 11th Foot 17 July 1771 till Jan. 1777, when he sold out as senior Ensign. Apptd. Cadet for Madras 1777; sailed for India in the *Duke of Portland* 30 Apr. 1777, aged 23. Arrived Calcutta 1777; detained there by illness; transfd. as Cadet to Bengal Est. 27 Feb. 1778. First Mahratta War 1779; Lieut. 2nd Bengal Eur. Regt. Lieut. 2/1st Eur. Regt. in Oct. 1779. Apptd. A.D.C. to Edward Wheler, actg. G.G., 12 July 1781; do. to Warren Hastings 11 Apr. 1783 till 1785.[1] Leave s.c. to C.G.H. 4 Dec. 1783. Apptd. Regulating Ofr. of Calcutta Mil. 17 Jan. 1785; removed by Cornwallis to make room for his nephew and apptd. to comd. escort with William Palmer, *q.v.*, Resdt. with Sindhia; comdd. this latter till resignation.
Refs.: Grier, pp. 353-4. *Hist. MSS. Commission,* vol. viii ("1790—Indian papers."). *B.M. MSS.* "29,173." Will dated 11 Aug. 1792; proved (P.C.C. 404 *Newcastle*) 30 June 1795.

[1] *Note:* Hastings was one of his exors.

PHIPPS, Wilton Frederick (1807-1832). Lieutenant, 35th N.I. *b.* Leighton 15 Feb. 1807. Cadet 1823. Arrived in India 2 Nov. 1824. Ensign 20 June 1824. Lieut. 10 Oct. 1825. *d.* in England 7 May 1832.[1]

bapt. Westbury, Wilts., 24 Dec. 1808. 5th son of Thomas Henry Hele Phipps, of Leighton House, nr. Westbury, J.P. and D.L., high sheriff 1804, and Mary his wife, only dau. of William Leckonby, of Gt. Eccleston and Hothersall Hall, Lancs.
Services: Posted Ensign to 35th N.I. 31 Mar. 1825. Siege and capture of Bhurtpore; Lieut. 35th N.I. Adjt. 35th N.I. 7 May till 27 Oct. 1829. Fur. 25 Nov. 1829 till death.
Refs.: Burke's *Landed Gentry,* 13th edn., p. 1410, *s.n.* Phipps, of Chalcot, Wilts.
[1] *Note:* "Date from *Dodwell & Miles,* but no report received from his relatives." (*I.O. Rec.*)

*PICKERING, John [1] (1752-1781). Fireworker, Artillery. (171) *b.* 1752. Country Cadet 1778. Fireworker 27 Sept. 1778.

Local Capt. 1780. *d.* Fort Marlbro', Sumatra, 1 Jan. 1781, "of a Bloody Flux," aged 28.
Services: Apptd. Condr. of Ord. 4 Apr. 1778; apptd. Cadet 11 Aug. 1778. Arrived at Fort Marlbro' from Bengal in Sept. 1780, and was promoted Local Capt. for service at that Settlement.
[1] *Note:* William in the bur. register.

*PICKERING, Thomas (*d.* 1763). Lieutenant, Infantry. Cadet (?) Ensign (?) Lieut. (?) *d.* 1 July 1763 : kld. in action at the battle of Manjhi.
Services: N.F.P.
Refs.: Firminger, p. 71. *Swinton of Kimmerghame Records,* p. 50.

PICKERSGILL, Joshua (1780-1818). Lieutenant, 24th N.I. *b.* 1780. Cadet 1804. Arrived in India 17 Mar. 1805. Ensign 21 July 1806. Lieut. 1 Feb. 1807. *d.* Saugor, C.P., 8 Sept. 1818, of fever.
Son of Joshua Pickersgill and Harriot his wife. Brother of William Pickersgill, *q.v.*
Services: Ensign H.M. 22nd Regt. 30 June 1804. Posted Ensign to 24th N.I. in 1807. Employed on survey work 1813-14. Nepal War 1814-15; surveying on Gorakhpur frontier.[1] Nepal War 1816; attached to Champaran L.I.; employed on survey work in Q.M.G. Dept., with Centre Column; discovered the track over the hills by which Sir D. Ochterlony's force was able to turn the main Chiriaghati position in Feb. 1816. D.A.Q.M.G. 1 cl. 1 Jan. 1817, with Left Div. of Grand Army. Third Mahratta War; Mandala; A.Q.M.G. Author of "The Three Brothers," 4 vols. 12mo, 1803.
Refs.: Cardew, pp. 123, 125. *N. & Q.* 2S. iv. 55. *The Hearseys,* pp. 206-7. *G.M.* 1804, ii. 1047.
[1] *Note:* On 19 Feb. 1815, he charged a body of 500 Gurkhas with a Troop of Gardner's Horse and dispersed them with the loss, so it is said, of over 100 kld.

PICKERSGILL, William (1787-1827). Captain, 31st N.I. *b.* Marylebone 24 Nov. 1787. Cadet 1803. Arrived in India 17 Mar. 1805. Ensign 12 Apr. 1805. Lieut. 13 Apr. 1805. Capt. 13 June 1817. *d.* Nimach 12 May 1827.
Son of Joshua Pickersgill and Harriot his wife. Brother of Joshua Pickersgill, *q.v. m.* Benares 8 Feb. 1807, Elizabeth, dau. of Francis Wilford, *q.v.* (*See also* William Baker (1775-1825).) (She *re-m.* William Vincent, *q.v.*)

Services: Posted Lieut. to 15th N.I. in 1806. Nepal War 1814-15; Lieut. 2/15th N.I., in 4th Div. Nepal War 1816; Lieut. 2/15th N.I., in 4th Bde. Centre Column. Capt. Lt. 15th N.I. 9 Aug. 1816. Siege and capture of Hathras 1817; Capt. Lt. 2/15th N.I. Leave to Mauritius 1817; to N.S.W. 1822. Transfd. to 30th N.I. (late 1/15th) May 1824; to 31st N.I. 31 Mar. 1825. Siege and capture of Bhurtpore; Capt. 31st N.I.

Refs.: Will dated 24 Feb. 1827; proved 30 May 1828.

PICKETT, William (1758-1796). Lieutenant, Infantry. *b.* 1758. Country Cadet 1779. Ensign 26 Aug. 1779. Lieut. 13 Apr. 1781. *d.* 29 Jan. 1796, aged 37 : kld. in action on board the *Triton* when returning from fur.[1]

Son of Alderman William Pickett, of the firm of Theed & Pickett, of London, goldsmiths, lord mayor of London 1790, and his wife, dau. of —— Pratten.

Services: Apptd. Cadet 19 Aug. 1779. Campaign against the Rajah of Benares 1781; Bijaigarh. Lieut. 14th Bn. Sepoys in July 1787. Third Mysore War; Arikera; operations before Savandrug; capture of Savandrug; Lieut. 14th Bn. Resigned 22 Feb. 1793 in order to go home on fur.

Refs.: Cal. Gaz. 11 Feb. 1796. *M.M.* 1796, ii. 909-10.

[1] *Note:* He sailed from Portsmouth on 9 July 1795 on board the *Triton*, 800 tons. This ship was captured by surprise by a French schooner off Puri, in the Bay of Bengal, 29 Jan. 1796, on her voyage from Madras to Calcutta.

PIERCY, Henry James (1816-1862). Lieut. Colonel. 49th N.I. *b.* Calcutta 28 Feb. 1816. Cadet 1833. Arrived in India 11 Dec. 1834. Ensign 24 Sept. 1834. Lieut. 17 July 1837. Capt. 22 Jan. 1847. Major 11 Oct. 1859. Retired 31 Dec. 1861. Hon. Lt. Col. 31 Dec. 1861. *d.* Cavendish Sq., London, 28 Feb. 1862.

Youngest son of Major Jeffrey Piercy, H.M. 53rd Regt., and Frances Rand his wife. Brother of Jeffrey Rand Piercy, *q.v.*, and of Mary, 2nd wife of George Acklom Smith, *q.v.* Addiscombe Cadet 10 Aug. 1832 till 13 June 1834.

Services: d.d. 10th N.I. 22 Dec. 1834. Posted to 49th N.I. 2 Mar. 1835. Actg. Adjt. 2nd L.I. Bn. 1 Dec. 1841; permanent do. 21 June 1842 till broken up in 1843. Second Sikh War; siege of Multan Aug. 1848 till Jan. 1849; Capt. 49th N.I. (Medal). Offg. Cantt. Joint Mgte. at Mian Mir in 1857. Fur. p.a. 21 Feb. 1860 till retirement.

Refs.: The Times, 7 Mar. 1862.

PIERCY, Jeffrey Rand (1808-1827). Ensign, 5th Extra Regt.
b. in India 12 Aug. 1808. Cadet 1825. Ensign 2 Mar. 1826.
d. Jubbulpore 17 Nov. 1827.

bapt. in India 16 Oct. 1809. Eldest son of Jeffrey Piercy, Capt. H.M. 53rd Regt., and Frances Rand his wife. Brother of Henry James Piercy, *q.v.*

Services: Posted Ensign to 29th N.I. 26 Sept. 1826; transfd. to 5th Extra Regt. 5 Oct. 1826. No record of active service.

Refs.: A.J. xxv. 683. M.I. at Mirzapur and at Jubbulpore.

PIERCY or PERCY, John. Lieutenant. Infantry. Country Cadet 1778. Ensign 12 Feb. 1780. Lieut. 23 Feb. 1781. Struck off 1788.

Services: Apptd. Cadet 6 Nov. 1778. Never arrived in India: shown as on fur. in July 1787.

PIERS, James (*d.* 1766). Lieutenant, Infantry. Lieut. 29 Oct. 1764. *d.* Patna 18 Sept. 1766.

Services: Ensign H.M. 51st Ft. (in Germany) 29 Sept. 1760. Apptd. in England 2 Mar. 1764, Lieut. on the Bengal Est.; transfd. as Lieut. to Bengal Army (G.O. 17 Apr. 1765); sailed for India in the *Lord Anson* 29 May 1764.

Refs.: Will dated Patna, 13 Sept. 1766; proved in 1766.

PIERSE, John James. Fireworker. Artillery. (247) Cadet 1783. Arrived in India 20 Sept. 1783. Fireworker 5 Jan. 1785. Resigned 1792.

Services: Apptd. Cadet 4 Mar. 1783; sailed for India in the *Halsewell* 11 Mar. 1783. Fireworker 3rd Bn. Art. in July 1787.

PIGG, Theodore (*d.* 1770). Ensign, Infantry. Cadet 1769. Ensign 3 Aug. 1769. *d.* Monghyr 24 Oct. 1770.

Services: N.F.P.

PIGOT, Henry Edward (1794-1830). Captain, 45th N.I. *bapt.* All Saints, Derby, 9 July 1794. Cadet 1811. Ensign 26 Feb. 1814. Lieut. 2 Mar. 1818. Capt. 8 Sept. 1825. *d.* Nasirabad 29 Oct. 1830.

3rd and youngest son of John Hollis Pigot, M.B., of Southwell, and Margaret his wife, dau. of Richard Turner Becher, of Southwell, J.P. *m.* Birbhum, Bengal, 17 May 1821, Miss Clementina Elizabeth Peres Geraldes. (She died Mussoorie 14 Mar. 1850.)

Services: Posted Ensign to 2/23rd N.I. in 1814; served with

THE BENGAL ARMY, 1758-1834   529

Rangpur Bn. 1815-22. Lieut. 1/23rd N.I.; Asst. Bk.Mr. 14th (Saugor) Div. 1822-5; transfd. to 45th N.I. (late 1/23rd) May 1824.
Refs.: Hunter's *Familiæ Minorum Gentium,* iii. 1026.

PIGOTT, Charles Cæsar (1809-1841). Lieutenant, 18th N.I. *bapt.* Taghmon, co. Wexford, 14 June 1809. Cadet 1826. Arrived in India 24 May 1827. Ensign 19 Nov. 1826. Lieut. 25 Dec. 1827. *d.* at sea 12 Apr. 1841, on board the *Plantagenet* off I. of Ascension.

4th and youngest son of William Pemberton Pigott, of Slevoy Castle, co. Wexford, Lt. Col. Wexford Mil., J.P., high sheriff 1794, and Ellen his wife, dau. of Henry Thomas Houghton, of Kilmannock, co. Wexford. His mother was sister of the wives of Goddard Richards and Lewis Thomas, *qq.v.   m.* Aligarh 12 Feb. 1834, Mary Madeline Fraser, 3rd dau. of Henry Hannah or Hannay, and sister of Simon Fraser Hannah, *q.v.*
Services: Ensign d.d. 2nd N.I. 2 June 1827; posted to 18th N.I. 19 June 1827. Leave to Hills 15 Jan. 1833 till 1 May 1834. Adjt. Recruit Depot at Meerut 8 Sept. 1838 till 29 Nov. 1839; Adjt. 18th N.I. 29 Nov. 1839. Fur. s.c. 22 Jan. 1841 till death. No record of active service.
Refs.: Burke's *Landed Gentry of Ireland,* p. 564, *s.n.* Pigott, of Slevoy Castle, co. Wexford. Burke's *Landed Gentry,* 4th edn., p. 726, *s.n.* Houghton, of Kilmannock House, co. Wexford. *G.M.* 1841, ii. 222. *The Times,* 22 June 1841, p. 7.

PIGOTT,[1] **John Pelling** (1754-1800). Lieut. Colonel, 6th N.C. *b.* 1754. Cadet 1778. Admitted 10 Dec. 1778. Ensign 1778. Lieut. 20 Oct. 1778. Capt. 1 June 1796. Major 1 Nov. 1798. Lt. Col. 29 May 1800. *d.* Ghazipur 12 Nov. 1800, aged 46.

(*Probably* son of John Pigott, of Windsor Castle, organist, and Isabella his wife, dau. of Col. Thomas Gillery, of Newcastle-on-Tyne.) Ed. Eton; admitted 24 Apr. 1763; left 1767.
Services: Sailed for India in the *Stafford* 27 May 1778, aged 23. Removed from Inf. and apptd. to 1st Regt. Cav. 19 Aug. 1779. First Mahratta War; Lieut. 1st Regt. Cav., with detachment under Thomas Goddard, *q.v.* Campaign against the Rajah of Benares 1781; Bijaigarh. Apptd. to G.G.'s Inf. Bodyguard under comd. of Thomas Polhill, *q.v.,* 23 Sept. 1783; Lieut. 13th Bn. Sepoys in July 1787; posted to 2nd N.C. 14 Dec. 1787; confirmed as Adjt. 1st N.C. 10 Feb. 1794. Second Rohilla War; battle of Bitaurah (w.); Lieut. 2nd N.C. Raised 4th N.C. at Moneah in

1797 ; Major 4th N.C. ; raised 6th N.C. at Ghazipur in May 1800 and comdd. till death.

Refs. : Burke's *Landed Gentry*, 2nd edn., iii. 259, *s.n.* Pigott, of Oxfordshire. *Austen-Leigh. Hickey*, iv. 122. *G.M.* 1801, i. 573. Portrait in Zoffany's "Col. Mordaunt's Cock Match." M.I. at Ghazipur.

[1] *Note* : His surname is usually spelt with only one 't' in official documents throughout his service.

*PIGOU, Robert (1816-1841). 1st Lieutenant, Engineers. *b.* Bengal 5 Oct. 1816. Cadet 1834. Arrived in India 1836. 2nd Lieut. 12 Dec. 1834. 1st Lieut. 25 Jan. 1841. *d.* Nazian valley, Afghanistan, 24 Feb. 1841 : kld. by a premature explosion.[1]

bapt. Dacca 13 Oct. 1816. Son of Henry Minchin Pigou, B.C.S., of Banwell Castle, Somerset, Comr. of Revenue at Jessore, and Elizabeth his 1st wife, *née* Bird. Ed. Rugby ; admitted Aug. 1830. Addiscombe Cadet 1833-4 ; Chatham till 1 Dec. 1835.[2]

Services : First Afghan War 1838-41 ; Ghazni 1839 ; unsuccessful storm of Pashut fort 18 Jan. 1840 ; 2nd Lt. Engrs. ; operations in Nazian valley against the Sangu Khel Feb. 1841 (kld.) ; 1st Lt. Engrs. ; Pol. employ with Shah Shuja's troops (*Cal. Gaz.* 1 Apr. 1841). See History of Bengal Engineers.

Refs. : *Rugby School Register. I.N.* No. 13, p. 288.

[1] *Note* : He cut his fuze too short when blowing open the principal gate of a fort with bags of powder, and was unable to make good his retreat before the explosion took place. At Pashut, three attempts by him to blow up the inner gate of the fort were foiled by heavy rain.

[2] *Note* : He saved a private from drowning at Chatham on 27 Aug. 1835, for which he was awarded the medal of the Royal Humane Soc. See acts of gallantry.

PILGRIM, George Mempers (1804-1825). Ensign, 40th N.I. *b.* Woburn, Beds., 9 Sept. 1804. Cadet 1823. Ensign 17 Jan. 1824. *d.* Ramree, Burma, 26 July 1825, of a bilious fever.

bapt. Woburn 24 Oct. 1804. Youngest son of Edward Trapp Pilgrim, of Alphington, nr. Exeter, and Dorothy his wife.

Services : First Burma War 1824-5 ; Ensign 40th N.I.
Refs. : *Bath Chron.* 12 Jan 1826.

PILLANS, John (*d.* 1769). Lieutenant, Infantry. Cadet (?) Ensign 1765. Lieut. 18 Dec. 1766. *d.* 1769.
Services : N.F.P.

PILLANS, William Soltau (1806-1873). Colonel. Artillery. (541) *b.* Leith 12 Mar. 1806. Cadet 1823. Arrived in India 26 Mar. 1824. 2nd Lieut. 6 June 1823. Lieut. 23 June 1827. Capt. 1 Sept. 1840. Major 25 Feb. 1853. Retired 25 July 1854. Hon. Col. 26 Oct. 1855. *d.* Broome Place, Norfolk, 2 Mar. 1873. Of Broome Hall, nr. Bungay, Suffolk. *bapt.* Leith 19 May 1806. 3rd son of James Pillans, of Myres Castle, Fife, merchant in Leith, and Anne his wife, dau. of John Wilson, of the Cleugh, co. Lanark. *m.* Chislehurst 26 June 1838, Maria Louisa, 2nd dau. of William Soltau, of Clapham. (She died Manuka, N.Z., 27 Oct. 1886, aged 79.) Ed. Edin. High School. Addiscombe Cadet 1821-3.

Services: With 1st Troop 3rd Bde. H.A. 1825-7. Siege and capture of Bhurtpore; 2nd Lieut. 1st Troop 3rd Bde. (India medal). With 2nd Troop 2nd Bde. 1831; 2nd Troop 3rd Bde. 1832. Fur. p.a. 7 Feb. 1835 till 20 Dec. 1838. A.D.C. to Presdt. of Council and Dy. Govr. of Bengal 17 June 1839; do. Lt. Govr. N.W.P. 3 Feb. till 8 Apr. 1840. Posted to 1st Troop 1st Bde. H.A 10 Nov. 1840; to 1st Coy. 1st Bn. 14 Mar. 1843. Dy. Comy. Ord. at Cawnpore 11 Mar. 1840; Comy. Ord. do. 22 Apr. 1840; do. Agra 9 Aug. 1844; do. Delhi 1845; do. Agra 1846; do. Cawnpore Dec. 1851. First Sikh War; Sobraon; Comy. Ord. at Ferozepore (Medal). Fur. s.c. 9 Feb. 1852 till retirement. Posted Major to 7th Bn. Foot Art. 17 May 1853; to 1st Bn. 27 July 1853; to 9th Bn. Aug. 1853.

Refs.: Burke's *Colonial Gentry*, i. 386, *s.n.* Pillans, of Myres. *A.J.* N.S. xxvi. 285. *The Times*, 4 Mar. 1873.

PILLICHODY, Charles (1782-1818). Ensign. Infantry. Subsequently Lieut. 24th Light Dgns. *b.* Yverdon, canton Vaud, Switzerland, 24 Mar. 1782. Cadet 1805. Admitted 20 July 1807. Ensign 10 July 1807. Resigned 26 July 1807. *d.* in India Jan. 1818.

Son of Henri Louis Pillichody.

Services: Ensign H.M. Swiss Regt. de Meuron 3 Apr. 1799; Lieut. do. 1802. Cornet 24th Light Dgns. 10 Apr. 1807; Adjt. do. 1811; Lieut. do. 30 Apr. 1812.

Refs.: *Livre d'Or.* Will dated 20 Nov. 1817; proved 25 July 1818.

PINDER, John Duefelle (1811-1832). Cadet (actg. Ensign), d.d. 38th N.I. *b.* Watford, Herts., 7 Aug. 1811. Cadet 1829. Arrived in India 6 Oct. 1830. Ensign (5 June 1830). *d.* nr. Midnapore 3 June 1832, of fever.

LIST OF THE OFFICERS OF

4th son of Richard Pinder, of York Pl., Brighton, and Elizabeth his wife.

Services: Cadet d.d. 11th N.I. 23 Oct. 1830; d.d. 7th N.I. 26 Apr. 1831; d.d. 38th N.I. 19 Oct. 1831. Was on service in Bhamanghati, B. & O., quelling an insurrection, as actg. Ensign d.d. 38th N.I., when his death occurred.

Refs.: *G.M.* 1833, i. 94 (where date of death is incorrectly given as 25 Nov. 1832). *A.J.* N.S. ix. 186. Will dated 2 June 1832; proved 18 Apr. 1833. M.I. at Midnapore.

PINE, George Hanbury (1765-1831). Major General. Colonel 58th N.I. *b.* Suffolk 20 July 1765. Cadet 1780. Arrived in India 6 Jan. 1781. Ensign 27 Apr. 1781. Lieut. 19 June 1781. Capt. 1 Nov. 1798. Major 27 Jan. 1804. Lt. Col. 12 June 1807. Col. 4 June 1814. Maj. Gen. 19 July 1821. *d.* Barrackpore 3 Nov. 1831.

Brother of Susannah Anne Pine, of Windsor, and of Mary Jane Hanbury Pine. *m.* Anne Antoinette, dau. of Mme Marie Jeanne Crouvezierl. (She died 21 Mar. 1858, aged 68.) His dau. *m.* Henry Perry Cotton, *q.v.*

Services: Arrived as a Cadet at Madras Jan. 1781 and did duty there for 2 mos. Posted Lieut. to 3rd Bengal Eur. Regt. June 1781; transfd. to 2/32nd N.I. Sept. 1781. Fur. 3 yrs. on full pay 13 Dec. 1785 till 1 Sept. 1790. Third Mysore War 1791-2; Seringapatam; Lieut. 2nd Vol. Bn. Second Rohilla War; battle of Bitaurah; Lieut. 32nd Bn. Capt. 11th N.I. Fur. s.c. 14 Jan. 1803; sailed in the *Culland's Grove*, which was captured by a French privateer in the English Channel; taken to France, and detained there a prisoner for several yrs., during the whole of which period he was continued on the strength of the Army (C.D. Mily. Letter to Bengal, 14 Feb. 1812). He returned to India 21 Jan. 1817, after an absence of 14 yrs.[1] Posted Lt. Col. to 25th N.I. 1807; to Bengal Eur. Regt. 1811; to 6th N.I. 1812; to 1/8th N.I. 1813; to Bengal Eur. Regt. 1817. Comdg. at Berhampore 1817. Posted Col. to 30th N.I. 24 Jan. 1819. Apptd. to comd. at Cuttack, with tempy. rank of Bdr., 6 Mar. 1820. Fur. p.a. 20 Mar. 1821 till 1826. Transfd. to 58th N.I. May 1824. Apptd. to Gen. Staff of Army and posted to Cawnpore 11 Oct. 1826; Presdy. Div. 23 Jan. 1827. Presdt. of Mily. Board 12 Feb. 1827. Tour on Gen. Staff expired 13 Oct. 1830; reapptd. to Gen. Staff and comd. Presdy. Div. 30 Nov. 1830.

Refs.: *E.I.M.C.* i. 280-1. *A.J.* N.S. viii. 41. Will dated 3 Dec. 1826; proved 14 Nov. 1831. M.I. in Barrackpore cemetery.

THE BENGAL ARMY, 1758-1834

¹ *Note :* Nearly one half of his service of 50 yrs. was spent out of India.

PIRIE, Patrick (1784-1858). Lieutenant. 6th N.I. *b.* Aberdeen 4 Dec. 1784. Cadet 1804. Arrived in India 5 Aug. 1804. Ensign 29 Aug. 1805. Lieut. 30 Aug. 1805. Struck off 28 Feb. 1810. *d.* 3 Aug. 1858.
bapt. Aberdeen 9 Dec. 1784. 3rd and youngest son of Patrick Pirie, merchant in Castle St., Aberdeen, and Margaret his wife, dau. of Alexander Smith. *m.* Eliza, dau. of Henry George Forsyth, Lieut. R.N., of Hart Hill.
Services : Posted Lieut. to 6th N.I. in 1806. Fur. 8 Sept. 1807 till struck off. No record of active service.
Refs. : Burke's *Landed Gentry*, 13th edn., p. 749, *s.n.* Pirie-Gordon, of Buthlaw, co. Aberdeen. *Thanage of Fermartyn*, p. 475.

*PITMAN, Frederick Cobbe (*c.* 1727-*c.* 1780). Lieutenant. Eur. Grenadiers. Afterwards Capt. on the Bencoolen Est. *b. c.* 1727. Lieut. 26 Apr. 1758. Capt. (Bencoolen) 2 Dec. 1761. Resigned 1762. *d. c.* 1780.
m. Trinity church, Newport, Rhode I., 26 Oct. 1765, Lydia, dau. of William Strengthfield, judge of the vice-admiralty court, by his wife Phebe Dyer. Father of Robert Pitman, *q.v.*, and of the mother of Robert Mathison, *q.v.*
Services : Ensign in Bdr.-Gen. Reade's Regt. (afterwards 9th Ft.) 26 Mar. 1744 ; resigned 5 Jan. 1751. Commissioned as Lieut. in a Coy. of Grens. raised for service in Bengal under Capt. Robert Delaval, 26 Apr. 1758 ; sailed for India in the *Prince George* in 1758, aged 29. Actg. Qmr. to troops under Clive in expedn. to Patna Feb. 1759 ; comdd. Gren. Coy. with force under Col. Forde at battle of Badara Nov. 1759, during absence of Capt. Henry Delaval at Madras. Resigned 29 Dec. 1759. Taken prisoner by Count D'Estaing at Bencoolen, Sumatra, Mar. 1760 ; released on parole 24 June 1760, and returned to England. Apptd. Capt. of a Mily. Coy. on Fort Marlbro' Est. 2 Dec. 1761 ; resigned 1762.
Refs. : Family information. *N. & Q.* 9S. iv. 417.

PITMAN, Robert (1777-1846). Major General, C.B. Colonel 54th N.I. *b.* Pershore 9 Oct. 1777. Cadet 1796. Admitted 15 Apr. 1798. Ensign 25 Sept. 1797. Lieut. 10 Sept. 1798. Capt. 26 Feb. 1805. Major 1 Oct. 1815. Lt. Col. 9 Aug. 1821. Col. 5 June 1829. Maj. Gen. 28 June 1838. *d.* Dumfries 26 Dec. 1846.

bapt. Holy Cross, Pershore, 8 Dec. 1777. 4th son of Frederick Cobbe Pitman, *q.v.*, and Lydia his wife. *m.* Edinburgh 26 Sept. 1827, Mary, 2nd dau. of John Anderson, of Inchyra, co. Perth, and niece of James Anderson (1757-1833), *q.v.* (She died Edinburgh 20 Jan. 1870, aged 72.)

Services: Lieut. 1/6th N.I.; transfd. to 2/6th N.I. 2 Oct. 1800. Expedn. to Egypt 1801; Lieut. Vol. Bn. Operations in Baghelkhand 1803; Chaukandi; Lieut. 2/6th N.I. Adjt. 2/6th N.I. 1804-6. Second Mahratta War; operations in Bundelkhand 1805-6. Comdd. escort of Mountstuart Elphinstone, Envoy to Kabul, 1809; wounded in a skirmish on his way back to India. Fur. p.a. 13 Feb. 1812 till 1 Nov. 1816. Served with Nizam's army 1817-25; apptd. to comd. whole of Regular Inf. in Berar 11 Apr. 1817. Third Mahratta War; Nagpur. Siege and capture of Nowah 8-31 Jan. 1819; Major comdg. the force. To comd. whole of Nizam's Regular Inf. 1 Oct. 1819; afterwards comdd. Aurangabad Div. Posted Lt. Col. to 2/20th N.I. 1821; to 2nd N.I. May 1824; as Lt. Col. Comdt. to 45th N.I. Jan. 1825. Leave s.c. 1 yr. to Cape 4 Jan. 1823; extended 9 mos. 26 Jan. 1824; fur. s.c. from Bombay 22 Jan. 1825 till death. Col. 54th N.I. 15 Mar. 1830. C.B. 27 Sept. 1831.

Refs.: Family information. Elphinstone's *Account of the Kingdom of Cabul*, introduction, 2 and 106. *Burton, passim.* *G.M.* 1827, ii. 365; 1847, i. 214. M.I. Warriston cemetery.

PITT, Henry (1789-1810). Lieutenant, 12th N.I. *b.* "on or about" 27 Jan. 1789. Cadet 1803. Arrived in India 2 Dec. 1804. Ensign 22 Oct. 1804. Lieut. 22 Oct. 1804. *d.* nr. Dinajpur, Bengal, 12 Aug. 1810: drowned when crossing a nullah.

bapt. Kensington, London, 1 Mar. 1791. Son of Henry Pitt and Mary his wife.

Services: Posted Lieut. to 12th N.I. in 1805. Operations in Oudh 1808; Lieut. 12th N.I.

PITTS, John Staniforth (1800-1833). Captain, Bengal Eur. Regt. *bapt.* Bridlington, Yorks., 1 May 1800. Cadet 1818. Admitted 2 Oct. 1819. Ensign 23 May 1819. Lieut. 29 Oct. 1821. Capt. 15 Dec. 1830. *d.* Cherrapunji, Assam, 2 July 1833, aged 33.

5th son of John Pitts, of Newcastle-on-Tyne, in the Customs, Lt. Col. Bridlington Vols., and Frances his wife, 8th dau. of James Heblethwayte. *m.* Chanda, nr. Nagpur, 14 Sept. 1823, Cornelia

THE BENGAL ARMY, 1758-1834 535

Harvey, 3rd dau. of William Dring, of Calcutta, merchant. (*See also* Gavin Ralston Crawfurd.) (She died 7 July 1886, aged 79.) Woolwich Cadet.
Services : Ensign d.d. Bengal Eur. Regt. ; posted Ensign to 1/7th N.I. ; transfd. to Bengal Eur. Regt. 12 July 1822 ; to newly-formed 2nd Bengal Eur. Regt. May 1824 ; exchanged to 1st Bengal Eur. Regt. 18 June 1824 ; Adjt. do. 22 June 1824 till Nov. 1829. Siege and capture of Bhurtpore ; Lieut. 1st Bengal Eur. Regt. Adjt. Bengal Eur. Regt. (on its formation into one Regt.) 13 Nov. 1829 till 15 July 1831.
Refs. : Misc. Gen. et Her. N.S. i. 419. *A.J.* N.S. xiii. 39. *G.M.* 1833, ii. 556. Will dated 1 Oct. 1823 ; proved 20 Sept. 1833. M.I. in Cherrapunji cemetery.

PLACE, James (1790-1812). Cadet, Infantry. *bapt.* St. Nicholas, Nottingham, 2 Aug. 1790. Cadet 1810. *d.* Berhampore 21 Sept. 1812, aged 22.
Eldest son of John Place, of Nottingham, saddler, and Susannah Gordon his wife. Cousin of Mary Ann Fincham.
Services : Cadet d.d. 2/9th N.I. 1811 till death.
Refs. : M.M. 1813, ii. 80.

PLAISTOW(E) or PLASTOW, Thomas (1739/40-?). Lieutenant. Infantry. *b.* co.[Bucks. 1739/40. Cadet 1764. Ensign 5 Feb. 1765. Lieut. 12 Dec. 1766.
Services : Sailed for India in the *Earl of Lincoln* 17 Mar. 1764, aged 24. Out of the Service before 1 Feb. 1767. Was still in Calcutta on 6 Apr. 1772, when he wrote requesting a passage to England in the *Clive* for himself and one servant.

PLATT, John (*d.* 1783). Cadet. Infantry. Subsequently Ensign Madras Est. Cadet 1782. *d.* Madras 25 Apr. 1783.[1]
Services : Apptd. Cadet 10 Oct. 1781 ; sailed for India in the *Kent* 6 Feb. 1782. Exchanged with Henry Robert Patton, *q.v.*, and was transfd. to Madras Est. Jan. 1783. Ensign 4 Apr. 1783.
[1] *Note : Bur.* St. Mary's cemetery, Madras, as Ensign John Plaitt.

PLATT, John (1802-1857). Bt. Colonel, 23rd N.I. *b.* King's Langley, Herts., 24 Apr. 1802. Cadet 1819. Admitted 1 July 1820. Ensign 31 Dec. 1819. Lieut. 17 May 1823. Capt. 28 July 1833. Major 8 Aug. 1847. Lt. Col. 7 June 1853. Bt. Col. 18 May 1856. *d.* Mhow 1 July 1857 : kld. by mutineers of his own Regt.

Son of Rev. Alexander Platt and Charlotte Henrietta his wife. Brother of William Platt, *q.v.* *m.* Bengal 8 Sept. 1825, Miss Charlotte Atkinson. (She died 4 Aug. 1853.)

Services: Posted Ensign to 2/5th N.I. in 1820; transfd. to 4th N.I. July 1823, but remained with 2/5th for some months longer.[1] Transfd. to 23rd N.I. (late 2/4th) May 1824. Actg. Adjt. 1st L.I. Bn. 2 Oct. 1824. Leave s.c. Nov. 1824 till 12 Feb. 1825, when he rejoined 23rd N.I. Siege and capture of Bhurtpore; Lieut. 23rd N.I. (India medal). Intr. & Qmr. 23rd N.I. 3 Feb. 1829 till 6 June 1834. Fur. s.c. 6 Feb. 1836 till 28 Sept. 1839. Attached to 2nd Vol. Bn. for China 1 Feb. 1840 till 1 Mar. 1843, when it was broken up. First China War 1842; Capt. Vol. Bn. (Medal). Comdt. 2nd Regt. Oudh Local Inf. 26 Dec. 1843 till 3 Dec. 1847. Operations against Afridis of Kohat Pass Feb. 1850; Major 23rd N.I. Posted Lt. Col. to 23rd N.I. 4 Aug. 1853, and was comdg. when that Regt. mutinied at Mhow on evening of 1 July 1857.

Refs.: *I.M.* 16 Oct. 1857, p. 696. M.I. Mhow old cemetery.

[1] *Note:* He was wounded by dacoits on the night of 6/7 May 1823 whilst a guest of George Ravenscroft, an indigo planter (late B.C.S.), at his house nr. Bhinga. His host was killed.

PLATT, William (1806-1830). Lieutenant, 18th N.I. *b.* King's Langley, Herts., 25 May 1806. Cadet 1824. Arrived in India 1 June 1825. Ensign 11 Dec. 1824. Lieut. 13 June 1826. *d.* Mirzapur, U.P., 1 July 1830: drowned.

bapt. King's Langley 19 July 1806. Son of Rev. Alexander Platt, of Bushey, Herts., and Charlotte Henrietta his wife. Brother of John Platt, *q.v.*

Services: Ensign d.d. 2nd Bengal Eur. Regt. 11 June 1825; posted Ensign to 18th N.I. in 1825. Siege and capture of Bhurtpore; Ensign 18th N.I.

Refs.: M.I. Mirzapur cemetery.

PLAYDELL, James William (1770/71-1821). Major, Invalid Est. 14th N.I. Comdt. Saharanpur Provl. Bn. *b.* 1770/71. Country Cadet 1793. Ensign 27 Sept. 1794. Lieut. 1 June 1796. Capt. 10 May 1804. Major 12 Oct. 1812. Invalided 1 Mar. 1816. *d.* Saharanpur 24 Jan. 1821, aged 50.

Son of Charles Stafford Playdell, B.C.S., Supt. of Police in Calcutta, and Elizabeth his wife, dau. of John Zephaniah Holwell (*D.N.B.*). Cousin of James Holwell. *m.* Berhampore 11 Oct. 1799, Miss Mary Anne Dubois. (She died 1827.)

Services : Arrived in India in 1791, and was Dy. Purveyor to Dinapore hospital when apptd. Cadet 7 Mar. 1794. Lieut. 3rd Bengal Eur. Regt. in 1796. Second Mahratta War 1803-4 ; battle of Delhi ; Agra ; Gwalior ; Monson's retreat ; Lieut. 1/14th N.I. (? Nepal War 1814-15 ; Jitgarh ; Major 1/14th N.I., in 3rd Div.) Comdt. Saharanpur Provl. Bn. 15 Mar. 1816 till death.
Refs. : *A.J.* xii. 380. Will dated 28 Feb. 1820 ; proved 14 Feb. 1821.

PLAYFAIR, Sir Hugh Lyon (1786-1861). Lieut. Colonel, Kt. Artillery. (354) Provost of St. Andrews. *b.* Meigle, co. Perth, 18 Nov. 1786. Cadet 1804. Arrived in India 12 July 1805. Lieut. 14 May 1805. Capt. Lt. 17 Feb. 1815. Capt. 1 Sept. 1818. Major 28 Sept. 1827. Retired 10 Feb. 1834. Hon. Lt. Col. 28 Nov. 1854. *d.* St. Andrews, Fife, 12 Jan. 1861.

Of St. Leonards, St. Andrews. 3rd and youngest son of Rev. James Playfair, D.D., principal of St. Andrews, and formerly minister of Meigle, and Margaret his wife, sister of Hugh Lyon, *q.v.* Brother of William Davidson Playfair, *q.v.* ; uncle of Sir Lyon Playfair, 1st Baron Playfair, of Jessie Macdonald Playfair, 3rd wife of John Samuel Henry Weston, *q.v.*, and of Anne, wife of John Hickey, *q.v. m.* Scotscraig House, co. Fife, 7 Mar. 1820, Jane, youngest dau. of William Dalgleish, of Scotscraig. (She died 1872.) Ed. Dundee Grammar School and St. Andrews. Woolwich Cadet 1804 till 8 Jan. 1805.
Services : See *D.N.B.* To comd. Art. at Bareilly 22 Mar. 1807. 2nd Troop H.A. Nov. 1807 till 1817. Adjt. & Qmr. H.A. 5 Nov. 1809 till June 1816. Nepal War 1814-15 ; Kalanga (w.) ; Lieut. 3rd Troop (d.d. from 2nd Troop), with 2nd Div. (India medal). Fur. s.c. 31 Dec. 1816 till 27 Nov. 1820. Supt. of Calcutta—Benares road 1820 till Apr. 1828. Comdd. 4th Bn. Foot Art. till 4 July 1831. Fur. p.a. via China 25 July 1831 till retirement. Provost of St. Andrews 1842 till death. Revived and established the Golf Club.
Refs. : Burke's *Peerage*, 1923, p. 1778, *s.n.* Baron Playfair, of St. Andrews, Fife. *The Playfair Book*, by Rev. A. G. Playfair, 4th edn., 1932. *D.N.B. Boase. D.I.B. S.M.* 1820, i. 292. *G.M.* 1861, i. 333. *I.L.N.* x. (1847), 176 (portrait) ; xxxviii (1861), 103 *The Times*, 28 Jan. 1861. Portrait, by Sir J. Watson Gordon, in St. Andrews town hall.

PLAYFAIR, John (1786-1810). Ensign, 24th N.I. *b.* Edinburgh 10 Feb. 1786. Cadet 1805. Arrived in India 22 Jan. 1807.

Ensign 25 Dec. 1806. d. Hardwar, U.P., 28 Mar. 1810 : drowned whilst bathing in the Ganges.

bapt. Edinburgh 22 Mar. 1786. Eldest son of Robert Playfair, of Edinburgh, writer, and Margaret Macniven his wife.

Services : Posted Ensign to 24th N.I. in 1807. Settlement of Hariana 1809; capture of Bhawani (w.); Ensign 2/24th N.I.

Refs.: The Playfair Book, p. 7.

PLAYFAIR, William Davidson (1783-1852). Lieut. Colonel. 39th N.I. b. Meigle, co. Perth, 23 Sept. 1783. Cadet 1803. Arrived in India 2 Dec. 1804. Ensign 3 Nov. 1804. Lieut. 3 Nov. 1804. Capt. 19 Nov. 1817. Major 8 Apr. 1823. Lt. Col. 30 July 1824. Retired 27 Apr. 1831. d. 31 Jan. 1852.

2nd son of Rev. James Playfair, D.D., Principal of St. Andrews Univ., and Margaret his wife. Brother of Sir Hugh Lyon Playfair, q.v. m. Calcutta 3 Nov. 1812, Anne, eldest dau. of John Ross, of Castle Hill, Edinburgh, and sister of George Ross, q.v.

Services : Posted Lieut. to 8th N.I. in 1805. Expedn. to Mauritius 1810-11 ; Lieut. 8th N.I., with Vol. Bn. Dy. Paymr. Gen. in Mauritius 1811 ; Supt. of mily. roads 10 July 1813 till 1818. Lieut. 2/8th N.I.; transfd. as Capt. to 1/8th N.I. Third Mahratta War; Capt. 1/8th N.I., A.Q.M.G. Fur. 17 Feb. 1821 till 1824. Posted Lt. Col. to 55th N.I. in 1824 ; transfd. to 12th N.I. in 1825 ; to 62nd N.I. in 1826 ; to 39th N.I. 24 Jan. 1831.

Refs.: Burke's Peerage, 1923, p. 1778, s.n. Playfair, B. Family of Playfair, p. 39 (portrait). Scott's Fasti, vii. 415.

PLAYFORD, John (d. 1787). Ensign, Infantry. Cadet 1783. Arrived in India Aug. 1784. Ensign 25 Jan. 1785. d. Berhampore 27 Apr. 1787.

Services : Apptd. Cadet 26 Feb. 1783 ; sailed for India in the Valentine 6 Jan. 1784. N.F.P.

PLOWDEN, Arthur Wellington Chicheley (1814-1861). Bt. Lieut. Colonel, 1st Eur. L.C. b. Calcutta 1 Nov. 1814. Cadet 1832. Arrived in India 1 Dec. 1833.   Cornet 19 June 1833. Lieut. 23 Dec. 1841. Capt. 21 Oct. 1852. Bt. Major 22 Oct. 1852. Bt. Lt. Col. 13 Apr. 1860. d. Dehra Dun, U.P., 3 Jan. 1861.

4th son of Richard Chicheley Plowden, B.C.S., Salt Agent at Hijili, Bengal, and Sophia Span his wife, dau. of Richard Fleming, of Calcutta. Brother of Edmund Walter Chicheley Plowden, nephew of George Augustus Chicheley Plowden, and cousin-german of James Vansittart Law, *qq.v. m.* Karnal 7 May 1840, Caroline Charlotte, 5th dau. of Charles Mackenzie, B.C.S., and niece of the wife of Lyttleton Lyster, *q.v.* (She died Rajpore, U.P., 3 Nov. 1848.)

Services: Cornet d.d. 5th L.C. 17 Dec. 1833; posted to 3rd L.C. 9 June 1836. First Afghan War 1838-9; capture of Ghazni; Cornet 3rd L.C. (Medal). First Sikh War; Badhowal; Aliwal; Sobraon (horse shot); Lieut. 3rd L.C. (Medal with clasp). Intr. & Qmr. 3rd L.C. 13 May 1846 till Nov. 1852, but continued to act as such for many months subsequently. Was tempy. comdg. 3rd L.C. during the absence of Lt.-Col. G. M. Carmichael-Smyth, *q.v.*, and was placed in arrest for not reading to his Regt. G.O.G.G. No. 470 of 27 Mar. 1857, relating to the disbanding of 19th N.I. Posted to Left Wing of newly-raised 1st Eur. L.C. in 1858.

Refs.: Burke's *Landed Gentry*, 12th edn., p. 1515, *s.n.* Plowden, of Plowden, Salop. *Records of the Chicheley Plowdens*, by W. F. C. Chicheley Plowden (London, 1914), ptely. printed.

*PLOWDEN, Edmund Walter Chicheley (1817-1866). Captain. 5th L.C. Afterwards Local Major in Turkey. *b.* Calcutta 4 Oct. 1817. Cadet 1834. Arrived in India 8 Nov. 1834. Cornet (8 Nov. 1834) 9 June 1836. Lieut. 1 July 1841. Dismissed by G.C.M. 18 Mar. 1848; reinstated as Capt. 16 Nov. 1853 (G.O. 7 Mar. 1854). Retired 16 Nov. 1853. *d.* 1866.

bapt. Calcutta 10 Nov. 1817. 5th son of Richard Chicheley Plowden, B.C.S., and Sophia Span his wife. Brother of Henry Gordon Chicheley Plowden, *q.v.*, and 2nd cousin of James Chicheley Plowden, *q.v. m.* Cawnpore 24 Apr. 1837, Harriet, only dau. of Capt. Henry Bond, 11th Light Dgns.

Services: Supy. Cornet d.d. 10th L.C. 3 Dec. 1834; d.d. 5th L.C. 16 June 1835. Posted Cornet to 5th L.C. 9 June 1836. Leave s.c. to Mussoorie 20 Apr. till 20 Dec. 1839. First Afghan War 1840-2; Jalalabad, under Sale (Medal); Gandamak (*Lond. Gaz.* 11 Feb. and 9 Aug. 1842); Kabul 1842; Lieut. 5th L.C. (Medal). Second in comd. 5th Irreg. Cav. 2 Feb. 1843 till 19 Apr. 1844. First Sikh War; Mudki; Ferozshahr; Aliwal; Sobraon; Lieut. 5th L.C. (Medal with 3 clasps). After dismissal from the Service he was apptd., in 1848, an Asst. in the Accountant Gen.'s office in Calcutta. Crimean War; Local Major in Turkey 27 Mar. 1855. Order of the Medjidie, 4 cl. (*Lond. Gaz.* 2 Mar. 1858).

Refs.: Burke's *Landed Gentry*, 12th edn., p. 1515, *s.n.* Plowden, of Plowden, Salop. *I.M.* 2 May 1848, pp. 263-4; 26 Sept. 1848, p. 551.

PLOWDEN, George Augustus Chicheley (1785-1804). Cadet. Infantry. Afterwards Writer, B.C.S. *b.* 17 Dec. 1785. Cadet 1800. Resigned 1802. *d.* Calcutta 16 Nov. 1804.

bapt. Calcutta 29 July 1786. 4th son of Richard Chicheley Plowden, of Devonshire Pl., London, Dir. E.I. Co., formerly B.C.S., and Elizabeth Sophia his wife, dau. of George Augustus Prosser, of Portsea, Hants. Nephew of Henry Chicheley Plowden, *q.v.*, and uncle of Henry Gordon Chicheley Plowden, *q.v.*

Services: Never joined the Mily. Service. Apptd. a Writer, B.C.S., 14 July 1802. Admitted to Coll. of Ft. Wm. Dec. 1803. Arrived in India 2 Apr. 1804.

Refs.: Burke's *Landed Gentry*, 12th edn., p. 1516, *s.n.* Plowden, of Plowden, Salop. M.I. in S. Park St. cemetery, Calcutta.

PLOWDEN, Henry Chicheley (1754-1821). Ensign. Infantry. Subsequently Senior Mercht., B.C.S. *b.* 14 Mar. 1754. Cadet 1771. Ensign 26 Jan 1773. Resigned 1773. *d.* Lymington, Hants, 12 Jan. 1821.

Of Newton Park, Lymington. 5th son of Rev. James Plowden, of Ewhurst House, and Susanna his wife, dau. of Rev. Thomas Durnford, rector of Ewhurst and Rochbourne, Hants. Uncle of George Augustus Chicheley Plowden, *q.v.*, and grand-uncle of James Chicheley Hyde, *q.v.*, Arthur Wellington Chicheley Plowden, *q.v.*, and James Chicheley Plowden, *q.v. m.* Calcutta 14 July 1781, Eugenia, dau. of "Major William Brooke, H.E.I.C.S., of Bath" (*probably* Robert Brooke, *q.v.*), and sister of William Augustus Brooke, B.C.S. (She died Newton Grove, nr. Lymington, 1 June 1845, aged 88.)

Services: Transfd. as Writer to B.C.S. in 1773. His last appt. before finally returning to England in 1819 was that of Salt Agent for the Chittagong Div. Promoted Lieut. in Calcutta Native Mil. 3 Jan. 1802.

Refs.: Burke's *Landed Gentry*, 12th edn., p. 1515, *s.n.* Plowden, of Plowden, Salop. *Records of the Chicheley Plowdens.* Burke's *Visitation of Seats & Arms*, 1S. i. 9. *G.M.* 1821, i. 187.

PLOWDEN, Henry Gordon Chicheley (1811-1855). Captain, 9th L.C. *b.* Calcutta 17 Aug. 1811. Cadet 1831. Arrived in India 23 June 1832. Cornet 23 June 1832. Lieut. 10 Dec. 1841. Capt. 28 Nov. 1854. *d.* Calcutta 13 Jan. 1855, suddenly.

bapt. Calcutta 13 Nov. 1811. 3rd son of Richard Chicheley Plowden, B.C.S., and Sophia Span his wife. Brother of Arthur Wellington Chicheley Plowden, *q.v. m.* Simla 27 Mar. 1841,

Caroline, dau. of Rev. William Stafford. (She died Bayswater, London, 5 Mar. 1852.)

Services : Cadet d.d. 6th L.C. 13 Nov. 1832 ; d.d. 5th L.C. 15 Dec. 1832.; Supy. Cornet d.d. 10th L.C. Oct. 1834 ; do. 5th L.C. 2 Dec. 1835. Posted to 9th L.C. 9 June 1836. Served with 5th Inf., Nizam's army, 7 Jan. 1836 till 1839, and 1840-2. Adjt. 9th L.C. 18 Feb. 1843 till Dec. 1849. Campaign in Sind 1843 ; Miani (w.) (*Lond. Gaz.* 11 Apr. 1843) ; Hyderabad ; Lieut. 9th L.C. (Medal). Leave s.c. to Cape and N.S.W. 28 Mar. 1845. Second in comd. 11th Irreg. Cav. 18 Dec. 1849. Offg. Bde. Major at Meerut 27 Sept. 1850 ; Bde. Major on the Est. at Barrackpore 7 Dec. 1850. Fur. s.c. 3 Mar. 1851 till Dec. 1854.

Refs. : Burke's *Landed Gentry*, 12th edn., p. 1515, *s.n.* Plowden, of Plowden, Salop. *I.M.* 3 Mar. 1855, p. 95.

PLOWDEN, James Chicheley (1804-1871). Colonel. 17th N.I. *b.* London 9 Oct. 1804. Cadet 1820. Arrived in India Nov. 1821. Ensign 4 July 1821. Lieut. 11 Feb. 1824. Capt. 8 Oct. 1839. Major 10 Dec. 1854. Bt. Lt. Col. 28 Nov. 1854. Retired 9 Sept. 1856. Hon. Col. 9 Sept. 1856. *d.* at his residence, Chale, I.W., 17 Sept. 1871.

bapt. Lambeth 7 July 1805. Only son of James Chicheley Plowden, sometime sheriff of Calcutta, and Elizabeth his wife, dau. of William Lee, of Kennington. Grand-nephew of Henry Chicheley Plowden, *q.v.*, and 2nd cousin of Arthur Wellington Chicheley Plowden, *q.v. m.* 12 Nov. 1833, Mary Elizabeth Cadoux, dau. of James Hudson, of Cumberland, and of St. Paul's House, Camberwell. Ed. Christ's Hospital.

Services : Posted Ensign to 11th N.I. Fur. p.a. 28 July 1822 till 23 Oct. 1823. Transfd. to 17th N.I. (late 2/11th) May 1824. Fur. p.a. 24 Mar. 1833 till 13 Sept. 1834. Actg. Adjt. 17th N.I. 23 Mar. 1836. Attached to L.I. Bn. with Army of Reserve (for Afghanistan) Oct. 1842 till Jan. 1843. Tempy. S.A.C.G. with Army of Reserve 21 Oct. 1842. In charge of Balasore Div., P.W.D., 17 June 1844 ; do. Midnapore 24 Apr. 1848 till Apr. 1850. Fur. s.c. Jan. 1850 till 31 May 1852. No record of active service. Assoc. Inst. C.E., 1851.

Refs. : Burke's *Landed Gentry*, 12th edn., p. 1515, *s.n.* Plowden, of Plowden, Salop. *The Times*, 4 Oct. 1871.

PLUMBE, Thomas (1806-1894). Colonel. 26th N.I. *b.* 14 July 1806. Cadet 1824. Arrived in India 15 May 1825. Ensign 14 Nov. 1824. Lieut. 15 June 1826. Capt. 8 Oct. 1839. Major

18 Apr. 1851. Lt. Col. 11 Nov. 1856. Retired 5 June 1858. Hon. Col. 5 June 1858. *d.* 10 Jan. 1894.

bapt. Wantage, Berks., 8 Aug. 1806. Son of Samuel Plumbe, of Wantage, and Mary Aldworth his wife. *m.* Trinity Church, Marylebone, 1 June 1841, Ellen, youngest dau. of D. Moss, of Portland St., London.

Services : Ensign d.d. 2nd Bengal Eur. Regt. 3 June 1825. Siege and capture of Bhurtpore ; Ensign d.d. 37th N.I. (India medal). Posted to 27th N.I. in 1826 ; Intr. & Qmr. do. 20 Nov. 1830 till 13 Feb. 1840. Fur. p.a. 25 Mar. 1840 till 28 Oct. 1842. Comdg. at Aligarh 11 Mar. 1843. First Sikh War ; Capt. 27th N.I. (Medal). Posted Lt. Col. to 27th N.I. 5 Feb. 1857, and was comdg. when that Reg. was disarmed at Peshawar 22 May 1857. Transfd. to 26th N.I. Sept. 1857.

PLUMER, James (*d.* 1818). Bt. Colonel. 2nd N.I. Country Cadet 1780. Ensign 29 Jan. 1781. Lieut. 9 Oct. 1781. Capt. 3 Aug. 1799. Major 25 Aug. 1804. Lt. Col. 30 Sept. 1808. Bt. Col. 4 June 1814. Retired 24 Apr. 1816. *d.* at his house, Walcot Terr., Bath, 26 June 1818.

(*Probably* brother of John Plumer, *q.v.*) *m.* 1st, Gaya, B. & O., 5 Mar. 1794, Miss Sophia Dwyer. (She died Chunar 21 Oct. 1803.) *m.* 2nd, London, June 1806, a dau. of Robert Trueman, of Bread St., London (? and sister of William Louis Trueman, *q.v.*). (She died Balasore 23 Nov. 1809, aged 23.)

Services : Apptd. a Gent. Vol. in the Coy. of Art. 3 Apr. 1780. Lieut. 13th Bn. Sepoys in July 1787. Third Mysore War ; Arikera ; operations before Savandrug ; Seringapatam ; Lieut. 13th Bn. Second Rohilla War ; battle of Bitaurah ; Lieut. 13th Bn. Bt. Capt. 1/8th N.I. in Aug. 1798 ; Capt. Lt. 2nd N.I. in Jan. 1799 ; Capt. 1/2nd N.I. in 1802. Operations in Jumna Doab 1803 ; Sasni ; Capt. 1/2nd N.I. Fur. 18 Dec. 1804 till 25 Nov. 1807. Major 2/2nd N.I. ; posted Lt. Col. to 1/2nd N.I. Fur. 13 Feb. 1813 till retirement.

Refs. : *G.M.* 1810, ii. 89 ; 1818, i. 643. *M.M.* 1806, p. 570. *Bath Chron.* 2 July 1818. Will dated 12 Mar. 1816 ; codicil dated Freshford Cottage, 18 May 1818 ; proved 20 Apr. 1820.

PLUMER, John (*d.* 1794). Lieutenant, 13th Bn. Sepoys. Country Cadet 1780. Ensign 6 Feb. 1781. Lieut. 8 Oct. 1781. *d.* 26 Oct. 1794 : kld. in action at the battle of Bitaurah. (*Probably* brother of James Plumer, *q.v.*)

Services : Apptd. a Gent. Vol. in the Coy. of Art. 3 Apr. 1780.

Lieut. 13th Bn. Sepoys in July 1787. Third Mysore War ; Arikera ; operations before Savandrug ; Seringapatam ; Lieut. 13th Bn. Second Rohilla War ; battle of Bitaurah (kld.) ; Lieut. 13th Bn.
Refs. : M.I. in St. John's churchyard, Calcutta.

PLUMPTRE, Kaye Francis (1784-1810). Lieutenant, 9th N.I.
b. 9 July 1784. Cadet 1800. Arrived in India 24 Oct. 1801. Ensign 8 Dec. 1801. Lieut. 30 Sept. 1803. *d. unm.* Calcutta 17 May 1810.[1]
bapt. Teversall, Notts., 16 Aug. 1784. Elder son of Rev. Charles Plumptre, rector of Teversall, and afterwards of Long Newton, co. Durham, and Mary his wife, dau. of Joseph Mellar, of Mansfield.
Services : Second Mahratta War ; Lieut. 9th N.I.
Refs. : Burke's *Landed Gentry,* 13th edn., p. 1422, *s.n.* Plumptre, of Fredville, Kent.
[1] *Note :* " Died in Calcutta jail." *(Philippart MS.)*

PLUNKETT, William Walter (1781-1804). Lieutenant, 4th N.I.
b. St. Mary's, Dublin, 14 Sept. 1781. Cadet 1800. Arrived in India 23 Aug. 1801. Ensign 7 Jan. 1802. Lieut. 30 Sept. 1803. *d.* Delhi 1 Nov. 1804.
Son of Thomas Plunkett, of Portmarnock, co. Dublin, and Christina his wife.
Services : Posted Ensign to 4th N.I. Second Mahratta War ; Aligarh ; (? defence of Delhi) ; Lieut. 4th N.I.
Refs. : Burke's *Landed Gentry of Ireland,* p. 567, *s.n.* Plunkett, of Portmarnock, co. Dublin. *Pester,* p. 342.

POCKLINGTON, William Thomas (1811-1843). Bt. Captain, 38th N.I. *b.* Swansea 6 Jan. 1811. Cadet 1827. Arrived in India 1 Aug. 1828. Ensign 3 Mar. 1828. Lieut. 1 June 1832. Bt. Capt. 3 Mar. 1843. *d.* Meerut 4 Sept. 1843.
Son of Henry Sharpe Pocklington and Anne Harvey his wife. *m.* St. James's, Delhi, 12 Aug. 1843, Mary Appeline, only dau. of Abraham Fuller, *q.v.* (She *re-m.* 7 Oct. 1844, Robert Bridge, 72nd N.I.)
Services : Ensign d.d. 24th N.I. 8 Sept. 1828 ; posted to 38th N.I. 4 Nov. 1828. Fur. s.c. 7 Feb. 1833 till 28 May 1836. Actg. Adjt. 38th N.I. 2 Jan. 1841. First Afghan War 1840-2 ; operations against Ghilzais 1841 ; action at Ilmi, nr. Kalat-i-Ghilzai, under Lt.-Col. G. P. Wymer, *q.v.*, 29 May 1841 ; Kandahar ; Ghazni ; Kabul 1842 ; Lieut. 38th N.I., with Gen. Nott's force (Medal).
Refs. : Burke's *Landed Gentry,* 13th edn., p. 1424, *s.n.* Pocklington, of Chelsworth, Suffolk.

POETT, John Joseph (1807-1879). Major. 27th N.I. *bapt.* Booterstown, co. Dublin, 25 Mar. 1807. Cadet 1826. Arrived in India 30 Nov. 1827. Ensign 14 June 1827. Lieut. 28 Sept. 1831. Capt. 14 Jan. 1842. Retired 5 July 1849. Hon. Major 28 Nov. 1854. *d.* 10 Jan. 1879.

Son of Joseph Poett, surgeon, Rathfarnham dispensary. *m.* Meerut 17 Apr. 1843, Rebecca, dau. of Don Marianna Castelli, of Lima, and widow of Henry Charles Eddy, Asst. Surg. Bengal. (*See also* Bernard Cary.)

Services : Ensign d.d. 46th N.I. 22 Jan. 1828; posted to 27th N.I. 20 Feb. 1828. Leave s.c. 18 mos. to Mauritius and N.S.W. 12 Sept. 1831. Fur. u.p.a. 24 Apr. 1833 till 16 June 1834. First Afghan War 1840-2; Nazian valley; defence of Ghazni (s.w.); taken prisoner on surrender of that garr. Mar. 1842; released Sept. 1842; Capt. 27th N.I. First Sikh War; Ferozshahr; Capt. 27th N.I. (Medal).

POGSON, Wredenhall Robert (1787-1843). Lieut. Colonel, 47th N.I. *b.* Sutton, Surrey, 1 July 1787. Cadet 1803. Arrived in India 17 Mar. 1805. Ensign 25 Apr. 1805. Lieut. 26 Apr. 1805. Capt. 15 Sept. 1819. Major 20 Apr. 1833. Lt. Col. 8 Oct. 1839. *d.* Sikraul, Benares, 6 Aug. 1843.[1]

bapt. 30 July 1787. 4th son of Bedingfield Pogson, of Sutton, and Elizabeth Philadelphia his wife. Grandson of John Pogson, late of Deep Bay estate, St. Kitts, and of Downsal Hall, Essex. His sister *m.* John MacInnes, *q.v. m.* Lucknow 28 Mar. 1815, Ann Cordelia, dau. of Joseph Queiros, of Lucknow, merchant, and sister of Joseph Queiros, *q.v.* (*See also* Rowland Cotton Dickson and Joseph Nesbitt.)

Services : Posted Lieut. to 24th N.I. in 1806. Settlement of Hariana 1809; Bhawani; Lieut. 2/24th N.I. Adjt. 2/24th N.I. 1811 till May 1815. Intr. & Qmr. do. 4 May 1815 till 1 Nov. 1819. Third Mahratta War; Lieut. 24th N.I. Transfd. as Capt. to 1/24th N.I. d.d. 2/9th N.I. 26 Jan. till 28 Oct. 1822. Transfd. to 47th N.I. (late 1/24th) May 1824. On this Regt. mutinying in Nov. 1824, he was posted to newly-raised 69th N.I. (became 47th in 1828). Bde. Major at Presdy. 4 June 1824; do. Agra and Muttra frontier 22 Jan. till 12 July 1825. D.A.A.G. on Est. at Meerut 12 July 1825 till 16 Oct. 1826. A.A.G. 1st Inf. Div., Bhurtpore force, 3 Dec. 1825. Siege and capture of Bhurtpore; Capt. 69th N.I., A.A.G. Agent for family money, and Paymr. pensioners at Barrackpore 16 Oct. 1826 till 8 Feb. 1834. Major comdg. 47th N.I. in Jan. 1837. Posted Lt. Col. to 47th N.I.

THE BENGAL ARMY, 1758-1834 545

29 Jan. 1840; 25th N.I. 19 July 1842; 47th N.I. Nov. 1842. Author of "History of the Boondelas, . . ." Calcutta, 1824, 8vo; also wrote poetry.
Refs.: *Caribbeana*, i. 9. *A.J.* 3S. ii. 217. *I.M.* No. vii. 211. *G.M.* 1843, ii. 669. *The Times*, 18 Nov. 1843. Will dated Barrackpore, 11 Oct. 1841; admon. 26 Mar. 1844. M.I. Benares Cantt., nr. rly.
¹ *Note*: "He was a man of learning, and author of some rather eccentric writings. He was buried by a roadside, according to a direction in his will, the adjt. reading the service, as the chaplain of the station refused to officiate under such circumstances." (*I.M.*)

POLGRAVE, Thomas (*d.* 1768). Cadet, Infantry. Cadet 1768. *d.* 1768.
Services: N.F.P.

POLHILL, Thomas (1746/47-1804). Lieut. Colonel, 1st N.I.
b. 1746/47. Cadet 1772. Admitted 18 July 1772. Ensign 14 July 1776. Lieut. 3 July 1778. Capt. 30 Dec. 1792. Major 31 Aug. 1798. Lt. Col. 4 Jan. 1801. *d.* Kalpi, U.P., 9 May 1804, aged 57.
Eldest son of David Polhill, one of the Jurats of Maidstone, Kent. *m.* Calcutta 4 Oct. 1783, Miss Ann Smyth. (She died Valenciennes, France, 3 Dec. 1856, aged 96. "One of the *détenues* of Napoleon.") (*Probably* father of Thomas William Polhill, *q.v.*) Ed. Tonbridge School 1761-2.
Services: First Rohilla War; battle of St. George; Cadet in the Select Picket. Adjt. Nawab-Wazir of Oudh's bodyguard in Nov. 1777; reapptd. to d.d. with do. 6 Jan. 1778. Campaign against the Rajah of Benares 1781; operations nr. Chunar; Latifpur; Lora; Sukrut Pass; Lieut. comdg. Nawab's bodyguard, with force under Major Crabbe, *q.v.* Lieut. in G.G.B.G. in Apr. 1782; posted to Inf. body-guard of G.G. 4 July 1782 till reduced 1 Mar. 1785. Lieut. 1st Eur. Bn. in July 1787; posted to 34th Bn. Sepoys 31 Oct. 1787; Adjt. do. 15 Dec. 1787 till 30 Dec. 1792. Capt. 4th Eur. Bn. in Oct. 1793, when posted to P.W.I. detachment; apptd. to comd. troops at P.W.I. 30 Jan. 1797. Major 7th N.I. Posted Lt. Col. to 1/1st N.I. in Jan. 1801. Operations in Bundelkhand 1804; Lt. Col. comdg. 1/1st N.I.
Refs.: Burke's *Landed Gentry*, 14th edn., p. 30, *s.n.* Polhill-Drabble, of Woodside, Sundridge, Kent. *V.B.G. N. & Q.* 10S. xi. 314. *G.M.* 1805, ii. 877.

POLHILL, Thomas William (1791-1808). Ensign, 13th N.I. *b.* Fatehgarh 1 Mar. 1791. Cadet 1805. Arrived in India 13 Dec. 1806. Ensign 8 Dec. 1806. *d.* Benares (? Chunar) 4 Nov. 1808.
Ward of W. Polhill. (*Probably* son of Thomas Polhill, *q.v.*, and Ann his wife.)
Services: Posted as Ensign to 13th N.I. in 1807.

POLIER, Antoine Louis Henri (1741-1795). Lieut. Colonel. Infantry. *bapt.* Lausanne, Switzerland, 28 Feb. 1741. Cadet 1758. Ensign 1 May 1759. Lieut. 18 Sept. 1761. Capt. 16 Oct. 1763. Major 3 May 1766. Lt. Col. 12 Apr. 1782. Retired 1789. *d.* Rosetti, nr. Avignon, 9 Feb. 1795: assassinated by robbers.
Younger son of Jacques Henri Etienne Polier (branche de Bottens), of a French Protestant family which had emigrated to Switzerland in the 17th century, and Jeanne Françoise Moreau de Brosses his wife. Nephew of Paul Philippe Polier, Comdt. of Fort St. George, Madras. *m.* in France 20 Jan. 1791, Anne Rose Louise Berthoudt, dau. of Jacob, Baron Van Berchem. Father of Pierre Amédée Charles Guillaume Adolphe, Comte de Polier. Ed. Neufchâtel.
Services: Sailed for Madras in the *Hardwicke* in 1757, intending to join his uncle at Madras. Madras Cadet 1757. Saw active service under Clive against the French. Transfd. as Lieut. to Bengal in 1761. Succeeded Thomas Amphlett, B.C.S., as Chief Engr. in Oct. 1762, and was employed on the construction of the new fort in Calcutta till superseded in 1764 by Fleming Martin, *q.v.* Apptd. Field Engr. to the Army in the field under Major Hector Munro 21 Nov. 1764, having probably taken part in the battle of Buxar the preceding month. Permitted by C.D. in 1765 to succeed Martin as Chief Engr., and he acted in that capacity for two yrs. In 1766, the year he was promoted Major, the C.D. issued an order that no foreigner was to rise to higher rank in their Service than that of Major. Apptd. in 1773 to proceed to Oudh in capacity of Engr. and architect to Nawab Shuja-ud-daulah, who had applied for such a person. In 1774, incurred displeasure of majority of Council for having assisted Najaf Khan at head of a body of Wazir's troops at siege of Agra, and was recalled to Presdy. Board permitted him to resign in 1775. Returned to Oudh, without permission, to settle his affairs. In May 1780 he informed the G.G. and Council that, with the approval of Sir Eyre Coote, he had been restored by the Wazir to his former station of Engr. and architect: the Board agreed to this. In Mar. 1782, his appt. having been

annulled, he was readmitted into the Service with the rank of Bt. Lt. Col., but not to serve in any Corps. Settled at Lucknow. In Oct. 1785 he applied to superintend the surveys of Upper Provinces. Returned to canton Vaud in 1789, and shortly afterwards accompanied his father-in-law, who had been banished by the Bernese, into exile at Rosetti. Pensd. on Lord Clive's fund 14 Mar. 1792.[1] His death at the hands of robbers (or revolutionaries) said to have been due to his Oriental display of wealth. Author of "Mythologie des Indous," pub. posthumously 1809. Collected MSS., and was the first European to obtain a complete copy of the *Vedas*, now in B.M.

Refs. : Dict. biog. des Genevois et des Vaudois. D.I.B. Forrest, i. 190, 200. *Recueil de Généalogies vaudoises*, fasc. ii, 153 (Lausanne, 1912). Portrait in Zoffany's ' Col. Mordaunt's Cock Match,' and in the same artist's ' Claude Martin and his Friends.'

[1] *Note :* He can have possessed no legitimate claim to its benefits on the score of poverty.

POLLARD, John (1798-1827). Lieutenant, 1st Extra Regt. N.I. *b.* W. Grinstead, Sussex, 21 May 1798. Cadet 1819. Ensign 14 Feb. 1820. Lieut. 11 July 1823. *d.* Nimach, C.I., 25 Nov. 1827.

bapt. W. Grinstead chapel 22 May 1798. Son of James Pollard and Elizabeth his wife. Nephew of John Laker, farmer in Sussex. *m.* (before 1819) Elizabeth ——, niece of Major J. Brown. (She died 4 Mar. 1834.)

Services : Posted Ensign to 1/10th N.I. in 1820. Fur. 1822-3. Transfd. as Lieut. to 26th N.I. July 1823 ; to 51st N.I. (late 1/26th) May 1824 ; to newly-raised 1st Extra Regt. May 1825. Operations against the Bhils 1827 ; Lieut. 1st Extra Regt.

POLLOCK, David Taylor (1808-1843). Bt. Captain, 74th N.I. *b.* London 5 Oct. 1808. Cadet 1826. Arrived in India 23 Sept. 1827. Ensign 13 May 1827. Lieut. 23 June 1835. Bt. Capt. 13 May 1842. *d.* Erinpura, Rajputana, 16 Feb. 1843.

Eldest son of Sir David Pollock, Kt., C.J. Bombay, and Elizabeth Gore his wife, dau. of John Atkinson, of London. Nephew of Sir George Pollock, Bart., *q.v. m.* Calcutta 9 Jan. 1832, Georgiana Margaret, youngest dau. of M. Smith. (She *re-m.* 14 Oct. 1844, Lieut. J. F. Hall, 22nd B.N.I.) Ed. St. Paul's ; admitted 3 Oct. 1818 ; Eton ; in 5th Form, Upper School, in 1826.

Services : Posted Ensign to 6th Extra Regt. (became 74th N.I.) 3 Jan. 1828. Intr. & Qmr. 74th N.I. 26 Feb. 1835 till 16 Jan. 1839 ;

S.A.C.G. 14 Dec. 1838. Granted leave to Bombay 11 Jan. 1843, and was on his way there when his death occurred.

Refs.: Foster's *Baronetage*, p. 506, *s.n.* Pollock, Bart., of Hatton, Middlesex. *Gardiner. Eton School Lists. G.M.* 1843, i. 556. *The Times*, 15 Apr. 1843, p. 7. Will dated 3 Mar. 1838 ; admon. 30 Aug. 1844. M.I. Erinpura.

POLLOCK, Sir George, first baronet (1786-1872). Field Marshal, G.C.B., G.C.S.I. Colonel Comdt. Royal (late Bengal) Artillery. (323) Constable of the Tower of London. *b.* Piccadilly, London, 4 June 1786. Cadet 1800. Arrived in India 14 Dec. 1803. Lieut. 3 Sept. 1803. Capt. Lt. 3 Oct. 1805. Capt. 1 Mar. 1812. Major 4 May 1820. Lt. Col. 1 May 1824. Col. Comdt. 3 Mar. 1835. Maj. Gen. 28 June 1838. Lt. Gen. 11 Nov. 1851. Gen. 17 May 1859. F.M. 24 May 1870. *d.* Walmer 6 Oct. 1872.

1st Bart., " of the Khyber Pass." *cr.* 26 Mar. 1872. *bapt.* Down St. 2 July 1786. 5th son of David Pollock, of Charing Cross, saddler, and Sarah Homeria his wife, dau. of Richard Parsons. Brother of the Rt. Hon. Sir Frederick Pollock, 1st Bart., Lord Chief Baron, and uncle of David Taylor Pollock, *q.v. m.* 1st, Cawnpore 6 Aug. 1810, Frances Webb, dau. of Sheriff John Barclay, of Tain. (She died 12 Sept. 1849.) Father of Sir Frederick Montagu-Pollock, 2nd Bart., *q.v. m.* 2nd, Battersea 15 Jan. 1852, Henrietta, elder dau. of George Hyde Wollaston, of Clapham Common. (She died 14 Feb. 1873.) Woolwich Cadet 21 Jan. 1801 till 7 May 1803.

Services : See *D.N.B.* Second Mahratta War ; Deig ; Bhurtpore ; Lieut. 3rd Coy. 1st Bn. (India medal). Nepal War 1814-15 ; Capt. 3rd Coy. 3rd Bn., in 3rd Div. First Burma War 1824-6 ; Lt. Col. comdg. Bengal Art. with Sir A. Campbell's force in Burma from Dec. 1824 (clasp to India medal). Fur. s.c. 10 Jan. 1827 till 18 Nov. 1830. First Afghan War 1842 ; Maj. Gen. comdg. the " Army of Retribution " which forced the Khyber, relieved Jalalabad, and reoccupied Kabul (Medal). Actg. Resdt. at Lucknow 1843. Mily. Member of Supreme Council at Calcutta 20 Sept. 1844 till 31 Mar. 1847. Fur. s.c. 21 Feb. 1847. Govt. Dir. of E.I.C. 1854-6. C.B. 2 Jan. 1827 ; G.C.B. 2 Dec. 1842 ; K.S.I. 19 Aug. 1861 ; G.C.S.I. 24 May 1866. Constable of the Tower of London 14 Nov. 1871 till death. *Bur.* in Westminster Abbey.

Refs.: Burke's *Peerage*, 1923, p. 1790, *s.n.* Montagu-Pollock, Bart. *Walford. D.N.B. D.I.B. Boase. Vibart*, pp. 166-84. *E.I.M.C.* i. 277. *I.L.N.* lix (1871), 441 (portrait). Painting by

THE BENGAL ARMY, 1758-1834 549

Sir Francis Grant, P.R.A., in Council reading room at I.O. Portrait, F. Grant—J. J. Chant, pub. H. Graves & Co., 1857.

POLLOCK, Hugh. Cadet. Infantry. Cadet 1783. Arrived in India 11 July 1784. Resigned 1 Sept. 1784.
Services: Apptd. Cadet 13 Mar. 1783; sailed for India in the *Berrington* 2 Feb. 1784. In 1790 was Asst. Accountant, Board of Revenue; sometime a shopkeeper at Calcutta.

POLLOCK, Montgomery (1780-1803). Cornet, 1st N.C. *b.* Irvine, co. Ayr, 31 May 1780. Cadet 1799. Arrived in India 12 Jan. 1801. Cornet 13 Apr. 1801. *d.* 13 Mar. 1803: kld. in action at Kachaura.[1]
2nd son of Rev. Thomas Pollock, minister of Kilwinning, co. Ayr, 1770-98, and Margaret his wife, 2nd dau. of Alexander Hamilton, of Grange, surgeon at Saltcoats. Brother of Robert Pollock, *q.v.*
Services: Posted Cornet to 1st N.C. Operations in Jumna Doab 1803; Sasni; Bijaigarh; Kachaura (kld.); Cornet 1st N.C.
Refs.: Scott's *Fasti*, iii. 118. *Pester*, pp. 67, 68. *S.M.* 1804, p. 79.
[1] *Note:* According to Pester's *Journal* (op. cit.) both he and Major Robert Nairne, *q.v.*, were kld. on 21 Feb. Official records, however, give 13 Mar. as the date of his death, and 12 Mar. for Major Nairne.

POLLOCK, Robert (1786-1806). Lieutenant, 22nd N.I. *b.* Kilwinning, co. Ayr, 7 Jan. 1786. Cadet 1800. Arrived in India 14 Oct. 1801. Ensign 3 Dec. 1801. Lieut. 30 Sept. 1803. *d.* 16 Mar. 1806, on board the *Eliza Ann*, in Madras Roads.
bapt. Kilwinning 12 Jan. 1786. 4th son of Rev. Thomas Pollock, minister of Kilwinning, and Margaret his wife. Brother of Montgomery Pollock, *q.v.*
Services: Ensign d.d. 7th N.I. in 1802. Second Mahratta War; operations in Bundelkhand 1803; Ensign 18th N.I. Transfd. as Lieut. to 2/22nd N.I. Sept. 1803. Second Mahratta War 1804-5; battle and capture of Deig; Bhurtpore (w. in 2nd assault 21 Jan. 1805); Lieut. 2/22nd N.I. Adjt. Etawah Provl. Bn. 1805-6.
Refs.: Scott's *Fasti*, iii. 118. Will dated 1 Oct. 1804; codicils dated 28 Jan. and 22 Sept. 1805; proved 22 May 1806.

POLLOCK, Robert McCully (1791-1828). Lieutenant, 3rd Extra Regt. *b.* Newtownards, co. Down, June 1791. Cadet

1811. Ensign 15 June 1814. Lieut. 17 Aug. 1816. *d. unm.* Bhopalpur, C.I., 20 June 1828.

Son of James Pollock, of Newtownards, farmer on Lord Londonderry's estate, and Alice his wife. Brother of John, and of Rachel, wife of Thomas Glass, of Portaferry.

Services : Was for many yrs. an Ofr. in one of the Irish Yeo. Regts. Posted Ensign to 2/7th N.I. in 1815 ; transfd. as Lieut. to Bengal Eur. Regt. Aug. 1816 ; retransfd. to 2/7th N.I. 3 Feb. 1819 ; to newly-formed 32nd N.I. July 1823 ; to 63rd N.I. (late 1/32nd) May 1824 ; to 64th N.I. July 1824. Adjt. 64th N.I. 6 July 1824 ; do. newly-raised 3rd Extra Regt. 12 July 1825 till death. No record of active service.

Refs. : *A.J.* xxvii. 93. Will dated 21 Aug. 1827 ; proved 12 Sept. 1828.

*MONTAGU-POLLOCK, Sir Frederick, second baronet (1815-1874). Lieutenant. Bengal Engrs. *b.* Benares 27 Feb. 1815. Madras Cadet 1833. 2nd Lieut. (Madras Engrs.) 13 Dec. 1833. 2nd Lieut. (Bengal Engrs.) 14 Dec. 1833. Lieut. 12 Aug. 1840. Retired 5 Sept. 1844. *d.* Thurlow, Clapham, 17 June 1874.

2nd Bart. *s.* 6 Oct. 1872. Assumed by R. L. 11 Aug. 1873, the additional surname and arms of Montagu. Eldest son of Sir George Pollock, 1st Bart., *q.v.*, and Frances Webb his 1st wife. *m.* Clapham 9 July 1861, Laura Caroline, dau. of Henry Seymour Montagu, of Westleton Grange, Suffolk, *q.v.* (She died 26 May 1900.) Ed. Eton. Addiscombe Cadet 1832-3.

Services : On fur. in England in 1839, when he was transfd. from the Madras to the Bengal Est. In charge of Delhi canal 1841-2. Fur. s.c. 5 Mar. 1842 till retirement. No record of active service.

Refs. : Burke's *Peerage*, 1923, p. 1791, *s.n.* Montagu-Pollock, Bart. *Eton School Lists.* Boase. *The Times*, 19 June 1874. *I.L.N.* 27 June 1874, p. 619.

POLSON, William (1811-1832). Ensign, 58th N.I. *b.* Acton. Middlesex, 23 Feb. 1811. Cadet 1828. Arrived in India 31 Aug, 1829. Ensign 5 June 1829. *d.* Sultanpur, U.P., 16 Nov. 1832.

3rd son of William Gray Polson, of New Sq., Lincoln's Inn, barr.-at-law, stipendiary mgte. of I. of St. Vincent, sometime Capt. H.M. 59th Regt., and Charlotte Sarah his wife, *née* McConnell. Addiscombe Cadet 1829.

Services : Ensign d.d. 60th N.I. 15 Mar. 1830 ; posted to 58th N.I. 26 June 1830. No record of active service.

Refs. : *G.M.* 1833, i. 574.

THE BENGAL ARMY, 1758-1834   551

POLWHELE, Thomas (1797-1885). General. Colonel 17th N.I. *b.* Manaccan vicarage, Cornwall, 4 Oct. 1797. Cadet 1814. Arrived in India Sept. 1815. Ensign 22 Aug. 1815. Lieut. 1 Feb. 1818. Capt. 26 July 1830. Major 21 Aug. 1843. Lt. Col. 17 Jan. 1850. Col. 26 May 1859. Maj. Gen. 1 May 1858. Lt. Gen. 18 Mar. 1870. Gen. 13 Dec. 1876. *d.* Tivoli Lodge, Cheltenham, 23 May 1885.

bapt. Manaccan 1 June 1798. 5th son of Rev. Richard Polwhele, J.P., Dy. Warden of the Stanneries, vicar of Newlyn (*D.N.B.*), and Mary his 2nd wife, dau. of Richard Tyrrell, of Starcross, Devon. *m.* St. Mary's, Truro, Feb. 1830, Edith Edgecumbe Hoskins, dau. of John James, of Truro. Woolwich Cadet 1813-14.

Services : Posted Ensign to 1/21st N.I. in 1815. Nepal War 1816 ; Ensign 1/21st N.I., in 1st Bde. Rt. Column (India medal). With 1st Ceylon Vol. Bn. Oct. 1818 till Mar. 1820, when he rejoined 1/21st N.I. Adjt. 2/21st N.I. 16 Jan. 1823 ; transfd. to 41st N.I. (late 1/21st) May 1824. Exchanged to 42nd N.I. 21 Aug. 1824 ; Intr. & Qmr. do. 21 Aug. 1824 ; Adjt. do. 6 Jan. 1826 till 15 Jan. 1828. First Burma War ; Arakan 1825 ; Lieut. 42nd N.I. (clasp to India medal). Fur. s.c. 30 Dec. 1827 till 13 Sept. 1830. d.d. 9th N.I. 17 Nov. 1831 till 5 Oct. 1832. Apptd. Bde. Major 2nd Bde., 1st Div., Army of Indus 10 Sept. 1838. First Afghan War 1838-42 ; capture of Ghazni 1839 (Medal) ; recapture of Kalat (*Lond. Gaz.* 12 Feb. 1841) ; operations of Kandahar force under Nott ; action of 12 Jan. 1842 (*Lond. Gaz.* 24 Nov. 1842). Apptd. Bde. Major 2nd Bde. in Afghanistan 28 Jan. 1841 ; actg. A.A.G. to troops in Kandahar 14 May 1842. First Sikh War ; Mudki ; Ferozshahr ; Sobraon (w.) ; Major comdg. 42nd N.I. (Medal with 2 clasps). Posted as Lt. Col. to 42nd N.I. Apr. 1850 ; to 54th N.I. 27 Feb. 1851 ; to 36th N.I. 1856. Apptd. Bdr. on the Est. 14 Feb. 1856, and posted to Lahore ; to Delhi 7 Mar. 1856 ; to Agra 9 Aug. 1856. Was comdg. Agra Div. at outbreak of the Mutiny, and was superseded. Col. 17th N.I. 1857 till 4 May 1858. Fur. p.a. 3 yrs. Apr. 1858.

Refs. : Burke's *Landed Gentry*, 13th edn., p. 1427, *s.n.* Polwhele, of Polwhele, Cornwall. Boase. *The Times*, 26 May 1885. Vivian's *Visitations of Cornwall*, p. 378.

POND, James Ruthven (1812-1857). Bt. Lieut. Colonel, 1st Eur. Bengal Fus. *b.* Edinburgh 28 Mar. 1812. Cadet 1827. Arrived in India 29 Sept. 1828. Ensign (22 May 1828) 3 June 1829. Lieut. 11 May 1832. Capt. 1 Nov. 1844. Major 5 Dec. 1855. Bt. Lt. Col. 20 June 1854. *d.* Sydenham 17 Apr. 1857.

Son of Samuel Pond, of Circus Pl., Edinburgh, merchant, and Elizabeth Sutherland Ruthven his wife. Brother of Samuel Pond, *q.v. m.* Benares 9 Apr. 1847, Maria, dau. of Richard Radford Hughes, *q.v.* Ed. Edin. High School.

Services: Ensign d.d. 51st N.I. 19 Nov. 1828; do. 24th N.I. 16 Feb. 1829. Posted Ensign to 67th N.I. 4 Mar. 1829; transfd. to 2nd Bengal Eur. Regt. 3 June 1829. Actg. Adjt. Bengal Eur. Regt. 9 July 1838. First Afghan War 1838-40; Ghazni 1839 (Medal); occupation of Kabul; Pashut Jan. 1840; capture of Kajja fort; Lieut. 1st Bengal Eur. L.I. With Army of Reserve (for Afghanistan) Oct. 1842 till Jan. 1843. First Sikh War; Ferozshahr; Sobraon; A.A.G. to Gen. Sir Robert Dick's Div. (Medal with clasp). D.A.A.G. Benares Div. 24 July 1846; A.A.G. Sirhind Div. 28 Oct. 1848; do. Benares Div. 1849; do. Peshawar 1852; do. Lahore Aug. 1853 till Feb. 1854. Second Burma War 1852-3; capture of Pegu; Bt. Major 1st Eur. Bengal Fus. (Medal). Fur. s.c. 3 Feb. 1854 till death.

Refs.: I.M. 29 Apr. 1857, p. 290. *G.M.* 1857, i. 631. Name on mural tablet in Winchester cathedral (where his second name is mis-spelt Ruther).

POND, Samuel (1814-1844). Lieutenant, 46th N.I. *b.* Edinburgh 2 Aug. 1814. Cadet 1831. Arrived in India 17 June 1832. Ensign 17 June 1832. Lieut. 10 July 1838. *d.* Barrackpore 22 Dec. 1844.

Son of Samuel Pond and Elizabeth Sutherland Ruthven his wife. Brother of James Ruthven Pond, *q.v.* Ed. Edin. High School.

Services: Cadet d.d. Bengal Eur. Regt. 27 June 1832; do. 63rd N.I. 5 Aug. 1833. Posted Ensign to 46th N.I. 19 Dec. 1833. Adjt. 46th N.I. 12 Dec. 1838 till death. No record of active service.

Refs.: I.M. 25 Feb. 1845, p. 86. M.I. in Barrackpore cemetery.

PONEY, Robert. (*See* **POWNEY, Robin.**)

PONSONBY, Carrique [1] (1757/58-1779). Lieutenant, Infantry. *b.* in Ireland 1757/58. Cadet 1777. Ensign 21 Feb. 1778. Lieut. 27 Sept. 1778. *d.* 1779, on active service with the Bombay detachment; *bur.* Surat 19 Aug.

Services: Sailed for India in the *Duke of Kingston* 24 Mar. 1777, aged 19. N.F.P.

[1] *Note:* The surname, after all, is probably Carrique not

Ponsonby. (*See* Part I. p. 310.) (Cf. *The Ponsonby Family*, by Maj.-Gen. Sir John Ponsonby, K.C.B., London 1929, Table M.)

PONSONBY, Frederick. (*See* **SYSONBY, Frederick.**)

PONSONBY, George Connolly (1799-1866). Major General. 2nd Bengal Eur. L.C. *b*. psh. of St. Mark's, Dublin, 9 Feb. 1799. Cadet 1819. Admitted 15 Nov. 1820. Cornet (19 May 1820) 1 Nov. 1820. Lieut. 14 Sept. 1822. Capt. 19 May 1838. Major 28 Nov. 1854. Bt. Lt. Col. 7 June 1849. Bt. Col. 28 Nov. 1854. Retired 25 Feb. 1860. Hon. Maj. Gen. 25 Feb. 1860. *d*. Harrow 3 June 1866, of paralysis.

Son of Rt. Hon. George Ponsonby, Lord Chancellor of Ireland (*D.N.B.*). *m*. Karnal 30 Aug. 1832, Harriet Milling, eldest dau. of Capt. Mathew William Ford, H.M. 16th Regt. (*See also* Sir Arthur Mitford Becher.)

Services : Posted Cornet to 2nd L.C. in 1820. Adjt. do. 28 Aug. 1823 till 5 Sept. 1825. Siege and capture of Bhurtpore ; Lieut. 2nd L.C., d.d. 10th L.C. (India medal). Fur. s.c. 21 Mar. 1826 till 8 July 1828. First Afghan War 1838-40 ; Ghazni (Medal) ; Kohistan 1840 ; Parwandara (w.) ; Capt. 2nd L.C. D.A.A.G. Saugor Div. 17 Feb. 1841 ; A.A.G. Meerut Div. 14 Apr. 1841 till 1855 ; do. to British troops in Afghanistan 16 Apr. 1841. First Afghan War 1842 ; A.A.G. to Gen. Pollock 5 Jan. 1842 ; Khyber (*Lond. Gaz.* 7 June 1842) ; reoccupation of Kabul ; Tazin (ib. 24 Nov. 1842) ; A.A.G. (Medal). Granted wound pension. Posted to newly-raised 11th L.C. (became 2nd L.C. in 1850) 1842. Second Sikh War ; Sadulapur ; Chilianwala ; Gujerat ; A.A.G. of Div. (Medal with 2 clasps). Bdr. on the Est. 29 Apr. 1857, and was comdg. Benares Bde. on outbreak of the Mutiny. Fur. s.c. Aug. 1857 till retirement. Transfd. to newly-raised 2nd Bengal Eur. L.C. 1 May 1858. Durani 3 cl.

Refs. : Burke's *Peerage*, 1923, p. 267, *s.n.* Bessborough, E. *The Ponsonby Family*, p. 68. *G.M.* 1866, ii. 120. *The Times*, 7 June 1866.

PONTON, John (1781-1801). Lieutenant, 12th N I. *b*. Edinburgh 20 Apr. 1781. Cadet 1798. Arrived in India 26 Aug. 1799. Ensign 21 Jan. 1800. Lieut. 29 May 1800. *d*. Cawnpore 6 Oct. 1801.

Son of Alexander Ponton, wright and burgess, and Isobel his wife, dau. of John Anderson, surgeon in Linlithgow.

Services : Posted Lieut. to 2/12th N.I. 15 Apr. 1801. No record of active service.
Refs. : S.M. 1802, p. 708.

POOLE, Benjamin Francis (*d.* 1774). Ensign, Infantry. Cadet 1773. Ensign 30 Oct. 1773. *d.* Berhampore 11 Jan. 1774. *m.* Mary.
Services : N.F.P.

POOLE, Charles (1777-1843). Lieut. Colonel Comdt., Invalid Est. 51st N.I. *b.* Little Stanmore, *alias* Whitchurch, Middlesex, 28 Oct. 1777. Cadet 1797. Arrived in India 28 Aug. 1799. Ensign 27 Sept. 1798. Lieut. 1 Nov. 1798. Capt. 5 Oct. 1806. Major 15 Nov. 1817. Lt. Col. 11 July 1823. Lt. Col. Comdt. 30 Sept. 1827. Invalided 30 May 1828. *d. unm.* Chunar 24 Nov. 1843.

bapt. Whitchurch 27 Nov. 1777. Son of Rev. Henry Poole, rector of Whitchurch, and Susanna Millar his 2nd wife. Brother of Mary Jane and Lettice Poole, and cousin-german of Samuel Rowlands, of Anglesey. His dau. *m.* Joseph Corfield, *q.v.* Ed. Merchant Taylors' Oct. 1785-Mar. 1796. St. John's Coll., Oxon.; matric. 5 July 1796, aged 18.

Services : Lieut. 6th N.I. Fur. 20 Feb. 1801 till 27 Sept. 1804. Operations in Bundelkhand 1805-6; Lieut. 6th N.I. Capt. 2/6th N.I. With 6th Vol. Bn. 1811-16. Capture of Java 1811; Capt. 6th Vol. Bn. Transfd. to 1/6th N.I. 1816. (? Third Mahratta War; Capt. 1/6th N.I., in Reserve Div.) Major 1/6th N.I. Posted Lt. Col. to 1/6th N.I. (became 3rd N.I.) July 1823. Tempy. comdg. 69th N.I. 12 Feb. 1825. Transfd. to 14th N.I. 21 Nov. 1826. Leave s.c. 6 mos. to Singapore 26 Jan. 1827. Posted Lt. Col. Comdt. to 51st N.I. 18 Feb. 1828. Comdt. Farrukhabad Provl. Bn. 30 May 1828 till 1 May 1831, when disbanded. At Fatehgarh 1831-4; at Presdy. 1834-9; Comdt. of Chunar 1839 till death.

Refs. : Robinson. Alumni Oxon. I.M. 9 Feb. 1844, p. 307. Will dated Chunar 11 Nov. 1842; proved 16 Dec. 1843. M.I. at Chunar and in Bath Abbey.

POOLE, Edward (1801-1822). Lieutenant, 22nd N.I. *b.* Spaxton, Somerset, 24 Feb. 1801. Cadet 1818. Ensign (?) Lieut. 29 Sept. 1820. *d.* Nagpur 26 Sept. 1822.

bapt. Spaxton 4 June 1801. Son of John Evered Poole, of Bridgwater, solicitor, and Elizabeth his wife. Addiscombe Cadet 1817-18.

Services: Ensign d.d. Bengal Eur. Regt. 1819. Posted Lieut. to 2/22nd N.I. in 1820. No record of active service.
Refs.: M.I. Kamptee.

POOLE, George (1787-?). Ensign. 22nd N.I. *bapt.* Nettlecombe, Somerset, 8 July 1787. Cadet 1805. Arrived in India 11 July 1806. Ensign 11 Sept. 1806. Struck off 1 Aug. 1807. Son of Thomas Poole, of Huish, Somerset, and Eleanor his wife. Ed. Blundell's; admitted 5 Feb. 1798, aged 11; left 29 June 1803.
Services: Posted Ensign to 22nd N.I. whilst still at Barasat C.C. Struck off the List of the Army 1 Aug. 1807 for absenting himself without leave from the Cadet Coy. since 10 Dec. 1806.
Refs.: *Blundell's School Register.*

POPE, Alexander (1787-1849). Lieut. Colonel, C.B., 6th L.C. *b.* Ipswich 9 Sept. 1787. Cadet 1805. Arrived in India 22 Jan. 1807. Cornet 1 Jan. 1807. Lieut. 7 Dec. 1812. Capt. 13 May 1825. Major 12 Apr. 1836. Lt. Col. 4 Nov. 1839. *d.* Kasauli 20 Apr. 1849, of wounds received at the battle of Chilianwala on 13 Jan.

bapt. St. Mary at Quay, Ipswich, 14 Sept. 1787. Son of John Pope and Sarah his wife, *née* Read. *m.* Benares 2 Nov. 1819, Frances, dau. of William Cracroft. (She died 16 Nov. 1889, aged 92.)

Services: Posted Cornet to 8th N.C. 1 Feb. 1807. Operations in Bundelkhand against marauders 1810-11; Cornet 8th N.C. Nepal War 1814-15; Lieut. 8th N.C., in 3rd Div. Third Mahratta War 1817-18; Jubbulpore 19 Dec. 1817 (s.w.—spear thrust); Lieut. 8th N.C., with Bdr.-Gen. Hardyman's Div. " He charged steadily under a heavy fire from the heights, penetrated to the enemy's guns, received a spear thrust into his body, and continued the pursuit with vigour." (Gen. Hardyman's Desp.; *Lond. Gaz.* 14 Jan. and 7 Aug. 1819.) Adjt. Native Invalids, and Paymr. Native pensioners at Allahabad, 1 Aug. 1819. Executive Ofr. Purnea Div., P.W.D., 18 Sept. 1820 till Nov. 1822. Leave s.c. to N.S.W. 10 Aug. 1822 till Jan. 1825. Transfd. to newly-raised 2nd Extra Regt. (became 10th L.C.) 17 June 1825 and joined Jan. 1826, too late to take part in capture of Bhurtpore. Actg. D.J.A.G. 28 Dec. 1829. Comdd. 10th L.C. from 8 Sept. 1829; posted Lt. Col. to 10th L.C. Jan. 1840. On sick leave to Simla Apr. 1841 till Dec. 1842, thus missing the First Afghan War. Gwalior campaign; Maharajpur (*Lond. Gaz.* 8 Mar. 1844); Lt. Col. comdg. 10th L.C. (Bronze star). Transfd. to 6th L.C. 24 July 1847; to comd. 2nd Bde. Cav., Army of the Punjab, 13 Oct. 1848; transfd.

to 8th L.C. Oct. 1848; to 6th L.C. Dec. 1848. Second Sikh War; passage of Chenab; Chilianwala (s.w.—sabre cut on head); Bdr. comdg. 2nd Cav. Bde. (Medal with clasp). Leave s.c. to Simla Apr. 1849, but died before reaching that place. C.B. 2 May 1844.
Refs.: De Rhé-Philipe. Fortescue, xii. 455-6, 459. Will dated 26 Mar. 1849; proved 28 Aug. 1849. M.I. at Kasauli.

POPE, William. Ensign. Infantry. Cadet 1781. Ensign 14 Aug. 1782. Resigned 29 Nov. 1784.
Services: Dy. Paymr. to 1st Bde. 21 Jan. 1782 till 7 Oct. 1783. Leave p.a. 6 mos. 1 Dec. 1783. (? After resigning the Service he became a silk and indigo manufacturer at Kasim Bazar, Bengal; later at Mahomedpur. His name appears for the last time in *E.I.R.* for Jan. 1804.)

POPHAM, George Munro (1779-1824). Lieut. Colonel Comdt., C.B., 23rd N.I. *bapt.* Madras 1 May 1779. Cadet 1794. Arrived in India 22 Oct. 1796. Ensign 19 Oct. 1795. Lieut. 15 Mar. 1797. Capt. 26 Feb. 1805. Major 1 June 1813. Lt. Col. 1 Mar. 1818. Lt. Col. Comdt. 1 May 1824. *d. unm.* Chichester 22 Oct. 1824.

Eldest son of Stephen Popham, of Madras, and Anne his wife, sister of Sir George Thomas, 3rd Bart., of Yapton. Brother of Louisa Maria, wife of John Goldingham, Coy.'s Astronomer at Madras, and nephew of William Popham, *q.v.* Inherited £100,000 from his father whilst at Westminster School. Ed. Westminster; K.S. 1795.

Services: Apptd. Cadet 24 Feb. 1795; sailed for India in the *Dublin* 17 May 1796. Expedn. to Egypt 1800; Lieut. 10th N.I., with Vol. Bn. Fur. 1801 till 3 May 1803. Transfd. to newly-raised 23rd N.I. 9 Nov. 1803. Operations against Dhundia Khan 1807; Komona; Ganauri; Capt. 1/23rd N.I. In comd. of Mr. Metcalfe's escort which was attacked by Akhali Sikhs nr. Amritsar 16 Feb. 1809. Major 1/23rd N.I. Comdd. 3rd Gren. Bn. 1814-15; do. 2nd Bde. Nagpur Subsdy. Force in 1817. Third Mahratta War; Chanda; comdd. one of the two columns of assault; Lt. Col. 1/23rd N.I. Bdr. comdg. Dacca Force 1823. Fur. 1824. C.B. 23 July 1823.
Refs.: *Westminster School Register*. *A.J.* xviii. 649. Will dated Barrackpore 9 Sept. 1822; proved 11 May 1825.

POPHAM, William (1739/40-1821). Lieut. General. 7th N.I.
b. Cork "11 June 1739/40, 20 min. past 8 in the evening on

Friday." Capt. 7 Aug. 1768. Major 4 Sept. 1780. Lt. Col.
8 Dec. 1782. Resigned 21 Dec. 1784. Readmitted 7 Feb. 1794.
Col. 7 Dec. 1793. Maj. Gen. 26 Feb. 1795. Lt. Gen. 29 Apr.
1802. Retired 1 Jan. 1803. *d.* York St., London, 20 Feb. 1821.
Eldest son of Joseph Popham, of Cork, sometime H.B.M. consul
at Tetuan, Morocco, and Mary Riggs, of Waterford, his 1st wife.
Half-brother of Adm. Sir Home Riggs Popham, K.C.B. (*D.N.B.*),
and brother of Stephen, father of George Munro Popham, *q.v.*,
and of Anne, mother of Charles Wyndham Humphreys, *q.v.* *m.* 1st,
20 July 1785, Mary, 3rd dau. of Sir William Thomas, 2nd Bart.,
of Yapton Pl., nr. Bognor, M.P. (She died at sea 25 Jan. 1803.)
m. 2nd, Jane, widow of John Simpson and mother of Frederick
John Simpson, *q.v.* (She died Chippenham House, nr. Slough,
11 Jan. 1849, aged 69.)

Services : Ensign H.M. 24th Ft. 29 July 1757 ; Ensign 64th Ft.
(renumbered 79th in 1758) 30 Nov. 1757 ; Lieut. 79th (Draper's)
Ft. 1 May 1759. Siege and capture of Manila Sept.-Oct. 1762 ;
Lieut. 79th Ft., with expedn. under Gen. Draper. h.p. 1763-7.
Capt. 13th Ft. 4 Feb. 1767 ; sold out 27 May 1768. Was the senior
of 12 officers who were transfd. from H.M.S. by M.C. of 1 Sept. 1768.
Comdg. in Cooch Behar in Jan. 1776. First Mahratta War ; comdd.
2nd N.I. with Bombay detachment under Goddard ; sent with a
force at end of 1779 to assist the Rana of Gohad against the
Mahrattas ; capture of Lahar fort ; storm and capture of Gwalior
3 Aug. 1780 ; relieved by Lt.-Col. Jacob Camac, *q.v.*, at end of 1780.
Campaign against Rajah of Benares 1781 ; Major comdg. 35th
Regt. Sepoys ; capture of Patita and Bijaigarh, C.I. ; Major comdg.
the force.[1] His Regt. mutinied at Berhampore in 1782 and was
disbanded (G.G.O. of 20 Mar. 1782). Apptd. to comd. 23rd Regt.
Sepoys 17 July 1782. Fur. 21 Dec. 1784 till 7 Feb. 1794. M.P. for
Milborne Port, Somerset, 1787-90 ; defeated candidate for Queens-
boro' 1790. Apptd. to comd. at Fatehgarh and ordered to join
army in the field 26 Oct. 1794. Fourth Mysore War 1799 ; comdd.
a column consisting of 3 Coys. Art. and 3 Bns. Vols. which proceeded
to Madras by sea ; storm and capture of Seringapatam ; Maj.
Gen. comdg. Left Wing of the Army (Gold medal). Maj. Gen.
comdg. at the Presdy. and 1st M.M.B. in 1802. Fur. 24 Dec.
1802.

Refs. : E.I.M.C. ii. 93-100. *D.I.B. Williams,* p. 88. *Hickey,*
iv. 110. *N. & Q.* 11S. v. 136. *S.M.* 1821, i. 399. Portrait by
Sir Martin Archer Shee in Nat. Portrait Gallery, London.

[1] *Note :* His share of the prize-money at Bijaigarh amounted
to Rs. 2,94,000.

PORTEOUS, Charles (1776-1816). Major, 20th N.I. *b.* Perth 8 June 1776. Cadet 1795. Arrived in India 3 Mar. 1797. Ensign 2 Nov. 1796. Lieut. 30 Oct. 1797. Capt. 30 Nov. 1804. Major 1 Oct. 1815. *d.* Fort Marlbro', Sumatra, 8 Apr. 1816.
bapt. 9 June 1776. Son of Alexander Porteous, of Perth, merchant, and Helen Bell his wife. *m.* Berhampore 24 Apr. 1802, Elizabeth, dau. of Lawrence Rawstorne, *q.v.* (She died Calcutta 27 Jan. 1842, aged 63.) His daus. *m.* James Hay and William Innes (1803-1832), *qq.v.*
Services: Adjt. 1st Bn. Marine Regt. (became 20th N.I.) in 1803. Serving at P.W.I. in 1806; Malacca 1811; Bencoolen 1814. Major 2/20th N.I.
Refs.: Will dated Barrackpore 30 Jan. 1814; proved 2 Nov. 1816. M.I. Bencoolen.

PORTER, John (1761/62-?). Lieutenant. Infantry. *b.* in Scotland 1761/62. Cadet 1779. Ensign 1780. Lieut. 17 Aug. 1781. Struck off 1793.
Half-brother of Samuel Kilpatrick, *q.v.*
Services: Sailed for India in the *Neptune* 3 June 1780, aged 18. Leave s.c. to sea 7 May 1783; fur. 28 Oct. 1785 till struck off.

*PORTER, —— (*d.* 1772). Cadet in the Select Picket. *d.* Benares 3 June 1772.
Services: N.F.P.
Refs.: Macpherson, p. 95.

*PORTSMOUTH, William (*d.* 1769). Lieutenant, Engineers. Ensign 1 Nov. 1767. Lieut. (?) *d.* in India Apr. 1769.
Cousin of Ann Molineux; brother-in-law of John and James Pitt, of London. *m.* (?)
Services: Employed on survey in the Midnapore district, 1767-8.
Refs.: Will dated 27 Aug. 1768; proved 27 June 1769.

POTT, David (1812-1881). General, C.B. 7th (late 47th) N.I.; now 3rd Bn. (Duke of Connaught's Own) 7th Rajput Regt. *b.* Littleham, Exmouth, 9 Feb. 1812. Cadet 1828. Arrived in India 23 May 1829. Ensign 20 Jan. 1829. Lieut. 6 June 1833. Capt. 8 Oct. 1839. Major 31 Jan. 1854. Lt. Col. 1 May 1858. Bt. Col. 22 Aug. 1857. Maj. Gen. 15 Feb. 1866. Lt. Gen. 14 Apr. 1874. Gen. 1 Oct. 1877. *d.* Borthwickshiels, Hawick, 2 Oct. 1881.
Of Todrig and Borthwickshiels. 2nd son of George Pott, of

Todrig, co. Selkirk, and Borthwickshiels, co. Roxburgh, J.P. and D.L., Convener of Selkirk, and Katherine his wife, dau. of David Reid, and sister of Stephen Reid, *q.v.* Brother of George Pott, *q.v. m.* 1st, Cawnpore 12 Mar. 1850, Mary Anne Sophia, dau. of John Peter Ripley, *q.v.* (She died 1870.) *m.* 2nd, 1876, Anna Frances, dau. of A. Boyle, of Dublin.

Services : Served in R.N. 1824-8. Ensign d.d. 55th N.I. 13 July 1829 ; posted to 47th N.I. 14 Sept. 1829. Insurrection in Cuttack 1832-3 ; Ensign 47th N.I. Actg. Adjt. 47th N.I. 25 July 1838. Leave s.c. 2 yrs. to Aust. and Cape 18 Nov. 1840 ; fur. s.c. 11 June 1842 till 14 June 1844. First Sikh War ; Mudki ; Ferozshahr ; comdg. 47th N.I. ; Badhowal ; Aliwal ; Sobraon (horse shot under him) ; Capt. 47th N.I. (Medal with 3 clasps). Second Burma War ; comdd. a force of 1,800 men against insurgents in Pegu 1854 ; Major 47th N.I. (Medal). Mutiny campaign ; was comdg. 47th N.I. on outbreak of Mutiny and kept the Regt. loyal ; against rebels in Mirzapur district 1857-8 ; Lt. Col. 47th N.I. (Medal). Posted Lt. Col. to 47th N.I. 24 July 1858. Second China War 1858-9 ; Lt. Col. comdg. 47th N.I. (Medal). Comdg. 7th B.N.I. (late 47th N.I.) 1861-3 ; Comdt. do. 1 Jan. till Dec. 1864 ; Bdr. comdg. Dinapore Bde. Dec. 1864 till Oct. 1866. Transfd. to Staff Corps 12 Sept. 1866. Fur. p.a. 11 Dec. 1868, and 1 Nov. 1872 till death. C.B. 29 May 1875.

Refs. : Burke's *Landed Gentry*, 13th edn., p. 1432, *s.n.* Pott, of Todrig, co. Selkirk. *Boase. The Times*, 5 Oct. 1881.

POTT, George (1811-1877). Lieut. Colonel. 3rd N.I. *b.* Roberton, co. Selkirk, 3 Feb. 1811. Cadet 1827. Arrived in India 26 Oct. 1828. Ensign 19 May 1828. Lieut. 1 Jan. 1837. Capt. 24 Jan. 1845. Major 21 Oct. 1857. Retired 1 Feb. 1858. Hon. Lt. Col. 1 Feb. 1858. *d.* Borthwickshiels House, nr. Hawick, 15 Nov. 1877.

Of Todrig and Borthwickshiels. Eldest son of George Pott and Katherine his wife. Brother of Stephen Pott, *q.v. m.* 1840, Julia, youngest dau. of Rev. Robert Sparke Hutchings, sometime chaplain at Penang. Ed. Edin. Acad. 1825-6.

Services : Ensign d.d. 13th N.I. 20 Nov. 1828 ; posted to 3rd N.I. 4 Mar. 1829. Intr. & Qmr. 3rd N.I. 13 Oct. 1832 till 9 Jan. 1845. Shekhawat expedn. 1834 ; Ensign 3rd N.I. Actg. S.S.O. at Mainpuri 17 Mar. 1835, and 25 May 1837. Leave s.c. 2 yrs. to Cape 19 Sept. 1838. Leave s.c. 1844 till 1 Nov. 1845. Comdt. Inf. of Malwa Contingent 11 Nov. 1845 till 5 Feb. 1856. Fur. s.c. to Cape and Europe Feb. 1854 till Nov. 1856.

Refs.: Burke's *Landed Gentry*, 13th edn., p. 1432, *s.n.* Pott, of Todrig, co. Selkirk. *The Times*, 19 Nov. 1877.

*POTT, John. Ensign. Infantry. Cadet 1764. Ensign 2 Nov. 1765.

Services: N.F.P.

POTT, Stephen (1813-1885). Major General. Colonel Royal (Bengal) Engineers. *b.* Borthwickshiels 21 Sept. 1813. Cadet 1833. Arrived in India 11 Sept. 1834. 2nd Lieut. 14 Dec. 1832. Lieut. 31 Mar. 1840. Capt. 15 Feb. 1854. Lt. Col. 24 Aug. 1859. Bt. Col. 30 June 1862. Retired 31 Dec. 1862. Hon. Maj. Gen. 31 Dec. 1862. *d.* The Priory, Melrose, 9 Oct. 1885.

bapt. Roberton 30 Sept. 1813. 3rd and youngest son of George Pott and Katherine his wife. Brother of David Pott, *q.v.* Ed. Edin. Acad. 1825-8. Addiscombe Cadet 4 Feb. 1831 till 14 Dec. 1832. Chatham 11 Feb. 1833 till 4 Feb. 1834.

Services: Posted to S. & M. at Delhi 22 Sept. 1834. Surveying in Cawnpore district 14 May 1835. Asst. Executive Ofr. Ramgarh Div., P.W.D., 6 Aug. 1835; Asst. Supt. new Benares road 1 Aug. 1836; Asst. to Supt. of Feroze Shah's canal 16 Oct. 1837; Asst. to Supt. Burdwan–Benares road 19 Feb. 1838. Gwalior campaign; Maharajpur (Bronze star). Fur. 10 Mar. 1845 till 1847. Executive Engr. 5th (Benares) Div., P.W.D., 28 Jan. 1848; do. Hijli Div. 24 Apr. 1848; Cawnpore Div. 21 Dec. 1850; Prome 1854; Meerut 14 Feb. 1855. Fur. m.c. 29 Dec. 1858.

Refs.: Burke's *Landed Gentry*, 13th edn., p. 1531, *s.n.* Pott, of Todrig, co. Selkirk. *The Times*, 14 Oct. 1885.

POTTER, Peter [1] (*d.* 1782). Captain, 2nd Bengal Eur. Regt. Cadet 1770. Ensign 30 Dec. 1772. Lieut. 26 Mar. 1777. Capt. 24 Mar. 1781. *d.* Cawnpore June 1782.

Services: N.F.P.

Refs.: Will dated Cawnpore, 17 June 1782; proved 30 Dec. 1782.

[1] *Note*: (or John.)

POTTINGER, Thomas (1783-1845). Lieutenant. 13th N.I. Afterwards Lieut. 8th Light Dgns. *b.* Florida, Killinchy, co. Down, 3 Nov. 1783. Cadet 1803. Arrived in India 17 Mar. 1805. Ensign 11 May 1805. Lieut. 12 May 1805. Resigned 17 Apr. 1806. *d.* Oct. 1845.

Of Mount Pottinger, co. Down. *bapt.* Killinchy 17 Nov. 1783. Eldest son of Eldred Curwen Pottinger, of Mount Pottinger, and

THE BENGAL ARMY, 1758-1834   561

Ann his wife, dau. of Robert Gordon, of Florida House, co. Down. Brother of Rt. Hon. Sir Henry Pottinger, 1st Bart. *m.* 1st, Charlotte Jane, dau. of James Moore, of Castle Lesby, co. Down. Father of Eldred Pottinger, the "Hero of Herat" (*D.N.B.*). *m.* 2nd, Calcutta 7 June 1814, Eliza, dau. of John Williamson Fulton, and half-sister of Joseph Hennessy Fulton, *q.v.*
Services : Posted Lieut. to 13th N.I. in 1805. Lieut. 8th Light Dgns. (13 July 1806) 27 Aug. 1807 ; retired 21 May 1818.
Refs. : Burke's *Peerage*, 1905, p. 1304, *s.n.* Pottinger, Bart. Foster's *Families of Royal Descent*, i. 427.

POVOLERI, Charles Wills Robert (1781-1843). Lieut. Colonel, Invalid Est. 23rd N.I. *bapt.* Lambeth, Surrey, 13 Sept. 1781. Cadet 1796. Arrived in India 23 Oct. 1797. Ensign 24 Sept. 1797. Lieut. 10 Sept. 1798. Capt. 11 Sept. 1806. Major 1 Mar. 1818. Lt. Col. 11 July 1823. Invalided 3 June 1824. *d. unm.* at sea 17 Jan. 1843, on board the *Ellenborough.*
Son of John Povoleri and Elizabeth his wife. (*Perhaps* related to the wife of Arnold Nesbit Mathews, *q.v.*)
Services : Posted Ensign to 7th N.I. in 1797 ; transfd. as Lieut. to 5th N.I. in 1798 ; to 3rd N.I. ; to newly-raised 23rd N.I. in 1804. Served with 1st Vol. Bn. 1804-5. Capt. Lt. 23rd N.I. 12 Jan. 1806. Operations in Hariana 1809 ; Bhawani ; Capt. 2/23rd N.I. Third Mahratta War ; Major 1/23rd N.I. Comdg. Dacca Provl. Bn. 24 July 1829 till 1831. Regulating Ofr. of Invalid Tannah Ests. 1832.
Refs. : Will dated 26 Nov. 1839 ; codicils dated 7 May and 21 Nov. 1840, and 31 Oct. 1842 ; admon. 12 Mar. 1845.

*POWELL, Caleb (1730-1797). Captain. Infantry. *b.* 1730. Capt. 12 Dec. 1757. Resigned Oct. 1759. *d.* 1797.
Of Clonshavoy, co. Limerick. Collector of the port of Limerick 1765, high sheriff of the county 1773. 5th and youngest son of Robert Powell, of Newgarden, and Anne his wife, dau. of Col. Samuel Eyre, M.P. for town of Galway. *m.* 1st, 1760, Frances, dau. of John Bowen, of Frankville, co. Westmeath. (She died 1781.) Father of Stratford Powell, *q.v. m.* 2nd, 1783, Sarah, dau. of Thomas Westropp, of Ballystreen, co. Limerick. (She died 1805.)
Services : Ensign H.M. 39th (Adlercron's) Ft. 25 Aug. 1749 ; Lieut. do. 21 Feb. 1755. Transfd. as Capt. to Bengal Army in 1757. Operations against the French under Clive and Francis Forde, *q.v.*, 1757-9 ; Rajamundry 1758 ; Masulipatam 1759. " Acted as A.D.C. to Cols. Clive and Ford, and was on the staff

of the latter at the decisive battles of Rajamindery and Masulipatam." (*Burke*.) h.p. 39th Ft. on reduction 25 Dec. 1758; do. addl. from 11 Nov. 1760 till death.

Refs.: Burke's *Landed Gentry*, 7th edn., p. 1491, *s.n.* Powell, of Clonshavoy, co. Limerick. Will proved P.C. Dublin, 1797.

POWELL, James (*d*. 1805). Lieut. Colonel, 24th N.I. Country Cadet 1778. Admitted 2 Mar. 1778. Ensign 4 June 1778. Lieut. 2 Sept. 1779. Capt. 3 Oct. 1796. Major 14 Dec. 1802. Lt. Col. 21 Sept. 1804. *d*. Manchester Sq., London, 18 Oct. 1805.

Brother of Joseph and Samuel Powell. *m.* Calcutta 31 Mar. 1795, Elizabeth, sister of Henry Leadbeater. (*See also* John Boujannar.) (She died 1 Nov. 1843, aged 70.) His natural daus. *m.* John Pitt Griffin and Thomas Newton, *qq.v.*

Services: Sergt. Major 3rd Bengal Eur. Regt.; apptd. Adjt. 2nd do. 2 Mar. 1778; apptd. Cadet 4 June 1778. Lieut. 1/2nd Bengal Eur. Regt. in Oct. 1779; apptd. Adjt. do. 22 Mar. 1780. 1st Eur. Bn. in July 1787; transfd. to 3rd do. Feb. 1790. Capt. 2/12th N.I. Transfd. to 19th N.I. 29 May 1800; to newly-raised 24th N.I. in 1804. Fur. 11 Feb. 1803 till death.

Refs.: *G.M.* 1805, ii. 982. Will dated 11 Mar. 1805; proved 11 Oct. 1806.

*POWELL, James. Cadet. Infantry. Apptd. Cadet 5 Sept. 1783. Declined the appt.

POWELL, John (1758/59-1804). Colonel, 19th N.I. *b.* 1758/59. Cadet 1770. Arrived in India 30 July 1770. Ensign 12 Nov. 1771. Lieut. 27 July 1776. Capt. 20 Feb. 1781. Major 1 Mar. 1794. Lt. Col. 31 Aug. 1798. Col. 30 Sept. 1803. *d*. Fatehgarh, U.P., 14 Jan. 1804, " of fatigue after Lord Lake's campaigns," aged 45.

Brother of Peregrine Powell, *q.v. m.* Berhampore 1 Nov. 1790, Prudence (Prudentia), younger dau. of Major Jerome Noble. (She *re-m.* her cousin Samuel Noble, *q.v.*)

Services: (? Went out to India as Midshipman in the *Admiral Pocock*.) Apptd. Adjt. 39th Bn. Sepoys 22 Mar. 1780. Fur. 27 Sept. 1785 till 23 July 1788. Capt. 5th Bengal Eur. Bn. in 1790; 2nd do. in 1792; to comd. 17th Bn. Sepoys 22 Sept. 1794. Major 1/8th N.I. in Aug. 1798. Operations in Jumna Doab 1803; Sasni; Bijaigarh; Kachaura; Lt. Col. 1/8th N.I. Second Mahratta War; Aligarh; Agra; Laswari; Lt. Col. 8th N.I. Bdr. comdg. 4th Inf. Bde. of Lake's Grand Army 26 Aug. till

16 Dec. 1803, when he went sick. Posted Col. to 19th N.I. Sept. 1803.
Refs.: Burke's *Landed Gentry of Ireland,* p. 513, *s.n.* Noble, of Glassdrummond. *Pester, passim.* *G.M.* 1804, ii. 1071. Will dated Dinapore 17 Mar. 1792; admon. 27 Aug. 1804. M.I. Fatehgarh.

POWELL, John (1804-1881). Colonel. 55th N.I. *b.* Marylebone 13 Nov. 1804. Cadet 1823. Arrived in India 19 May 1824. Ensign 16 Jan. 1824. Lieut. 9 July 1825. Capt. 30 Nov. 1840. Major 15 Nov. 1852. Lt. Col. 27 June 1857. Retired 15 Feb. 1861. Hon. Col. 15 Feb. 1861. *d.* 1 Apr. 1881.
Son of Col. John Powell and Lucy his wife, 5th sister of Pownoll Phipps, *q.v.*
Services: Posted Ensign to 17th N.I. Transfd. as Lieut. to 28th N.I. 10 Oct. 1825. Adjt. 28th N.I. 19 Nov. 1831 till 21 Nov. 1841. Bde. Major at Barrackpore 23 Feb. till 18 Nov. 1842; do. Multan 1 Mar. 1850 till Feb. 1853. Was comdg. 58th N.I. at Shahjahanpur when that Regt. mutinied on 31 May 1857, but was temporarily absent from the station. Posted Lt. Col. to 55th N.I. in 1857. Fur. 1858 till retirement.
Refs.: *Life of Col. Pownoll Phipps.*

POWELL, Peregrine (1754/55-1835). Lieut. General. Colonel 23rd N.I. *b.* 1754/55. Cadet 1770. Arrived in India 30 July 1770. Ensign 17 Nov. 1771. Lieut. 31 July 1776. Capt. 22 Feb. 1781. Major 1 Mar. 1794. Lt. Col. 1 Nov. 1798. Col. 13 July 1803. Maj. Gen. 25 July 1810. Lt. Gen. 4 June 1814. *d.* Weymouth 7 May 1835, aged 80.
Brother of John Powell (1758/59-1804), *q.v.*, and of the wife of John Fenwick, *q.v.* *m.* Cawnpore 11 June 1798, Jennett, dau. of Dr. James Collie, surgeon at Burdwan. (*See also* William Francklin.)
Services: Apptd. Adjt. 19th Bn. Sepoys 22 Mar. 1780. Second Mysore War 1781-4; Pollilur; Cuddalore; Capt. comdg. 1/13th N.I., with Col. Pearse's detachment. Capt. 5th Bengal Eur. Bn. in July 1787 and in 1790; transfd. to 1st do. Apptd. to comd. 13th Bn. Sepoys 14 Nov. 1794; Lt. Col. 7th N.I. in 1798; to comd. 1/13th N.I. 1799. This Bn. was called after him "*Poel-ki-Paltan.*" Employed for some months in 1799 under Col. Morris in the Gorakhpur district in pursuit of Vizier Ali. In 1800 comdd. 13th N.I. at Captainganj, in newly-ceded province of Gorakhpur, and captured several mud forts. Second Mahratta War; operations in

Bundelkhand against Rajah Shamsher Bahadur 1803; Kapsa; Kalpi; Col. comdg. the force (*Cal. Gaz.* 3 Nov. 1803). Relinquished his comd. owing to ill health. Granted Bdr.'s allowances 25 July 1805. Col. 20th N.I. 1805; 7th N.I. 1807; 19th N.I. 1808; 23rd N.I. 1819-23, when he was transfd. to the Senior Officers' List. Fur. 8 Feb. 1807 till death.

Refs.: A.J. N.S. xvii. 185. *G.M.* 1835, ii. 322.

POWELL, Richard (*d.* 1766). Ensign, Infantry. Country Cadet 1765. Ensign 25 Aug. 1765. *d.* in India 19 Jan. 1766.

Son of Elizabeth Powell, of Cornwall. Brother of Capt. James Powell, Madras Est., and Margaret Powell.

Services: Was already in Bengal when apptd. Cadet with effect from 6 Feb. 1765. (G.O. 19 Mar. 1765.) Posted to 1st Bengal Eur. Regt. 13 Aug. 1765.

Refs.: Will dated 12 Jan. 1766; proved 13 Jan. 1767.

POWELL, Stratford (1761-1793). Lieutenant, 36th Bn. Sepoys. *b.* Dublin 1761. Cadet 1780. Ensign 6 Oct. 1780. Lieut. 19 Aug. 1781. *d. unm.* Calcutta 18 Dec. 1793, in the insane hospital.

Eldest son of Caleb Powell, of Clonshavoy, co. Limerick, *q.v.* Ed. Winchester. T.C.D.; Pensioner 24 May 1777.

Services: Sailed for India in the *Contractor* 3 Apr. 1780, aged 19. Was Adjt. of Sepoy Corps in 3rd Bde. in Mar. 1786; Lieut. 36th Bn. Sepoys in July 1787.

Refs.: Burke's *Landed Gentry*, 7th edn., p. 1491, *s.n.* Powell, of Clonshavoy, co. Limerick. *Alumni Dub.*

POWELL, William (*d.* 1766). Lieutenant, Infantry. Lieut. 6 Aug. 1765. *d.* in India 21 Dec. 1766.

Son of Capt. William Powell, H.M. 54th Ft.

Services: Ensign H.M. 54th Ft. 27 May 1763; reduced on h.p. with its 10th Coy. 1763. Apptd. in England an Ensign on the Bengal Est. 9 Nov. 1764; Lieut. 28 Dec. 1764; sailed in the *Pacific* 14 Apr. 1765.

POWNEY, Richard (1786-1864). Lieut. General, Artillery. (347) *b.* July 1786. Cadet 1804. Arrived in India 21 June 1806. Lieut. 7 May 1805. Capt. Lt. 23 Oct. 1811. Capt. 7 Oct. 1817. Major 25 Mar. 1826. Lt. Col. 3 Mar. 1835. Col. 12 July 1844. Col. Comdt. 22 July 1844. Maj. Gen. 20 June 1854. Lt. Gen. 21 Sept. 1859. *d.* in England 23 Dec. 1864.

Of Ockwells. *bapt.* Bray 14 Aug. 1786. 2nd son of Penyston

Powney, of Grovebury, Ives Place and Ockwells, M.P. for New Windsor 1780, 1788 and 1790, and Elizabeth his wife, dau. of Peter Flowyer, of Worcester. Woolwich Cadet; nominated to R.M.A. 13 Apr. 1802; obtained his certificate 31 Jan. 1805.
Services : Present at capture of Cape Jan. 1806 as a Cadet. Fur. u.p.a. via China 13 July 1813 till 21 July 1818. Comy. Ord. in charge of Delhi mag. 27 Feb. 1819 till 7 June 1824. In charge of gun carriage factory at Kasipur 18 June 1829. Offg. Dy. Principal Comy. Ord. 26 Dec. 1829. Offg. Town and Fort Major at Ft. Wm. 5 Dec. 1831 till 11 Sept. 1832. Gunpowder Agent at Ichapur 1 Sept. 1832 till 28 July 1835. Offg. Principal Comy. Ord. 19 Mar. till 22 Dec. 1835; permanent do. 13 Feb. 1838 till 18 Oct. 1844. Transfd. from 1st Bn. Foot Art. to 3rd Bde. H.A. 16 Dec. 1831; to 6th Bn. 1 Aug. 1835; to 7th Bn. 12 Apr. 1836; to 1st Bn. 23 Jan. 1838; to 3rd Bn. 30 Jan. 1844; to 6th Bn. 14 Aug. 1844. Posted Lt. Col. Comdt. to 7th Bn. 24 July 1845. Fur. 18 Feb. 1847 till death.
Refs. : *History of the Hundred of Bray*, p. 148. Boase. *G.M.* 1865, i. 386.

POWNEY, Robin (1731-1773). Ensign. Infantry. Subsequently Lieutenant Bombay Est. *b.* Madras 15 Feb. 1731. Country Cadet 1763. Ensign 26 Aug. 1763. Resigned 12 Oct. 1763. *d.* Anjengo, Travancore, 16 July 1773.
bapt. Madras 24 Mar. 1731. 11th son of John Powney, of Madras, a sea captain, and Mary his wife, dau. of Capt. George Heron, Madras pilot. Uncle of Rumbold Charles Powney, *q.v. m.* Anne.
Services : Permitted to proceed to India as a free merchant 9 Dec. 1762. Lieut. Bombay Est. 9 Oct. 1769.
Refs. : Family information. Intestate; admon. (Bombay) 31 Jan. 1774.

POWNEY, Rumbold Charles (1778-1800). Lieutenant, 15th N.I. *bapt.* Madras 16 July 1778. Cadet 1794. Arrived in India 27 Sept. 1795. Ensign 29 Sept. 1794. Lieut. 1 June 1796. *d.* in India 10 Aug. 1800.
4th son of Thomas Powney, of Madras, free merchant, and Catherine his wife, dau. of Quintan de la Metrie, a French merchant of Pondicherry. Nephew of Robin Powney, *q.v.*
Services : Apptd. Cadet 16 Apr. 1794; sailed for India in the *Nonsuch.*
Refs. : Burke's *Landed Gentry*, 13th edn., p. 1439, *s.n.* Powney, of Milden Hall, Suffolk. Family information.

POWNOLL, Philemon Devert (1794-?). Lieutenant. 26th N.I. *bapt.* E. Stonehouse, Devon, 23 Mar. 1794. Cadet 1811. Ensign 2 Jan. 1814. Lieut. 1 Feb. 1817. Cashiered by G.C.M. 25 Dec. 1821.

Son of Philemon Pownoll, late Capt. R.M., and Susan Paxton his wife. Ed. Plymouth Grammar School. Marlow and Woolwich Cadet.

Services : Posted Ensign to 2/26th N.I. Operations against the Bhattis of Hariana 1818 ; Lieut. 2/26th N.I. Cashiered for having sent a written challenge to fight a duel to P. P. Morgan, *q.v.*, on 13 Sept. 1821.

Refs.: Misc. Gen. et Her. 4S. iii. 45. *N. & Q.* clxxxviii. 273.

POWYS, Hon. Robert Vernon (1802-1854). Captain, Invalid Est. 12th N.I. *b.* 3 Dec. 1802. Cadet 1823. Arrived in India 10 Aug. 1824. Ensign 18 Feb. 1824. Lieut. 13 June 1825. Capt. 24 Aug. 1842. Invalided 1 Jan. 1846. *d.* Binsur, nr. Almora, U.P., 26 May 1854.

bapt. Lilford, Northants, 17 Jan. 1803. 2nd son of Thomas Powys, 2nd Baron Lilford, and Henrietta Maria his wife, eldest dau. of Robert Vernon Atherton, of Atherton Hall, Lancs. *m.* Koil, Aligarh, 14 Apr. 1825, Jane, 3rd dau. of William Beckett, *q.v.* (*See also* James Glencairn Burns.) (She died 10 Nov. 1842.)

Services : Posted Ensign to 12th N.I. ; Intr. & Qmr. do. 22 Sept. 1832 till Jan. 1836. Fur. p.a. 7 Jan. 1836 till 19 Dec. 1838. Offg. Intr. & Qmr. 58th N.I. 26 Jan. 1839 ; Intr. & Qmr. 12th N.I. 30 Nov. 1839 till 3 Dec. 1842 ; offg. Bde. Major in Oudh 15 Nov. 1842 till 1844. No record of active service.

Refs.: Burke's *Peerage*, 1923, p. 1398, *s.n.* Baron Lilford, of Lilford, Northants. *G.M.* 1854, ii. 313. Will dated Almora, 15 Feb. 1851 ; proved 7 Aug. 1854.

PRATT, John Backhouse (1784-1837). Major. 7th N.I. *bapt.* St. Nicholas, Durham, 11 June 1784. Cadet 1803. Arrived in India 27 Sept. 1804. Ensign 16 Sept. 1804. Lieut. 21 Sept. 1804. Capt. 1 Jan. 1819. Major 27 Apr. 1831. Retired 12 Dec. 1831. *d.* Harbledown, nr. Canterbury, 20 Nov. 1837.

Son of John Pratt, of Hurworth, co. Durham, and Mary Backhouse his wife. Cousin-german of Edward Barnes Backhouse, *q.v.*

Services : Ensign N. Riding Mil. 7 Apr. 1795 ; Lieut. do. 1801. Posted Lieut. to 4th N.I. in 1805. Operations in Bundelkhand 1809 ; Rajaoli ; Ajaigarh ; Lieut. 1/4th N.I. Actg. Adjt. 1/4th N.I. 1811-13 ; with 4th Gren. Bn. 1815 ; transfd. to 2/4th N.I. Fur. s.c. 22 Aug. 1816 till 16 Sept. 1819. Capt. 2/4th N.I. ; ordered to raise 500 recruits 26 Aug. 1823, and 16 Feb. 1824 ; transfd. to 7th N.I. (late 1/4th) May 1824. Apptd. D.J.A.G. on the Est. 21 Feb. 1825 ; posted to Cawnpore Div. 30 Mar. 1825. Leave s.c. 18 mos. to Mauritius and N.S.W. 2 May 1826. D.J.A.G. Sirhind Div. 31 Oct. 1827. Leave s.c. 18 mos. to Cape 16 Jan. 1830 till 23 Dec. 1831.

Refs. : G.M. 1837, ii. 658. M.I. St. Dunstan's church, Canterbury.

PRENDERGAST, William Grant (1815-1858). Bt. Lieut. Colonel, 8th L.C. *b.* Madras 24 June 1815. Cadet 1834. Arrived in India 13 Aug. 1835. Cornet (9 Feb. 1835) 13 Nov. 1835. Lieut. 24 July 1838. Capt. 19 May 1850. Bt. Major 20 May 1850. Bt. Lt. Col. 28 Nov. 1854. *d.* Alipore, Calcutta, 15 Sept. 1858, of cholera.

bapt. Madras 2 Aug. 1815. 4th son of Lt.-Gen. Sir Jeffrey Prendergast, Kt., Mily. Auditor Gen. Madras (who was 4th son of Thomas Prendergast, of Clonmell), and Elizabeth his wife, sister of James Dalrymple, *q.v. m.* Hove, Sussex, 30 Sept. 1857, Eliza, youngest dau. of John T. Hensley, of Harewood Pl., Hanover Sq., London. (She died Brighton 23 May 1894.) Ed. Charterhouse 1828-30. Trin. Coll., Camb. ; matric. 1833.

Services : Leave p.a. 6 mos. to Madras 31 Aug. 1835. d.d. 8th L.C. 20 Apr. 1836. Posted Cornet to 8th L.C. 11 Nov. 1836 ; Intr. & Qmr. do. 16 Jan. 1839 till 16 Oct. 1843. Bde. Qmr. to troops in Bundelkhand under Bdr. Young 25 Nov. 1842. Insurrection in Bundelkhand 1842-3 ; Lieut. 8th L.C. Fur. s.c. 16 Nov. 1843 till 1845. Second in comd. 16th Irreg. Cav. 24 Jan. till 24 Mar. 1846. Persian Intr. to C.-in-C. 23 Nov. 1846 till 18 May 1849. Second Sikh War ; Ramnagar ; Chilianwala ; Gujerat ; Lieut. 8th L.C., Persian Intr. to C.-in-C. (Medal with 2 clasps). Raised at Lahore 18 May 1849, 3rd Punjab Cav.,[1] and comdd. this Regt. for some years. Offg. Bdr., Punjab Irreg. Force, 1 Mar. 1854. Operations on N.W. frontier. Resumed comd. of 3rd Punjab Cav. 31 Jan. 1856. Fur. s.c. 20 Mar. 1856 till 1858.

Refs. : Foster's *Families of Royal Descent*, i. 250. *Charterhouse School List. G.M.* 1858, ii. 647. *The Times*, 3 Nov. 1858.

[1] *Note :* Late 23rd Cav., F.F. ; now 11th P.A.V.O. Cav. (F.F.)

PRESGRAVE, Duncan (1785-1841). Lieut. Colonel, 24th N.I. *b.* 30 Apr. 1785. Cadet 1803. Arrived in India 2 Dec. 1804. Ensign 16 Nov. 1804. Lieut. 16 Nov. 1804. Capt. 1 Aug. 1818. Major 8 Feb. 1828. Lt. Col. 4 Feb. 1833. *d.* Rondebosch, Cape Town, 11 July 1841.

bapt. Bourne, Lincs., 25 July 1785. Son of Edward Presgrave
and Ann his wife. Brother of Robert Presgrave, of the firm of
Presgrave & Co., Calcutta merchants. m. Saugor 18 Jan. 1831,
Susannah, widow of —— Leigh. (She died 9 June 1844.) His
ward m. William Phillips Bignell, q.v.

Services: Posted Lieut. to 26th N.I. in 1805. Operations in
Bundelkhand 1807; Sehlehuganj; Lieut. 1/26th N.I. Adjt.
Cawnpore Provl. Bn. 2 Jan. 1816 till 1818. Transfd. to 2/26th
N.I.; as Capt. to 1/26th N.I.; to 52nd N.I. (late 2/26th) May
1824. Assay Master, Saugor Mint, 10 Feb. 1820 till 23 Dec. 1835.
Constructed in 1828-30 the first iron suspension bridge in India,
over the Beas, 12 m. from Saugor. Posted as Lt. Col. to 18th N.I.
25 Oct. 1833; to Left Wing, Bengal Eur. Regt., 21 Dec. 1833.
Comdd. 1st N.I. 1 July 1836 till Feb. 1839. Supt. Kasipur foundry
5 Mar. 1839 till death. Transfd. to 66th N.I. 19 Feb. 1839 (? to
24th N.I. in 1841). Leave s.c. 2 yrs. to Cape and Aust. 9 Sept.
1840.

Refs.: *Life of Lt.-Col. John Haughton*, by Major A. C. Yate,
1900. Will dated 18 Jan. 1840; admon. 8 Feb. 1842. M.I. in
Cape Town cemetery.

PRESTON, D'Arcy (1803-1827). Lieutenant, 65th N.I. bapt.
Titchfield, Hants, 27 Mar. 1803. Cadet 1821. Ensign 26 Feb.
1822. Lieut. 13 May 1825. d. Barrackpore 20 Sept. 1827.

5th son of D'Arcy Preston, Adm. R.N., of Askham Bryan, Yorks.,
and Sophia his wife, 4th dau. of Sir George Nares, one of the judges
of the Common Pleas. Cousin-german of George Walter Adam
Nares, q.v. m. Calcutta 30 June 1827, Miss Jane Forrest, natural
dau. of William Forrest, q.v.

Services: Posted Ensign to 16th N.I.; transfd. to newly-raised
33rd N.I. July 1823; to 65th N.I. (late 1/33rd) May 1824. No
record of active service.

Refs.: Burke's *Landed Gentry*, 13th edn., p. 1443, s.n. Preston,
of Askham Bryan Hall, Yorks. Foster's *Families of Royal Descent*,
ii. 584. G.M. 1828, i. 285. A.J. xxv. 378.

PRESTON, George (1789-1822). Bt. Captain, 9th N.I. bapt.
Warcop, Westmorland, 19 Feb. 1789. Cadet 1806. Arrived in
India 25 Nov. 1807. Ensign 26 Oct. 1807. Lieut. 13 June 1812.
Bt. Capt. 14 Apr. 1822. d. Korge, Bengal, between Titalia and
Dinajpur, 17 Oct. 1822, of jungle fever.

2nd son of William Stephenson Preston, of Warcop Hall, Penrith,
and Sarah his wife, *née* Todd. Brother of Rev. William Michael

Stephenson Preston, rector of Warcop. *m.* St. Helena 24 Feb. 1813, Lydia Rachel, dau. of Thomas Adams. (She *re-m.* 27 Aug. 1824.)
Services: Barasat C.C. Posted Ensign to 9th N.I. in 1808. Operations in Hariana 1809; Bhawani; Ensign 1/9th N.I. Operations in Oudh 1809-10; Pragpur; Ensign 1/9th N.I. Fur. 1812-13. Bt. Capt. 1/9th N.I. Was actg. Adjt. Rangpur Local Bn. at time of his death.
Refs.: Burke's *Landed Gentry*, 15th edn., p. 1845, *s.n.* Preston (*now* Wild), of Warcop Hall. *G.M.* 1823, ii. 477. Will dated 3 Mar. 1813; proved 22 Feb. 1823.

PRESTON, Henry (*d.* 1791). Ensign, 6th Bengal Eur. Bn. Cadet 1783. Ensign 29 Jan. 1785. *d.* Dinapore 19 Feb. 1791. Of Wolborough, Devon. Brother of Capt. William Preston, Madras Est., and of Fitzgerald Preston, of Dublin.
Services: Apptd. Cadet 11 Feb. 1783; sailed for India in the *York* 11 Mar. 1783; landed at Madras 21 July. Second Mysore War 1783-4; joined Col. Pearse's detachment in Madras and accompanied it to Bengal in 1785. Unposted Ensign in July 1787 and Dec. 1788; posted to 6th Eur. Bn. 5 Feb. 1790.
Refs.: *Palk MSS.* (*Hist. MSS. Commn.* No. 74).

*PRESTON, James. Lieutenant. Infantry. Lieut. 23 Dec. 1766.
Services: N.F.P. (*Perhaps* identical with the next, although both are given in a MS. *A.L.* of 1 Feb. 1767.)
Refs.: *B.M. Addl. MS.* 6050, p. 90.

PRESTON, Thomas (*d.* 1768). Lieutenant, Infantry, 2nd Bde. Ensign 15 Aug. 1765. Lieut. 11 Dec. 1766. *d.* in India 5 Oct. 1768.
Son of Mary Preston, of Lancaster.
Services: Apptd. in England 28 Dec. 1764, Ensign on Bengal Est.; sailed in the *Falmouth* 10 May 1765; cast ashore east of Saugor sands at mouth of Ganges R. 13 June 1766.
Refs.: *B.M. Addl. MS.* 23,679, p. 3. Will dated 1 Oct. 1768; proved 12 Feb. 1771.

PRESTON, Thomas (*d.* 1807). Capt. Lieutenant, Engineers. Cadet 1782. Arrived in India 23 Sept. 1783. Ensign 3 Feb. 1785. Lieut. 14 Dec. 1796. Capt. Lt. 1806. *d. unm.* at sea 9 May 1807, on the voyage to England.

3rd son of Thomas Preston, of Beeston. Brother of Rev. George Preston, of Windham (? Wymondham), Norfolk, and cousin of Benjamin Booty.

Services: Apptd. Cadet for Inf. 5 Dec. 1782; sailed for India in the *Lord Macartney* 11 Mar. 1783. Transfd. as Cadet to Engrs. 6 Oct. 1783. Fur. 23 Feb. 1807.

Refs.: *G.M.* 1807, ii. 977. Will dated Calcutta 10 Feb. 1807; proved 15 Oct. 1807.

PRESTON, William (*d.* 1797). Captain, Infantry. Country Cadet 1772. Admitted 11 Oct. 1772. Ensign 11 Aug. 1776. Lieut. 27 July 1778. Capt. 7 Sept. 1793. *d.* Cawnpore 4 Oct. 1797.

m. Chunar 10 Nov. 1795, Miss Charlotte Hervey, late of Golden Sq., London. (She *re-m.* 20 May 1798, George Prager, of Serampore, merchant.)

Services: Apptd. Cadet 1 Oct. 1772. First Rohilla War; battle of St. George; Cadet in the Select Picket. Ensign 14th Bn. Sepoys in June 1778; apptd. Adjt. of Sepoys, 2nd Bde.; 17 July 1778. Bde. Major 2nd Bde. in 1781; reapptd. Bde. Major 2nd Bde. 12 June 1786; do. 5th Bde. in July 1787; do. at Cawnpore 1790 till death. Capt. 3rd Bengal Eur. Regt. in 1796.

Refs.: Macpherson, p. 364. *G.M.* 1796, i. 350.

PRESTON, William (1783-1803). Lieutenant, 15th N.I. *b.* Dublin 1783. Cadet 1798. Admitted 11 Sept. 1800. Ensign 26 Jan. 1800. Lieut. 11 Aug. 1800. *d.* Patparganj 11 Sept. 1803: kld. in action at the battle of Delhi.

bapt. Dublin *c.* 10 Nov. 1783. Younger son of William Preston, of Dublin, barr.-at-law (*D.N.B.*).

Services: " Well versed in the best Latin and Greek authors . . . originally designed for one of the learned professions; but an ardent mind, and the prospect of more rapid advancement, led him to the profession of arms." (*M.M.*) Posted Lieut. to 2/15th N.I. 15 Apr. 1801. Operations in Jumna Doab 1803; Sasni; Bijaigarh; Kachaura; Lieut. 2/15th N.I. Second Mahratta War; battle of Delhi (kld.); Lieut. 2/15th N.I.

Refs.: *M.M.* 1804, p. 404. *Pester*, p. 170. M.I. Patparganj.

PRICE, Francis Nicholas (1798-1821). Lieutenant, Artillery. (467) *b.* Dublin *c.* 1 June 1798, during the rebellion. Cadet 1816. Fireworker 25 Sept. 1817. Lieut. 1 Sept. 1818. *d.* Sujanpore, Nadia district, Bengal, 13 Jan. 1821.

THE BENGAL ARMY, 1758-1834 571

Son of a mily. officer. Ward of J. Nicholas Price. *m.* 2 Nov. 1819, Anna Helena, dau. of Henry Grace, *q.v.* (She *re-m.* 1838, William Nettleton Boyce, Lieut. R.N.) Addiscombe Cadet 1813-16. *Services :* With 6th Troop H.A. in 1819. No record of active service.

PRICE, Howell John Roderick (1757/58-1781). Lieutenant, Infantry. *b.* co. Hereford 1757/58. Cadet 1780. Ensign 1780. Lieut. 28 Jan. 1781. *d.* Ganjam, Madras, 28 Mar. 1781.

Services : Sailed for India in the *Earl of Dartmouth* 3 June 1780, aged 22. Second Mysore War 1781 ; with detachment under Col. T. D. Pearse, *q.v.*

PRICE, James (1757/58-1842). Lieut. General. Colonel 47th N.I. *b.* 1757/58. Country Cadet 1779. Admitted 21 May 1779. Ensign 1 Sept. 1779. Lieut. 19 Apr. 1781. Capt. 1 July 1798. Major 21 Sept. 1804. Lt. Col. 22 Feb. 1809. Col. 12 Aug. 1819. Maj. Gen. 22 July 1830. Lt. Gen. 23 Nov. 1841. *d.* 16 Queen's Sq., Bath, 3 Oct. 1842, aged 84.

(? Father of Mary, wife of James Oram Clarkson, *q.v.*, and grandfather of Louisa, wife of Edward Biddulph, *q.v.*)

Services : Lieut. 2nd Bn. Sepoys in July 1787 and in 1792. Capt. 5th N.I. With Invalid Tannah Ests. at Chittagong 1804-6 ; Regulating Ofr. do. 1806-12. Posted Lt. Col. to 20th N.I. 1809 ; 8th N.I. 1810 ; 25th N.I. 1813 ; 5th N.I. 1815 ; 2/21st N.I. 1815. (? Nepal War 1816 ; Lt. Col. comdg. 2/21st N.I.) Transfd. to 2/28th N.I. 1817. Third Mahratta War ; Dhamoni ; comdd. supporting column at siege of Mandala (*Lond. Gaz.* 7 Dec. 1818) ; Lt. Col. comdg. 6th Inf. Bde., 3rd Div. Transfd. to 22nd N.I. 1818. Posted Col. to 18th N.I. 1820. Apptd. to comd. of Rohilkhand with tempy. rank of Bdr. 6 Mar. 1820. Transfd. to 47th N.I. May 1824. On this Regt. mutinying Nov. 1824, he was transfd. to newly-raised 69th N.I. (became 47th in 1828). Apptd. to Gen. Staff with rank of Bdr. Gen. 24 Dec. 1824 ; to comd. Benares Div. 22 Jan. 1825 ; do. Dinapore 9 Feb. 1828. Tour on Staff expired 24 Dec. 1828. Fur. p.a. 31 Jan. 1829 till death.

Refs. : *Bath Chron.* 6 Oct. 1842. *G.M.* 1842, ii. 556. *The Times,* 8 Oct. 1842. Will dated Bath, 22 Apr. 1842 ; codicil dated 5 Aug. 1842 ; proved 1 Mar. 1843.

PRICE, James (1789-1826). Captain, 5th Extra Regt. *b.* Hatherop, Gloucs., 8 Feb. 1789. Cadet 1807. Arrived in India 14 Aug. 1808. Ensign 12 Sept. 1808. Lieut. 16 Dec. 1814. Capt. 13 May 1825. *d. unm.* Sulkea, Bengal, 22 Sept. 1826.

Son of Elizabeth Price. Brother of Joseph Price, of Fairford, Gloucs., merchant, and John Price, of Fairford, draper.
Services: Barasat C.C. Posted Ensign to 26th N.I. in 1809. Operations against the Bhattis of Hariana 1818 ; Lieut. 2/26th N.I. Supt. of salt *golahs* [1] at Sulkea 1822 till death. Transfd. to 51st N.I. (late 1/26th) May 1824 ; to newly-raised 5th Extra Regt. May 1825.
Refs.: A.J. xxiii. 529. Will dated 17 July 1824 ; proved 29 Sept. 1826.

[1] *Note:* i.e. store-houses.

PRICE, John (1731/32-1760). Lieutenant, Infantry. *b.* co. Montgomery 1731/32. Cadet (?) Ensign 30 Dec. 1757. Lieut. 30 Apr. 1759. *d.* Calcutta 2 Oct. 1760.
Services: Sailed for India in the *Calcutta* in 1759, aged 27.

PRICE, Robert (1813-1853). Captain, 67th N.I. *b.* London 13 July 1813. Cadet 1829. Arrived in India 1 June 1830. Ensign 23 Apr. 1830. Lieut. 15 Feb. 1836. Capt. 28 Feb. 1850. *d.* Donabyu, Burma, 4 Feb. 1853, of wounds received in action the same day.
bapt. London 13 Aug. 1813. 3rd son of Ralph Price, of Sydenham, merchant, and Charlotte Savery his wife, dau. of Thomas Carteret Hardy. *m.* 1st, Kyaukpyu, Arakan, 25 Aug. 1838, Ellen Anne, dau. of J. Robinson. (She died 24 Nov. 1838.) *m.* 2nd, Sultanpur, Benares, 29 Feb. 1840, Sophia Catharine, youngest dau. of Robert Lindsay Anstruther, *q.v.* (She died Allahabad 8 Oct. 1845, aged 23.) *m.* 3rd, Sydenham 16 May 1850, his cousin Harriet, 3rd dau. of Sir Charles Price, of Spring Grove, Richmond, 2nd Bart. (She died Sydenham 11 May 1880, aged 75.) Ed. Elizabeth Coll., Guernsey, 1826-8. Sandhurst Cadet.
Services: Cadet d.d. 13th N.I. 12 June 1830. Actg. Ensign (having been over 2 yrs. in India) 2 July 1832. Posted Ensign to 67th N.I. 20 Aug. 1833 ; Intr. & Qmr. 67th N.I. 10 Jan. 1840 till 17 Mar. 1841. Fur. p.a. 23 Feb. 1841 till 8 Aug. 1842. Actg. Intr. & Qmr. 18th N.I. 31 Aug. 1842 ; do. 37th N.I. 16 May 1843. Adjt. 67th N.I. 29 Jan. 1844 till 19 Jan. 1849. Fur. s.c. 23 Dec. 1848 till 25 Dec. 1851. Second Burma War 1852-3 ; Pegu 1852 ; repulse at Donabyu 4 Feb. 1853 (kld.) ; Capt. 67th N.I.
Refs.: Burke's *Peerage*, 1923, p. 1821, *s.n.* Rugge-Price, Bart., of Spring Grove, Surrey. *Howard & Crisp*, xv. 150, *s.n.* Price. *G.M.* 1853, i. 560.

THE BENGAL ARMY, 1758-1834 573

PRICE or PRYCE, Thomas (1738/39-1776). Lieutenant, Infantry. *b.* in Wales 1738/39. Bombay Cadet 1761. 2nd Lieut. (Bo.) 5 July 1762. 1st Lieut. (Bo.) 1 June 1765. Lieut. (Bengal) Oct. 1765. *d.* Chittagong 7 Oct. 1776.
m. Martha.
Services: Sailed for India in the *True Briton* 26 May 1761, aged 22. Served with the Bo. Detachment in the campaign in Bengal, 1764, under Major Hector Munro; transfd. to Bengal Army 1765. Resigned his Commission during the " Batta mutiny " May 1766 and returned to England; readmitted 1 Feb. 1774.

PRICE, Thomas Smith (1805-1866). Lieut. Colonel. 8th N.I. *b.* Richmond, Surrey, 11 Nov. 1805. Cadet 1823. Arrived in India 3 Sept. 1824. Ensign 13 Apr. 1824. Lieut. 2 Nov. 1825. Capt. 9 Mar. 1842. Bt. Major 11 Nov. 1851. Retired 25 Feb. 1852. Hon. Lt. Col. 28 Nov. 1854. *d.* at his residence nr. Bath 29 June 1866.
bapt. Richmond 6 Dec. 1805. Son of Thomas Price, Comdr. of *Lord Duncan* Indiaman, and Eliza his wife. Nephew of William Price, *q.v. m.* Walcot, Somerset, 24 July 1838, Mary, eldest dau. of R. Dickerson, of Kensington Pl., Bath. (She died Midnapore 18 Jan. 1842, of cholera, aged 23.)
Services: Posted Ensign to 8th N.I. Actg. Intr. & Qmr. 18th N.I. 7 June 1828; do. 1st Bengal Eur. Regt. 3 Sept. 1829; do. 10th N.I. 9 Nov. 1829; Intr. & Qmr. 8th N.I. 22 Oct. 1831 till Jan. 1836. Jodhpur demonstration 1834. Fur. s.c. 28 Jan. 1836 till 19 Jan. 1839. Intr. & Qmr. 8th N.I. 20 Nov. 1839 till 2 Oct. 1840. Offg. in Comst. Dept. at Barrackpore 1844-5; actg. D.J.A.G. June 1845. Second Sikh War; Multan; Gujerat; Capt. 8th N.I. (Medal with 2 clasps).
Refs.: G.M. 1866, ii. 275. *The Times,* 2 July 1866.

PRICE, William (1788-1888). Lieut. Colonel. 20th N.I. *b.* Kingston-upon-Thames 3 Sept. 1788. Cadet 1804. Arrived in India 6 Apr. 1806. Ensign 9 Mar. 1806. Lieut. 3 Feb. 1807. Capt. 11 July 1823. Major 22 Apr. 1831. Retired 20 May 1834. Hon. Lt. Col. 28 Nov. 1854. *d.* at his residence, Egerton House, Richmond, Surrey, 7 Feb. 1888, in his 100th year.
bapt. Kingston-upon-Thames 25 Sept. 1788. Son of Thomas Price and Anne his wife. Uncle of Thomas Smith Price, *q.v.*
Services: Barasat C.C. Posted Lieut. to 5th N.I. in 1807. Reduction of Kalinjar 1812; Lieut. 2/5th N.I. Transfd. to 1/5th N.I. 1816; to 2/5th N.I. 7 Jan. 1820; to 20th N.I. (late

2/5th) May 1824. Coll. of Fort William 1813-31 ; Asst. Professor of Sanskrit, Bengali, and Hindi 18 Dec. 1813 ; Examiner do. 23 July 1821 ; Professor of Hindi 12 Dec. 1823. Sec. to Hindu Coll. at Calcutta 27 Jan. 1826. Placed at disposal of C.-in-C. for regtl. duty 22 Aug. 1831. Fur. p.a. 17 Jan. 1832 till retirement.
Refs.: Boase. *The Times*, 9 Feb. 1888.

PRICE, William Phillips (1776-1844). Major General. Colonel 1st N.I. *bapt.* St. Martin's, Birmingham, 1 Jan. 1777. Cadet 1794. Arrived in India 3 Mar. 1796. Ensign 3 Nov. 1795. Lieut. 25 Apr. 1797. Capt. 15 Aug. 1806. Major 1 Apr. 1818. Lt. Col. 11 July 1823. Col. 5 June 1829. Maj. Gen. 28 June 1838. *d.* Triley Cottage, Abergavenny, 7 May 1844, aged 68.

Son of Rev. Thomas Price, headmaster of the Birmingham Free Grammar School 1775-97, and Ann his wife. *m.* (before 1834) (?)
Services: Apptd. Cadet 22 Apr. 1795 ; sailed for India in the *Berrington* 9 July 1795. Lieut. 5th N.I. ; Capt. Lt. 5th N.I. 21 Sept. 1804 ; Capt. 2/5th N.I. (? Reduction of Kalinjar 1812 ; Capt. 2/5th N.I.) Comdd. 6th Gren. Bn. 1815-16. Transfd. as Major to 1/5th N.I. in 1818. Operations in Kotah 1821 ; comdd. rt. column of attack on Mongrol (*Lond. Gaz.* 20 Mar. 1822). Posted Lt. Col. to 5th N.I. 1823 ; to 11th N.I. (late 1/5th) May 1824. Siege and capture of Bhurtpore ; Lt. Col. comdg. 11th N.I. Transfd. to 21st N.I. 29 Feb. 1828 ; as Lt. Col. Comdt. to 65th N.I. 22 Apr. 1828. Fur. p.a. 21 Jan. 1828 till death. Col. 65th N.I. 1829 ; 36th N.I. 1834 ; 1st N.I. 1839.
Refs.: G.M. 1844, i. 666. *The Times*, 11 May 1844.

*PRICE, ——. Lieutenant. Infantry. Cadet 1778. Never arrived in India. Ensign 14 Aug. 1779. Lieut. 6 Apr. 1781. Struck off ——.
Services: N.F.P.

PRICHARD, Richard (1786-1815). Lieutenant, 7th N.I. *bapt.* Brecon 28 July 1786. Cadet 1805. Arrived in India 11 Nov. 1806. Ensign 30 Sept. 1806. Lieut. 24 Oct. 1809. *d.* in England June 1815.

Son of Charles Prichard, apothecary, and Elizabeth his wife.
Services: Barasat C.C. Posted Ensign to 7th N.I. ; Lieut. 2/7th N.I. Fur. 8 Jan. 1811 till death. No record of active service.

PRIDEAUX, Sir John Wilmot, eighth baronet (1791-1833). Captain. 37th N.I. *b.* Farway, Devon, 29 Sept. 1791. Cadet

1808. Arrived in India 11 Mar. 1809. Ensign 9 Feb. 1809.
Lieut. 15 Nov. 1813. Capt. 13 May 1825. Retired 31 Mar.
1831. *d. unm.* Calcutta 13 May 1833.

8th Bart. of Netherton, Devon. *s.* 3 Mar. 1826. Elder son of
Sir John Wilmot Prideaux, 7th Bart., and Anne Phœbe his 2nd
wife, dau. of William Priddle, of Farway.

Services : Barasat C.C. Posted Ensign to 18th N.I. in 1810.
Nepal War 1816 ; Lieut. 1/18th N.I., in 1st Bde. Rt. Column.
Cuttack insurrection 1816 ; Khurda. Third Mahratta War ;
Jawad ; Lieut. 1/18th N.I. Actg. Adjt. Rt. Wing 1/18th N.I.
5 Oct. 1821 ; do. Left Wing 22 Oct. 1821. (? Operations in Jodhpur
1823 ; Lamba ; Lieut. 1/18th N.I.) Transfd. to 37th N.I. (late
2/18th) May 1824. Siege and capture of Bhurtpore ; Bt. Capt.
37th N.I. d.d. 53rd N.I. 12 Sept. 1829.

Refs. : Burke's *Peerage*, 1859, p. 822, *s.n.* Prideaux, Bart., of
Netherton, Devon. Vivian's *Visitation of Devon*, p. 623, *s.n.*
Prideaux of Solden and Netherton. *A.J.* N.S. xii. 191. *G.M.*
1833, ii. 478. M.I. Farway church, Devon.

PRINGLE, Andrew (*d.* 1803). Captain. 3rd Bengal Eur. Bn.
Cadet 1770. Ensign 22 Nov. 1771. Lieut. 5 Aug. 1776. Capt.
26 Feb. 1781. Resigned 17 Dec. 1792. *d.* Argyle St., London,
1803.

3rd and youngest son of Mark Pringle, of Crichton, Midlothian,
consul in Spain, and Veronica Rennie his 2nd wife. *m.* Cawnpore
5 June 1790, Cordelia Ann, 2nd dau. of John Fortnom, *q.v.* (*See
also* Samuel Cox.) (She died London 22 Nov. 1854, aged 82.)
Father of Robert Pringle, *q.v.*

Services : On survey in Cooch Behar under James Rennell, *q.v.*,
in 1777 ; to survey Rotas Nov. 1783. Capt. 3rd Bengal Eur.
Regt. in 1782 ; 1st Eur. Bn. in July 1787 ; 3rd do. in 1791. Became
a merchant at Lucknow after resigning the Service. Sailed from
Calcutta Jan. 1803.

Refs. : The Records of the Pringles, by Alex. Pringle (Edin., 1933),
pp. 177, 320. Burke's *Landed Gentry*, 4th edn., p. 1229, *s.n.* Pringle,
of Clifton and Haining. *S.M.* 1791, p. 100. Will dated Cawnpore
5 June 1790 ; codicil dated Lucknow July 1801 ; proved (P.C.C.)
7 Nov. 1803 ; proved Calcutta 20 Aug. 1804.

PRINGLE, David (1790-1876). Lieut. Colonel. 10th N.I. *b.*
Cranston, Midlothian, 21 Mar. 1790. Cadet 1805. Arrived in
India 19 Sept. 1806. Ensign 13 Oct. 1806. Lieut. 2 Jan. 1810.

Capt. 1 May 1824. Major 10 Jan. 1833. Retired 5 Mar. 1835. Hon. Lt. Col. 28 Nov. 1854. d. 16 May 1876.

Of Carriber, to which he s. 11 Mar. 1836. *bapt.* Cranston 30 Mar. 1790. Son of John Pringle, tenant in Pardovan (of the family of Pringle of Carriber), and Mary Walker his wife. His sister *m.* David Sherriff, *q.v.*

Services: Barasat C.C. Posted Ensign to 7th N.I. in 1807. Nepal War 1814-15; Lieut. 7th N.I., in 2nd Div. (India medal). Third Mahratta War; Lieut. 2/7th N.I. Adjt. Rampura Local Bn. 4 May 1818 till 4 Feb. 1822. Disturbances in Jhabua country, C.I., July 1821. On political duty in Nizam's service; Asst. to Capt. Spears, Madras Est., at Chikalda, Berar, 13 May 1822. Operations against the Bhils Apr. 1824. Transfd. to 10th N.I. (late 2/7th) May 1824. Placed at disposal of C.-in-C. 24 Sept. 1824. First Burma War; Arakan 1825; Capt. 2nd Gren. Bn. (clasp to India medal). Returned to his duties at Indore Oct. 1826. Fur. s.c. 8 Mar. 1829 till 29 Oct. 1832; leave p.a. 6 mos. to Madras 21 Aug. 1834.

Refs.: Annals of a Border Club, by George Tancred, p. 371.

PRINGLE, James (1746/47-1810). Major General. Colonel 11th N.I. *b.* 1746/47. Country Cadet 1769. Admitted 16 Aug. 1769. Ensign 10 Oct. 1769. Lieut. 1 Apr. 1773. Capt. 28 Jan. 1781. Major 1 Mar. 1794. Lt. Col. 30 Oct. 1797. Col. 16 Nov. 1802. Maj. Gen. 25 Oct. 1809. *d.* The Circus, Bath, 20 May 1810, aged 63; *bur.* Bath Abbey 29 May.

3rd and youngest son of Robert Pringle, Lord Edgefield, of the Court of Session (who was grandson of Sir Robert Pringle, 1st Bart., of Stichill), and Elizabeth his wife, dau. of Sir John Clerk, of Penicuik. *m.* Edinburgh 5 Apr. 1800, Sholto Charlotte, 7th and youngest dau. of Sir John Wedderburn Halkett, of Pitfirrane, 4th Bart., and niece of Henry Wedderburn, *q.v.* (She *re-m.* 1818, Stewart Boone Inglis and died 8 Oct. 1853, aged 79.) His dau. *m.* John Nicholas O'Halloran, *q.v.*

Services: First Rohilla War 1774. Leave s.c. to sea 12 May 1781. Capt. 1st Eur. Bn. in July 1787; D.J.A.G. Chunar and Dinapore in Dec. 1788; actg. D.Q.M.G. in 1790; D.Q.M.G. (with annexed rank of Major) 24 Oct. 1792. Fur. 22 Jan. 1798 till 8 Dec. 1802. Lt. Col. 13th N.I. Q.M.G. Bengal 1803-4. Posted Col. to 11th N.I. 1803. Fur. 4 Mar. 1804 till death.

Refs.: Records of the Pringles, p. 316. Burke's *Peerage*, 1904, p. 725, *s.n.* Halkett, Bart., of Pitfirrane, co. Fife. *The Wedderburn Book*, i. 389. *G.M.* 1800, i. 589; 1810, i. 594. M.I. Bath Abbey.

THE BENGAL ARMY, 1758-1834 577

PRINGLE, Robert (1791-1824). Bt. Captain, 18th N.I. Comdt. Magh Levy. *b.* Cawnpore 21 Sept. 1791. Cadet 1806. Arrived in India 1 Aug. 1807. Ensign 11 Aug. 1807. Lieut. 8 Aug. 1812. Bt. Capt. 5 Feb. 1822. *d.* Ramu, Burma, 16 May 1824 : kld. in action.
bapt. Cawnpore 1 Nov. 1791. Son of Andrew Pringle, *q.v.*, and Cordelia Ann his wife.
Services: Barasat C.C. Posted Ensign to 6th N.I. in 1808. Adjt. 6th Vol. Bn. Nov. 1811 till 1816. Capture of Java 1811 ; Ensign 6th Vol. Bn. Lieut. 1/6th N.I. Served with Pioneers 1817-24. (? Third Mahratta War ; Lieut. Pioneers.) Transfd. to 18th N.I. (late 2/6th) May 1824. First Burma War ; Ramu (kld.) ; Comdt. Magh Levy.

PRINSEP, John (1746-1830). Cadet. Infantry. Afterwards a merchant in London. *b.* Tamworth 23 Apr. 1746. Cadet 1771. Resigned 26 Nov. 1771. *d.* London 30 Nov. 1830.
Of Thoby Park, Essex. Only son who survived infancy of Rev. John Prinsep, rector of Bicester, and Sarah his wife, dau. of John Bossum, bursar of Balliol, Oxon. *m.* Calcutta 22 Jan. 1782, Sophie Elizabeth, dau. of James Auriol (who was son of Jean Louis Auriol, of Geneva, who settled in London) and Charlotte Russell his wife, of the family of the Duke of Bedford. (She died 6 Gt. Cumberland St., London, 21 Feb. 1850, aged 90.) Father of Thomas Prinsep, *q.v.*, and of Charles Robert Prinsep, Advocate Gen. Bengal (*D.N.B.*).
Services: " Was regularly bred to the profession of a cloth merchant in the City of London, . . . In 1769, he received the thanks of a committee of directors appointed to examine his information relative to the improvement of the Coy.'s fabrics." (*Cal. Review*). Never joined the Army. Sailed for India as a Cadet in the *Rochford* 2 Apr. 1771. Apptd. an alderman of the mayor's court, Calcutta, 1773 ; Asst. Supt. of Investments 1778-85. Introduced the cultivation and manufacture of indigo into Bengal at a factory at Nilganj, nr. Barasat, 1779. Opened a copper mint at Palta, nr. Barrackpore, under the authority of Govt. in 1780, and contracted with Govt. for the supply of the first copper coinage ever struck in Bengal. This mint he conducted till 1784, when he surrendered it to Govt. for an indemnity. Left India in 1788. M.P. for Queensborough 1802-6 ; Alderman of the city of London 1804-9 ; high bailiff of Southwark 1817-24. Was one of the founders of the Westminster Life Insurance Society.
Refs.: D.I.B. *Notices généal. sur les familles genevoises*, par

Galiffe, tome iv. (1857), f. 27, *s.n.* Auriol. *Personal Reminiscences of Augusta Becher, 1830-1888*, ed. by H. G. Rawlinson. *B. : P.P.* No. 52, p. 154. *I.M.* 25 Sept. 1845, p. 570. Will dated London 2 Mar. 1826 ; proved (Bombay) 11 Nov. 1834.

PRINSEP, Thomas (1800-1830). Captain, Engineers. *b.* London 15 Sept. 1800. Cadet 1818. Ensign (?) Lieut. 5 Sept. 1823. Capt. 28 Sept. 1827. *d.* Calcutta 24 Jan. 1830, in consequence of a fall from his horse.

bapt. St. Peter's, Cornhill, 17 Oct. 1800. 8th son of John Prinsep, of Gt. Cumberland St., London, *q.v. m.* Calcutta 18 Feb. 1829, Lucy Anne, 2nd dau. of Robert Campbell, of Calcutta, and sister of James Hunter Campbell, *q.v.* (She died 13 Mar. 1891, aged 83.) Addiscombe Cadet 1816-19.

Services: Surveyor with Comrs. in the Sundarbans 1821-4 ; to proceed to Chittagong under orders of Bdr. Morrison 30 Dec. 1824. First Burma War ; Arakan 1825. At Chittagong till 1826. Supt. of canals, with a salary of Rs. 1,000 *p.m.*, exclusive of his mily. pay, 30 Oct. 1826 till death.

Refs. : Family information. *A.J.* xxviii. 113 ; N.S. ii. 160. *G.M.* 1830, i. 651. M.I. in S. Park St. cemetery, Calcutta.

PRIOR, Charles (1807-1881). General. Comdt. 1st Goorkha Regt., now 1st King George's Own Gurkha Rifles (The Malaun Regt.). *b.* Plymouth 17 June 1807. Cadet 1823. Ensign 13 Apr. 1824. Lieut. 13 May 1825. Capt. 17 Jan. 1841. Major 10 July 1857. Lt. Col. 25 Apr. 1858. Col. 10 June 1862. Maj. Gen. 6 Mar. 1868. Lt. Gen. 8 Feb. 1877. Gen. 20 Aug. 1878. Retired 1 Oct. 1877. *d.* Jullundur 21 Apr. 1881.

bapt. Plymouth 10 Feb. 1808. Son of John Harris Prior, of Chippenham, Wilts., solicitor, and Elizabeth Bridget Minifie his wife. *m.* Dinapore 18 Nov. 1833, Charlotte Denham, youngest dau. of Charles William Hamilton, *q.v.* (*See also* T. V. Lysaght.)

Services: Posted Ensign to 64th N.I. Oct. 1824. Adjt. 64th N.I. 12 Mar. 1829 till 26 Mar. 1840. First Afghan War 1842 ; operations under Bdr. Wild ; retreat from Ali Masjid in Jan. ; forcing of Khyber ; relief of Jalalabad in Apr. ; Capt. 64th N.I., with Gen. Pollock's force (Medal). Returned to India on sick leave June 1842. Against Hill tribes in Sind 1845 ; Capt. 64th N.I. Offg. in Comst. Dept. Dec. 1845 till Oct. 1847. A.D.C. to his father-in-law, Maj.-Gen. C. W. Hamilton, *q.v.*, comdg. Saugor Div., 1 Oct. 1847 till Mar. 1852. Offg. D.A.A.G. Lahore Div. Dec. 1852 ; permanent do. 24 Mar. 1854 ; A.A.G. Lahore 27 June 1856

THE BENGAL ARMY, 1758-1834   579

till Aug. 1857, but continued to officiate in that appt. till Jan. 1859.
Fur. p.a. Mar. 1859 till Dec. 1860. Apptd. to comd. 1st Gurkha
L.I. (now 1st K.G.O. Gurkha Rifles) Nov. 1861 ; Comdt. do. 1 Jan.
1864 till Aug. 1868. Bhutan expedn. 1865 ; comdg. 1st Gurkha L.I.
(Medal with clasp). After vacating comd. of his Regt. he resided
continuously in India.
Refs. : Boase. De Rhé-Philipe. M.I. in Art. cemetery at
Jullundur.

PRITCHARD, James (*d.* 1796). Lieutenant, Infantry. Country
Cadet 1781. Admitted 10 May 1781. Ensign 22 Sept. 1781.
Lieut. 26 June 1783. *d.* Cawnpore 27 Feb. 1796.
Services : Lieut. 4th Bn. Sepoys in July 1787, and in 1792.

PROBIN, James. Cadet. Infantry. Cadet 1768. Resigned
1768.
Services : N.F.P.

PROCTOR, Richard (1806-1824). Ensign, Infantry. Unposted.
b. Cawnpore 24 Jan. 1806. Cadet 1823. Never arrived in India.
Ensign 4 May 1824. *d.* at sea 8 Aug. 1824, on board the *Lord
Amherst* on the voyage to India.
bapt. Cawnpore 4 Apr. 1807. Son of George Proctor, Surg.
8th Light Dgns., and Elizabeth Anne his wife. Sandhurst Cadet.

PROLE, George (1756/57-1835). Lieut. General. Colonel 14th
N.I. *b.* 1756/57.[1] Cadet 1776. Arrived in India 12 Sept. 1776.
Ensign 12 Mar. 1777. Lieut. 9 Aug. 1778. Capt. 28 Oct. 1794.
Major 14 July 1799. Lt. Col. 30 June 1802. Col. 4 June 1811.
Maj. Gen. 4 June 1814. Lt. Gen. 22 July 1830. *d.* Cheltenham
6 Aug. 1835.
Of Belle Vue, Clifton, formerly of Spa, nr. Gloucester. *m.*
Calcutta 16 Mar. 1800, Miss Lydia Whish. Father of George
Newton Prole, *q.v.*, and of William Sandys Prole, *q.v.*
Services : Apptd. Cadet 10 Nov. 1775 ; sailed for India in the
Shrewsbury 14 Mar. 1776. Served for 8 mos. in the Select Picket.
First Mahratta War 1778-84 ; siege of Ahmedabad Feb. 1780 (s.w.) ;
retreat down the Bhor Ghaut Apr. 1781 (w.) ; Lieut. with Gen.
Goddard ; latterly as Paymr. to the Bombay detachment. Apptd.
Sub-Sec. Mily. Dept. of Inspection 2 Aug. 1786 ; Lieut. 3rd Bn.
Sepoys in Dec. 1788. Transfd. from 5th Eur. Bn. to 28th Bn.
Sepoys 25 Feb. 1790. Third Mysore War 1790-2 ; Lieut. 28th Bn.,
with Col. Cockerell's detachment. Second Rohilla War ; battle

of Bitaurah. Posted Capt. to 2nd Eur. Bn. 28 Nov. 1794; 1st
N.I. in 1798. Fur. p.a. 18 Jan. 1796 till 23 Dec. 1798. Second
Mahratta War 1803-5; operations in Bundelkhand under Lt.-Col.
Gabriel Martindell, *q.v.*; Lt. Col. 1/1st N.I. Col. 1st N.I. Comdd.
Delhi and Rewari frontier 27 Feb. 1813 till Nov. 1814. Fur. p.a.
2 Jan. 1815 till death. Transfd. to 4th N.I. (late 2/1st) May 1824;
to 46th N.I. 10 Sept. 1828; to 14th N.I. 22 July 1833.

Refs.: *E.I.M.C.* iii. 209-11. *Bath Chron.* 20 Aug. 1835. *G.M.*
1836, i. 202.

[1] *Note:* Aged 62 in Aug. 1819.

PROLE, George Newton (1801-1839). Major, 3rd N.I. *b.*
Calcutta 8 June 1801. Cadet 1818. Admitted 26 June 1819.
Ensign 6 Feb. 1819. Lieut. 14 June 1820. Capt. 11 Oct. 1827.
Major 8 July 1839. *d.* at sea off Kedgeree 15 Sept. 1839, on
board the *Larkins*, on his passage to the Cape.

bapt. Calcutta 5 July 1801. Elder son of George Prole, *q.v.*,
and Lydia his wife. Brother of William Sandys Prole, *q.v. m.*
Cawnpore 7 Nov. 1826, Margaret Tierney, dau. of Benjamin
Fergusson, and sister of John Tierney Fergusson, *q.v.* (*See also*
John Lealand Mowatt.) Addiscombe Cadet 1817-18.

Services: Ensign d.d. 13th N.I. 1820. Posted Lieut. to 2/6th
N.I. 21 Nov. 1820. Transfd. to 3rd N.I. (late 1/6th) May 1824.
First Burma War; Arakan 1825; with 26th N.I. Actg. Adjt.
Left Wing 3rd N.I. 23 Sept. 1825; actg. Intr. & Qmr. do. 27 Aug.
1826. Fur. p.a. 7 Feb. 1832 till 2 Dec. 1834. Leave s.c. 2 yrs.
to Cape 12 Aug. 1839.

Refs.: *G.M.* 1840, i. 110.

PROLE, William Sandys (1802-1846). Captain, 37th N.I.
b. Calcutta 14 Nov. 1802. Cadet 1818. Admitted 26 June
1819. Ensign 6 Feb. 1819. Lieut. 12 July 1820. Capt. 4 Apr.
1832. *d.* Nasirabad 27 June 1846.

bapt. Calcutta 23 Jan. 1803. Younger son of George Prole,
q.v., and Lydia his wife. Brother of George Newton Prole, *q.v.*
m. Stainton, nr. Milford, 3 Mar. 1835, Harriet, youngest dau. of
William Dobbin, Capt. R.N., of Milford. Addiscombe Cadet
1817-18.

Services: Ensign d.d. 13th N.I. 1820; d.d. 2/19th N.I. Nov.
1820. Posted Lieut. to 2/18th N.I. 21 Nov. 1820. Actg. Intr.
& Qmr. do. 21 Oct. 1823. Transfd. to 36th N.I. (late 1/18th)
May 1824; to 37th N.I. 31 Mar. 1825. Siege and capture of
Bhurtpore; Lieut. 37th N.I. Fur. p.a. 10 Sept. 1832 till 5 Oct.

1835. First Afghan War 1838-40 ; action in Khyber Pass 19 Nov. 1839 (s.w.) ; Capt. 37th N.I. Granted a gratuity of 6 mos. pay for wound. d.d. 33rd N.I. at Meerut 11 Nov. 1841 ; d.d. 3rd Inf. Levy at Delhi 11 Feb. 1842 till 1 Mar. 1843, when it was broken up. Fort Adjt. Allahabad 17 Nov. 1843 till Oct. 1845, when he rejoined his Regt. at Nasirabad.
Refs. : *A.J.* N.S. xvi. 303. M.I. Nasirabad.

PRYCE, Edward (1788-1832). Captain. Artillery. (350) *bapt.* W. Ham, Essex, 7 May 1788. Cadet 1804. Arrived in India 12 July 1805. Lieut. 10 May 1805. Capt. Lt. 26 Mar. 1813. Capt. 1 Sept. 1818. Retired 12 Dec. 1821. *d.* Grenada Pl., Old Kent Rd., London, 14 Feb. 1832, aged 44.

Son of Josiah Pryce, late E.I.C.S., and Catherine his wife. Brother of Elias Bird Pryce, *q.v.* Art. Cadet at Marlow 27 Apr. 1803 till 11 Jan. 1805.

Services : Operations against Dhundia Khan 1807 ; Komona ; Ganauri ; Lieut. 3rd Coy. 1st Bn. Art., d.d. from 2nd Coy. 2nd Bn. Settlement of Hariana 1809 ; Bhawani ; Lieut. 3rd Bn. Reduction of Kalinjar 1812. Siege and capture of Hathras 1817 ; Capt. Lt. comdg. 4th Coy. 2nd Bn. Third Mahratta War ; Capt. 4th Coy. 2nd Bn.

Refs. : *G.M.* 1832, i. 185.

PRYCE, Elias Bird (1791-1825). Captain, 52nd N.I. *bapt.* W. Ham, Essex, 14 Jan. 1791. Cadet 1807. Arrived in India 28 Oct. 1808. Ensign 11 Feb. 1807. Lieut. 27 Apr. 1809. Capt. 1 May 1824. *d.* Dacca 24 Oct. 1825.

Son of Josiah Pryce, late E.I.C.S., and Catherine his wife. Brother of Edward Pryce, *q.v.* Marlow Cadet.

Services : Posted to 2/26th N.I. in 1808. (? Operations in Bundelkhand 1808-10 ; Hirapur ; Rajaoli ; Ajaigarh ; Lieut. 2/26th N.I.) With 6th Gren. Bn. 1815-16. Operations against the Bhattis of Hariana 1818 ; Lieut. 2/26th N.I. Fur. 1822-3. Transfd. to 52nd N.I. (late 2/26th) May 1824. (? First Burma War ; Cachar 1825 ; Capt. 52nd N.I.)

Refs. : Will undated ; proved 10 Nov. 1825. M.I. Dacca.

PRYOR, William (*d.* 1805). Captain, 22nd N.I. Cadet 1783. Arrived in India 17 Sept. 1783. Ensign 1 Feb. 1785. Lieut. 13 Nov. 1791. Capt. 5 Mar. 1804. *d.* Agra 4 Sept. 1805, of fever.

Services : Apptd. Cadet 11 Dec. 1782 ; sailed for India in the

Barwell 11 Mar. 1783. Supy. Ensign, unposted, in July 1787; posted to 2nd Bengal Eur. Bn. 5 Feb. 1790; Lieut. 1st Eur. Regt. in 1796. Bt. Capt. 1st N.I.; transfd. as Capt. Lt. to newly-raised 2/22nd N.I. 22 Dec. 1803. Second Mahratta War; battle and capture of Deig; Bhurtpore; Capt. comdg. 2/22nd N.I.
Refs.: Pester, p. 428.

PRYOR, William Springham (*d.* 1831). Major. 21st N.I. Country Cadet 1781. Admitted 15 Oct. 1781. Ensign, 15 July 1782. Lieut. 12 Jan. 1785. Capt. 13 July 1803. Major 2 Feb. 1809. Retired 15 Mar. 1814. *d.* at his house in Regency Sq., Brighton, 5 May 1831.

m. Clifton, Gloucs., July 1815, Catherine, dau. of Rev. Anthony Starling, of Waterford.

Services: Posted to 1st Bengal Eur. Regt. Aug. 1782. Adjt. 17th Bn. Sepoys in July 1787; Adjt. & Qmr. 6th Bde. Sepoys in Dec. 1788 and in Mar. 1793. Lieut. 6th N.I. in 1798; Capt. Lt. 6th N.I.; transfd. as Capt. to newly-raised 1/21st N.I. July 1803. Fort Adjt. & Qmr. at Chunar 14 Aug. 1798 till 1809. Fur. 1811 till retirement.

Refs.: A.J. N.S. v. 118. G.M. 1831, i. 477.

PUDNER, John (1760/61-1836). Captain. 6th N.I. Subsequently Paymr. H.E.I.C. Depot at Chatham. *b.* London 1760/61. Cadet 1796. Was already in India when apptd. Cadet. Ensign 22 Oct. 1797. Lieut. 10 Sept. 1798. Capt. 11 July 1805. Retired 23 June 1809. *d.* at his residence, New Rd., Rochester, 19 Sept. 1836, aged 75.

m. Cawnpore 21 June 1801, Elizabeth, dau. of George Birch, of Sheiksarai. (She died Kensington 3 Jan. 1852, aged 70.)

Services: Conductor of Ord. in 1785; apptd. Dy. Comy. of Ord. 4 Nov. 1793; Dy. Comy. of Ord. at Allahabad 25 Nov. 1793 till 1806, with the exception of a short period (1796-7) at Ft. Marlbro'. Fur. 22 Sept. 1806 till retirement. Employed on H.E.I.C. recruiting service in the London and afterwards the Manchester district; subsequently (1821 till death) Paymr. at H.E.I.C. depot at Chatham.

Refs.: A.J. N.S. xxi. 121.

PUGH, James (1740/41-1797). Captain, 8th N.I. *b.* 1740/41. Country Cadet 1779. Ensign 31 Aug. 1779. Lieut. 18 Apr. 1781. Capt. 7 Jan. 1796. *d.* Chunar 16 Apr. 1797, aged 56.

Brother of Margaret Pugh, of Bie St., Hereford.

Services: Apptd. Cadet 19 Aug. 1779. Lieut. 20th Bn. Sepoys

THE BENGAL ARMY, 1758-1834 583

in July 1787 and in Dec. 1790 ; Adjt. 33rd Bn. in Mar. 1793 ; Capt. 2/8th N.I. at death.
Refs.: M.I. Chunar (Shamspur) old cemetery. Will dated 12 Sept. 1796 ; proved 19 July 1797.

PULLER, Henry (1782-1813). Lieutenant. Infantry. Subsequently B.C.S. *b.* 15 Apr. 1782. Cadet 1798. Admitted 23 Oct. 1800. Ensign 7 Dec. 1799. Lieut. 29 May 1800. Transfd. as Writer to B.C.S. 21 Aug. 1801. *d.* Rangpur, Bengal, 15 Nov. 1813.
bapt. St. Peter le Poor, London, 11 May 1782. Son of Richard Puller, of London, and Selina his wife, dau. of Thomas Wall, of Albury Park, Surrey. Brother of Sir Christopher Puller, Kt., C.J. Bengal *(D.N.B.).*
Services: Admitted to Coll. of Ft. Wm. Dec. 1801. Judge and mgte. at Rangpur 1 Feb. 1813.
Refs.: Burke's *Landed Gentry,* 13th edn., p. 1458, *s.n.* Giles-Puller, of Youngsbury, Herts. M.I. at Rangpur.

PURCELL, Theobald (*d.* 1791). Lieutenant, 6th Bn. Sepoys. Country Cadet 1780. Ensign 12 Feb. 1781. Lieut. 10 Oct. 1781. *d.* Jogi-Ghopa, Assam, 14 June 1791 : kld. by dacoits.
m. (before 1788) Rachel.
Services: Apptd. a Gent. Vol. in the Coy. of Art. 3 Apr. 1780 ; given a Cadetship for his services in procuring recruits in England for the Coy. Second Mysore War 1781-4 ; Lieut. 24th Bn. Sepoys. Lieut. 6th Bn. Sepoys in July 1787.

PUREFOY, William Albert (*d.* 1825). Ensign. Infantry. Subsequently Capt. h.p. 79th Ft. Cadet 1783. Arrived in India 5 July 1784. Ensign 5 Feb. 1785. Transfd. to H.M.S. 1789. *d.* Walworth 21 Aug. 1825.
Eldest son of James Purefoy, of Woodfield, co. Galway, and Jane his wife, dau. of Thomas Burrowes, of Stradone, co. Cavan.
Services: Apptd. Cadet 28 Nov. 1783 ; sailed for India in the *Foulis* 27 Dec. 1783. Fur. s.c. on his staff pay 5 Dec. 1785 till Oct. 1788. Transfd. to H.M.S. Ensign 76th Ft. 8 Nov. 1788 ; Lieut. 36th Ft. 24 Oct. 1789 ; Addl. Capt. 46th Ft. (13 Nov. 1799) 5 May 1800 ; Capt. h.p. 79th Ft. 9 July 1803 till death. Wounded at siege of Bangalore Mar. 1791.

PURVIS, Barrington (1792-1822). Lieutenant, 13th N.I. *b.* Beccles, Suffolk, 21 Mar. 1792. Cadet 1808. Arrived in India

27 Oct. 1809. Ensign 19 May 1810. Lieut. 15 Dec. 1814. d. in England 28 Mar. 1822.

bapt. Beccles 22 Mar. 1792. Of Porter's Hall, Essex. 4th and youngest son of Richard Purvis, of Porter's Hall, Essex, and Bockenden Grange, co. Warwick, Post Capt. R.N. (who was cousin-german of T. D. Pearse, *q.v.*), and Lucy his wife, dau. of Rev. John Leman, rector of Wenhaston, Suffolk. Brother of George Thomas Purvis and cousin-german of Richard Fortescue Purvis, *qq.v.* *m.* 11 Sept. 1820, Amy Letitia, eldest dau. of Rev. Nathaniel Colvile, rector of Lawshall. (She died Hawkesley Park, Essex, 9 Apr. 1850.)

Services : Barasat C.C. Posted Ensign to 13th N.I. in 1810. Lieut. 2/13th N.I. ; transfd. to 1/13th N.I. after 1817. Fur. 1820 till death. No record of active service.

Refs. : Burke's *Landed Gentry*, 7th edn., p. 1515, *s.n.* Purvis, of Darsham, Suffolk.

PURVIS, George Thomas (1789-1819). Bt. Captain, 4th N.I. *b.* Beccles, Suffolk, 7 Nov. 1789. Cadet 1804. Arrived in India 10 Sept. 1805. Ensign 7 May 1805. Lieut. 8 May 1805. Bt. Capt. 8 Jan. 1818. *d. unm.* at sea 28 Apr. 1819, on board the *Sovereign*, on his passage to England.

bapt. Beccles 7 Nov. 1789. 3rd son of Richard Purvis, Post Capt. R.N., and Lucy his wife. Brother of John Leman Purvis, *q.v.* Marlow Cadet.

Services : Posted Lieut. to 1/4th N.I. in 1806. (? Operations in Bundelkhand 1809 ; Rajaoli ; Ajaigarh ; Lieut. 1/4th N.I.) Nepal War 1815 ; operations in Kumaon ; Sitauli ; capture of Almora ; Lieut. 1/4th N.I. Adjt. Saharanpur Provl. Bn. 11 Jan. 1816 till 1819. Fur. s.c. 1819.

Refs. : Burke's *Landed Gentry*, 7th edn., p. 1515, *s.n.* Purvis, of Darsham, Suffolk.

PURVIS, John Leman (1786-1805). Lieutenant, 15th N.I. *b.* Beccles 1 Mar. 1786. Cadet 1802. Arrived in India 16 Oct. 1803. Ensign 12 Sept. 1803. Lieut. 28 June 1804. *d. unm.* Rampura, C.I., 17 Mar. 1805.

bapt. Beccles 4 Mar. 1786. 2nd son of Richard Purvis, Post Capt. R.N., and Lucy his wife. Brother of Barrington Purvis, *q.v.*

Services : Second Mahratta War ; with Col. Monson's force 1804 ; operations in Rampura district 1805 ; capture of Khataoli (w.) ; Lieut. 15th N.I., with detachment under Capt. Charles Hutchinson, *q.v.* Fort Adjt. of Rampura.

THE BENGAL ARMY, 1758-1834

Refs.: Burke's *Landed Gentry*, 7th edn., p. 1515, *s.n.* Purvis, of Darsham, Suffolk. *Stubbs,* i. 237. Intestate ; admon. 14 May 1805.

PURVIS, Richard Fortescue (1789-1868). Captain. 30th N.I. Subsequently rector of Whitsbury, Hants. *b.* Wickham, Hants, 4 Jan. 1789. Cadet 1803. Arrived in India 31 Aug. 1804. Ensign 18 Aug. 1804. Lieut. 21 Sept. 1804. Bt. Capt. 1 Jan. 1818. Capt. 1820. Retired 31 May 1820. *d.* at the Rectory, Whitsbury, 27 May 1868.

B.C.L., J.P. *bapt.* Wickham 5 Mar. 1789. 2nd son of John Child Purvis, of Vicar's Hill House, Hants, Adm. R.N., and Catherine his 1st wife, only dau. of John Sowers, Clerk of the Cheque of H.M. Dockyard, Deptford. Cousin-german of Barrington Purvis, *q.v. m.* 19 Jan. 1824, Elizabeth Helen, eldest dau. of Rev. Thomas Baker, of Little Cressingham, Norfolk, rector of Rollesby. (*See also* James Cock.) Ed. R.N. Coll., Portsmouth. Jesus Coll., Camb. ; 1st Cl. Law Tripos 1821-2 ; LL.B. 1825.

Services : Posted Lieut. to 21st N.I. in 1805. (? Operations in Bundelkhand 1809-12 ; Lieut. 2/21st N.I.) Intr. & Qmr. 2/21st N.I. 1 July 1814. Transfd. to newly-raised 1/30th N.I. 1815 ; Intr. & Qmr. do. 4 May 1815 till 1818. Nepal War 1816 ; Makwanpur ; Lieut. 1/30th N.I., in 4th Bde. Centre Column (India medal). Fur. 1818 till retirement. Took holy orders ; Deacon 1820 ; Priest 1821. Vicar of Whitsbury 10 Mar. 1824 till death. Domestic chaplain to Earl of Limerick 1846.

Refs.: Burke's *Landed Gentry*, 7th edn., p. 1515, *s.n.* Purvis, of Darsham, Suffolk. *Walford. Graduati Cantab. The Times,* 2 June 1868.

PYEFINCH, Herbert (1765-1793). Lieutenant, 12th Bn. Sepoys. *b.* 4 July 1765. Country Cadet 1781. Admitted June 1781. Ensign 2 July 1782. Lieut. 2 Jan. 1785. *d.* Cawnpore 16 Nov. 1793 : kld. in a duel.

(*Probably* son of Herbert Pyefinch [1] and Sarah his wife, dau. of Mrs. Sophia Aratoon.) Ed. Merchant Taylors' Sept. 1776 till Oct. 1779.

Services : Lieut. 12th Bn. Sepoys in July 1787.

Refs. : Robinson.

[1] *Note :* He was either a Writer or a private merchant at Calcutta during the siege in 1756. He served in the Mil., and afterwards escaped to Fulta ; E.I. Co.'s cooper till Sept. 1760. He was probably of the family of Pyefinch of Wegnall and Presteign, co. Radnor. (Cf. *Misc. Gen. et Her.* 5S. iii. 155.)

PYNE, Arthur Thomas (1791-1818). Lieutenant, 11th N.I. *b.* S. Weald, Essex, 27 June 1791. Cadet 1809. Ensign 19 Dec. 1812. Lieut. 27 Nov. 1817. *d.* in India 25 July 1818.

bapt. S. Weald 16 July 1791. Son of Francis Pyne and Elizabeth his wife. *m.* Dinapore 3 May 1813, Miss Sarah Long. (She died Calcutta 27 May 1833, aged 32—*sic.*)

Services : Was already in Bengal in the Pilot Service when apptd. Cadet. Posted Ensign to 1/2nd N.I. in 1813; with 2nd Gren. Bn. 1815-16; transfd. as Lieut. to 11th N.I. Nov. 1817. (? Third Mahratta War 1817-18; Lieut. 2/11th N.I.)

PYNE, John (1795-1881). Major. 32nd N.I. *b.* Somerton, Somerset, 16 Jan. 1795. Cadet 1810. Admitted 27 Aug. 1811. Ensign 12 Feb. 1813. Lieut. 1 June 1818. Capt. 30 Jan. 1828 Retired 18 July 1837. Hon. Major 28 Nov. 1854. *d.* Burnham, Somerset, 4 May 1881.

bapt. Somerton 31 July 1795. Eldest son of Rev. Anthony Pyne, of High Ham, Somerset, rector of Pitney and Kingsweston, and Catherine his wife, dau. of Simon Wetherell.

Services : Cadet d.d. 25th N.I. 1811-13; posted Ensign to 1/16th N.I. in 1813. Fur. p.a. 5 Feb. 1822 till 21 May 1825. Transfd. to 32nd N.I. (late 1/16th) May 1824; ordered to rejoin 2nd Gren. Bn. at Chittagong 5 Sept. 1825. First Burma War; Arakan 1825; Lieut. 2nd Gren. Bn. Intr. & Qmr. 32nd N.I. 6 Jan. 1826 till 12 Aug. 1828. Actg. Intr. & Qmr. 2nd Gren. Bn. 12 Apr. 1826. Offg. 1st Asst. Mily. Auditor Gen. 18 Feb. 1832; apptd. 2nd Asst. Mily. Auditor Gen. 23 Oct. 1832; 1st do. 7 Dec. 1834 till 31 Dec. 1835. Fur. p.a. 15 Jan. 1836 till retirement. Retired on full pay of 10/6 *p.d.*

Refs. : Burke's *Landed Gentry*, 4th edn., p. 1242, *s.n.* Pyne, of Curry Mallett, Somerset. Burke's *Visitation of Seats and Arms*, 2S. ii. 57. *The Times*, 9 May 1881.

Q

*QUEIROS, Joseph (Mary Francis) (c. 1788-1824). Ensign. Infantry. Afterwards Cornet 24th Light Dgns., then a merchant at Lucknow, finally in the service of the King of Oudh at Lucknow. b. Calcutta c. 1788. Cadet 1805. Arrived in India 1 Sept. 1806. Ensign 8 Sept. 1806. Resigned 11 Sept. 1806. d. Lucknow 15 Mar. 1824.

Son of Joseph Queiros, of Lucknow, merchant,[1] and Teresa Le Blanc his wife. His sisters m. Rowland Cotton Dickson, Joseph Nesbitt, and Wredenhall Robert Pogson, qq.v. m. 17 Feb. 1816, Miss Rozalia Vrignon (probably dau. of Gabriel Vrignon, of Calcutta, merchant). (She re-m. 25 July 1828, Major Nicholas Brutton, H.M. 11th Light Dgns.)

Services: Cornet 24th Light Dgns. 13 July 1806; resigned 11 Oct. 1810. Joined his father's business at Lucknow c. 1818.

Refs.: Will dated 4 Oct. 1823; proved 16 Apr. 1825.

[1] Note: A Portuguese native who, having acted as clerk to Claud Martin, q.v., was by him apptd. one of the Exors. to his Will. Was an auctioneer in Calcutta 1785-8; afterwards in the service of the King of Oudh.

*QUIN, Patrick (1728/29-1795). Bt. Ensign, Infantry. b. 1728/29. Bt. Ensign 17 Aug. 1781. d. Monghyr 22 Apr. 1795, aged 66.

Services: Apptd. Condr. of Ord. 4 Apr. 1778; commissioned as Bt. Ensign of Militia 17 Aug. 1781.

Refs.: M.I. at Monghyr.

*QUIN, Thomas (1805-1857). Bt. Lieut. Colonel, 4th L.C. b. Dublin 30 Sept. 1805. Cadet 1825. Arrived in India 16 May 1826. Cornet (5 Nov. 1825) 16 May 1826. Lieut. 21 Nov. 1828. Capt. 20 Apr. 1848. Bt. Major 21 Apr. 1848. Bt. Lt. Col. 28 Nov. 1854. d. Simla 7 Nov. 1857.

3rd son of Rev. Thomas Quin, of St. Stephen's Green, Dublin, preby. of Tynan, co. Armagh, and Ellen his wife, dau. of William Wilson, of Caherconlish, co. Limerick. m. Nasirabad 2 June 1828, Henrietta Wynetta, eldest dau. of Capt. Richard Phillips, Madras Eur. Regt. (See also George Tebbs.) His dau. m. William Charles Alexander, q.v. Ed. Royal School, Armagh. T.C.D.; Fellow Commoner 18 Oct. 1824.

Services : Posted Cornet to 4th L.C. 24 May 1826. Offg. Bde. Major at Meerut June-Nov. 1830. Shekhawat expedn. 1834 ; Lieut. 4th L.C. Comdg. escort of C.-in-C. 15 Nov. 1838 till Jan. 1839. Apptd. 2nd in comd. of Bundelkhand Legion, then about to be raised, 7 Jan. till 6 Sept. 1839. Intr. & Qmr. 4th L.C. 20 Sept. 1842 till July 1846. Gwalior campaign ; Maharajpur (Bronze star). Apptd. D.A.Q.M.G. of Cav. Div., Army of the Sutlej, 13 Dec. 1845. First Sikh War ; Mudki ; D.A.Q.M.G. ; Ferozshahr ; Aliwal ; Sobraon ; actg. Comdt. G.G.B.G. (Medal with 3 clasps). Offg. Comdt. G.G.B.G. 18 Dec. 1845 till 25 June 1846. Apptd. Comdt. 12th (became 13th) Irreg. Cav., the raising of which had then been ordered, 3 Jan. 1846, and comdd. till 21 July 1855, when he resigned the comd. owing to ill health. Second Sikh War Feb. 1849 ; comdg. 13th Irreg. Cav., with force which held Wazirabad and the fords of the Chenab during the battle of Gujerat (Medal with clasp). Operations against the Baizais Dec. 1849 ; comdg. 13th Irreg. Cav. Leave s.c. 2 yrs. to Cape Mar. 1851. Leave s.c. to hills Apr. 1855 till death.

Refs. : *Register of the R. School, Armagh* (1933). *Alumni Dub. De Rhé-Philipe. V.B.G. I.M.* 13 Jan. 1858, p. 14. M.I. in new cemetery, Simla.

R

RABAN, George Higgins (*d*. 1829). Lieut. Colonel, C.B. Artillery. (238) Country Cadet 1782. Admitted 28 Oct. 1782. Fireworker 26 Apr. 1783. Lieut. 25 Nov. 1790. Capt. Lt. 8 Jan. 1798. Capt. 10 Mar. 1803. Major 17 Sept. 1807. Lt. Col. 27 Aug. 1813. Retired 6 May 1817. *d*. at his brother's house, Beauchamp Lodge, Somerset, 8 July 1829, of apoplexy.

Of Savile Row, London. Son of John Caspar Raban, of London, and Elizabeth Evans his wife. Brother of William Raban, *q.v.*, uncle of Henry Tilman Raban, *q.v.*, and cousin of George Evans and of Emily, mother of Charles Welland, *q.v.*

Services: Originally a Lieut. on the Bombay Est. First Mahratta War 1782-4; with Col. Goddard's detachment. To comd. 1st Coy. Sepoys (? Golandaz) at P.W.I. 23 Dec. 1786, and served there till 18 Sept. 1793, holding also the appt. of Garr. Storekeeper. Expedn. to Kedah, Penang, Apr. 1791. Fur. 4 Feb. 1794 till 20 Feb. 1798. Second Mahratta War; Aligarh; Delhi; Agra; Laswari; Rampura; siege of Deig; Bhurtpore; Capt. comdg. 2nd Coy. 1st Bn. Art. Operations against the Rana of Gohad 1806; capture of Gohad; Capt. comdg. 2nd Coy. 1st Bn. Operations in Rewah 1811-13. Fur. 2 Jan. 1815 till retirement. C.B. 4 June 1815.

Refs.: *E.I.M.C.* i. 76-7. *Bath Chron.* 16 July 1829. *G.M.* 1829, ii. 180. Will dated London 25 Feb. 1826; proved 28 June 1831.

RABAN, Henry Tilman (1799-1838). Bt. Captain, 47th N.I. *b*. Calcutta 8 May 1799. Cadet 1817. Admitted 11 Aug. 1818. Ensign 15 Mar. 1818. Lieut. 3 Sept. 1818. Bt. Capt. 15 May. 1833. *d*. Agra 16 Apr. 1838, of cholera.

bapt. Calcutta 7 Aug. 1799. Son of Thomas Raban, of Calcutta, atty., and Catherine his wife, dau. of William Jones, of Swansea. Brother of Richard Raban, *q.v.*, of Emma Maria, wife of Charles Thomas Higgins, *q.v.*, and of Anne, wife of Edward Cave-Browne, *q.v. m.* Secrora, U.P., 7 Nov. 1834, Miss Theodosia Mahon.[1] (She died *c*. 1849.)

Services: Ensign R. Eastern Regt. of Middlesex Mil. 26 June 1815. Posted Lieut. to 2/24th N.I. in 1818. Actg. Adjt. Left Wing 2/24th N.I. 17 Nov. 1823. Transfd. to 47th N.I. (late 1/24th) May 1824. On this Regt. being disbanded for mutiny in Nov. 1824, was transfd. to newly-raised 69th N.I. (became 47th in 1828);

actg. Adjt. do. 1 Sept. 1826; permanent 22 Jan. 1831 till 4 Dec. 1833. No record of active service.

Refs.: A.J. N.S. xxvi. 244. M.I. Agra Cantt. cemetery.

¹ *Note:* She was a beneficiary under the Will of James Price (1757/58-1842), *q.v.*

RABAN, Richard (1801-1840). Captain, 48th N.I. *b.* Swansea 2 Nov. 1801. Cadet 1817. Admitted 5 Sept. 1818. Ensign 21 Apr. 1818. Lieut. 17 Dec. 1818. Capt. 30 June 1838. *d.* Kila Kazi, Kohistan, 16 Oct. 1840.

bapt. St. Mary's, Swansea, 2 Nov. 1801. Son of Thomas Raban and Catherine his wife. Brother of Thomas Uvedale Stephen Raban, *q.v.*, uncle of Winifred Emma, wife of George Young (1789-1860), *q.v.*, and cousin-german of Mary Elizabeth, wife of Charles Henry Baines, *q.v.* *m.* Emma Walmesley, of London. (She died 6 Dec. 1876.)

Services: Posted Lieut. to 2/24th N.I.; transfd. to 48th N.I. (late 2/24th) May 1824. Intr. & Qmr. 48th N.I. 13 July 1824 till 17 Dec. 1832. Fur. s.c. 29 Nov. 1832 till 4 May 1837. First Afghan War 1838-40; capture of Ghazni 1839 (Medal); Capt. 48th N.I.; to remain in Afghanistan and posted to 1st Bde. 25 Nov. 1839; operations in Kohistan under Bdr. Sale Sept.-Oct. 1840; storm of Julgah fort (*Lond. Gaz.* 9 Jan. 1841); Comst. Ofr. and A.D.C. to Sale.

Refs.: M.I. Afghan Memorial Church, Bombay.

RABAN, Thomas Uvedale Stephen (1787-1832). Major, Invalid Est. 14th N.I. *bapt.* Calcutta 26 June 1787. Cadet 1803. Arrived in India 27 Sept. 1804. Ensign 19 Sept. 1804. Lieut. 21 Sept. 1804. Capt. 1 Jan. 1819. Major 23 May 1828. Invalided 30 May 1829. *d.* Dinajpur, Bengal, 14 Mar. 1832.

Son of Thomas Raban and Catherine his wife. Brother of William Raban, *q.v.*, and nephew of William Raban, *q.v.* Ed. Eton; in Fourth Form in 1802.

Services: Posted Lieut. to 10th N.I. in 1805. Third Mahratta War; Lieut. 1/10th N.I. Transfd. as Capt. to 2/10th N.I.; to 14th N.I. (late 1/10th) May 1824. Posted to 1st Bn. Native Invalids 25 Aug. 1829.

Refs.: Eton School Lists.

RABAN, William (1764-1843). Lieut. Colonel. Bengal Eur. Regt. *b.* London 1764. Cadet 1781. Admitted 6 May 1782. Ensign 10 July 1781. Lieut. 10 Oct. 1782. Capt. 21 Feb. 1801.

Major 14 Nov. 1805. Lt. Col. 11 Sept. 1811. Retired 20 July 1814. *d.* Hatch Beauchamp, Somerset, 1 May 1843, aged 78.
Of Beauchamp Lodge. Son of John Caspar Raban, of London, and Elizabeth Evans his wife. Brother of George Higgins Raban, *q.v.*, uncle of William Raban, *q.v.*, and related to (? cousin-german of, Thomas Evans (*d.* 1809), *q.v.* *m.* 31 Oct. 1816, Ellen, dau. of Rev. William Calton, of Bramford Speke, Devon. His dau. *m.* William Raban, *q.v.*
Services : Appt. Cadet 14 Dec. 1780, aged 16 ; sailed for India in the *Hinchinbrooke* 13 Mar. 1781, aged 16. Lieut. 12th Bn. Sepoys in July 1787. Second Rohilla War ; battle of Bitaurah ; Lieut. 12th Bn. Capt. Lt. 12th N.I. 29 May 1800. Capt. 2/12th N.I. Fur. 24 Dec. 1802 till 12 Sept. 1805. Comdt. Barasat C.C. on its reopening in 1806 till July 1807. Capture of Java 1811 ; Weltervreden ; Cornelis ; Major comdg. 6th Vol. Bn. (Gold medal). Expedn. to Palembang, Sumatra, 1812. Posted Lt. Col. to Bengal Eur. Regt. in 1811. Resdt. at Cheribon, Java, 1812 till July 1814, when he sailed from Java for England on retirement. Pub. Calcutta, 1819, " Origin of the Pindaries . . ."
Refs. : *E.I.M.C.* i. 90-1. *G.M.* 1843, i. 669.

RABAN, William (1792-1864). Ensign. 21st N.I. Subsequently Major 22nd Ft. *b.* Calcutta 11 Feb. 1792. Cadet 1806. Arrived in India 3 Oct. 1807. Ensign 20 Oct. 1807. Resigned 5 Aug. 1808. *d.* Old Burlington St., London, 20 Feb. 1864.
bapt. Calcutta 23 June 1792. Son of Thomas Raban and Catherine his wife.[1] Brother of Henry Tilman Raban, *q.v.* *m.* Emma, dau. of his uncle William Raban, *q.v.*
Services : Posted Ensign to 21st N.I. Ensign H.M. 22nd Ft. 3 Jan. 1811 ; Lieut. do. 2 June 1813 ; Capt. do. 14 Feb. 1828 ; Major do. 18 Dec. 1840 ; Major on retired full pay of 22nd Ft. 23 Feb. 1844 till death. Bt. Lt. Col. 28 Nov. 1854.
Refs. : *G.M.* 1864, i. 537.
[1] *Note :* She was related to Lt.-Gen. William Jones, *q.v.*

RADCLIFFE, James (1761/62-1805). Major, 12th N.I. *b.* London 1761/62. Cadet 1779. Admitted 19 Nov. 1779. Ensign 26 June 1779. Lieut. 17 Feb. 1781. Capt. 30 Oct. 1797. Major 1 May 1804. *d.* Bhurtpore 26 Feb. 1805, of wounds received in action.
Brother of Charles Moss Radcliffe.
Services : Apptd. Cadet 18 Nov. 1778 ; sailed for India in the *Gen. Barker* 7 Mar. 1779, aged 17. Lieut. 21st Bn. Sepoys in July

1787 and Dec. 1792; d.d. 26th Bn. 12 Feb. 1794; Lieut. 3rd Bengal Eur. Regt. in 1796; Capt. 9th N.I. in 1798; transfd. to 1/12th N.I. as Capt. Second Mahratta War; Agra; Laswari; capture of Deig, comdd. left storming party; siege of Bhurtpore (s.w. in 3rd assault 20 Feb. 1805); Major 1/12th N.I.
Refs.: Pester. Intestate; admon. granted 23 May 1805.

RAGULL, Thomas (*d.* 1772). Major, Artillery. (31) Fireworker (Madras) 28 June 1759. 2nd Lieut. 18 June 1760. Lieut. 9 Feb. 1762. Capt. Lt. 1 Aug. 1765. Transfd. to Bengal Art. 5 Apr. 1766. Capt. (Bengal) 15 Sept. 1766. Major 30 Oct. 1769. *d.* Monghyr 8 Nov. 1772.
Brother of Jean, wife of Samuel Humphries, of Westminster, and of Catherine Dawn.
Services: N.F.P.
Refs.: Leslie, No. 40. Will dated 20 Oct. 1772; proved 26 Jan. 1773.

RAIKES, Charles Lewis Napier (1818-1837). Lieutenant, 67th N.I. *b.* Drayton, Norfolk, 29 Jan. 1818. Cadet 1834. Ensign (12 Dec. 1834) 3 Jan. 1835. Lieut. 3 Aug. 1837. *d.* Akyab, Burma, 5 Aug. 1837, of remittent fever.
3rd son of Rev. Robert Napier Raikes, vicar of Longhope and Old Sodbury, Gloucs., and Caroline his wife, dau. of Very Rev. John Probyn, dean of Llandaff. Brother of Robert Napier Raikes, *q.v.*, grandson of Robert Raikes, founder of Sunday Schools (*D.N.B.*), and 2nd cousin of Robert Raikes Kinleside, *q.v.* Addiscombe Cadet 2 Feb. 1833 till 12 Dec. 1834.
Services: d.d. 67th N.I. 8 Aug. 1835; posted Ensign to 70th N.I. 24 Sept. 1835; transfd. to 67th N.I. 30 Oct. 1835. No record of active service.
Refs.: Burke's *Landed Gentry*, 13th edn., p. 1471, *s.n.* Raikes, of Bennington, Herts. *A.J.* N.S. xxv. 37.

RAIKES, Robert Napier (1813-1909). General, u.s.l. 67th N.I. *b.* Drayton, Norfolk, 13 Oct. 1813. Cadet 1829. Arrived in India 15 May 1830. Ensign (19 Nov. 1829) 23 Apr. 1830. Lieut. 28 June 1836. Capt. 20 Feb. 1852. Major 28 Nov. 1857. Lt. Col. 18 Feb. 1861. Col. 18 Feb. 1866. Maj. Gen. 1 Oct. 1877. Lt. Gen. 18 Dec. 1879. Transfd. to u.s.l. 1 July 1881. Gen. 22 Jan. 1889. *d.* at his residence, 8 Hartfield Sq., Eastbourne, 23 Mar. 1909, aged 95.
Of Bennington, Stevenage, Herts. 2nd son of Rev. Robert Raikes

and Caroline his wife. Brother of Charles Lewis Napier Raikes, *q.v.*
m. Mussoorie 25 Sept. 1854, Harriette, dau. of William Beckett (1798-1844), *q.v.* (*See also* Thomas Riddell and Daniel Stansbury.) Ed. Bury Grammar School 1821-2. Addiscombe Cadet 1828-9.
Services: Cadet d.d. 24th N.I. 7 June 1830 ; 44th N.I. 28 Mar. 1831 ; 10th N.I. 22 Oct. 1831. Actg. Ensign (having been 2 yrs. in India) 16 July 1832. d.d. 68th N.I. 27 Jan. 1833 ; 70th N.I. 15 May 1833. Posted Ensign to 36th N.I. 20 Aug. 1833 ; to 67th N.I. 18 Oct. 1833. Adjt. Arakan Local Bn. 28 Aug. 1837 till 30 Aug. 1838. Actg. Adjt. Inf., Sindhia's Contingent, 12 May 1841 ; permanent do. 10 Nov. 1841 till 1844. Gwalior campaign ; Paniar (Bronze star). Adjt. 1st Cav., Sindhia's Contingent, 13 Jan. 1844 ; 2nd in comd. 15th Irreg. Cav. 24 Jan. 1846 ; do. 1st Cav., Sindhia's Contingent, 3 July 1846 till 1857, when it mutinied. Rejoined 67th N.I. tempy. for Burma 9 Mar. 1852. Second Burma War 1852 ; capture of Rangoon ; Pegu ; Capt. 67th N.I. (Medal with clasp). Mutiny campaign 1857 ; served as Field Engr. Remount Agent 1858-9.
Refs.: Burke's *Landed Gentry*, 13th edn., p. 1471, *s.n.* Raikes, of Bennington, Herts. Ruvigny's *Plantagenet Roll of the Blood Royal*, Essex Vol., p. 650. *The Times*, 24 Mar. 1909.

RAINEY, Arthur Crowe (1811-1891). Captain. 25th N.I. Afterwards in holy orders. *b.* Ludhiana 7 Feb. 1811. Cadet 1827. Arrived in India 22 Nov. 1828. Ensign 18 June 1828. Lieut. 17 Jan. 1834. Capt. 24 Nov. 1839. Retired 12 Feb. 1846. *d.* 6 Dec. 1891.
2nd son of James Rainey, *q.v.*, and Anne his wife. *m.* Calcutta 12 Dec. 1836, Louisa Hester, eldest dau. of Henry Minchin Pigou, B.C.S., and sister of Robert Pigou, *q.v.*
Services: Ensign d.d. 13th N.I. 13 Dec. 1828 ; do. 29th N.I. 8 Jan. 1829 ; do. 13th N.I. 10 Feb. 1829 ; posted Ensign to 25th N.I. Intr. & Qmr. 25th N.I. 26 May 1831. Offg. Junior Asst. to Comr. of Arakan 12 May 1834 ; permanent do. 30 Oct. 1834. In charge of public bldgs. at Kyaukpyu 14 Feb. 1833 till 13 May 1834. Offg. Senior Asst. in Sandoway, Lower Burma, 14 Feb. till 28 Sept. 1835. Leave s.c. to China 13 Aug. 1836 till 8 Jan. 1837. Received charge of district of Ramri 1 Feb. 1837. Leave s.c. to Mussoorie 27 Nov. 1837 till 31 Mar. 1838. Offg. Asst. to P.A. Sabathu 19 Feb. 1838 ; permanent do. 25 Aug. 1838 till 17 Feb. 1843, when that office was abolished. Postmr. at Sabathu 26 Sept. 1838 till 15 Apr. 1840. Leave s.c. 8 Apr. 1841 ; s.c. 18 mos. to Cape 8 Oct. 1841 ; fur. s.c. 12 Aug. 1843 till retirement. No record of active service. Took holy orders.

Refs.: Burke's *Landed Gentry of Ireland*, p. 599, *s.n.* Rainey-Robinson.

RAINEY, James (1782/83-1816). Bt. Captain, 7th N.C. *b.* co. Down 1782/83 (aged 17 on Mar. 13 1800). Cadet 1799. Arrived in India 9 Dec. 1800. Cornet 15 Apr. 1801. Lieut. 11 Mar. 1805. Bt. Capt. 8 Jan. 1816. *d.* Partabgarh, U.P., 29 Nov. 1816.

3rd son of William Rainey, of Greenville, co. Down, sometime Capt. Royal Welch Fus., and Henrietta Maria his 1st wife, dau. of Rev. James Hutchinson. Brother of William Henry Rainey, *q.v. m.* Anne Loring. (She died Bedford 8 Apr. 1860, aged 76.) Father of Arthur Crowe Rainey, *q.v.*

Services: Posted Cornet to 2nd N.C. Operations in Jumna Doab 1803. Qmr. 2nd N.C. 1804-5. Second Mahratta War 1803-4; battle of Delhi ; Laswari ; battle of Deig ; Cornet 2nd N.C. Transfd. to newly-raised 7th N.C. Apr. 1805 ; Qmr. do. 16 May 1805 till death. Operations in Oudh 1808. Settlement of Hariana 1809-10. Nepal War 1814-15 ; Lieut. 7th N.C., in 2nd Div.

Refs.: Burke's *Landed Gentry of Ireland*, p. 599, *s.n.* Rainey-Robinson. Will dated 25 Jan. 1809 ; codicil dated 19 May 1816 ; proved 9 Jan. 1817.

RAINEY, William Henry (1780-1830). Major. 4th L.C. *b.* 1780. Cadet 1797. Arrived in India 21 Sept. 1798. Cornet 1 Nov. 1798. Lieut. 29 May 1800. Capt. 1 Sept. 1818. Major 16 Mar. 1820. Retired 7 Mar. 1823. *d.* in Ireland 15 July 1830.

Of Mount Panther, co. Down ; J.P. co. Down. 2nd son of William Rainey and Henrietta Maria his 1st wife. Brother of James Rainey, *q.v. m.* Kaitha, U.P., 28 Nov. 1809, Margaret, dau. of Robert Macan, of Carriff, co. Armagh, and sister of Thomas Macan, *q.v.* His dau. *m.* John Theodore Wilcox, *q.v.* (*See also* John Richardson.)

Services: Served as a boy under his father in the Yeomanry Cav. during the Irish Rebellion. Posted Ensign to Bengal Eur. Regt. Oct. 1798 ; transfd. as Cornet to 4th N.C. Operations in Jumna Doab 1803 ; Sasni ; Bijaigarh ; Kachaura ; Lieut. 4th N.C. Second Mahratta War ; Laswari (horse shot under him) ; Lieut. 4th N.C. Adjt. 4th N.C. 16 May 1805 till Aug. 1811 ; Qmr. do. 25 Aug. 1811 till 1817. (? Nepal War 1814.) Capt. Lt. 4th N.C. 18 May 1816. Offg. Comdt. G.G.B.G. 17 Feb. 1817 ; permanent do. 21 June 1818 till 14 Oct. 1820. Third Mahratta War 1817-18 ; comdg. G.G.B.G., in Centre Div. Fur. 14 Oct. 1820 till retirement.

Refs.: Burke's *Landed Gentry of Ireland*, p. 599, *s.n.* Rainey-

Robinson. Family information. *V.B.G.* (portrait). *A.J.* N.S. iii.
43. Will dated 25 May 1830 ; proved 5 June 1832.

RAINSFORD, Frederick. (*See* **RAINSFORD-HANNAY.**)

RAINSFORD, Randolph (1743/44-1783). Lieutenant, 1st Bengal Eur. Regt. *b.* 1743/44. Country Cadet 1777. Ensign 24 Sept. 1777. Lieut. 8 Oct. 1778. *d.* Buxar 19 Apr. 1783, aged 39.
" The son of a gentleman of some family." (Mily. Cons.)
Services : Apptd. Cadet from Condr. of Ord. 19 May 1777 ; posted to 1st Bde. Sept. 1777 ; transfd. to 2nd Bde. 16 Oct. 1777 ; Lieut. 2/1st Bengal Eur. Regt. in Oct. 1779.
Refs. : M.I. at Buxar.

RAKER, James. (*See* **ROKER.**)

RALEIGH, Frederick (1808-1856). Bt. Major, 1st N.I. Comdt. Calcutta Native Mil. *b.* Cullompton, Devon, 9 June 1808. Cadet 1825. Arrived in India 6 July 1826. Ensign 15 Mar. 1826. Lieut. 20 June 1833. Capt. 24 Jan. 1845. Bt. Major 20 June 1854. *d.* off Calcutta 25 Apr. 1856, on board the steam packet *Andrew Henderson*, whilst proceeding down the Hooghly R.
Son of —— Raleigh and Esther his wife. Brother of Edward Ward Raleigh, and brother-in-law of Charles Vine, of Shepherd's Bush. *m.* (before 1842) Mary.
Services : Ensign d.d. 7th N.I. 27 July 1826 ; posted Ensign to 1st N.I. 26 Sept. 1826. Fur. s.c. 7 Jan. 1832 till 26 Nov. 1836, and 14 Oct. 1837 till 23 Sept. 1841. Adjt. 1st N.I. 22 Sept. 1843 ; do. Calcutta Native Mil. 13 June 1844 ; Comdt. do. 24 Jan. 1845 till death. No record of active service.
Refs. : *I.M.* 16 June 1856, p. 346. Will dated 7 Sept. 1852 ; proved 28 Apr. 1856.

RALFE, Charles (1806-1842). Captain, 3rd N.I *b.* Southampton 5 July 1806. Cadet 1825. Arrived in India 20 Nov. 1826. Ensign 17 July 1826. Lieut. 11 Sept. 1835. Capt. 18 Nov. 1841. *d.* in camp at Malthon, C.P., 19 Apr. 1842, of wounds received in action on 16 Apr.
Son of James Ralfe, of Winchester, solicitor and steward to the Coll., and Elizabeth Tredgold his wife. Brother of Henry Ralfe, *q.v.*, and nephew of Henry Ralfe, *q.v. m.* Chunar 13 Sept. 1841, Mary Hicks, dau. of Thomas Little, of Biddlestone, and sister of William Little, *q.v.* (She *re-m.* Henry Wilson, *q.v.*)

Services: Ensign d.d. 67th N.I. 13 Jan. 1827; posted to 3rd N.I. 10 May 1827. Shekhawat expedn. 1834; Ensign 3rd N.I. Disturbances in Bundelkhand 1842; skirmish with insurgents on the Narhut road nr. Malthon 16 Apr. (s.w.); Capt. 3rd N.I.

Refs.: Family information. M.I. old cemetery, Saugor.

RALFE, Henry (1791-1869). Captain. Artillery. (416) *b.* Petersfield, Hants, 23 July 1791. Cadet 1809. Admitted 3 Oct. 1810. Fireworker 5 Nov. 1809. Lieut. 25 Sept. 1817. Capt. 1 May 1824. Retired 3 Feb. 1830. *d.* Winchester 18 Sept. 1869.

Sometime of Bovey Tracey, Devon. *bapt.* Petersfield 9 Nov. 1791. Son of Rev. William Ralfe,[1] rector of Maulden, Beds., and Anabella Gauntlett his wife. Uncle of Henry Ralfe, *q.v. m.* Greenock 27 Aug. 1828, Margaret, widow of W. A. Clubley. Woolwich Cadet; nominated to R.M.A. 31 Jan. 1806.

Services: Capture of Java 1811; Lieut. F. 7th Coy. 1st Bn. (Medal). Expedn. to Palembang, Sumatra, Apr. 1812. Comdt. Art. and Comy. Ord. I. of Banca 1812. Expedn. to Palembang Sept. 1812. Comdt. Art. in Bantam district, Java, 1813. Fur. s.c. Mar. 1815 till Nov. 1818. Comdt. Art. at Singapore 1819 till Nov. 1821, when he returned to Bengal. Fur. s.c. 1822-5. Served at P.W.I. 1826-8; Mily. Sec. and A.D.C. to Govr. of P.W.I. Aug. 1826. Fur. s.c. from Penang 15 Feb. 1828 till retirement.

Refs.: Family information. *E.I.M.C.* iii. 289-90. *G.M.* 1828, ii. 270. *The Times,* 23 Sept. 1869.

[1] *Note:* Granted by Warrant, 2 Sept. 1784, a pension of £182 10/- *p.a.,* charged on the revenues of Gibraltar.

RALFE, Henry (1810-1837). Ensign, 38th N.I. *bapt.* Holy Rhood, Southampton, 17 Mar. 1810. Cadet 1827. Ensign 24 Oct. 1827. *d.* Delhi 9 Mar. 1837.[1]

Son of James Ralfe, of Winchester, solicitor, and Elizabeth his wife. Brother of Charles Ralfe, *q.v.*

Services: Ensign d.d. 66th N.I. Feb. 1828. Posted to 3rd N.I. 1 July 1828. Transfd. to 38th N.I. 2 July 1832, but did not join till Aug. 1833; d.d. in the meantime at Nasirabad with 3rd, 54th and 66th N.I. No record of active service.

Refs.: De Rhé-Philipe. A.J. N.S. xxiii. 317. M.I. in Rajpura cemetery, Delhi.

[1] *Note:* Both *A.J.* and the inscription on his tombstone give the date of his death, incorrectly, as 29 Mar.

THE BENGAL ARMY, 1758-1834 597

RALPH, Benjamin (*d.* 1795). Fireworker. Artillery. (261) Afterwards Lieut. 73rd Ft. Cadet 1783. Arrived in India Aug. 1784. Fireworker 12 Apr. 1785. Transfd. to H.M.S. 1788. *bur.* Madras 26 Nov. 1795.

Services: Apptd. Cadet 5 Nov. 1783 ; sailed for India in the *Hillsborough* 28 Jan. 1784. In 3rd Bn. Art. in July 1787. Ensign H.M. 76th Ft. (12 Apr. 1785) 4 Nov. 1788 ; Lieut. 73rd (Highland) Ft. 16 Aug. 1790 till death.

RALPH, James (1782-1857). Lieutenant, 8th N.C. Subsequently Paymr. Aurangabad Div., Nizam's army. *b.* Upton, Berks., 30 Aug. 1782. Cadet 1798. Arrived in India 5 Sept. 1799. Cornet 14 June 1800. Lieut. 26 July 1803. Cashiered by G.C.M. 23 June 1808.[1] Restored 30 May 1810. Resigned and entered H.M.S. *d.* Aurangabad 11 Apr. 1857.

Son of —— Ralph and Jane his wife, " of Upton, nr. Eton, Bucks." *m.* (before 1811) Anna. (She died Aurangabad 27 Mar. 1850, aged 68.)

Services: Posted Cornet to 6th N.C. Operations in Jumna Doab 1803 ; Sasni ; Bijaigarh ; Kachaura ; Lieut. 6th N.C. Second Mahratta War ; Laswari ; Lieut. 6th N.C. (India medal). Transfd. to newly-raised 8th N.C. in 1805. On restoration to the Service was reposted to 8th N.C. Ensign H.M. 59th Ft. 17 June 1813 ; Lieut. do. 26 May 1814 ; h.p. in 1816 ; 30th Ft. 18 Dec. 1819 ; Capt. 19th Ft. 5 June 1827 ; h.p. (unattached) 5 Feb. 1829 ; 22nd Ft. 9 July 1829 ; sold out 16 July 1829. Apptd. to Nizam's army 30 Apr. 1833 ; Paymr. Aurangabad Div. till after 1852. Appears to have edited *The Mirror* in Calcutta, *c.* 1808 ; also edited the *Bengal Hurkaru c.* 1813.

Refs.: Officers of the Green Howards. I.M. 2 June 1857, p. 345. M.I. nr. railway station, Aurangabad.

[1] *Note:* " For disorderly and mutinous conduct on the parade, in front of the regt., . . . and for endeavouring by words and gestures to excite the men of the corps to mutiny, and release a prisoner under sentence of a regtl. ct.-mar., . . ." (G.O.C.C. 27 June 1808.)

RALPH, John (*d.* 1795). Lieutenant, Infantry. Country Cadet 1778. Ensign 4 June 1778. Lieut. 4 Sept. 1779. *d.* Cawnpore 29 Mar. 1795.

(*Probably* brother of Richard Ralph, *q.v.*)

Services: Apptd. Cadet 27 Feb. 1778. Lieut. 2/1st Bengal Eur. Regt. in Oct. 1779 ; 13th Bn. Sepoys in July 1787 ; transfd.

to 20th Bn. 1790. Third Mysore War; Lieut. Bengal Vols., detached from 20th Bn. Sepoys.

RALPH, Richard (1748/49-1804). Lieut. Colonel, 22nd N.I. *b.* 1748/49. Country Cadet 1778. Admitted 9 Mar. 1778. Ensign 31 Mar. 1778. Lieut. 1 Sept. 1779. Capt. 27 Sept. 1796. Major 5 Aug. 1802. Lt. Col. 30 June 1804. *d.* Allahabad 18 Nov. 1804, aged 55.

(*Probably* brother of John Ralph, *q.v.*)
Services: Apptd. Cadet 27 Feb. 1778. Lieut. 13th Bn. Sepoys in July 1787; transfd. to 20th Bn. 1790. Third Mysore War; Lieut. Bengal Vols., detached from 20th Bn. Sepoys. Capt. 2/11th N.I.; transfd. to 1/18th N.I. 29 May 1800; to newly-raised 1/22nd N.I. Nov. 1803.

Refs.: Intestate; admon. 30 July 1805. M.I. Kydganj cemetery, Allahabad.

Note: " Ensign Ralph, senr., be apptd. Practitioner Engr. to rank in the Corps from this day." (*Bengal Mily. Cons.* 30 Mar. 1779.) No record of his service with Engrs. has been traced.

RAMSAY, Allan (1801-1841). Lieutenant. 8th N.I. *b.* London 24 Sept. 1801. Cadet 1817. Admitted 15 Sept. 1818. Ensign (?) Lieut. 1 Aug. 1818. Resigned in India 11 Mar. 1831. *d.* off Berhampore 21 June 1841.

bapt. St. Mary-at-Hill, London, 28 Oct. 1801. Son of Thomas Ramsay, of London, wine merchant, and Jane his wife. *m.* Agra 15 Feb. 1830, Anne Louisa, *née* Liddington.[1] Addiscombe Cadet 1817-18.

Services: Posted Lieut. to 2/9th N.I.; transfd. to 8th N.I. (late 1/9th) May 1824. Actg. Adjt. Left Wing 8th N.I. 30 Nov. 1826. No record of active service. Committed to gaol in Calcutta 24 June 1831, on a charge of being an accessory before the fact to his wife's attempt to murder Lieut. George Richard Talbot, *q.v.* Subsequently went to England, returning later to India.

Refs.: *A.J.* xxvi. 738; N.S. ii. 157; viii. 67; xiii. 229; xxxvi. 57. *I.N.* 7 Sept. 1841, p. 386. *Good old days of Hon. John Company* (1906 edn.), i. 255-6.

[1] *Note:* She had been previously married to a Dr. O'Neal, and secondly to Dr. John Patterson.

RAMSAY, Andrew (1809-1840). Lieutenant, 34th N.I. *b.* Arbirlot, co. Forfar, 7 Sept. 1809. Cadet 1825. Arrived in India 6 May 1826. Ensign 12 Jan. 1826. Lieut. 17 Dec. 1832. *d.* Almora 1 July 1840.

4th son of Lt.-Gen. Hon. John Ramsay and Mary his wife, dau. of Philip Delisle, of Calcutta. Brother of George, 12th Earl of Dalhousie, and of David Ramsay (1812-1839), *q.v.*, and cousin-german of George Ramsay, *q.v.*, and of William Edmund (Maule Ramsay) Hay, *q.v.*
Services : Posted Ensign to 34th N.I. 26 Sept. 1826. Fur. s.c. 17 Jan. 1829 till 5 Dec. 1831. d.d. 30th N.I. 21 Mar. 1832. A.D.C. to his father, comdg. Meerut Div., 9 Oct. 1834 till 11 Dec. 1837. Apptd. Asst. to Comr. in Kumaon 11 Dec. 1837, but did not join this appt. Leave s.c. 2 yrs. to Cape 23 Mar. 1838. No record of active service.
Refs. : Burke's *Peerage*, 1923, p. 653, *s.n.* Dalhousie, E. Will dated 27 June 1840 ; proved 24 Dec. 1840. M.I. Almora.

RAMSAY, David (1808-1828). Lieutenant, 14th N.I. *b.* Edinburgh 19 May 1808. Cadet 1824. Arrived in India 21 May 1825. Ensign 7 Dec. 1824. Lieut. 23 Feb. 1827. *d.* on the river nr. Chinsura, Bengal, 22 July 1828, of liver complaint.
bapt. St. Cuthbert's, Edinburgh. Son of George Ramsay, of Craigleith, Edinburgh, and Ann Rigg his wife. Brother of Patrick Rigg Ramsay, *q.v.* Ed. St. Andrews Univ.
Services : Posted Ensign to 43rd N.I. in 1825 ; transfd. to 14th N.I. in 1826. No record of active service.
Refs. : A.J. xxvii. 358.

RAMSAY, David (1812-1839). Lieutenant, 37th N.I. *b.* Arbroath, co. Forfar, 14 July 1812. Cadet 1828. Arrived in India 10 Dec. 1829. Ensign (15 July 1829) 14 Mar. 1833. Lieut. 14 Nov. 1833. *d.* 26 Mar. 1839, on the march through the Bolan Pass.
6th son of Lt.-Gen. Hon. John Ramsay and Mary his wife. Brother of Hon. Sir Henry Ramsay, *q.v.* Addiscombe Cadet 1828.
Services : Ensign d.d. 2nd N.I. 8 Jan. 1830. Operations against the Kols in Chota Nagpur 1832 ; d.d. 2nd N.I. Actg. Ensign (having been 2 yrs. in India) 12 Mar. 1832. d.d. 28th N.I. 11 July 1832. Posted to 37th N.I. 14 Mar. 1833. A.D.C. to his father 2 Oct. 1833 till 9 Oct. 1834. Leave s.c. to Simla 16 Apr. till 16 Oct. 1834. Actg. Adjt. 3rd Local Horse 2 Mar. 1835. First Afghan War 1838-9 ; Lieut. 37th N.I.
Refs. : Burke's *Peerage*, 1923, p. 653, *s.n.* Dalhousie, E. *A.J.* N.S. xxix. 306. M.I. Afghan Memorial Church, Bombay.

RAMSAY, George (1813-1887). General. 10th N.I. Resdt. in Nepal. *b.* Bengal 22 Aug. 1813. Cadet 1829. Arrived in India

6 Oct. 1830. Ensign 6 Oct. 1830. Lieut. 23 Aug. 1834. Capt. 5 May 1841. Major 10 Sept. 1852. Lt. Col. 27 June 1857. Col. 1 Jan. 1862. Maj. Gen. 6 Mar. 1868. Lt. Gen. 1 Oct. 1877. Gen. 1 Oct. 1877. *d.* at his residence, Eccleston Sq., London, 3 July 1887.

Elder son of Hon. Andrew Ramsay, of Cheltenham, formerly B.C.S., and Rachel his wife, dau. of James Cock, of Rampur. Cousin-german of Hon. Sir Henry Ramsay and William Edmund (Maule Ramsay) Hay, *qq.v.* *m.* Sikraul 5 Aug. 1830, Eleanor Mary, eldest dau. of David Williamson, *q.v.* (*See also* Christopher George Fagan.) (She died 12 Oct. 1902.)

Services: Cadet d.d. 37th N.I. 19 Oct. 1830; 43rd N.I. 17 Mar. 1831. Actg. Ensign (having been 2 yrs. in India) 9 Nov. 1832. Posted Ensign to 25th N.I. 19 Oct. 1833. Fur. s.c. 4 July 1835 till 16 Dec. 1837. A.D.C. to Bdr.-Gen. J. Cock, *q.v.*, 11 May 1838. Asst. to Resdt. at Nagpur 6 Oct. 1842; Resdt. in Nepal 10 Apr. 1853 till 1867. Posted Lt. Col. to 10th N.I. in 1857. Transfd. to Staff Corps 18 Feb. 1861. Fur. 4 Jan. 1868 till death. No record of active service.

Refs.: Burke's *Peerage*, 1923, p. 653, *s.n.* Dalhousie, E. Burke's *Royal Families*, ped. lxii. Boase. *The Times*, 7 July 1887.

RAMSAY, Gilbert (*d.* 1793). Lieutenant, 23rd Bn. Sepoys. Cadet 1782. Arrived in India Sept. 1783. Ensign 13 Jan. 1783. Lieut. 1 Feb. 1789. *d.* Diamond Harbour, Bengal, 25 June 1793: drowned in the *Mary*.

Brother of Alexander Ramsay.

Services: Apptd. Cadet 22 May 1782, with permission to remain in England till the following year. Ensign 6th Bengal Eur. Bn. in July 1787; transfd. to 23rd Bn. Sepoys.

Refs.: Intestate; admon. 26 Nov. 1793.

RAMSAY, Graham (1807-?). Lieutenant, Pension Est. 61st N.I. *b.* Yarmouth 28 Feb. 1807. Cadet 1824. Ensign 6 Sept. 1825. Lieut. 11 July 1828. Pensioned in England 2 Mar. 1829. (Pension ceased after 1 Aug. 1860.)

bapt. Anstruther Wester. Son of Robert Ramsay, C.B., Rear Adm. R.N., and Janet Navall his wife. Brother of Robert Ramsay, *q.v.*, and of Margaret, wife of William Milner Neville Sturt, *q.v.* Ed. St. Andrews Univ.; matric. 3 Apr. 1821.

Services: Posted Ensign to 61st N.I. in 1826. Fur. s.c. 1 Sept. 1826 till pensioned. No record of active service.

THE BENGAL ARMY, 1758-1834   601

RAMSAY, Hon. Sir Henry (1816-1893). General, K.C.S.I., C.B. 53rd N.I. Comr. in Kumaon. *b.* Arbirlot, co. Forfar, 21 Sept. 1816. Cadet 1833. Arrived in India 26 Sept. 1834. Ensign (14 June 1834) 30 Oct. 1834. Lieut. 8 Jan. 1840. Capt. 15 Dec. 1849. Major 15 July 1857. Lt. Col. 2 Nov. 1861. Col. 18 Feb. 1866. Maj. Gen. 1 Oct. 1877. Lt. Gen. 1 Jan. 1880. Gen 22 Jan. 1889. *d.* 4 Turnham Rd., Gipsy Hill, Norwood, 16 Dec. 1893. Raised to the rank of an Earl's son in 1874. *bapt.* Arbirlot 4 Oct. 1816. 7th son of Lt.-Gen. Hon. John Ramsay and Mary his wife. Brother of George, 12th Earl of Dalhousie, and of James Ramsay, *q.v. m.* Naini Tal 11 Nov. 1850, Laura, dau. of Sir Henry Lushington, 3rd Bart., and niece of Matthew Lushington, *q.v.* (She died 29 July 1914.) Ed. Edinburgh Academy 1829-32.

Services : Ensign d.d. 69th N.I. 9 Oct. 1834 ; 13th N.I. 17 Oct. 1834. Posted to 30th N.I. 2 Mar. 1835 ; to 7th N.I. 23 Apr. 1835 ; to 53rd N.I. 16 Aug. 1837. A.D.C. to his father 23 Dec. 1837 till 1839. Adjt. Kumaon Local Bn. and Junior Asst. to Comr. in Kumaon 5 Aug. 1840, and spent the next 44 yrs. in Kumaon and Garhwal. Senior Asst. to Comr. in Garhwal 23 Nov. 1845 ; Comr. in Kumaon 20 Feb. 1856 till 1884. Was called the "King of Kumaon." Rejoined his Regt. tempy. Oct. 1848. Second Sikh War ; Capt. 53rd N.I., in garr. at Lahore (Medal). C.B. (Civil) 18 May 1860. K.C.S.I. 31 Dec. 1875. Transferred to Staff Corps 18 Feb. 1861.

Refs. : Burke's *Peerage*, 1923, p. 653, *s.n.* Dalhousie, E. Boase. *D.I.B. I.L.N.* lxviii (1876), 305 (portrait). *The Times*, 21 Dec. 1893.

***RAMSAY, James.** Ensign. Infantry. Cadet 1766. Ensign 5 Jan. 1767.
Services : N.F.P.
Refs. : B.M. Add. MSS. 6050, p. 90.

RAMSAY, James (1808-1868). Major General. 35th N.I. Comy. Gen. Bengal. *b.* co. Forfar 3 Oct. 1808. Cadet 1824. Arrived in India 3 Oct. 1825. Ensign 13 May 1825. Lieut. 16 July 1829. Capt. 24 Jan. 1845. Bt. Major 7 June 1849. Bt. Lt. Col. 28 Nov. 1854. Retired 11 Nov. 1858. Hon. Maj. Gen. 11 Nov. 1858. *d.* 46 Bryanston Sq., London, 26 Dec 1868.

3rd son of Lt.-Gen. Hon. John Ramsay and Mary his wife. Brother of William Maule Ramsay, *q.v. m.* Calcutta 3 Feb. 1840, Florence Harriet Charlotte, dau. of William Robert Burlton-Bennet,

B.C.S., and sister of Francis Edward Burlton-Bennet, *q.v.* (She died 13 Dec. 1889.) Addiscombe Cadet 1823-5.

Services: Posted Ensign to 23rd N.I. Actg. Adjt. 23rd N.I. 29 Feb. 1828. Exchanged to 35th N.I. 16 July 1829. Adjt. Dacca Provl. Bn. 31 Dec. 1829 till 5 Feb. 1830. S.A.C.G. 27 May 1830; D.A.C.G. 2 cl. 30 June 1835; 1 cl. 12 Apr. 1837. Comst. Ofr. 1st Div., Army of Indus, 6 Jan. 1839. Leave in India 16 Feb. 1839 till 17 Jan. 1840. First China War 1840-2; in Comst. Dept. at Singapore depot Apr. 1840 till Aug. 1841; Hong Kong depot Sept. 1841 till Nov. 1842 (Medal). A.C.G. 2 cl. 20 Dec. 1842. Gwalior campaign; Maharajpur (*Lond. Gaz.* 8 Mar. 1844); Principal Executive Comst. Ofr. (Bronze star). A.C.G. 1 cl. 2 May 1845; Joint Dy. Comy. Gen. 5 Feb. 1848. To conduct Comst. duties of Army of the Punjab 13 Oct. 1848. Second Sikh War; Ramnagar; passage of Chenab; Chilianwala; Gujerat (Medal with 2 clasps). Comy. Gen. and M.M.B. 9 Nov. 1852 till retirement. Fur. 1857 till 15 Feb. 1858. Bailiff *ad honores* of order of St. John of Jerusalem.

Refs.: Burke's *Peerage*, 1923, p. 653, *s.n.* Dalhousie, E. *Walford. Boase. I.L.N.* xxxvi. 397, 410. *The Times*, 29 Dec. 1868.

RAMSAY, John (1780-1818). Captain, 21st N.I. *b.* Whalsay, Shetland Is., 1780. Cadet 1798. Arrived in India 20 Aug. 1799. Ensign 29 Dec. 1799. Lieut. 29 May 1800. Capt. 16 Dec. 1814. *d.* Brijetolla, Calcutta, 20 Aug. 1818.

m. Calcutta 2 Feb. 1811, Elizabeth, dau. of William Hunter, M.D., Surg. Bengal Medical Est. (*D.N.B.*). (She died 7 Feb. 1856, aged 67.)

Services: Posted Lieut. to 1/10th N.I. 15 Apr. 1801. Transfd. to newly-raised 21st N.I. in 1803. Second Mahratta War 1804-5; Lieut. 21st N.I. Adjt. Calcutta Native Mil. 1807-11. Bk.Mr. at Ft. Wm. 22 Feb. 1811 till death. Capt. 2/21st N.I.; transfd. to 1/21st N.I. in 1817.

Refs.: S.M. 1819, i. 480.

RAMSAY, Jonathan (*d.* 1788). Captain. Infantry. Ensign (Madras) 27 Mar. 1764. Lieut. (Madras) 1 Dec. 1765. Capt. (Bengal) 7 Apr. 1769. Resigned 18 Jan. 1772. *d.* 15 Apr. 1788.

Services: Probably transfd. to Madras Army from H.M.S. (not traced), or commissioned from the ranks, as he is stated to have served for 17 yrs. when pensd. on Lord Clive's fund from 20 Oct. 1772, the date of his arrival in England, owing to wounds received on active service. Transfd. to Bengal Est. c. 1766.

RAMSAY, Michael (1788-1851). Colonel, 24th N.I. *b.* Falkirk 15 Nov. 1788. Cadet 1807. Arrived in India 21 Mar. 1809. Ensign 5 Feb. 1809. Lieut. 16 Dec. 1814. Capt. 25 Feb. 1825. Major 19 Sept. 1833. Lt. Col. 18 July 1840. Col. 17 Feb. 1851. *d.* 113 George St., Edinburgh, 15 Sept. 1851.
bapt. Falkirk 23 Nov. 1788. Son of Alexander Ramsay, of Mungal, co. Stirling, postmaster of Falkirk, and Christian Rattray his wife. Cousin of Robert Rankine (and *probably* related to William Rattray (1759-1819), *q.v.*). *m.* (before 1821) Helen. (She died 15 June 1888, aged 87.) His dau. *m.* James Knox Spence, *q.v.*
Services: Ensign 28th Regt. of Mil. Posted Ensign to 8th N.I. in 1809; Lieut. 2/8th N.I. Nepal War 1816; Lieut. 5th Gren. Bn., in 2nd Bde. Left Column (India medal). Fur. s.c. 2 Sept. 1817 till 19 Dec. 1820. Attached to Champaran L.I. 16 Apr. till 22 Aug. 1821. Actg. Garr. Engr. and Executive Ofr. at Hansi 22 May 1822; Asst. to Capt. J. Colvin, *q.v.*, 31 Mar. 1823; Asst. Supt. of Feroze Shah's canal 30 July 1823 till 7 June 1834. Transfd. to 24th N.I. (late 2/8th) May 1824. Posted Lt. Col. to 57th N.I. 11 Aug. 1841; to 5th N.I. 15 Feb. 1848; to 57th N.I. 12 Apr. 1848; to 67th N.I. 1849; to 57th N.I. 27 Mar. 1850. Fur. s.c. 5 July 1849 till death. Posted Col. to 24th N.I. 29 Apr. 1851.
Refs.: Boase. *I.M.* 19 Sept. 1851, p. 564. *G.M.* 1851, ii. 554.

RAMSAY, Patrick Rigg (1810-?). Ensign. 26th N.I. *b.* Edinburgh 15 Aug. 1810. Cadet 1827. Ensign 3 June 1829. Resigned in India 18 Sept. 1829.
Son of George Ramsay, of Craigleith, and Ann Rigg his wife. Brother of David Ramsay (1808-1828), *q.v.*
Services: Ensign d.d. 43rd N.I. 14 Jan. 1829; posted to 26th N.I. June 1829.

RAMSAY, Richard. Captain. Cavalry. Cadet 1770. Ensign 15 Nov. 1771. Lieut. 29 July 1776. Capt. 21 Feb. 1781. Deserted Jan. 1795. (? Living in Dec. 1828.)
m. Mary, eldest dau. of Samuel Skardon, *q.v.* (*See also* Thomas Wharton.)
Services: First Rohilla War; battle of St. George; Ensign Inf. Transfd. to Cav. 6 Apr. 1778; apptd. Adjt. 1st Cav. 30 Nov. 1778. "Served with distinction in all the campaigns under Gen. Goddard." Capt. comdg. 2nd Rissalah of Cav. in July 1787 and in 1792.

Second Rohilla War; battle of Bitaurah; Capt. comdg. two regts. of Cav.[1]

Refs.: *Cardew*, pp. 64, 65. *Hickey*, iv. 123-4. *Tours in Upper India*, by Major Archer (1833), ii. 12.

[1] *Note:* The cavalry on this occasion, owing to a faulty movement, got into disorder, in which state they were charged in flank by the Rohilla horse. Completely routed, both regts. fled in confusion, galloping through the ranks of 13th Bn. Sepoys in their flight and throwing them also into disorder. At a court of inquiry held subsequently, the two regts. were acquitted of any misconduct, but the trial of the C.O. was ordered in Jan. 1795. Ramsay, rather than face trial by C.M., absconded. According to one account, he afterwards entered the French service and served under Napoleon as a Comst. ofr. Hickey, however, states that two yrs. after his escape from close arrest he was seen and recognized in Scotland, where he was residing under an assumed name. Major Archer writes, " The officer who thus acquired a deathless infamy is still (Dec. 1828) alive and recently resided on the Continent." Thomas Edwards (*d.* 1815), *q.v.*, stated that he saw him " at his residence near Brussels," but does not give the date. He was living in or near Brussels with his family from 1805 till 1816, or later. (*Letters of John Orrok*, p. 198.)

RAMSAY, Robert (1803-1863). Colonel. 74th N.I. Dy. Mily. Auditor Gen., Bengal. *b.* Chelsea 16 June 1803. Cadet 1824. Arrived in India 29 June 1825. Ensign 8 Jan. 1825. Lieut. 9 Dec. 1825. Capt. 17 Mar. 1841. Major 14 July 1853. Lt. Col. 18 Nov. 1857. Retired 14 July 1859. Hon. Col. 14 July 1859. *d.* Ipswich 21 Feb. 1863.

bapt. Chelsea 1 Jan. 1804. Eldest son of Rear-Adm. Robert Ramsay, C.B., and Janet his wife. Brother of Graham Ramsay, *q.v. m.* 6 Apr. 1849, Caroline, dau. of S. Thomas, Esq., Ord. Dept. (She died Tower of London 24 Mar. 1851, aged 29.) Ed. St. Andrews Univ.[1]

Services: Posted Ensign to 10th N.I. Siege and capture of Bhurtpore; Lieut. d.d. 36th N.I. (India medal). Actg. Adjt. detachment of 10th N.I. on escort duty with C.-in-C. 27 Jan. 1832. Actg. Intr. & Qmr. 10th N.I. 8 Apr. 1835; do. 43rd N.I. 9 Aug. 1835; do. 71st N.I. 16 Dec. 1836 till 18 July 1837; do. 10th N.I. 28 July 1837; permanent do. 21 Mar. 1838 till 1841. Leave s.c. to Simla 1 Apr. till 30 Nov. 1839; fur. s.c. 4 Feb. 1841 till 10 Dec. 1843. Offg. 3rd Asst. Mily. Auditor Gen. 1 Nov. 1844; 2nd do. 10 Feb. 1845; 1st do. 20 Mar. 1846 till Sept. 1857. Second

Burma War 1852-3 ; Pegu ; Bt. Major 10th N.I. (Medal). Dy. Mily. Auditor Gen. 17 Sept. 1857. Fur. p.a. 15 Dec. 1858 till retirement.
Refs.: *The Times*, 24 Feb. 1863. *G.M.* 1863, i. 529.
¹' *Note :* His name is not in the matriculation roll.

RAMSAY, Silvester (*d.* 1810). Major. 3rd Bengal Eur. Bn. Cadet 1766. Ensign 6 Jan. 1767. Lieut. 23 Feb. 1769. Capt. 1 Apr. 1777. Major 5 Feb. 1781. Struck off 1791. *d.* Gt. Russell St., London, 13 Aug. 1810.
Services : Transfd. from 2/1st Bengal Eur. Regt. to comd. a Bn. of Sepoys 13 Sept. 1779 ; to comd. 1st Bn. Sepoys 28 Mar. 1781. Major 3rd Bengal Eur. Bn. in July 1787. On fur. in Dec. 1788.
Refs.: *G.M.* 1810, ii. 196.

RAMSAY, Sir Thomas, eighth baronet (*c.* 1765-1830). Colonel, 43rd N.I. *b. c.* 1765. Cadet 1783. Admitted 1783. Ensign 13 Apr. 1785. Lieut. 28 Oct. 1793. Capt. 30 June 1804. Major 6 Mar. 1814. Lt. Col. 1 June 1818. Lt. Col. Comdt. 1 May 1824. Col. 5 June 1829. *d.s.p.m.* Edinburgh 26 June 1830, when the assumption of this baronetcy ceased.

8th Bart. of Balmain. *s.* 1807. " Only surviving brother and heir of Sir James Ramsay, 7th Bart., sometime resident in Barbadoes, whose parentage and descent is unknown." (*G.E.C.*) ¹

m. 1st, St. James's, Westminster, 29 June 1809, Anne, youngest dau. of Rev. Dr. James Steele, of Jamaica, and of Mrs. Hardie, of St. James's St., London. (She died· Batavia 13 Oct. 1812, aged 35.) *m.* 2nd, 1819, Elizabeth, 2nd dau. of Duncan Macdonnell, of Glengarry, and widow of The Chisholm. (She died Thorn Faulcon, Somerset, 7 Oct. 1859, aged 82.)

Services : First Mahratta War 1782-4 ; as a Vol. in 6th Bn., with detachment under Lt.-Col. Charles Morgan, *q.v.* Posted to 14th Bn. Sepoys 8 Feb. 1790. Third Mysore War ; Seringapatam ; Ensign 14th Bn., with Col. Cockerell's detachment. Transfd. from 6th Eur. Bn. to 3rd do. 26 Mar. 1793 ; to 4th do. 21 Nov. 1793. Comdd. troops in Andaman Is. 24 Dec. 1793 till 1795. Transfd. to Bengal Eur. Regt. in 1799 ; Adjt. do. till Sept. 1804. Second Mahratta War ; Bundelkhand 1803-4 ; siege of Bhurtpore (w. 7 Jan. 1805 ; s.w. in 4th assault 21 Feb. 1805) ; Capt. Bengal Eur. Regt. Fur. s.c. 25 Aug. 1805 till 7 ·Dec. 1809. Served in the Moluccas 1810-17 ; as Comdt. there from Dec. 1811 till Apr. 1817. Fur. 1817-21. Posted Lt. Col. to 27th N.I. 1818; to 22nd N.I. 1820 ;

to 1/3rd N.I. 1821; as Lt. Col. Comdt. to 19th N.I. (late 2/3rd)
May 1824; to 28th N.I. 4 Aug. 1826; to 16th N.I. 30 Oct. 1826;
to 43rd N.I. 22 Apr. 1828. Fur. p.a. 31 Oct. 1828 till death.
Refs.: *G.E.C.*: *Complete Baronetage*, ii. 302. Scott's *Fasti*, i.
307. *E.I.M.C.* i. 106-8. *G.M.* 1809, ii. 676; 1813, i. 386. *A.J.*
N.S. ii. 244.

[1] *Note*: Served heir general to his grandfather, Andrew Ramsay
of Abbotshall, 26 Oct. 1807.

RAMSAY, Thomas (1806-1836). Ensign, 22nd N.I. *b.* St.
Andrew's psh., Edinburgh, 7 Aug. 1806. Cadet 1826. Arrived
in India 20 May 1827. Ensign 17 Jan. 1827. *d.* nr. Udaipur,
Jaipur, 27 Mar. 1836.

Son of Thomas Ramsay, of the W.I., and of Princes St., Edinburgh.
m. Jane. Ed. Edinburgh High School.
Services: Posted Ensign to 22nd N.I. 19 June 1827. Fur. s.c.
14 Mar. 1828 till 22 Oct. 1831. Shekhawat expedn. 1834; Ensign
22nd N.I.
Refs.: *A.J.* N.S. xxi. 109.

RAMSAY, Thomas Kennedy (1788-1807). Lieutenant, 11th
N.I. Pioneers. *b.* Kirkmichael, co. Ayr, 7 Jan. 1788. Cadet
1803. Arrived in India 2 Dec. 1804. Ensign 31 Oct. 1804.
Lieut. 31 Oct. 1804. *d.* 18 Nov. 1807, of wounds received at the
assault of Komona fort on 30 Oct.

bapt. Kirkmichael 10 Jan. 1788. 2nd son of Rev. John Ramsay,
minister of Kirkmichael 1766-1801, and Margaret M'Fadzean his
wife.
Services: Posted Lieut. to 2/11th N.I. in 1805. Operations
against the Rana of Gohad 1806; capture of Gohad; Lieut. 2/11th
N.I. Operations against Dhundia Khan 1807; siege of Komona
(s.w.); Lieut. 2/11th N.I., serving with Pioneers.
Refs.: Scott's *Fasti*, iii. 45. *A.A.R.* x. 21. *G.M.* 1808, ii. 851.
Will dated camp, Camoona, 21 Oct. 1807; proved 2 Jan. 1808.

RAMSAY, William Maule (1804-1871). Lieut. General. 35th
N.I. *b.* Brechin Castle 20 May 1804. Cadet 1820. Arrived in
India Oct. 1821. Ensign 21 Mar. 1821. Lieut. 21 July 1823.
Capt. 4 Jan. 1836. Major 5 July 1844. Lt. Col. 28 Sept. 1850.
Col. 25 Oct. 1859. Maj. Gen. 1 July 1862. Lt. Gen. 11 May
1871. *d. unm.* 32 St. James's St., London, 13 Dec. 1871.

Eldest son of Lt.-Gen. Hon. John Ramsay and Mary his wife.
Brother of Andrew Ramsay, *q.v.* Sandhurst Cadet.

Services: Posted Ensign to 2/4th N.I.; transfd. as Lieut. to 31st N.I. July 1823; to 62nd N.I. (late 2/31st) May 1824. First Burma War; Arakan 1825; Lieut. 62nd N.I. (India medal). Adjt. Dinajpur Local Bn. 12 July 1825. Intr. & Qmr. 62nd N.I. 14 June 1827. Extra A.D.C. to Earl of Dalhousie, C.-in-C., 3 Feb. 1829; Persian Intr. do. 1 Jan. 1830; do. to Sir Edward Barnes, G.C.B., C.-in-C., 10 Jan. 1832. Intr. & Qmr. 62nd N.I. 18 Mar. 1834. Asst. in *Thagi* Dept. in Bihar 5 Oct. 1835. Leave s.c. to Cape 25 Jan. till 23 Dec. 1840. D.C. 3 cl., Saugor & Narbada, 9 Mar. 1843. Fur. s.c. 2 Mar. 1845 till 12 Dec. 1849. Posted Lt. Col. to 62nd N.I. Nov. 1850. Fur. s.c. 22 Feb. 1853 till Dec. 1855. Bdr. comdg. Gwalior Contingent 17 Mar. 1856 till 1857, when it mutinied. Transfd. to 70th N.I. June 1856; to 35th N.I. in 1857. Fur. 3 yrs. Mar. 1858.

Refs.: Burke's *Peerage*, 1923, p. 653, *s.n.* Dalhousie, E. *Boase. The Times*, 15 Dec. 1871.

RAMSEY, William (1793-1847). Major, Invalid Est. 41st N.I. *bapt.* St. Martin's, Beverley, Yorks., 19 Mar. 1793. Cadet 1808. Admitted 25 Sept. 1809. Ensign 22 Mar. 1810. Lieut. 16 Dec. 1814. Capt. 2 Aug. 1828. Major 28 June 1838. Invalided 10 July 1846. *d.* Fatehgarh, U.P., 7 Feb. 1847.

Son of Robert Ramsey (? Purser R.N.) and Harriet his wife. *m.* 1st, Delhi 5 May 1832, Miss Susan Hay Crichton. (*See also* Charles Devaynes Blair.) (She died Delhi 26 May 1837, aged 24.) *m.* 2nd, Delhi 1 Jan. 1838, Harriet Doveton, 2nd dau. of George Wayland Moseley, *q.v.* (*See also* Charles Finch Farmer.)

Services: Posted Ensign to 21st N.I.; Lieut. 2/21st N.I. Transfd. to 41st N.I. (late 1/21st) May 1824. Fort Adjt. at Delhi 9 July 1825. Actg. Adjt. & Qmr. newly-raised 3rd Extra N.I. 12 July 1825. Siege and capture of Bhurtpore; Bt. Capt. Rt. Wing 41st N.I. Leave s.c. to Simla 1 Apr. till Dec. 1835. Dy. Postmr. at Delhi 25 Nov. 1837.

Refs.: *G.M.* 1838, i. 654. Will dated Dehra Dun 26 Nov. 1846; proved 26 Apr. 1847.

RAMUS, William Pickering (1784-1817). Captain, 6th N.I. *bapt.* St. James's Palace, Westminster, 31 Aug. 1784. Cadet 1799. Arrived in India 10 Dec. 1800. Ensign 18 Dec. 1800. Lieut. 25 Sept. 1802. Capt. 28 Nov. 1814. *d.* Bareilly, U.P., 8 Sept. 1817.

Son of Charles Ramus [1] and Mary his wife.
Services: Posted Ensign to 1/6th N.I. 17 Apr. 1801. Adjt.

2/6th N.I. 14 Feb. 1807 till 1812. Capt. Lt. 6th N.I. 31 May 1813. Nepal War 1814-15; Capt. 2/6th N.I., in 1st Div.

[1] *Note:* "On board his yacht, off Penzance, 21 June 1823, Charles Ramus, Esq., aged 82." (*S.M.* 1823, ii. 255.) He was probably a brother of Nicholas Ramus, page of the backstairs at St. James's Palace, who was father of the beautiful Miss Benedetta Ramus (afterwards Lady Day), painted by Romney. (Cf. Busteed's *Echoes from Old Calcutta*, and *Hickey*, iii. 301.) This family was of Dutch extraction.

RANDALL, George (1786-1857). Lieutenant. 12th N.I. *b.* Orford, Suffolk, 28 May 1786. Cadet 1800. Arrived in India 6 Feb. 1802. Ensign 22 Nov. 1801. Lieut. 30 Sept. 1803. Resigned 17 Aug. 1814. *d.* Middleton, Suffolk, 12 May 1857.

Several times mayor of the boroughs of Orford and Aldeburgh. *bapt.* Orford 13 Aug. 1786. 4th son of John Randall, Chamberlain of Orford 1822-30, and Mary his wife, dau. of John Webber, of Friston, Suffolk. Brother of Samuel Randall, gentleman usher to George III, IV, William IV and Victoria, and groom of the privy chamber to Victoria. *m.* Gretna Green, Mary Ann Todd. (She died Aldeburgh 1 May 1865, aged 73.)

Services: Posted Ensign to 12th N.I. in 1802. Operations in Jumna Doab 1802-3; Sasni; Ensign 2/12th N.I. Second Mahratta War 1803-5; Aligarh; battle of Delhi; Laswari; Monson's retreat (w. 25 Aug. 1804); Bhurtpore; Lieut. 2/12th N.I. (India medal). Operations in Oudh 1807-8; Akbarpur; Pathar-serai; Lieut. 2/12th N.I. Fur. 1811 till resignation.

Refs.: Howard & Crisp, iii. 175, *s.n.* Randall. *G.M.* 1857, ii. 100.

RANKEN, Charles (1751/52-1802). Captain. Infantry. *b.* Antrim 1751/52. Cadet 1769. Ensign 1769. Lieut. 12 Nov. 1772. Capt. 15 Nov. 1780. Struck off 1793. *d.* Highgate, Middlesex, 9 Apr. 1802, aged 50; *bur.* St. Mary's churchyard, Hornsey.

Eldest son of Rev. John Rankin,[1] Presbyterian minister at Antrim for 40 yrs., and Sarah his wife, dau. of Charles Lynd or Lind. Brother of John Rankin, *q.v. m.* 18 Jan. 1787, Mary, dau. of Rev. Moses Grant, rector of Nolton, co Pembroke, and preby. of St. David's, and niece of Henry Grant, *q.v.* (She died Clifton 1 Apr. 1849, aged 82.) Father of John Grant Ranken, *q.v.*, and of Alicia, wife of Evan Thomas, of Llwyn Madoc, co. Brecon.

Services: Surveying under James Rennell, *q.v.*, in 1776; do.

in Ramgarh district in Jan. 1779. Capt. comdg. a Coy. of 3rd Bengal Eur. Regt. in 1782. Constructed mily. road Calcutta—Chunar 1781-5. Fur. 2 Nov. 1785 till struck off. Resided in Calcutta for some time after retirement and continued to draw his salary as Supt. of the mily. road. Most of his service appears to have been spent in surveying and civil engineering.

Refs.: *Gen. Scrap Book* 4, fol. 53, Bodleian. *Macpherson*, p. 377. Will at Somerset House, dated 25 Mar. 1802; proved 19 May 1802. M.I. St. Mary's churchyard, Hornsey.

[1] *Note:* He spelt his name with an 'i', as did all his sons throughout their service in the Bengal army. Charles, however, appears to have altered the spelling to Ranken after his return from India, and the Rev. John Rankin's name is spelt Ranken on his tombstone, probably from information supplied by Charles.

RANKEN, George (1807-1874). Lieut. Colonel. 69th N.I.
b. Edinburgh 30 Jan. 1807. Cadet 1826. Arrived in India 31 Oct. 1827. Ensign 25 May 1827. Lieut. 3 Mar. 1837. Capt. 29 May 1848. Bt. Major 1854. Retired 17 July 1854. Hon. Lt. Col. 28 Nov. 1854. *d.* suddenly, 3 Windsor Terr., Portobello, 7 Sept. 1874.

Son of William Ranken, currier ("Annuitant, Stirling"), and Catherine McNish or McNeish his wife. His sister *m.* Robert Chalmers, *q.v.* Cousin-german of the wife of W. D. Playfair, *q.v. m.* 26 Aug. 1856, Sophia, only dau. of Patrick Moir Davidson, R.N. and E.I.C.N.S. (She *re-m.* 1876, Dr. William MacGrath, of Bayswater.)

Services: Posted Ensign to 1st Extra Regt. (became 69th N.I.) 3 Jan. 1828; transfd. to 72nd N.I. 24 Sept. 1835; reposted to 69th N.I. 5 Apr. 1836. Apptd. to Vol. Regt. for China 15 Feb. 1840; Adjt. do. 6 Nov. 1840 till 22 May 1841, when broken up. First China War 1840-1; Chusan; Lieut. 1st Bengal Vols. (Medal). Fur. s.c. 24 Jan. 1842 till 12 Oct. 1844. Operations in Sind against Hill tribes 1845; Bt. Capt. 69th N.I. Second Sikh War; passage of Chenab; Chilianwala; Gujerat; Capt. 69th N.I. (Medal with 2 clasps).

Refs.: *Family of Playfair,* by Rev. A. G. Playfair, 3rd edn., 1913. *The Families of Moir and Byres,* by A. G. Mitchell Gill (Edin., 1885), p. 35. *The Times,* 11 Sept. 1874.

RANKEN, John Grant (1789-1812). Lieutenant, 18th N.I.
b. Holywood, co. Down, 26 July 1789. Cadet 1803. Arrived

in India 17 Mar. 1805. Ensign 30 Apr. 1805. Lieut. 1 May 1805. *d.* Cheltenham 6 Aug. 1812.

Eldest son of Charles Ranken, *q.v.*, of Richmond Lodge, nr. Holywood, and Mary his wife. Ed. Charterhouse June 1801-Feb. 1802.

Services: Posted Lieut. to 18th N.I. With Ramgarh Bn. 1810-11. Fur. s.c. 1811 till death.

Refs.: *Charterhouse School List*. *G.M.* 1812, ii. 193. Will dated 23 July 1812; proved Aug. 1812.

RANKIN, John (1762/63-1839). Captain. 2nd N.I. *b.* Antrim 1762/63. Cadet 1780. Arrived in India 26 Aug. 1780. Ensign 27 Sept. 1780. Lieut. 18 July 1781. Capt. 15 Jan. 1799. Retired 27 May 1801. *d.* Vienna 21 June 1839, aged 76.

Son of Rev. John Rankin, Presbyterian minister at Antrim, and Sarah his wife. Brother of William Rankin, *q.v.*

Services: Actg. Adjt. Ramghur L.I. 1781-2. Lieut. 31st Bn. Sepoys in July 1787 and in 1792. Supt. of new road, Chunar to Calcutta, 24 Jan. 1785 till 1788; Supt. of new mily. road, Midnapore to Berhampore, 1788-90. Postmr. at Chas, B. & O., 1793-4. Fur. 27 Mar. 1797 till retirement.

Refs.: *G.M.* 1839, ii. 438.

RANKIN, Thomas (*d.* 1766). Cadet, Infantry. Cadet 1764. *d.* 1766: drowned nr. Suti, Bengal.

(*Possibly* brother of William Rankin, *q.v.*)

Services: Sailed for India in the *Asia* 16 May 1764.

RANKIN, William (*d.* 1831). Major. 1st N.I. Cadet 1782. Admitted 22 Jan. 1783. Ensign 20 Jan. 1783. Lieut. 3 Mar. 1789. Capt. 13 July 1803. Major 1 July 1810. Retired 9 June 1814. *d.* Charles St., Berkeley Sq., London, 20 Oct. 1831.

Son of Rev. John Rankin, of Antrim, and Sarah his wife. Brother of Charles Ranken and cousin of David Ruddell, *qq.v.* *m.* (?)

Services: Apptd. Cadet 17 Oct. 1781; sailed for India in the *Warren Hastings* 6 Feb. 1782. Ensign 1st Bengal Eur. Bn. in July 1787; transfd. from 2nd Eur. Bn. to 15th Bn. Sepoys 5 Feb. 1790; from 6th Eur. Bn. to 11th Bn. Sepoys 9 Nov. 1792. Postmr. at Chas, B. & O., 1798 till 1800 or later. Lieut. 1st N.I. With Ramgarh Bn. 1802-5; Supt. of mily. roads 1805-10. Fur. 1811 till retirement.

Refs.: *G.M.* 1831, ii. 473. Will dated 25 Jan. 1830; codicil dated 6 July 1831; admon. 6 Mar. 1841.

THE BENGAL ARMY, 1758-1834 611

RANNIE, Hugh. (*See* **RENNY.**)

RAPER, Felix Vincent (1778-1849). Major General. Colonel 1st N.I. A.G.G. Murshidabad. *b.* Macao, China, 1778. Cadet 1796. Arrived in India 18 Feb. 1798. Ensign 29 Sept. 1797. Lieut. 10 Sept. 1798. Capt. 24 Jan. 1809. Major 1 Aug. 1819. Lt. Col. 1 May 1824. Col. 1 Dec. 1829. Maj. Gen. 28 June 1838. *d.* Norfolk Cresc., Hyde Pk., London, 14 Nov. 1849.

Lord of the manors of Kingshall, Brandhall, Rousehall and Wascolies, nr. Clopton, and owned estates nr. Blythborough and Alderton, Suffolk. (*Probably* son of Matthew Raper, H.C. Canton Est., Chief of Council 1777-81.) *m.* Fatehgarh 5 May 1820, Elizabeth, 2nd dau. of Charles Fraser, *q.v.* (*See also* Richard Home.)

Services: Posted Ensign to 1st Bengal Eur. Regt. in 1798; Lieut. 10th N.I. d.d. Ramgarh Bn. 1802. Capt. Lt. 10th N.I. 13 Sept. 1807. Comdd. a Coy. 10th N.I. on escort duty to Kabul in 1809. To survey cantts. in Delhi and Rewari Comds. 16 Jan. 1810; to survey S. and W. frontiers of Bihar and Bengal 1 Oct. 1813. Tempy. S.A.C.G. in the field 27 Oct. 1814. Nepal War 1814-15; tempy. S.A.C.G.; Capt. 1/10th N.I. 2nd Asst. to Resdt. at Lucknow 9 Nov. 1816; 1st do. 1818; Dy. Postmaster at Lucknow 12 May 1818. P.A. at Jaipur 1 Mar. 1824. Posted Lt. Col. to 34th N.I. May 1824; to 40th N.I. 24 May 1825. Fur. p.a. 4 June 1826 till 16 Sept. 1831, and 11 Jan. 1832 till 30 Nov. 1835. Posted Col. to 42nd N.I. 24 Jan. 1831; to 70th N.I. 28 Dec. 1835. Fur. p.a. 20 Jan. 1837 till 14 Nov. 1838. Offg. A.G.G. Murshidabad 1 July 1840; permanent do. 11 Feb. 1841 till death. Col. 1st N.I. 1844. Fur. s.c. 28 Jan. 1849 till death.

Refs.: *G.M.* 1850, i. 105. Will dated 13 July 1835; proved 13 Mar. 1851.

*RASHFIELD, Albert (*d.* 1767). Lieut. Fireworker, Artillery. Cadet 1765. Fireworker (? May 1766). *d.* 1767.

m. Anna.

Services: Apptd. Cadet and Conductor of Art. 7 Feb. 1765. (G.O. 19 Mar. 1765.) Shown as Lieut. F. (no date) in *A.L.* of 1 Feb. 1767. He is perhaps to be identified with the Mr. Rashfield, a Conductor, who was one of those whom Sir Robert Fletcher, *q.v.*, offered to appoint to act as officers on 14 May 1766. (*Broome*, appendix BB, p. lxxii.) He is not given by Stubbs.

Refs.: *B.M. Add. MS. 6050.* Will dated 26 Feb. 1766; proved 24 Apr. 1767.

RATHBORNE, Joseph (*d.* 1777). Ensign, Infantry. Cadet 1773. Ensign 14 Aug. 1776. *d.* Berhampore 22 Dec. 1777.

N.B.—The following is conjectural only : (? Eldest son of William Rathborne, of Dublin, and Anne his wife, dau. of Robert Billing. *m.* June 1774, Anne, dau. of Robert Madden, of Meadesbrook, co. Meath.) (? T.C.D. ; Pensioner 8 July 1763 ; B.A. 1768.)

Services : First Rohilla War ; battle of St. George ; Cadet with 2nd Regt.

Refs. : (? Burke's *Landed Gentry of Ireland*, p. 583, *s.n.* Rathborne, late of Scripplestown, co. Dublin.)

RATTRAY, Alexander (1746-1782). Lieutenant, Artillery. (163) *b.* 28 May 1746. Cadet 1778. Fireworker 19 Sept. 1778. Lieut. 17 Sept. 1779. *d.* in the China Seas 1782.

3rd son of James Rattray, of Ranagullon,[1] and Jean his wife, 4th dau. of Sir James Kinloch, 2nd Bart., of that ilk. Brother of William Rattray (1759-1819), *q.v.*, cousin-german of Francis Peregrine Kinloch, *q.v.*, and grand-uncle of Charles Rattray, *q.v.*

Services : Apptd. Cadet in India 17 July 1778.

Refs. : Family information. Burke's *Landed Gentry*, 4th edn., p. 1253, *s.n.* Rattray, of Barford House, co. Warwick. *Anderson*, iii. 734. Burke's *Peerage*, 1923, p. 1298, *s.n.* Kinloch, Bart., of Kinloch. Will dated July 1781 ; proved 29 Apr. 1782.

[1] *Note :* Ran(n)agullion, Runnygullion or Ranagulzeon.

RATTRAY, Charles (1810-1841). Lieutenant, 20th N.I. *b.* Daventry, Northants, 29 Aug. 1810. Cadet 1826. Arrived in India 23 Sept. 1827. Ensign 13 May 1827. Lieut. 20 May 1834. *d.* 3 Nov. 1841 : assassinated at Lughmani, nr. Charikar, Afghanistan.[1]

bapt. Daventry 7 Dec. 1810. Son of Charles Rattray, M.D., and Marianne his wife, dau. of Thomas Freeman, of Whilton, Northants. Grand-nephew of Alexander Rattray, *q.v.*, and nephew of the wife of Charles Wedderburn, *q.v.* Ed. Rugby ; admitted 1821.

Services : Posted Ensign to 20th N.I. 3 Jan. 1828. Actg. Adjt. to a detachment of British troops proceeding with the Mission to Peshawar 29 Mar. 1839. P.A. in Turkestan 6 Sept. 1839. Apptd. to Shah Shuja's army 1 Oct. 1839 ; selected for employment under the Envoy, Sir W. Macnaghten ; apptd. A.P.A. to Major Eldred Pottinger (*D.N.B.*) in Kohistan. First Afghan War 1839-41 ; Bamian 1840, under Bdr. W. H. Dennie (*Lond. Gaz.* 9 Jan. 1841) ; A.P.A. at Charikar. Durani 3 cl. 7 Sept. 1841.

THE BENGAL ARMY, 1758-1834   613

Refs.: Family information. Burke's *Landed Gentry*, 4th edn., p. 1253, *s.n.* Rattray, of Barford House, co. Warwick. *Rugby School Register.* M.I. Afghan Memorial Church, Bombay.

[1] *Note:* He was treacherously cut down at the end of a conference with some of the insurgent chiefs besieging Charikar.

RATTRAY, George Herbert (1801-1822). Lieutenant, 21st N.I. *b.* India Jan. 1801. Cadet 1817. Ensign (?) Lieut. 1 Aug. 1818. *d.* Kamptee, C.P., 7 Aug. 1822 : kld. in a duel.

Only son of James Rattray, B.C.S., 2nd Judge of the Provl. Court of Appeal at Dacca, and Charlotte his wife, *née* Vaughan. Nephew of William Rattray (1785-1813), *q.v.*

Services: Ensign H.M. 87th Ft. (in India) 1 Sept. 1816. Admitted a Cadet and promoted Ensign (G.O. 5 Sept. 1818); posted Lieut. to 1/21st N.I. 1818.

Refs.: Family information. M.I. Kamptee.

RATTRAY, John (*d.* 1798). Colonel. 17th N.I. Cadet 1768. Arrived in India 30 May 1769. Ensign 26 July 1769. Lieut. 14 Nov. 1772. Capt. 7 Oct. 1780. Major 179-. Lt. Col. 1 Mar. 1794. Col. 8 Jan. 1796. Retired 1798. *d.* Craighall, co. Perth, 26 Nov. 1798.

Of Craighall-Rattray. 2nd son of John Rattray, of Craighall-Rattray, surgeon in Edinburgh, and Christian his 1st wife, dau. of George Main, jeweller in Edinburgh. *m.* St. Andrew's, Holborn, 11 Jan. 1798, Julia, dau. of James Simpson, of Chancery Lane.

Services: Fur. 30 Nov. 1775 till 2 Oct. 1778. First Mahratta War 1779-84 ; surprised and defeated a band of Kathis nr. Ahmedabad in Dec. 1780 ; retreat down Bhor Ghaut 24 Apr. 1781 (w.) ; succeeded Thomas Harding, *q.v.*, in comd. of 5th N.I. with the Bombay detachment in 1782, and returned to Bengal in comd. of that Regt. in 1784. Capt. 2nd Bengal Eur. Bn. in July 1787 ; Capt. comdg. 7th Bn. Sepoys in Dec. 1788. Third Mysore War ; Arikera ; Penagra ; Seringapatam ; Major comdg. 7th Bn. Fur. 18 Jan. 1797 till retirement.

Refs.: Family information. Burke's *Landed Gentry*, 15th edn., p. 1894, *s.n.* Burn-Clerk-Rattray, of Craighall Rattray, Douglas' *Duronuye*, p. 278. *Williams*, pp. 97, 103. *India Gazette*, 9 June 1781. *G.M.* 1798, i. 83. *S.M.* 1799, p. 908.

RATTRAY, William (1759-1819). Bt. Lieut. Colonel. Artillery. (138) *b.* 30 Oct. 1759. Country Cadet 1772. Admitted 24 Dec. 1774. Fireworker 24 Dec. 1774. Lieut. 20 June 1778. Capt.

Lt. 22 June 1783. Capt. 25 May 1786. Major 5 Nov. 1796. Bt. Lt. Col. 1 Jan. 1798. Retired 6 June 1798. *d.s.p.* at his residence, Downie Park, 20 Dec. 1819.

Of Downie Park. 5th son of James Rattray, of Ranagullon, and Jean Kinloch his wife. Brother of Alexander Rattray, *q.v.* (*Probably* related to Michael Ramsay, *q.v.*) *m.* Dundee 22 Dec. 1796, Henrietta Janet, dau. of John Rankine, of Dudhope.

Services : First Mahratta War May 1779 till 1781 ; retreat down the Bhor Ghaut Apr. 1781 (w.). 1st Bn. Art. in July 1787. Apptd. a member of the gun carriage committee 31 Jan. 1794. Fur. 1 Feb. 1796 till retirement.

Refs. : Family information. Burke's *Landed Gentry*, 4th edn., p. 1253, *s.n.* Rattray, of Barford House, co. Warwick. *S.M.* 1796, p. 864 ; 1820, i. 190. *G.M.* 1820, i. 90.

RATTRAY, William (1785-1813). Lieutenant, 11th N.I. *b.* 3 Mar. 1785. Cadet 1802. Arrived in India 15 Oct. 1803. Ensign 13 Sept. 1803. Lieut. 10 Sept. 1804. *d. unm.* Kunch, U.P., 19 Aug. 1813.

bapt. St. George the Martyr, Queen's Sq., London, 7 Apr. 1785. 3rd son of James Rattray, of Arthurstone (a branch of the Rannagullion family), and Henrietta his wife, 2nd dau. of Robert Heronshaw. Uncle of George Herbert Rattray, *q.v.*

Services : Originally a Cav. Cadet. Ensign d.d. 12th N.I. in 1804 ; transfd. as Lieut. to 11th N.I. in 1805. Adjt. Murshidabad Provl. Bn. 1808-10. Reduction of Kalinjar 1812 ; Lieut. 11th N.I. Lieut. 2/11th N.I.

Refs. : Family information.

RAVENSCROFT, Edward William (1809-1856). Lieutenant, Invalid Est. 72nd N.I. *b.* Kingston-upon-Hull, Yorks., 14 Jan. 1809. Cadet 1826. Arrived in India 5 Oct. 1827. Ensign 20 May 1827. Lieut. 29 July 1834. Invalided 5 Feb. 1835. *d.* Chunar 22 Dec. 1856.

bapt. Holy Trinity, Kingston-upon-Hull, 24 Feb. 1809. Son of William Ravenscroft and Marianne his wife. Stepson of William Alexander Urquhart, of Fenchurch St., London, merchant. *m.* 1st, Calcutta 17 Dec. 1832, Miss Georgiana Oram (? dau. of Alfred Oram, of Faridpur, indigo planter). (She died Kishunnagar, B. & O., 19 Jan. 1838.) *m.* 2nd, Serampore 20 June 1839, Caroline, eldest dau. of E. M. Sandford, of Arrah, B. & O., indigo planter.

Services : Posted Ensign to 4th Extra Regt. (became 72nd N.I.) 3 Jan. 1828. Fur. s.c. 14 Sept. 1830 till 23 June 1832. To do duty

at Chunar 31 Mar. 1841 ; actg. Adjt. & Qmr. to Eur. Invalids at Chunar 29 Sept. 1842 ; Postmr. at Hooghly ; Adjt. & Qmr. to Eur. Invalids at Chunar May 1851 till death. No record of active service.
Refs.: *I.M.* 17 Feb. 1857, p. 115. Will dated 21 Dec. 1856 ; proved 31 Jan. 1857. M.I. Chunar.

RAWLINS, Henry Brotherson (1782-1817). Capt. Lieutenant, 7th N.I. *b.* Aldershot 4 May 1782. Cadet 1800. Arrived in India 17 Sept. 1801. Ensign 27 Oct. 1801. Lieut. 30 Sept. 1803. Capt. Lt. 16 Dec. 1814. *d.* in India 24 May 1817.
bapt. Aldershot 11 Nov. 1782. Son of Henry Rawlins and Mary Hill his wife. Stepson of James McKenzie and brother of Maria Loscombe. *m.* Calcutta 11 Nov. 1806, Miss Marianna Fitzgerald.
Services: Ensign d.d. 18th N.I. in 1802. Posted Ensign to 7th N.I. Capture of Java 1811 ; Lieut. 4th Bn. Bengal Vols. Capt. Lt. 2/7th N.I.
Refs.: Will dated, " My birthday, 4 May 1817 ; " proved 30 May 1817 ; P.C.C. (471, Cresswell).

RAWLINS, John (1791-1847). Lieut. Colonel, Artillery. (411) *b.* Overton, Hants, 12 Mar. 1791. Cadet 1808. Arrived in India 21 Oct. 1809. Fireworker 27 Oct. 1809. Lieut. 1 Oct. 1816. Capt. 1 May 1824. Major 31 Dec. 1839. Lt. Col. 3 July 1845. *d.* on R. Ganges, nr. Calcutta, 31 Mar. 1847.
Son of John Rawlins, of Overton, and Mary his wife. Nephew of Henry Wilkins Hicks, *q.v.* Woolwich Cadet.
Services: Capture of Mauritius 1810-11 ; Lieut. F. 6th Coy. 1st Bn. Foot Art. First Burma War ; Arakan 1825 ; Capt. comdg. 3rd Coy. 2nd Bn. Major 3rd Bn. 4 June 1841 ; posted as Lt. Col. to 8th Bn. 4 July 1845.
Refs.: *A.J.* xxvii. 599 ; N.S. xxi. 105-6. *I.M.* 2 June 1847, p. 328.

RAWLINSON, Abraham Beck (1754-1781). Lieutenant, Infantry. *b.* 1754. Cadet 1780. Ensign 1780. Lieut. 1781. *d.s.p.* at sea Mar. 1781, on the voyage out to India.
7th and youngest son of Abraham Rawlinson, of Lancaster, and Ellen his wife, dau. of William Godsalve.
Services: Sailed for India in the *Earl of Dartmouth* 3 June 1780, aged 25.
Refs.: Burke's *Landed Gentry*, 9th edn., p. 1241, *s.n.* Rawlinson,

of Duddon Hall, Cumberland ; *Peerage*, 1923, p. 1854, *s.n.* Rawlinson, B. Foster's *Lancs. Peds.*

RAWLINSON, George Hutton (1795-1856). Major. Artillery. (449) *bapt.* St. Anne's, Manchester, 16 Sept. 1795. Cadet 1813. Admitted 5 Aug. 1814. Fireworker 30 Nov. 1814. Lieut. 1 Sept. 1818. Capt. 25 July 1831. Retired 4 Aug. 1841. Hon. Major 28 Nov. 1854. *d.* London 2 Jan. 1856, aged 60.

Son of William Rawlinson and Sarah his wife. (*Probably* of the family of Rawlinson, of Duddon Hall.) Addiscombe Cadet 1811-14.

Services : Comdg. Art. in Cuttack in 1823. First Burma War 1824-6 ; Adjt. Bengal detachment of Art. with Sir A. Campbell's force in Burma, and offg. in Comst. Dept. (India medal). Asst. to Comr. Tenasserim province 16 Mar. 1833 till 1839. In charge of Police at Moulmein 1836. Fur. s.c. 4 Feb. 1839 till retirement.
Refs.: I.M. 15 Jan. 1856, p. 51. *G.M.* 1856, i. 213.

RAWNSLEY, Charles (1786-1811). Lieutenant, 18th N.I. *bapt.*, Bourne, Lincs., 30 May 1786. Cadet 1806. Arrived in India 25 Nov. 1807. Ensign 29 Oct. 1807. Lieut. 1811. *d.* Fatehgarh. 4 July 1811.

Son of Thomas Rawnsley, of Bourne, and Deborah his wife. Brother of Rev. Thomas Hardwicke Rawnsley, of Halton Holgate, Lincs.

Services : Barasat C.C. Posted Ensign to 18th N.I. in 1808. Operations in Bundelkhand 1809 ; Rajaoli ; Ajaigarh ; Ensign 1/18th N.I.
Refs.: G.M. 1812, i. 497. M.I. Fatehgarh fort cemetery.

RAWSTORNE, Edward (1745/46-1801). Major General. Colonel Comdt., Cavalry. *b.* 1745/46. Cadet 1764. Admitted 1 Sept. 1764. Ensign 6 Mar. 1765. Lieut. 14 Dec. 1766. Capt. 14 Oct. 1769. Major 9 Jan. 1781. Lt. Col. 14 Feb. 1787. Col. 3 May 1796. Maj. Gen. 1800. *d.* Berhampore 7 July 1801.

Eldest son of Rev. William Rawstorne, 52 yrs. rector of Badsworth, Yorks., and Elizabeth his wife, dau. of Samuel Walker, of Stapleton Park, Yorks. Brother of Lawrence Rawstorne, *q.v.* His daus. *m.* William Innes and Thomas Ward, *qq.v.*

Services : Sailed for India in the *Vansittart* 4 Mar. 1764, aged 18. Ensign 1st Bengal Eur. Regt. ; resigned his Commission during the " Batta mutiny " 15 May 1766 ; restored 1766. Dismissed

Jan. 1767 for his mutinous support of Sir Robert Fletcher *q.v.*; restored 7 July 1767. Capt. comdg. 28th Bn. Sepoys in Dec. 1777; Capt. Comdt. of Kalpi fort in 1778. Apptd. to comd. 21st N.I. 1 Jan. 1781; comdg. at Fatehgarh in June 1781; comdg. 27th N.I. in Apr. 1786. Fur. 30 Oct. 1786 till 20 Aug. 1790. Lt. Col. comdg. 6th Eur. Bn. in Feb. 1796; transfd. as Col. to 2nd Bengal Eur. Regt. 1796. Apptd. Col. Comdt. of newly-formed Cav. Bde. of four regts. 2 June 1797; comdg. at Berhampore May 1799 till death.

Refs.: Burke's *Landed Gentry*, 4th edn., p. 1255, *s.n.* Rawstorne, of Penwortham Priory, Lincs. *G.M.* 1802, i. 584.

RAWSTORNE, Lawrence (1750/51-1805). Lieut. Colonel, 4th N.I. *b.* 1750/51. Cadet 1778. Arrived in India 2 Oct. 1778. Ensign Oct. 1778. Lieut. 20 Nov. 1778. Capt. 1 June 1796. Major 10 Aug. 1801. Lt. Col. 30 June 1804. *d.* Aligarh 16 Oct. 1805.

2nd son of Rev. William Rawstorne and Elizabeth his wife. Brother of Edward Rawstorne, *q.v. m.* (?) His dau. *m.* Charles Porteous, *q.v.*

Services: Sailed for India in the *Nassau* 1 Mar. 1778, aged 27. Apptd. Adjt. 28th Bn. Sepoys 22 Mar. 1780. Fur. 16 Dec. 1784 till Nov. 1788. Lieut. 5th Bengal Eur. Bn. in Dec. 1788 and in 1790; 12th Bn. Sepoys in 1792; 6th Eur. Bn. in Feb. 1796. Transfd. as Capt. to 5th N.I.; as Major to Bengal Eur. Regt.; as Lt. Col. to 2/4th N.I. (? Second Mahratta War; defence of Delhi Oct. 1804; Lt. Col. comdg. 2/4th N.I.)

Refs.: Burke's *Landed Gentry*, 4th edn., p. 1255, *s.n.* Rawstorne, of Penwortham Priory, Lincs.

RAYMOND, Charles Henry (1787-1837). Captain. 28th N.I. *b.* Berks. 21 or 22 Nov. 1787. Cadet 1803. Arrived in India 2 Sept. 1804. Ensign 27 Aug. 1804. Lieut. 21 Sept. 1804. Capt. 14 Jan. 1819. Retired 8 Jan. 1820. *d.* Cirencester 21 Aug. 1837.

Of Sherborne Villas, Spa, Gloucs. Natural son of David Fell, of Caversham Grove, Oxon. *m.* 1st, Augusta Sophia. (She died Spa 28 Feb. 1828.) *m.* 2nd, Gloucester 20 May 1829, Miss Warner, of the Spa.

Services: Posted Lieut. to 18th N.I. in 1805. (Either operations in Bundelkhand 1809; Rajaoli; Ajaigarh; Lieut. 1/18th N.I.; or operations in Hariana 1809; capture of Bhawani; Lieut. 2/18th N.I.) Comdg. escort of Board of Comrs. in Sundarbans

1812-16. Transfd. to newly-raised 2/28th N.I. in 1815. Fur.
27 Jan. 1817 till retirement.
Refs.: A.J. xxv. 568; N.S. xxiv. 123. G.M. 1829, i. 556.

RAYNE, Robert (1752/53-1810). Major General. Colonel Bengal
Eur. Regt. *b.* 1752/53. Cadet 1769. Admitted 3 Aug. 1769.
Ensign 11 Aug. 1769. Lieut. 23 Jan. 1773. Capt. 16 Jan. 1781.
Major 1 Mar. 1794. Lt. Col. 25 Apr. 1797. Col. 8 Jan. 1801.
Maj. Gen. 25 Apr. 1808. *d.* Sydney Pl., Bath, 5 Aug. 1810,
aged 57.

m. 1st, (?) (She died London 31 Aug. 1791.) *m.* 2nd, Skieviog,
co. Flint, 21 Aug. 1802, Anne, *née* Taylor, widow of William Allen,
of Coedybrain, co. Flint. Stepfather of William Taylor Allen who
changed his name to Rayne 21 July 1807.

Services: Sailed for India in the *Havannah* 2 Jan. 1769. To
d.d. as Ensign 27 Oct. 1769; A.D.C. to Col. A. Champion, *q.v.*,
in Jan. 1770; Adjt. in June 1773. First Rohilla War; battle
of St. George. Fur. 8 Feb. 1775 till 2 Aug. 1777, and 8 Feb. 1782
till 22 Feb. 1786, returning to India overland. Transfd. to Cav.
6 Apr. 1778; Capt. in Cav.; retransfd. to Inf. Jan. 1782. Capt.
3rd Bengal Eur. Bn. in July 1787; comdg. 34th Bn. Sepoys 1789-97;
Lt. Col. comdg. 2/1st N.I. in Mar. 1798; transfd. to 1/1st N.I.
21 Apr. 1800. Fur. 14 Mar. 1800 till death. Posted Col. to 18th
N.I. Jan. 1801; to Bengal Eur. Regt. in 1804.

Refs.: Macpherson, pp. 26, 133. G.M. 1810, ii. 194.

READ, Henry (*d.* 1795). Lieutenant, Infantry. Country Cadet
1778. Ensign 31 Mar. 1778. Lieut. 31 Aug. 1779. *d.* Berhampore 13 Mar. 1795.

m. Calcutta 1 June 1780, Catherine, dau. of Rev. Richard Penneck,
keeper of the reading-room at the B.M., rector of St. John's,
Horsleydown, 1765-1803. Father of John Peregrine Read, Mary
Penneck, wife of Charles Becher, and Catherine, wife of James
Edwards, *qq.v.*

Services: Apptd. Cadet 27 Feb. 1778. Lieut. 2/3rd Bengal
Eur. Regt. in Oct. 1779; 16th Bn. Sepoys in June 1781. Bk.Mr.
at Berhampore Oct. 1782 till death; also, in addition, Dy. Postmr.
there from *c.* 1793.

Refs.: S.M. 1795, p. 817. Will dated 11 Aug. 1794; proved
20 Mar. 1795.

READ, James (1789-1826). Captain, 1st N.I. *b.* 92 Aldersgate
St., London, 3 Sept. 1789. Cadet 1806. Arrived in India

THE BENGAL ARMY, 1758-1834   619

21 July 1807. Ensign 2 Aug. 1807. Lieut. 31 July 1810. Capt. 1 May 1824. d. New Anchorage, Kedgeree, Bengal, 23 Sept. 1826, on board the *Dunira*.
Son of —— Read and Bradley his wife. m. Calcutta 6 Nov. 1813, Henrietta, 3rd dau. of H. L. Christiana, of Southampton. (She re-m. 1832.)
Services : Barasat C.C. Posted Ensign to 12th N.I. in 1808. (? Operations in Oudh 1808 ; Ensign 12th N.I.) With Mirzapur Local Bn. 1813-16. Nepal War 1816 ; actg. Intr. & Qmr. 5th Gren. Bn., in 2nd Bde. Left Column. Adjt. Hill Rangers 1817-18 ; do. 1/12th N.I. 20 Nov. 1818 till 1822. A.D.C. to Maj.-Gen. Lewis Thomas, *q.v.*, 1822 ; Agent for family money at Barrackpore 1822 till death. Transfd. to 1st N.I. (late 2/12th) May 1824.
Refs. : A.J. xxiii. 529. M.I. at Kedgeree.

*READ or REID, John (*d.* 1763). Lieut. Fireworker, Artillery. (27) Cadet 1762. Fireworker 29 Jan. 1763. *d.* 25 June 1763 : kld. in action during the assault of Patna.
Services : N.F.P.
Refs. : Firminger, p. 71.

READ, John. Ensign. Infantry. Cadet 1782. Never arrived in India. Ensign 6 Mar. 1783. Struck off 1788.
Services : Apptd. Cadet 3 July 1782 ; should have sailed for India in H.M.S. *Cato.*

READ or REID, John Lewis (*d.* 1782). Lieutenant, Invalid Est. Infantry. Cadet 1770. Ensign 1 Dec. 1771. Lieut. 10 Aug. 1776. Invalided July 1781. *d.* Calcutta 12 May 1782.
m. Rozina ——.
Services : Was Capt. Lt. comdg. the garr. of the Coy.'s settlement on Balambangan I., N. of Borneo, till its capture by Suluans in 1775. After trial by C.M. in 1776 for the loss of the island, he returned to England and was apptd. Cadet on the Bencoolen Est. 29 Jan. 1777. Resided unemployed in Calcutta for some time before his death. Promoted to rank of Lieut. on Invalid Est., but not to rise higher, 24 July 1781.
Refs. : Will dated Dec. 1781 ; admon. 30 July 1782.

READ, John Peregrine (1781-1802). Lieutenant, Marine Regt. N.I. *b.* Berhampore 18 May 1781. Cadet 1795. Admitted 22 Sept. 1797. Ensign 14 Aug. 1797. Lieut. 10 Aug. 1798. *d.* Barrackpore 23 July 1802.

bapt. Berhampore 8 June 1781. Son of Henry Read, *q.v.*, and Catherine his wife.
Services: Apptd. a Minor Cadet 7 June 1781, aged 3 weeks. Lieut. 2nd Bengal Eur. Regt.; on the reduction of this Bn. was transfd. in May 1802 to the Marine Regt. Granted leave s.c. 6 mos. to sea 20 May 1802, but did not live to embark.
Refs.: Will (letter only) dated Berhampore, 27 May 1802; admon. 17 Apr. 1806.

READ, Stephen (*d.* 1774). Lieutenant, Infantry. Cadet 1768. Ensign 7 Feb. 1769. Lieut. 6 June 1770. *d.* Berhampore 20 Aug. 1774.
Services: Lieut. 1st Bn. Sepoys in May 1772.

READE, Henry Jonathan (1801-1821). Lieutenant, 4th L.C. *b.* Ipsden, Oxon., 25 Feb. 1801. Cadet 1817. Cornet (?) Lieut. 13 May 1819. *d.* Mangrol, Kotah, 1 Oct. 1821: kld. in action.
bapt. Ipsden 30 Mar. 1801. 3rd son of John Reade, of Ipsden, J.P. and D.L., and Anna Maria his wife, eldest dau. of John Scott-Waring, *q.v.* Brother of William Barrington Reade, *q.v.* Ed. Charterhouse 1811-18; scholar 3 May 1811.
Services: Posted Lieut. to 4th L.C. in 1819. Operations against Maharao Kishor Singh of Kotah 1821; Mangrol (kld.); Lieut. 4th L.C. (*See* note to William Mactier.)
Refs.: Burke's *Landed Gentry*, 13th edn., p. 1488, *s.n.* Reade, of Ipsden House, co. Oxford. *A Record of the Redes*, by Compton Reade, Hereford, 1899. *Alumni Carthusiani.* M.I. Mangrol.

READE, John (1753/54-1814). Lieut. Colonel, Invalid Est. 13th N.I. *b.* 1753/54. Country Cadet 1779. Admitted 19 Aug. 1779. Ensign 3 Sept. 1779. Lieut. 21 Apr. 1781. Capt. 11 July 1798. Major 10 June 1804. Lt. Col. 22 Sept. 1808. Invalided 15 Jan. 1814. *d.* Calcutta 25 June 1814, aged 60.
Natural son of Sir John Reade, 5th Bart., of Shipton Court, Oxon., by Jane Day, spinster. Half-brother of Sir John Reade, 6th Bart., and of Mary, wife of Sir Elijah Impey. *m.* St. George's, Hanover Sq., 9 Apr. 1807, Elizabeth, only dau. of Thomas Reade, of Stoke Marmyon, Oxon. (She died 1816, aged 39.)
Services: Lieut. 3rd Bengal Eur. Bn. in July 1787; 1st do. in 1790; 4th do. in 1792. Comdg. troops at Padang, Sumatra, in 1797, and was still serving at Bencoolen in 1802. Capt. and Major 1/7th N.I. Fur. 1 Dec. 1805 till 4 Oct. 1809. Posted as Lt. Col. to 1/13th N.I.

Refs.: *G.E.C.*; *Complete Baronetage. A Record of the Redes. G.M.* 1807, i. 375; 1815, i. 88. Will undated; codicil dated Rewari, 1810; proved 30 June 1814.

READE, William Barrington (1803-1881). Lieutenant. 1st L.C. *b.* Ipsden 30 Jan. 1803. Cadet 1823. Arrived in India 7 June 1824. Cornet 7 May 1824. Lieut. 13 May 1825. Resigned 8 Mar. 1833. *d.* Ipsden 11 Dec. 1881.

Of Ipsden House, Oxon., J.P. and D.L. *bapt.* 24 Feb. 1803. 4th son of John Reade, of Ipsden, and Anna Maria his wife. Brother of Henry Jonathan Reade, *q.v. m.* 1st, Benares 10 May 1827, Elizabeth, 2nd dau. of John Griffin, of Sloane St., London. (She died 1836.) *m.* 2nd, Ryde 12 Apr. 1837, Elizabeth, only child of John Murray, of Ardbennie, co. Perth, Capt. R.N. (She died 10 Sept. 1895, aged 84.)

Services: " Midshipman in Indian Navy, and made three voyages, being shipwrecked on the coast of Spain." (*A Record of the Redes.*) Posted Cornet to 7th L.C. in 1824; transfd. as Lieut. to 1st L.C. May 1825; actg. Adjt. do. 13 July 1829. No record of active service.

Refs.: Burke's *Landed Gentry*, 13th edn., p. 1488, *s.n.* Reade, of Ipsden House, co. Oxford. Foster's *Baronetage*, p. 523, *s.n.* Reade, Bart. *Walford. A.J.* xxv. 103.

REDDIE, George Burd (1809-1880). Major General. 29th N.I. Dy. Comy. Gen. *b.* Glasgow 21 Apr. 1809. Cadet 1825. Arrived in India 4 Sept. 1826. Ensign 15 Apr. 1826. Lieut. 24 Apr. 1833. Capt. 6 Dec. 1845. Major 11 July 1861. Lt. Col. 16 July 1864. Col. 18 Feb. 1866. Retired 1 Jan. 1870. Hon. Maj. Gen. 1 Jan. 1870. *d.* 10 Somerset Pl., Bath, 17 Mar. 1880.

3rd son of James Reddie, of Glasgow, advocate, town clerk and legal assessor for that city (*D.N.B.*), and Charlotte Marion his wife, dau. of J. Campbell, saddler, Glasgow. (*Probably* nephew of John Campbell (1764-1833), *q.v.*) *m.* Nimach 10 Nov. 1846, Sarah Abbott, dau. of George Harriott. (She died 15 Sept. 1892, aged 70.) Ed. Glasgow Grammar School and Univ.; matric. 1821.

Services: Posted Ensign to 29th N.I. 5 Oct. 1826. Fur. s.c. 26 Feb. 1831 till 24 Oct. 1834. Intr. & Qmr. 29th N.I. 4 Jan. 1836; S.A.C.G. 17 Apr. 1837; Comst. Ofr. with Cav. Bde., Army of the Indus, 13 Sept. 1838. First Afghan War 1838-9; Ghazni; S.A.C.G. (Medal). Leave s.c. to Cape and Tasmania 24 Feb. 1841 till 28 Dec. 1842. D.A.C.G. 2 cl. 10 Jan. 1845; 1 cl. Dec. 1847. Second Sikh War; D.A.C.G. (Medal). A.C.G. 2 cl. 9 June 1851;

1 cl. 19 Jan. 1853 ; Dy. Comy. Gen. 29 Nov. 1858 till retirement. Fur. s.c. June 1857 till Oct. 1858, and 19 Feb. 1868 till retirement.
Refs. : *The Times*, 22 Mar. 1880.

REDDISH, Charles (1778-1810). Captain, Invalid Est. 22nd N.I. *b.* London 1778. Cadet 1797. Arrived in India 20 Aug. 1799. Ensign 20 Oct. 1798. Lieut. 1 Nov. 1798. Capt. 22 Nov. 1807. Invalided 16 Jan 1809. *d.* Chunar 8 June 1810, aged 32.

bapt. St. Paul's, Covent Gdn., London, 3 Jan. 1779. Youngest natural (twin) son of Samuel Reddish, the actor (*D.N.B.*), by Mary Ann,[1] the actress, dau. of Jordan Costello and widow of George Canning, barr.-at-law. Half-brother of Rt. Hon. George Canning, Prime minister 1827 (*D.N.B.*). *m.* Calcutta 28 Feb. 1805, Miss Beatrice Caroline Manning.

Services : Operations in Jumna Doab 1803 ; Sasni ; Bijaigarh ; Lieut. 8th N.I. Transfd. to newly-raised 22nd N.I. 9 Nov. 1803 ; Capt. Lt. 22nd N.I. 9 Sept. 1806.

Refs. : *N. & Q.* clvii. 203 ; clxiii. 294-5. *Bath Chron.* 1811. M.I. at Chunar.

[1] *Note :* She is described as his wife in the bapt. register.

REDING, Walter (1787-1830). Major, 53rd N.I. *b.* Jan. 1787. Cadet 1803. Arrived in India 17 Mar. 1805. Ensign 1 May 1805. Lieut. 2 May 1805. Capt. 12 May 1820. Major 27 May 1828. *d.* at the Cape 12 Feb. 1830.

bapt. Andover, Hants, 27 June 1787, aged 5 mos. Son of William Reding and Grace his wife.

Services : Posted Lieut. to 27th N.I. in 1806. Operations against Dhundia Khan 1807 ; Komona ; Ganauri ; Lieut. 27th N.I. With 7th Gren. Bn. 1815-16. Third Mahratta War ; Madhurajpura ; Bt. Capt. 1/27th N.I. Transfd. to 53rd N.I. (late 1/27th) May 1824. Leave s.c. 18 mos. to N.S.W. and Cape 13 Feb. 1829 till death.

Refs. : *A.J.* N.S. ii. 185. Will dated Cape Town 31 Jan. 1830 ; proved 2 Dec. 1830.

REDMAN, James (*d.* 1811 ?). Lieutenant. Artillery. (83) Cadet 1766. Fireworker 15 Sept. 1767. Lieut. 9 Mar. 1770. Deserted from camp Apr. 1774. '(? *d.* in England 19 Oct. 1811, from a kick by a cow on the calf of the leg.)

Services : Sailed for India in the *Hector* 27 Nov. 1766. Tried by C.M. at Allahabad on a complaint of Capt. Edward Roach, *q.v.*, for challenging him to a duel at Bilgram 3 Apr. 1774. Both were dismissed by Govr. and Council 18 Apr. 1774. He had been tried by C.M. on a similar charge in Mar. 1774 and acquitted. Letter from Camp, 8 June 1774, " surmised that Lieut. Redman, in place of proceeding down the country from Cawnpore, had deserted, and I now have holograph proof of his Infamy." Letter dated 24 June 1774, " Redman is at Nigibabad (another name for Pettergur) in the service of Nabob Koolah Khan, brother to Tabiz Cann." On 6 July 1781, the Board in Calcutta agreed to pardon him if he would surrender himself to the Fort Major at Calcutta before 1 Jan. 1782. He was subsequently apprehended and deported from India. Held a Warrant as Cadet in R.A. in 1767.

Refs.: Macpherson, p. 186. (? *G.M.* 1811, ii. 489.)

REDSHAW, Christopher (*d.* 1773). Lieutenant, Infantry. Cadet 1768. Ensign 21 Feb. 1769. Lieut. 16 May 1770. *d.* Dinapore 28 Jan. 1773.

Services: N.F.P.

REED, Charles (1785-?). Ensign. 2nd N.I. *b.* Woodford, Essex, 25 May 1785. Cadet 1805. Arrived at Madras 21 Feb. 1807. Ensign 22 Sept. 1806. Resigned 28 Mar. 1808.

bapt. Woodford 22 June 1785. Son of James Reed, of Warlies Park, Essex, and Charlotte his wife. Nephew of Thomas Reed, of Copthal Court, Throgmorton St., London.

Services: On arrival at Madras in Feb. 1807, was detained there on duty. Posted Ensign to 2nd N.I.

REES, Crawford Mitford (1814-1850). Captain, 65th N.I. *b.* Calcutta 8 May 1814. Cadet 1833. Arrived in India 15 Aug. 1834. Ensign (13 Dec. 1833) 30 Apr. 1834. Lieut. 15 Sept. 1838. Capt. 10 June 1845. *d.* Ambala 13 Dec. 1850.

bapt. Calcutta 30 Dec. 1814. Son of John Mitford Rees, Senior Merchant B.C.S., and Harriet Anne his wife, eldest dau. of C. Stokes, Receiver Gen. of Inland Revenue, I. of France. *m.* 1st, Allahabad 8 Nov. 1838, Eleanor Margaret, youngest dau. of Samuel Austen, of Dublin, and sister of George Powell Austen, *q.v.* (*See also* Edward Sunderland.) (She died Nowgong 2 Aug. 1847.) *m.* 2nd, Chunar 23 Nov. 1849, his cousin, Elizabeth Mary, dau. of William Edward Rees, B.C.S. (She died Mian Mir 16 Nov. 1850.) Addiscombe Cadet 29 Apr. 1832 till 13 Dec. 1833.

Services: Ensign d.d. 50th N.I. 20 Aug. 1834. Posted to 65th N.I. 5 Nov. 1834. Apptd. to 1st Regt. Inf., Oudh Auxy. Force (became 1st Oudh Local Inf.), 21 Apr. 1838 ; Adjt. do. 17 Jan. 1840 till Aug. 1845. Rejoined 65th N.I. Sept. 1845. Offg. Fort Adjt. at Chunar Feb. 1849 ; Comdt. do. Aug.-Dec. 1849, when he rejoined his Regt. Was on his way from Lahore to Calcutta preparatory to applying for fur. s.c. when his death occurred. No record of active service.

Refs.: De Rhé-Philipe. *I.M.* 18 Feb. 1851, p. 92. Will dated Ferozepore 3 Dec. 1850 ; admon. 4 July 1851. M.I. at Ambala.

REES, Walter Williams (*d.* 1839). Captain. 50th N.I. Country Cadet 1808. Admitted 26 May 1810. Ensign 13 Aug. 1811. Lieut. 4 June 1815. Capt. 23 Aug. 1826. Invalided 12 Dec. 1833. Retired 15 Dec. 1835. *d.* Delhi 14 Feb. 1839.[1]

Services: As he had resided in Bengal since 1808 he was, in June 1810, excused from attendance at Barasat C.C. and was attached to a Native Corps. Posted Ensign to 16th N.I. in 1811 ; transfd. to 1/25th N.I. Sept. 1812. S.A.C.G. 9 Feb. 1816 ; in executive charge at Karnal 1817-20. Third Mahratta War ; S.A.C.G. in 2nd Div. Leave s.c. 12 mos. to Cape 21 Nov. 1820. S.A.C.G. 1 cl. 5 Sept. 1823 ; D.A.C.G. 1 cl. 12 Dec. 1823. Transfd. to 50th N.I. (late 2/25th) May 1824. Fur. s.c. 28 Oct. 1824 till 6 Nov. 1827, and 8 Jan. 1829 till 23 June 1832. Apptd. tempy. to Comst. Dept. with Jungle Mehals F.F. 30 Dec. 1832. Fur. s.c. 17 Jan. 1834 till retirement.

Refs.: A.J. N.S. xxix. 140.

[1] *Note:* Also said to have *d.* in London 14 Nov. 1838. (*G.M.* 1839, i. 104 ; *A.J.* N.S. xxvii. 340.)

REEVES, Francis Carleton (1804-1862). Major. 9th N.I. *b.* Cork 22 July 1804. Cadet 1819. Arrived in India Feb. 1821. Ensign 23 Aug. 1820. Lieut. 11 July 1823. Capt. 24 Dec. 1841. Retired 1 Jan. 1845. Hon. Major 28 Nov. 1854. *d.s.p.* 1862.

Of Ballyglissane, co. Cork. Elder son of Edward Hoare Reeves and Dorothea his 2nd wife, dau. of John Carleton, of Cork, and niece of Lord Carleton.

Services: Posted Ensign to 2/5th N.I. ; transfd. as Lieut. to 8th N.I. July 1823 ; to 9th N.I. (late 1/8th) May 1824. Actg. Adjt. 9th N.I. 3 Aug. 1824. First Burma War ; Arakan 1825 ; Lieut. 1st L.I. Bn. (? India medal). Tempy. charge of Comst. Dept. at Nimach in 1830. Actg. Adjt. 9th N.I. 24 Feb. 1831. Fur. p.a. 3 Feb. 1832 till 26 Oct. 1835. Adjt. 9th N.I. 14 Mar. 1836 till 2 Feb. 1842. Bde. Major 2nd Inf. Bde., Army of Reserve (for Afghanistan), 14 Oct. 1842.

Refs. : Burke's *Landed Gentry of Ireland,* p. 584, *s.n.* Reeves, of Besborough, co. Clare.

REID, Andrew Gildart (1815-1876). Captain. 47th N.I. *b.* 26 May 1815. Cadet 1833. Arrived in India 8 Dec. 1834. Ensign 22 Aug. 1834. Lieut. 12 Mar. 1838. Capt. Mar. 1850. Retired 3 Aug. 1849. *d.* 1 Jan. 1876 ; *bur.* Kensal Green cemetery.

bapt. Chipping Barnet 24 Dec. 1815. Eldest son of Nevile Reid, of Suffolk Lane, Cannon St., London, wine merchant, and of Runnymede, Berks., and Eliza Maria his 1st wife. *m.* Calcutta 20 Oct. 1840, Eliza Philadelphia Margaret, dau. of Lewis Wiggins, *q.v.* (*See also* Anthony Highmore Jellicoe.) (She died 11 Oct. 1891.) Ed. Charterhouse Jan. 1826-1829. Ed. Rugby ; admitted 1829. Addiscombe Cadet 3 Aug. 1832 till 13 June 1834.

Services : d.d. 10th N.I. 22 Dec. 1834 ; posted to 47th N.I. 2 Mar. 1835. Actg. Intr. & Qmr. 7th L.C. 8 Sept. 1838. Intr. & Qmr. 47th N.I. 21 Feb. 1839 till Feb. 1847. First Sikh War ; Badhowal ; Aliwal ; Sobraon ; Lieut. 47th N.I. (Medal with clasp). Fur. p.a. 3 Feb. 1847 till retirement.

Refs. : *Charterhouse School List. Rugby School Register. Tom Brown's School Days,* Ch. iv. *The Times,* 5 Jan. 1876.

REID, Charles Samuel (1807-1876). Lieut. General, Artillery. (566) *b.* Muttra 20 Nov. 1807. Cadet 1824. Arrived in India 12 May 1825. 2nd Lieut. 16 Dec. 1824. Lieut. 4 Apr. 1829. Capt. 16 Dec. 1843. Major 31 Dec. 1854. Lt. Col. 25 Sept. 1857. Col. 18 Feb. 1861. Maj. Gen. 24 Jan. 1865. Lt. Gen. 5 Apr. 1873. *d.* Barrackpore 9 Apr. 1876.

bapt. Muttra 13 Feb. 1808. Son of John Reid, Surgeon Bengal Est., and Ann his wife, dau. of Solomon Boileau, of Dublin. Brother of Henry Solomon Reid and nephew of Samuel Davis, *qq.v. m.* Cawnpore 13 July 1830, Katherine Cecilia, 4th dau. of Major Robert Durie, 11th Light Dgns. (*See also* William Beckett (1798-1844).) Addiscombe Cadet 1822-4.

Services : Dy. Comy. Ord. at Saugor 5 Aug. 1840 ; Comy. Ord., Army of Reserve (for Afghanistan), 6 June 1842 till 10 Jan. 1843 ; Dy. Comy. Ord. Ferozepore Sept. 1843 ; do. Cawnpore 9 Aug. 1844 ; Comy. Ord. Cawnpore 14 Jan. 1845 ; do. Ajmer 25 Jan. till 22 July 1848. Second Burma War 1852-3 ; capture of Rangoon 1852 ; comdd. Art. with Sir John Cheape's force Feb.-Mar. 1853 ; Donabyu (s.w.—rt. arm amputated) ; Bt. Major 2nd Coy. 5th Bn. (Medal). Fur. p.a. Feb. 1854 till Jan. 1855. Posted to 9th Bn.

Mar. 1855; offg. Town Major Ft. Wm. Mar. 1855; 11th Bn. May 1855; 2nd Bn. July 1856; 9th Bn. 19 Nov. 1856; 2nd Bn. 29 Sept. 1859; 3rd Bde. H.A. 27 Aug. 1860.
Refs.: Boase. *The Times*, 10 May 1876.

REID, David. Lieutenant. 22nd Bn. Sepoys. Country Cadet 1779. Ensign 4 Sept. 1779. Lieut. 22 Apr. 1781. Resigned 14 Dec. 1789.

(? *m.* Berhampore 23 Mar. 1788, Johanna D'Rozario, widow.)
Services: Apptd. Cadet 19 Aug. 1779. Granted leave s.c. to sea 29 Nov. 1784. Was Adjt. 22nd Bn. Sepoys in July 1787 and on resignation.

REID, David (1789-1861). Captain. 1st L.C. *b.* St. Andrew's kirk psh., Edinburgh, 6 Feb. 1789. Cadet 1804. Arrived in India 6 Apr. 1806. Cornet 25 Mar. 1806. Lieut. 27 Oct. 1808. Bt. Capt. 1 Jan. 1819. Capt. 1822. Retired 29 May 1822. *d.* Tours, France, 4 Dec. 1861.

Son of David Reid, Comr. of Customs, and Jean his wife, dau. of Capt. Renny or Rainey, of Montrose. Brother of Stephen Reid, *q.v.*, and of Katherine, mother of David Pott, *q.v. m.* (before 1822) (?)

Services: Barasat C.C. Posted Cornet to 1st N.C. in 1807. Operations in Bundelkhand against Gopal Singh 1810-11; Bichaund; Lieut. 1st N.C. Intr. & Qmr. 1st N.C. 12 Feb. 1813 till 10 Apr. 1819. Leave to Cape 1817-18; fur. 11 Oct. 1818 till retirement.

Refs.: G.M. 1862, i. 108. *The Times*, 9 Dec. 1861.

REID, David (1813-1876). Major General, Artillery. (646) *b.* Greenock 28 Aug. 1813. Cadet 1830. Arrived in India 5 June 1831. 2nd Lieut. 10 Dec. 1830. Lieut. 13 Dec. 1839. Capt. 26 Oct. 1848. Bt. Major 12 Oct. 1857. Lt. Col. 23 Dec. 1858. Col. 13 Jan. 1864. Maj. Gen. 21 July 1874. *d.* at sea off Madras 29 Feb. 1876, on board the *Australia*.

Eldest son of James Reid, of 21 Minto St., Edinburgh, Comptrolling Searcher of the Customs, and Helena his wife. Cousin-german of Alexander David Beatson, *q.v.* Ed. Edin. Acad. 1825-8. Addiscombe Cadet 1829-30.

Services: Actg. 2nd Lieut. (having been 2 yrs. in India) 25 June 1833. Posted to Foot Art. 18 Sept. 1835. Fur. s.c. 4 Dec. 1836 till 30 Jan. 1840. To comd. local corps of Art. forming in Assam 20 May 1840, and comdd. for over 20 yrs.; in addition served in

P.W.D. in Upper Assam. Abor expedn. 1859, under Col. S. F. Hannah, q.v.; capture of Pashi 27 Feb. Posted Lt. Col. to 2nd Bn. 9 May 1859. Comdg. R.A. and Bde., Allahabad Div., 1867-72; do. Gwalior district 1872-4.
Refs.: Boase. *The Times,* 29 Mar. 1876.

REID,[1] **George** (1807-1875). Bt. Captain. 5th L.C. *b.* Glanmire, co. Cork, 25 Oct. 1807. Cadet 1825. Arrived in India 19 Jan. 1826. Cornet (?) Lieut. 16 Sept. 1825. Bt. Capt. 9 Aug. 1840. Resigned in India 1 July 1841. *d.* Cheltenham 2 Apr. 1875. Of Deer Park, co. Cork. Son of David Reid, of Millbank, nr. Fermoy, and Jane his wife. *m.* 1842, Elizabeth Cecilia, eldest dau. of Sir James Caleb Anderson, 1st Bart., of Buttevant. (She died Cheltenham 3 Apr. 1880.)
Services: Posted Lieut. to 5th L.C. 25 May 1826. Fur. s.c. 15 Dec. 1837 till 17 Apr. 1841. No record of active service.
Refs.: The Times, 6 Apr. 1875.
[1] *Note:* This man has been confused with the following in both "Service Army Lists, Bengal" (*I.O. Rec.*), and in *Westminster School Register.*

REID, George (1808-1845). Bt. Captain, 1st L.C. *b.* Shrewsbury 29 Apr. 1808. Cadet 1824. Arrived in India 18 Mar. 1826. Cornet 28 Sept. 1825. Lieut. 7 Dec. 1827. Bt. Capt. 28 Sept. 1840. *d.* Calcutta 16 Oct. 1845.
bapt. Holy Cross, Shrewsbury, 15 May 1808. Son of George Reid, of Jamaica, later of Watlington Hall, Norfolk, and Louisa his wife, 4th dau. of Sir Charles Oakeley, 1st Bart., Govr. of Madras 1792-4. Brother of Gen. Sir Charles Reid, G.C.B. Ed. Westminster 17 Jan. 1821 till 1823.
Services: Posted Cornet to 1st L.C. Adjt. 1st L.C. 10 Jan. 1828 till 17 July 1830; Intr. & Qmr. do. 5 Apr. 1832 till 1836. Fur. s.c. 5 Apr. 1836 till 11 Apr. 1839. Intr. & Qmr. 1st L.C. 30 July 1839 till 1843. Bde. Major to Marwar F.F. for reduction of Jhansi 5 Aug. till 14 Oct. 1839. Actg. Bde. Major to Cav. Bde., troops W. of Indus, 1 Apr. 1842. First Afghan War 1842; advance on Kabul; Lieut. 1st L.C., with Gen. Pollock's force (Medal). D.A.Q.M.G. 2 cl. at Saugor 17 Jan. 1843. A.Q.M.G. of Army of Exercise 17 Nov. 1843. Gwalior campaign; Paniar (*Lond. Gaz.* 8 Mar. 1844); A.Q.M.G. (Bronze star). Hon. A.D.C. to Lord Ellenborough, the G.G., 1 Feb. 1844; to William Wilberforce Bird, actg. G.G., 15 June 1844; to Sir Henry Hardinge, G.G., 23 July 1844. Supt. of Mysore Princes 23 July 1845.

Refs.: Burke's *Peerage,* 1923, p. 1628, *s.n.* Oakeley, Bart. *Westminster School Register.* A.J. N.S. xix. 33. Will dated Calcutta, 12 Oct. 1845; admon. 3 Feb. 1846.

REID, Henry Solomon (1792-1852). Lieutenant. 17th N.I. *b.* Calcutta 16 Feb. 1792. Cadet 1808. Arrived in India 27 Oct. 1809. Ensign 22 Mar. 1810. Lieut. 16 Dec. 1814. Resigned in India 1 Jan. 1823. *d.* Darlington, Canada, 28 Nov. 1852.

bapt. Calcutta 7 Mar. 1792. Son of John Reid, Surgeon Bengal Est., and Ann his wife. Brother of Frances Charlotte, mother of George Duncan Mercer, and of Charles Samuel Reid, *qq.v. m.* 1st, St. John's, Calcutta, 1 Nov. 1821, Jane Caroline, dau. of Sir Robert Blair, *q.v.* (*See also* Henry Clayton.) *m.* 2nd, Elizabeth ———. (She died Ontario 8 Nov. 1892.) Ed. Charterhouse Sept. 1803-Dec. 1808.

Services: Barasat C.C. Posted Ensign to 17th N.I. in 1810; with escort to Resdt. with Sindhia 1812 [1]; Adjt. 2/17th N.I. 4 May 1815 till 25 May 1820. Nepal War 1814-15; Lieut. 2/17th N.I., in 3rd Div. (India medal). S.A.C.G. 1820. Joined his brother-in-law's firm, Mercer & Co., at Calcutta in 1823. Commissioned as Local Lieut. in Nizam's army 11 Apr. 1828; resigned 21 Jan. 1830, and went to civil employ.

Refs.: *Charterhouse School List.* G.M. 1853, i. 217.

[1] *Note:* His sister's brother-in-law, Dr. Graeme Mercer, had been Resdt. with Sindhia 1807-10.

REID, Hugh Atkins (1810-1849). Captain, Invalid Est. 71st N.I. *b.* London 1 Apr. 1810. Cadet 1827. Arrived in India 16 Oct. 1828. Ensign 16 Apr. 1828. Lieut. 5 Feb. 1835. Capt. 16 Apr. 1843. Invalided 1 Apr. 1847. *d.* at sea 9 Feb. 1849, on board the *Monarch,* on the voyage to England.

bapt. St. George's, Bloomsbury, 4 Mar. 1813. Son of Capt. Hugh Atkins Reid, shipowner, formerly E.I.C.N.S., and Margaret Sophia his wife. His sister *m.* Charles Henry Spencer Freeman, *q.v. m.* Fatehgarh 25 July 1840, Rose Maria, youngest dau. of Stephen Birch, formerly Major in the Mahratta service. (*See also* John Baldock.)

Services: Ensign d.d. 55th N.I. 20 Nov. 1828; posted to 71st N.I. 4 Mar. 1829; d.d. 47th N.I. in Cuttack 15 Mar. till 1 Nov. 1831. Leave s.c. 15 Apr. till 15 Oct. 1839. Intr. & Qmr. 71st N.I. 8 Aug. 1844 till 16 Dec. 1846. Fur. s.c. 25 Jan. 1849. No record of active service.

Refs.: Will dated Mainpuri 1 May 1848; admon. 27 June 1850.

THE BENGAL ARMY, 1758-1834   629

REID, John (1753/54-1833). Lieut. Colonel. 13th N.I.   *b.*
1753/54. Cadet 1777. Admitted 1777. Ensign 11 Feb. 1778.
Lieut. 21 Sept. 1778. Capt. 21 Jan. 1796. Major 21 Apr. 1800.
Lt. Col. 13 July 1803. Retired 7 Sept. 1803. *d.* Ayr 6 Dec.
1833.
Son of Thomas Reid, merchant in Saltcoats, co. Ayr. Brother
of Robert Boyd Reid, laird of Adamton. *m.* 1st, Elizabeth, 3rd
dau. of John McKerrell, of Hillhouse, co. Ayr, and aunt of Robert
McKerrell, *q.v.* (*See also* Moses Crawfurd and John Fulton
(1807-1887).) *m.* 2nd, Cunninghamhead, co. Ayr, 21 July 1806,
Christina, eldest dau. of Neil Snodgrass, of Cunninghamhead.
(She died 1820.)
Services : Apptd. Cadet 29 Jan. 1777 ; sailed for India in the
Besborough 15 July 1777, aged 23. Lieut. 1/1st Bengal Eur.
Regt. in Oct. 1779. Second Mysore War 1781-5 ; Lieut. 24th N.I.
(formerly 31st Bn.), with Col. Pearse's detachment. Adjt. 1st
Bn. Sepoys in Mar. 1786 till after Mar. 1795. Transfd. to 7th N.I.
1796 ; Capt. 13th N.I. in 1798 ; Major 1/13th N.I. Fur. 20 Feb.
1801 till retirement.
Refs. : Burke's *Landed Gentry*, 13th edn., p. 1174, *s.n.* McKerrell,
of Hillhouse. *S.M.* 1806, p. 725. *A.J.* N.S. xiii. 67. *G.M.* 1834,
i. 118. Will dated Ayr, 6 Apr. 1833 ; proved 13 Mar. 1835.

REID, Stephen (1780-1841). Colonel, 10th L.C. *b.* Edinburgh
27 Jan. 1780. Cadet 1798. Arrived in India 31 Aug. 1799.
Cornet 31 May 1800. Lieut. 21 Feb. 1801. Capt. 15 Feb. 1816.
Major 26 Feb. 1820. Lt. Col. 13 May 1825. Col. 18 June 1831.
d. unm. at sea 10 Mar. 1841, on board the *Reliance.*
bapt. Edinburgh 5 Mar. 1780. Son of David Reid, of St. Andrew's
psh., Edinburgh, Comr. of Customs. Brother of David Reid
(1789-1861), *q.v.*
Services : Ensign 2/2nd R. Edin. Vols. 29 June 1797. Operations in Jumna Doab 1803 ; Sasni ; Bijaigarh ; Kachaura ; Lieut.
4th N.C. Second Mahratta War ; Laswari (w.) ; Lieut. 4th N.C.
Transfd. to newly-raised 8th N.C. in 1805 ; Adjt. do. 14 Jan. 1807
till 30 Sept. 1812 ; Qmr. do. Sept. 1812 till Dec. 1814. Capt. Lt.
8th N.C. 27 Feb. 1812. Fur. p.a. 2 Jan. 1815 till 5 Sept. 1818.
Posted Lt. Col. to 2nd L.C. in 1825 ; to 8th L.C. in 1827 ; to 7th
L.C. 4 Sept. 1828. Fur. s.c. 24 Dec. 1825 till 6 Oct. 1830. Transfd.
to 1st L.C. 13 Oct. 1830. Posted Col. to 1st L.C. 10 Sept. 1834 ;
to 6th L.C. 24 Nov. 1834 ; to 10th L.C. 7 Apr. 1835. Apptd. Bdr.
to comd. station of Barrackpore 9 Aug. 1839. Fur. s.c. 27 Nov.
1840 till death.

Refs.: *G.M.* 1841, i. 670. Will dated Barrackpore, 8 Apr. 1840; proved 30 June 1841.

REILLY, Bradshaw York (1807-1853). Lieut. Colonel, Invalid Est. Engineers. *bapt.* St. Michael's, Bath, 25 Mar. 1807. Cadet 1823. Arrived in India 21 May 1825. 2nd Lieut. 16 Oct. 1823. Lieut. 1 May 1824. Capt. 20 Apr. 1835. Major 30 Nov. 1844. Lt. Col. 19 June 1846. Invalided 4 Nov. 1848. *d.* Landour, U.P., 5 Nov. 1853, aged 46.

Son of Bradshaw Lewis Reilly, of Bath, and Maria his wife, née Grimes. *m.* (before 1844) Emily. Addiscombe Cadet 13 Mar. 1821 till 6 June 1823; Chatham 1823-4.

Services: Posted to S. & M. at Cawnpore 10 June 1825. Siege and capture of Bhurtpore; Lieut. S. & M. (India medal). Actg. Adjt. S. & M. 21 Jan. 1826; permanent do. 3 Feb. 1827 till 25 Apr. 1829. Executive Engr. 13th Div., P.W.D., 2 Mar. 1829 till 26 Apr. 1834; 14th (Saugor) Div. 10 Jan. 1834. Fur. p.a. 17 Feb. 1836 till 7 Jan. 1839. Offg. Garr. & Executive Engr. at Delhi, and superintend building of Hindaun bridge, 6 Mar. 1839. Suptg. Engr. S.E. Provinces Dec. 1840. Gwalior campaign; Maharajpur (Bronze star). First Sikh War; Sobraon (Medal). Leave s.c. 1 yr. to Landour 8 Nov. 1847.

Refs.: *I.M.* 28 Dec. 1853, p. 775. *G.M.* 1854, i. 217. Will dated 13 Sept. 1840; proved 16 Jan. 1854. M.I. Landour.

REILY, Leeson (1760/61-1797). Ensign. Infantry. Subsequently Bt. Captain, Madras Est. *b.* 1760/61. Country Cadet 1780. Ensign 10 Feb. 1781. Transfd. to Madras 15 Oct. 1781. *d.* Samulcotta, Madras, 16 Aug. 1797, aged 36.

Services: Apptd. a Gent. Vol. in Coy. of Art. 7 Apr. 1780. Ensign (Madras) 14 Dec. 1780; Lieut. 17 Apr. 1786; Bt. Capt. 7 Jan. 1796.

Refs.: M.I. at Samulcotta, Godavari district, Madras.

REINAGLE, Charles Edward (1803-1826). Lieutenant, 40th N.I. *b.* St. Clement Danes, London, 8 Dec. 1803. Cadet 1821. Ensign 16 May 1823. Lieut. 26 Sept. 1824. *d.* at sea 4 Feb. 1826, on board the hospital ship *Edward Strettell.*

Son of Ramsay Richard Reinagle, A.R.A., animal and landscape painter (*D.N.B.*), and Oriana his wife.

Services: Posted Ensign to 40th N.I. in 1824. First Burma War; Chittagong 1824; Ramu; Lieut. 40th N.I.

REMINGTON, James (1808-1842). Bt. Captain, 12th N.I. *b.* Clapham, Surrey, 11 June 1808. Cadet 1823. Arrived in India 12 Mar. 1825. Ensign 15 Aug. 1824. Lieut. 4 Sept. 1825. Bt. Capt. 25 Aug. 1838. *d.* Cawnpore 16 Sept. 1842.

bapt. Clapham 12 July 1808. Eldest son of David Robert Remington, of London, banker, and Martha his wife, *née* Copland. *m.* Calcutta 3 Mar. 1830, Louisa Jessie, dau. of Archibald Watson, *q.v.* (*See also* Robert Guthrie Macgregor.) (She *re-m.* 23 Sept. 1854, George Ramsden.) His dau. *m.* Augustus Turner, *q.v.*

Services: Ensign d.d. 28th N.I. 12 Apr. 1825 ; posted Lieut. to 12th N.I. in 1825 ; d.d. 60th N.I. 11 Apr. till 1 Oct. 1828. Fur. s.c. 22 June 1834 till 20 Aug. 1836. Actg. Intr. & Qmr. 58th N.I. 23 June 1841 ; do. 40th N.I. 8 Dec. 1841 till death. No record of active service.

Refs.: G.M. 1843, i. 111. *The Times*, 9 Nov. 1842, p. 6.

REMINGTON, Thomas (1786-1814). Lieutenant, Invalid Est. 17th N.I. *b.* Croydon 18 Aug. 1786. Cadet 1803. Arrived in India 31 Aug. 1804. Ensign 26 Aug. 1804. Lieut. 21 Sept. 1804. Invalided 1 May 1813. *d. unm.* Bankipore, B. & O., 18 Aug. 1814.

bapt. Croydon 29 Sept. 1786. Eldest son of Thomas Remington, of Guildford, M.D., and Anne Read his 1st wife.

Services: Posted Ensign to 17th N.I. in 1805 and served throughout with that Regt. No record of active service.

Refs.: Genealogist, N.S. xxvii. 148. M.I. Eastry church, Kent

RENNELL, James (1742-1830). Major. Engineers. Surveyor Gen. Bengal. *b.* Upcot, Devon, 3 Dec. 1742. Cadet 1764. Arrived in India Sept. 1760. Ensign 9 Apr. 1764. Lieut. 14 Jan. 1765. Capt. 1 Jan. 1767. Major 20 Jan. 1775. Resigned 9 Apr. 1777. *d.* Harrow 29 Mar. 1830, in consequence of a fracture of the neck of the thigh bone 12 weeks earlier ; *bur.* in Westminster Abbey.

bapt. Chudleigh, Devon, 21 Dec. 1742. Son of John Rennell, Capt. R.A., and Ann his wife, dau. of —— Clarke, of Chudleigh. *m.* Calcutta 15 Oct. 1772, Jane, 3rd dau. of Archdeacon Thomas Thackeray, D.D., headmaster of Harrow, and aunt of Thomas Thackeray, *q.v.* (She died Brighton Feb. 1810, aged 70.)

Services: See *D.N.B.* Entered R.N. ; joined *Brilliant* frigate, Capt. Hyde Parker, as Capt.'s servant in Jan. 1756 ; attack on Cherbourg 6 Aug. 1758 ; arrived at Madras as Midshipman in *America* frigate in Sept. 1760 ; employed in surveying ; siege of

Pondicherry 1761. Left R.N. and entered E.I.C.N.S. July 1763; comdd. yacht *Neptune* in which he executed survey of Palk Strait and Pamhen Channel. Ordered to make a survey of Bengal in 1764, and started work on 7 May. Surveyor Gen., on a salary of Rs. 300 *p.m.*, 8 Jan. 1767. On 20 Feb. 1766, his party was attacked by Saniyasis and he was s.w.; in Mar. 1771, was again in action against the Saniyasis, in comd. of a force in the Rangpur district. Engaged for 13 yrs. in surveying. Sailed from India in Mar. 1777. Granted a pension of £600 *p.a.* by E.I. Co. "The father of Indian geography." Pub. *Bengal Atlas*, 1779; *Memoir and Map of Hindostan*, 1783, 3rd edn. 1793; and various other works. F.R.S. 1781.

Refs.: Burke's *Family Records*, p. 594, *s.n.* Thackeray. *D.N.B. B.*: *P.P.* No. 53, pp. 1-11 (portrait). *D.I.B. Thackeray*, pp. 11-20 (portrait). *Ency. Brit.* (11th edn.) xxiii. 100. *Major James Rennell*, by Sir Clements Markham. *A.J.* N.S. ii. 56. *G.M.* 1830, i. 561. Portrait, E. Scott—A. Cardon. Crayon portrait by George Dance in Nat. Portrait Gallery. Bust nr. western door of Westminster Abbey.

Note: He appears as "Rennett, ——" (No. 32) in *Stubbs's List*.

RENNIE, George (*d.* 1784). Captain, Invalid Est. 1st Bengal Eur. Regt. Country Cadet 1766. Ensign May 1766. Lieut. 1 Sept. 1767. Capt. 29 Nov. 1772. Invalided (?) *d.* at sea June 1784.

Services: Came out to India in a private capacity and was given a Commission during the "Batta mutiny." Capt. 1st Bengal Eur. Regt. at Berhampore in Dec. 1774, when he was found guilty by a G.C.M. of entering into mercantile transactions with a sutler to the army and suspended for 6 mos. Capt. 1/1st Eur. Regt. in Oct. 1779. Leave s.c. to sea 23 Nov. 1780.

RENNIE, William (*d.* 1800). Bt. Captain, 14th N.I. Cadet 1782. Ensign 13 Apr. 1783. Lieut. 13 Mar. 1790. Bt. Capt. 7 Jan. 1796. *d.* at the Cape 1800, on his way home.

Services: Posted to 2nd Bengal Eur. Bn. 5 Feb. 1790; transfd. to 14th Bn. Sepoys 6 Nov. 1793. Second Rohilla War; battle of Bitaurah; Lieut. 14th Bn. Fur. 29 Jan. 1800.

RENNY or RANNIE, Hugh (*d.* 1778). Capt. Lieutenant, Artillery. (108) Cadet (?) Fireworker 31 Mar. 1770. Lieut. 17 May 1772. Capt. Lt. 30 Mar. 1778. *d.* Calcutta 21 Aug. 1778.

THE BENGAL ARMY, 1758-1834

(*Possibly* son of Capt. David Rannie, of Melville Castle, nr. Edinburgh, formerly of Calcutta,[1] and Elizabeth Bayley his wife, whose dau. Elizabeth *m.* Henry Dundas, 1st Viscount Melville.) *m.* (?)
Services : Was Adjt. of Art. in Tempy. Bde. at his death.
Refs. : S.M. 1779, p. 455. Will dated 21 Aug. 1778 ; proved 31 Aug. 1778.
[1] *Note :* cf. *Hill's Calcutta,* p. 76 ; also *S.M.* 1764, p. 632.

RENNY, Thomas. (*See* **RENNY-TAILYOUR.**)

REPEAN, Thomas. (*See* **NEPEAN.**)

REVELL, John Raithby (1804-1850). Captain, Invalid Est. Artillery. (521) *b.* London 13 Dec. 1804. Cadet 1820. Arrived in India 16 Jan. 1822. 2nd Lieut. 9 June 1821. Lieut. 1 May 1824. Capt. 1 Aug. 1838. Invalided 23 Dec. 1840. *d.* Serampore 4 May 1850.
bapt. St. Olave, Jewry, 24 Feb. 1805. Son of Henry Read (who changed his name to Revell, by Sign Manual, 10 Mar. 1809), of Round Oak, Englefield Green, and Louisa his wife. Brother of Joseph Leverton Revell, *q.v.,* of Anne Matilda, wife of Reymond Hervey De Montmorency, *q.v.,* and of Emily, wife of John Handcock Low, *q.v.* Uncle of Henry Patch, *q.v.* Addiscombe Cadet 20 Aug. 1819 till 9 June 1821.
Services : Siege and capture of Bhurtpore ; Lieut. 3rd Coy. 1st Bn. Foot Art. Fur. s.c. 26 May 1826 till 5 Sept. 1829 ; leave s.c. to Simla 19 Feb. 1834 till 19 Feb. 1835 ; leave s.c. 2 yrs. to Tasmania 23 Jan. 1836 ; fur. s.c. 14 May 1838 till 29 Mar. 1840, and 30 Jan. 1846 till Nov. 1849.
Refs. : I.M. 1 July 1850, p. 387.

REVELL, Joseph Leverton (1802-1881). Lieut. Colonel. 2nd Bengal Eur. Regt. *b.* London 12 Feb. 1802. Cadet 1817. Admitted 30 Jan. 1819. Ensign 6 Aug. 1818. Lieut. 21 Jan. 1820. Capt. 8 Oct. 1839. Major 8 Jan. 1847. Retired 21 July 1848. Hon. Lt. Col. 28 Nov. 1854. *d.* 2 Langford Pl., London, 13 Dec. 1881.
Of Round Oak, Englefield Green. *bapt.* St. Olave's, Jewry, 20 Mar. 1802. Son of Henry Revell, of Round Oak, and Louisa his wife. Brother of John Raithby Revell, *q.v. m.* 1st, Mary Jane Ward. (She died 1 Nov. 1829.) *m.* 2nd, Gorakhpur, U.P., 15 July 1834, Louisa, 2nd dau. of Charles Wale Lamborne, *q.v.*

(*See also* Stephen Moody.) (She died 11 Aug. 1879.) Sandhurst Cadet.
Services : Lieut. d.d. 2/13th N.I. 28 Oct. 1820 ; posted to 2/4th N.I. 3 Nov. 1820. Second in comd. Rohilla Cav. 21 Mar. 1822 till 1826. Transfd. to 7th N.I. (late 1/4th) May 1824. Fur. s.c. 12 Feb. 1826 till 11 Nov. 1828. Adjt. 7th N.I. 2 Mar. 1836 till 16 May 1838. Transfd. to 2nd Bengal Eur. Regt. 8 Oct. 1839. D.A.G. 2nd Inf. Div., Army of Reserve (for Afghanistan), 14 Oct. 1842. Bde. Major at Meerut 18 Feb. till 27 Oct. 1843 ; offg. do. at Ludhiana 16 Oct. 1844. No record of active service.
Refs. : *The Times*, 15 Dec. 1881.

REYNOLDS, Henry Coffin (1808-1844). Bt. Captain, 40th N.I. *b.* 1 Mar. 1808. Cadet 1825. Arrived in India 30 June 1826. Ensign 20 Dec. 1825. Lieut. 24 May 1829. Bt. Capt. 28 Dec. 1840. *d.* Mussoorie 12 Sept. 1844, of dysentery, aged 36.

bapt. Lympstone, Devon, 15 Apr. 1808. Of Dowry Parade, Clifton. 5th son of William Reynolds, of Malpass House, Newport, Mon., clerk in the admiralty and inspr. of lighthouses, and Georgiana Grueber his wife, 2nd dau. of William Larkins, B.C.S., accountant gen. Bengal. *m.* E. Budleigh, Devon, 20 Aug. 1839, Elizabeth Ann, 2nd dau. of Thomas Hunter, of Salterton.
Services : Ensign d.d. 4th Extra Regt. 8 July 1826 ; posted to 25th N.I. 26 Sept. 1826 ; transfd. to 40th N.I. 2 Mar. 1827. Adjt. 40th N.I. 16 Aug. 1833 till 7 Apr. 1837. S.S.O. at Aligarh 1 May 1834 ; actg. do. in Arakan 24 Nov. 1834. Volunteered his services in pursuit of dacoits in Arakan Jan. 1836. Fur. s.c. 30 Jan. 1837 till 3 Feb. 1840. Actg. Adjt. 40th N.I. 18 Apr. 1842 ; permanent do. 4 Nov. 1842 till 20 Jan. 1844.
Refs. : *G.M.* 1844, ii. 670. Family information.

REYNOLDS, Thomas (*d.* 1770). Ensign, Infantry. Cadet 1769. Ensign 18 Oct. 1769. *d.* Berhampore 2 June 1770.
Services : N.F.P.

REYNOLDS, Thomas (1788-1873). Lieut. Colonel. 63rd N.I. *b.* Kilbarron, co. Donegal, 7 Mar. 1788. Cadet 1804. Arrived in India 21 June 1806. Ensign 11 Nov. 1805. Lieut. 16 Aug. 1806. Capt. 1 July 1823. Major 5 Apr. 1834. Invalided 25 Sept. 1834. Retired 10 Oct. 1838. Hon. Lt. Col. 28 Nov. 1854. *d.* 176 Oakley St., Chelsea, 10 June 1873.

6th son of Hewetson Reynolds (of the family of Reynolds, of Kilbarron and Coolbeg) and Mary Ann his wife, dau. of John

Smyth, of Ballyshannon, co. Donegal. *m.* 1st, Calcutta 18 July 1811, Mary, dau. of Sir Robert Blair, *q.v.* (*See also* Henry Clayton.) (She died Hansi 16 Apr. 1827, aged 38.) His dau. *m.* Ninian Lowis, *q.v. m.* 2nd, Mellington Hall, co. Montgomery, 13 May 1839, his cousin Barbara, younger dau. of Michael Reynolds, M.D., of Ballyshannon, and of the Donegal Mil.

Services : Served as Cadet at capture of Cape in 1806. Posted Lieut. to 2nd N.I. in 1806. Adjt. 1/2nd N.I. 28 Feb. 1817 till July 1823. Leave s.c. 10 mos. to sea 7 Mar. 1817. Actg. Intr. & Qmr. 1/2nd N.I. 12 Feb. 1822. Transfd. as Capt. to newly-formed 32nd N.I. July 1823 ; to 63rd N.I. (late 1/32nd) May 1824. First Burma War ; Arakan 1825 ; Capt. 2nd Gren. Bn. (India medal). Fur. s.c. 15 Dec. 1827 till 22 Dec. 1830. Transfd. to Invalid Est. owing to loss of his voice. Fur. p.a. 17 Jan. 1836 till retirement. Retired on pension of 16/- *p.d.*

Refs. : Family information. Burke's *Landed Gentry*, 15th edn., p. 2667, *s.n.* Reynolds, of The Mullens. *N. & Q.* 12S. ix. 7. *A.J.* N.S. xxix. 158. *The Times*, 13 June 1873.

REYNOLDS, Thomas Conway. Lieutenant. Infantry. Country Cadet 1778. Ensign 19 May 1779. Lieut. 22 Jan. 1781. Struck off 12 Feb. 1781. *d.* in India (?)

Services : Apptd. Cadet for Inf. 11 Aug. 1778 ; transfd. as Cadet to Art. (III.-10) 6 Feb. 1779 ; retransfd. to Inf. Struck off, never having joined his Corps.

REYNOLDS, William (1784-1815). Captain, 6th N.I. *b.* London 13 Apr. 1784. Cadet 1799. Arrived in India 1 Dec. 1800. Ensign 26 Oct. 1800. Lieut. 6 May 1803. Capt. 1 Sept. 1815. *d.* Fatehgarh 12 Sept. 1815.

bapt. St. John Zachary, Aldersgate, 12 May 1784. Son of Edward Reynolds and Mary his wife.

Services : Posted Ensign to 1/6th N.I. 17 Apr. 1801. Capt. Lt. 6th N.I. 28 Nov. 1814. Civil architect for W. provinces of Bengal 1812 till death. No record of active service.

Refs. : G.M. 1816, i. 564. *Cal. Gaz.* 23 Oct. 1823. M.I. Fatehgarh fort cemetery.

RICE, James George Allerton (1809-1871). Colonel. 4th Bengal Eur. Inf. *b.* Stondon Massey, Essex, 28 Dec. 1809. Cadet 1825. Arrived in India 24 June 1826. Ensign 5 Feb. 1826. Lieut. 9 July 1828. Capt. 6 Mar. 1846. Major 18 Apr. 1853. Lt. Col. 29 July 1857. Retired 31 Dec. 1861. Hon. Col. 31 Dec. 1861. *d.* Lawn Villa, Bognor, 13 May 1871.

bapt. Stondon Massey 21 June 1820. Son of James George Rice, of 38 Hans Pl., Chelsea, and Sarah Dunning his wife. His sister *m.* Robert James Latter, *q.v.* *m.* Allahabad 18 Sept. 1832, Mary Charlotte, 3rd dau. of Henry Hawes Harington, of Madras, and sister of Sir Henry Byng Harington, *q.v.* (She died 26 July 1879, aged 66.)

Services: Ensign d.d. 4th Extra Regt. 8 July 1826; posted to 6th N.I. 26 Sept. 1826; Adjt. do. 30 July 1832 till Mar. 1846. First Afghan War 1842; Bt. Capt. 6th N.I., on lines of communication (Medal). Garr. Staff at Jalalabad 21 Aug. 1842. Actg. S.S.O. at Ludhiana 24 May 1843. First Sikh War; Capt. 6th N.I., on escort duty. 2nd Asst. Sec. to Govt., Mily. Dept., Mar. 1851; 1st do. Mar. 1856. Fur. s.c. 6 mos. Apr. 1857. Posted Lt. Col. to 11th N.I. in 1857; Mily. Sec. to Presdt. in Council 1 June 1858; to comd. 4th Bengal Eur. Inf. 19 July 1858.

Refs.: Howard & Crisp, x. 124, *s.n.* Harington. *The Times*, 23 May 1871.

RICE, John Howard (1803-1859). Lieutenant. 44th N.I. Pensioner on Lord Clive's fund. *b.* Petersham, Sussex, 24 May 1803. Cadet 1824. Ensign 18 Apr. 1825. Lieut. 25 Jan. 1828. Pensioned 9 Mar. 1831. *d.* Sutton Courtenay, Berks., 30 Aug. 1859.

Only son of Rev. Edward John Howard Rice, D.C.L., rector of St. Luke's, Old St., London, and Charlotte his wife. Brother of Jane, wife of Joseph Whiteford and afterwards of Edward Thomas Tierney, *qq.v.* *m.* Mary. Father of Rev. Richard John Howard Rice, vicar of Sutton Courtenay 1856. Ed. Charterhouse Oct. 1815-May 1818.

Services: Served for a time in R.N. Posted Ensign to 44th N.I. in 1825. Fur. s.c. 1825 till Nov. 1828, and 27 Feb. 1829 till pensioned. No record of active service.

Refs.: Charterhouse School List. *G.M.* 1859, ii. 430. *The Times*, 2 Sept. 1859.

***RICE, Richard** (1740/41-?). Ensign, Infantry. *b.* co. Carmarthen 1740/41. Cadet 1764. Ensign 1765.

Services: Sailed for India in the *Fort William* 17 May 1764, aged 23. Posted Ensign to 1st Bengal Eur. Regt. 13 Aug. 1765. Was Ensign in 2nd Eur. Regt. when, on 7 May 1766, he was one of the signatories to a letter to the C.-in-C. on the subject of Batta; resigned his Commission during the "Batta mutiny," but was restored later. Not in *A.L.* of 1 Feb. 1767.

Refs. : Broome, p. 597. *Caraccioli*, iii. 198. Will dated 19 Mar. 1765 ; proved 6 Mar. 1767.

RICE, William Henry (*d.* 1773). Captain, Infantry. Cadet 1764. Ensign 22 Apr. 1765. Lieut. 16 Dec. 1766. Capt. 17 Oct. 1769. *d.* Dinapore 4 Sept. 1773.
Services : Posted Ensign to 1st Bengal Eur. Regt. 13 Aug. 1765 ; resigned during the " Batta mutiny " ; reinstated 1766.

RICH, John (1789-1856). Lieutenant. 15th N.I. Subsequently rector of Newtimber, Sussex. *b.* 27 Sept. 1789. Cadet 1805. Arrived in India 19 Sept. 1806. Ensign 25 Sept. 1806. Lieut. 13 Apr. 1809. Resigned 12 Jan. 1813. *d.* at the Rectory, Newtimber, 24 June 1856.
bapt. Farnham, Surrey, 27 Oct. 1789. 4th son of Rev. Sir Charles Bostock Rich, 1st Bart., of Shirley House, Hants (who assumed the surname of Rich 23 Dec. 1790), and Mary Frances his wife, only dau. and heir of Lt.-Gen. Sir Robert Rich, 5th Bart. *m.* 3 Aug. 1825, Georgiana, dau. of Charles Gordon. (She died 1889.) Ed. Harrow 1799-1803. Woolwich Cadet. St. John's Coll., Camb. ; B.A. 1816 ; M.A. 1819.
Services : Posted Ensign to 15th N.I. in 1807, and served throughout with that Regt. Fur. 1811 till resignation. No record of active service. Took holy orders. Rector of Cheddington, Bucks., 12 Jan. 1819 ; subsequently rector of Newtimber till death.
Refs. : Burke's *Peerage*, 1923, p. 1869, *s.n.* Rich, Bart., of Shirley House, Hants. Berry's *Hants Peds.*, p. 13. *Harrow School Register. Graduati Cantab. G.M.* 1856, ii. 254.

RICH, Robert (1787-1852). Colonel, 6th N.I. Comdg. Benares Div. *b.* London 7 Mar. 1787. Cadet 1803. Arrived in India 17 Mar. 1805. Ensign 21 Mar. 1805. Lieut. 22 Mar. 1805. Capt. 1 Jan. 1819. Major 11 Feb. 1826. Lt. Col. 21 Jan. 1831. Col. 19 Dec. 1842. *d.* Naini Tal, U.P., 25 May 1852.
bapt. St. Olave's, Hart St., London, 12 Apr. 1787. Son of Robert Rich and Anne his wife. *m.* 1st, Cawnpore 26 Sept. 1809, Maria Ann, dau. of Frederick Trench, *q.v.* (She died Nasirabad 13 Apr. 1837.) *m.* 2nd, Emma. (She died 4 Sept. 1882.)
Services : Served in E. London Mil. Posted Lieut. to 3rd N.I. in 1805 ; actg. Adjt. Rt. Wing 2/3rd N.I. 30 June 1812. Nepal War 1814-15 ; Lieut. 2/3rd N.I., in 1st Div. (India medal). Capt. 1/3rd N.I. 2nd Asst. Sec. and 1st Asst. Accountant, Mily. Board, 13 Aug. 1821 ; tempy. 1st Asst. Sec. 22 Mar. till 3 Nov. 1823.

Transfd. to 19th N.I. (late 2/3rd) May 1824. Fort Adjt. at Allahabad 4 June 1824 till 7 Oct. 1826. To assume charge of 6th N.I. 10 Nov. 1830. Posted Lt. Col. to 6th N.I. 24 Sept. 1831 ; to 23rd N.I. 7 Dec. 1833 ; to 22nd N.I. 9 Dec. 1836. Bdr. 2 cl. and comd. 2nd Bde. for service in Marwar 5 Aug. 1839 ; comdd. at occupation of Jodhpur ; force broken up 14 Oct. 1839. Transfd. to newly-raised 3rd Bengal Eur. Regt. 7 Nov. 1839 ; to 5th N.I. 15 Jan. 1840 ; to 8th N.I. 25 Feb. 1840 ; to 53rd N.I. 3 Oct. 1840 ; to 74th N.I. 20 July 1841 ; to 6th N.I. 21 Jan. 1843. Col. 6th N.I. 19 Dec. 1842 till death. Fur. s.c. 9 Apr. 1846 till 6 Dec. 1851. Apptd. to Divl. Staff of Army 31 Dec. 1851 ; posted to Cis-Jhelum Div. 10 Jan. 1852 ; to Benares Div. Apr. 1852.

Refs. : Boase. *Bombay Times*, 5 June 1852. M.I. Naini Tal.

RICH, Thomas Thynne[1] (*d.* 1768). Ensign, Infantry. Cadet 1767. Ensign 1 Dec. 1767. *d.* Calcutta 2 Aug. 1768.

Services : N.F.P.

[1] *Note :* His christian name is given as James in the burial register.

RICHARDS, Alfred (1781-1852). Lieut. General, C.B. Colonel 31st N.I. *bapt.* Cowbridge, co. Glam., 12 July 1781. Cadet 1794. Arrived in India 1 Mar. 1797. Ensign 1 Dec. 1795. Lieut. 30 Oct. 1797. Capt. 13 June 1805. Major 19 Sept. 1816. Lt. Col. 13 Feb. 1823. Col. 5 June 1829. Maj. Gen. 28 June 1838. Lt. Gen. 11 Nov. 1851. *d.* Summerlands, Exeter, 17 Nov. 1852.

Son of William Richards, *q.v.*, and Elizabeth his wife. Brother of Scipio Edward Richards, *q.v. m.* St. Michael's, Bath, 30 Jan. 1812, Miss Rhoda Cecilia Howell, of Carmarthen, sister of Ilted Howell.

Services : Apptd. Cadet 21 June 1796 ; sailed for India in the *Lascelles* 11 Aug. 1796. Lieut. 5th N.I. in 1798 ; transfd. to 19th N.I. ; to newly-raised 2/23rd N.I. 9 Nov. 1803. Fur. p.a. 5 Aug. 1809 till 26 Nov. 1812. Comdd. 7th Gren. Bn. 1815-16. Third Mahratta War ; comdd. column of Inf. in successful action nr. Gadarwara in Jan. 1818 (*Lond. Gaz.* 14 July and 7 Dec. 1818) ; Major 2/23rd N.I. Posted Lt. Col. to 2/23rd N.I. in 1823 ; to 46th N.I. (late 2/23rd) May 1824. First Burma War ; conquest of Assam 1824-5 ; succeeded to comd. of force on death of Lt.-Col. George Macmorine, *q.v.* ; action nr. Rangpur 29 Jan. 1825 (w.) (*Lond. Gaz.* 22 Feb. and 9 July 1825) ; Lt. Col. comdg. Assam force (India medal). Fur. 1 Feb. 1826 till death. Posted Lt. Col.

THE BENGAL ARMY, 1758-1834 639

Comdt. to 51st N.I. 30 Oct. 1826; to 33rd N.I.; to 31st N.I. 28 Dec. 1827. Col. 31st N.I. 5 June 1829 till death. C.B. 26 Dec. 1826.
Refs.: Boase. *G.M.* 1852, ii. 663.

RICHARDS, Charles James (1815-1875). Lieut. Colonel. 25th N.I. *bapt.* Tenby 30 May 1815. Cadet 1832. Arrived in India 5 Mar. 1833. Ensign 7 Nov. 1832. Lieut. 15 May 1837. Capt. 12 Feb. 1846. Bt. Major 1 May 1858. Retired 31 Dec. 1861. Hon. Lt. Col. 31 Dec. 1861. *d.* Ferryside, co. Carmarthen, 29 Nov. 1875.
Son of Jacob Richards, of Tenby, and Susannah his wife. Addiscombe Cadet 30 Aug. 1830 till 14 June 1832.
Services: d.d. 25th N.I. 23 Mar. 1833; posted to 10th N.I. 11 Feb. 1834; transfd. to 25th N.I. 2 Mar. 1835. Second in comd. Arakan Local Bn. 14 Nov. 1840 till Mar. 1847. Fur. s.c. 10 Mar. 1847 till 14 Jan. 1850, and 1857 till retirement. No record of active service.
Refs.: *The Times*, 7 Dec. 1875.

RICHARDS, Goddard (1764-1833). Colonel, 59th N.I. *b.* 1764. Cadet 1782. Arrived in India 2 Nov. 1782. Ensign 26 Feb. 1783. Lieut. 14 Feb. 1790. Capt. 30 Sept. 1803. Major 11 Mar. 1811. Lt. Col. 1 Sept. 1815. Lt. Col. Comdt. 1 May 1824. Col. 5 June 1829. *d.* at his residence, Cavendish Cresc., Bath, 19 Oct. 1833.
Of Gath, Ireland, and of Cavendish Cresc., Bath. 3rd son of Goddard Richards, of Grange, co. Wexford, and Anne his wife, dau. of Ven. Nicholas Hewetson, archdeacon of Killaloe. *m.* in Ireland 24 Sept. 1802, Anne, 2nd dau. of Henry Thomas Houghton, of Kilmannock House, co. Wexford. (*See also* Charles Caesar Pigott and Lewis Thomas.) (She died Versailles 3 Oct. 1865.) His daus. *m.* George Burges and Arthur Wheatley, *qq.v.*
Services: Approved as Cadet 7 Nov. 1781; sailed for India in the *Norfolk* 6 Feb. 1782. Posted Ensign to 3rd Bengal Eur. Regt. 28 Feb. 1783. Supy. Ensign, unposted, in July 1787; 1st Eur. Bn. in Dec. 1788. Reposted to 1st Eur. Bn. 5 Feb. 1790; transfd. to 30th Bn. Sepoys 9 Sept. 1791; to 7th N.I. Aug. 1793; Bt. Capt. 7th N.I. in June 1798; transfd. to 2nd Eur. Regt. 1798. Fur. s.c. 1800 till 8 Sept. 1803. Capt. Lt. Marine Regt.; posted Capt. to newly-raised 2/22nd N.I. Sept. 1803. Second Mahratta War 1804-5; battle and capture of Deig; Bhurtpore; Capt. comdg. 2/22nd N.I. Operations in Bundelkhand against Gopal

Singh 1810-11 ; Major comdg. 1/22nd N.I. Nepal War 1816 ; Makwanpur ; Lt. Col. comdg. 2/22nd N.I., in 3rd Bde. Centre Column. Transfd. to 27th N.I. in 1820 ; to 1/13th N.I. 1821 ; to 12th N.I. 1822 ; as Lt. Col. Comdt. to 59th N.I. May 1824. Fur. p.a. 7 Mar. 1823 till 11 Mar. 1825. Bdr. comdg. Rohilkhand district 27 May 1825 till Feb. 1828. Fur. p.a. 22 Feb. 1828 till death. Col. 59th N.I. June 1829.

Refs. : Burke's *Landed Gentry of Ireland*, p. 590, *s.n.* Richards, of Monksgrange, co. Wexford. Burke's *Landed Gentry*, 4th edn., p. 726, *s.n.* Houghton, of Kilmannock House, co. Wexford. *E.I.M.C.* ii. 358-9. Faulkner's *Dublin Journal*, 28 Sept. 1802. *Bath Chron.* 24 Oct. 1833. Will dated Calcutta, 31 Jan. 1828 ; proved 25 Apr. 1834.

*RICHARDS, Robert (1738/39-?). Cadet. *b.* Tiverton 1738/39. Cadet 1764.

Services : Sailed for India in the *Devonshire* 20 Feb. 1764, aged 25. N.F.P.

RICHARDS, Scipio Edward (1784-1854). Captain. 11th N.I. *bapt.* Cowbridge, co. Glam., 25 Oct. 1784. Cadet 1799. Arrived in India 9 Mar. 1800. Ensign 20 Aug. 1800. Lieut. 30 Nov. 1800. Capt. 16 Dec. 1814. Retired 12 July 1820. *d.* Pettistree, Suffolk, 7 Jan. 1854, aged 69.

Of Java Lodge, Pettistree. Son of William Richards, *q.v.*, and Elizabeth his wife. Brother of Sir William Richards, *q.v. m.* Easter. (She died 2 Oct. 1883, aged 75.)

Services : Posted Lieut. to 2/11th N.I. 17 Apr. 1801. Second Mahratta War ; Bundelkhand 1803 ; Kapsa ; Kalpi ; Gwalior ; Lieut. 2/11th N.I. Capture of Gohad 1806 ; Lieut. 2/11th N.I. Capture of Java 1811 ; Lieut. & Qmr. Vol. L.I. Bn. (Medal). (? Nepal War 1814-15 ; Capt. L.I. Bn., in 2nd Div.) Fur. 1817 till retirement.

Refs. : *G.M.* 1854, i. 330. *I.M.* 31 Jan. 1854, p. 51.

RICHARDS, William. Captain. Engineers. Cadet 1764. Fireworker (Art.) (72) 10 Dec. 1764. Ensign (Engrs.) 10 Dec. 1764. Lieut. 6 Aug. 1768. Capt. 1 Apr. 1769. Resigned 2 Dec. 1776.

(? Son of William Richards, of Cardiff. Oriel Coll., Oxon. ; matric. 21 May 1762, aged 17.) *m.* Elizabeth. Father of Alfred, Scipio Edward, and Sir William, *qq.v.*

Services : Sailed for India as Art. Cadet in the *Caernarvon* 20 Feb.

THE BENGAL ARMY, 1758-1834   641

1764. Transfd. to Engrs. and employed in surveying Bengal under James Rennell, *q.v.*, from Dec. 1764. In action against the Saniyasis 20 Feb. 1766 (w.). At Dacca in 1774; at Ft. Wm. in 1775. The whole of his service was spent in survey work and he appears to have officiated as Surveyor Gen. for a short period. Apptd. Surveyor Gen. by C.D. in England 25 Nov. 1778, but apparently did not return to India to take up the appt.; wrote from St. Helena 15 Jan. 1781, resigning his Commission and the post of Surveyor Gen. of Bengal.

Refs.: (? *Alumni Oxon.*)

RICHARDS, Sir William (1778-1861). General, K.C.B. Colonel 26th N.I. *b.* Tichborne, Hants, 2 Jan. 1778. Cadet 1793. Arrived in India 18 Oct. 1794. Ensign 26 Sept. 1794. Lieut. 8 Jan. 1796. Capt. 21 Sept. 1804. Major 7 Aug. 1814. Lt. Col. 3 Sept. 1818. Lt. Col. Comdt. 1 May 1824. Col. 5 June 1829. Maj. Gen. 10 Jan. 1837. Lt. Gen. 9 Nov. 1846. Gen. 20 June 1854. *d.* Naini Tal, U.P., 1 Nov. 1861.

Son of William Richards, *q.v.*, and Elizabeth his wife. Brother of Alfred Richards, *q.v.* *m.* 1st, a natural dau. of Andrew Wilson Hearsey, *q.v.*, by an Indian lady. (*See also* James Oram Clarkson and Arthur Owen.) *m.* 2nd, Agra 15 Oct. 1830, Henrietta Herd (aged 18, spinster), " a native lady of the Jat tribe." (She died Agra 28 Nov. 1845.)

Services: Apptd. Cadet 5 Mar. 1794; sailed for India in the *Essex* 2 May 1794. Posted Ensign to 5th Eur. Bn. 8 Nov. 1794; Lieut. 1st Bengal Eur. Regt. in 1796; transfd. to newly-raised 1/13th N.I. in Dec. 1797. Fourth Mysore War Jan. 1799-July 1800; Seringapatam; Lieut. 3rd Bn. Bengal Vols. (Medal). Adjt. 3rd Bn. Vols. May 1799 till July 1800. Second Mahratta War 1803-6; operations in Bundelkhand; storm and capture of Jaitpur; Capt. 13th N.I.; Suptg. Ofr. with Mohd. Jiwan Khan's native bde. in Bundelkhand Dec. 1804 till May 1806. Operations against Dhundia Khan 1807; Komona; Ganauri; Capt. 1/13th N.I. Nepal War 1814-15; Kalanga; Jampta (*Lond. Gaz.* 19 Aug. 1815); affair on 2 Apr. 1815; Major 1/13th N.I. (India medal). Bareilly insurrection 1816; made a forced march of 63 miles in 41 hours from Moradabad to Bareilly; Major comdg. 1/13th N.I. Posted Lt. Col. to 1/13th N.I.; transfd. to 2/14th N.I. 1821; to 1/19th 20 Sept. 1822. Operations against Larka Kols 1821; comdg. the force. Comdt. Asirgarh fortress 12 Nov. 1821 till 1824. Posted Lt. Col. Comdt. to 26th N.I. (late 1/13th) May 1824; Col. 26th N.I. 1829 till death. First Burma War; comdd. storming party

at assault of Arakan heights 30 Mar. 1825 ; comdg. 1st Bde. of
Bdr.-Gen. Morrison's force from 23 Nov. 1824. Resigned comd.
of S.E. Div. of Army owing to ill health 9 Jan. 1826. Comdt.
fortress of Agra 1 Feb. 1826 ; apptd. Bdr. on the Est. 8 Oct. 1828 ;
comdd. Agra and Muttra frontier 14 Nov. 1828 till Dec. 1833.
Apptd. to Gen. Staff of Army as Bdr. Gen. 24 Dec. 1833, and comdd.
Dinapore Div. till 24 Dec. 1838 when his tour on the Staff expired.
Resided continuously in India for 67 yrs. C.B. 2 Jan. 1827 ;
K.C.B. 20 July 1838.

Refs. : Walford. Boase. D.I.B. E.I.M.C. ii. 473-7. *A.J.*
N.S. xxii. 153. *G.M.* 1862, i. 237. *The Times*, 23 Dec. 1861, p. 4.
M.I. Naini Tal.

RICHARDS, William (1778-1843). Bt. Major. Artillery. (302)
b. 2 Jan. 1778. Cadet 1793. Admitted 25 Sept. 1794. Fireworker 17 Sept. 1794. Lieut. 14 Feb. 1802. Capt. Lt. 21 Sept.
1804. Capt. 11 June 1808. Bt. Major 4 June 1814. Retired
29 Dec. 1815. *d.s.p.* Argyll St., London, 6 Sept. 1843.

bapt. ptely. Cardiff Jan. 1778. Younger son of John Richards,
of Cardiff, and Jane his 1st wife, dau. of William Richards. Brother
of Mary, wife of Sir Jeremiah Homfray, Kt., of Llandaff House,
co. Glam., and of Charlotte, 2nd wife of Sir Robert Lynch-Blosse,
8th Bart. Nephew of Rev. George Richards, and uncle and cousin
of Ann Maria, wife of John Homfray, of Llandaff House.

Services : Apptd. Inf. Cadet 7 Feb. 1793 ; sailed for India in
the *Lord Camden* 2 May 1794. Transfd. to Art. 1795. Fourth
Mysore War ; operations in Hyderabad 1798 ; capture of
Seringapatam 1799 ; Lieut. F. 3rd Coy. 1st Bn. Second Mahratta
War ; operations in Bundelkhand 1803 ; Kapsa ; Kalpi ; siege of
Gwalior (w.) ; Lieut. 1st Coy. 3rd Bn. Comdt. Art. at P.W.I.
1807-9. Capture of Java 1811 ; Cornelis [1] ; Capt. comdg. 7th
Coy. 1st Bn. Comy. Ord. at Allahabad 3 Mar. 1812 till 1814.
Fur. s.c. 1814 till retirement. Retired on h.p. and pension for
wounds.

Refs. : Genealogies of Morgan and Glamorgan, by G. T. Clark,
p. 552, *s.n.* Richards, of Roath. *E.I.M.C.* iii. 107-9. *A.J.* 1843,
3S. i. 667. Will dated 2 May 1843 ; admon. 5 Jan. 1844.

[1] *Note :* He was severely injured on 24 Aug. by the explosion
of some cartridges in the 18-pdr. battery, and was subsequently
obliged to return to Bengal on this account.

RICHARDSON, Charles John (1808-1857). Bt. Major, 57th N.I.
b. Madras 15 June 1808. Cadet 1824. Arrived in India 4 Oct.

THE BENGAL ARMY, 1758-1834 643

1825. Ensign 13 May 1825. Lieut. 18 July 1828. Capt. 7 Jan. 1841. Bt. Major 11 Nov. 1851. *d.* St. Leonards-on-Sea 17 Feb. 1857.

bapt. Negapatam, Madras, 30 Sept. 1808. Son of Francis Richardson, of Devonshire St., Portland Pl., London, formerly M.C.S., Commercial Resdt. at Nagore, and Elizabeth his wife, 10th dau. of Edward, 1st Earl Winterton. Grandson of William Richardson, Accountant Gen. E.I.C., and brother of Francis Turnour Richardson, *q.v.* Cousin-german of Sir John Larkins Cheese Richardson, *q.v.*

Services : Posted Ensign to 57th N.I.; Intr. & Qmr. do. 22 May 1833; Adjt. do. 22 June 1836 till 21 May 1841. Insurrection in Bundelkhand 1842; engagement nr. Jaitpur (s.w.). Asst. to A.G.G. Bundelkhand, specially attached to Jhansi State, 20 Feb. 1843. Second in comd. 5th Inf., Gwalior Contingent, 13 Jan. 1844; Comdt. 4th Inf. do. 9 Nov. 1849 till 1856. Fur. s.c. 29 Apr. 1856 till death.

Refs. : *I.M.* 3 Mar. 1857, p. 139. Will dated 12 Feb. 1857; admon. 4 Feb. 1859.

RICHARDSON, Charles Welstead (1806-?). Lieutenant. 5th L.C. *b.* London 4 Sept. 1806. Cadet 1825. Arrived in India 20 Mar. 1826. Cornet 25 Oct. 1825. Lieut. 26 Mar. 1829. Resigned 2 Dec. 1831.

Son of George Richardson, of Barnstaple, Capt. *United Kingdom*, Indiaman, and Susanna his wife. *m.* Dinapore 19 Mar. 1829, Mary Margaret Woolmer, eldest dau. of Capt. Tristram Charnley Squire, H.M. 13th L.I.

Services : Posted Cornet to 5th L.C.; d.d. 1st L.C. 21 Feb. 1829. Sailed from India without leave 28 Aug. 1830, and remained absent nearly 12 mos. No record of active service. Settled at the Cape.

Refs. : *A.J.* xxviii. 475.

RICHARDSON, David Lester (1801-1865). Captain. 56th N.I. *b.* London 22 Jan. 1801. Cadet 1819. Admitted 22 Apr. 1820. Ensign 13 Nov. 1819. Lieut. 11 July 1823. Capt. 29 Oct. 1832. Invalided 19 Feb. 1833. Retired 12 July 1858. *d.* at his residence, 1 Lambourne Rd., nr. The Grange, Clapham, 17 Nov. 1865.

Natural son of David Thomas Richardson, *q.v.*, by Sarah Lester. *m.* Dinapore 8 Jan. 1821, Marian, dau. of William Scott (1763-1808), *q.v.*, by " a Persian princess." (She died Pimlico 15 Dec. 1865, aged 64.)

Services: Ensign d.d. 1/23rd N.I. 22 Aug. 1820; posted to 1/2nd N.I. in 1820; d.d. Bhagulpur Hill Rangers 22 Nov. 1822 till 1824; transfd. as Lieut. to 28th N.I. July 1823; to 56th N.I. (late 2/28th) May 1824. Fur. s.c. 19 Jan. 1824 till 28 June 1829. Readmitted to the Service 1 Sept. 1830, from 28 June 1829, the date of his arrival, having been absent from sickness more than 5 yrs. No record of active service. A.D.C. to G.G. 25 Feb. 1835. Professor of English Literature in Hindu Coll., Calcutta, Feb. 1836; Principal of Hindu Coll. 1839. A.D.C. on personal staff of Presdt. in Council 12 Mar. 1839. Fur. s.c. 18 Apr. 1843 till 3 July 1845. Principal of new Krishnagar Coll. 1845; do Hooghly Coll.; do. Hindu Coll. 1848-50. Edited *Calcutta Literary Gazette*, which appeared in 1825; editor of *Bengal Hurkara* 1850. Returned to England Feb. 1861, and assisted in editing *Allen's Overland Mail*, and *Homeward Mail*, and edited the *Court Circular*. Author of several literary works.

Refs.: Boase. D.I.B. *Men of the Times*, 1865, p. 693. *I.M.* 21 May 1850, pp. 285-6. *The Times*, 21 Nov. 1865.

RICHARDSON, David Thomas (*d.* 1808). Lieut. Colonel. 17th N.I. Country Cadet 1779. Admitted 2 Aug. 1779. Ensign 13 Oct. 1779. Lieut. 23 May 1781. Capt. 31 Aug. 1798. Major 1 July 1803. Lt. Col. 27 Feb. 1805. Retired 29 Sept. 1808. *d.* at sea 22 Nov. 1808; perished, together with his wife, in the *Lord Nelson*, which was lost in a storm nr. Mauritius.

"Son-in-law" of Mrs. Stewart of Langholm. Brother of Jane, wife of Peter Littlejohn, *q.v.*, of Maria, wife of James Doddington Sherwood, *q.v.*, and of Susan Ramsay. Father of David Lester Richardson, *q.v.*, by Sarah Lester. *m.* 15 Aug. 1800, Violet, 2nd dau. of William Oliver, of Dinlabyre, and sister of Archibald Oliver, *q.v.*

Services: Apptd. Cadet by Bdr.-Gen. Goddard 12 May 1779. First Mahratta War; (w. Apr. 1781, in atk. on Col. Brown's convoy). Lieut. 5th Bn. Sepoys in July 1787; apptd. Adjt. 3rd Bengal Eur. Bn. 5 Dec. 1793; in 3rd Bengal Eur. Regt. in 1796. Intr. to C.M., and Paymr. of Marine families 1797-8. Fur. 14 Mar. 1799 till 22 May 1801. A.D.C. to V.P. 1802. First Comdt. of the newly-established Barasat C.C. 1802-5. Major 2/17th N.I. Mily. Sec. to Sir George Hilaro Barlow, Bart., G.C.B., during the whole of his administration as G.G. 17 Oct. 1805 till July 1807. Lt. Col. 17th N.I. Member of the Asiatic Soc., and pub. in the 7th vol. of the *Researches* of the Soc. an account of the *Bazeegurs* (certain tribes of Indian gypsies).

THE BENGAL ARMY, 1758-1834

Refs.: List of Mily. Secs. to G.G. S.M. 1800, p. 575. Will dated Calcutta, Sept. 1808; proved 22 Mar. 1810.
Note: In *List of Mily. Secs.* it is stated that, " He commanded a force which endeavoured to carry the fort of Toorkapoona by storm, but was repulsed by unforseen accidents with a heavy loss, nearly all the Europeans at the guns being destroyed." This incident has not been identified.

RICHARDSON, Edward Josiah (1801-1822). Lieutenant, 21st N.I. *b.* Streatham, Surrey, 3 Aug. 1801. Cadet 1817. Ensign (?) Lieut. 1 Aug. 1818. *d.* Kamptee, C.P., 25 Apr. 1822.
bapt. Streatham 24 Nov. 1801. Son of Rowland Richardson, of Streatham, and Sarah his wife, eldest dau. of Paul Prickett, of London. Brother of Marmaduke Richardson, *q.v.* Addiscombe Cadet 1816-18.
Services: Posted Lieut. to 1/21st N.I. in 1811. Served with Narbada F.F. 1820-2.
Refs.: Burke's *Landed Gentry*, 2nd edn., p. 1070, *s.n.* Prickett, of Octon Lodge, Yorks. M.I. Kamptee.

RICHARDSON, Francis Turnour (1800-1824). Lieutenant, 46th N.I. *bapt.* Madras 5 Feb. 1800. Cadet 1817. Ensign (?) Lieut. 1 Aug. 1818. *d.* in Assam 27 Dec. 1824.
Eldest son of Francis Richardson, M.C.S., and Elizabeth his wife. Brother of Charles John Richardson, *q.v.*
Services: Posted Lieut. to 2/23rd N.I. in 1819; transfd. to 46th N.I. (late 2/23rd) May 1824. First Burma War; Assam; Lieut. 46th N.I.
Refs.: G.M. 1825, ii. 190.

RICHARDSON, Sir James, eleventh baronet (1782-1804). Lieutenant, 17th N.I. *b.* London 13 Sept. 1782. Cadet 1800. Arrived in India 24 Oct. 1801. Ensign 16 Dec. 1801. Lieut. 9 Mar. 1804. *d. unm.* Gorakhpur 10 Nov. 1804.

11th Bart. *s.* his elder brother, Sir George Preston Richardson, 10th Bart., 21 Oct. 1803. *bapt.* St. John the Evangelist, Westminster, 4 Mar. 1783. 2nd son of Sir George Richardson, 9th Bart., Comdr. of the *Pigot* Indiaman, and Mary his wife, dau. of David Cooper, R.N.
Services: Posted Ensign to 17th N.I.; Lieut. 1/17th N.I. No record of active service.[1]
Refs.: Burke's *Peerage*, 1923, p. 1870, *s.n.* Stewart-Richardson,

Bart., of Pitfour, co. Perth. Foster's *Baronetage*, p. 691, *s.v.* 'Chaos.' Admon. Mar. 1808.

[1] *Note:* According to G.E.C.'s *Complete Baronetage* he "*d.* of wounds received in Lord Lake's action."

RICHARDSON, John (*d.* 1829). Lieutenant. Cavalry. Subsequently Senior Merchant, B.C.S. Cadet 1782. Admitted 3 Feb. 1783. Ensign 8 Apr. 1783. Lieut. 9 Mar. 1790. Resigned 2 Jan. 1796. d. May 1829.

Of Mount Panther, co. Down. *m.* 1st, Fatehgarh 15 Sept. 1793, Jane Louisa, dau. of John Debonnaire. (*See also* Sir Thomas Theophilus Metcalfe, Bart.) (She died Calcutta 26 Sept. 1808, aged 42.) *m.* 2nd, 28 Nov. 1809, Miss Elizabeth Macan, sister of Thomas Macan, *q.v.* (*See also* W. H. Rainey.) (She died Brighton Feb. 1855, aged 67.)

Services: Posted Ensign to 1st Bengal Eur. Regt. 28 Feb. 1783 ; posted Lieut. to 1st Eur. Bn. Mar. 1790; transfd. to 31st Bn. Sepoys 1790. Third Mysore War 1791-2; Lieut. Bengal Vols., detached from 31st Bn. Posted to 1st Regt. Cav. 10 Feb. 1794. Second Rohilla War; battle of Bitaurah (w.); Lieut. 1st Cav. Transfd. to B.C.S. with rank as Writer from 14 Sept. 1794. Arrived in India 14 Sept. 1795. Comr. of Cuttack 1813 ; at home in 1816 ; out of the Service in 1819.

Refs.: *Misc. Gen. et Her.* N.S. iii. 248. *Hickey*, iv. 122. *S.M.* 1794, p. 373.

RICHARDSON, Sir John Larkins Cheese (1810-1878). Major. Artillery. (622) Subsequently Speaker of the Legislative Council of N.Z., Kt. *b.* Howrah, Calcutta, 4 Aug. 1810. Cadet 1828. Arrived in India 23 May 1829. 2nd Lieut. 12 Dec. 1828. Lieut. 19 Aug. 1837. Capt. 6 Oct. 1846. Retired 18 Mar. 1852. Hon. Major 28 Nov. 1854. *d.* Dunedin, Otago, N.Z., 6 Dec. 1878.

Of Willowmead, Otago. *bapt.* Calcutta 10 Sept. 1810. Son of Robert Richardson, B.C.S., Commercial Resdt. at Kumarkhali, Bengal, and Mary Anne Romney his wife. Brother of Robert Edward Turnour Richardson, *q.v.*, and of Eliza Maria, 1st wife of James Stainbank Winfield, *q.v.* Cousin-german of Charles John Richardson, *q.v. m.* Agra 15 Feb. 1834, Charlotte, 3rd dau. of James Bruce Laing, B.C.S., Collector of Purnea. Addiscombe Cadet 1827-8.

Services: See *D.N.B.* Posted to 2nd Coy. 5th Bn. Foot Art. 14 Mar. 1833 ; actg. Adjt. 5th Bn. 15 Sept. 1837 ; transfd. to

4th Troop 1st Bde. H.A. 10 May 1839. Bde. Major Art. for service in Marwar 5 Aug. till 14 Oct. 1839. First Afghan War 1842 ; capture of Istalif (w.) (*Lond. Gaz.* 6 Dec. 1842) ; Lieut. 3rd Troop 1st Bde., with Gen. Pollock's force (Medal). Dy. Comy. Ord. at Ferozepore 6 Dec. 1844 till Aug. 1848. First Sikh War ; Ferozshahr (? w.) ; Dy. Comy. Ord., and part-time A.D.C. to Gen. Sir Harry Smith (Medal). Comy. Ord. at Dum-Dum 21 Aug. 1848 till Feb. 1851. Fur. s.c. Feb. 1851 till retirement. Settled at Otago 1856. Supt. of Otago Province May 1861 till 1863 ; P.M.G., N.Z., Nov. 1864 ; Member of Legislative Council 1867 ; Speaker 1868 till death. First Chancellor of Otago Univ. Author of " A Summer Excursion to New Zealand," 1852. Kt. 14 Aug. 1875.

Refs.: *D.N.B.* Boase. *The Times*, 13 Feb. 1879.

RICHARDSON, John Luther (1763/64-1848). Lieut. General. Colonel 70th N.I. *b.* Suffolk 1763/64. Cadet 1780. Admitted 8 May 1781. Ensign 1780. Lieut. 27 Aug. 1781. Capt. 8 Feb. 1800. Major 24 Feb. 1807. Lt. Col. 12 Oct. 1812. Lt. Col. Comdt. 11 July 1823. Col. 5 June 1829. Maj. Gen. 10 Jan. 1837. Lt. Gen. 9 Nov. 1846. *d.* 95 Sydney St., Bath, 10 Nov. 1848, aged 84.

Of the extinct family of Lord Cramond. (*Possibly* son of Rev. Anthony Luther Richardson (1739-1810), rector of Kennet, Cambs.) *m.* Cawnpore 5 Feb. 1808, Eliza Mary, 3rd dau. of John Fagan, of Kiltallagh, and sister of Christopher Sullivan Fagan, *q.v.* (*See also* Christopher Fagan.) (She died Bath 27 Apr. 1841.)

Services: Sailed for India in the *Rochford* 3 June 1780, aged 16. Arrived Madras 10 Jan. 1781 and served in the Cadet Coy. at that Presdy. till the following May, when he proceeded to Bengal. Second Mysore War 1783-4 ; Cuddalore ; with Col. Pearse's detachment. Lieut. 25th Bn. Sepoys in July 1787 and Dec. 1792. Fur. s.c. 4 Dec. 1797 till 7 Jan. 1801. Capt. Lt. 14th N.I. in 1798. Second Mahratta War 1803-6 ; defence of Delhi ; action at Shamli 30 Oct. 1804 ; and various operations under Lt.-Col. William Burn, *q.v.* ; pursuit of Holkar ; Capt. 2/14th N.I. Lt. Col. 2/14th N.I. Fur. s.c. to Cape and Europe 10 Feb. 1817. Transfd. to 2/27th N.I. in 1821 ; to 13th N.I. 1823. Fur. p.a. 11 Jan. 1824 till death. Transfd. as Lt. Col. Comdt. to 52nd N.I. May 1824 ; Col. do. June 1829 ; 70th N.I. 1846.

Refs.: Burke's *Landed Gentry*, 13th edn., p. 1800, *s.n.* Van Straubenzee, of Spennithorne, Yorks. *E.I.M.C.* iii. 80-2. *Bath Chron.* 16 Nov. 1848. *G.M.* 1849, i. 108.

RICHARDSON, Joseph (d. 1794). Lieutenant, 13th Bn. Sepoys. Country Cadet 1781. Admitted 26 Feb. 1781. Ensign 25 Aug. 1781. Lieut. 9 June 1783. d. 26 Oct. 1794 : kld. in action at the battle of Bitaurah.
Services : Apptd. Cadet 19 Dec. 1781. Lieut. 2nd Bengal Eur. Bn. in July 1787 ; transfd. to 13th Bn. Sepoys 1790. Third Mysore War ; Lieut. 13th Bn. Second Rohilla War ; battle of Bitaurah (kld.) ; Lieut. 13th Bn.
Refs. : M.I. in St. John's churchyard, Calcutta.

RICHARDSON, Marmaduke (1804-1825). Lieutenant, 3rd N.I. 2nd Gren. Bn. *b.* Streatham, Surrey, 3 Feb. 1804. Cadet 1819. Ensign 14 Feb. 1820. Lieut. 11 July 1823. *d.* at sea 11 Dec. 1825 : drowned whilst proceeding to Arakan.
Son of Rowland Richardson, of Streatham, and Sarah his wife. Brother of Edward Josiah Richardson, *q.v.* Addiscombe Cadet 1819.
Services : Posted Ensign to 2/4th N.I. Fur. 17 Aug. 1821 till 1823. Transfd. as Lieut. to 6th N.I. July 1823 ; to 3rd N.I. (late 1/6th) May 1824. First Burma War ; Arakan 1824-5 ; Lieut. 2nd Gren. Bn.
Refs. : Burke's *Landed Gentry*, 2nd edn., p. 1070, *s.n.* Prickett, of Octon Lodge, Yorks. *A.J.* xxiii. 86.

RICHARDSON, Robert Edward Turnour (1808-1891). Colonel. 62nd N.I. *b.* Bengal 13 Oct. 1808. Cadet 1825. Arrived in India 19 Sept. 1826. Ensign 21 May 1826. Lieut. 30 Mar. 1832. Capt. 30 May 1841. Major 28 Sept. 1850. Lt. Col. 9 Apr. 1856. Retired 18 May 1858. Hon. Col. 18 May 1858. *d.* 102 Westbourne Grove, London, 29 May 1891.
bapt. Calcutta 11 Nov. 1808. Eldest son of Robert Richardson, B.C.S., and Marian (Mary Anne) his wife. Brother of Taylor Campbell Richardson, *q.v.*
Services : Ensign d.d. 62nd N.I. 7 Oct. 1826 ; posted Ensign to 62nd N.I. and served throughout with that Regt. Fur. p.a. 3 Sept. 1838 till 15 Jan. 1842. Gwalior campaign ; Maharajpur ; Capt. 62nd N.I. (Bronze star). Posted Lt. Col. to 62nd N.I. 16 June 1856, and was comdg. it at Multan when it mutinied 31 Aug. 1857, having previously been disarmed on 10 June.
Refs. : *A.J.* N.S. ii. 96. *The Times*, 1 June 1891.

RICHARDSON, Taylor Campbell (1812-1857). Captain, 18th N.I. *b.* on board the *Sovereign*, in Saugor Roads, 25 Dec. 1812. Cadet 1831. Arrived in India 19 May 1832. Ensign (8 Dec.

THE BENGAL ARMY, 1758-1834   649

1831) 19 May 1832. Lieut. 3 Sept. 1839. Capt. 13 Apr. 1852. d. nr. Bareilly 6 June 1857 : murdered by the villagers of Rampati. (*See* note to Henry Edward Pearson.)

Son of Robert Richardson, B.C.S., and Marian his wife. Brother of Sir John Larkins Cheese Richardson, *q.v.* Addiscombe Cadet 5 Feb. 1830 till 8 Dec. 1831.

Services : Cadet d.d. 28th N.I. 28 June 1832 ; 64th N.I. 24 Aug. 1832. Posted Ensign to 18th N.I. 19 Dec. 1833. Posted to Vol. Regt. for China 15 Feb. 1840. First China War 1840 ; capture of Chusan ; Lieut. Vol. Regt. (Medal). Fur. s.c. 23 Feb. 1841 till 1843. Second Sikh War ; Bt. Capt. 18th N.I. in garr. at Lahore (Medal). Fur. p.a. 20 Feb. 1851 till Jan. 1854.

RICHARDSON, Thomas (1761-1786). Lieutenant, Infantry. *b.* Cheshire 1761. Cadet 1780. Ensign 1781. Lieut. Sept. 1782. *d.* Chittagong 18 June 1786.

Services : Apptd. Cadet 19 Dec. 1780, aged 19 ; sailed for India in the *Rodney* 11 Sept. 1782. N.F.P.

RICHARDSON, William. Ensign. Infantry. Cadet 1771. Ensign 9 Feb. 1773. Struck off Feb. 1774.

Services : N.F.P.

RICHARDSON, William (1811-1888). Major General, C B. 44th B.N.I. (now 8th Gurkha Rifles). *b.* Wapping 1 Mar. 1811. Cadet 1827. Arrived in India 4 July 1828. Ensign 19 Jan. 1828. Lieut. 2 Aug. 1839. Capt. 19 Jan. 1843. Major 20 June 1854. Lt. Col. 25 Oct. 1859. Col. 18 Feb. 1866. Retired Mar. 1869. Maj. Gen. Mar. 1869. *d.* 1 Campden Hill Gdns., Kensington, 18 Apr. 1888..

bapt. St. George's, Middlesex, 26 Apr. 1811. 4th son of James Richardson, of Wapping, slop seller, and Fanny his wife, *née* Kirkby.

Services : Ensign d.d. 42nd N.I. 31 July 1828 ; posted to 73rd N.I. 4 Nov. 1828. Actg. Intr. & Qmr. 73rd N.I. 30 Jan. 1838 ; do. 3rd N.I. 5 Oct. 1838. Intr. & Qmr. 73rd N.I. 2 Sept. 1839 till 1842. Actg. Adjt. 1st Irreg. Cav. 11 Feb. till 16 July 1842 ; actg. 2nd in comd. 7th Irreg. Cav. 26 Aug. 1842. First Sikh War ; Mudki ; Ferozshahr ; Sobraon ; Capt. 73rd N.I. (Medal with 2 clasps). Second Sikh War ; Capt. 73rd N.I., in garr. at Lahore (Medal). Fur. s.c. 24 Nov. 1853 till 26 Sept. 1856. Offg. Comdt. 2nd Assam L.I. 6 Feb. 1857. Mutiny campaign 1857 ; Major comdg. 2nd Assam L.I. Comdt. Sylhet L.I. Bn. (became 44th B.N.I. in 1861) 27 Jan. 1858 till 6 Oct. 1866. Transfd. to Staff

Corps 18 Feb. 1861. Operations in the Khasiah and Jaintiah hills of Assam Dec. 1862-Feb. 1863 ; capture of stockaded village of Umkai ; Umkiang 5 Jan. (s.w.) ; Lt. Col. comdg. 44th B.N.I. Bhutan War 1864-6 ; comdd. Advance Column of the Bhutan F.F. at recapture of Dewangiri Apr. 1865 ; comdd. Rt. Column in operations in Bhutan in Feb. 1866 ; Col. 44th B.N.I. (India medal with clasp " Bhootan "). Fur. 10 Sept. 1866 till retirement. C.B. 13 Oct. 1863. Good Service Pension 23 Aug. 1865.

Refs.: Family information. *Cardew*, pp. 305, 316. *The Times*, 20 Apr. 1888.

RICHMOND, Archibald Fullerton (1789-1866). Lieut. General, C.B. Colonel 24th N.I. *b.* Edinburgh 3 Dec. 1789. Cadet 1808. Arrived in India 27 Oct. 1809. Ensign (27 Oct. 1809) 10 Apr. 1810. Lieut. 16 Dec. 1814. Capt. 1 May 1824. Major 13 May 1833. Lt. Col. 24 Jan. 1840. Col. 28 Mar. 1850. Maj. Gen. 28 Nov. 1854. Lt. Gen. 21 Oct. 1864. *d.* The Tower, Lawrie Pk., Sydenham, 25 Aug. 1866.

Son of Matthew Richmond, at Leith Walk, Edinburgh, nurseryman, and Janet Wilson his wife. *m.* Barrackpore 23 Oct. 1824, Mary Anne Frances, dau. of Nathaniel Altham Cumberlege, *q.v.*, by his 1st wife. (*See also* W. J. B. Knyvett.) (She died 31 Dec. 1889, aged 86.)

Services: Barasat C.C. Posted Ensign to 16th N.I. in 1810. Reduction of Kalinjar 1812 ; Ensign 2/16th N.I. Nepal War 1814-15 ; Kalanga (w.) (*Lond. Gaz.* 19 Aug. 1815) ; Nalagarh ; Nahan ; Lieut. 2/16th N.I., in 2nd Div. (India medal). Adjt. 2/16th N.I. 28 Feb. 1817 till 13 July 1824. Transfd. to 33rd N.I. (late 2/16th) May 1824. Siege and capture of Bhurtpore ; Capt. 33rd N.I. (clasp to India medal). Actg. D.J.A.G. Rajputana and Meywar forces 27 Oct. 1828. Sec. to Board of Superintendence for improving the breed of cattle 15 Oct. 1829 ; Comdt. Calcutta Native Mil. 1 Jan. 1831 till 4 June 1835. Leave p.a. to Mauritius 22 Sept. till 10 Dec. 1831. Fur. s.c. 9 Sept. 1835 till 22 Jan. 1839. Comdg. 13th N.I. from 6 Mar. 1839 ; posted Lt. Col. to 33rd N.I. 4 Feb. 1840. First Afghan War 1842 ; Tazin valley, comdg. Rear Guard (*Lond. Gaz.* 24 Nov. 1842) ; Jagdalak (ib. 17 Mar. 1843) ; advance on Kabul ; Lt. Col. comdg. 33rd N.I. (Medal). A.G.G., N.W.F., 14 June 1843 ; Resdt. at Lucknow 27 Sept. 1844 till 11 Jan. 1849. Transfd. to 15th N.I. 1846 ; to 41st N.I. ; to 33rd N.I. Feb. 1848. Fur. s.c. 10 Feb. 1849 till death. Posted Col. to 42nd N.I. June 1850 ; to 24th N.I. 31 Mar. 1852. C.B. 24 Dec. 1842.

Refs.: Boase. *The Times*, 29 Aug. 1866.

RICKARDS, William Henry (1809-1884). Lieut. Colonel. 14th N.I. *bapt.* Woodbridge, Suffolk, 23 Mar. 1809. Cadet 1824. Arrived in India 6 Oct. 1825. Ensign 13 May 1825. Lieut. 23 May 1828. Capt. 1 Mar. 1844. Major 4 May 1858. Retired 12 Apr. 1859. Hon. Lt. Col. 12 Apr. 1859. *d.* 10 Courtfield Gdns., S. Kensington, 8 Dec. 1884, aged 74.

Son of William Rickards, Northants Mil., Capt. 64th Ft., and Emma his wife, *née* Elton. *m.* Nimach 10 Aug. 1843, Catherine Georgiana, elder dau. of Francis Farington Gardner, Rear Adm. R.N., and sister of Stewart William Gardner, *q.v.* Ed. Christ's Hospital.

Services : Posted Ensign to 14th N.I. Intr. & Qmr. 14th N.I. 27 Aug. 1828 till 8 Mar. 1843. D.J.A.G. Nimach Div. 7 Jan. 1843 till 1848. Offg. P.A. Jaipur Dec. 1847 ; permanent do. 24 Mar. 1848 till Aug. 1856. Fur. s.c. 5 Feb. 1855 till 23 Jan. 1856. P.A. Bhopal 15 Aug. 1856 till 29 Mar. 1859.

Refs.: I.M. 16 June 1856, p. 352. *The Times,* 10 Dec. 1884.

RICKETTS, George Poyntz (1808-1885). Lieut. Colonel. 1st L.C. *b.* Patna 28 Oct. 1808. Cadet 1824. Arrived in India 25 Nov. 1825. Cornet 18 Apr. 1825. Lieut. 13 May 1825. Capt. 1 Jan. 1844. Bt. Major 11 Nov. 1851. Retired 30 Nov. 1853. Hon. Lt. Col. 28 Nov. 1854. *d.* at his residence, 13 Lansdown Cresc., Bath, 25 Apr. 1885.

Only son of George Poyntz Ricketts, B.C.S., judge at Mirzapur, and Sophia Sarah Jane his wife, youngest dau. of Capt. Richard Pierce, of the *Halsewell* East Indiaman, and sister of the wife of William Flemyng, *q.v.* Brother of Frances Isabella, 1st wife of Sir Abraham Roberts, *q.v. m.* 1st, Cawnpore 30 Sept. 1833, Isabella Victoria, youngest dau. of Peter Begbie, and sister of Arthur Pitt Begbie, *q.v.* (She died 16 Dec. 1853, aged 40.) *m.* 2nd, Costock, Notts., 21 Feb. 1860, Martha Anne, only dau. of Rev. William Kirby, rector of Caldecote, Hunts. (She died Bath 28 July 1869, aged 57.) *m.* 3rd, 10 June 1879, Eliza Catherine, dau. of Lt.-Col. Edmund Craster, Madras Est. (She died Bath 5· May 1904, aged 75.)

Services : Posted Lieut. to 1st L.C. in 1825 and served throughout with that Regt. First Afghan War 1842 ; advance on Kabul ; Bt. Capt. 1st L.C., with Gen. Pollock's force (Medal). First Sikh War ; Aliwal ; Capt. 1st L.C. (Medal). Second Sikh War ; passage of Chenab ; Chilianwala ; Gujerat ; Capt. 1st L.C. (Medal with clasp).

Refs.: Burke's *Landed Gentry,* 5th edn., p. 1168, *s.n.* Ricketts, of Combe, co. Hereford. Foster's *Peerage*, p. 590, *s.n.* St. Vincent, V. Berry's *Hants Peds.* p. 165. *The Times*, 28 Apr. 1885. M.I. Lansdown cemetery, Bath.

RICKETTS, John Henry (1767-1792). Ensign, Engineers. *b.* 17 Mar. 1767. Cadet 1783. Ensign 3 Jan. 1785. *d.* in the Carnatic 11 Apr. 1792.

Eldest son of John Ricketts, surgeon, and Harriet Grace his wife, sister of Roger Elliot Roberts, *q.v.* Elder brother of Vice-Adm. Sir Robert Tristram Ricketts, 1st Bart. Father, by an Indian woman, of John Ricketts, the "East Indian Patriot," founder of the Doveton Coll. in Calcutta.

Services: Apptd. Cadet 20 Dec. 1782; sailed for India in H.M.S. *Elizabeth.* Transfd. as Cadet from Inf. to Engrs. Nov. 1783; employed on survey in Bengal 1787-8. Third Mysore War; Ensign Engrs.

Refs.: *Howard & Crisp (Notes)*, iii. 89.

RIDDELL, Robert (1804-1864). Lieutenant. 33rd N.I. *b.* Edinburgh 14 Mar. 1804. Cadet 1821. Arrived in India 13 Sept. 1822. Ensign 13 Sept. 1822. Lieut. 7 Jan. 1825. Resigned 28 Apr. 1830. *d.* Château d'Outreau, nr. Boulogne, 18 Nov. 1864.

Of Glen Riddell. 3rd and youngest son of Michael Riddell and Janet his 2nd wife, dau. of Robert Hunter, of Thurston. Cousin-german of James Hunter Campbell, *q.v.* *m.* 6 Apr. 1836, Elizabeth, dau. of Vice-Adm. Henry Vansittart. (She died 8 Aug. 1873.)

Services: Posted Ensign to 16th N.I. in 1822; transfd. to 33rd N.I. (late 2/16th) May 1824. Actg. Adjt. 33rd N.I. 13 Sept. 1824; Intr. & Qmr. do. 7 Jan. 1825 till 14 Nov. 1828. Siege and capture of Bhurtpore; Lieut. 33rd N.I. (India medal). Fur. p.a. 21 Dec. 1827 till 2 Jan. 1833, when he resigned with effect from 28 Apr. 1830.

Refs.: Burke's *Peerage*, 1923, p. 1874, *s.n.* Buchanan-Riddell, Bart., of Riddell, co. Roxburgh. *The Times*, 25 Nov. 1864.

RIDDELL, Thomas (1810-1854). Major, 60th N.I. *b.* Edinburgh 6 Oct. 1810. Cadet 1826. Arrived in India 11 June 1827. Ensign 13 Feb. 1827. Lieut. 30 Apr. 1833. Capt. 24 Jan. 1845. Major 15 Nov. 1849. *d.* Mussoorie 23 May 1854.

4th son of Thomas Riddell, of Camieston, co. Roxburgh, and Jane his wife, dau. of Capt. Walter Ferrier, of Somerford. Brother of William Riddell, *q.v.* *m.* Cawnpore 24 July 1848, Ann Ellen,

THE BENGAL ARMY, 1758-1834   653

dau. of William Beckett (1798-1844), *q.v.* (*See also* Robert Napier Raikes.) (She *re-m*. Capt. George Corham Huxham, Bengal Est., and died Bexhill 2 Feb. 1925, aged 95.) Ed. Edin. High School.
Services : Posted Ensign to 60th N.I. Leave s.c. 15 Apr. 1834 till 10 Feb. 1836. Adjt. 2nd L.I. Bn. 21 Nov. 1840 till 1 Dec. 1841. First Afghan War 1842 ; advance on Kabul ; Bt. Capt. 60th N.I., with Gen. Pollock's force (Medal). To comd. Karnal Police Bn. 18 Apr. 1844 ; afterwards comdd. Rohilkhand Police Bn. Joint Cantt. Mgte. at Cawnpore 30 June 1847 till death. Rejoined 60th N.I., with Reserve Div. for Second Sikh War, Oct. 1848 for a few months.
Refs. : Burke's *Peerage*, 1923, p. 1876, *s.n.* Buchanan-Riddell, Bart., of Riddell, co. Roxburgh. Burke's *Landed Gentry*, 13th edn., p. 1501, *s.n.* Riddell, of Camieston, co. Roxburgh. *G.M.* 1854, ii. 313. *The Times*, 5 Feb. 1925. Will dated Mussoorie, 1 May 1854 ; proved 3 July 1854. M.I. Mussoorie.

RIDDELL, William (1805-1875). Major General, C.B. 3rd Bengal Eur. Inf. *b.* Edinburgh 12 Dec. 1805. Cadet 1821. Arrived in India 21 June 1823. Ensign 28 May 1823. Lieut. 13 May 1825. Capt. 1 Dec. 1836. Major 15 Nov. 1849. Lt. Col. 25 Feb. 1855. Bt. Col. 5 Dec. 1855. Retired 31 Dec. 1861. Hon. Maj. Gen. 31 Dec. 1861. *d.* The Anchorage, Melrose, 22 June 1875.
Of Camieston, co. Roxburgh, J.P. Eldest son of Thomas Riddell, of Camieston, and Jane his wife. Brother of Thomas Riddell, *q.v. m.* Bhopal 9 Apr. 1837, Margaret, youngest dau. of John Wilkie, *q.v.* (*See also* Cosby Burrowes.) (She died 27 Feb. 1905, aged 85.) Ed. Edin. High School and Coll.
Services : Posted Ensign to 30th N.I. ; transfd. to 60th N.I. (late 2/30th) May 1824. Siege and capture of Bhurtpore ; Lieut. 60th N.I. (India medal). Adjt. 60th N.I. 1 Sept. 1828 till 25 Jan. 1837. To comd. Bhopal Contingent 3 Jan. 1839 ; offg. P.A. Bhopal 5 Feb. till 27 June 1840 ; Asst. in *Thagi* Dept., Malwa, 27 June 1840 ; Asst. to Resdt. at Nagpur 11 Dec. 1841. Dy. Paymr. to Gen. Pollock's force 12 Mar. 1842 till 21 June 1843. First Afghan War 1842 ; advance on Kabul ; Tazin (*Lond. Gaz.* 24 Nov. 1842) ; Dy. Paymr. (Medal). Offg. S.A.C.G. to Pollock's force 12 Sept. 1842. Served in *Thagi* Dept. 1843 till 4 Oct. 1848, when he rejoined 60th N.I. Second Sikh War ; Bt. Major 60th N.I., in Reserve Div. Fur. 1850 till Mar. 1852. Posted Lt. Col. to 60th N.I. May 1855 ; transfd. to 3rd Bengal Eur. Regt. in 1857. Mutiny campaign 1857-8 ; Bt. Col. comdg. 3rd Eur. Inf. (Medal).

Fur. p.a. 15 mos. 8 Oct. 1859. C.B. 28 Feb. 1861. Served as a private in 3rd Roxburgh Rifle Vols. (Melrose) 26 Feb. 1861 till 30 Apr. 1871 and never aspired to promotion.

Refs.: Burke's *Peerage*, 1923, p. 1875, *s.n.* Buchanan-Riddell, Bart., of Riddell, co. Roxburgh. *Boase. The Times*, 25 June 1875.

RIDDING, Thomas (1799-1818). Lieutenant, 1st N.I. *bapt.* St. Thomas's, Winchester, 3 Jan. 1799. Cadet 1816. Ensign (?) Lieut. 1818. *d.* Saugor 7 Dec. 1818.

Son of John Ridding, of Winchester, and Harriet his wife, *née* Durnford.

Services : Posted Lieut. to 2/1st N.I. in 1818. (? Third Mahratta War ; Dhamoni ; Lieut. 2/1st N.I.)

RIDEOUT, Richard (1793-1828). Captain, 10th N.I. Comdt. 5th Regt. Nizam's Cav. *bapt.* Mountfield, Sussex, 18 Dec. 1793. Cadet 1810. Ensign 14 Nov. 1813. Lieut. 1 Aug. 1818. Capt. 9 Dec. 1825. *d.* Ellichpur, Berar, 2 Oct. 1828, aged 34.

Son of Rev. Richard Rideout, of Framfield, Sussex, and Sarah his wife. *m.* Meerut 26 Aug. 1819, Miss Isabella Clark(e). (She died Forres 24 May 1856.)

Services: Posted Ensign to 1/7th N.I. Nepal War 1814-15 ; Ensign 1/7th N.I., in 2nd Div. Third Mahratta War 1817-19 ; Lieut. 1/7th N.I. Served in Nizam's army 1821 till death. Transfd. to 10th N.I. (late 2/7th) May 1824.

Refs.: Will dated 5 Dec. 1823 ; proved 19 Mar. 1829. M.I. at Ellichpur.

RIDER, Richard. Cadet. Infantry. Cadet 1772. Resigned 1 Feb. 1773.

Services: Sailed for India in the *Triton* 1 Jan. 1772. N.F.P.

RIDER, Thomas. Cadet. Infantry. Cadet 1772. Resigned 2 Apr. 1773.

Services: Sailed for India in the *Prince of Wales* 1 Apr. 1772. N.F.P.

RIDGE, Charles John (1777-1820). Major, 4th L.C. *bapt.* Kilmeston, Hants, 22 Jan. 1777. Cadet 1794. Arrived in India 1 Nov. 1795. Cornet 7 Nov. 1795. Lieut. 25 Apr. 1797. Capt. 11 Mar. 1805. Major 27 July 1819. *d.* Bombay 16 Mar. 1820.

Son of Thomas Ridge,[1] J.P. Southampton and distributor of

THE BENGAL ARMY, 1758-1834   655

stamps for E. Div. of Hants, and Mary his wife. Brother of Edward Jervoise Ridge and uncle of Henry Penton Ridge, qq.v.
Services: Apptd. Cadet 25 Mar. 1795; sailed for India in the *Marquess of Lansdowne* 19 June 1795. Adjt. 4th N.C. 29 May 1800 till 16 May 1805. Operations in Jumna Doab 1803; Sasni; Bijaigarh; Kachaura; Lieut. 4th N.C. Second Mahratta War; Laswari; Lieut. 4th N.C. Fur. 31 Dec. 1816 till 1819.
Refs.: Will dated 9 May 1819; proved 1 Feb. 1821 and 23 May 1834.
¹ *Note:* Although the father of 21 children, including Lt.-Col. Henry Ridge who fell at the head of 5th Foot at the storm of Badajos, he kept and hunted a pack of hounds, 1749-95. This he did at his own expense until 1783, when the name of this pack was changed from the Kilmeston Hunt to the H.H.

RIDGE, Edward Jervoise (1780-1833). Major, C.B. 4th L.C. *bapt.* Kilmeston, Hants, 26 Dec. 1780. Cadet 1797. Arrived in India 6 Nov. 1798. Cornet 1 Nov. 1798. Lieut. 29 May 1800. Capt. 18 May 1816. Major 27 July 1819. Retired 3 Nov. 1824. *d.* Blackbrook cottage, Hants, 13 July 1833.
Of Bishops Waltham, Hants. Son of Thomas Ridge and Mary his wife. Brother of James Brooke Ridge, *q.v.*
Services: Posted Cornet to newly-raised 4th N.C. in 1798 and served throughout with that Regt. Operations in Jumna Doab 1803; Sasni; Bijaigarh; Kachaura. Second Mahratta War; Laswari. Capt. Lt. 29 Aug. 1810. Fur. s.c. 25 Dec. 1809 till Nov. 1813. Third Mahratta War 1817-18; action against Pindaris 11 Apr. 1817; storm and capture of Jawad 1818. Operations against Maharao Kishor Singh of Kotah 1821; action at Mangrol (s.w.—sabre cut on head); Major comdg. two Sqdns. 4th L.C.¹ Fur. s.c. 1822 till retirement. C.B. 23 July 1823.
Refs.: E.I.M.C. iii. 185-90. *Pester,* p. 84. G.M. 1833, ii. 370. A.J. N.S. xi. 279. Will dated 12 July 1823; proved 23 May 1834.
¹ *Note:* See note to William Mactier.

RIDGE, George (1804-1831). Captain, 9th L.C. *b.* 11 Apr. 1804. Cadet 1821. Arrived in India 25 June 1822. Cornet 12 Jan. 1822. Lieut. 31 Jan. 1825. Capt. 6 Jan. 1830. *d. unm.* Nimach 29 Nov. 1831.
bapt. London 10 May 1804. Eldest son of Benjamin Ridge, of 1 Bridge St., Lambeth, Surrey, surgeon, and Maria Pope his 1st wife. Brother of Benjamin Ridge, of Chichester, F.R.C.S.
Services: Posted Cornet to 2nd L.C. in 1822. Adjt. 4th Local

Horse 14 Feb. 1825 ; 2nd in comd. do. 24 Mar. 1828 till 7 Dec. 1829. Transfd. to newly-raised 9th L.C. 13 May 1825 ; Adjt. do. 7 Dec. 1829 till death. No record of active service. An amateur artist in water colour.

Refs.: Family information. *Pedigree Register*, iii. (Dec. 1915), 334. *G.M.* 1832, i. 575. Will dated Nimach, 7 Aug. 1830 ; proved 3 Feb. 1832. M.I. Nimach.

RIDGE, Henry Penton (1800-1825). Lieutenant, 39th N.I.
b. Dover 5 Nov. 1800. Cadet 1817. Ensign (?) Lieut. 4 Apr. 1820. *d.* Dinapore 16 Sept. 1825.

bapt. St. Mary the Virgin, Dover, 20 Nov. 1800. 2nd son of Thomas Roger Ridge, of Fyning, Rogate, Sussex (of Petersfield), farmer, and Sarah Margaret his wife. Nephew of James Brook Ridge, *q.v.* Ed. Merchant Taylors' Mar. 1812 till 1816. Addiscombe Cadet 1817-18.

Services: Ensign d.d. Muttra Levy 1819-20. Posted Lieut. to 1/19th N.I. in 1820. Transfd. to 39th N.I. (late 2/19th) May 1824 ; Adjt. do. 13 July 1824 till death. First Burma War ; Cachar 1824-5 ; Lieut. 39th N.I.

Refs.: Robinson.

RIDGE, James Brook (1783-1818). Bt. Captain, 21st N.I.
bapt. Kilmeston, Hants, 4 May 1783. Cadet 1800. Arrived in India 19 Aug. 1801. Ensign 16 Oct. 1801. Lieut. 30 Sept. 1803. Bt. Capt. 8 Jan. 1816. *d.* Southampton 22 Sept. 1818, aged 34.

Son of Thomas Ridge and Mary his wife. Brother of Charles John Ridge, *q.v. m.* Calcutta 19 Feb. 1812, Harriet Essex, dau. of William Nicholl, *q.v.*

Services: Posted Ensign to 15th N.I. in 1801. Operations in Jumna Doab 1803 ; Sasni ; Bijaigarh ; Kachaura ; Ensign 15th N.I. Transfd. as Lieut. to newly-raised 2/21st N.I. in 1803 ; Adjt. do. 19 Jan. 1804 till 6 Aug. 1817. Second Mahratta War 1804-5. Operations in Bundelkhand 1809-12 ; in Rewah 1811 ; Bhapawi. (? Nepal War 1816 ; Harriharpur.) Fur. 1817 till death.

Refs.: *A.J.* vi. 445. *G.M.* 1819, i. 186 (where date of death is incorrectly given as 28 Jan. 1819).

RIDLEY, John George (1809-1834). Lieutenant, 2nd N.I.
bapt. Verdun-sur-Meuse 3 Aug. 1809. Cadet 1824. Arrived in India 24 Feb. 1826. Ensign 6 Sept. 1825. Lieut. 22 May 1829. *d.* Saugor 12 Aug. 1834 : drowned whilst bathing in the lake.

Son of John Ridley, Major R.M., and Marie Anne Thomas his wife. (*Probably* of the family of Viscount Ridley.[1])

THE BENGAL ARMY, 1758-1834 657

Services : Posted Ensign to 2nd N.I. Operations against the Kols in Chota Nagpur 1832 ; Lieut. 2nd N.I.
Refs. : A.J. N.S. xvi. 137. Will dated 7 June 1828 ; proved 12 Jan. 1835. M.I. old cemetery, Saugor.
¹ *Note :* He mentions in his Will his " worthy friend " Rev. Henry Colborne Ridley, of Henley-on-Thames, and Matthew Ridley, of Verdun.

RIDLEY, William (1759/60-1794). Lieutenant, 32nd Bn. Sepoys.
b. Hexham, Northumberland, 1759/60. Cadet 1781. Ensign 24 July 1781. Lieut. 22 Oct. 1782. *d.* Calcutta 12 Apr. 1794.
Son of —— Ridley and Elizabeth his wife, of Hexham. Brother of Elizabeth Garbet. *m.* Dinapore 16 Mar. 1793, Mary, dau. of Hercules Skinner, *q.v.* (*See also* James Oldham Oldham.) (She *re-m.* William Henry Cooper, *q.v.*)
Services : Apptd. Cadet 23 Jan. 1781, aged 21 ; sailed for India in the *Chapman* 13 Mar. 1781. Lieut. 4th Bengal Eur. Bn. in July 1787 ; 32nd Bn. Sepoys in Dec. 1788.
Refs. : Will undated ; proved 19 May 1794.
Note : He is incorrectly described in the burial register as Lieut. of Art.

*RIGGE, Isaac. Cadet. Infantry. Apptd. Cadet 9 Jan. 1783. Declined the appt.
(? Of Kendal. *m.* 9 Apr. 1806, Dorothy, dau. of Nathan Gough, of Kendal.)

RIGHY, Henry (1811-1881). General. Colonel Comdt. Royal (late Bengal) Engrs. *b.* Gt. Marlow, Bucks., 10 May 1811. Cadet 1829. Arrived in India 23 Dec. 1830. 2nd Lieut. 12 June 1829. Lieut. 20 May 1839. Capt. 1 Dec. 1847. Major 20 Sept. 1857. Lt. Col. 27 Aug. 1858. Col. 12 Mar. 1861. Col. Comdt. 31 Mar. 1875. Maj. Gen. 6 Mar. 1868. Lt. Gen. 31 Mar. 1875. Gen. 15 Aug. 1878. *d.* 31 Clanricarde Gdns., Bayswater, 14 Sept. 1881.
bapt. Barking, Essex, 13 June 1815. Son of Joseph Righy, of 14 Golden Sq., London, solicitor and atty., and Elizabeth his wife. *m.* Staines 3 June 1833, Georgiana Emma, eldest dau. of John Reynolds, of Knowle Green. (She died 5 Jan. 1890.) Addiscombe Cadet 1828 till 12 June 1829.
Services : Fur. s.c. 28 Aug. 1831 till 10 Dec. 1833. Asst. to Garr. Engr. at Ft. Wm. 21 Dec. 1833. Adjt. Engrs. 7 Feb. 1835. Offg. Executive Engr. at Balasore 28 Apr. 1835 ; do. Benares Div.

20 May 1836. Superintended construction of lighthouse at False Point, B. & O. Executive Engr. 17th Div., P.W.D., 2 July 1838; do. Cuttack 18 Dec. 1839; do. Midnapore 17 Oct. 1851; do. Benares Div. 30 May 1854. Offg. Suptg. Engr. 2nd circle, N.W.P., 24 Sept. 1856; do. 1st circle, Lahore, 28 Oct. 1856; permanent do. 14 Apr. 1857 till 1864. No record of active service.
Refs.: Boase. *A.J.* N.S. xi. 202. *The Times,* 20 Sept. 1881, p. 4; 22 Sept., p. 7.

RILEY, Stephen Davis (1787-1867). Lieut. General. Colonel 7th N.I. (now 3rd Bn. 7th Rajput Regt.). *b.* London 9 Nov. 1787. Cadet 1804. Arrived in India 10 Sept. 1805. Ensign 1 Jan. 1804. Lieut. 2 July 1806. Capt. 29 Aug. 1822. Major 3 July 1832. Lt. Col. 19 Apr. 1839. Col. 9 Apr. 1849. Maj. Gen. 28 Nov. 1854. Lt. Gen. 6 Oct. 1862. *d.* Kidderpore, Calcutta, 29 May 1867.

bapt. St. James's, Westminster, 11 Nov. 1787. Son of Stephen Riley and Mary Anne his wife.
Services: Posted Lieut. to 6th N.I. in 1806. Intr. & Qmr. 1/6th N.I. 1 July 1814 till 1822. Nepal War 1814-15 (w.); Lieut. 1/6th N.I., in 2nd Div. (India medal). Third Mahratta War; Bde. Qmr. 7th Inf. Bde., 4th Div. Transfd. to 3rd N.I. (late 1/6th) May 1824. A.D.C. to Maj.-Gen. R. B. Gregory, *q.v.,* 13 Sept. 1824. Shekhawat expedn. 1834; Major comdg. 3rd N.I. Comdd. 3rd N.I. 1 Nov. 1834 till 1 Feb. 1838. Posted Lt. Col. to 3rd N.I. 14 June 1839; to 30th N.I. 20 Jan. 1840; 62nd N.I. Dec. 1840. To comd. 6th Bde., 3rd Div., Army of Exercise, with rank of Bdr. 2 cl. 20 Oct. 1843. Gwalior campaign; Maharajpur (*London Gaz.* 8 Mar. 1844); Bdr. comdg. 6th Bde. Comdg. escort of G.G. 4 Feb. 1844. Apptd. Persian translator under Govt. 7 June 1844; Examiner at Coll. of Ft. Wm. 21 June 1844. Transfd. to 39th N.I. 9 Aug. 1844; to 22nd N.I. 6 June 1845; to 14th N.I. 11 Oct. 1847; to 5th N.I. 12 Apr. 1848; to 49th N.I. 18 July 1848. Col. 47th N.I. (became 7th in 1861) 1849 till death.
Refs.: Boase.

RIND, James Nathaniel (*d.* 1814). Major. 18th N.I. Country Cadet 1778. Admitted 17 Aug. 1778. Ensign 21 May 1779. Lieut. 24 Jan. 1781. Capt. 6 Aug. 1797. Major 30 Sept. 1803. Retired 15 Jan. 1804. *d.* 21 Mar. 1814.

Of Wester Livelands, co. Stirling. Son of William Rind, of Livelands, psh. of St. Ninian's, Stirling, and Mrs. Jean Don. *m.* Anne, dau. of Maurice Evans and sister of Thomas Evans (1776-

1812), *q.v.* (She died Bath 4 Dec. 1855.) Father of James Nathaniel Rind and William James Rind, *qq.v.*

Services : Lieut. Bombay Marine 17 Aug. 1778 ; apptd. Cadet 10 Sept. 1778. Was one of the Assts. to Major James Browne, *q.v.*, at Delhi in Apr. 1785, and surveyed the Sikh country and neighbourhood of Delhi 1785-7 ; Lieut. 17th Bn. Sepoys in July 1787 ; employed on survey duty 1788-9. Transfd. from 17th Bn. to Adjt. & Qmr. 1st Sepoy Bde. 18 Nov. 1793 ; Bde. Major 1st Bde. 15 Nov. 1794 till Jan. 1801. Capt. 14th N.I. in 1798 ; transfd. to 2/17th N.I. ; to 2/18th N.I. 29 May 1800. Fur. 4 Apr. 1801 till retirement.

Refs. : Will dated Stirling 8 June 1814 ; proved 16 Nov. 1816.

RIND, James Nathaniel (1809-1842). Captain, 37th N.I. *b.* Wester Livelands, St. Ninian's, Stirling, 24 Dec. 1809. Cadet 1825. Arrived in India 2 Aug. 1826. Ensign 30 Jan. 1826. Lieut. 22 Oct. 1827. Capt. 23 Nov. 1841. *d.* Gandamak 13 Jan. 1842 : kld. in the retreat from Kabul.

2nd son of James Nathaniel Rind, *q.v.*, and Anne his wife. Brother of William James Rind, *q.v.* *m.* 20 Dec. 1827, Mrs. Marian Rose.

Services : Ensign d.d. 3rd N.I. 12 Aug. 1826 ; posted to 37th N.I. 26 Sept. 1826. Served with Pioneers 23 May 1831 till Nov. 1833. Offg. Asst. Revenue Surveyor 8 Nov. 1833 ; permanent do. at Bareilly 4 Apr. 1834. Rejoined 37th N.I. for active service Nov. 1838. First Afghan War 1838-42 ; Ghazni 1839 (Medal) ; operations in Kohistan under Sale 1840 ; Parwandara (*Lond. Gaz.* 9 Jan. 1841) ; outbreak at Kabul ; retreat from Kabul (kld.) ; Capt. 37th N.I. Durani 3 cl. 3 Dec. 1841.

Refs. : Bath Chron. 7 July 1842. Will dated Kabul 30 Sept. 1839 ; proved 26 Apr. 1843. M.I. Afghan Memorial Church, Bombay.

RIND, William James (1806-1869). Captain, Invalid Est. 71st N.I. *b.* St. Ninian's, Stirling, 13 July 1806. Cadet 1823. Arrived in India 20 May 1824. Ensign 7 Jan. 1824. Lieut. 4 July 1825. Capt. 6 Aug. 1839. Invalided 7 Dec. 1849. *d.* Mussoorie 20 Aug. 1869.

bapt. St. Ninian's 1 Sept. 1806. Eldest son of James Nathaniel Rind, *q.v.*, and Anne his wife. *m.* Bathwick, Somerset, 8 Aug. 1840, Anne, eldest dau. of Jonathan Johnson, of Bathwick. (She died Mussoorie 25 July 1872, aged 59.)

Services : Posted Ensign to 20th N.I. in 1824 ; transfd. to newly-raised 3rd Extra Regt. (became 71st N.I.) May 1825. (? Siege and capture of Bhurtpore; Ensign 3rd Extra Regt.[1]) Actg. Adjt. 71st N.I. 4 Nov. 1829. Fur. s.c. 8 Mar. 1838 till 28 Dec. 1840. Second Sikh War; Capt. 71st N.I., in Jullundur Doab.

Refs.: Howard & Crisp, viii. 4, s.n. Heathcote. The Times, 28 Sept. 1869. M.I. Mussoorie.

[1] Note: He is shown in the India M.R. as having received the medal for siege of Bhurtpore, at that time an Ensign in 3rd Extra Regt. Neither this Regt. nor his former Corps, 20th N.I., was engaged in this campaign, and he is not credited with this service by any other authority.

RING, George (d. 1775). Lieutenant, Infantry. Cadet 1767. Ensign 12 June 1767. Lieut. 11 Apr. 1769. d. Calcutta 3 Apr. 1775.

Services: N.F.P.

RIPLEY, John Peter (1801-1857). Lieut. Colonel, 54th N.I. b. Kelvedon, Essex, early in 1801. Cadet 1818. Arrived in India Mar. 1820. Ensign 20 Sept. 1819. Lieut. 7 May 1822. Capt. 19 June 1831. Major 1 Mar. 1850. Lt. Col. 5 Dec. 1855. d. Delhi 11 May 1857: mortally wounded at the head of his Regt. by mutineers.

bapt. Kelvedon 29 Sept. 1801. 4th son of Rev. Thomas Ripley, vicar of Wootton Bassett, Wilts., and Mary his wife. m. Ghazipur 24 Feb. 1822, Amelia Jane, dau. of Edward Pitches Wilson, q.v. His dau. m. David Pott, q.v. Woolwich Cadet.

Services: Ensign d.d. 2/18th N.I. 3 Apr. 1820. Posted to Bengal Eur. Regt. Jan. 1821. Transfd. to newly-formed 2nd Bengal Eur. Regt. May 1824. Intr. & Qmr. do. 17 June 1824 till 14 June 1832. Staff Ofr. to Garr. of Cheduba I. Dec. 1825 till Nov. 1826, during First Burma War (India medal). Offg. Sec. to Clothing Board at Calcutta Dec. 1832 till Oct. 1833. Fur. s.c. 27 Oct. 1833 till 4 Dec. 1836. First Afghan War; at Kandahar 1839-42; sometime Fort Adjt., Postmr., and A.D.C. to Gen. Nott; Goaine; recapture of Ghazni; operations of Kandahar force under Nott (Lond. Gaz. 11 Sept. 1842, 17 Mar. 1843); Capt. 1st Eur. L.I. (Medal—Kandahar, Ghazni, Kabul). In charge of Kandahar treasure chest 31 July 1842 till 14 Mar. 1843. Fur. s.c. 9 Jan. 1844 till 24 Oct. 1847. Offg. A.A.G., Cawnpore Div., Oct. 1848 till Feb. 1850. Comdd. 1st Eur. Bengal Fus. Mar. 1851 till June 1852. Fur. s.c. Jan. 1853 till Jan. 1856. Posted Lt. Col. to 54th N.I. 18 Mar. 1856, and was

THE BENGAL ARMY, 1758-1834   661

comdg. the Regt. at Delhi when the mutiny broke out at that station on 11 May 1857.[1]
Refs. : *De Rhé-Philipe.* G.M. 1857, ii. 346.
[1] *Note :* Having been cut down by men of 3rd L.C. and his own regt. and left for dead with 17 wounds, he was eventually found by the garr. surgeon and removed to the Flag Staff Tower on the Ridge. Late in the evening he was despatched, in a dying condition, towards Karnal. Nothing further was ever heard of him. Promoted Bt. Col. posthumously on 17 May 1859, with effect from 22 Aug. 1855.

RITSO, George Frederick (1810-1836). Lieutenant, 40th N.I. *b.* Somerton, Somerset, 22 Sept. 1810. Cadet 1828. Arrived in India 2 Oct. 1829. Ensign (12 Dec. 1828) 14 Sept. 1829. Lieut. 16 Nov. 1835. *d.* Kyaukpyu, Arakan, 6 July 1836.

Of Polish extraction. *bapt.* Somerton 20 July 1815. Son of John Ritso, of Bath, Capt. 76th Foot, and sometime A.D.C. to Marquess Wellesley when G.G., and Charlotte his wife. Addiscombe Cadet 1827-8.
Services : Posted Ensign to 40th N.I. in 1829. d.d. 6th N.I. 31 Mar. till 15 Oct. 1830. No record of active service.

ROACH, Edward [1] (1734-?). Captain. Infantry. *b.* Portsmouth 1734. Cadet (Bo.) 1761. Ensign (Bo.) 5 July 1762. 2nd Lieut. (Bo.) 18 Feb. 1764. Lieut. (Bengal) 26 Sept. 1764. Capt. 30 May 1767. Dismissed by the Govr. and Council 24 Apr. 1774.

Services : Sailed as a Cadet for Bombay in the *Gen. Lawrence* in 1761. Served with the Bo. detachment in the campaign in Bengal, 1764, under Major Hector Munro ; transfd. to Bengal Army 21 Aug. 1765. Passed over for comd. of a Bn. in 1773 as being an invalid. Dismissed in consequence of his quarrel with James Redman, *q.v.* Was in England in Aug. 1768.
Refs. : *Forrest,* i. 84.
[1] *Note :* His name is given as William in both embarkation roll and MS. Bo. *A.L.* of 1763 and 25 Jan. 1766, in the latter of which he is noted as being in Bengal. His name is absent from Bo. *A.L.* of 15 Jan. 1767. In these circumstances, though Edward and William may, of course, be separate individuals, it is believed that they are one and the same person.

ROACH, James (1752/53-1787). Lieutenant, Infantry. *b.* Norwich 1752/53. Cadet 1781. Ensign 1 June 1781. Lieut. 15 Sept. 1782. *d.* Rangpur, Bengal, 21 Apr. 1787, aged about 33.

Services : Apptd. Cadet 6 Dec. 1780, aged 28 ; sailed for India in the *Chapman* 13 Mar. 1781, aged 28. N.F.P.
Refs. : B : P.P. vi. 402.

ROACH, John. (*See* **ROCH, John Odell.**)

ROACH, Maurice (*d*. 1763). Lieutenant, Bengal Eur. Bn. Cadet (?) Ensign Oct. 1759. Lieut. 1761. *d*. 5th, 6th or 11th Oct. 1763 ; massacred at or near Patna by order of Nawab Mir Muhammad Kasim. (*See* note to Hugh Mackay.)

Services : Assault of Patna city 25 June 1763.

Refs. : Broome, p. 365. *Swinton of Kimmerghame Records*, p. 50. *Innes*, p. 169.

ROATS or ROOTS, Anthony. Captain. Artillery. (26) Cadet (?) Fireworker 18 Sept. 1762. 2nd Lieut. 2 Jan. 1763. Lieut. 4 Dec. 1763. Capt. Lt. 25 Jan. 1765. Capt. 20 Oct. 1765. Resigned May 1766.

Services : Comy. of Ord. in 1764, and was present at the battle of Buxar in Oct. Resigned his Commission during the " Batta mutiny " ; petitioned the C.D. in England in Jan. 1770 to be restored to the Service.

ROBB, Ferris Charles (1791-1855). Major. 22nd N.I. *b*. Deptford, Kent, 24 Feb. 1791. Cadet 1809. Arrived in India 3 Oct. 1810. Ensign 20 Aug. 1811. Lieut. 31 May 1816. Capt. 6 Sept. 1826. Major 20 June 1836. Retired 26 Nov. 1836. *d*. Beaulieu House, Southsea, 23 Jan. 1855.

bapt. St. Paul's, Deptford, 24 May 1791. Son of Charles Robb, Master R.N., Master Attendant of Deptford Yard. *m*. Calcutta 15 Jan. 1827, Eliza, dau. of —— Mercer, and widow of Andrew Suter, Lieut. H.M. 1st or Royal Scots.

Services : Barasat C.C. Posted Ensign to 1/2nd N.I. in 1811. Operations against the Bhils in Khandesh district, Bombay, 1820 ; Lieut. 1/2nd N.I. D.A.Q.M.G. 3 cl. 2 Jan. 1821 ; 2 cl. 25 Apr. 1823 ; 1 cl. 7 June 1824. Transfd. to 22nd N.I. (late 2/2nd) May 1824. Employed on survey work in Saugor district 1824-5. Siege and capture of Bhurtpore ; D.A.Q.M.G. (India medal). Leave s.c. 18 mos. to N.S.W. 17 June 1826. Survey work in Saugor district. Fur. s.c. 6 Jan. 1834 till 12 Nov. 1836.

Refs. : A.J. xxiii. 857. *G.M.* 1855, i. 333.

ROBBINS, William Pitt (1809-1862). Major General. 15th N.I. *b*. London 10 Sept. 1809. Cadet 1826. Arrived in India

THE BENGAL ARMY, 1758-1834 663

11 May 1827. Ensign 20 June 1827. Lieut. 31 May 1834.
Capt. 1 Feb. 1843. Major 28 Nov. 1854. Lt. Col. 9 Oct. 1858.
Bt. Col. 28 Nov. 1857. Retired 31 Dec. 1861. Hon. Maj. Gen.
31 Dec. 1861. *d.* St. Kilda, nr. Melbourne, N.S.W., 14 Feb. 1862.
bapt. St. Giles-in-the-Fields 16 Nov. 1809. Son of Robert Robbins and Anne Eliza his wife. Ward of Joseph Pitt, M.P., of East Court, nr. Cirencester.
Services: Ensign d.d. 14th N.I. 28 May 1827; posted to 3rd Extra Regt. 19 June 1827; transfd. to 15th N.I. 29 Feb. 1828. Fur. s.c. 28 Feb. 1832 till 27 Jan. 1835; leave s.c. to Cape 30 Aug. 1837 till 18 Jan. 1839. Second Sikh War; Chilianwala; Gujerat; Capt. 15th N.I., Orderly Ofr. to Sir W. R. Gilbert, *q.v.*; pursuit of Sikhs and Afghans to Peshawar, A.D.C. to Gilbert (Medal with 2 clasps). Offg. Comdt. 17th Irreg. Cav. 6 Dec. 1849. Comdt. Ramgarh L.I. 18 July 1851 till 31 July 1857, when the Bn. mutinied. To do general duty at Barrackpore 20 Aug. 1860; do. at Ambala 27 Oct. 1860.
Refs.: Boase. *The Times,* 17 Apr. 1862.

ROBE, George Mountain Sewell (1802-1825). Lieutenant, 27th N.I. *b.* Quebec 25 Oct. 1802. Cadet 1819. Ensign 14 Feb. 1820. Lieut. 1 July 1823. *d.* Chittagong 30 Dec. 1825.
bapt. Quebec 21 Dec. 1802. Son of Col. Sir William Robe, K.C.B., R.A. (*D.N.B.*), and Sarah his wife. Woolwich Cadet.
Services: Posted Ensign to 1/15th N.I. in 1820. Transfd. as Lieut. to 13th N.I. July 1823; to 26th N.I. (late 1/13th) May 1824. First Burma War; Arakan 1825; Lieut. 26th N.I. Transfd. to 27th N.I. 3 June 1825.

ROBE, William Green James (1800-1848). Lieutenant. 58th N.I. *bapt.* St. Mary's, Lambeth, 9 Nov. 1800. Cadet 1819. Arrived in India 6 Jan. 1821. Ensign 16 July 1820. Lieut. 11 July 1823. Name removed from *A.L.* 19 Mar. 1834. *d.* Frogs Hall, Takeley, Essex, 18 Apr. 1848, aged 48.
Son of James Robe, Clerk to the House of Commons, and Ann his wife.
Services: Ensign 2/10th N.I.; transfd. as Lieut. to 29th N.I. July 1823; to 58th N.I. (late 2/29th) May 1824. To take charge of detachment of Hill Rangers at Berhampore 10 Mar. 1825; Adjt. do. 2 Nov. 1825; exchanged to Adjt. Bundelkhand Provl. Bn. 13 June 1827 till disbanded 1 Mar. 1831. Fur. p.a. 18 Oct. 1831 till 14 Oct. 1835, when his name was removed from *A.L.* with effect from 19 Mar. 1834 for having overstayed his leave. Bt. Capt.

16 July 1835, but this promotion was cancelled on his being struck off. No record of active service.
Refs.: *G.M.* 1848, i. 675.

ROBERDEAU, James William (1789-1847). Lieut. Colonel. 10th L.C. *b.* Bromley St. Leonard, Middlesex, 2 May 1789. Cadet 1805. Arrived in India 13 Dec. 1806. Cornet 13 Dec. 1806. Lieut. 31 July 1816. Capt. 16 Mar. 1820. Major 9 Apr. 1833. Lt. Col. 15 Nov. 1837. Invalided 4 Nov. 1839. Retired 13 July 1841. *d.* Sloane Sq., London, 15 June 1847.

bapt. Bromley St. Leonard 23 Aug. 1789. 3rd and youngest son of John Peter Roberdeau, the dramatist (*D.N.B.*), and Mary his wife, dau. of Rev. John Townley, rector of St. Benet's, Gracechurch St. Nephew of Paul Le Mesurier, Director E.I.C. *m.* Muirfield, Inverness, 10 May 1831, Eliza Raper, 2nd dau. of Arthur Cooper, of Inverness, J.P. (She died Chelsea 6 May 1884, aged 79.)

Services: "Renounced the hazardous blank-abounding lottery of a Naval life." (*G.M.* 1815, i. 275.) Posted Cornet to 4th N.C. in 1807. Promoted Lieut. in 1818 with effect from 14 Aug. 1815, subsequently altered to 31 July 1816. Third Mahratta War; Jawad; Lieut. 4th N.C. Siege and capture of Bhurtpore; Capt. 4th L.C. Fur. s.c. 21 Dec. 1826 till 1831. Shekhawat expedn. 1834; Major 4th L.C. Posted Lt. Col. to 1st L.C. 26 Feb. 1838; transfd. to 10th L.C. 14 Feb. 1839. Fur. s.c. 31 Oct. 1838 till 1 Nov. 1839, and 12 Jan. 1840 till retirement.

Refs.: *Misc. Gen. et Her.* 5S. i. 178. *G.M.* 1831, i. 463; 1847, ii. 217.

ROBERTON, William (1764-?). Lieutenant. Infantry. *b.* Hants 1764. Cadet 1780. Ensign 8 Apr. 1782. Lieut. 30 July 1782. Resigned 15 Nov. 1789.

Services: Apptd. Cadet 29 Dec. 1780, aged 16. Lieut. 5th Bengal Eur. Bn. in July 1787. Fur. on h.p. 3 Oct. 1788 till resignation.

ROBERTS, Sir Abraham (1784-1873). Lieut. General, G.C.B. Colonel 101st Royal Bengal Fus. *b.* Waterford 11 Apr. 1784. Cadet 1803. Arrived in India 18 Mar. 1805. Ensign 18 Mar. 1805. Lieut. 19 Mar. 1805. Capt. 27 Aug. 1822. Major 24 Sept. 1826. Lt. Col. 28 Sept. 1831. Col. 10 Nov. 1843. Maj. Gen. 20 June 1854. Lt. Gen. 13 Oct. 1857. *d.* at his residence, 25 Royal York Cresc., Clifton, 28 Dec. 1873.

bapt. St. Olave's, Waterford, 23 Apr. 1785. 4th son of Rev. John

THE BENGAL ARMY, 1758-1834

Roberts, rector of Ballymacward, co. Galway, J.P. co. Waterford, and Anne his wife, dau. of Rev. Abraham Sandys, of Dublin. Uncle of Thomas Roberts, *q.v.* *m.* 1st, Moidapore 20 July 1820, Frances Isabella, dau. of George Poyntz Ricketts, B.C.S., and sister of George Poyntz Ricketts, *q.v.* (She died 14 May 1827, aged 24.) *m.* 2nd, Benares 2 Aug. 1830, Isabella, dau. of Abraham Bunbury, of Kilfeacle, co. Tipperary, and widow of Hamilton George Maxwell, *q.v.* (She died Hampton Court Palace 7 Mar. 1882, aged 83.) Father of F.M. Earl Roberts.

Services : See *D.N.B.* Ensign Waterford Mil. 1801 ; Ensign H.M. 48th Regt. 1803. Second Mahratta War 1805-6 ; operations in Bundelkhand ; Lieut. 1/13th N.I. Operations against Dhundia Khan 1807 ; Komona ; Ganauri ; Lieut. 1/13th N.I. Adjt. 1/13th N.I. 29 Mar. 1807 till 1819. Nepal War 1814-15 ; Kalanga ; Jaithak ; Lieut. 1/13th N.I., in 2nd Div. (India medal). Bareilly insurrection 1816. Posted Lt. Col. to Rt. Wing Bengal Eur. Regt. 10 Aug. 1832. Fur. s.c. 3 Jan. 1834 till 5 Dec. 1836. First Afghan War 1838-41 ; capture of Ghazni 1839 (Medal) ; Bdr. comdg. 4th Bde. ; comdd. Shah Shuja's force in 1840, but resigned and returned to India. Comdd. 4th Bde., Army of Reserve (for Afghanistan) 1842. Posted Col. to 48th N.I. 11 Feb. 1844. Fur. p.a. 16 Feb. 1844 till 8 Jan. 1852. Bdr. Gen. comdg. Lahore Div. 20 Mar. 1852 ; do. Peshawar Div. June 1852 till Mar. 1854. Fur. s.c. 3 Mar. 1854 till death. Col. 13th N.I. 1848 till 1859 ; do. 1st Eur. Bengal Fus. (became 101st Royal Bengal Fus.) 1859 till death. C.B. 20 Dec. 1839 ; K.C.B. 28 Mar. 1865 ; G.C.B. 24 May 1873. Durani 2 cl. 15 June 1841.

Refs.: Burke's *Peerage*, 1923, p. 1884, *s.n.* Roberts, E. *Howard & Crisp*, xi. 10, *s.n.* Roberts, E. *D.N.B.* *D.I.B.* Boase. *I.L.N.* lxiv (1874), 23. *The Times*, 1 Jan. 1874.

ROBERTS, Browne (1782-1854). Captain. 25th N.I. Afterwards a Calcutta merchant. *b.* Stradbally, Queen's Co., 17 Feb. 1782. Cadet 1801. Arrived in India 6 Sept. 1802. Ensign 8 Aug. 1802. Lieut. 30 Nov. 1803. Capt. 1 Aug. 1818. Resigned 1 Aug. 1820. *d.* Brighton 11 Nov. 1854.

Of Ravensbourne Pk., Lewisham. 6th son of Arthur Roberts, of Stradbally, and Elizabeth Brown his wife, of Portarlington. Cousin-german of Walter Fitzgerald, of Piccadilly, London, hosier. *m.* Calcutta 22 Nov. 1814, Mary Margaret, youngest dau. of John Anderson (*d.* 1812), *q.v.* (*See also* Archibald Oliver.) His niece *m.* Charles Vivian Swinton, *q.v.*

Services : One of the first Cadets at the newly-established Barasat

C.C. 1802-3. Posted Lieut. to 1st N.I. in 1803 ; transfd. to newly-raised 25th N.I. Sept. 1804. Capture of Gohad 1806 ; Lieut 2/25th N.I. Capture of Mauritius 1810 ; Lieut. & Adjt. 1st Vol. Bn. Actg. S.A.C.G. 24 July 1813 ; permanent do. 22 Dec. 1815 till resignation. Joined mercantile house of Mackintosh & Co., Calcutta, 1820-8 ; afterwards in Rickards, Mackintosh & Co., London. Sheriff of Calcutta 1828.

Refs.: Burke's *Landed Gentry*, 13th edn., p. 1574, *s.n.* McMillan-Scott. *Journal of the Irish Memorials Assn.* vol. vii (1908), p. 503. *A.J.* N.S. xviii. 36-40. *G.M.* 1855, i. 106.

ROBERTS, Charles Morrissey (1781-1845). Captain. 5th N.C. *b.* Cawnpore 21 Aug. (? 10 Mar.) 1781. Cadet 1795. Arrived in India 26 Sept. 1796. Cornet 8 Nov. 1796. Lieut. 29 May 1800. Capt. 11 Mar. 1805. Retired 15 Sept. 1815. *d.* Everton House, nr. Lymington, Hants, 5 May 1845.

bapt. ptely. 8 Sept. 1781. 2nd son of William Roberts, *q.v.*, and Elizabeth his wife. Brother of Henry Tufnell Roberts, *q.v.*, and nephew of Shearman Bird, B.C.S. *m.* Lymington 29 Dec. 1819, Maria Louisa, dau. of Mappe Allen, of Lymington, and of The Valley, Barbados. (She *re-m.* 20 Jan. 1849, Henry Stackpole de Linnee Peers.)

Services: Apptd. a Minor Cadet 22 Oct. 1781 ; struck off 2 May 1786. Posted Ensign to 1st Bengal Eur. Regt. in 1796 ; transfd. as Cornet to 1st N.C. ; as Lieut. to newly-raised 5th N.C. 29 May 1800 ; Adjt. do. 29 May 1800 till 16 May 1805. Second Mahratta War 1803-4 ; Lieut. 5th N.C. Fur. 7 Nov. 1812 till retirement.

Refs.: *Misc. Gen. et Her.* 4S. ii. 105 ; iv. 214-18. *I.M.* 24 May 1845, p. 298.

ROBERTS, Edward (*d.* 1767). Lieutenant, 3rd Bengal Eur. Regt. Cadet 1764. Ensign 12 Oct. 1764. Lieut. 25 Oct. 1765. *d.* Allahabad 10 June 1767.[1]

Services: Lieut. 2nd Bengal Eur. Regt. in 1766 ; transfd. to 3rd Regt.

[1] *Note*: "The troops had been out that morning to attend an execution. . . . Lieut. Roberts, on returning to his tent, feeling himself excessively warm, ordered a few pots of cold water to be thrown over him, which checked perspiration, and brought on a high fever that terminated his existence in less than an hour." (*Williams*, p. 156 *n.*)

ROBERTS, Henry Tufnell (1785-1859). Lieut. General, C.B. Colonel 7th L.C. *b.* Newport, I.W., 30 July 1785. Cadet 1798.

Arrived in India 8 Nov. 1799. Cornet (8 Nov. 1799) 1 June 1800. Lieut. 17 July 1801. Capt. 1 Sept. 1818. Major 13 May 1825. Lt. Col. 2 Oct. 1828. Col. 19 May 1838. Maj. Gen. 23 Nov. 1841. Lt. Gen. 11 Nov. 1851. *d.* Beauchamp Lodge, Leamington, 3 Feb. 1859.

Of Lymington. 3rd son of William Roberts, *q.v.*, and Elizabeth his wife. Brother of Charles Morrissey Roberts, *q.v. m.* Lymington 17 June 1823, Jane, 2nd dau. of Thomas Beckley, of Lymington. (She died 16 July 1890, aged 89.)

Services: Ensign Milford Mil. Vols. 24 May 1798. Cornet 5th N.C. On service in Baghelkhand in 1803. Second Mahratta War; occupation of Bundelkhand 1803-4; Kapsa; Kalpi; Lieut. 5th N.C. Operations in Bundelkhand and Rewah 1809-10; Bde. Major. Tempy. Bde. Major to Cav. Bde. for service in Bundelkhand 27 Dec. 1809. Qmr. 5th N.C. 22 May till Nov. 1814. Baghelkhand 1813; storm and capture of Entauri. ⸀Raised 1st Rohilla Cav. (known as Roberts' Rohilla Horse) 14 Nov. 1814, and comdd. till Jan. 1822. Capt. Lt. 5th N.C. 16 Sept. 1815. Nepal War 1815 and 1816 (India medal). Siege and capture of Hathras 1817. Third Mahratta War 1817-18; with Div. under Col. J. W. Adams, *q.v.*; Satanwari (*Lond. Gaz.* 10 Aug. 1819 and 20 Jan. 1821). Fur. p.a. 11 Jan. 1822 till 17 July 1826. Transfd. to 1st Extra Cav. Regt. 17 June 1825. Posted Lt. Col. to 2nd L.C. 7 Nov. 1828; to 5th L.C. 18 Oct. 1833. Fur. p.a. 16 Feb. 1832 till 24 Dec. 1836. Bdr. 1 cl., Nizam's army, comdg. Aurangabad Div. 23 Jan. 1837 till 20 Feb. 1839. Col. 7th L.C. 19 Sept. 1838. Fur. p.a. 8 May 1839 till death. C.B. 27 Sept. 1831.

Refs.: Misc. Gen. et Her. 4S. iv. 214-18. *E.I.M.C.* ii. 430-8. Boase. *A.J.* xvi. 105. *G.M.* 1859, i. 332. *The Times*, 8 Feb. 1859.

ROBERTS, Ralph Gore (1801-1876). Major. Artillery. (474) *bapt.* Eton, Bucks., 2 Dec. 1801. Cadet 1817. Admitted 4 Aug. 1818. 2nd Lieut. 28 July 1818. Lieut. 8 Nov. 1818. Capt. 31 May 1833. Retired 1 Aug. 1838. Hon. Major 28 Nov. 1854. *d.* 31 Mar. 1876.

4th son of Rev. William Roberts, vice-provost of Eton Coll. and rector of Worplesdon, Surrey, and Anne his wife, dau. of Col. John Gore, lt. govr. of Tower of London. Brother of Jane, last Countess of Egremont, nephew of Sir John Gore, K.C.B., Vice Adm. R.N. (*D.N.B.*), and cousin-german of Thomas George Mesham, *q.v.* (? and of George William Molyneux Gore, *q.v.*). *m.* Benares 11 Sept. 1828, Isabella, 4th dau. of Rev. George Holgate, rector of Theydon Bois, Essex. (She died Upper Norwood 7 Feb. 1865, aged 67.) Ed. Eton; in Remove in 1814. Addiscombe Cadet 1816-18.

Services : With 2nd Troop H.A. 1821-3 ; posted to newly-formed 2nd Troop 1st Bde. H.A. in 1825. Dy. Comy. Ord. 1 May 1824, and posted to Chunar ; Comy. Ord. at Cawnpore 22 Nov. 1828 till 1838. Leave s.c. 2 yrs. to Cape 30 Dec. 1835. Offg. Dy. Principal Comy. Ord. 1 Jan. 1838. No record of active service.

Refs. : Bradney's *Hist. of Monmouthshire,* Vol. I, Pt. i, p. 179. *Eton School Lists.*

ROBERTS, Robert (1741/42-1763). Ensign, 9th Bn. Sepoys.[1] *b.* in Wales 1741/42. Cadet 1760. Ensign 18 Sept. 1761. *d.* 14 (or 17) July 1763 : kld. in action nr. Katwa.

Services : Sailed for India in the *Royal Duke* in 1759, aged 17. War with Mir Muhammad Kasim 1763 ; defence of a convoy (kld.) ; Ensign 9th Bn., 2nd in comd. to William Glenn, *q.v.*

Refs. : Fortescue, iii. 71.

[1] *Note :* He may possibly have belonged to Bengal Eur. Bn.

ROBERTS, Roderick (1791-1843). Major, Artillery. (402) *bapt.* Aberystwith 19 Jan. 1791. Cadet 1807. Arrived in India 21 Mar. 1809. Fireworker 28 Mar. 1809. Lieut. 23 Aug. 1813. Capt. 7 Mar. 1824. Major 20 Oct. 1839. *d.* Sukkur, Sind, 8 Oct. 1843, of paralysis.

Son of Thomas Roberts and Mary his wife. Brother of Rev. Richard Roberts, of Stewkley, Bucks. *m.* Cawnpore 20 July 1832, Isabella, youngest dau. of Capt. Ryder Mowatt, and sister of John Lealand Mowatt, *q.v.* (She *re-m.* George Campbell, *q.v.,* and died 10 Dec. 1865.) Woolwich Cadet; nominated to R.M.A. 11 June 1806.

Services : Nepal War 1814-15 ; Lieut. 6th Coy. 2nd Bn., with 4th Div. ; afterwards with detachment in Tirhut under Col. R. B. Gregory, *q.v.* Siege and capture of Hathras ; Lieut. 6th Coy. 2nd Bn. Third Mahratta War ; Lieut. 2nd Troop, afterwards 1st Troop H.A. With 1st Troop 1818 ; 4th Troop 1819-20 ; 6th Troop 1821-3 ; 3rd Troop 1824. To comd. newly-formed 2nd Troop 1st Bde. H.A. 1825. Siege and capture of Bhurtpore ; Capt. comdg. 2nd Troop 1st Bde. Fur. s.c. 7 Jan. 1838 till 5 Jan. 1841. To join 2nd Troop 3rd Bde. Aug. 1842 ; to comd. Art. at Ludhiana 30 Dec. 1842 ; at Ferozepore 1843 ; to comd. Art. for Sind at Sukkur 22 Mar. 1843.

Refs. : I.M. 6 Dec. 1843. Will dated 17 Aug. 1840 ; admon. 16 Apr. 1844. M.I. Afghan Memorial Church, Bombay.

THE BENGAL ARMY, 1758-1834   669

ROBERTS, Roger Elliot (1753/54-1831). Colonel. 2nd Bengal Eur. Regt. Subsequently Lieut. of H.M. band of gentlemen-pensioners. *b.* 1753/54. Country Cadet 1767. Admitted 25 Nov. 1767. Ensign 6 Dec. 1767. Lieut. 14 Oct. 1769. Capt. 26 Feb. 1778. Major 21 Feb. 1782. Lt. Col. 1 Mar. 1794. Col. 1 Jan. 1798. Retired 21 Apr. 1800. *d.* Upper Grosvenor St., London, 9 Aug. 1831, aged 77.

Son of Rev. Robert Roberts, vicar of Aldford, co. Chester, and Harriett Lawrence his wife. His sisters *m.* Gilbert Ironside, *q.v.*, and John Ricketts, the father of John Henry Ricketts, *q.v.* Related to William Chauncy Lawrence, *q.v.*, and to Charles Herbert White (*d.* 1798), *q.v. m.* in England 15 Oct. 1801, Marianne, 4th dau. of Sir William Wake, 8th Bart.

Services : Apptd. Persian Intr. to Col. A. Champion, *q.v.*, 19 Jan. 1774 ; A.D.C. to Sir John Clavering in 1777. Apptd. to comd. a Bn. of Sepoys 22 Mar. 1780 ; Sec. and Persian Intr. to Col. Ironside's detachment 9 Feb. 1781. Major comdg. 30th N.I. till Dec. 1783. Fur. 9 Jan. 1786 till 13 Aug. 1791. Acted as second to Major James Browne, *q.v.*, in his duel with Sir John Macpherson, the ex-G.G., in Hyde Park, London, 10 Aug. 1787. Transfd. from 5th Bengal Eur. Bn. to 4th do. 7 Nov. 1793 ; Lt. Col. comdg. 2nd Bengal Eur. Regt. in 1796. Fur. 6 Dec. 1797 till retirement. Pub. in 1785 a Vocabulary of Persian and English Words.

Refs. : Family information. Burke's *Peerage*, 1923, p. 2243, *s.n.* Wake, Bart., of Clevedon, Somerset. *Macpherson*, p. 176. *Selections from Calcutta Gazettes*, i. 236. *A.J.* N.S. vi. 43. *G.M.* 1801, ii. 959.

ROBERTS, Thomas (1800-1850). Captain. 51st N.I. *b.* Waterford 28 Oct. 1800. Cadet 1818. Admitted 11 Sept. 1819. Ensign 20 May 1819. Lieut. 12 May 1821. Capt. 6 May 1833. Invalided 25 Apr. 1836. Retired 16 Jan. 1846. *d.* at his residence, Montpelier Sq., S. Kensington, 29 Oct. 1850.

bapt. Waterford cathedral 23 Apr. 1819 (*sic*). 2nd son of John Roberts, of Waterford, atty.-at-law, and Grace his wife, eldest dau. of William Dobbyn, of Waterford. Nephew of Sir Abraham Roberts, *q.v. m.* St. Mary's, Bath, 8 Apr. 1835, Harriet, 3rd dau. of William Lowndes, of Chesham, Bucks. (She died London 6 Apr. 1882, aged 70.)

Services : Ensign d.d. Bengal Eur. Regt. 1819 ; posted Lieut. to 2/26th N.I. 24 Sept. 1821 ; Adjt. do. 3 Nov. 1823. Transfd. to 51st N.I. (late 1/26th) May 1824 ; Adjt. do. 17 June 1824 till 7 Jan. 1832. Leave s.c. to Hills 1829-30 ; s.c. 18 mos. to Cape and N.S.W. 13 Feb. 1830 ; fur. s.c. 10 Dec. 1831 till 5 Sept. 1835 No record of active service.

Refs.: *Howard & Crisp*, xi. 2, *s.n.* Roberts, E. Burke's *Landed Gentry*, 11th edn., p. 1054, *s.n.* Lowndes (*now* Frith), of Chesham. *G.M.* 1850, ii. 672.

ROBERTS, Walter. Lieutenant. Artillery. (104) Cadet (?) Fireworker 28 Feb. 1770. Lieut. 6 Dec. 1771. Dismissed by G.C.M. Oct. 1776.

m. Mary.

Services: Lieut. 3rd Coy. Art. Fur. 30 Dec. 1772 till 1776. Tried by G.C.M. at Calcutta Oct. 1776.

*ROBERTS, William (1742/43-?). Lieutenant, Infantry. *b.* Herts. 1742/43. Cadet 1764. Ensign 4 Oct. 1764. Lieut. 23 Oct. 1765.

(*Probably* brother of Edward Roberts, *q.v.*)

Services: Sailed for India in the *Calcutta* 2 Apr. 1764, aged 21. N.F.P.

ROBERTS, William (1746-1809). Major. 30th Bn. N.I. *b.* I. of Wight 20 Nov. 1746. Country Cadet 1766. Ensign 2 Sept. 1766. Lieut. 15 Sept. 1767. Capt. 5 Apr. 1773. Major 25 Jan. 1781. Resigned 7 Dec. 1793. *d.* Lymington, Hants, 23 June 1809.

4th and youngest son of Henry Roberts, of Standen, I. of Wight, and Elizabeth his wife, dau. of Samuel Tufnell, of London. *m.* Lymington 25 Mar. 1776, Elizabeth, eldest dau. of James Morrissey, of Ireland, Purser of H.M.S. *Bedford*. (She died Lymington Oct. 1814.) Father of Charles Morrissey Roberts and Henry Tufnell Roberts, *qq.v.* Uncle of Sir Henry Worsley, *q.v.*

Services: Arrived in Bengal in 1766 as a Free Merchant. Resigned and went home sick in Dec. 1773 ; returned to India July 1778. Apptd. to comd. one of the three newly-raised Sepoy Bns.[1] 11 Aug. 1778 ; Capt. 2/3rd Bengal Eur. Regt. in Oct. 1779 ; to comd. 30th N.I. 1 Jan. 1781. Campaign against the Rajah of Benares 1781 ; Major comdg. 30th N.I. Fur. Jan. 1784 till 1791.

Refs.: *Misc. Gen. et Her.*, 4S. iv. 214-18.

[1] *Note*: 37th Bn., raised at Benares, became 30th N.I. in 1781, 33rd N.I. in 1784, disbanded 1785.

ROBERTS, William Maitland (1813-1845). Lieutenant, 30th N.I. *b.* Isla de Leon, Spain, 16 Oct. 1813. Cadet 1829. Arrived in India 22 Nov. 1830. Ensign (11 June 1830) 23 Oct. 1833.

Lieut. 8 Oct. 1839.   d. nr. Kalna, Bengal, 12 Feb. 1845, on board the Jalangi flat.
bapt. Cadiz 21 Nov. 1813. Son of Lt.-Col. William Roberts, comdg. R.A. in Upper Canada, and Caroline his wife. Addiscombe Cadet 1828-30.
Services : Cadet d.d. 37th N.I. 5 Jan. 1831 ; 13th N.I. 30 Oct. 1832. Actg. Ensign (having been 2 yrs. in India) 5 Dec. 1832. Actg. Adjt. 3rd Local Horse 4 Apr. 1833. Posted Ensign to 18th N.I. 18 Oct. 1833 ; transfd. to 30th N.I. 19 Dec. 1833. Fur. p.a. 22 Dec. 1840 till 29 Jan. 1844. No record of active service.
Refs. : *G.M.* 1845, ii. 102.

*ROBERTSON, Alexander (*d.* 1797). Bt. Captain, Artillery. Comy. of Ord. Bt. Lieut. Fireworker 10 Apr. 1783. Bt. Capt. (? 7 Jan. 1796). *d.* Cawnpore 6 July 1797.
Uncle of John Duff, of Pitlochry, and of John and Andrew, sons of Robert Clapperton, surgeon at Lochmaben. .Related to Patrick Duff (1742-1803) and James Lawtie, *qq.v.*
Services : Promoted Comy. of Ord. from Dy. Comy. 6 Sept. 1781. Comy. of Ord. at Cawnpore 5 Feb. 1788 till death.
Refs. : Will dated 5 June 1797 ; proved 30 Oct. 1797.

ROBERTSON, David (1766/67-1847). Major. 23rd N.I. *b.* 1766/67. Cadet 1783. Admitted 25 Oct. 1783. Ensign 8 Apr. 1785. Lieut. 9 Oct. 1793. Capt. 21 Sept. 1804. Major 28 Sept. 1810. Retired 1 June 1813. *d.* Cheltenham 14 Jan. 1847, aged 80.
m. Camnethan House 17 July 1809, Caroline, 4th dau. of James Lockhart, of Castlehill, Cambusnethan, co. Lanark, and cousin-german of Harry Nisbet, *q.v.*
Services : Apptd. Cadet 10 Dec. 1782 ; sailed for India in the *Vansittart* 11 Mar. 1783. Transfd. from Supy. Ensign 5th Eur. Bn. to 1st do. 30 Jan. 1791 ; to 2nd do. 12 Nov. 1793. Apptd. Adjt. 5th Bn. Sepoys 5 Oct. 1794 ; Adjt. 3rd Bengal Eur. Regt. in 1796 ; Lieut. 13th N.I. in 1798 ; transfd. to 15th N.I. Transfd. to 2/18th N.I. 29 May 1800 ; Adjt. do. 29 May 1800 till 1803. Transfd. to newly-raised 23rd N.I. in 1803 ; Capt. Lt. do. 1 Oct. 1803. Second Mahratta War ; Bde. Major in Bundelkhand. Fur. 24 Feb. 1807 till 9 Dec. 1810. Major 1/23rd N.I.
Refs. : *Farley's Bristol Journal,* 5 Aug. 1809. *G.M.* 1847, i. 329.

ROBERTSON, Edward (1808-1827). Ensign, 52nd N.I. *b.* psh. of St. James's, Middlesex, 24 Feb. 1808. Cadet 1825. Ensign

5 Nov. 1825. *d.* Akyab, Burma, 22 June 1827, of Arakan fever. Son of —— Robertson, of Ross by Hamilton, Capt. E.I.C.S.
Services: Posted Ensign to 52nd N.I. in 1826. No record of active service.
Refs.: A.J. xxiv. 792.

ROBERTSON, Francis (*c.* 1737/38-1791). Lieut. Colonel. 6th Bengal Eur. Bn. *b. c.* 1737/38. Cadet 1764. Ensign 7 Jan. 1765. Lieut. (13 Dec. 1766) 6 Apr. 1773. Capt. (12 Oct. 1769). Major 8 Jan. 1781. Lt. Col. 1 Dec. 1786. Resigned 16 July 1787. *d.* London 11 Sept. 1791, aged about 53.

Brother of Sarah, 2nd wife of Rev. Henry Barnard, D.D., the father of Gen. Sir Andrew Francis Barnard, G.C.B. (*D.N.B.*). Cousin of Miss Rebecca Forbes.

Services: Sailed for India in the *Success* 17 May 1764. Adjt. 3rd Bde. at Bankipore under Col. Sir Robert Barker, *q.v.* Cashiered as one of the ringleaders of the " Batta mutiny " in 1766 ; restored by C.D. in Mar. 1776, with rank of Capt., without prejudice to his original standing in the Service. Comdd. 8 Coys. Mil. Sepoys at Murshidabad 14 May 1777 till 30 Jan. 1784, when he was granted leave s.c. in India. Lt. Col. comdg. 6th Eur. Bn., and Comdt. at Dinapore, in July 1787.

Refs.: Will dated 5 Sept. 1790 ; proved 23 Aug. 1792. M.I. in Grosvenor chapel, S. Audley St., London. Portrait, by Carlo Van Loo, was offered for sale at Sotheby's, 16 May 1928, by the owner, Mrs. O'Neill Daunt, of Kilcascan, Ballineen, co. Cork.

ROBERTSON, James (*c.* 1775-1810). Captain, Engineers. *b. c.* 1775. Cadet 1790. Arrived in India 17 Aug. 1792. Ensign 19 Aug. 1793. Lieut. 31 July 1800. Capt. 8 Oct. 1806. *d.* on board his budgerow at Ghazipur 4 Nov. 1810, aged 35.

Son of Charles Robertson, of Edinburgh, and Margaret his wife, dau. of Alexander Stirling, of Edinburgh, and sister of Sir James Stirling, Bart. His sister was mother of William Bell, *q.v. m.* Chinsura 13 Feb. 1803 (a runaway match), Sarah Anne Catherine, dau. of Thomas Whinyates, *q.v.* (She *re-m.* Calcutta 8 June 1811, Robert Younghusband, Capt. 53rd Ft., and uncle of Oswald John Younghusband, *q.v.*, and died 23 Aug. 1860, aged 80.)

Services: Apptd. Cadet 8 Feb. 1792 ; sailed for India in the *Melville Castle* 8 Mar. 1792. Adjt. Engrs. 1805-8. At Allahabad 1808-10. Operations in Bundelkhand against Lachman Dawa 1809 ; Ajaigarh ; Field Engr. Fur. s.c. Oct. 1810.

Refs.: Betham's *Baronetage*, iv. (1804) 249, *s.n.* Stirling, Bart.

Whinyates Family Records. A St. Helena Who's Who, p. 140.
S.M. 1811, p. 398. Will dated Allahabad 20 Jan 1809 ; proved 18 Dec. 1810. M.I. at Ghazipur.

ROBERTSON, James (1778-1834). Colonel, 46th N.I. *b.* Aberdeen 28 May 1778. Cadet 1796. Arrived in India 29 Jan. 1798. Ensign 30 Sept. 1797. Lieut. 10 Sept. 1798. Capt. 17 Aug. 1808. Major 20 Feb. 1821. Lt. Col. 1 May 1824. Col. 10 Jan. 1833. *d.* Nimach 18 Dec. 1834.

Son of Andrew Robertson, of Foveran, stocking merchant, and Jane Davidson his wife, dau. of Mr. Davidson, of Newton.

Services : Posted Ensign to 2nd Bengal Eur. Regt. in 1798 ; as Lieut. to 8th N.I. Sept. 1798 ; to 2nd N.I. Dec. 1798 ; to 1/11th N.I. Cantt. Adjt. & Qmr. at Ghazipur June 1801 till 1809.[1] Leave s.c. 4 mos. to sea 2 Sept. 1802. Fur. p.a. 12 Feb. 1812 till 28 Nov. 1814. Nepal War 1815 ; Capt. 1/11th N.I. Major 2/11th N.I. Posted Lt. Col. to 17th N.I. (late 2/11th) May 1824 ; to 33rd N.I. 3 Apr. 1828 ; to 45th N.I. 7 Mar. 1831 ; to 46th N.I. 15 Sept. 1832. Posted Col. to 46th N.I. 22 July 1833. Tempy. comdg. Meywar F.F. Dec. 1832, and 15 Jan. till 21 Feb. 1834.

Refs. : Scottish N. & Q., 1S. ix. 97. *E.I.M.C.* iii. 384-7. *A.J.* N.S. xvii. 131. M.I. at Nimach.

[1] *Note :* It was in his bungalow at Ghazipur that Marquis Cornwallis, the G.G., died in Oct. 1805.

ROBERTSON, James Court (1811-?). Lieutenant. 21st N.I. *b.* Kennington, London, 15 Sept. 1811. Cadet 1831. Arrived in India 25 Jan. 1833. Ensign (18 July 1832) 25 June 1833. Lieut. 3 Oct. 1840. Name removed from the *A.L.* 8 Dec. 1841.[1]

bapt. St. Mary's, Lambeth, 21 May 1828. Younger son of Harry Robertson, chief clerk of the ballot office, Trinity House, and Julia his wife, widow of Charles Pennick. Nephew of John Robertson (1775-1807), *q.v.*

Services : Allowed to rank from 18 July 1832, the day he would have sailed but for an accident. Supy. Ensign d.d. 2nd N.I. 11 Feb. 1833 ; 34th N.I. 3 Oct. 1833. Posted Ensign to 21st N.I. 24 May 1834. Fur. s.c. 22 Apr. 1841. No record of active service.

Refs. : Burke's *Landed Gentry*, 12th edn., p. 1610, *s.n.* Robertson, of Kindeace, co. Ross.

[1] *Note :* G.O. 23 Feb. 1842.

ROBERTSON, James Wells (1809-1847). Captain, Engineers. *b.* Georgetown, W.I., 10 Dec. 1809. Cadet 1827. Arrived in

India 23 Oct. 1828. Lieut. 28 Sept. 1827. Capt. 3 Apr. 1842. d. Simla 23 May 1847.

Son of Jane Robertson, of Bath, widow. (*Probably* brother of John Robertson (1804-1833), *q.v.*) Addiscombe Cadet 1826; Chatham 1827.
Services: d.d. S. & M. at Aligarh 20 Nov. 1828. Actg. Executive Engr. at Mhow 21 Nov. 1829; permanent do. 7 Apr. 1830 till 13 June 1833. With S. & M. at Delhi 29 July 1833. Asst. to Executive Engr., P.W.D., at Agra 27 Dec. 1833 till 7 Sept. 1836. First Afghan War 1842; Adjt. Engrs. 15 June 1842; operations in Shinwari valley (*Lond. Gaz.* 11 Oct. 1842) (Medal). Executive Engr. Delhi Div., P.W.D., 1 Feb. 1843; in charge of Nimach Div. 1 Nov. 1845 till 1846. First Sikh War; Sobraon (Medal).
Refs.: *I.M.* 24 Aug. 1847, p. 489.

ROBERTSON, James William John (1802-1827). Lieutenant, 33rd N.I. b. Berhampore, Bengal, 16 Oct. 1802. Cadet 1819. Ensign 2 Feb. 1820. Lieut. 22 Feb. 1822. d. in England 25 May 1827.

bapt. Berhampore 25 Dec. 1802. Son of James Robertson, Asst. Surg., Bengal Est., and Eliza his wife.
Services: Posted Ensign to 1/16th N.I. in 1820; transfd. to 33rd N.I. (late 2/16th) May 1824. First Burma War; Arakan 1825; Lieut. 1st Gren. Bn. Fur. s.c. 1826 till death.

ROBERTSON, John (1775-1807). Captain, 21st N.I. b. Fearn, co. Ross, 7 Apr. 1775. Cadet 1794. Arrived in India 26 Sept. 1796. Ensign 18 Oct. 1795. Lieut. 15 Mar. 1797. Capt. 21 Sept. 1804. d. 16 Nov. 1807: kld. in action at the siege of Komona.

bapt. 11 Apr. 1775. 9th and youngest son of Charles Robertson, of Kindeace, co. Ross, and Janet his wife, only dau. of Hugh Rose, Clava, co. Nairn. Uncle of James Court Robertson, *q.v.*
Services: Apptd. Cadet 8 Mar. 1796; sailed for India in the *Europa* 17 May 1796. Posted Ensign to 1st Bengal Eur. Regt. in 1796. Lieut. 9th N.I. Transfd. to newly-raised 2/21st N.I. in 1803. Second Mahratta War 1804-5; Rampura; Monson's retreat; operations nr. Tonk Rampura; Capt. 2/21st N.I. Operations against Dhundia Khan 1807; Komona (kld.); Capt. 2/21st N.I., with Gren. Bn.
Refs.: Burke's *Landed Gentry*, 12th edn., p. 1610, *s.n.* Robertson, of Kindeace, co. Ross. *A.A.R.* x. 21.

THE BENGAL ARMY, 1758-1834 675

*ROBERTSON, John (1791-?). Cadet. Infantry. *b.* Axminster 17 Apr. 1791. Cadet 1809. Admitted 2 Aug. 1810. Suspended and sent to England (G.O. 12 Mar. 1811).
2nd son of Robert Robertson, grocer, and Elizabeth his wife, dau. of John Perham, of Widworthy, yeoman.
Services : Suspended for fighting a duel at Barasat C.C. with Cadet Kennedy on 27 Feb. 1811.

ROBERTSON, John (1804-1833). Lieutenant, 70th N.I. *b.* Grenada 29 June 1804. Cadet 1823. Arrived in India 11 Oct. 1824. Ensign 9 May 1824. Lieut. 8 Sept. 1825. *d.* Marionburn, Tasmania, 15 Dec. 1833.
(*Probably* brother of James Wells Robertson, *q.v.*) *m.* Calcutta 25 Feb. 1830, Miss Fanny Beaumont Rogers. Ward and brother-in-law of Richard Purcell, of 28 Montagu Sq., London.
Services : Posted Ensign to 14th N.I. 31 Mar. 1825 ; transfd. as Lieut. to 2nd Extra Regt. (became 70th N.I.) Sept. 1825. Fur. s.c. 4 Aug. 1826 till 12 Feb. 1830. d.d. 53rd N.I. 23 Feb. till 1 Nov. 1830. Leave s.c. to N.S.W. via Mauritius 12 Sept. 1831 till death. No record of active service.
Refs. : A.J. N.S. xv. 37.

ROBERTSON, Lewis Alexander (1800-1818). Ensign, Infantry. Unposted. *b.* co. Aberdeen 8 Jan. 1800. Cadet 1817. Ensign (?) *d.* Calcutta 13 Sept. 1818.
Son of James Robertson, in Balletroch (? Balaterach), Glenmuick, an Ofr. in H.E.I.C.S., and Helen Macdonald his wife.
Services : N.F.P.

ROBERTSON, Patrick (*d.* 1781). Captain, Infantry. Cadet 1769. Ensign 1 Aug. 1769. Lieut. 27 Nov. 1772. Capt. Nov. 1780. *d.* at sea 1781 ; *bur.* Bombay 31 May 1781.
Services : Leave s.c. to sea Jan. 1781.

ROBERTSON, Roderick (1814-1869). Major. 70th N.I. *b.* Calcutta 25 May 1814. Cadet 1832. Arrived in India 30 Sept. 1833. Ensign (14 Dec. 1832) 18 June 1833. Lieut. 15 Mar. 1839. Capt. 9 Aug. 1851. Retired 10 Jan. 1859. Hon. Major 10 Jan. 1859. *d.* Worthing, Sussex, 8 Oct. 1860.
Son of Roderick Robertson, of Calcutta, merchant, of the firm of Stewart & Robertson, and Anne his wife, sister of Sir Archibald Galloway, *q.v.* London Univ., Gower St. Addiscombe Cadet 4 Feb. 1831 till 14 Dec. 1832.
Services : d.d. 55th N.I. 19 Oct. 1833 ; posted to 70th N.I.

24 May 1834. Posted to newly-raised 1st Cav., Oudh Auxy. Force, 29 Jan. 1838. Junior Asst. to Comr. Saugor Div. 17 Jan. 1840. Fur. s.c. 3 Oct. 1840 till 11 Oct. 1842. Actg. Intr. & Qmr. 31st N.I. 27 Jan. 1843 till 1845; do. 7th L.C. 1846. Comdd. Delhi Palace Gds. 1847-9. Comr. Cis-Sutlej States 22 Dec. 1849; Supt. of Bhatti territories 26 Feb. 1852 till 1858. Fur. 1858 till retirement. No record of active service.

Refs.: *The Times*, 12 Oct. 1869.

ROBERTSON, Thomas (*d.* 1761). Captain, Infantry. Bombay Cadet (?) Ensign (Bo.) (?) Lieut. (Bengal) 11 Nov. 1757. Capt. 8 Apr. 1759. *d.* 1761.[1]

Services: Served in Bengal under Clive from Mar. 1757; battle of Plassey; Ensign Bo. Est. Transfd. to Bengal Est. 1757.

[1] *Note*: Living in June 1761.

ROBERTSON, Thomas (1762/63-1831). Colonel, Engineers. *b.* 1762/63. Country Cadet 1781. Admitted 26 Nov. 1781. Ensign 17 July 1782. Lieut. 1 Mar. 1793. Capt. Lt. 31 July 1800. Capt. 1 Jan. 1806. Major 25 Apr. 1808. Lt. Col. 4 July 1818. Lt. Col. Comdt. 1 Dec. 1826. Col. 5 June 1829. *d.* Garden Reach, Calcutta, 18 June 1831, aged 68.

2nd son of William Robertson, of Inshes, and Jean his 1st wife, dau. of Col. William Murray. *m.* 1st, Edinburgh 4 Nov. 1799, Christian, dau. of William Hamilton, of Hill St. (She died at sea July 1807, on board the *Cirencester*.) *m.* 2nd, (?) (She died Selkirk Manse 18 Nov. 1822.)

Services: Asst. Engr. at Cawnpore in July 1787; employed surveying in Chittagong in 1795. Fur. p.a. 17 Jan. 1797 till 12 Dec. 1800. On duty in Burdwan 1801-2; surveying Sundarbans 1803-4. Second Mahratta War; siege of Deig (*Cal. Gaz.* 8 Jan. 1805); Bhurtpore. Engr. and Surveyor at P.W.I. 20 Mar. 1806 till 1811. Conducted disembarkation of troops at Macao under Weguelin, *q.v.*, Oct. 1808. Comdd. troops for occupation of Moluccas on death of Major Wright (Cons. 19 Sept. 1809). Fur. s.c. 5 Sept. 1811 till 9 Dec. 1814. Garr. Engr. and Executive Ofr. at Chunar 1 Apr. 1815 till 1830.

Refs.: Burke's *Landed Gentry*, 5th edn., p. 1174 *s.n.* Robertson, of Inshes, co. Inverness. Douglas's *Baronage*, p. 412. *Pester*, p. 364.[1] *G.M.* 1799, ii. 1192. *A.J.* N.S. vi. 191. M.I. in S. Park St. cemetery, Calcutta.

[1] *Note*: Pester gives his name as Robinson, as also do all *E.I.R.* down to 1812.

THE BENGAL ARMY, 1758-1834 677

ROBERTSON, William. (See **ROBERTON.**)

ROBERTSON, William Elphinstone (1803-1832). Lieutenant, 49th N.I. b. Edinburgh 1 Feb. 1803. Cadet 1823. Arrived in India 7 June 1824. Ensign 21 Feb. 1824. Lieut. 28 Jan. 1825. d. Calcutta 24 Nov. 1832.
bapt. St. Andrew's, Edinburgh, 28 Feb. 1803. Son of Duncan Robertson, hairdresser, and Jane Cameron his wife, natural dau. of Charles, 10th Lord Elphinstone. Ed. Edin. High School.
Services : Posted Ensign to 26th N.I. in 1824. First Burma War ; Arakan 1825 ; Lieut. 26th N.I., d.d. 49th N.I. Transfd. to 49th N.I. 11 Feb. 1826 ; d.d. 45th N.I. 8 May 1826 ; actg. Adjt. Left Wing 49th N.I. 20 Nov. 1826. Fur. s.c. 5 Mar. 1830 till 21 Sept. 1832.
Refs. : A.J. N.S. x. 157.

ROBESON, John (1789-1836). Captain. 24th N.I. Subsequently a merchant in Calcutta. bapt. Thurso 6 July 1789. Cadet 1805. Arrived in India 20 July 1807. Ensign 9 July 1807. Lieut. 8 July 1812. Capt. 8 Apr. 1823. Resigned 1 Aug. 1825. d. Calcutta 13 July 1836, aged 47.
Eldest son of Donald Robeson, writer in Thurso, and Elizabeth his wife, dau. of William Manson. Cousin of John Sutherland, q.v. m. Calcutta 8 Aug. 1814, Elizabeth, dau. of Capt. Thomas Dunbar, of Westfield. (See also James Murray MacGregor.) His dau. m. Charles James Horton Perreau, q.v.
Services : Barasat C.C. Posted Ensign to 8th N.I. in 1808. Nepal War 1814-15 ; Lieut. 1/8th N.I., in 4th Div. Adjt. Benares Provl. Bn. 2 Jan. 1816 till 1822 ; transfd. to 24th N.I. (late 2/8th) May 1824. First Burma War ; Arakan 1825 ; Capt. 1st Gren. Bn. Joined firm of Robertson & Co., merchants in Calcutta ; afterwards a merchant at Fatehgarh.
Refs. : Caithness Family Hist., p. 315. A.J. N.S. xxi. 267. Will dated Calcutta 3 Sept. 1829 ; proved 6 Sept. 1836. M.I. in Scots cemetery, Calcutta.

ROBINETT, Richard (d. 1795). Lieutenant, Infantry. Country Cadet 1780. Admitted 3 Apr. 1780. Ensign 19 Feb. 1781. Lieut. 14 Oct. 1781. d. in camp 10 Oct. 1795.
Services : Apptd. a Gent. Vol. in the Coy. of Art. 3 Apr. 1780. Lieut. 16th Bn. Sepoys in July 1785 and Dec. 1792.
Note : He may perhaps be identified with the 4th and youngest son of James Robinett, atty., of Saffron Walden, and Susannah his

wife, dau. of Thomas Rayner, of Duxford ; *b.* 7 Nov. ; *bapt.* 6 Dec. 1743. (Cf. *Misc. Gen. et Her.* 3S. i. 99.)

ROBINS, George (1785-1805). Lieutenant, 12th N.I. *b.* London 1 Dec. 1785. Cadet 1803. Arrived in India 27 Sept. 1804. Ensign 28 Sept. 1804. Lieut. 28 Sept. 1804. *d.* Muttra 18 June 1805.

bapt. St. Dunstan-in-the-West 29 Dec. 1785. Son of William Robins, of Fleet St., London, goldsmith, and in the common council for Farringdon Without, and Mary his wife.

Services : Posted Lieut. to 12th N.I. in 1805.

Refs. : G.M. 1806, i. 477. Will dated Futtipoor, 21 Apr. 1805 ; proved 5 June 1806.

ROBINS, John Gregory. Ensign. Infantry. Subsequently Lieut. H.M.S. Cadet 1783. Ensign 18 Jan. 1785. Resigned 1789.

Services : Ensign N. Devon Regt. of Mil. 25 Apr. 1781 ; Lieut. do. 3 Aug. 1782 till 23 Mar. 1783. Apptd. Cadet 31 Dec. 1783 ; sailed for India in the *Berrington* 2 Feb. 1784. Fur. 20 Sept. 1786. Ensign H.M. 76th Ft. 2 Nov. 1788 ; Lieut. 77th Ft. 1 Apr. 1789. Retired 13 Dec. 1792.

ROBINSON, Anthony (1761/62-?). Lieutenant. Infantry. *b.* Westmorland 1761/62. Cadet 1780. Ensign 1780. Lieut. 3 June 1781. Struck off 1793. *d.s.p.*

3rd and youngest son of Daniel Robinson, sheriff of co. Westmorland, and Mary his wife, eldest dau. of John Hilton. Brother of Christopher Robinson and kinsman of John Stables, *qq.v.*

Services : Sailed for India in the *Royal Admiral* 3 June 1780, aged 18. Arrived Bombay in 1781, and served with Col. Morgan's detachment in Bombay during First Mahratta War. Lieut. 33rd Bn. Sepoys in July 1787. On fur. in Dec. 1788.

Refs. : Patrician, vi. 404.

ROBINSON, Christopher (1757-1809). Lieutenant. Infantry. *b.* 1757. Cadet 1776. Ensign 9 Mar. 1777. Lieut. 6 Aug. 1778. Struck off 1793. *d.* Penrith Dec. 1809, aged 52.

Of Skersgill, Cumberland. 2nd son of Daniel Robinson and Mary his wife. Brother of Anthony Robinson, *q.v. m.* (before 1789) Mary Bradley.

Services : Apptd. Cadet 19 Dec. 1775 ; sailed for India in the *Earl of Sandwich* 6 Jan. 1776. Qmr. at Chunar fort in 1785. Fur. 19 Dec. 1785 till struck off.

Refs. : Patrician, vi. 404. *M.M.* xxviii. 636.

THE BENGAL ARMY, 1758-1834

ROBINSON, David (1810-1834). Lieutenant, 65th N.I. *bapt* Drumcree, co. Armagh, 14 Jan. 1810. Cadet 1826. Arrived in India 5 June 1827. Ensign 3 Feb. 1827. Lieut. 2 Nov. 1827. *d.* Bhopawar, C.I. (or Bhusawar, Rajputana), 15 Oct. 1834.
Son of Thomas Robinson, of Drumcree, " gentleman farmer."
Services : Posted Ensign to 65th N.I. 19 June 1827. Actg. Adjt. 5th Local Horse 27 Jan. 1834. No record of active service.
Refs. : A.J. N.S. xvi. 272.

ROBINSON, Edward (*d.* 1781). Captain, Engineers. Cadet (?) Ensign 23 Oct. 1773. Lieut. 14 Dec. 1775. Capt. 29 Jan. 1781. *d.* Bhagulpur Nov. 1781, of dropsy.
Services : Employed on survey work in 1780. First Mahratta War 1780-1 ; on survey with Major William Popham's detachment.
Refs. : India Gazette, 8 Dec. 1781. M.I. at Bhagulpur.

ROBINSON, Edward Innes (1811-1856). Major. 7th L.C. *b.* London 13 Oct. 1811. Cadet 1828. Arrived in India 7 Sept. 1829. Cornet 27 Aug. 1829. Lieut. 3 Sept. 1838. Capt. 13 Jan. 1849. Retired 1 Nov. 1853. Hon. Major 28 Nov. 1854. *d. unm.* Victoria St., Pimlico, 3 Dec. 1856, of bronchitis.
5th and youngest son of Sir George Abercrombie Robinson, Bart., *q.v.*, and Margaret Southwell his wife.
Services : Leave s.c. 7 mos. to Hills 5 Apr. 1830. Actg. Cornet (having been 2 yrs. in India) 4th L.C. 27 Oct. 1831 ; d.d. 10th L.C. 14 Nov. 1832 ; posted Cornet to 7th L.C. 20 Aug. 1833. Second in comd. 3rd Local Horse 28 Sept. 1833. Leave s.c. to Simla 15 Apr. 1834 till 31 Jan. 1836. Asst. in *Thagi* Dept. 24 Feb. 1836. Leave s.c. to Simla 1 Oct. 1836 till 1 Oct. 1837. Asst. to Comr. at Delhi 9 Dec. 1837 ; offg. Asst. to P.A. Ludhiana 3 Nov. 1838 ; resumed appt. at Delhi 9 Feb. 1839. Offg. Supt. of Bhatti territories 3 Aug. 1839 ; permanent do., and Asst. to A.G.G. Rajputana, 1 Sept. 1842 till 1852. Fur. s.c. 2 yrs. to Egypt and S. Europe 13 Dec. 1843. Leave s.c. 2 yrs. to N.S.W. 18 Apr. 1852 till retirement. No record of active service.
Refs. : Burke's *Peerage*, 1923, p. 1887, *s.n.* Robinson, Bart., of Batts House. *G.M.* 1857, i. 122.

ROBINSON, George (*d.* 1768). Fireworker, Artillery. (80) Cadet 1767. Fireworker 15 Sept. 1767. *d.* in India 1768.
Services : Held a Warrant as Cadet in R.A.

ROBINSON, Sir George Abercrombie, first baronet (1758-1832). Captain. 2nd Bengal Eur. Regt. Mily. Auditor Gen.

b. 29 Mar. 1758. Country Cadet 1779. Admitted 19 Aug. 1779. Ensign 8 Oct. 1779. Lieut. 18 May 1781. Capt. 31 Aug. 1798. Retired 27 Oct. 1802. *d.* Dyrham rectory, nr. Bath, 13 Feb. 1832. 1st Bart. of Batts House, Somerset. *cr.* 11 Nov. 1823. M.P. for Honiton ; Chairman E.I. Co. Son of John Robinson, of Calcutta, and Margaret his 2nd wife, dau. of George Leslie, of Kincraigie. *m.* Calcutta 27 Mar. 1794, Margaret Southwell, natural dau. of Thomas, 14th Earl of Suffolk and Berkshire. (She died 31 May 1824.) Father of Edward Innes Robinson, *q.v.*

Services : Ensign 1/3rd Bengal Eur. Regt, in Oct. 1779. A.D.C. to Maj.-Gen. Giles Stibbert, *q.v.*, 1783-5. Actg. Comy. Gen. Bengal 28 Feb. 1786 ; permanent do. 23 May 1786. A.D.C. to Lord Cornwallis, the G.G., 26 Sept. 1788. Head Asst. in Mily. Auditor Gen.'s office 1788-92. Ordered to embark for Madras 9 Nov. 1790, and make enquiries regarding stores, grain and cattle. Garr. Storekeeper at Ft. Wm. and Sec. to Mily. Board. Mily. Auditor Gen. 31 Oct. 1798. Accompanied Cornwallis to India on his second appt. as G.G. as his Pte. Sec., and held that office from 30 July till 5 Oct. 1805. Returned to England. Dir. E.I. Co. 13 Apr. 1808 till 20 Mar. 1829 ; Chairman 1820-1 and 1826-7. Sometime M.P. for Honiton.

Refs. : Burke's *Peerage*, 1923, p. 1887, *s.n.* Robinson, Bart., of Batts House. *D.I.B. List of Pte. Secs. to G.G. A.J.* N.S. vii. 166. *G.M.* 1832, i. 270.

ROBINSON, G—— Gowan. Captain. Infantry. Capt. 1762. Resigned 30 July 1762.

(*Probably* brother of John Gowan Robinson, *q.v.*)
Services : N.F.P.

ROBINSON, George Henry (1794-1850). Bt. Major. 34th N.I. *bapt.* Abergavenny 1 Dec. 1794. Cadet 1810. Admitted 21 Jan. 1812. Ensign 13 Dec. 1813. Lieut. 23 Jan. 1817. Capt. 19 May 1825. Bt. Major 28 June 1838. Retired 14 Aug. 1839. *d.* Clifton 19 Mar. 1850, aged 56.

3rd son of George Robinson, of Bath, J.P. and D.L. co. Surrey, Middlesex and Somerset, ex-Govr. of Senegal, and Elizabeth Grace his wife, dau. of Milward Rowe, chief clerk of the Treasury. *m.* Wimborne Minster 8 May 1838, Laura Maria, 2nd dau. of Frederick Nicolay, of the Treasury, and sister of Frederick Granville Nicolay, *q.v.* (She died Bath 8 Dec. 1881, aged 71.) Haileybury 1809-11.

Services : Posted Ensign to 1/17th N.I. in 1814. Served with Champaran L.I. 1814-20. Nepal War 1814-15 and 1816 ; Ensign

THE BENGAL ARMY, 1758-1834

Champaran L.I. d.d. escort to Resdt. in Nepal 15 Mar. 1820; comdd. do. at Katmandu 4 Feb. 1826 till 28 Nov. 1836. Transfd. to 35th N.I. (late 2/17th) May 1824; to 34th N.I. 13 May 1825. Fur. p.a. 14 Feb. 1837 till retirement.

Refs.: Burke's *Landed Gentry*, 13th edn., p. 1510, *s.n.* Robinson, of Poston Court, co. Hereford. *A.J.* N.S. xxix. 158. *I.M.* 2 Apr. 1850, p. 211. *G.M.* 1850, i. 554.

ROBINSON, James (*d.* 1806). Lieut. Colonel, Artillery. (184) Asst. Surg. 9 Mar. 1778. Cadet (Art.) 9 Sept. 1778. Fireworker 29 Oct. 1778. Lieut. 23 June 1783. Capt. 23 Jan. 1794. Major 28 May 1804. Lt. Col. 21 Sept. 1804. *d. unm.* Cawnpore 27 Feb. 1806.

Services: Second Mysore War 1781-5; Lieut. F. 5th Coy. 1st Bn. Lieut. 1st Bn. in July 1787. To Madras on service June 1794; Capt. 4th Coy. 2nd Bn. Operations in Jumna Doab 1803; Sasni; Capt. 4th Coy. 2nd Bn. Second Mahratta War 1803-5; Aligarh; Delhi; Agra; Capt. comdg. 4th Coy. 2nd Bn.

Refs.: Roll of I.M.S. No. B.218. Will dated 8 Dec. 1805; proved 12 Apr. 1806.

ROBINSON, John Brown (1805-1830). Lieutenant, 61st N.I. *b.* London 5 Nov. 1805. Cadet 1821. Ensign 19 Jan. 1822. Lieut. 3 Oct. 1824. *d.* Fatehgarh, U.P., 2 June 1830.

bapt. St. George's, Hanover Sq., 30 Nov. 1805. Son of George Robinson, of Margaret St., Cavendish Sq., London, and Frances Elizabeth his wife, *née* Brown. Brother of George and Richard Robinson. *m.* St. John's, Calcutta, 27 July 1825, Eliza, sister of William George Cooper, q.v. (*See also* Gordon Caulfeild and Hutton Watkins.) (She died Edinburgh 24 Feb. 1846, aged 48.) Ed. Christ's Hospital.

Services: Posted Ensign to 17th N.I. in 1822; transfd. to 31st N.I. July 1823; to 61st N.I. (late 1/31st) May 1824. Adjt. Farrukhabad Provl. Bn. 11 June 1829 till death. No record of active service.

Refs.: A.J. N.S. iv. 37. Will dated 2 June 1830; proved 29 July 1830. M.I. Fatehgarh fort cemetery.

ROBINSON, John Gowan (*d.* 1775). Captain, Infantry. Lieut. 14 Oct. 1763. Capt. Lt. 3 Aug. 1765. Capt. 20 July 1766. *bur.* Calcutta 14 June 1775.

(*Probably* brother of G. Gowan Robinson, *q.v.*)

Services: Ensign H.M. 84th Ft. 25 Oct. 1762; h.p. do. 25 Dec.

1764 till death. Transfd. to Bengal Eur. Regt. on disbandment of 84th Ft.[1] First Mysore War 1767-70 ; arrived Madras in comd. of a detachment of 240 men of Bengal Eur. Regt. c. Oct. 1767. Joined Col. Champion's Bde. with his Bn. 24 Feb. 1773. (? First Rohilla War ; battle of St. George ; Capt. 2nd Bengal Eur. Regt.) Comdg. a Sepoy Bn. at death.

Refs. : *Wilson,* i. 254. *Macpherson,* p. 124.

[1] *Note :* His name appears in a list of 84th Ft. on 24 June 1765. (*Orme MSS.—India,* vii.) " Gowan " often appears as " Gowin."

ROBINSON, Philip (*d.* 1768). Cadet, Artillery. (87) Cadet 1768. *d.* 17 Oct. 1768.

Services : N.F.P.

ROBINSON, Thomas (1760/61-1794). Lieutenant, Infantry. *b.* London 1760/61. Cadet 1780. Ensign 1780. Lieut. 30 Aug. 1781. *d.* Cawnpore 10 Sept. 1794.

Services : Apptd. Cadet 17 May 1780 ; sailed for India in the *Royal George* 27 July 1780, aged 19 ; captured by combined fleets of France and Spain Aug. 1780 ; returned to England from Spain Apr. 1781. Sailed for India in the *Montagu* Sept. 1782 ; arrived in India Aug. 1783. Lieut. 20th Bn. Sepoys in July 1787 and in 1792.

ROBINSON, Thomas (1788-1850). Lieut. Colonel, 23rd N.I. P.A. Meywar. *bapt.* Antrim 17 May 1788. Cadet 1803. Admitted 27 June 1805. Lieut. 29 Mar. 1805. Capt. 11 July 1823. Major 10 May 1834. Lt. Col. 17 Jan. 1841. *d.* Nimach 18 June 1850, aged 63.

b. 12 May 1788. Son of Samuel Robinson, of Antrim. Brother of Skeffington Robinson, of 1 Crown Court, London, of James, Samuel, Elizabeth and Martha, and nephew of John Robinson, of Rosalie and Brookhills estates, W.I.

Services : Posted Lieut. to 1/2nd N.I. in 1806. Comdd. guard of Resdt. at Indore 25 Sept. 1820 till 1827. Transfd. as Capt. to newly-formed 32nd N.I. July 1823 ; to 64th N.I. (late 2/32nd) May 1824. Apptd. to a civil situation at Indore 26 Oct. 1827 ; 2nd Asst. to Resdt. at Indore 21 Feb. 1828 ; 1st do. 10 June 1831 till 1838 ; in charge of Indore Residency 2 Dec. 1833 till 8 Apr. 1834. Offg. P.A. Meywar 22 Dec. 1838 ; P.A. Kotah 5 June 1839 ; do. Meywar 24 Feb. 1841 till death. Posted Lt. Col. to 1st Eur. L.I. 1841 ; to 39th N.I. 14 Nov. 1843 ; to 23rd N.I. in 1844. No record of active service.

THE BENGAL ARMY, 1758-1834

Refs. : I.M. 19 Aug. 1850, p. 485. Will dated Nimach, 27 June 1844 ; proved 29 Oct. 1850. M.I. Nimach.

ROCH or ROACH, John Odell (1759/60-?). Captain. 10th N.I. *b.* in Ireland 1759/60. Cadet 1781. Ensign 1 June 1781. Lieut. 28 Aug. 1782. Capt. 7 Jan. 1796. Retired 31 Oct. 1798. (In *E.I.R.* for Dec. 1821, not in Aug. 1822.)

(*Probably* son of James Roch, of Odell Lodge and Woodbine Hill, co. Waterford, and Isabella his wife, dau. of John Osborne Odell, of Mount Odell, co. Waterford.)

Services : Apptd. Cadet 11 May 1781 ; sailed for India in the *Earl of Chesterfield* 26 June 1781, aged 21. Lieut. 3rd Bn. Sepoys in July 1787. Third Mysore War ; Bangalore ; operations before Savandrug ; Seringapatam ; Lieut. 3rd Bn. Sepoys. 2nd Bengal Eur. Regt. in 1796.

Refs. : (? Burke's *Landed Gentry of Ireland,* p. 599, *s.n.* Roch, of Woodbine Hill, co. Waterford. Burke's *Family Records,* p. 512.)

ROCHE, Robert (1787-1820). Lieutenant, 25th N.I. *bapt.* Rotterdam, Holland, 1 Aug. 1787. Cadet 1805. Arrived in India 11 July 1806. Ensign 9 Aug. 1806. Lieut. 21 Apr. 1809. *d.* Chinsura 14 Dec. 1820, aged 33.

Son of Peter Roche, merchant, and Elizabeth his wife. *m.* Chinsura 31 May 1809, Margaretha Louisa, youngest dau. of Dr. Jacob Plusker. (*See also* George Holroyd Alley.) His daus. *m.* Samuel Robinson Bagshawe and John Finnis, *qq.v.*

Services : Barasat C.C. Posted Ensign to 25th N.I. in 1807. Nepal War 1814-15 ; Lieut. 2/25th N.I., in 4th Div. Nepal War 1816 ; Chirriaghati ; Makwanpur ; Lieut. 2/25th N.I., in 3rd Bde. Centre Column. d.d. Rangpur Bn. 1817-19.

Refs. : M.I. in Chinsura cemetery.

ROCHFORD, Henry. Captain. Infantry. Cadet 1780. Admitted 1780. Ensign 27 Sept. 1780. Lieut. 2 July 1781. Capt. 7 Jan. 1796. Struck off 14 Mar. 1798.

(*Perhaps* Henry Rochfort, 4th and youngest son of William Rochfort, of Clontarf (who was younger brother of Robert, 1st Earl of Belvidere), and Henrietta his wife, dau. of Col. John Ramsay. His sister *m.* Edward Ellerker, *q.v.* *d.* in Surrey 1821.)

Services : Apptd. Cadet 3 Dec. 1779 ; sailed for India in the *Duke of Portland* 12 Feb. 1780. Lieut. 6th Bn. Sepoys in July 1787 and in 1792. Fur. 15 Feb. 1793 (? till struck off).

Refs. : (? Ruvigny's *Plantagenet Roll of the Blood Royal,* Essex Vol., p. 210. Will proved 8 Sept. 1821.)

ROCK, Thomas B—— (*d.* 1793). Lieutenant, 16th Bn. Sepoys. Country Cadet 1780. Ensign 31 Jan. 1781. Lieut. 6 Oct. 1781. *d.* Dacca 8 Oct. 1793.

Services: Apptd. a Gent. Vol. in the Coy. of Art. 3 Apr. 1780. Lieut. 2nd Bengal Eur. Bn. in July 1787; transfd. to 16th Bn. Sepoys Mar. 1790.

ROCKE, Frederick Becher (1799-?). Lieutenant. 5th L.C. *b.* Calcutta 6 Nov. 1799. Cadet 1819. Cornet 2 Feb. 1820. Lieut. 1 May 1824. Resigned in India 12 Feb. 1830.

bapt. Calcutta 4 Feb. 1800. Son of Richard Rocke, B.C.S., Senior Member, Board of Revenue, Calcutta, and Sarah Susannah Pattle his wife. Brother of Thomas James Rocke, *q.v.* (Perhaps nephew of Henry John Pattle, *q.v.*) *m.* St. John's, Calcutta, 17 Jan. 1825, Eliza Mary, youngest dau. of John Scott (1781-1832), *q.v.* Ed. Harrow 1810-15. Sandhurst Cadet.

Services: Cornet 24th Light Dgns. 15 Feb. 1816; Lieut. do. 24 June 1819. To do duty with G.G.B.G. 21 July 1820. Intr. & Qmr. 5th L.C. 27 Feb. 1821 till 18 Oct. 1824. Fur. 1825-7.

Refs.: Harrow School Register. V.B.G.

ROCKE, Thomas James (1803-1881). Lieutenant. 69th N.I. Subsequently vicar of Littleham with Exmouth. *b.* Berhampore, Bengal, 22 Nov. 1803. Cadet 1821. Ensign 3 Dec. 1821. Lieut. 2 May 1824. Struck off 15 Aug. 1826. *d.* Guildford, Surrey, 30 Aug. 1881.

bapt. Berhampore 16 Jan. 1804. Son of Richard Rocke, B.C.S., and Sarah Susannah his wife. Brother of Frederick Becher Rocke, *q.v. m.* 1st, Hallow 18 June 1828, (? his cousin) Lucy, eldest dau. of Very Rev. Thomas Hill Peregrine Furye Lowe, dean of Exeter. (She died Exmouth 6 Aug. 1865, aged 56.) *m.* 2nd, Kensington 7 Dec. 1876, Emily Adelaide, youngest dau. of Maj.-Gen. George Mackie, C.B., and widow of Arthur Dewes. Ed. Westminster 5 Apr. 1815 till 2 Nov. 1821. Downing Coll., Camb.; B.A. 1829; M.A. 1849.

Services: Posted Ensign to 6th N.I. in 1822. Transfd. to 24th N.I. in 1823; to 47th N.I. (late 1/24th) May 1824; to newly-raised 69th N.I. (late 47th) Nov. 1824. Fur. u.p.a. 1 yr. without pay 28 Jan. 1825 till struck off. No record of active service. Took holy orders; Deacon 1829; Priest 1830. Rector of Holy Trinity, Exeter, 5 Oct. 1839. Vicar of Littleham with Exmouth 1843-77.

Refs.: Howard & Crisp, xvi. 149, *s.n.* Lowe. Burke's *Landed Gentry*, 2nd edn., p. 767, *s.n.* Lowe, of Bromsgrove. *Westminster*

THE BENGAL ARMY, 1758-1834   685

School Register. Graduati Cantab. Crockford. The Times, 2 Sept. 1881.

RODBER, John (Pole) (1786-1858). Colonel. Artillery. (334) *bapt.* Melcombe Regis, Dorset, 5 June 1786. Cadet 1803. Arrived in India 27 Sept. 1804. Lieut. 23 Aug. 1804. Capt. Lt. 16 Sept. 1807. Capt. 1 Oct. 1816. Major 1 May 1824. Lt. Col. 27 Sept. 1830. Retired 27 Jan. 1837. Hon. Col. 28 Nov. 1854. *d.* Hotel Metropole, Geneva, 6 Nov. 1858, aged 73.

Son of Thomas Rodber and Catharine his wife. Woolwich Cadet; nominated to R.M.A. 14 Feb. 1804; obtained his certificate 2 Mar. 1804.

Services: Posted to 3rd Troop H.A. 4 Oct. 1809. Nepal War 1814-15; Kalanga; Capt. Lt. 3rd Troop, in 2nd Div. (? India medal). Siege and capture of Hathras; Capt. 3rd Troop. Third Mahratta War; action at Seoni, Berar, 17 Apr. 1818; storm and capture of Chanda; Capt. 6th Troop. Fur. s.c. 15 Dec. 1826 till 11 Nov. 1831. Posted to 3rd Bde. H.A. 22 Oct. 1830; to 2nd Bde. 27 Sept. 1831; to 3rd Bde. 1 Oct. 1832.

Refs.: G.M. 1859, i. 73. *I.M.* 29 Nov. 1858, p. 960. *The Times*, 24 Nov. 1858.

ROEBUCK, Benjamin (1797-1818). Lieutenant, 6th N.I. *b.* Edinburgh 18 Jan. 1797. Cadet 1813. Ensign 28 Nov. 1814. Lieut. 16 Nov. 1817. *d.* Agra 31 Dec. 1818.

Son of John Roebuck, of Baxter's Bldgs., Edinburgh, later of London, civil engineer, and Jane Livingstone his wife. Grandson of John Roebuck, M.D., the inventor (*D.N.B.*), and brother of George Douglas Roebuck, *q.v.*, and Capt. Thomas Roebuck, 17th Madras N.I., the orientalist (*D.N.B.*).

Services: Posted Ensign to 1/6th N.I. in 1815. No record of active service.

ROEBUCK, George Douglas (1800-1846). Major, 71st N.I. *b.* Edinburgh 19 Oct. 1800. Cadet 1817. Admitted 26 Sept. 1818. Ensign 16 Mar. 1818. Lieut. 9 Sept. 1818. Capt. 3 June 1830. Major 7 Sept. 1845. *d.* Mainpuri, U.P., 9 July 1846.

Son of John Roebuck and Jane Livingstone his wife. Brother of Benjamin Roebuck, *q.v.* *m.* Edinburgh 15 Apr. 1830, Henrietta, 2nd dau. of T. Andrew.

Services: Posted Lieut. to 2/23rd N.I. in 1818. Adjt. Mhairwara Local Bn. 18 July 1822 till 7 June 1823, and 16 July 1823 till 13 Apr. 1826. Transfd. to newly-raised 33rd N.I. July 1823; to 65th N.I.

(late 1/33rd) May 1824; to 3rd Extra Regt. (became 71st N.I.)
13 May 1825. Fur. p.a. 7 Oct. 1828 till 14 Sept. 1830. No record
of active service.
Refs.: *A.J.* N.S. ii. 56.

ROGERS, Charles (1788-1861). Lieut. Colonel. 20th N.I.
b. Liverpool 16 Jan. 1788. Cadet 1806. Arrived in India 2 Dec.
1807. Ensign 4 Nov. 1807. Lieut. 3 Dec. 1813. Capt. 22 Oct.
1824. Major 8 Feb. 1841. Retired 14 Mar. 1843. Hon. Lt.
Col. 28 Nov. 1854. *d.* Gloucester Terr., Hyde Pk., London,
19 Aug. 1861.

Son of ——— Rogers and Sarah his wife. Brother of Edward
Rogers. *m.* Shahjahanpur, U.P., 3 Feb. 1817, Charlotte, only dau.
of Alexander Wright, B.C.S. (She died Hazaribagh 1 Nov. 1817,
aged 23.)

Services: Barasat C.C. 7 mos. Posted Ensign to 5th N.I. in
1808. d.d. Ramgarh Bn. 1810; Adjt. do. 23 Aug. 1812 till 1818.
Leave s.c. 6 mos. to sea 1 Oct. 1813. Nepal War 1814-15; Lieut.
Ramgarh Bn., in 4th Div. Leave s.c. 10 mos. to Cape 27 Oct. 1815.
Comdd. escort to Resdt. at Katmandu 9 Oct. 1819 till 14 Sept. 1822.
Fur. p.a. 13 Oct. 1822 till 12 Dec. 1826. Transfd. to 20th N.I.
(late 2/5th) May 1824. Actg. Bde. Major to troops in Bundelkhand
3 Mar. 1830. D.J.A.G. on Est. 6 Apr. 1832; Saugor Div. 4 May
1832; Cawnpore Div. 21 Mar. 1835. Leave s.c. 2 yrs. to Cape
25 Nov. 1835. Postmr. at Cawnpore 24 Feb. 1840. Fur. s.c.
25 Jan. 1841 till retirement.
Refs.: *G.M.* 1861, ii. 336.

ROGERS, Charles (1805-1841). Captain, 3rd N.I. *b.* Clonanagh,
Queen's Co., 26 July 1805. Cadet 1824. Arrived in India
24 Nov. 1825. Ensign 13 May 1825. Lieut. 6 Jan. 1827. Capt.
8 July 1839. *d.* Barrackpore 18 Apr. 1841.

Brother of Joseph Rogers, of Mountrath, Queen's Co.
Services: Posted Ensign to 3rd N.I. and served throughout with
that Regt. Shekhawat expedn. 1834; Lieut. 3rd N.I.

ROGERS, John (1813-1839). 2nd Lieutenant, Artillery. (658)
bapt. Lewes, Sussex, 3 Dec. 1813. Cadet 1832. Arrived in
India 19 June 1833. 2nd Lieut. 14 Dec. 1832. *d.* Sabathu,
Punjab, 23 May 1839.

Son of Thomas Attree Rogers and Mary Elizabeth his wife.
Addiscombe Cadet 1 Feb. 1831 till 14 Dec. 1832.
Services: Supy. 2nd Lieut. d.d. Art. at Dum-Dum. Fur. s.c.

15 Aug. 1834 till 8 July 1837. Brought on effective strength of Art. and posted to 3rd Troop 2nd Bde. H.A. May 1836 ; transfd. to 3rd Coy. 5th Bn. Art. 4 Aug. 1837. Leave s.c. to Simla and Sabathu 25 Apr. 1838 till death. No record of active service.
Refs.: De Rhé-Philipe. M.I. at Sabathu.

ROGERS, Levi (1785-1804). Lieutenant, 20th N.I. *bapt.* Maenclochog, co. Pembroke, 15 Apr. 1785. Cadet 1799. Arrived in India 9 June 1801. Ensign 4 Nov. 1800. Lieut. 13 July 1803. *d.* Trincomali, Ceylon, 7 Nov. 1804, of fever contracted in Kandy.
Son of John Rogers and Lettice his wife.
Services : Posted Ensign to 2/3rd N.I. 17 Apr. 1801 ; served with 2nd Vol. Bn. in Ceylon 1803 till death ; transfd. to 20th N.I. in 1804.
Refs.: Calcutta Monthly Journal, Dec. 1804, p. 931. Intestate ; admon. 9 Apr. 1805.

ROGERS, William (1810-1828). Cadet, Infantry. *bapt.* ptely. Feniton, Devon, 7 Nov. 1810. Cadet 1827. *d.* on the Ganges R. 14 Aug. 1828.
Son of Rev. John Rogers, rector of Feniton, and Lucy his wife.
Services : d.d. 42nd N.I. 31 July 1828.

ROKER, James (*d.* 1791). Lieutenant, 32nd Bn. Sepoys. Country Cadet 1778. Ensign 31 Mar. 1778. Lieut. 25 Aug. 1779. *d.* Dinapore 29 Aug. 1791.
m. Calcutta 4 Oct. 1788, Miss Ann Robinson. (She died Calcutta 16 Apr. 1841.)
Services : Apptd. Cadet 27 Feb. 1778. Was Adjt. 6th Regt. Sepoys in Mar. 1786 ; Adjt. 32nd Bn. 1786 till death.

ROLLAND, George (1783-1807). Lieutenant, 9th N.I. *b.* Alloa 1 Apr. 1783. Cadet 1799. Admitted 16 Apr. 1801. Ensign 13 Mar. 1801. Lieut. 21 Jan. 1803. *d.* 25 Nov. 1807, of wounds received at the siege of Komona.
bapt. Alloa 12 Apr. 1783. Son of William Rolland, of N. Burnside of Saline, merchant in Alloa, and Janet Stewart his wife. Brother of William Rolland, merchant in Dunfermline.
Services : Socond Mahratta War ; pursuit of Holkar 1805-6 ; Lieut. 1/9th N.I. Operations against Dhundia Khan 1807 ; siege of Komona (s.w.) ; Lieut. 1/9th N.I.
Refs.: A.A.R. x. 21. Will dated 1 Nov. 1807 ; proved 21 Jan. 1808.

ROLLAND, John (1760-1801). Bt. Captain, 7th N.I. *b.* Culross, co. Fife, 18 Feb. 1760. Cadet 1782. Admitted 23 July 1783. Ensign 5 Feb. 1783. Lieut. 17 Jan. 1790. Bt. Capt. 8 Jan. 1796. *d. unm.* Fatehgarh 19 Sept. 1801.

Eldest son of Rev. Robert Rolland, minister of Culross 1758-1815, and Antonetta his wife, dau. of Adam Rolland, of Gask and Luscar, W.S. Glasgow Univ.; matric. 1774; M.A. 1778.

Services: Apptd. Cadet 28 Mar. 1782; sailed for India in the *Busbridge* 11 Sept. 1782. Ensign 5th Bengal Eur. Bn. in July 1787; 29th Bn. Sepoys in Dec. 1788 and in 1792; Bt. Capt. 2/6th N.I. in July 1798; transfd. to 1/7th N.I. 1798.

Refs.: Scott's *Fasti*, v. 17. *S.M.* 1802, p. 446. Will dated Fatehgarh, 18 Sept. 1801; proved 29 Oct. 1801.

ROMAN, Joseph.[1] Captain. Infantry. Cadet 1764. Bt. Ensign 1766. Lieut. 2 Oct. 1769. Capt. 20 July 1772. Invalided 20 Jan. 1782. Resigned 29 Feb. 1792. (*d.* before 1796.) Born a subject of the King of Sardinia.

Services : Assault of Chunar fort Dec. 1764; Cadet under Major C. Pemble, *q.v.* Posted as tempy. Ensign to Pioneer Coy. 5 Dec. 1764. Campaign against the Rajah of Benares 1781; Bijaigarh. Capt. comdg. 1st Bn. Native Invalids at Chunar in July 1787. Letter from the Marquis de Cordon, Minister from the Court of Turin, to Lord Weymouth, dated Jan. 1777 : " Le nommé Roman, né sujet du Roi de Sardaigne, employé depuis long temps dans le Service militaire de la Comp. des Indes Orientales avec rang du Capitaine, a écrit une lettre dattée de Dacca au Bengal le 28 nov. 1775 à l'Envoye du Roi de Sardaigne à Londres pour lui demander son appuy et son interposition d'auprès des administrateurs de lade [*sic*] compagnie à fin de lui procurer quelque avancement."

Refs.: I.O. Rec., Home Misc. Series, 128 (2).

[1] *Note :* His christian name is given as James in the MS. *A.L.* for July 1787.

ROMNEY, Peter. Cadet. Cavalry. Country Cadet 1778. Resigned 9 Sept. 1778.

(*Possibly* nephew or cousin of George Romney, the artist, whose younger brother James was Lt. Col. on the Bombay Est.)

Services: Apptd. Cadet for Cav. 11 Aug. 1778, on the recommendation of Edward Wheler, Member of the Supreme Council.

ROOKE, George. Captain. Infantry. Country Cadet 1765. Ensign 13 Nov. 1765. Lieut. 28 May 1767. Capt. 26 June 1771. Resigned 17 Jan. 1774.

THE BENGAL ARMY, 1758-1834 689

m. Calcutta 25 Nov. 1769, Phillis, widow of Samuel Bartholomew Case, B.C.S. His dau. Phillis (*bapt.* Calcutta 16 Oct. 1770 ; *d.* 28 Dec. 1832) *m.* Capt. Edward Seymour Bailey, R.N., of Wheddon Park, Devon.
Services : Came out to India in a private capacity. Fur. Jan. 1774 ; permitted to return to India in the *York* via Bombay without prejudice to his rank, Oct. 1777. (? *d.* on the voyage out.)

ROOKE, Peter (*d.* 1770). Ensign, Infantry. Cadet (?) Ensign 1770. *d.* 1770.[1]
Services : N.F.P.
[1] *Note :* His death has not been traced. *Possibly* identical with the next.

*ROOKE,[1] **Robert** (*d.* 1769). Fireworker. Artillery. (62) Cadet 1763. Fireworker 23 Apr. 1764. Resigned (?) *bur.* Calcutta 1 June 1769.
Services : Apptd. Adjt. & Qmr. 2nd Coy. Art. 1 Sept. 1765. Not in *A.L.* of 1 Feb. 1767. *Probably* resigned his Commission in May 1766 during the " Batta mutiny."
Refs. : Stubbs's List.
[1] *Note :* Rook in the burial register.

ROOPE, Benjamin (1780-1855). Lieut. General. Colonel 23rd N.I. *bapt.* Churston Ferrers, Devon, 16 Oct. 1780. Cadet 1798. Arrived in Bombay 6 Dec. 1799. Ensign 21 Nov. 1799. Lieut. 29 May 1800. Capt. 4 May 1812. Major 11 July 1823. Lt. Col. 13 May 1825. Col. (18 June 1831) 29 Nov. 1834. Maj. Gen. 3 Nov. 1841. Lt. Gen. 11 Nov. 1851. *d.* Kittery Court, Kingswear, Devon, 5 Dec. 1855, aged 75.
Son of Roope Harris Roope, of Chipton, Devon, and Mary his wife. *m.* Cawnpore 30 Jan. 1812, Maria, dau. of James Rotton, *q.v.*
Services : Posted Lieut. to 1/6th N.I. 15 Apr. 1801 ; transfd. to newly-raised 23rd N.I. in 1804. Operations against Dhundia Khan 1807 ; Komona ; Ganauri ; Lieut. 1/23rd N.I. Capt. Lt. 23rd N.I. 28 Sept. 1810. Apptd. Bde. Major 2nd Inf. Bde., Nagpur Subsdy. Force 14 Nov. 1817. Third Mahratta War ; storm and capture of Chanda 1818 ; Capt. 1/23rd N.I., Bde. Major. With 3rd Ceylon Vol. Bn. 1819. Posted Major to newly-raised 31st N.I. July 1823 ; to 62nd N.I. (late 2/31st) May 1824 ; Lt. Col. to 49th N.I. May 1825. First Burma War ; Arakan 1825 ; Lt. Col. 49th N.I. (? India medal). Transfd. to 44th N.I. 5 Mar. 1828 ; to 52nd N.I. 29 Dec. 1828 ; to 12th N.I. ; to 19th N.I. 27 Oct. 1832. Posted

Col. to 19th N.I. 8 Jan. 1835 ; to 24th N.I. 11 Dec. 1837. Fur. p.a.
3 Feb. 1828 till death. Col. 23rd N.I. 1846 till death.
Refs. : Boase. G.M. 1856, i. 102.

ROPER, Thomas (*d.* 1769). Captain, Infantry. Lieut. 11 Oct.
1763. Capt. Lt. 11 Dec. 1764. Capt. 7 Aug. 1765. *d.* 1769.
Services : Ensign H.M. 84th (from Surgeon's Mate) 25 June 1762 ;
h.p. do. 25 Dec. 1764. Transfd. to Bengal Army as Capt. Lt.
11 Dec. 1764 ; Capt. 3rd Bengal Eur. Regt. in 1766. Resigned
during the " Batta mutiny " in May 1766 ; readmitted later.
Refs. : Broome, p. lix.

ROSAT, David (*d.* 1769). Captain, Artillery. (37) Fireworker
(R.A.) 15 Aug. 1760. 2nd Lieut. (R.A.) 12 Apr. 1768. Capt.
(Bengal Art.) 1 Sept. 1768. *d.* 1769.
Services : Was an instructor at R.M.A., Woolwich, in Dec. 1764.
Transfd. as Capt. to Bengal Art. Sept. 1768. " Capt. Rosatt [*sic*]
is to take rank in the Art. next below Capt. Bailey (W. A. Bailie,
q.v.), and in the Army next below Capt. Horsefall." [1] (M.C. 1 Sept.
1768.)
Refs. : Kane, No. 390.
[1] *Note :* Capt. Christopher Horsefall—see Appendix B.

ROSE, Alexander (1736/37-1769). Captain, Infantry. *b.*
1736/37.[1] Transfd. as Capt. from H.M.S. Arrived in India
Sept. 1768. Capt. 1 Sept. 1768. *d.* Calcutta 17 Oct. 1769.
A native of Scotland. Brother of Capt. Hugh Rose.[2]
Services : Ensign H.M. 54th Foot (renumbered 52nd in 1756)
1 Jan. 1756 ; Lieut. 52nd Foot 7 May 1757 ; renewed 27 Oct. 1760 ;
Capt. Lt. do. 25 Feb. 1767 ; left 27 Apr. 1768. Sailed for India
in the *Grenville* 7 Apr. 1768. Transfd. as Capt. to Bengal Army
(M.C. 1 Sept. 1768). Carried out surveys in Muzaffarpur and Saran
districts.
Refs. : Will dated 26 Dec. 1768 ; proved 31 Oct. 1769.
[1] *Note :* His age is given as 20 yrs. in a Return of H.M. 52nd Ft.,
dated 16 June 1757.
[2] *Note : Probably* related to the Kilravoch family : the present
head of the family is, however, unable to identify him.

ROSE, Bernard (1764/65-1801). Captain, 7th N.I. *b.* 1764/65.
Country Cadet 1781. Admitted 15 Oct. 1781. Ensign 16 July
1782. Lieut. 13 Jan. 1785. Capt. 7 Jan. 1796. *d. unm.* Fatehgarh 8 Sept. 1801, aged 36.

THE BENGAL ARMY, 1758-1834

Services : Lieut. 4th Bengal Eur. Bn. in July 1787 ; posted to 22nd Bn. Sepoys 31 Oct. 1787 ; transfd. to 1/7th N.I.
Refs. : G.M. 1802, ii. 785. Will dated Fatehgarh, 3 Sept. 1801 ; proved 12 Sept. 1801. M.I. Fatehgarh fort cemetery.

*ROSE, George Henry (1813-1837). Lieutenant, 72nd N.I. *b.* Croy, Nairn, 3 Feb. 1813. Cadet 1828. Admitted 5 Sept. 1829. Ensign (17 Feb. 1829) 14 Sept. 1829. Lieut. 3 Feb. 1835. *d. unm.* in camp at Bhopal 19 Nov. 1837, of cholera, after 12 hours' illness.

3rd son of Hugh Rose, of Kilravock Castle, co. Nairn, Vice-Lieut. co. Nairn, Col. of the Nairnshire Mil., and Katherine his 1st wife, dau. of Col. John Baillie, of Dunain, Inverness.
Services : Posted Ensign to 72nd N.I. Was on leave at the time of his death. No record of active service.
Refs. : Burke's *Landed Gentry*, 12th edn., p. 1627, *s.n.* Rose, of Kilravock Castle, Nairn. *A.J.* N.S. xxv. 257. M.I. Bhopal city and in Mhow church.

ROSE, Hugh (*d.* 1836). Lieut. Colonel. 5th N.C. Cadet 1783. Admitted 26 July 1784. Ensign 2 Jan. 1785. Lieut. 22 June 1790. Capt. 22 Jan. 1802. Major 1 Feb. 1806. Lt. Col. 18 Aug. 1814. Retired 25 May 1816. *d.* 26 Aug. 1836.

Of Holme, co. Inverness. Eldest son of John Rose, of Holme, and Jane his wife, dau. of Alexander Cumming, of Logie, co. Moray. Brother of Sir John Rose, *q.v.*, and of Jane, mother of Colin Troup, *q.v. m.* 10 Sept. 1791, Anne, dau. of Henry Topham, of Sunbury, Middlesex. (She died London 19 June 1856, aged 85.)
Services : Lieut. 76th Regt. of Highland Ft. 14 Jan. 1778. Apptd. Cadet 19 Mar. 1783 ; sailed for India in the *Contractor* 19 Jan. 1784. Fur. 10 May 1789 till 15 Aug. 1791. Transfd. from 2nd Eur. Bn. to 20th Bn. Sepoys 6 Oct. 1792. Lieut. 2nd N.C. in June 1798 ; 1st N.C. in Jan. 1799 ; Capt. Lt. 16 June 1800. Operations in Jumna Doab 1803 ; Sasni ; Bijaigarh ; Kachaura ; Capt. 1st N.C. Second Mahratta War 1803-4 ; Bde. Major. Dy. Paymr. at Cawnpore 1805-13. Major 1st N.C. Fur. 12 Dec. 1813 till retirement. Posted Lt. Col. to 5th N.C.
Refs. : Burke's *Landed Gentry*, 12th edn., p. 1628, *s.n.* Rose, of Holme Rose, co. Inverness. Will dated Holme, 14 Jan. 1836 ; proved 1 July 1837.

ROSE, James (1778-1812). Lieutenant, 5th N.I. *b.* 8 Oct. 1778. Cadet 1799. Arrived in India 6 Jan. 1801. Ensign

16 Oct. 1800. Lieut. 11 Aug. 1802. *d. unm.* Bundelkhand 10 June 1812.

bapt. Chipping Wycombe, Bucks., 12 Oct. 1778. 4th and youngest son of Thomas Rose, of Chipping Wycombe, many times mayor of that borough, and Honor Tett his wife. Uncle of Sir Philip Rose, 1st Bart. of Rayners, Bucks.

Services : Posted Ensign to 1/5th N.I. 17 Apr. 1801. Second Mahratta War ; operations in Cuttack 1804 ; (? capture of Khurda) ; Lieut. 1/5th N.I. Fur. 27 Nov. 1806 till 18 Mar. 1808. Operations in Bundelkhand against Gopal Singh 1810 ; Tirowa ; Lieut. 1/5th N.I.

Refs. : Burke's *Peerage*, 1923, p. 1902, *s.n.* Rose, Bart., of Rayners, Bucks.

ROSE, Sir John (1777-1852). Lieut. General, K.C.B. Colonel 63rd N.I. *b.* Croy, Nairn, 23 July 1777.[1] Cadet 1795. Arrived in India 6 Mar. 1797. Ensign 5 Oct. 1797. Lieut. 30 Oct. 1797. Capt. 18 July 1806. Major 1 May 1813. Lt. Col. 4 Nov. 1817. Lt. Col. Comdt. 1 May 1824. Col. 5 June 1829. Maj. Gen. 10 Jan. 1837. Lt. Gen. 9 Nov. 1846. *d.* Holme, co. Inverness, 9 Sept. 1852.

Of Holme Rose, J.P. 4th and youngest son of John Rose, of Holme, and Jane his wife. Brother of Hugh Rose, *q.v.* *m.* Prescot, Lancs., 16 Feb. 1811, Lilias, dau. of James Fraser, of Culduthel, Inverness, and sister of James Fraser (1800-1868), *q.v.* (She died Upton Park, Slough, May 1855, aged 65.)

Services : Lieut. 5th N.I. in June 1798 ; transfd. to 14th N.I. 1798. Fourth Mysore War ; Malavelli ; Seringapatam ; operations in Mysore ; Lieut. 2nd Vol. Bn. (Medal). Expedn. to Egypt 1801 ; Lieut. Vol. Bn. (Peninsula medal). With Bombay Army in Gujarat 1801-2. Adjt. & Qmr. 14th N.I. 1803-4 and 1806. Second Mahratta War ; Aligarh ; siege of Agra (s.w. 10 Oct. 1803) ; Gwalior ; Dholpur ; battle and defence of Delhi, comdd. a successful sortie 24 Oct. 1804 (*Cal. Gaz.* 8 Nov. 1804) ; pursuit of Holkar 1805 ; Lieut. 1/14th N.I. (India medal). Actg. Bde. Major to Lt.-Col. William Burn, *q.v.*, throughout the operations of 1803-5. Bde. Major at the Presdy. 15 May 1806 till 11 June 1807. Fur. p.a. 8 Feb. 1808 till 3 Dec. 1811. Major 2/14th N.I. Comdd. newly-raised Mirzapur Local Bn. 21 Aug. 1813 till 1816. Nepal War 1815. Posted Lt. Col. to 1/14th N.I. in 1817. Third Mahratta War ; Lt. Col. comdg. 1/14th N.I. Fur. 29 Dec. 1823 till death. Posted Lt. Col. Comdt. to 63rd N.I. May 1824 ; Col. do. 5 June 1829 till death. C.B. 27 Sept. 1831 ; K.C.B. 20 July 1838.

Refs.: Burke's *Landed Gentry*, 13th edn., p. 1523, s.n. Rose, of Holme Rose, co. Inverness. *Boase. D.I.B. E.I.M.C.* iii. 410-13. *Pester*, pp. 199, 337-8. *G.M.* 1811, i. 288; 1852, ii. 528. *Inverness Courier*, 16 and 30 Sept. 1852. Will dated Nairn, 7 Feb. 1852; admon. 7 Nov. 1853.

[1] *Note:* The year of his birth is incorrectly given by Burke as 1779.

ROSS, Andrew Hunter. (*See* **LOCKHART-ROSS, Andrew Hunter.**)

ROSS, Benjamin (*d.* 1790). Lieutenant, 6th Bengal Eur. Bn. Country Cadet 1779. Ensign 24 Aug. 1779. Lieut. 12 Apr. 1781. *d. unm.* Dinapore 19 Jan. 1790.

Younger son of George Ross (who was 6th son of Andrew Ross, VII of Shandwick), merchant at Gothenburg, and Dorothea Switzer his wife.

Services: Apptd. Cadet 19 Aug. 1779. Lieut. 22nd Bn. Sepoys in July 1787; 2nd Bengal Eur. Bn. in Dec. 1788; transfd. to 6th do. 1789.

Refs.: *The Earls of Ross*, by F. N. Reid (Edin. 1894), p. 34. *Scottish Antiquary*, iv. 71.

ROSS, Charles (*d.* 1765). Captain, Bengal European Regt. Capt. 27 July 1764. *d.* May 1765.

Services: Transfd. as Capt. from H.M.S. to Bengal Eur. Regt. Campaign against the Nawabs of Bengal and Oudh 1764-5; Capt. Bengal Eur. Regt.

ROSS, Charles (*d.* 1791). Ensign, 13th Bn. Sepoys. Cadet 1783. Arrived in India 16 Oct. 1783. Ensign 27 Mar. 1785. *d.s.p.* 15 May 1791; kld. in action at the battle of Arikera.

Younger son of William Ross, X of Invercharron, and Anne his wife, dau. of David Ross, II of Inverchasley.

Services: Apptd. Cadet 31 Dec. 1782; sailed for India in the *Atlas* 11 Mar. 1783. Posted to 13th Bn. Sepoys 8 Feb. 1790. Third Mysore War; battle of Arikera (kld.); Ensign 13th Bn.

Refs.: *Scottish Antiquary*, iv. 58. Name on cenotaph erected by Mysore Govt. in Bangalore fort.

ROSS, Charles (1780-1805). Lieutenant, 3rd N.I. *b.* Gladfield, co. Kincardine, 6 Feb. 1780. Cadet 1795. Arrived in India 4 Feb. 1797. Ensign 5 Nov. 1796. Lieut. 30 Oct. 1797. *d.* Bombay 7 June 1805.

Son of Simon Ross, of Gladfield (who was son of Hugh Ross, of Braelangwell).
Services : Leave s.c. 6 mos. to sea 1 Nov. 1804 till death. No record of active service.

ROSS, Charles George (1804-1853). Lieut. Colonel, 73rd N.I. *b.* Edinburgh 6 Oct. 1804. Cadet 1821. Arrived in India 31 Mar. 1823. Ensign 11 July 1823. Lieut. 13 May 1825. Capt. 21 Sept. 1835. Major 22 Nov. 1843. Lt. Col. 28 Mar. 1850. *d.* Biel, co. Haddington, 12 Jan. 1853.

2nd son of Davis Ross, of Calcutta, merchant (who was eldest son of David Ross, Lord Ankerville, one of the Senators of the Coll. of Justice), and Marian his wife, dau. of Lawrence Gall, *q.v.* Brother of David Ross, *q.v. m.* Lucknow, 3 Nov. 1827, Mary Anne, 2nd dau. of William George Maxwell, *q.v. (See also* Charles Henry Boisragon.) (She died 29 Nov. 1887, aged 77.) Ed. Edin. High School and Coll.

Services : Posted Ensign to 3rd N.I. in 1823 ; transfd. to 6th N.I. (late 1/3rd) May 1824 ; as Lieut. to 19th N.I. May 1825. A.D.C. to Bdr.-Gen. A. Knox, *q.v.*, 1 Apr. 1827. D.J.A.G. Nimach 20 Sept. 1830. Leave s.c. to Simla 1 Jan. 1836 till 1 Jan. 1838. D.J.A.G. to Marwar F.F. Aug. till 14 Oct. 1839. Fur. s.c. 2 Jan. 1843 till 1846. Second Sikh War ; Major 19th N.I., in Reserve Div. at Jagraon. Posted Lt. Col. to 19th N.I. in 1850 ; to 30th N.I. Dec. 1851 ; to 43rd N.I. 19 Jan. 1852 ; to 73rd N.I. Mar. 1852. Fur. p.a. 10 Mar. 1852 till death.

Refs. : Burke's *Landed Gentry*, 7th edn., p. 1581, *s.n.* Grove-Ross, of Invercharron, co. Ross. Mackenzie's *Munroes of Fowlis*, pp. 196-7. *A.J.* xxv. 518. *I.M.* 18 Jan. 1853, p. 20. *G.M.* 1853, i. 329.

ROSS, David (1801-1857). Lieut. Colonel, 11th N.I. Comr. at Leiah, Punjab. *b.* Calcutta 8 July 1801. Cadet 1821. Arrived in India 20 Aug. 1822. Ensign 10 Mar. 1822. Lieut. 1 May 1824. Capt. 18 Feb. 1838. Major 1 Oct. 1852. Lt. Col. 27 June 1857. *d.* Leiah 3 Sept. 1857.

Eldest son of David Ross, of Calcutta, merchant, and Marian his wife. Brother of Lawrence Ross, *q.v.*, and stepson of Alexander Mackay, 8th Baron Reay.

Services : Ensign d.d. Sindhia's Contingent Sept. 1822, and remained with it for 11 yrs. Posted Ensign to 1/2nd N.I. Oct. 1822. Transfd. to 1/26th N.I. Sept. 1823 ; to 51st N.I. (late 1/26th) May 1824, but never actually joined either of these Corps, although

THE BENGAL ARMY, 1758-1834

borne on the rolls of the latter for nearly 34 yrs. On active service with Sindhia's Contingent against rebels 1824-5 and 1828. Second in comd. Sindhia's Contingent 4 Mar. 1831. Apptd. Asst. to Resdt. at Gwalior 3 Apr. 1833 ; offg. Supt. Bhatti territory 10 Mar. 1838 ; Supt. Jhansi territory 22 Nov. 1838 till 1845. On service against fort Kairura, Bundelkhand, Apr. 1841. Supt. of Jalaun, U.P. Offg. Asst. to A.G.G. for affairs of Sindhia's dominions May 1848 till Mar. 1849. Comr. at Leiah 13 Apr. 1849 till death. Fur. p.a. Mar. till 23 Oct. 1855. Posted Lt. Col. to 11th N.I. 2 Sept. 1857, the day before his death.

Refs. : Burke's *Landed Gentry*, 7th edn., p. 1581, *s.n.* Grove-Ross, of Invercharron, co. Ross. Mackenzie's *Munroes of Fowlis*, pp. 196-7. *G.E.C.* x. (1945). 757, *s.n.* Reay, B. *De Rhé-Philipe. I.L.N.* 28 Nov. 1857, p. 523. M.I. at Leiah.

ROSS, George (1801-1825). Lieutenant, 20th N.I. *b.* Edinburgh 24 Dec. 1801. Cadet 1817. Ensign (?) Lieut. 19 Oct. 1818. *d.* Arakan 4 Sept. 1825.

Younger son of John Ross, of Castle Hill, Edinburgh, painter, and Janet his wife, only dau. of George Ranken, of Edinburgh, wine merchant. Brother of Agnes and Eliza Ross, and of Ann, wife of William Davidson Playfair, *q.v.* Cousin-german of George Ranken, *q.v.*

Services : Posted Lieut. to 2/5th N.I. in 1819 ; transfd. to 20th N.I. (late 2/5th) May 1824. First Burma War ; Arakan 1825 ; Lieut. 2nd L.I. Bn.

Refs. : *Family of Playfair*, by Rev. A. G. Playfair, 3rd (1913) edn. *S.M.* 1826, i. 511. Will dated 21 May 1819 ; codicil dated camp, 30 Jan. 1825 ; proved 5 Aug. 1826.

ROSS, Hugh (1788-1838). Lieut. Colonel, 2nd N.I. *b.* Kerse, Dalrymple, co. Ayr, 23 Apr. 1788. Cadet 1804. Arrived in India 1 Sept. 1805. Ensign 6 Oct. 1805. Lieut. 14 Nov. 1805. Capt. 18 Jan. 1822. Major 19 June 1831. Lt. Col. 24 July 1837. *d.* Cawnpore 3 Oct. 1838.

bapt. Dalrymple 26 Apr. 1788. 2nd son of Hugh Ross, III of Kerse and Skeldon, and Janet Campbell his wife. *m.* Dwarka Khan, U.P., 28 Feb. 1818, Eliza, 3rd dau. of William Watson (*d.* 1815), *q.v.* (She died London 19 June 1856, aged 65.)

Services : Posted Lieut. to 21st N.I. in 1806. Operations in Bundelkhand and Rewah 1809-12 ; Lieut. 2/21st N.I. Offg. Bk. Mr. at Ft. Wm. 5 Aug. 1814. Intr. & Qmr. 2/21st N.I. 4 May 1815 ; Adjt. do. 6 Aug. 1817 till 1822. Transfd. to 42nd N.I. (late 2/21st)

May 1824. First Burma War; Arakan 1825; Capt. 42nd N.I. Offg. Fort Adjt. Arakan 18 June 1825. Tempy. 2nd Extra A.A.G. 3 Oct. 1825 till 1 Dec. 1826. Fur. p.a. 8 Dec. 1827 till 12 Oct. 1832. d.d. 33rd N.I. 29 Oct. 1832. Offg. Town & Fort Major at Ft. Wm. 6 June till 18 Nov. 1833. Comdd. 33rd N.I. 7 Dec. 1833 till Jan. 1834; do. 42nd N.I. 10 Nov. 1835 till 6 Jan. 1838. Posted Lt. Col. to 7th N.I. 30 Dec. 1837; transfd. to 2nd N.I. 28 Sept. 1838.

Refs.: The Earls of Ross, by F. N. Reid (Edin. 1894), p. 30. A.J. N.S. xxviii. 42. Scottish Antiquary, iv. 67.

ROSS, Hugh Munro (1782-1815). Captain, 12th N.I. *b.* Dornoch, co. Sutherland, 10 May 1782. Cadet 1799. Arrived in India 12 Jan. 1801. Ensign 23 Oct. 1800. Lieut. 7 Jan. 1803. Capt. 11 Sept. 1811. *d. unm.* Natpur, Bengal, 28 June 1815.

Son of Hugh Ross, of Dornoch, atty.-at-law. Brother of Eliza Ross.

Services: Posted Ensign to 1/12th N.I. 17 Apr. 1801. Second Mahratta War 1803-5; Agra; Laswari; Monson's retreat (w. 24 Aug. 1804); capture of Deig; Bhurtpore; Lieut. 1/12th N.I. Operations in Oudh 1808; Bhadri; Samanpur; Gurha; Lieut. 1/12th N.I. Adjt. 1/12th N.I. 25 Dec. 1808 till 25 Oct. 1811. Capt. Lt. 12th N.I. 23 Sept. 1810.

Refs.: Will dated 10 Jan. 1815; proved 9 Nov. 1815.

*ROSS, John. Captain, Infantry. Capt. 27 July 1764.

Services: Apptd. in England 2 Mar. 1764, Capt. on the Bengal Est., " to rank between J. N. Parker and J. Tottingham," *qq.v.*; sailed in the *Fort William* 17 May 1764. N.F.P.

ROSS, John (1806-1824). Ensign, 67th N.I. *b.* Edinburgh 20 Mar. 1806. Cadet 1821. Ensign 2 Jan. 1823. *d.* Dinapore 14 Oct. 1824.

Son of Hugh Ross, of Buccleugh Pl., Edinburgh, and Janet Campbell his wife. Ed. Edinburgh High School.

Services: Posted Ensign to newly-raised 34th N.I. in 1823; transfd. to 67th N.I. (late 1/34th) May 1824. No record of active service.

ROSS, Lawrence (1807-1832). Ensign, 68th N.I. *b.* Edinburgh 26 May 1807. Cadet 1826. Arrived in India 6 Nov. 1827. Ensign 14 June 1827. *d.* 21 Apr. 1832 at the village of Bustanpur, at the entrance of the Jalangi R.

3rd and youngest son of David Ross, of Calcutta, and Marian

his wife. Brother of Charles George Ross, q.v. Ed. Edinburgh High School.
Services: Posted Ensign to 34th N.I. 20 Feb. 1828; transfd. to 68th N.I. 10 Oct. 1828. Actg. A.D.C. to Bdr.-Gen. A. Knox, q.v., 23 Feb. 1830. Actg. Adjt. Patna Provl. Bn. 6 May 1830. Leave s.c. 3 mos. to Presdy., to apply for fur., 22 Mar. 1832. No record of active service.
Refs.: Burke's *Landed Gentry*, 7th edn., p. 1581, *s.n.* Grove-Ross, of Invercharron, co. Ross. *A.J.* N.S. ix. 142.

ROSS, Robert (1789-1854). Colonel, 1st N.I. *b.* Perth 20 Jan. 1789. Cadet 1804. Arrived in India 10 Sept. 1805. Ensign 26 Sept. 1805. Lieut. 27 Sept. 1805. Capt. 1 Jan. 1819. Major 1 Dec. 1832. Lt. Col. 3 Sept. 1839. Col. 14 Nov. 1849. *d.* at the Cape 7 Nov. 1854.

Of Balshergo, co. Perth. *bapt.* Perth 28 Jan. 1789. Son of John Ross, of Perth, merchant, and Jean Richardson his wife. *m.* Rocklands, nr. Simon's Town, S.A., 15 May 1833, Wilhelmina Louisa Frederica, dau. of Francis Becker, of Rocklands. (She died Nice 23 Jan. 1878.)

Services: Posted Lieut. to 6th N.I. in 1806. (? Assault of Komona 1807.) To join escort of Resdt. with Sindhia 5 June 1810. Adjt. 2/6th N.I. 1812-14; Intr. & Qmr. do. 1 July 1814 till 1815. Nepal War 1814-15; Lieut. 2/6th N.I., in Intelligence Dept. (*Lond. Gaz.* 16 Nov. 1815) (India medal). Comdd. 1st Nassiri Bn.[1] 26 Aug. 1815 till 25 May 1822. Dy. Supt. of Sikh and Hill Affairs 11 Feb. 1822. 1st Asst. to Resdt. in Malwa and Rajputana, and comd. Resdt's guard 8 Mar. 1823. Transfd. to 18th N.I. (late 2/6th) May 1824. Fur. s.c. 11 Jan. 1825 till 29 Oct. 1828. Tempy. charge of Agra Provl. Bn. 22 Nov. 1828; Comdt. do. 5 Feb. 1829. Asst. to Resdt. at Hyderabad 8 Apr. 1831; P.A. Kotah and Bundi 30 Dec. 1831 till 1839. Leave s.c. to Cape 5 Jan. 1833 till 25 June 1834. P.A. Jaipur 18 Aug. 1839. Leave s.c. to Cape 20 Dec. 1839 till 3 Nov. 1841. Offg. P.A. Meywar 20 Dec. 1841 till 26 Apr. 1842. Lt. Col. 14th N.I.; 25th N.I.; 71st N.I. 1 Nov. 1847; 38th N.I. Dec. 1849. Posted Col. to 1st N.I. Feb. 1850. Fur. p.a. 7 Sept. 1842 till 1845; 18 Dec. 1846 till Nov. 1849; 12 Feb. 1850 till 1852.

Refs.: Boase. *A.J.* N.S. xii. 27.

[1] *Note:* This Bn. was raised by him at Subathu in 1815.

ROSS, William Hercules (1811-1849). Captain, 30th N.Ii *b.* 4 Sept. 1811. Cadet 1827. Arrived in India 11 Aug. 1828.

Ensign 21 Mar. 1828. Lieut. 28 Jan. 1833. Capt. 5 Feb. 1844. *d.* 13 Jan. 1849 : kld. in action at the battle of Chilianwala.

bapt. Macao, China, 30 Sept. 1811. Son of Capt. Daniel Ross,[1] Bombay Marine, sometime Marine Surveyor Gen., Bengal, afterwards Master Attendant of Bombay, and Maria his 1st wife. Brother of Eliza, wife of Francis Seaton, *q.v.*

Services : Ensign d.d. 51st N.I. 8 Sept. 1828 ; posted to 31st N.I. 4 Nov. 1828 ; transfd. to 30th N.I. 7 July 1830 ; Actg. Adjt. Kumaon Local Bn. 18 Nov. 1833 till Apr. 1834. Jodhpur demonstration Aug. 1839 ; Lieut. 30th N.I. With 3rd Depot Bn. 19 Oct. 1839 till Nov. 1840. First Afghan War 1842 ; action in Khyber Pass in Jan. ; forcing of Khyber in Apr. ; rearguard action nr. Garhi Lal Beg, on march to Ali Masjid, 3 Nov. (w.) [2] ; Lieut. 30th N.I., with Pollock's force (Medal). Offg. Adjt. 30th N.I. 13 Dec. 1842 till Apr. 1844. Leave 9 mos. to Malabar coast and Bombay 4 June 1847. Second Sikh War ; passage of Chenab ; Chilianwala (kld.) ; Capt. 30th N.I.

Refs. : *De Rhé-Philipe.* Monument on battle-field of Chilianwala. Will dated 2 July 1847 ; admon. 16 Feb. 1850.

[1] *Note* : A cadet of the family of Ross, of Rossie Castle, co. Forfar.

[2] *Note* : Knocked off his horse by a stone thrown by an Afghan and severely injured.

LOCKHART-ROSS, Andrew Hunter (1811-1869). Lieut. Colonel. 42nd N.I. *b.* Edinburgh 6 Oct. 1811. Cadet 1829. Arrived in India 14 May 1830. Ensign (20 Jan. 1830) 14 May 1830. Lieut. 6 Sept. 1839. Capt. 15 Nov. 1853. Bt. Major 28 Nov. 1854. Retired 31 Dec. 1861. Hon. Lt. Col. 31 Dec. 1861. *d.* 23 Hanover Sq., London, 3 Aug. 1869.

Took the surname of Lockhart before that of Ross by R.L. 17 July 1863. 2nd son of George Lockhart-Ross, advocate and judge of the consistorial court in Scotland, and Grace his wife, dau. of Rev. Andrew Hunter, D.D., of Barjarg, co. Dumfries. Edin. Univ.

Services : Cadet d.d. 63rd N.I. 7 June 1830 ; d.d. 59th N.I. 30 Mar. 1831 ; d.d. 71st N.I. 13 Dec. 1831. Actg. Ensign (having been 2 yrs. in India) 16 July 1832. Posted Ensign to 42nd N.I. 20 Aug. 1833. First Afghan War 1838-42 ; apptd. to Shah Shuja's army 3 Mar. 1839 ; Ghazni ; all operations of Kandahar force ; against Duranis 1841 ; action nr. Girishk on left bank of Helmand R. 3 July ; defeat of Akhtar Khan at Sikandarabad 17 Aug. 1841 ; Lieut. 42nd N.I., Shah's 5th Inf. (Medal). Adjt. 42nd N.I. 7 Apr. 1843 till Oct. 1848. First Sikh War ; Mudki ; Ferozshahr ; Sobraon ; Bt. Capt. 42nd N.I. (Medal with 2 clasps). Bde. Major

at Ferozepore 28 Oct. 1848 ; D.A.A.G. Presdy. Div. 30 Apr. 1849;
A.A.G. at Barrackpore 24 Mar. 1854 till 1860.
Refs.: Burke's *Peerage*, 1923, p. 1907, *s.n.* Ross, Bart., of Balnagowan, co. Ross. *The Times*, 5 Aug. 1869.

ROTH, John (1760/61-1796). Ensign. Infantry. Subsequently Lieut. Madras Est. *b.* 1760/61. Country Cadet 1780. Ensign 11 Feb. 1781. Transfd. to Madras 15 Oct. 1781. *d.* Pondicherry 1 June 1796, aged 35.

An Irishman.

Services: Apptd. a Gent. Vol. in the Coy. of Art. 3 Apr. 1780. Ensign (Madras) 13 Dec. 1780 ; Lieut. 17 Apr. 1786.

Refs.: *E.I.M.C.* ii. 293. Intest. ; Admon. 2 Jan. 1797. M.I. in English cemetery, Pondicherry.

ROTTON, James (1754/55-1831). Lieut. Colonel. 17th N.I. *b.* Somerset 1754/55. Cadet 1782. Admitted 6 May 1782. Ensign 19 Feb. 1783. Lieut. 9 Feb. 1790. Capt. 17 July 1801. Major 27 Feb. 1807. Lt. Col. 5 Nov. 1812. Invalided 9 Aug. 1816. Retired 17 Dec. 1822. *d.* Teignmouth 25 July 1831, aged 76.

Sometime of Howland St., Fitzroy Sq., London, later of Teignmouth. Brother of Jenny, wife of Richard Wormald, of Wells. Father of James Richard Rotton, Capt. 11th Light Dgns., and of Maria, wife of Benjamin Roope, *q.v.*

Services: Sailed for India in the *Worcester* 6 Feb. 1782, aged 24. Ensign 4th Bengal Eur. Bn. in Dec. 1788. Transfd. from 1st to 4th Eur. Bn. 5 Feb. 1790 ; 36th Bn. Sepoys in 1792 ; Lieut. 17th N.I. in 1798 ; Adjt. 1/17th N.I. in 1802. Operations in Jumna Doab 1803 ; Capt. 2/17th N.I. (? Second Mahratta War 1803-6 ; Capt. 2/17th N.I.) Nepal War 1814-15 ; Jitpur ; Lt. Col. 2/17th N.I., in 3rd Div. Comdg. at Gorakhpur 1815-16. Comdt. Gorakhpur Provl. Bn. 9 Aug. 1816 ; do. Dacca Provl. Bn. 17 Mar. 1818 till Feb. 1819. Fur. 27 Feb. 1819 till retirement.

Refs.: *A.J.* N.S. vi. 43. *G.M.* 1831, ii. 188. Codicil to Will dated 31 May 1825 ; proved 23 Jan. 1832.

ROTTON, John (*d.* 1795). Captain, 4th Bengal Eur. Bn. Comdt. at Bencoolen. Cadet 1770. Ensign 16 Feb. 1773. Lieut. 12 Mar. 1778. Capt. 7 Oct. 1781. *d.* at sea 27 Mar. 1795, on his passage to Bencoolen.

m. Barrackpore 12 Mar. 1793, Sarah, sister of John Staples Harriott, *q.v.* (She *re-m.* Walter Hawkes, *q.v.*) Father of John Stuart Rotton, *q.v.*

Services : Apptd. Adjt. 24th Bn. Sepoys 22 Mar. 1780. Sec. to Board in Mily. Dept. 1781 ; apptd. Mily. Sec. to Edward Wheler, actg. G.G., 12 July 1781 ; actg. Asst. Sec. to Board of Ord. in 1782 ; apptd. A.Q.M.G. 2nd Bde. 15 Mar. 1782. Capt. 29th Bn. Sepoys in July 1787 ; 4th Bengal Eur. Bn. in Dec. 1788. Fur. 1 yr. to Persia 1 Dec. 1788. Comdt. at Bencoolen.

Refs. : Will dated Ft. Wm., 1 July 1794 ; proved 19 Aug. 1795.

ROTTON, John Stuart (1795-1829). Lieutenant, Artillery. (448) *b.* Calcutta 17 July 1795. Cadet 1813. Fireworker 1 Aug. 1814. Lieut. 1 Sept. 1818. *d.* Luskintyre, N.S.W., 7 July 1829, after a severe and painful illness.

bapt. Calcutta 28 July 1795. Son of John Rotton, *q.v.*, and Sarah his wife. *m.* 1st, Cawnpore 23 Mar. 1821, Harriet, dau. of Sir Gabriel Martindell, *q.v.* (*See also* Henry Finch.) (She died Cawnpore 13 Nov. 1826, aged 27.) *m.* 2nd, Dinapore 16 Feb. 1828, Miss Ann Matilda Edwards. Ed. Westminster 1807-10. Addiscombe cadet 1811-14.

Services : Lieut. F. 3rd Coy. 1st Bn. Foot Art. A.D.C. to Major-Gen. Sir G. Martindell, *q.v.*, 1821-2. Apptd. Intr. & Qmr. to Golandaz Bn. 13 Apr. 1825. Siege and capture of Bhurtpore ; D.A.Q.M.G. of Art., and Intr. & Qmr. 6th Golandaz Bn. Leave s.c. to N.S.W. 1828.

Refs. : Westminster School Register. A.J. N.S. i. 103. Will dated 29 Apr. 1828 ; proved 23 Apr. 1830.

ROUGHSEDGE, Edward (1774-1822). Major, 26th N.I. Comdt. Ramgarh Bn. and P.A. Sambalpur. *b.* psh. of St. Peter, Liverpool, 21 Aug. 1774. Cadet 1794. Arrived in India 5 Feb. 1797. Ensign 17 Nov. 1795. Lieut. 30 Oct. 1797. Capt. 28 Feb. 1805. Major 6 Apr. 1818. *d. unm.* Sonpur, nr. Sambalpur, B. & O., 13 Jan. 1822, of fever.

Eldest son of Rev. Robert Hankinson Roughsedge, rector of Liverpool, and Elizabeth his wife, dau. of Joshua Wareing.

Services : Apptd. Cadet 7 Mar. 1796 ; sailed for India in the *Asia* 12 Apr. 1796. Lieut. 16th N.I. Second Mahratta War ; minor operations on frontier towards Nagpur ; Lieut. Ramgarh Bn. Adjt. Ramgarh Bn. 1804 ; Comdt. do. 3 Apr. 1806 till death. Transfd. as Capt. to 2/26th N.I. in 1815 ; as Major to 1/26th N.I. Nepal War 1814-15 ; Bt. Major comdg. Ramgarh Bn., in 4th Div. P.A. Sambalpur 1819 till death. Operations against Larka Kols in Singhbhum district 1820.

Refs. : Burke's *Landed Gentry*, 4th edn., p. 1300, *s.n.* Rough-

THE BENGAL ARMY, 1758-1834 701

sedge, of Foxghyll, Westmorland. Whellan's *Hist. of Cumberland and Westmorland*, p. 829. *G.M.* 1822, ii. 91. *A.J.* xiv. 232. Will dated 2 June 1821 ; proved 23 Mar. 1822. M.I. at Sambalpur.

ROUS, Thomas Hunter (1790-1816). Lieutenant, 11th N.I. *b.* Westminster, London, 25 Nov. 1790. Cadet 1806. Arrived in India 25 Nov. 1807. Ensign 16 Oct. 1807. Lieut. 27 Nov. 1811. *d.* Macassar 27 July 1816.

bapt. 26 Dec. 1790. Natural son of Thomas Bates Rous, of Moor Park, co. Hereford, M.P. for Worcs., by Mary Baldwin.

Services: Barasat C.C. Posted Ensign to 11th N.I. in 1808. Lieut. 1/11th N.I. Served with 4th Vol. Bn. 1811 till death. Capture of Java 1811 ; Ensign 4th Vol. Bn.

Refs.: Burke's *Landed Gentry*, 6th edn., p. 1384, *s.n.* Rous, of Courtyrala, co. Glam. Will dated 13 May 1816 ; proved 15 Feb. 1817.

ROUTLEDGE, Edward (1792-?). Lieutenant, Pension Est. 12th N.I. *b.* Norwich 10 Sept. 1792. Cadet 1810. Ensign 6 July 1813. Lieut. 7 Mar. 1818. Pensioned 15 Apr. 1820. (? *d.* 1821/22.[1])

bapt. ptely. St. Peter of Mancroft, Norwich, 17 Sept. 1792. Son of Edward Routledge, of Barrockside, Cumberland, farmer, and Sarah his wife, *née* Green.

Services: Cadet d.d. 9th N.I. 1811-13. Posted Ensign to 14th N.I. in 1813 ; transfd. to newly-raised 2/28th N.I. in 1815 ; to 12th N.I. in 1818. Fur. 19 May 1816 till 1818. No record of active service.

[1] *Note:* Pension last paid 31 Dec. 1821.

ROWCROFT, Francis (Rawdon Edward) (1802-1877). Lieut. General, C.B., 62nd N.I. *bapt.* St. Botolph, Bishopsgate, London, 29 Aug. 1802. Cadet 1818. Admitted 9 Oct. 1819. Ensign (26 May 1819) 7 Oct. 1819. Lieut. 14 Sept. 1821. Capt. 7 Aug. 1829. Major 26 May 1843. Lt. Col. 14 Nov. 1849. Col. 15 May 1859. Maj. Gen. 1 Jan. 1862. Lt. Gen. 25 June 1870. *d.* Holcombe, Dawlish, 22 Mar. 1877, aged 74.

Son of Thomas Rowcroft, of London, merchant, consul gen. at Lima, and Jennett Guest his wife. *m.* 27 Sept. 1830, Anne Josephine Félicité, natural dau. of Thomas Mathias Weguelin, *q.v.*, by Elizabeth Shaw. (She died Bath 31 July 1883, aged 71.)

Services: Ensign d.d. 18th N.I. 1819 ; posted to 1/12th N.I. in 1821 ; Intr. & Qmr. do. 7 Mar. 1822 ; Adjt. do. 14 Jan. 1823.

Transfd. to 1st N.I. (late 2/12th) May 1824; Adjt. do. 17 June 1824 till 22 Sept. 1829. Fur. p.a. 6 Mar. 1836 till 13 Nov. 1838. Offg. D.A.A.G. Saugor Div. 11 Nov. 1839; comdd. 1st N.I. 31 Mar. 1840 till 1 Jan. 1841; D.A.A.G. Presdy. Div. 5 June 1841 till 8 Sept. 1843. Fur. s.c. 3 Feb. 1847 till 4 Dec. 1849. Posted Lt. Col. to 27th N.I. 2 Feb. 1850; to 2nd N.I. Oct. 1852; to 69th N.I. 15 Nov. 1854; to 30th N.I. 22 Mar. 1855; to 31st N.I. Sept. 1855. Fur. s.c. Feb. 1854 till 13 Nov. 1855. Transfd. to 8th N.I. in 1856, and was comdg. that Regt. as Bt. Col. when it mutinied at Dinapore 25 July 1857. Transfd. to newly-raised 6th Bengal Eur. Inf. 1858. Mutiny campaign; with Saran F.F. 1857-8; defeated rebels at Sohanpur, Phulpur, and Amorha 5 Mar. 1858; comdd. Gorakhpur F.F. Oct. 1858 till Mar. 1859 (Medal). Col. 62nd N.I. Fur. 19 Jan. 1860. C.B. 16 Nov. 1858.

Refs.: Boase. *The Times*, 3 Apr. 1877.

*ROWE, George James. Cadet. Infantry. Cadet 1819. Declined the appt.

Son of George Rowe, of Woodbridge, Surgeon h.p., Royal Malta Regt.

ROWE, John Wilkinson (1801-1834). Captain, 31st N.I. Fort Adjt. of Calcutta. *bapt.* East Stonehouse, Devon, 6 Apr. 1801. Cadet 1819. Admitted 3 Aug. 1820. Ensign 4 Mar. 1820. Lieut. 11 July 1823. Capt. 30 July 1832. *d.* Calcutta 8 May 1834, of cholera, aged 33.

Son of Joshua Rowe, of Torpoint, Plymouth, merchant, and Hannah his wife. Brother of Sir Joshua Rowe, C.B., C.J. of Jamaica. *m.* Bishopsteignton, Devon, 14 June 1832, Harriet Meredith, dau. of James Bate, of Bishopsteignton. (She *re-m.* Calcutta 20 May 1835, John Swiney, M.D., Suptg. Surg. Bengal.) Sandhurst Cadet.

Services: Posted Ensign to 2/7th N.I.; transfd. as Lieut. to 2/15th N.I. July 1823. Offg. Adjt. Left Wing 2/15th N.I. 30 Jan. 1824. Transfd. to 31st N.I. (late 2/15th) May 1824. Intr. & Qmr. 31st N.I. 2 Oct. 1824 till 28 Sept. 1829. Siege and capture of Bhurtpore; Lieut. 31st N.I. Intr. & Qmr. 31st N.I. 2 July 1830. Fur. p.a. 14 Sept. 1830 till 20 June 1833. Offg. Fort Adjt. at Ft. Wm. 22 Nov. 1833 till death.

Refs.: Burke's *Landed Gentry*, 12th edn., p. 1074, *s.n.* Kennard. *A.J.* N.S. viii. 171; xv. 172. *G.M.* 1835, i. 221. M.I. in S. Park St. cemetery, Calcutta.

THE BENGAL ARMY, 1758-1834   703

ROWLAND, Alexander Mall (1774-1817). Captain, 17th N.I. *b.* Berwick-on-Tweed 22 May 1774. Cadet 1795. Arrived in India 6 Mar. 1797. Ensign 10 Oct. 1797. Lieut. 30 Oct. 1797. Capt. 27 Nov. 1805. *d. unm.* Gorakhpur, U.P., 9 Aug. 1817.

Son of Jonathan Rowland, of Berwick-on-Tweed, and Allison his wife. Brother of Walter and Mary Rowland.

Services : Lieut. 17th N.I. Fur. 1811-13. Nepal War 1814-15 ; Jitpur ; Capt. 2/17th N.I., in 3rd Div.

Refs. : Will dated camp Doorrah, 17 Mar. 1817 ; proved 26 Aug. 1817. M.I. at Gorakhpur.

*ROWLAND, Stephen (1753-?). Cadet. Infantry. *b.* in Scotland 1753. Cadet 1781. Did not proceed to India.

Services : Apptd. Cadet 2 Jan. 1781, aged 27.

ROWLAND, Thomas. Cadet. Infantry. Cadet 1770. Dismissed by C.M. 28 Oct. 1771.

Services : Cadet in the Select Picket in Apr. 1771, being then under arrest. Returned to England as a charter-party passenger in the *Ponsborne* at end of 1771.

ROWNING, Charles (1784-1813). Lieutenant, 14th N.I. *bapt.* St. Mary, Newmarket, Suffolk, 18 Aug. 1784. Cadet 1800. Arrived in India 4 Feb. 1802. Ensign 9 Dec. 1801. Lieut. 30 Sept. 1803. *d.* Allahabad 6 Apr. 1813.

Son of George Rowning and Sarah his 1st wife. *m.* Barrackpore 13 Jan. 1808, Sophia Jacoba, dau. of Jacob Plusker. (*See also* George Holroyd Alley.) (She *re-m.* Robert Blisset, *q.v.*)

Services : Posted Ensign to 14th N.I. Second Mahratta War 1803-4 ; battle of Delhi ; Agra ; Gwalior ; Monson's retreat ; Lieut. 1/14th N.I.

Refs. : Will dated Cuttack, 6 May 1812 ; proved 19 Apr. 1813. M.I. Kydganj cemetery, Allahabad.

ROXBURGH, Bruce (1797-1861). Captain. 6th L.C. *b.* Calcutta 12 Dec. 1797. Cadet 1813. Admitted 21 Apr. 1815. Cornet 4 Oct. 1816. Lieut. 1 Sept. 1818. Capt. 1 Dec. 1829. Invalided 12 Aug. 1831. Retired 13 Sept. 1832. *d.* Torquay, Devon, 14 June 1861.

3rd son of William Roxburgh, M.D., Supt. Calcutta botanical gdns. (*D.N.B.*), and Mary Hutteman his 2nd wife, sister of Alexander Boswell, of Edinburgh. Brother of George Roxburgh and cousin-german of Alexander Carre Boswell, *qq.v.* Ed. Charterhouse Sept. 1811-Feb. 1812. Addiscombe Cadet 1812-14.

Services: Posted Cornet to 6th N.C. in 1816. Third Mahratta War; Nagpur; Cornet 6th N.C. (India medal). Actg. Intr. & Qmr. 6th L.C. 10 Nov. 1824. Fur. s.c. 11 Nov. 1825 till 6 Oct. 1830, and 27 Mar. 1832 till retirement. Retired on a pension of 7/- *p.d.*
Refs.: Charterhouse School List. G.M. 1861, ii. 98. *The Times,* 18 June 1861.

ROXBURGH, George (1790-1815). Lieutenant, 6th L.C. *b.* Samalkot, Madras, 4 Apr. 1790. Cadet 1805. Arrived in India 11 July 1806. Cornet 18 July 1806. Lieut. 28 Aug. 1815. *d.* Sourabaya, Java, 6 Dec. 1815; struck by lightning.

bapt. Samalkot 1 Sept. 1792. Eldest son of William Roxburgh, M.D., and Mary his 2nd wife. Brother of James Roxburgh, *q.v.*
Services: Barasat C.C. Posted Cornet to 6th N.C. in 1807. Settlement of Hariana 1809; Bhawani; Cornet 6th N.C. Served with Java L.C. 1813 till death.
Refs.: Will dated Calcutta 26 Feb. 1813; proved 27 Nov. 1816.

ROXBURGH, James (1802-1884). Lieut. Colonel. 39th N.I. Subsequently Recruiting Ofr. at Newry. *b.* Calcutta 25 Feb. 1802. Cadet 1819. Admitted 17 July 1820. Ensign 14 Feb. 1820. Lieut. 11 July 1823. Capt. 12 June 1832. Major 18 Nov. 1846. Retired 28 Nov. 1849. Hon. Lt. Col. 28 Nov. 1854. *d.* at his residence, 1 Clarendon Rd., Kensington, 11 July 1884.

bapt. Calcutta 9 Aug. 1802. 4th son of William Roxburgh, M.D., and Mary his wife. Brother of Robert Roxburgh, *q.v. m.* Edinburgh 30 Apr. 1835, Isabella, eldest dau. of Nicholas Carnegie, *q.v.* (She died 30 June 1884.)

Services: Ensign 1/24th N.I.; transfd. as Lieut. to 19th N.I. July 1823; to 39th N.I. (late 2/19th) May 1824. Fur. p.a. 10 Jan. 1823 till 29 Sept. 1824. Intr. & Qmr. 39th N.I. 29 July 1825 till Sept. 1834. Junior Asst. to A.G.G., N.E. frontier, 18 July 1833. Fur. s.c. 18 Dec. 1833 till 3 Nov. 1835. 2nd Asst. Mily. Auditor Gen. 31 Dec. 1835; 1st do. 13 May 1840 till 20 Mar. 1846; offg. Dy. Mily. Auditor Gen. 8 Feb. 1841 till the post was abolished in Oct. 1842. Leave s.c. to Cape 5 Mar. 1844. Fur. p.a. 10 Apr. 1848 till retirement. Recruiting Ofr. at Newry, co. Down, Sept. 1850 till 1860. No record of active service.
Refs.: A.J. N.S. xvii. 144. *The Times,* 15 July 1884.

ROXBURGH, Robert (1796-?). Lieutenant. 4th N.C. *b.* Calcutta 4 May 1796. Cadet 1811. Cornet 8 July 1816. Lieut. 1 Sept. 1818. Resigned 31 Oct. 1818.

THE BENGAL ARMY, 1758-1834 705

bapt. ptely. Calcutta 13 Oct. 1796, being sick. 2nd son of William Roxburgh, M.D., and Mary his wife. Brother of Bruce Roxburgh, *q.v.* (? *m.* Glasgow 3 Dec. 1857, Marion Fairrie, dau. of David Johnstone.) Ed. Charterhouse ; admitted 1811 and left the same year.
Services : Posted Cornet to 4th N.C. in 1816. Third Mahratta War ; Jawad ; Cornet 4th N.C., in 2nd Div.
Refs. : Charterhouse School List. (G.M. 1858, i. 98.)

ROYLE, William Henry (1762/63-1806). Captain, 10th N.I. *b.* Surrey 1762/63. Cadet 1781. Admitted 21 Aug. 1783. Ensign 1781. Lieut. 10 July 1782. Capt. 21 Apr. 1800. *d.* Fatehgarh, U.P., 29 Oct. 1806.

m. Dinapore 18 Aug. 1797, Isabella, dau. of Maj.-Gen. John Forbes, *q.v.* (*See also* John Paton.) (She died Aligarh 4 Oct. 1828, aged 46.) Father of John Forbes Royle, surgeon and naturalist (*D.N.B.*).
Services : Lieut. Surrey Mil. 25 July 1780. Apptd. Cadet 9 Apr. 1782, aged 19. Lieut. 22nd Bn. Sepoys in July 1787 ; 3rd Bengal Eur. Bn. in Dec. 1788 ; transfd. to 24th Bn. Sepoys 26 Mar. 1783 ; Lieut. 10th N.I. in 1798. Raised at Fatehgarh in Oct. 1804, 1/25th N.I., called after him "*Rayle-ki-Paltan.*" Second Mahratta War 1805-6 ; pursuit of Holkar ; defeat of Rajah Khushal Rao at Adalatnagar 7 Apr. 1805 ; Capt. 1/10th N.I., comdg. the force.
Refs. : Cardew, p. 100. M.I. Fatehgarh fort cemetery.

RUDDELL, David (1786-1835). Captain, Bengal Eur. Regt. Sec. to the Persian Legation. *b.* Shankill, co. Armagh, 12 Dec. 1786. Cadet 1806. Arrived in India 22 Mar. 1808. Ensign 20 Mar. 1808. Lieut. 31 Aug. 1813. Capt. 13 May 1825. *d.* Shiraz, Persia, 16 Dec. 1835, of fever.

Younger son of John Ruddell, of Augha Common, Armagh, and Grace Bell his wife, sister of Charles Todd, Surg. Bengal Est. Stepson of —— Menethy, brother of James Ruddell Todd, of Ballintaggart,[1] uncle of Hugh Todd, *q.v.*, and cousin of William Rankin, *q.v.*
Services : Barasat C.C. 7½ mos. Ensign d.d. 9th N.I. 1811 ; posted Ensign to Bengal Eur. Regt. in 1811, and joined that Corps in Java at end of 1815. Served with Ramgarh Bn. 1811-15, and 1817-19. Nepal War 1814-15 ; Lieut. Ramgarh Bn., in 4th Div. Pte. Sec. to Lt. Govr. of Java 1815-16. Asst. Hindustani professor at Coll. of Ft. Wm. 25 Jan. 1820 ; Examiner do. 23 July 1821 ; offg. Sec. do. 8 Oct. 1821 ; permanent do. 11 Mar. 1824 till 11 Jan. 1832. A.D.C. to G.G. 14 Jan. 1823. Sec. and Supt. of Calcutta *Madrasa*

(Mohammedan Coll.) 27 Jan. 1826. Posted to 1st Bengal Eur. Regt. May 1824; to Rt. Wing Bengal Eur. Regt. 1830. Fur. p.a. 11 Jan. 1832; returned from fur. via Persia May 1835; permitted to remain in Persia on mily. duty 2 Nov. 1835; arrived at Shiraz 12 Dec. 1835 with despatches for India from the Brit. Ambassador at Court of Persia.

Refs.: A.J. N.S. xx. 54. Will dated 11 Apr. 1835; proved 16 Nov. 1836. M.I. at Shiraz.

[1] *Note:* Sometime an indigo planter at Rangpur, Bengal, who assumed the additional surname of Todd in compliance with the Will of his uncle, Charles Todd.

*RUMBOLD, Sir Thomas, first baronet ($173\frac{5}{6}$-1791). Captain. Infantry. Afterwards Govr. of Madras. *b.* Low Leyton, Essex, 4 Jan. $173\frac{5}{6}$. Lieut. (Madras) 19 Nov. 1753. Capt. (Bengal) 27 Sept. 1756. Resigned 31 Aug. 1758. *d.* Woodhall Park, Herts., 11 Nov. 1791.

1st Bart.; *cr.* 27 Mar. 1779. *bapt.* 25 Jan. $173\frac{5}{6}$. 3rd son of William Rumbold, 2nd in Council at Tellicherry, and Dorothy his wife, widow of John Mann, and dau. of Richard Cheney, of Hackney. *m.* 1st, Madras 22 June 1756, Frances, only dau. of James Berriman. (She died Calcutta 22 Aug. 1764, aged 26.) *m.* 2nd, 2 May 1772, Joanna, dau. of Rt. Rev. Edmund Law, D.D., bishop of Carlisle. (She died 4 Jan. 1823.)

Services: See *D.N.B.* Writer, M.C.S., 1752; transfd. to Madras Army 1753. Served under Stringer Lawrence at Trichinopoly 1754; accompanied Clive to Calcutta; wounded in the attack on the Nawab's camp 7 Feb. 1757; battle of Plassey (when he voted against coming to an immediate action), as A.D.C. to Clive. Transfd. to Bengal Est. Resigned owing to supercession by John Gowen, *q.v.* Reverted to civil service; Chief at Patna 1763; Member of Council in Bengal 1766-9, when he returned to England. M.P. for E. Shoreham 1770. Govr. of Madras 8 Feb. 1778 till 6 Apr. 1780, when he retired owing to ill health. M.P. for Yarmouth, I.W., 1781; for Weymouth 1784-90.

Refs.: Burke's *Peerage,* 1923, p. 1924, *s.n.* Rumbold, Bart. *D.N.B. D.I.B. Love, passim. Holzman. Eur. Mag.,* May 1782 (portrait). *G.M.* 1791, p. 1068. Will proved Dec. 1791.

RUSHWORTH, Edward (1802-?). Lieutenant. 2nd Bengal Eur. Regt. *bapt.* Holbeach, Lincs., 8 Mar. 1802. Cadet 1820.

THE BENGAL ARMY, 1758-1834   707

Was already in India when apptd. Cadet. Ensign 21 Feb. 1821.
Lieut. 11 July 1823. Discharged by G.C.M. 15 Feb. 1830.
Son of Edward Rushworth and Frances his wife. *m.* St. John's,
Calcutta, 9 July 1824, Miss Elizabeth Charter Conyers. (*See also*
John Selby Hele.)
Services : Posted Ensign to 1/16th N.I. in 1821 ; transfd. as
Lieut. to Bengal Eur. Regt. July 1823 ; to 2nd Eur. Regt. May
1824. No record of active service.
Refs. : A.J. xxvii. 740 ; N.S. ii. 215-16.

RUSSELL, Charles (or John, or Robert) (*d.* 1767). Lieutenant,
Infantry. Cadet 1764. Ensign 9 Oct. 1764. Lieut. 10 Jan.
1767. *d.* 1767.
Services : N.F.P. (? Ensign H.M. 68th Ft. 11 June 1760.)

RUSSELL, Charles (1786-1856). Captain. 21st N.I. Subsequently Chairman of Gt. Western Rly. Co. *b.* London 22 July
1786. Cadet 1800. Arrived in India 5 Feb. 1802. Ensign
9 Sept. 1801. Lieut. 13 July 1803. Capt. 1 Feb. 1818. Retired
18 Jan. 1822. *d. unm.* 9 Argyll St., London, 15 May 1856 :
committed suicide by shooting himself.
M.P. for Reading. *bapt.* St. Andrew's, Holborn, 21 Aug. 1786.
2nd son of Sir Henry Russell, 1st Bart. of Swallowfield, Berks.,
C. J. Bengal (*D.N.B.*), and Anna Barbara his 2nd wife, youngest
dau. of Sir Charles Whitworth, Kt., and sister of Charles, Earl
Whitworth, G.C.B. Cousin-german of Hon. James Thomas
Aylmer, *q.v.*
Services : Posted Ensign to 17th N.I. ; transfd. as Lieut. to newly-
raised 2/21st N.I. in 1803. (? Second Mahratta War 1804-5 ;
Monson's retreat ; Lieut. 2/21st N.I.) Apptd. to the escort to
Resdt. at Hyderabad where his brother Henry, afterwards 2nd Bart.,
was Sec., in 1805 ; comdd. the escort 28 July 1810 till Dec. 1817,
his brother then being Resdt. Capt. Lt. 2/21st N.I. 16 May 1815.
Fur. 6 Dec. 1817 till retirement. M.P. for Reading 12 Aug. 1830
till 17 July 1837, and 30 June 1841 till 23 July 1847. Chairman of
Gt. Western Rly. 1839-55.
Refs. : Burke's *Peerage*, 1923, p. 1927, *s.n.* Russell, Bart., of
Swallowfield, Berks. *Boaoc. Hardwicke's Annual Biog.,* 1857,
p. 61.

RUSSELL, George (1742/43-1827). Lieut. General. Colonel
13th N.I. *b.* 1742/43. Cadet 1767. Admitted 29 Jan. 1767.
Ensign 29 Jan. 1767. Lieut. 3 Apr. 1769. Capt. 2 Apr. 1777.
Major 7 Apr. 1781. Lt. Col. 1 Mar. 1794. Col. 30 Oct. 1797.

Maj. Gen. 1 Jan. 1805. Lt. Gen. 4 June 1813. *d.* George St., Portman Sq., London, 6 Dec. 1827, aged 84.

m. (?) His dau. *m.* Sir Daniel Eliott, K.C.S.I., M.C.S.; his grand-dau. *m.* John Hutcheson Fergusson-Home, *q.v.*

Services: " Acquired a very handsome fortune by building the Barrackpore barracks and other public edifices." (*Hickey.*) Carried out some surveys in the Buxar district 1767-71, which were embodied in Rennell's Maps; Supt. of Works at Berhampore 1771-4. Resigned 30 Dec. 1774; [1] readmitted 20 Feb. 1783. Supt. of Works at Berhampore 1783-4. Major comdg. 13th Bn. Sepoys in July 1787; posted to 1st Bde. Sepoys 20 Nov. 1787. Third Mysore War; 2nd in comd. of Bengal detachment under Lt.-Col. John Cockerell, *q.v.* Posted to 6th Bde. Sepoys 2 Nov. 1793; to 5th do. 25 Jan. 1794. Posted Col. to 13th [2] N.I.; to 3rd N.I.; to 20th N.I. 1804; to 13th N.I. 1805-17. Fur. 21 Dec. 1803 till death.

Refs.: Burke's *Peerage*, *s.n.* Eliott, Bart., of Stobs. *Hickey*, ii. 315; iii. 62-3, 350-1. *A.J.* xxv. 146. *G.M.* 1827, ii. 571.

[1] *Note:* " Returned from Bengal with a fortune of upwards of forty thousand pounds, the whole of which he had squandered away or lost at the gaming table, . . ." (*Hickey.*)

[2] *Note:* He raised both Bns. of this Regt. at Benares in Nov. 1797.

RUSSELL, Henry (1810-1835). Ensign, 20th N.I. *b.* N. Leith, Edinburgh, 22 June 1810. Cadet 1827. Arrived in India 24 May 1828. Ensign 1 Feb. 1828. *d.* Calcutta 9 Nov. 1835.

bapt. Leith 8 Aug. 1810. Son of Michael Russell, of the Customs, Leith, and Janet his wife, 5th dau. of William Mainwaring, a Govr. of Hudson's Bay Co., and cousin-german of Edward Henry Mainwaring, *q.v.*

Services: Posted Ensign to 20th N.I. 4 Nov. 1828. Asst. in Thagi Dept. 30 June 1835. Granted fur. s.c. 3 Nov. 1835, but did not live to embark.

Refs.: Burke's *Family Records*, p. 415, *s.n.* Mainwaring. *A.J.* N.S. xix. 296. *G.M.* 1836, i. 567. M.I. in S. Park St. cemetery, Calcutta.

RUSSELL, John (1804-1860). Lieutenant, Pension Est. 46th N.I. *b.* Edinburgh 2 Sept. 1804. Cadet 1820. Arrived in India May 1821. Ensign 16 Jan. 1821. Lieut. 11 July 1823. Discharged 31 Dec. 1829. Pensioned 13 May 1831. *d.* Agra 8 May 1860.

Son of Patrick Russell, W. S., and Rebecca Thomas (*sic*) his wife, dau. of Michael Carmichael, of Hazelhead. *m.* Agra 15 July 1831,

Ellen, 8th and youngest dau. of Col. Pedron, late of the Mahratta service, and grand-dau. of Gen. Pierre Cuiller Perron, of the same service.

Services : Posted Ensign to 1/13th N.I. in 1821 ; transfd. as Lieut. to 23rd N.I. July 1823 ; to 46th N.I. (late 2/23rd) May 1824. No record of active service. In 1848 was employed as an Asst. in the office of Sec. to Govt. in general and financial depts.

Refs. : Foster's *Baronetage*, p. 547, *s.n.* Russell, Bart., of Charlton Park. *I.M.* 26 Sept. 1848, p. 551 ; 20 June 1860, p. 458. Will dated 26 June 1838 ; proved 25 Sept. 1860. *M.I.* Agra Cantt. cemetery.

*RUSSELL, Lockhart (1735 or 1742-1798). Captain. Engineers. *b.* 1735 or 1742. Capt. (Bo. Art.) 2 Mar. 1768. Transfd. to Bengal as an Engr. Dec. 1770. Resigned 1772. *d.s.p.* at his house in Southampton 8 Jan. 1798, aged 62.

Brother of Elizabeth Russell and uncle of the wife of John Innes. *m. c.* 1773 (as her 3rd husband) Mrs. Rachel Woodley, dau. of William Yeamans, of Millhill, Antigua. (She died Sept. 1809, aged 78.)

Services : Ensign 45th Ft. 15 Aug. 1759 ; Lieut. do. 27 Sept. 1762 ; Addl. Lieut. h.p. on reduction 1763. Apptd. in England 10 Feb. 1768, an Engr. on the Bombay Est. Employed on the fortifications of Ft. Wm. Jan. 1771 till Jan. 1772 ; in charge of an expedn. to Mauritius early in 1772 for the purpose of reconnoitring the harbour of Port Louis and its defences ; returned to England July 1772. Local Major in E.I. 24 Sept. 1772.

Refs. : Oliver's *Antigua*, iii. 61. *Caribbeana*, iii. 281. *Spring*, No. 77. *G.M.* 1798, i. 87. Will dated 2 Dec. 1797 ; sworn 9 Feb. 1798. M.I. All Saints' church, Southampton.

RUSSELL, Samuel Stone (1783-1814). Lieutenant, 14th N.I. *b.* Ballintoy, co. Antrim, 4 Mar. 1783. Cadet 1804. Arrived in India 10 Sept. 1805. Ensign 7 Sept. 1805. Lieut. 8 Sept. 1805. *d. unm.* Allahabad 19 Nov. 1814.

Son of Rev. Richard Russell, vicar of Armoy and Lochguile, co. Antrim.

Services : Posted Lieut. to 1/14th N.I. in 1806. Adjt. & Qmr. 14th N.I. 1812 till death. No record of active service.

Refs. : Will dated Cuttack 26 Sept. 1811 ; codicils dated Allahabad 23 May 1813 and 7 May 1814 ; proved 11 May 1815.

*RUSSELL, ——. Lieutenant, Artillery. (53) 1st Lieut. Feb. 1767.

Services : According to Capt. Buckle was transfd. from Madras

Est. N.F.P. Not in *Leslie*. Perhaps identical with Lockhart Russell, *q.v.*
Refs.: Buckle, p. 31 *n*.

RUTHERFORD, Henry (1802-1874). Lieut. Colonel. Artillery. (482) *b.* St. Martin's, London, 6 Dec. 1802. Cadet 1818. Admitted 30 Oct. 1819. 2nd Lieut. 9 Apr. 1819. Lieut. 30 June 1820. Capt. 25 Sept. 1834. Major 3 July 1845. Retired 5 July 1846. Hon. Lt. Col. 28 Nov. 1854. *d.* Anderson's Bay, Dunedin, Otago, N.Z., 25 Dec. 1874.

Grandson of John Rutherford, of Bowland Stow, nr. Edinburgh, and Frances his wife, widow of Gabriel Johnson, Govr. of N. Carolina. Nephew of William Gordon Rutherford, C.B., Capt. of H.M.S. *Swiftsure* at the Battle of Trafalgar, afterwards Capt. of Greenwich Hospital. *m.* Frances, elder dau. of his cousin-german John Sauchie Schaw, of Douglas, I. of Man, sometime Lieut. R.A. (She died 1894, aged 70.) Addiscombe Cadet 1817-19.

Services: First Burma War; Arakan 1825 (India medal). Asst. to P.A. Upper Assam 10 June 1830; employed in surveying Assam boundary. Junior Asst. to A.G.G., N.E. frontier, 3 Apr. 1833; Principal Asst. to Comr. Assam 14 Mar. 1835 till 2 June 1840. Leave s.c. to Cape 25 Nov. 1835 till 26 Oct. 1837. Offg. Pte. Sec. to Lt. Govr., N.W.P., 4 Feb. 1840; permanent do. 2 June 1840. Fur. s.c. 1 Apr. 1842 till 4 Oct. 1845. Posted Major to 5th Bn. Foot Art. 24 July 1845.

Refs.: Misc. Gen. et Her. 4S. iii. 324. *The Times*, 15 Apr. 1875.

RUTHERFORD, Robert (*d.* 1784). Cadet, Artillery. (III.-18) Cadet 1783. *d.* Chunar 25 Oct. 1784.

Services: Apptd. Cadet for Art. 9 Jan. 1783; sailed for India in the *Lascelles* 11 Mar. 1783.

RUTHERFURD, Walter (1801-1856). Lieut. Colonel, 11th N.I. *b.* Jedburgh 25 July 1801. Cadet 1819. Admitted 17 July 1820. Ensign 14 Feb. 1820. Lieut. 11 July 1823. Capt. 23 Oct. 1831. Major 17 Sept. 1846. Lt. Col. 14 Aug. 1852. *d.* Allahabad 22 May 1856.

4th and youngest son of John Rutherfurd, Capt. 42nd Regt. and Major Dumfries Mil., and Agnes his 2nd wife, dau. of J. Chatto, of Mainhouse. *m.* Mar. 1835, Margaret, dau. of Capt. Knight, R.N., of Gordonstoun, co. Perth. (She died Napier, N.Z., 25 May 1887, aged 70.) Edinburgh Univ.

Services: Posted Ensign to 1/14th N.I. Comdd. escort to John Crawfurd, M.R.C.S., Surg. Bengal Est., on his mission to Siam and

Cochin China 8 Oct. 1821 till 1823. Adjt. 2nd L.I. Bn. 2 Oct. 1824 till 5 Sept. 1825. First Burma War; Arakan 1825; Lieut. 2nd L.I. Bn. (India medal). Transfd. to 28th N.I. (late 1/14th) May 1824; Adjt. do. 12 July 1825 till 19 Nov. 1831. Fur. p.a. 17 Jan. 1832 till 19 Sept. 1835. Comdd. 28th N.I. Mar.-Dec. 1841. Offg. Asst. Sec. to Govt., Mily Dept. 1 Feb. 1842; 2nd Asst. Sec. Mily. Board 30 June till 29 Dec. 1843. Asst. to Civil Architect at Presdy. 3 Nov. 1843; Executive Ofr. in charge of circular and eastern canals 14 Feb. 1845 till Jan. 1852. Rejoined 28th N.I. for a short time 4 Oct. 1848. Fur. p.a. 21 Jan. 1852 till Dec. 1854. Posted Lt. Col. to 16th N.I.; transfd. to 11th N.I. Oct. 1854.

Refs. : Burke's *Landed Gentry*, 12th edn., p. 1644, *s.n.* Rutherfurd, of Fairnington, co. Roxburgh. Tancred's *Annals of a Border Club*, p. 395. *I.M.* 18 July 1856, p. 418. *M.I.* Kydganj cemetery, Allahabad.

HORE-RUTHVEN, Hon. Walter (1814-1856). Bt. Major, 25th N.I. *b.* Harperstown, co. Wexford, 25 Feb. 1814. Cadet 1830. Arrived in India 29 Jan. 1831. Ensign (30 Aug. 1830) 29 Jan. 1831. Lieut. 5 Sept. 1834. Capt. 16 Nov. 1841. Bt. Major 20 June 1854. *d.* at sea between Calcutta and London 5 Mar. 1856.

6th and youngest son of Walter Hore, of Harperstown, and Mary Elizabeth Thornton, Baroness Ruthven, his wife, only surviving dau. of James, 6th Lord Ruthven. Assumed the additional surname of Ruthven and the prefix Hon. 27 July 1853, when the barony devolved on his mother. Cousin-german of William Hore and Charles Boyd, *qq.v.*

Services: Cadet d.d. 64th N.I. 4 Mar. 1831. Actg. Ensign (having been 2 yrs. in India) 9 Feb. 1833. Posted Ensign to 25th N.I. 19 Oct. 1833. Fur. s.c. 8 Apr. 1837 till 11 Aug. 1840. Actg. Adjt. 25th N.I. 30 June till 17 Nov. 1841. Fur. p.a. 10 Apr. 1847 till 1850; s.c. 18 mos. Feb. 1856. No record of active service.

Refs. : Burke's *Peerage*, 1923, p. 1931, *s.n.* Ruthven, B. *I.M.* 16 June 1856, p. 368. *G.M.* 1856, ii. 122.

RUTLEDGE, Francis (1760-1817). Colonel, 26th N.I. *b.* in Ireland 1760. Cadet 1778. Admitted 2 Oct. 1778. Ensign Oct. 1778. Lieut. 26 Nov. 1778. Capt. 1 June 1796. Major 8 Sept. 1802. Lt. Col. 21 Sept. 1804. Col. 22 June 1816. *d.* Barrackpore 3 Nov. 1817, aged 56.

(Son of either Thomas Rutledge, of Killala, or of Peter Ruttledge, of Cornfield.) Kinsman of William Knox, *q.v.* Father of Francis Rutledge, *q.v.*, and of Eliza, wife of Thomas Gamon, *q.v.*

Services : Sailed for India in the *Shrewsbury* 7 Mar. 1778, aged 18. Lieut. 2/2nd Bengal Eur. Regt. in Oct. 1779 ; 15th Bn. Sepoys in July 1787 and Dec. 1792. Capt. and Major 3rd N.I. Posted Lt. Col. to 1/3rd N.I. in 1805. Operations in Bundelkhand 1809 ; Rajaoli ; Ajaigarh ; Lt. Col. comdg. 1/3rd N.I. Dismissed by G.C.M. 12 Feb. 1816, but sentence remitted. Transfd. as Col. to 26th N.I. in 1816.

Refs.: *Hickey*, iv. 262-3. *A.J.* i. 513. M.I. in Barrackpore cemetery.

RUTLEDGE, Francis (1787-1871). Major, Invalid Est. 38th N.I. *b.* Patna 15 May 1787. Cadet 1805. Arrived in India 11 July 1806. Ensign 18 July 1806. Lieut. 26 Mar. 1807. Capt. 1 May 1824. Major 1 Dec. 1830. Invalided 31 Dec. 1830. *d.* Calcutta 30 May 1871.

bapt. Cawnpore 28 Oct. 1789. Natural son of Francis Rutledge, *q.v.*, by an Englishwoman.

Services : Barasat C.C. for $15\frac{1}{2}$ mos. Posted Lieut. to 19th N.I. in 1807. Siege and capture of Ajaigarh 1809. Nepal War 1814-15 ; Malaun (*Lond. Gaz.* 16 Nov. 1815) ; Lieut. 1/19th N.I., in 1st Div. (India medal). Third Mahratta War ; Nagpur ; Lieut. 1/19th N.I. (clasp to India medal). Actg. Adjt. 1/19th N.I. 6 Nov. 1823 ; transfd. as Capt. to 38th N.I. (late 1/19th) May 1824. After transfer to the Invalid Est. he resided for more than 30 yrs. at Chinsura, Bengal.

RYAN, Bernard (1775-1811). Captain, 12th N.I. *b.* Newtown, co. Kildare, 7 Mar. 1775. Cadet 1794. Arrived in India 6 Mar. 1797. Ensign 11 Dec. 1796. Lieut. 28 Jan. 1798. Capt. 27 Aug. 1805. *d.* Calcutta 17 Oct. 1811.

bapt. Newtown 9 Mar. 1775. Son of Edward Ryan, of Ballinakill, co. Kildare, farmer, and Catherine his wife, eldest dau. of Philip O'Reilly, of Ballymorice, co. Longford. *m.* Farrukhabad, U.P., 26 Aug. 1805, Jane (Jean), youngest dau. of Maj.-Gen. John Forbes, *q.v.* (*See also* John Paton.) (She *re-m.* May 1815, George G. Mills, of the Army Pay Office.)

Services : Lieut. 1st Bengal Eur. Regt. in June 1798 ; transfd. to 12th N.I. 1798. Operations in Jumna Doab 1803 ; Sasni ; Lieut. 2/12th N.I. Second Mahratta War ; Agra (w.) ; Laswari (w.) ; Bhurtpore (w. in 3rd assault on 20 Feb. 1805) ; Lieut. 2/12th N.I. Capt. Lt. 14 Nov. 1805 ; Capt. 10 Sept. 1807, subsequently (1809) antedated to 27 Aug. 1805. Operations in Oudh 1807-8 ; Akbarpur ; Pathar-serai ; Capt. 2/12th N.I.

Refs.: Will undated ; proved 2 Nov. 1811.

THE BENGAL ARMY, 1758-1834   713

RYAN, Charles (1782-1850). Lieut. Colonel. 12th N.I. *bapt.*
St. Mary's, Limerick, Aug. 1782. Cadet 1799. Arrived in India
9 Dec. 1800. Ensign 13 Nov. 1800. Lieut. 16 Jan. 1803. Capt.
18 Oct. 1811. Major 4 Sept. 1823. Lt. Col. 14 July 1825.
Retired 6 Mar. 1826. *d.* 6 July 1850.
Son of George Ryan.
Services: Posted Ensign to 2/12th N.I. 17 Apr. 1801, and served
throughout with that Regt. Operations in Jumna Doab 1803;
Sasni. Second Mahratta War; battle of Delhi; Agra; Laswari
(w.); Bhurtpore. Operations in Oudh 1807-8; Akbarpur; Pathar-
serai. Nepal War 1816; Capt. 5th Gren. Bn., in 2nd Bde. Left
Column. Siege and capture of Hathras. Third Mahratta War
1818; Dhamoni; against the Bhattis of Hariana. Transfd. as
Major to 12th N.I. (late 1/12th) May 1824. Fur. 1824 till retirement. Stood his trial at the Supreme Court of Calcutta on
4 Dec. 1806 for the murder of Lieut. John Corry, *q.v.*, in a duel
at Cawnpore on 21 May 1806. A verdict of manslaughter was
returned, and he was sentenced to a fine of Rs. 100 and 6 mos.
imprisonment.
Refs.: Cal. Gaz. 11 Dec. 1806.

RYDER, Charles (1781-1821). Major, 3rd L.C. *b.* Hendon,
Middlesex, 30 July 1781. Cadet 1797. Arrived in India 6 Nov.
1798. Cornet 1 Nov. 1798. Lieut. 29 May 1800. Capt. 5 Dec.
1807. Major 1 Sept. 1818. *d.* Muttra 7 May 1821.
bapt. Hendon 27 Aug. 1781. 2nd son of Thomas Ryder, Registrar
of Charterhouse 1789-1835, and Mary his wife. His sister *m.* Rev.
Alexander John Scott (*D.N.B.*) and was mother of Margaret Gatty,
author of *Parables from Nature* (*D.N.B.*). Ed. Charterhouse;
admitted Feb. 1791.
Services: Posted Cornet to 3rd N.C. and served throughout with
that Regt. Operations in Jumna Doab 1803; Sasni; Bijaigarh;
Kachaura. Second Mahratta War 1803-6; battle of Delhi;
Laswari; Rampura; battle of Deig; pursuit of Holkar. Operations against Dhundia Khan 1807; Komona; Ganauri. Fur.
14 Jan. 1816 till 1819.
Refs.: G.M. 1821, ii. 378. Will dated Muttra 22 Apr. 1821;
proved 7 July 1821. M.I. Muttra Cantt. cemetery.

RYLEY, John Sheffield Gilbert (1808-1891). Lieut. Colonel.
5th L.C. *b.* London 16 Aug. 1808. Cadet 1825. Arrived in
India 24 June 1826. Cornet 16 Feb. 1826. Lieut. 4 Sept. 1835.
Capt. 21 Aug. 1849. Bt. Major 20 June 1854. Retired 31 Dec.

1854. Hon. Lt. Col. 16 Mar. 1855. *d.* Seaview, Uphill, Weston-super-Mare, 31 May 1891.

bapt. Marylebone 17 Feb. 1809. Son of John Ryley, J.P. and D.L. co. Herts., and Charlotte Catherine his wife. *m.* Delhi 20 Sept. 1838, Marianne Christian Walker, only dau. of Hutton Watkins, *q.v.* Ed. Harrow 1823-5.

Services: Cornet d.d. 1st L.C. 8 July 1826; posted to 2nd L.C. 25 Sept. 1826. Adjt. 2nd L.C. 22 Mar. 1834 till 23 Jan. 1839. Jodhpur demonstration 1834. First Afghan War 1839-40; Ghazni; Lieut. 2nd L.C. (Medal). On disbandment of 2nd L.C., d.d. 3rd L.C. 6 May 1841. Posted to newly-raised 11th L.C. in 1842; transfd. to 5th L.C. 14 Dec. 1842. S.S.O. at Landour 11 Oct. 1844 till 1848. First Sikh War; Sobraon; Bt. Capt. 5th L.C. (Medal). Second Sikh War; Ramnagar (s.w.); Capt. 5th L.C.

Refs.: Harrow School Register. The Times, 5 June 1891.

RYVES, William Henry (1812-1873). Bdr. General. Comdt. 8th Bengal Cav. (now 3rd Cav.). *b.* Stoke Damerel, Devon, 9 Jan. 1812. Cadet 1828. Arrived in India 27 Aug. 1829. Ensign 5 June 1829. Lieut. 11 Oct. 1838. Capt. 24 Jan. 1845. Major 15 July 1859. Lt. Col. 18 Feb. 1861. Col. 18 Feb. 1866. Bdr. Gen. 2 Dec. 1870. *d.* Agra 30 Sept. 1873.

bapt. Plymouth end of 1812. Son of Peter Thomas Ryves, of Brussels, Lt. Col. h.p. H.M.S., and Matilda Elizabeth his wife, 2nd dau. of W. Pirner, of Arlington St., St. James's. *m.* Nimach 19 Oct. 1838, Emma, youngest dau. of William George Maxwell, *q.v.* (*See also* Charles Henry Boisragon.) (She died 1 June 1896, aged 78.)

Services: Posted Ensign to 61st N.I. 22 Sept. 1830. Shekhawat expedn. 1834; comdg. 3rd Local Horse. Actg. Intr. & Qmr. 9th L.C. 7 Feb. till 22 Oct. 1835. Adjt. 3rd Local Horse 22 Apr. 1836; Adjt. 4th Local Horse 27 Sept. 1838 till 1 June 1841. First Afghan War 1839; Ghazni; Adjt. 4th Local Horse (Medal). Second in comd. 7th Irreg. Cav. 1 June 1841 till Jan. 1846. Insurrection in Bundelkhand 1842-3. Raised 17th Irreg. Cav. (became 18th Irreg. Cav. in 1847; 8th Bengal Cav. in 1861; 3rd Cav. 1922) at Sultanpur in 1846, and comdd. that Regt. 24 Jan. 1846 till Dec. 1870. Operations against Hindustani fanatics and Khudu Khel; Sitana 22 Apr. 1858; Bt. Major comdg. 18th Irreg. Cav., under Maj.-Gen. Sir Sydney John Cotton (Medal). Transfd. to Staff Corps 18 Feb. 1861. Bdr. Gen. comdg. at Agra 2 Dec. 1870 till death.

Refs.: The Times, 30 Oct. 1873.

CORRIGENDA

Vol. I

p. xlii, l. 11 : *for* Oct. 16 *read* Oct. 13.
p. 1, l. 40 : *delete* ' H.M.S.' after Stevenson.
p. lii, l. 14 : *for* Weyland *read* Wayland.
p. liv, l. 42 ; *for* as *read* at.

*ADAMSON, Benjamin.
p. 9. There would appear to be no authority for the inclusion of his name by Broome, and by Stubbs who follows Broome, amongst those who lost their lives on this occasion. It is absent from all the three contemporary lists.

ALEXANDER, Samuel.
p. 20, l. 35 : *for* Sept. *read* Nov.

ALEXANDER, William.
p. 21, l. 6 : *for* Drumsang *read* Drumraney.
ll. 10 and 11 : *delete* William Minto.

*ALSTON, George.
p. 26. There would appear to be no authority for the inclusion of his name by Broome, and by Stubbs who follows Broome, amongst those who lost their lives on this occasion. It is absent from all the three contemporary lists.

ANDERSON, George.
p. 30, l. 5 : *for* Strand *read* Strand St.
(*See also* Vol. ii. p. 618.)

ANDERSON, Henry (1779-1810).
p. 30, l. 17 : *for* W.I. *read* N.I.

ANDERSON, James (Cadet 1775).
p. 30 : *delete* this biog. and *substitute* the following :—

ANDERSON, James (1757-1833). Lieutenant. Infantry. Pol. Resdt. with Sindhia. *b.* 23 Oct. 1757. Cadet 1775. Ensign 29 July 1776. Lieut. 16 July 1778. Struck off 1791. *d.* 3 Oct. 1833.

Of Wilton Lodge, Hawick. 5th son of David Anderson, of Stoneyhill, nr. Musselburgh, and Mary his wife, dau. of John Mitchelson, of Middleton, advocate. Brother of David Anderson,

B.C.S., Presdt. of the Committee of Revenue, cousin-german of Robert Swinton, *q.v.*, and uncle of the wife of Robert Pitman, *q.v. m.* Catherine, dau. of Andrew Grant, younger son of Lord Elchies.

Services : Sailed for India in the *Duke of Albany* 18 Feb. 1772. Obtained a Persian translatorship ; A.D.C. to Lt.-Col. Matthew Leslie, *q.v.*, 1774 ; Adjt. Sepoy Corps 1st Bde. 1775. First Mahratta War 1778-80 ; capture of Ahmedabad ; siege of Bassein ; on staff of Col. Thomas Goddard, *q.v.* Attached to staff of Warren Hastings in 1781, and was with him at Benares in Aug. on the outbreak of the insurrection. Apptd. on 5 Nov. 1781, A.D.C. to Hastings with effect from 1 July. Asst. to his brother David as Pol. Resdt. with Sindhia 1782 ; succeeded him as Resdt. 23 Nov. 1783 till 20 Dec. 1786. Fur. 1787 till struck off.

Refs. : Family information. *D.I.B.* (*s.n.* David Anderson). *N. & Q.* cliv. 265.

ARDEN, Samuel.

p. 47, ll. 23 and 24 : *delete* ' James Franklyn . . . city ' and *substitute* George Franklyn, of Hanbury Hill and of Bristol, merchant.

ARROW, George.

p. 54, l. 9 : *delete* ' (or Jones).'

ARROW, James.

p. 54, l. 21 : *delete* ' (or Jones).'
l. 24 : *for* Delhi *read* Oudh.

ATKINS, Robert.

p. 57 : *for* **ATKINS** *read* **AITKENS or AITKINS**.

AUBERT, Jeremiah.

p. 60, ll. 1 and 2 : *for* 1785 *read* 1786.

AULDJO, Thomas.

p. 60, l. 35 : *for* 4th son of Day George Auldjo *read* 4th son of George Auldjo, sometime provost of Aberdeen, and Susan Beauvais his wife.

BADENACH, Walter.

p. 69, ll. 1 and 2 : *for* 1786 *read* 1784.

BAILEY, Abraham Jennings.

p. 71 : *for* Abraham *read* Ephraim.

BAILLIE, William (1752/53-1799).

p. 74, l. 26 : *for* Major *read* Lieut.
l. 28 : *delete* ' Capt. (?). Major (?).'

CORRIGENDA

BALFOUR, Arthur.
 p. 84, l. 30 : *for* Services *read* Refs.

BARBOR, George Alexander.
 p. 89, ll. 21 and 22 : *for* b. 28 Feb. 1805 *read* b. 20 Feb. 1804.

BARKER, Sir Robert.
 p. 92, l. 25 : *for* 18 June 1774 *read* 22 Dec. 1773.

BARRAT, Savage.
 p. 96 : The name probably should be **BARRELL**. If so, perhaps son of Savage Barrell, of Warfield, Berks. (Cf. *Eton Coll. Register, 1698-1752*, by R. A. Austen-Leigh.)

BAYLDON, Richard.
 p. 105, l. 6 from bottom : *for* 1780 *read* 1789.

*BECHEATON, John.
 p. 114 : *delete* the whole of this biog.

BECHER, George.
 p. 116, l. 8 : *delete* m. 2nd, Harriot Gildart. The full name of his wife was Harriet Geldart Barclay.

BENETT, Frederick.
 p. 129, l. 7 : *for* m. 1811 *read* m. St. Helena 5 Feb. 1812.

BENTLEY, Forster Parkes.
 p. 132 : *for* **BENTLEY, F—— P——** *read* **BENTLEY, Forster Parkes.**

BERGUER, John Frederick.
 p. 133, l. 19 : *for* 9 June *read* 20 June.

BIRD, John Jenkins.
 p. 147 : *delete* m. Marie L'Herondell . . . Mary Le Clere his wife) and *substitute* m. Mary le Clere, widow of Francis L'Herondell (formerly de la Tremouille), of Calcutta, atty. *Note :* It was almost certainly her dau. by her first husband who m. Robert Francis, *q.v.*

BISHOP, Henry.
 p. 152, l. 31 : *delete* 'probably.'

BLACKALL, Robert.
 p. 155, ll. 34 and 35 : *delete* m. 1st (before 1809), Catherine, dau. of W. Lewis, Bo.C.S.

BLAKE, George.
    p. 163, l. 2 : *for* d. nr. Darjeeling, *read* d. nr. Ghazipur on his way to Darjeeling.

BOLTON, George.
    p. 175, l. 39 : *for* Landown *read* Landour.

BOYD, Robert.
    p. 192 : *delete* ll. 40-1 and *substitute* Executed by the Spanish at Malaga 11 Dec. 1831, together with Gen. José Maria Torrijos and 47 others, for promoting an insurrection in favour of the constitution.
    Refs.: *Some Pages of my Life*, by Bishop Boyd-Carpenter (London, 1911), pp. 95-106 (portrait). *G.M.* 1832, i. 84. *La Unión Mercantil*, of Malaga, 11 Dec. 1930, p. 5. Monument in Malaga cemetery.

BOYES, Robert.
    p. 193, l. 17 : *for* Willhall, Hanullen *read* Wellhall, Hamilton.

BRADBY, Edward Taylor.
    p. 195, l. 32 : *for* Sept. *read* Oct.

BRADLEY, John.
    p. 197, l. 24 : *for* 24th *read* 21st.

BREMNER, John.
    p. 200, l. 11 : *for* Infantry *read* 2nd Bengal Eur. Regt.

BRIGGS, William Thomas.
    p. 204, l. 17 : *for* Nyagaon, Bengal *read* Nyagaon, nr. Nasirabad, Rajputana.

BRISCOE, John.
    p. 206 : *delete* ll. 20, 21, 22, 25, 26.

BRISCOE, William Musgrave.
    p. 206 : *delete* ll. 36, 37, 38 and *substitute* the following : 2nd son of Rev. William Brisco, M.A., rector of Distington and minister of Trinity Church, Whitehaven, and Margaret his wife and cousin, dau. of George Langstaffe, of Carlisle, and widow of William Gilpin. Cousin-german of Horton Briscoe, *q.v.*

BROADBROOK, John.
    p. 209, l. 35 : *delete* ' Lieut. in England (H.M. 39th) 1758.'

BROOKE, Francis Cissen.
    p. 213, l. 35 : *for* Miss Brabazon his 2nd wife *read* Anne his wife, sister of Col. Alexander Wright, of St. Helena.

BROWNE, John.
p. 232, l. 22: *for* d. 15 Apr. *read* bur. 13 Apr.

BUCK, John.
p. 243, l. 26: *for* Queen's *read* Queens'.

BURLTON, William.
p. 252, l. 18: *for* Capt. William Knipe *read* Lieut. Samuel Knipe.

BURTON, Charles Æneas.
p. 263, last l.: *delete* (She died Aligarh 18 Nov. 1833.) *m.* 2nd (?)

BYNG, Hon. Robert Barlow Palmer.
p. 271, l. 12: *for* 1830 *read* 1839.

CAMPBELL, Robert (1800-1889).
p. 296, l. 6: *delete* Sir Hugh Massy Wheeler, K.C.B.

CAREY, Charles.
p. 301, l. 25: *for* Merwara *read* Mewar.

CARMICHAEL, Charles Montauban.
p. 305, ll. 26 and 27: *delete* Author of " A History . . . 1848.
l. 29: *for* (? Paris 1854) *read* (Paris, 1847).

CARNEGIE, John William.
p. 306, l. 22: *for* (1814-1874) *read* (1812-1874).
l. 23: *for* b. Aberdeen 21 Apr. 1814 *read* b. in India 13 July 1812.
l. 27: *for* bapt. Fetteresso 13 June 1814 *read* bapt. Bombay 21 Dec. 1812.

CARTER, Thomas.
p. 314, l. 8: *for* d. Belgaum, Bombay *read* d. Bilgram, Oudh.

CARY, Bernard.
p. 316, l. 16: *for* 1820 *read* 1920.

CASEMENT, Sir William.
p. 318, l. 30: *for* dau. *read* natural dau.

CATHCART, James.
p. 320, l. 5: *for* Lieut. 1796 *read* Lieut. 1 Apr. 1795.

CAULFEILD, James Gordon.
p. 321, l. 2 from bottom: *for* 1815 *read* 1816.

CHRISTIE, John.
p. 343, ll. 6 and 7: *for* 1806 *read* 1805.

CLARK, William.
p. 345, l. 34: *for* 1787 *read* 1784.
l. 35: *for* July 1787 *read* 11 July 1784.

CLERKSON, John.
p. 352, l. 3 from bottom: *for* Miss *read* Mrs.

COCKERELL, John.
p. 358, ll. 16 and 17: *for* 1753 *read* 1752.

COKE, Sir John.
p. 360, l. 14: *for* Ludow Castle *read* Ludlow Castle.

COLLIER, Charles.
p. 363, ll. 23 and 24: *for* 1782 *read* 1792.

CONYNGHAM or CONINGHAM, Daniel.
p. 376, l. 37: *for* 2 Sept. *read* 4 Sept.

CORFIELD, Alfred Henry.
p. 386, ll. 26 and 27: *for* 1810 *read* 1809.

COSBY, William.
p. 392, l. 4: *for* 1760 *read* 1768.
l. 7: *delete* 'Probably.'

CRUIKSHANK, John.
p. 419, l. 26: *for* Aug. 1818 *read* 24 Sept. 1818.

Vol. II

D'AGUILAR, George Thomas.
p. 2, l. 22: *for* Or. *read* Ofr.

DALLAS, Charles.
p. 3, l. 33: *for* Jane *read* Janet; *for* Robert *read* George.
l. 36: *for* Long *read* Young.

DALY, Frederick.
p. 6, l. 11: *for* 25th N.I. *read* 20th N.I.

*DARE, William.
p. 11, l. 26: *for* (d. 1774 ?) *read* (d. 1776).
l. 27: *delete* d. 1774 ?; shipwrecked and drowned off the Coromandel Coast and *substitute bur.* Calcutta 25 Nov. 1776.

DAVIDSON, Robert (1782-1804).
p. 19, l. 5: *for* 1/12th *read* 2/12th.

LLOYD-DAVIES, Thomas Dolman.
  p. 23, l. 25; *for* Part St. *read* Park St.

DEAS, John.
  p. 33 : *for* **DEA** *read* **DEAS**. Remove this biog. to bottom of p. 34.

DICKSON, James.
  p. 61, l. 29 : *for* 1829, i. 873 *read* 1829, i. 373.

DONALDSON, James.
  p. 68, ll. 22 and 23 : *for* 1781 *read* 1780.

DONNETT, Nevill.
  p. 70 : His name probably was **DOMETT, Newell.**

DORNBUST, Joseph.
  p. 70 : *for* **DORNBUST** *read* **DORNBUSH**.

DOWNES, William.
  p. 81, l. 11 : *for* (? *d.* Charlotte St., Portland Pl., London, 3 Nov. 1793.) *read d.* Cheadle, Cheshire, 20 May 1789, aged 48. M.I. Cheadle churchyard.

DRUMMOND, John Philip.
  p. 88, l. 25 : *for m.* Mary Harriet Cridland *read m.* Edinburgh 7 Apr. 1791, Mary Heriot, dau. of Capt. Simonides Creedland, 4th (? 44th) Regt.

DUDGEON, Patrick.
  p. 90, l. 27 : *for* Drem *read* Dam.

DU FEU, John.
  p. 90, ll. 6 and 5 from bottom : *for* 1785 *read* 1784.

DUNBAR, Matthew Charles.
  p. 96, ll. 10 and 11 : *for* 1787/88 *read b.* St. Nicholas Acons, London, 18 Feb. 1789.

DYER, ———.
  p. 112 : *delete* this biog. and *substitute* the following :—

***DYER, John.** Captain. Infantry. Capt. 6 June 1758. Resigned 29 Dec. 1759.

Services : Was one of eleven signatories to a Memorial, dated Calcutta, 28 Aug. 1758, complaining of supercession by John Gowen, *q.v.* He was not, however, among the eight who resigned their Commissions on that occasion.

Refs.: *Orme MSS.—India,* xiii. 3639. *I.O. Rec., Home Misc. Series,* 90 (1), pp. 1-21.
This biog. should follow David Dyce on p. 111.

EDMONSTONE, Archibald.
p. 121, l. 16 : *for d.* Bengal Feb. 1776 *read d.* Lucknow 14 Mar. 1777.

ELDRIDGE, Ambrose.
p. 127, bottom l. : *for* 1856 *read* 1846.

ELLIOT, George.
p. 129 : *delete* this biog. and *substitute* the following :—

ELLIOT, George (1760/61-1794). Lieutenant. Infantry. Afterwards Junior Merchant, B.C.S. *b.* 1760/61. Cadet 1779. Ensign 21 July 1779. Lieut. 12 Mar. 1781. Resigned 31 Aug. 1782. *d.* Bhagulpur 17 Oct. 1794, aged 33.

Son of George Elliot, of Laugharne, co. Carmarthen, and Margaret his wife, *née* Grant. Related to Elliot Voyle, *q.v.*, who *m.* his elder dau. *m.* Calcutta 10 July 1792, Rachel, sister of Edward Dunkin, *q.v.*

Services : Apptd. Writer 1 Oct. 1781 ; Dy. Postmr. 1783 ; Paymr. to the Art. Garr. and Ord. 17 May 1793.

Refs. : *Hickey,* iv. 70, 73-4. Will dated Calcutta, 7 May 1794 ; proved 31 Oct. 1794. M.I. Bhagulpur.

EVORS, Pryce John.
p. 145, ll. 30 and 33 : *for* **EVERS** *read* **EVORS**.
l. 30 : *for* Pryse *read* Pryce.

EWART, Richard Sheridan.
p. 147, l. 24 : *for née* Bennet *read née* Berner, dau. of a Prussian General.

FANE, William John Jervis.
p. 161, top l. : *for* Jarvis *read* Jervis.
l. 3 : *for* 13 July *read* 16 July.

FARLEY, William Johnson.
p. 162, l. 5 : *for* George *read* Thomas.

FARMER, Charles Finch.
p. 162, l. 21 : *for* Weyland *read* Wayland.

FARQUHARSON, George.
p. 164, ll. 31-3 : *delete* ' Bdr. 2 cl. . . . mutiny at Multan)'

and *substitute* Was comdg. 46th N.I. at Sialkot when it mutinied 9 July 1857.

FENTON, Albert.
p. 170, l. 15 : *for* bapt. Sheffield 25 Apr. 1802 *read* b. 26 Mar. 1802 ; bapt. Sheffield 25 Apr. 1804.

FENWICK, John.
p. 171, l. 33 : *for* dau. (? sister) *read* sister.

FERRIER, Alexander.
p. 176, l. 25 : *for* Kintrockal *read* Kintrockat.

FETHERSTON, Thomas.
p. 178, l. 19 : *for* Mary *read* Hannah.
Note : Both Burke and Lodge give the name incorrectly as Mary.

FIELD, George Brydges Plantagenet.
p. 180, l. 5 : *for* Dec. *read* Feb.

FINNIS, John.
p. 182, l. 2 from bottom : *delete* ' Was comdg. at Allahabad on outbreak of Mutiny.'

FISHER, Thomas.
p. 185, l. 23 : *delete* ' probably.'

FLEMING, George.
p. 191, l. 31 : *for* Ensign *read* Fireworker (Art.).

FORBES, William.
p. 202, l. 2 : *for* (d. 1877-9 ?) *read* d. Dover 6 May 1877, suddenly, of heart disease. *The Times*, 9 May 1877.

DINGWALL-FORDYCE, Arthur.
p. 204, l. 3 from bottom : *for* Youngest *read* Third.

FOREMAN, James.
p. 205, l. 26 : *delete* ' Probably.'

FORSTER, Ralph.
p. 208, l. 8 : *for* High Brunton *read* High Burton, Warkworth, Northumberland.

FORTNOM, John.
p. 209, l. 5 : *for* Erstone *read* Enstone.

FOWLE, Henry.
p. 212, l. 16 : *for* (1820-?) *read* (1804-?).

FRASER, Andrew.
p. 215, l. 37 : *for* Libieton *read* Liberton.

FRASER, Richard.
p. 219, l. 1 from bottom : *for* Oram *read* Ord.

FRUSHARD, James.
p. 230, l. 2 : *for* Southwick *read* Southwark.

GALLIEZ, Primrose.
p. 244, l. 12 : *for* G.M. 1810 *read* G.M. 1819.

GARDINER, Robert.
p. 247, l. 14 : *delete* (? co. Donegal).

GILPIN, Martin.
p. 270 : *delete* ll. 35 and 36 and *substitute* Ensign H.M. 61st Ft. 18 Jan. 1760 ; Lieut. 107th Ft. 22 Oct. 1761 ; h.p. do. 1763 till death. Transfd. as Lieut. to Bengal Army (M.C. 1 Sept. 1768). Major comdg. 20th N.I. in Aug. 1781.

GOLDIE, Andrew.
p. 280, l. 21 : *for* William *read* George.

GOULD, James (*d.* 1772).
p. 296, l. 37 : *delete* 'Possibly.'

GRAND, George François.
p. 308, l. 8 : *for* John Peregrine Reed *read* Lieut. Thomas Reid, H.M. 76th Ft.

GRANGE, Richard George.
p. 309, l. 15 : *for d.* 1866 ? *read d.* 66 Gt. Portland St., London, 2 Feb. 1861 ; *bur.* Kensal Green.

GRANT, Alexander (*d.* 1822 ?).
p. 310, l. 26 : *for* (*d.* 1822 ?) *read* (1753-1816).
l. 29 : *for d.* 1822 ? *read d.* 16 July 1816.

GRANT, John.
p. 315, l. 7 from bottom : *delete* the whole of this biog. and *substitute* the following :—

GRANT, John (*d.* 1804). Major. Infantry. Lieut. 13 July 1764. Capt. 1 Dec. 1767. Major 1769. Resigned Sept. 1775. *d.* Waltham Place, Berks., 8 Jan. 1804.

Of Hill St., London, and White Waltham, nr. Maidenhead. J.P. Berks. Son of Rev. John Grant and Elizabeth his wife. Brother of Henry Grant, q.v. (? m. 1st, Ann, who died in India.) m. 2nd, Miss Alice Gilbert, of Salisbury. (She died Waltham Place 16 Nov. 1785.) m. 3rd, St. George's, Hanover Sq., London, 30 June 1788, Hon. Charlotte Bouverie, 3rd dau. of Sir Jacob Bouverie, 1st Viscount Folkestone.

Services : Surgeon's Mate H.M. 84th Regt. in 1759 ; Ensign do., from Surgeon's Mate, 27 May 1760 ; Lieut. do. 31 Aug. 1761. Lieut. in comd. of 300 Sepoys in association with Major John Carnac in July 1761. Sec. to Major Adams in 1763 : employed as Field Engr. at battle of Udhua Nullah ; Paymr. H.M. 84th in Mar. 1764 ; battle of Buxar ; h.p. 84th Ft. 24 Sept. 1765 till death. Transfd. to Bengal Army in 1764. Returned to England, but in 1769 went out to Madras as Sec. to Eyre Coote, ' with permission to remain there while the Gen. does and to have the rank of Major, but not to be apptd. to any Corps in the Coy.'s troops.' Sailed for England in the *Asia* 2 Feb. 1772. Became a partner in the banking firm of Pybus & Co., Old Bond St., London. M.P. for Fowey 1784-6. The writer of " Mr. Grant's Journal, 1761-4," among the *Orme MSS.* in I.O. library.

Refs. : Burke's *Peerage*, 1923, p. 1835, *s.n.* Radnor, E. *G.M.* 1784, i. 369 ; 1788, p. 658 ; 1804, i. 91. *Holzman.* Wylly's *Eyre Coote*, p. 126. Will dated 1 Aug. 1787 ; proved in London 15 Mar. 1804. M.I. in Nolton church and Roch church, co. Pembroke, and in White Waltham church, Berks.

GRAVELEY, Thomas Milton.

p. 323, l. 29 : *for* d. Belgaum, Bombay *read* d. Bilgram, Oudh.

GRAVES, Harry Meggs.

p. 324, l. 7 : *for* Katharine *read* Sarah Catharine. (She died Derby 18 Aug. 1894, aged 72.)

GREEN, Valentine Henry Frederick.

p. 327, l. 28 : *for* Robert *read* Rupert.

GREEN, William Horatio.

p. 327, l. 4 from bottom : *for* (*possibly* sister *read* dau.

GREENE, Robert.

p. 331, l. 23 : *for* Gemtry *read* Gentry.

GREENSTREET, John.

p. 332, l. 40 : *for* d. Hitchin *read* b. Hitchin.

GREGORY, Robert Bourke.

p. 333 : *delete* Eldest son of Robert Gregory of Coole Park, co. Galway, Chairman E.I. Co., and Maria Nimmo his wife.

p. 334, l. 13 : *delete* Burke's *Landed Gentry of Ireland*, p. 280, *s.n.* Gregory, of Coole Park.
l. 15 : *delete* Burke's *Landed Gentry*, 14th edn., p. 43, *s.n.* Gregory, of Ashfordbye and West Court, co. Kilkenny.
l. 18 : *delete* Portrait in Zoffany's " Cock Fight."

GREY, John.
p. 336, l. 12 : *for* b. 1760 *read* b. 8 Apr. 1761.

GRIFFITH, Joseph.
p. 339 : *delete* this biog. and *substitute* :—

GRIFFITHS, Joseph. Cadet 1783. Struck off 1784.
Services : Exchanged into h.p. of H.M. 102nd Ft. (disbanded 1783) with Thomas Stamford, *q.v.*, 28 Dec. 1784. Was still on h.p. in 1808, not in 1809.

GRIGG, Mark.
p. 341, l. 27 : *for* 1794 *read* 1793.

GUINAND, Alexander.
p. 346, l. 5 from bottom : *for* Perretta (? Perette or Mary) Ranby *read* Perrette Rauly his wife, dau. of Mrs. Carten Rauly.

HAIR, Joseph.
p. 356, l. 17 : *for* William *read* Willoughby.

HAIR, Thomas F——.
p. 356, l. 25 : It is thought that this entry should read : **HAIR, Willoughby Francis (or Fraser).**

HALDANE, Robert.
p. 358, l. 5 : *delete* (*Probably* uncle of Charles Haldane, *q.v.*)

HALL, Hawkesley.
p. 364 : *for* Hawkesby *read* Hawkesley.

HAMILTON, Anthony.
p. 368, ll. 14 and 15 : *for* 1753/54 *read* 1752.
l. 18 : *for* d. 29 Dec. 1830 *read* d. Whitehaven, Cumberland, 25 June 1830.

HAMILTON, John (1808-?).
p. 373, l. 22 : *delete* ' Probably.'

HAMMOND, George.
p. 377, l. 18 : *for Probably* nephew of *read* Brother of.

HARRIOTT, Frederick Joseph.

p. 392, l. 5 : *for* One of the judges who presided *read* As D.J.A.G. conducted the prosecution.

HARRISON, James.

p. 398, l. 3 : *for d.* 4 Jan. 1782 *read d.* in camp at Bijaigarh Dec. 1781, of jungle fever.

HAWKINS, Thomas.

p. 410, l. 6 : *delete* ' his deceased wife's sister.'

HAY, Edward.

p. 413, ll. 26 and 27 : *for* 1806 *read* 1808.

HEARSEY, Andrew.

p. 422, l. 3 from bottom : *for* Only son *read* 2nd son.

*HEATH, Joseph Barnaby.

p. 424 : *delete* the whole of this biog. and *substitute* :—

*HEATH, Joseph Barnabas. (*See* ***SLEATH, Joseph Barnabas.**)

HELLIER, Thomas.

p. 426 : *delete* the whole of this biog. and *substitute* :—

HELLYER, Thomas. Cadet, Infantry. Cadet 1778.

Services : Apptd. Cadet 9 Dec. 1778 ; sailed for India in H.M.S. *Superbe.* N.F.P.

HEPBURN, David.

p. 431, l. 16 : *for* Miller *read* Mylne.

HERBERT, James Dowling.

p. 434, l. 17 : *for* Joseph *read* James.

HERBERT, Philip.

p. 434, ll. 36 and 38 : *for* 1782 *read* 1781.

HESSMAN, William.

p. 438, l. 14 : *for d.* Oct. or Nov. 1779 *read d.* 3 Nov. 1777.

HICKS, William Charles.

p. 447, l. 10 : *for b.* Hadbury (?), Worcs. *read b.* Fladbury, Worcs.

HILL, Rowley John.

p. 453, ll. 11 and 12 : *for* 5th *read* 6th.

*HINCLES, William.

p. 455 : *delete* the whole of this biog. There would appear to be no authority for the inclusion of his name by Broome, and by Innes who follows Broome, amongst those who lost their lives on this occasion. No officer of this name can be traced in *I.O. Rec.*

HODGES, Charles Wyndham.

p. 457, l. 39 : *for* Ashton *read* dau. of Henry Hervey Aston, of Aston, sheriff of Cheshire 1768, which marriage was dissolved by Act of Parliament in 1795.

HOGG, Roger.

p. 464, l. 8 : *delete* ' Probably transfd. as Capt' and *substitute* Transfd. as Capt. Lt. 1 Sept. 1768.

HOLBROW, John.

p. 466, l. 15 : *for* Stonehouse, Devon *read* Stonehouse, Gloucs.

HOLLINGS, George Edward.

p. 467, l. 36 : *delete* ' probably.'

HOOKE, Archibald.

p. 477, l. 6 : *for* 1763 *read* 1768.

HUDLESTON, Henry.

p. 492, l. 35 : *for* Holy Walton *read* Isley Walton.

HUDSON, George Isaac.

p. 493, l. 13 : *for* Rev. C. A. Brock *read* Rev. Charles Abraham Brook.

HULL, John Watson.

p. 496, l. 29 : *for* (She died 6 May 1844) *read* (She died Mount Ida 31 Jan. 1877, aged 78.) (M.I. to husband and wife in Magherally Old Churchyard, co. Down.)

*HUMPHRIES or HUMPHREYS, Isaac.

p. 502 : *delete* ll. 9, 10, 11 and *substitute* d. 5 Aug. 1763, of wounds received in action at the battle of Gheria on 2 Aug.

HUNTER, Thomas.

p. 508, l. 32 : *for* Robert *read* Herbert.

HUTCHINSON, Charles (1768/69-1805).

p. 512, l. 11 : *for* a dau. of Anthony Lambert (1759/60-1800), *q.v. read* a sister of Anthony Lambert (1785-1803), *q.v.*

HYDE, John.
p. 519, l. 16 : *for* Ensign *read* Bt. Ensign.

INSLEY, John.
p. 527, l. 17 : *for* d. 18 Sept. *read* bur. Madras 30 Sept.

IRONSIDE, Charles.
p. 527 : *delete* this biog. and *substitute* :—

IRONSIDE, Charles (1748-1790). Lieut. Colonel. Infantry.
b. Bedlington, Surrey, 1748. Cadet 1763. Ensign 20 Aug. 1763. Lieut. 13 Apr. 1764. Capt. 27 July 1766. Major 24 Feb. 1778. Lt. Col. 3 Dec. 1781. Resigned 28 Jan. 1782. *d*. Charlotte St., Rathbone Pl., London, 4 May 1790.

Youngest son of Edward Ironside, of Lombard St., banker, and Anne his wife, dau. of Charles Newman, of Atford, Wilts. Brother of Gilbert Ironside, *q.v. m.* 1st, Charlotte St. chapel, Marylebone, 26 June 1768, Anne, dau. of Herman Nail, of Cornhill, London. *m*. 2nd, in England 26 Aug. 1784, Miss Neil.

Services : Major 2/3rd Bengal Eur. Regt. in Aug. 1781.

Refs. : Hutchins' *Dorset* (3rd edn.), ii. 282. *G.M.* 1790, i. 478.

IRVING, James (1807-?).
p. 531, top l. : *delete* ' co.' before Galloway.

JACKSON, James Nesbitt.
p. 538, l. 7 : *for* Nicholson *read* Nicolson.

JACKSON, William Hill.
p. 541, l. 34 : *for* Barrington *read* Burrington.

JACOB, Vickers.
p. 542, l. 20 : *for* Aghadoe *read* Aghaboe.

JACQUES, Henry.
p. 542, l. 35 : *delete* ' Probably.'

JAMES, William (1803-1833 ?).
p. 545 : *delete* the whole of this biog. and *substitute* :—

JAMES, William, afterwards WALLACE (1803-?). (*See* WALLACE, William James.)

JAMIESON, James William Henry.
p. 546, l. 2 : *for* Apparently still living in 1895 *read* d. 10 Oct. 1866.

JELLICOE, Anthony Highmore.
   p. 548, l. 29 : *for* Elizabeth his wife *read* Anne his wife, dau. of Robert Nash.

JESSUP, John Henry Bowes.
   p. 555, l. 9 : *for* Nov. *read* Dec.

JEWEL, F——.
   p. 555 : *delete* the whole of this biog. and *substitute* :—

*JEWEL, Ishmael. Lieut. Fireworker. Artillery. Lieut. F. 1764.
   Services : Apptd. by C.D. in England a Lt. F. to rank next Lt. F. John Stone, *q.v.* (G.O. 17 Feb. 1764.) N.F.P.
   Refs. : B.M. Add. MSS. 6050.

JOHNSON, Hugh.
   p. 556, l. 5 : *for* Weyland *read* Wayland.

KEATING, Michael (D.).
   p. 574, l. 25 : *for* Den *read* Don.

KENNEDY, James.
   p. 584, ll. 20 and 21 : *delete* William Minto.

KENNEDY, William Drummond.
   p. 587, l. 7 : *for* d. Calcutta *read* d. Muzaffarpur district, B. & O.

KIRCHOFFER, Thomas.
   p. 600, l. 1 from bottom : *for* (1801-1822) *read* (1786-1822).

KYD, Alexander.
   p. 613, l. 9 : *for* Related to *read* Nephew of.

ADDENDA

Vol. I

Add to Bibliography, pp. xvii-xx:

Caraccioli. The Life of Robert, Lord Clive, by Charles Caraccioli, gent. 4 vols., London, 1777.

A Catalogue of British Family Histories. Compiled by T. R. Thomson, M.A. London, 1928; 2nd edn., 1935.

Clan Donald, by Rev. A. Macdonald and Rev. A. Macdonald, 3 vols., Inverness, 1896-1904.

Clan Maclean. An Account of the Clan Maclean, by a Seneachie (John Campbell Sinclair or Neil Maclean). London, 1838.

Mackay. The Book of Mackay, by Angus Mackay. Edin., 1906.

Mackenzie's *Macdonalds.* History of the Macdonalds, by Alexander Mackenzie. Inverness, 1881.

Mackenzie. History of the Clan Mackenzie, by Alexander Mackenzie. Inverness, 1894.

Mackenzie's *Macleods.* History of the Macleods, by Alexander Mackenzie. Inverness, 1889.

MacInnes. The Brave Sons of Skye, by Lt.-Col. John MacInnes. Edin., 1899.

Macpherson. Soldiering in India, 1764-87, edited by W. C. Macpherson, C.S.I. Blackwood, 1928.

Memoir of James Young, Merchant Burgess of Aberdeen, . . ., by Alex. Johnston, 1861: ed. Lt.-Col. W. Johnston (Aberdeen, 1894).

Roll of I.M.S. Roll of the Indian Medical Service, 1615-1930, by Lt.-Col. D. G. Crawford. London, 1930.

Scottish Family History, by Margaret Stuart. Edin., 1930.

Scott's *Fasti. Fasti Ecclesiæ Scoticanæ,* by Hew Scott: new edn., 7 vols., Edin., 1915-28.

Westminster School Register. Refs. are to the new 1928 edn. in 2 vols., " Records of Old Westminsters." (Supplt., 1938.)

Inscriptions on Tombs, B. & O. ; Govt. of B. & O., 1926.

p. xxi : *add* as a footnote to the para. on " Minor Cadets " : One hundred and five Minor Cadets were struck off on 2 May 1786, pursuant to orders contained in C.D. Letter of 21 Sept.

1785, para. 11. Of this long list [1] a mere dozen eventually obtained regular cadetships. The following extract from *Soldiering in India, 1764-87*, proves that these Cadets drew, through their parents, from Govt. a monthly allowance of Rs. 50 : " On 10th November 1784 Col. Macpherson writes to Maj.-Gen. Giles Stibbert, Commander-in-Chief, ' Sir, I shall esteem myself much obliged to you if you will do me the favour to recommend my son, William Macpherson, to the Honble. the Governor-General and Council to be appointed a minor cadet on this establishment. He is now about 2 months and a half old, and I hope they will be pleased to grant me this indulgence. . . .' No answer to this letter is forthcoming, but household accounts show that an allowance of Rs. 50 a month was paid to Master William Macpherson by the Paymaster to the Garrison of Fort William from December 1784."

It may be added that the name William McPherson figures in the list referred to above.

[1] *Note :* See Appendix C.

p. liv, between ll. 15 and 16 : *add (Fortescue,* vol. xiii. pp. 238-402).

Between ll. 38 and 39 : *add (Fortescue,* vol. xiii. pp. 404-21).

p. lv, between ll. 24 and 25 : *add (Fortescue,* vol. xiii. pp. 423-45).

ADAMS, John.

p. 8, l. 12 : *add* Fur. to Madras 1764, and took part with Madras army in siege of Madura.

p. 8 : *add* as a new entry after the foregoing :—

*ADAMS, John (*d.* 1788). Lieutenant, Infantry. Cadet 1780. Ensign 1781. Lieut. 18 Sept. 1782. *d.* Chapra, B. & O., 23 Apr. 1788.

Services : Apptd. Cadet 8 Dec. 1780 ; sailed for India in the *Queen* 13 Mar. 1781. Lieut. 31st Bn. Sepoys on 1 July 1787.

ADAMS, O. George.

p. 8 : His name was **George Osborne ADAMS.**

ADAMS, Samuel.

p. 9, l. 20 : *add* Ed. Westminster.

l. 21 : *add* Lieut. in Leicestershire Mil. 27 Apr. 1778.

l. 25 : *add Refs. : Westminster School Register.*

ADDERLEY, Thomas.

p. 9, l. 36 : *add b.* Aug. 1748.

p. 10, top l. : *add* Ed. Merchant Taylors' Mar. 1760-Oct. 1763.
l. 4 : *add* to *Services* Major comdg. 3rd Regt. Sepoys on the Mahratta frontier in Aug. 1781.

ADDISON, Edmund.
p. 10, l. 12 : *add* Elder son of Richard Addison, of Preston, Lancs., upholsterer. Ed. Manchester Grammar School; admitted 14 June 1763.
Add *Refs.* : *Manchester School Register*, i. 113.

*ADNETT, Joseph.
p. 10, l. 6 from bottom : *add* Ensign 39th Ft. 14 Feb. 1754. (*See also* Vol. ii. 617.)

AGG, James.
p. 12 : *add b.* 1746/47. *d.* Prestbury, Gloucs., 14 Jan. 1827, aged 80.
l. 5 : *add* Of Hewletts, in psh. of Prestbury. *m.* (before 1802) Edith, dau. of James Gardner, of Cheltenham. (She died 19 Sept. 1851, aged 83.)
l. 22 : *add* to *Refs*. M.I. in Prestbury psh. church.

AINSLIE, John (1807-1844).
p. 14 : *add* Eldest son of John Ainslie, of Teviot Grove, Minto, *q.v.* Admitted an Advocate in 1833. *d.* 13 June 1844. Glasgow Univ.; matric. 1824.

AIRE, James Ritchie.
p. 14, l. 3 from bottom : *add d.* Agra 2 May 1827.
l. 2 from bottom : *add* bapt. Leith 21 Dec. 1792.
p. 15, l. 7 : *add* to *Refs*. M.I. at Agra.

AITCHISON, James.
p. 15, l. 29 : *add* bapt. S. Leith 17 Mar. 1793.
l. 31, after ' Militia ' : *add* 26 June 1809.

AITKEN, Robert.
p. 16, l. 4 : *add* 4th and youngest son of George Aitken, Col. of the Cupar Mil. in 1815, sometime of Tod Hall, co. Fife, and Janet Paton his wife. Brother of John Aitken, writer in Cupar, who *m.* a sister of Andrew Christie, *q.v.*
l. 11 : *add* to *Refs. Genealogical Mag.* iv. 206 (Sept. 1900).

AITKENS or AITKINS, Robert.
p. 57 : *add* to *Services* Had held a Commn. of Qmr. in H.M. 3rd D.G.

ALCOCK, Thomas.
  p. 17, l. 34 : *add* Treasurer of the Ordnance Jan. 1810 till 1818.

ALEXANDER, James.
  p. 19, l. 25 : *add m.* Bombay 18 Nov. 1802, Miss Harriet Bowles. (*See also* Vol. ii. p. 617.)

ALEXANDER, Sir James.
  p. 20, l. 9 : *add* Son of J. Alexander, M.D., of London.

ALEXANDER, Samuel.
  p. 20 : *add b.* 1772/73. *bur.* Fort Marlbro' 13 Nov. 1794, aged 21. *Note:* According to the burial register he was an Ensign.

ALLAMAND, John Peter.
  p. 22, line 18 : *add bapt.* St. Margaret's, Leicester, 1 Feb. 1787. Son of John Peter Allamand and Barbara Hayes his wife.

ALLAN, David.
  p. 22, l. 23 : *add* Only surviving son of David Allan, the Scottish painter (*D.N.B.*), of Tron Kirk psh., and Shirley his wife, yst. sister of Thomas Welsh, *q.v.*
  Refs.: Anderson, i. 116.

ALLARDYCE, James George.
  p. 23, l. 12 : *add* Son of James Allardyce, M.D., Surg. H.M. 34th Ft., and Dorothy his wife.

ALLINGHAM, Edward.
  p. 25, l. 20 : *add m.* St. George's, Hanover Sq., London 7 Oct. 1824, Miss Margaret Graham.

ALSTON, James Millar.
  p. 26, l. 27 : *add* and Mary Dennistoun his wife. Ed. Glasgow Grammar School and Glasgow Univ.

ALVES, Gilmour.
  p. 28, l. 4, after 'Castle' : *add* and Elizabeth his wife, dau. of Martin Eccles, surgeon in Edinburgh. Cousin-german of David Bethune Lindesay, *q.v.*

ANBURY, Sir Thomas.
  p. 28, l. 35 : *add* Son of Obadiah Anburey, of the Accountant's Office, E.I. House, 1745-85.
  l. 38 : *add* Served in the Accountant's Office, E.I. House, 1777-83. *Note:* His name usually appears as Anburey.

ANDERSON, Henry (1784-1805).
p. 30 : *add* 8th son of Dr. James Anderson, LL.D., and Margaret Seton his wife, of Mounie, co. Aberdeen.
Refs.: N. & Q. clxv. 46.

ANDERSON, James.
p. 30, l. 30 : *add* Of Wilton Lodge, Hawick. *b.* 1757. Son of David Anderson (Stoneyfield), W.S., and Mary, dau. of John Mitchelson, of Middleton, advocate.

ANDERSON, Robert.
p. 33, l. 34 : *add* Son of Robert Anderson, of Edinburgh, seedsman, and Grizel Callender his wife.

ANDREWS, James Richard Benson.
p. 36, l. 1 from bottom : *add* (She died Simla 29 July 1860.)

ANGELO, Richard Frederick.
p. 38, l. 26 : *add m.* 26 Apr. 1831.
l. 28 : *add* His sister *m.* G. R. Pemberton, *q.v.*

ANSON, Frederick Walpole.
p. 40, l. 2 : *add* His sister *m.* James John Kinloch, *q.v.*

ANSTRUTHER, Ashford John.
p. 41, l. 7 : *add m.* Harriet. (She died Boulogne 31 May 1870, aged 78.)
l. 12 : *add* to *Refs. Anstruther of that Ilk*, by A. W. Anstruther (Blackwood, 1923), p. 119 (where date of birth is given as 1792, and name as John Ayshford Anstruther).

ANSTRUTHER, Hon. David.
p. 41, l. 16 : *add* Said to have *d.* Reading *c.* 1825.
l. 21 : *add* His widow *d.* 27 July 1827.
l. 23 : *add* Ensign 1/1st Royal Regt. of Foot 25 June 1773.
l. 28 : *add* to *Refs. Anstruther of that Ilk*, p. 111. (*See also* Vol. ii. p. 614.)

ANSTRUTHER, Robert Lindsay.
p. 41, l. 36 : *add m.* 1st, 2 Aug. 1808, Miss Eliza Holt.
p. 42, line 6 : *add* to *Refs. Anstruther of that Ilk*, p. 118. (*See also* Vol. ii. p. 614.)

ARDEN, Russell.
p. 47, l. 15 : *add* Transfd. as Lieut. from H.M.S. 1 Sept. 1768.

ARDING, Cecil.
p. 48, l. 11 : *add* d.s.p. St. Helier, Jersey, 23 Oct. 1889.
l. 12 : *add* Eldest son of Rev. Isaac Richard Arding and Juliana his wife, eldest dau. of Sir Christopher Willoughby, 1st Bart. of Baldon House, Oxon.
l. 19 : *add to Refs.* Family information. Will dated 17 Oct. 1872 ; proved (P.C.C.) 8 Jan. 1890.

ARMSTRONG, Augustus.
p. 49, l. 30 : *add* Ed. Merchant Taylors' Mar. 1819-Mar. 1822.

ARMSTRONG, David.
p. 49, l. 38 : *add* Son of Edward Armstrong, advocate, and Helen his wife, dau. of William Mirtle, of Calcutta.

ARMSTRONG, George Craven.
p. 50, l. 12 : *add* Ed. Merchant Taylors' Oct. 1816-Oct. 1818.

ARMSTRONG, Richard Boswell.
p. 51 : *add to Services* Ensign S. Carolina Rangers 27 June 1780 ; served in this Regt. in America and Jamaica till July 1783.

ARNAUD, Henry Hawker.
p. 52, l. 4 : *add* Apptd. Major comdg. 5th Vol. Bn. R. Scots 6 Dec. 1859. (*See also* Vol. ii. p. 619.)

ARROW, George.
p. 54, l. 9 : *add bapt.* St. John Evang., Westminster, 23 Sept. 1792. Son of Jordan James Arrow and Elizabeth his wife.

ARROWSMITH, Joseph.
p. 54, l. 32 : *delete* parentheses and ' ?.'
l. 37 : *add to Services* Ensign 2/14th N.I.

ASHE, Benjamin.
p. 55, l. 4 : *add* Volunteer, to be Ensign 8th Ft. 28 Sept. 1757 ; Lieut. do. 27 Jan. 1760 ; h.p. 1763. Lieut. 6th Ft. 15 July 1766 till 8 Jan. 1768. He afterwards bought the h.p. of Lieut., late 101st Ft., and appears as such in *A.L.* down to 1815, when he presumably died. (*See also* Vol. ii. p. 619.)

ASHE, Benjamin (1792-1868).
p. 55, l. 10 : *add* Nephew of Simeon Droz, B.C.S.

ATKINS (*recte* AITKENS), Robert.
p. 57, l. 16 : *add to Services* Was Qmr. H.M. 3rd Dgn. Gds. before receiving appt. as Cadet.

ATKINSON, Henry.
p. 58, l. 13 : *add* Ensign H.M. 69th Ft. 15 Oct. 1759 ; Lieut. do. (?) ; h.p. as Lieut. ' Additional Officers' of 69th Ft., reduced in 1763, till death. Transfd. as Lieut. to Bengal Army (M.C. 1 Sept. 1768).

AUBERT, Jeremiah.
p. 60, line 7 : *add m.* Hannah Elizabeth ——. (She died Purnea 26 Mar. 1825, aged 35.)

BADDELEY, William Clinton.
p. 68, l. 23 : *add* dau. of Davis Sloane, *q.v.*

BAGNOLD, John Henry.
p. 69 : *add* Youngest son of Thomas Bagnold and Thomasin his wife, 7th dau. of James Burrough, of Alton Priors and Devizes, bell-founder. *m.* Marianne, sister of Robert Cauty, *q.v.* (*See also* Charles Cornwallis Chesney.)
Add to *Refs*. Family information.

BAGSHAW, Robert Morris.
p. 70, l. 16 : *add* Son of Stephen Bagshaw, *q.v.*
Add to *Refs.* Will dated 27 July 1805 ; proved 17 Mar. 1807.

BAGSHAW, Stephen.
p. 70 : *add m.* Sarah ——, of Greenwich. Father of Robert Morris Bagshaw, *q.v.*
Refs. : *B.* : *P.P.* xxxviii. 102. Will dated 17 Aug. 1785 ; codicil 6 June 1786 ; proved 21 Sept. 1786. (*See also* Vol. ii. p. 619.)

BAGSHAWE, Samuel Robinson.
p. 70, bottom l. : *add* Ed. Repton ; admitted Aug. 1815.
p. 71, l. 8 : *add* to *Refs*. *Repton School Register*. (*See also* Vol. ii. p. 619.)

BAILEY, Charles Drummond.
p. 71, l. 24 : *add* and Henrietta his wife.
l. 25 : *add* Ensign 64th Ft. 7 Nov. 1822 ; h.p. same day ; Ensign 66th Ft. 15 Dec. 1825.

BAILLIE, William (1752/53-1799).
p. 74 and Vol. ii. p. 619, l. 20 : *add m.* Chinsurah 22 Mar. 1789, Miss Ann Mary Roddy. Granted fur. without pay for 3 yrs. Apr. 1785. Supt. of the Calcutta Free School. Author of a " Plan of Calcutta " ; 12 Views of Calcutta (1794-5) ; and Views of Gour and Rajmahal.

Add to *Refs. Calcutta Gazette,* 13 June 1799.
Note : Though described as Major on M.I., he was only a Lieut. when he left the Army.

BAINBRIDGE, Thomas Drake.
p. 75 : *add* Trinity Coll., Camb. ; admitted Pensioner 4 Feb. 1824 ; matric. 1824. Ensign H.M. 82nd Regt. 1827. *d.* Down Hall, Epsom, 8 Feb. 1870.

BAINBRIDGE (or BAINBRIGGE), William Dixon.
p. 75, bottom l. : *add* Apptd. Lieut. F. in England 3 Mar. 1775.

*BAINBRIDGE, William Isacke Parnell.
p. 76 : *add Probably* son of Ensign William Arthur Henry Bainbridge and Clarissa Isacke his wife (*m.* Madras 19 Feb. 1798).

BAKER, Godfrey Evan.
p. 77, l. 34 : *add* Eldest brother of William Massy Baker, *q.v. m.* Margaret, 2nd dau. of Hugh, 1st Lord Massy. (She *re-m.* Capt. Hugh Wheeler, E.I.C.N.S., by whom she became mother of Sir Hugh Massy Wheeler, *q.v.*, and died 1838.)

BAKER, Richard.
p. 79, l. 24 : *add bapt.* 30 Oct. 1785. Son of James Baker, proctor, and Elizabeth his wife, dau. of Benjamin Earnshaw, of Pontefract.

BAKER, William (1810-1877).
p. 80, l. 8 : *add m.* St. James's, Piccadilly, 1 Aug. 1844, Frances Roupell, 2nd dau. of James Alexander Simpson, of Queen Sq., London.

BALCETTI, Joseph Gilbert.
p. 81, line 10 : *add* eldest dau. of Mr. J. D. Conyers.

BALDERSTON, Dugald.
p. 82, l. 5 : *add* and Helen his wife, dau. of William Little Gilmour, of Liberton and Craigmillar. Ed. Edin. Univ.

BALDOCK, Christopher.
p. 82, l. 28 : *add* youngest dau. of John Carey by Judith Dobree.

BALFOUR, Arthur.
p. 84, l. 30 : *add Services :* Major comdg. 19th N.I. in Aug. 1781.

ADDENDA

BALFOUR, Francis.
 p. 84, l. 38 : *add m*. Madras 6 Aug. 1776, Miss Emilia Balfour.
 p. 85, l. 5 : *add* to *Refs. Scots Peerage*, i. 545, *s.n.* Lord Balfour of Burleigh. Burke's *Landed Gentry*, 15th edn., p. 89, *s.n.* Balfour of Fernie Castle.

BANNERMAN, Alexander.
 p. 88, l. 11 : *add* to *Services* Nepal War ; S.A.C.G. and i/c. Pay Dept. of Ochterlony's Div.

BARBER, Charles.
 p. 88 : *add* Natural son and heir of W. Barber, of London, merchant, by Margaret, dau. of Philip Matthews, of the psh. of High Ercoll, Salop, by Mary Means his wife.

BARING, James Drummond.
 p. 91, l. 16 : *add* Ed. Charterhouse June 1822-June 1823.

BARKER, George.
 p. 92, l. 3 : *add m*. 1847, Mary Catherine, dau. of Gen. Vaughan Worsley, R.A. (She died 1896, aged 88.)
 l. 11 : *add* to *Refs*. Burke's *Landed Gentry*, 14th edn., p. 7, *s.n.* Barker, of Salt Hill, Chichester.

BARKER, Sir Robert, Bart.
 p. 92 : *add* Only son of Robert Barker, M.D., of Drayton, Salop, and St. Anne's, Soho, London, and Hannah his wife, dau. of —— Whitehead, of Coleman St., London. *bapt.* at his father's house, Soho, *c.* 1732. His dau. Juliana was mother of John Dethick Crommelin, *q.v.*
 Add to *Refs.* Hunter's *Familiæ Minorum Gentium*, i. 408. (*See also* Vol. ii. p. 620.)

BARLAND, Walter.
 p. 92, l. 32 : *add* 1st Lieut. H.M. 87th Regt. 20 Dec. 1760 ; h.p. do. 1763 till death. (*See also* Vol. ii. p. 620.)

BARLOW, Andrew Samuel.
 p. 92, line 2 from bottom : *add* His sister *m*. Rt. Hon. Sir James Parke, Baron Wensleydale (*D.N.B.*).

BARNARD, John Gilbert.
 p. 93, l. 36 : *add* to *Refs. Howard & Crisp*, xix. 161 ; (*Notes*), vii. 169.

BARNETT, William.
   p. 95, l. 15 : *add* Son of William Barnett, of Little Abbey, Bucks., formerly a W.I. planter, by his 1st wife. Ed. Westminster 1803-7. Marlow Cadet.
   l. 23 : *add* to *Refs. Westminster School Register.*

BARR, William.
   p. 95, l. 36 : *add m.* Meerut 8 Mar. 1836, Marcia Louisa Johnstone, eldest dau. of William Lamb (1779-1826), *q.v.* (*See also* George O'Bryen Ottley.) (She died 30 July 1888, aged 70.)

*BARRELL, George.
   p. 96 : The name should be prefixed with an asterisk.

BARSTOW, John Anderson.
   p. 98, l. 19 : *add bapt.* Morpeth 4 Sept. 1795. Son of Thomas Barstow, King's Falconer for Scotland, and Jane his wife, dau. of Samuel Mitchelson, W.S., Clerk to the Signet. Ed. Edin. High School.
   Add to *Refs.* Family information.

BARWELL, Augustus Leycester.
   p. 101, l. 13 : *add* Ed. Eton ; in 4th Form in 1817. Stepson of Edward Miller Mundy, of Shipley Hall, co. Derby, M.P.
   l. 16 : *add* to *Refs.* Burke's *Landed Gentry,* 13th edn., p. 1283, *s.n.* Mundy, of Shipley Hall. *Eton School Lists* (where his 2nd name is wrongly given as 'Luter').

BARWELL, Henry Montague.
   p. 101, l. 21 : *add* Ed. Winchester.

BATTINE, William.
   p. 104 : *add* to *Refs.* Will dated Cheltenham, 18 Sept. 1849 ; proved 17 Nov. 1851.

BAWDWIN, Thomas.
   p. 105, line 32 : *add m.* Mary.

BAYLDON, Richard.
   p. 105, bottom l. : *add* Nephew by marr. of Sir George Wood, Kt., Baron of the Exchequer 1807-23 (*D.N.B.*).

BAYLEY, William.
   p. 106, l. 30, after '4 May 1788' : *add* aged 29 days.

BEAN, John Dickson Dyke.
   p. 108, line 22 : *add m.* 1st, Chinsura 8 Nov. 1823, Magdelina, only dau. of Mr. Nasier Elias.

BEATSON, William Fergusson.
p. 111, l. 15 : *add* to *Refs. Genealogical Mag.* iii. 436-8 (Feb. 1900) (portrait). Portrait (from an engraving by D. J. Pound) in *King George's Own Central India Horse*, by Maj.-Gen. W. A. Watson, C.B., Blackwood, 1930.

BEAUMONT, Ernest Charles Francis.
p. 113, l. 5 : *add* and Sophia his wife. Ed. St. Paul's ; admitted 10 May 1815.

BECHER, Charles.
p. 115 : *add* Son of Richard Becher, B.C.S., and Ann Haselby his 2nd wife. Brother of George Becher, *q.v.* *b.* London 5 Feb. 1777 ; *bapt.* Marylebone 7 Mar. 1777.
Add to *Refs.* M.I. Speldhurst church, Kent.

BECHER, George.
p. 116, l. 6 : *add* 7th son of Richard Becher, B.C.S., and Ann Haselby his 2nd wife.
Add to *Refs. Personal Reminiscences in India and Europe, 1830-1888, of Augusta Becher*, edited by Professor H. G. Rawlinson, London, 1930 (portrait, with wife and family).

BECHER, George Richard Prendergast.
p. 116, l. 30 : *add* Ed. Charterhouse 1820.

BECHER, Henry Murray.
p. 117, l. 4 : *add m.* Lydia Reed.

BECHER, Septimus Harding.
p. 118, l. 15 : *add* (She died 1909.)

BECKETT, William.
p. 119, l. 39 : *add m.* Mary, dau. of John and Mary Ostlife.

BEDELL, William.
p. 120, l. 27 : *add m.* 1st, Ambur, Madras, 7 Feb. 1782, Anne Isherwood.
l. 28 : *add* eldest dau. of Robert Young, of Durham. (*See also* Charles Gatley.)
Add to *Services* Second Mysore War.
Add to *Refs. Howard & Crisp* (*Notes*), iv. 141, *s.n.* Young.

*BEDINGFIELD, John George.
p. 121 : *add d.* 8 Aug. 1841 : kld. in action in Afghanistan.
Refs. : Name on Afghan Memorial, St. John the Evang., Colaba, Bombay. (*See also* Vol. ii. p. 620.)

BEEK, William George.
 p. 121 : *add d.* Lionel Villa, Brixton, 19 June 1873, aged 68. *m.* Ann. (She died Camberwell 7 June 1885, aged 70.) Late of Leghorn and Messina, and sometime in the service of H.M. Fatteh Ali Shah, of Persia. K.L.S.
 Refs.: The Times, 24 June 1873.

BEGBIE, Arthur Pitt.
 p. 122, l. 16 : *add* Son of Peter Begbie and Frances his wife, youngest dau. of Arthur Jones, of The Priory, Reigate.

BELL, Charles Hamilton.
 p. 123, l. 7 : *add* 4th son of Rev. Dr. James Bell, minister of Coldstream 1778-94, and Anna his wife, dau. of Rev. Thomas Clark, minister of Eaglesham.
 l. 20 : *add* to *Refs.* Scott's *Fasti*, ii. 42.

BELL, John.
 p. 124, l. 4 : *add* (1759/60-1835).
 l. 6 : *add d.* at his residence, 17 Bryanston St., Portman Sq., London, 6 May 1835, aged 75.
 Add to *Refs. A.J.* N.S. xvii. 144.

BELL, Robert (1792-?).
 p. 125, l. 5 : *add* Ed. Charterhouse 1807-10.

BELL, William.
 p. 125, l. 23 : *add* and Elizabeth Robertson his wife.
 l. 29 : *add* Ed. Charterhouse 1800-06. (*See also* Vol. ii. p. 621.)

BELLASIS, Joseph Harvey.
 p. 126 : *add* to *Services* Lieut. Berks. Mil. 25 Apr. 1780.

BENDLEY, Thomas.
 p. 128 : *add b.* 4 Mar. 1763. Ed. Charterhouse June-Dec. 1774.

BENNETT, John William.
 p. 130, line 7 : *add b.* 21 June 1808.
 l. 9 : *add* Ed. Westminster 13 Jan. 1817 till 7 Dec. 1818.
 l. 17 : *add Refs.: Westminster School Register.*

BENNETT, Simon William.
 p. 130, l. 23 : *add* widow of Robert Scott, of Logie.

BENNETT, Thomas.
 p. 130, l. 31 : *add* Ed. Merchant Taylors' Mar. 1819-Mar. 1823.

BENSON, George.

p. 131, l. 11 : *add* 2nd son of George Fowls Benson, of Salisbury, and Martha his wife, eldest dau. of Edmund Abbot, of Winterbourne Dauntsey, Wilts.
Add to *Refs.* Hunter's *Familiæ Minorum Gentium*, iii. 1136.

BENT, Richard.

p. 132, l. 19 : *add* Fourth Mysore War 1799 ; storm and capture of Seringapatam (Medal).

BENTLEY, F—— P——.

p. 132. His full name was **Forster Parkes BENTLEY.**

BERKELEY, Henry Nicholas Lionel.

p. 133, l. 30 : *add b*. 12 Jan. 1757.
l. 34 : *add* Held a Commission in Lancashire Mil. before entering E.I.C.S. Posted to 28th Bn. Sepoys Mar. 1780.
Add to *Refs.* M.I. in old cemetery below Chunar fort.

BIE, George.

p. 139 : *add bapt.* Trondhjem, Norway, 17 Oct. 1762. Son of Jacob Bie, *q.v.*, and Mette Margarethe his wife. Arrived in India 1775.
Refs. : Family information.

BIE, Jacob.

p. 139 : *add bapt.* Trondhjem, Norway, 11 July 1738. Brother of Col. Ole Bie, Danish Govr. of Serampore. *m.* Mette Margarethe Lemmal. Father of George Bie, *q.v. d.* Serampore 1798. Arrived in Tranquebar 1778.
Refs. : Family information.

BIGGE, James Rundell.

p. 140, l. 15 : *add* 3rd son of Thomas Bigge and Maria his wife, dau. of Thomas Rundell, of Bath.
l. 20 : *add Refs.* : Burke's *Landed Gentry*, 4th edn., p. 99, *s.n.* Bigge, of Linden, Northumberland.

BIGGS, John Andrew.

p. 140, l. 28 : *add m.* Barbara. (She died 2 Feb. 1863, aged 70.)

BIGNELL, William Phillips.

p. 141, l. 37 : *add* Ed. Charterhouse 1814.

BINGLEY, Thomas Brooke.

p. 142, l. 13 : *add* Son of Thomas Bingley, of 3 Tavistock St., Covent Gdn., linendraper.

BINNS, Isaac.
　p. 142, l. 28 : *add* (She *re-m*. James Frushard, Supt. of the silk investment in Bengal, and died Barrackpore 17 Nov. 1820.) His dau. by his 2nd wife *m*. Charles Ramsay Skardon, *q.v.*

BIRCH, John Zephaniah Mill.
　p. 144, l. 39 : *add* to *Services* Ensign H.M. 26th Ft. 12 Dec. 1781, but never actually served with that Regt. as he was apptd. Cadet in Jan. 1782.

BIRD, Edward.
　p. 146, l. 25 : *add b*. 11 June 1762. Ed. Charterhouse Feb. 1772-June 1773. *m*. Elizabeth. (She died Mortimer St., Cavendish Sq., 1 Mar. 1845.)

BIRD, Robert Wilberforce.
　p. 148, l. 36 : *add m*. Elizabeth Maria, 3rd dau. of Henry Cloete, of Westerford, C.G.H.

BIRD, William Charles Lewis.
　p. 149, l. 14 : *add* (She *re-m*. 9 Feb. 1852, Sir Hector Maclean Hay, 7th Bart., and died 24 July 1888.)

BIRRELL, George.
　p. 150, l. 34 : *add m*. 31 July 1797, Helen, younger dau. of Rev. William Pairman, minister of Elie 1761-98.

BIRRELL, Thomas.
　p. 151, l. 12 : *add d*. 22 Sept. 1791.

BISHOP, George William.
　p. 152, l. 18 : *add* Ed. Merchant Taylors' Oct. 1823-Oct. 1825.

BLACK, Andrew.
　p. 153, l. 34 : *add* Lieut. 5th Bn. Sepoys.

BLACK, Charles.
　p. 154, l. 5 : *add* Ed. Merchant Taylors' Oct. 1821-Mar. 1822.

BLACK, Patrick.
　p. 154, l. 11 : *add b*. Aberdeen 17 Mar. 1763.
　l. 15 : *add* Only surviving son of Bailie Alexander Black, mgte. of Aberdeen, and Mary Leslie his wife. His sister was mother of Gavin Young, *q.v. m*. Aberdeen 30 Apr. 1811, Jane, 3rd dau. of William Young, and cousin-german of Gavin Young, *q.v.*
　l. 25 : *add* to *Refs*. *Memoir of James Young*, p. 148.

BLACKBURN, Richard Edward.
p. 156, l. 12 : *add* Maria his wife, sister of W. C. P. Collinson, *q.v.*

BLACKNEY, James.
p. 157, l. 15 : *add m.* M. M. (She died Meerut 11 Jan. 1825, aged 24.)

BLAGRAVE, George.
p. 158, l. 32 : *add* 5th son of John Blagrave, of Watchfield. *Add* to *Refs.* Berry's *Berks. Peds.* p. 146.

BLAIR, William.
p. 162, l. 7 : *add* Capt. H.M. 121st Foot. On h.p. in 1764. (*See also* Vol. ii. p. 622.)

BLAKE, William.
p. 164, l. 5 : *add m.* in England 1807, Mary Anne Wolsey, dau. of Col. Benjamin Wolsey Muirson, and sister of the mother of Henry John Childe Shakespear, *q.v.*
l. 10 : *add* Nepal War 1814-15 ; Capt. 1/13th N.I.

*BLAKE, William Powney.
p. 164 : *add* Son of Benjamin Blake, of Lamb's Conduit St., London, and Mary his wife. *b.* 12 June 1796 ; *bapt.* St. George the Martyr, London, 4 Oct. 1796.

BLANE, Robert.
p. 165 : *add* to *Services* Transfd. as Ensign from Bombay Est. 5 Aug. 1765.

BLANSHARD, John.
p. 166, l. 9 : *add* to *Services* Apptd. 3rd Mate of the *Royal George* East Indiaman in 1804 ; Comdr. of the *James Sibbald* 1811 ; of the *Carnatic* 1815 ; of the *Marquis Wellington. d.* Cheltenham 8 Sept. 1828.

BLANSHARD, John Henry.
p. 166, l. 17 : *add* Son of Richard Blanshard, of Patrick Brompton Hall, Yorks. *m.* Emily Edwards, dau. of Rev. William Peacock, LL.B.

BLOIS, Thomas Francis.
p. 168, l. 16 : *add* Ed. Charterhouse June 1820-Apr. 1821.

BLUNT, Henry James.
p. 170, l. 5 : *add b.* 14 Dec. 1806. Son of John Blunt and Lydia his wife.
l. 7 : *add* Ed. Charterhouse Jan. 1817-June 1822. (*See also* Vol. ii. p. 623.)

BLUNT, James Tillyer.
p. 170, l. 16 : *add* Ed. Merchant Taylors' Oct. 1774-Mar. 1776.

BOILEAU, Alexander Henry Edmonstone.
p. 171 : *add* His widow *m*. 2nd, Lt.-Gen. Alexander Todd Cadell, Madras Art.

BOMFORD, Robert.
p. 177, l. 11 : *add d*. 18 Apr. 1817.

BOURDIEU, James.
p. 184, l. 22 : *add* dau. of Henry Jacques, *q.v.* (She died Dehra Dun 1 Jan. 1858, aged 58.)

BOURKE, Walter.
p. 185, l. 18 : *add* Edmund Burke, the statesman (*D.N.B.*), in a letter to John Stewart, dated 30 Oct. 1772, refers to him as, ' my relation and namesake Walter Bourke, a Capt. of Seapoys.'
Add to *Services* Succeeded Major R. E. Roberts, *q.v.*, in comd. of 30th Regt. Sepoys in 1784.
Add to *Refs.* Will, written in Persian, undated (? on his deathbed) ; proved 15 Aug. 1788.

BOWIE, Robert.
p. 187, l. 8 : *add b*. 1760/61.
l. 13 : *add m*. Springfield, nr. Douglas, 10 Feb. 1809, Elizabeth, dau. of James Coventry.
Add to *Refs.* M.I. Agra Cantt. cemetery.

BOYDELL, Thomas.
p. 193, l. 12 : *add* Son of Thomas Boydell.

BRADLEY, Matthew.
p. 197, l. 29 : *add m*. Bombay 20 Sept. 1782, Miss Isabella Hay.

BRADLEY, Thomas.
p. 197, l. 32 : *add d*. 25 Nov. 1788.

BRETON, Thomas.
p. 201, l. 11 : *add* to *Services* Major comdg. 2nd Regt. of Sepoys at Chandernagore in Aug. 1781.

BRICE, James.
p. 202, top l. : *add* Son of Edward Brice, of Berners St., London. His sister *m*. Rt. Hon. Sir John Anstruther, 4th and 1st Bart., C.J. Bengal.
Add to *Refs.* Burke's *Peerage*, 1923, p. 120, *s.n.* Carmichael-Anstruther, Bart. *Hickey*, iv. 230. *B. : P.P.* No. 76, p. 106.

BRIDGE, George.
p. 202, l. 10 : *add d.* Calcutta.

BRIGGS, William Thomas.
p. 204, l. 19 : *add bapt.* St. Anne's, Westminster, 16 Oct. 1809. 2nd son of Sir John Thomas Briggs, Kt., Accountant Gen. of the Navy (*D.N.B.*), and Frances his wife, dau. of Thomas Lewis, of Cadiz. Ed. Westminster ; admitted 23 Sept. 1822.
Add to *Refs. Westminster School Register.* (*See also* Vol. ii. p. 623.)

BRIND, Frederick.
p. 204, l. 32 : *add* and Susannah Sowley his wife.
l. 33 : *add m.* 1st, Dinapore 27 June 1833, Elizabeth Stewart, widow.

BRISBANE, Thomas.
p. 205 : *add* the following : *Note :* " Capt. Thomas Brisbane, late from the East Indies," *m.* Bath June 1780, Cordelia, dau. of Fleming Martin, *q.v.* This was a runaway match which so displeased the bride's father that he refused to have anything further to do with the couple. Four months later Brisbane committed suicide by poison at Romsey. " Some attribute this rash action to his (Col. Martin's) inflexibility." (*Bath Chron.* 29 June and 26 Oct. 1780.)

BRISCOE, Horton.
p. 206, l. 6 : *add* only dau. of Sutton Banks, M.D., of the City of Lincoln. (She died Oct. 1794.)
l. 10 : *add* Major comdg. 10th Regt. Sepoys in Aug. 1781.

BRISCOE, John Jessop.
p. 206 : his second christian name was Jessop.
Add to *Services* Lieut. S. Devon Mil. 25 Dec. 1781.

BRISTOW, George William Grant.
p. 208, l. 12 : *add* (She died Benares 14 Mar. 1843, aged 33.)

BROADBENT, James.
p. 209, l. 8 : *add* Reduced by G.C.M. ; restored to his rank as Lieut. of Inf. 22 Nov. 1773.

BROADBENT, Thomas Wheeler.
p. 209, l. 14 : *add* Eldest son of Thomas Broadbent, of Sheffield, merchant and banker, and —— his wife, dau. of —— Wheeler.
Add to *Refs.* Hunter's *Familiæ Minorum Gentium,* ii. 428.

BROADBRIDGE, John.
    p. 209, l. 31 : *add to Services* Apptd. Ensign 39th Ft. from 9 Aug. 1755, and was also in R.A. at the same time.

BROADFOOT, William.
    p. 210, l. 7 : *add* and Helen his wife, dau. of James Sutherland. Ed. Westminster; admitted 12 Jan. 1824.
    Add to *Refs. Westminster School Register.*

BROADHURST, Thomas.
    p. 210, l. 23 : *add m.* (?) (Wife died Aug. 1812.)

BRODHURST, John.
    p. 211, l. 15 : *add* Ed. Repton; admitted Mar. 1802.
    l. 20 : *add* to *Refs. Repton School Register.*

BRODIE, David Hay.
    p. 211, l. 25 : *add* and Ann Taap his wife.

BROMLEY, Nathaniel Barrett.
    p. 212, bottom l. : *add d.* Belfast 15 Nov. 1829.
    p. 213, top l. : *add bapt.* St. James's, Clerkenwell, 17 July 1785.
    l. 3 : *add* dau. of Thomas Morgan (1760/61-1814), *q.v.*
    Add to *Services* Admitted to Gray's Inn 5 June 1804.
    Add to *Refs. Howard & Crisp (Notes),* vi. 45.

BROOKE, Charles William.
    p. 213, l. 28 : *add* Portrait of him as a boy, playing with the Nawab of Murshidabad, by Zoffany, was sold at Sotheby's 3 July 1929.

BROOKE, Henry Stuart.
    p. 215, l. 16 : *add bapt.* Calcutta 4 Jan. 1799.
    l. 18 : *add* Ed. Harrow 1811-14.

BROOKE, James Henry.
    p. 216, l. 7 : *add* widow of James Patton, B.C.S.

BROOKE, Robert.
    p. 216, l. 24 : *add m.* Mrs. Ann Maria Wynne, *née* Mapletoft.

BROWN, George (1790-1806).
    p. 224, l. 16 : *add bapt.* St. James's, Westminster, 21 June 1790. Son of Joseph Brown and Sarah his wife.

BROWN, Henry.
    p. 224, l. 24 : *add* Lord of the Manor of Horbling. Only son of Richard(s) Brown, M.D., of Huntingdon, and Lavinia his wife, only dau. of William Broff, Govr. of Ft. Marlbro'.
    l. 34 : *add* to *Refs. Genealogist,* iii. 73.

BROWN, James (*d.* 1788).
 p. 224 : *add m.* Margaret Lidderdale, niece of Lt.-Gen. Robert Fullerton of Dudwick. (*See also* James Williamson (1752-1792).)

BROWN, Sir Thomas.
 p. 227, l. 34 : *add b.* Monaghan 15 Aug. 1761.
 p. 228, l. 12 : *add* to *Refs. G.M.* 1839, ii. 668. M.I. Walton-on-Thames churchyard.

BROWN(E), Ulysses.
 p. 228, l. 25 : *add* Sub-Brigadier and Cornet 2nd Troop of Horse Gds. 18 Nov. 1764 ; Bdr. and Lieut. do. 12 Sept. 1766 ; Exempt and Capt. do. 6 Mar. 1771 ; left 23 Jan. 1778.
 l. 26 : *add* to *Refs.* M.I. at Bhagulpur.

BROWNE, Clement Read.
 p. 229, l. 39 : *add* Son of John Browne, Surg., Bengal Medical Est., and Charlotte Isabella Swinton his wife, of Swinton, co. Berwick. Brother of Gen. Sir Sam Browne, V.C. (*D.N.B.*), and of Charlotte Isabella, wife of Sir George St. Patrick Lawrence, *q.v.*

BROWNE, James.
 p. 232, top l. : *add* Major comdg. 31st N.I. in Aug. 1781.
 l. 4 : *add Probably* author of " History of the origin and progress of the Sikhs," dated 1781, pub. 1788.

BROWNE, John.
 p. 232, l. 21 : *add b.* 1764/65.
 l. 22 : *add d.* of a hectic fever, aged 25.
 l. 23 : *add Note :* Name given as Brown in burial register.

BROWNLOW, George Arthur.
 p. 234, l. 38 : *add* T.C.D. ; Fellow Commoner 18 Oct. 1824.

BRUCE, Michael.
 p. 237 : *add* 4th son of Sir Michael Bruce, 6th Bart. of Stenhouse, co. Stirling, and Mary his wife, eldest dau. of Gen. Sir Andrew Agnew, Bart. of Lochnaw.
 l. 28 : *add* Lieut. of an Independent Coy. in N. America 28 Oct. 1760 ; Lieut. 74th Ft. 5 July 1761 ; h.p. do. 1763 till death. Transfd. as Lieut. to Bengal Army (M.C. 1 Sept. 1768).

BRUCE, Robert.
 p. 237, l. 34 : *add* Younger son of Andrew Bruce, of Grangemyre or Grangehill, shipmaster in Kinghorn, and Jean his wife, dau. of Rev. John Squyre, minister of Forres. Father (*not*

brother) of Margaret Stuart, afterwards Mrs. Tyndale Bruce of Falkland, by a native lady.

p. 238, l. 4 : *add* to *Refs. Genealogist*, vii. 141. Scott's *Fasti*, vi. 422.

BRUCE, Robert Robertson.

p. 238, l. 32 : *add* Eldest son of Daniel Bruce and Anne his wife, dau. of John Robertson, farmer in Strathleck, co. Perth.

BRYANT, Edward Pinckard.

p. 240, l. 32 : *add* Ed. Merchant Taylors' Mar. 1820-Mar. 1823.

BRYANT, Sir Jeremiah.

p. 241, l. 15 : *add* (She died London 24 May 1866.)

BUCHAN, Alexander.

p. 242, l. 4 : *add b.* 3 Mar. 1760.
Add to *Refs.* Family information. Intest. ; admon. (Madras) 19 June 1794.

BUCKLEY, Frederick.

p. 244, l. 31 : *add* dau. of William Beckford Cox, *q.v.* Ed. Harrow ; admitted Jan. 1796.

BUCKLEY, William.

p. 245, l. 14 : *add* Ed. Harrow ; admitted Jan. 1796.

BUIST, George.

p. 246, l. 16 : *add* and Margaret his wife, dau. of William Fernie (*not* Fermie), of Tillywhonland.

BULLER, William.

p. 246, bottom l. : *add* Exeter Coll., Oxon.; matric. 7 Dec. 1821.

BUNBURY, Matthew Alexander.

p. 247, l. 24 : *add* Son (twin with Margaret Isabella) of Abraham Bunbury and Christian his wife (? *née* Jones).

BUNCE, Thomas.

p. 248, l. 11 : *add* Son of Rev. John Bunce.
l. 12 : *add Refs.* Will dated 26 May 1766 ; proved 1766.

BURGES, George.

p. 249, l. 30 : *add* 2nd son of Daniel Burges, burgess of Bristol and city solicitor, and Catherine his wife, dau. of Mr. Hudgson, of Baldwin St., Bristol.

l. 31 : *add* (She died 13 July 1843.)

BURGES(S), Thomas.
p. 250, l. 9 : *add* d. Calcutta Mar. 1798. *m*. Elizabeth Kerr. Reputed father of George Burges (*D.N.B.*).
Services : After quitting the Service he engaged in trade at Neshal Bagh, Bengal, and later at Calcutta.
Refs. : Will dated Calcutta, 24 June 1797 ; cod. 23 Mar. 1798 ; proved 11 Apr. 1798.

BURGH, Andrew.
p. 250, l. 15 : *add* Son of Burgh of Newhalls.

BURLTON, Philip Bowles.
p. 252, l. 3 : *add* Ed. Winchester ; Scholar 1815. *Add* to *Refs.* Kirby.

BURN, William.
p. 253, l. 14 : *add b*. N. Berwick 1745.

BURNE, William.
p. 253, l. 25 : *add b*. 24 Jan. 1795.
l. 26 : *add bapt.* St. Mary Newington, Surrey, 17 Apr. 1795. Son of Thomas Burne and Mary his wife.

BURRINGTON, George.
p. 259, l. 6 from bottom : *add* Ensign 2nd Bn. 32nd Ft. 3 Sept. 1756 ; formed into 71st Ft. 21 Apr. 1758 ; h.p. 71st Ft. 1763. Lieut. 56th Ft. 23 Sept. 1763 till 25 Feb. 1768. (*See also* Vol. ii. p. 624.)

BURROWES, Alexander.
p. 261, l. 22 : *add* Lieutenant, 10th Bn. Sepoys.
l. 24 : *add* accidentally kld. by sepoys of 29th Bn.
Refs. : M.I. Fatehgarh.

BURT, James Ranald.
p. 263, l. 11, after ' wife ' *add* dau. of Norman Macdonald, of Scalpa. Cousin-german of Malcolm Nicolson (1805-1835), *q.v.*

BURT, Thomas Seymour.
p. 263, l. 25 : *add m*. Elizabeth, widow of Thomas Seaton Forman, of Pepperbrook House, Dorking, M.P. for Bridgwater. (She died 5 July 1889.)

BURTON, Charles Æneas.
p. 264, l. 2 : *add* Ed. Charterhouse June 1820-1825/6.
Add to *Refs.* M.I. Kotah.

BUSH, James Tobin.
p. 265, l. 37 : *add* dau. of Gen. James Tobin.

BUTLER, Edward William.
p. 267, l. 11 : *add* b. 1769/70.
l. 14 : *add* d. Agra 1 Aug. 1819, aged 49.
Add to *Refs.* M.I. at Agra.

BUTLER, Whitwell.
p. 268, l. 36 : *add* to *Services* Fort Adjt. and Bk. Mr. at Chunar at death.
Add to *Refs.* M.I. old cemetery below Chunar fort.

BYNG, Hon. Robert Barlow Palmer.
p. 271, l. 11 : *add* Cousin-german of Arthur Hall, *q.v.*

CADDELL, Walter.
p. 273, l. 5 : *add* Son of Dr. Philip Caddell.
l. 7 : *add* Ed. Charterhouse Jan. 1818-May 1822.

CAILLAUD, John.
p. 274, l. 10 : *add* Son of Reuben Caillaud and Marguerita his wife. *b.* Dublin 5 Feb. 1726. *m.* 1763, Mary, only dau. of Jacob Pechell and sister of Sir Paul Pechell, 1st Bart. (*D.N.B.*).
l. 13 : *add* Ensign 8th Ft. 4 Oct. 1743 ; Lieut. do. 17 Feb. 1745/6 ; retired 31 Oct. 1751.
Add to *Refs. Huguenot Peds.*, by C. E. Lart, Vol. ii. (1928), p. 40. Burke's *Peerage*, 1923, p. 1745, *s.n.* Brooke-Pechell, Bart.

CALCRAFT, Henry Fox.
p. 274, l. 32 : *add* Ed. Westminster.
Add to *Refs. An Apology for the Life of George Anne Bellamy* (1785), iv. 187.

p. 275 : *add* as a new entry, after Sir Alexander Caldwell :—

*CALDWELL, Arthur (*d.* 1786). Captain, Engineers. Capt. 25 Jan. 1779. *d.* Benares 26 Jan. 1786.

Son of William Caldwell. Brother of Sir Alexander Caldwell, *q.v. m.* Elizabeth. (She died Glos. Pl., Portman Sq., 30 Dec. 1832.) Father of Gen. Sir James Lillyman Caldwell, G.C.B., Madras Engrs. (*D.N.B.*).

Services : First Mahratta War 1778-80, under Col. Thomas Goddard (w.) ; Capt. Engrs. Tried by C.M. in camp nr. Surat, 2 Aug. 1780, for insubordination to Col. Goddard, and dismissed ; restored to the Service by the Board at Calcutta 21 May 1781. Chief Engr. at Chunar.

Refs.: Burke's *Landed Gentry*, 4th edn., p. 198, *s.n.* Caldwell, of Beachlands, I.W.

CALL, Thomas.
p. 276, l. 38 : *add d.* at sea 12 Dec. 1788, on board the *William Pitt*, aged 39.
Add. to *Refs.* M.I. Exeter cathedral.

CALLANDER, Adam.
p. 277, l. 11 : *add* Cornet in Army 20 Mar. 1759 ; Cornet 2nd D.G. (in Germany) 29 Sept. 1759 ; Lieut. new 124th Ft. 13 Feb. 1762. On Irish h.p. of Lieut. late 124th Ft. on reduction in 1763 till transfd. (probably 1785 or 1786) to Brit. h.p. of Lieut., Donkin's Garr. Bn. ; still on its h.p. in 1799 ; not in *A.L.* for 1800.

CAMAC, Jacob.
p. 278, top l. : *add* Son of John Camac, of Maralin, co. Down, and Elizabeth his wife, dau. of Jacob Turner, of Lurgan, co. Down. Said to have *m.* " an Indian Princess."

CAMAC, Turner.
p. 278, l. 17 : *add m.* Marylebone 27 Jan. 1795, Miss Sarah Masters.
l. 18 : *add Refs.: G.M.* 1793, ii. 1148 ; 1795, i. 82.

CAMPBELL, John (*c.* 1745-1770).
p. 291, l. 6 : *add d.* Monghyr 12 Nov. 1770 : kld. in a duel by Dennis Morrison, *q.v.*

CAMPBELL, Neil.
p. 294, l. 13 : *add* to *Services* Served 2 or 3 yrs. in H.M.S. *Texel* before joining the Army.
l. 19 : *add* to *Refs. Memorials of Four Old Families*, by Capt. D. Wimberley (Inverness, 1893), p. 40.

CANHAM, Robert Spencer.
p. 299 : His christian names were Robert Spencer.

CARDEN, William.
p. 300, l. 31 : *add bur.* Madras 6 Aug. 1781.

CARNAC, John.
p. 305, bottom l. : *add* 2nd Lieut. 8th Marines 4 Feb. 1739/40 ; 1st Lieut. do. 30 Nov. 1745 ; transfd. to h.p. on their disbandment from 25 Dec. 1748. Exchanged to Lieut. 39th Ft. 18 Feb. 1754. Local Bdr. Gen. in E.I. 12 May 1764. (*See also* Vol. ii. pp. 616, 625.)

CARNAC, Scipio.

p. 306, l. 6: *add* Ensign 5th Ft. 2 Nov. 1745; h.p. 6 Jan. 1748/9. Ensign 1st Bn. 1st Ft. 16 Feb. 1756; Lieut. 3rd Ft. 29 Aug. 1756; exchanged to h.p. 99th Ft. 26 Feb. 1764. Lieut. of an Independent Coy. of Invalids at Plymouth 6 Oct. 1779; Adjt. of these 6 Coys. 25 Jan. 1795, and on their reduction was placed on full pay thereof 1802 till death. (*See also* Vol. ii. p. 625.)

CARNE, John Camin.

p. 306, l. 13: *add* after 'wife' dau. of Henry Wilmot, of Exeter.

CARNEGIE, John William.

p. 306, l. 30: *add* Ed. Edin. Acad.; in the Rector's class in 1824.

CARNEGY, Patrick Ogilvy.

p. 307: *add b.* 11 Oct. 1804. Son of James Carnegy, of P.W.I., merchant. Ed. Glasgow Grammar School Oct. 1813-June 1818.

CARROLL, Thomas.

p. 310, l. 21: *add* to *Services* 2nd Lieut. 18th Coy. Marines 31 July 1762; h.p. do. 1763 till death. Transfd. as Lieut. to Bengal Army 1 Sept. 1768.

CARRUTHERS, John.

p. 311, l. 4: *add* Son of John Carruthers, of Denbie.

CARSTAIRS, Peter.

p. 311: *add* 4th son of James Carstairs, who added the surname of Bruce (eldest son of Sir John Carstairs, of Kilconquhar), and Christian his wife, 3rd dau. of Sir Peter Wedderburn, afterwards Halkett, 1st Bart. of Gosford. Cousin-german of Henry Wedderburn, *q.v. b.* 5 June 1736.

Add to *Refs. The Wedderburn Book*, i. 379.

CARSTAIRS, Thomas.

p. 311, l. 38: *add* and Mary his 1st wife, dau. of William Dickson, of Prestonpans.

CARTE, Edward.

p. 312, l. 3: *add* 2nd son of Edward Carte, of The Castle, Newcastle, co. Limerick, and Margaret his 1st wife, dau. of Alexander Elliott. *m.* Miss Wyatt.

Add to *Refs.* Foster's *Families of Royal Descent*, ii. 640.

ADDENDA

CARTER, Samuel.
p. 314, top l.: *add bapt.* 1 Nov. 1794. Cousin-german of Sir John Peter Boileau, 1st Bart.

CARTER, William Charles.
p. 314, l. 15: *add* Nephew of W. B. Davis, *q.v.*

CATES, John.
p. 319, l. 22: *add* Ed. Charterhouse June 1813-Dec. 1814.

CATHCART, James.
p. 319, l. 1 from bottom: *add d. unm.* 17 Nov. 1810.
p. 320, l. 6: *add* Retired 17 Nov. 1808.

CAUTLEY, Richard.
p. 323, l. 5: *add d.* Jubbulpore, C.P.
l. 15: *add* M.I. Jubbulpore.

CHAIGNEAU, Christopher Theophilus.
p. 325, l. 18: *add b.* 1734/35. *d.* Madura, Madras, 16 May 1773, aged 38.
l. 22: *add* to *Refs.* M.I. Madura town cemetery. (*See also* Vol. ii. p. 626.)

CHALMERS, Robert.
p. 326, l. 16: *add* younger sister of George Ranken, *q.v.*

CHAMBRÉ, Christopher.
p. 328, l. 12: *add* 3rd son of Christopher Chambré, of Llanfoist, sometime Lieut. 53rd Ft.
l. 15: *add* to *Services* Capt. R. Monmouth and Brecon Mil. 25 Mar. 1813.
Add to *Refs.* Sir Joseph Bradney's *Hist. of Monmouth*, i. 284, 362.

CHAPMAN, Charles.
p. 330, l. 12: *add m.* (?) (His widow died Bath 20 Nov. 1807.) (? Father of Charles Chapman, of Bathford, Somerset, M.P. Newtown, Hants, in 1802 till he resigned in 1805—or himself the M.P.)
l. 13: *add* to *Services* Ensign H.M. 30th Ft. 19 May 1742; 2nd Lieut. do. 21 June 1745; Lieut. do. 1 Oct. 1755; Capt. 69th Ft. 1 May 1759. Junior Major 96th Ft. 6 Feb. 1761; on its h.p. 1763; do. 1807, but not in *A.L.* 1808. Bt. Lt. Col. 25 May 1772. Appears to have resigned the Coy.'s Service at some period, and to have been reapptd. a Lt. Col. in Sept. 1768. (M.C. 1 Sept. 1768—' Lt.-Col. Chapman is to take rank agreeable to his former Commission in the Coy.'s Service.')

CHARLTON, Andrew.
p. 331 : *add* to *Refs. Englishman*, 1 Sept. 1835.

CHEAPE, Harry.
p. 335 : *add* 5th son of Harry Cheape, 4th Baron of Rossie, and Alice his wife, 2nd dau. of John Landales, of Ardes, co. Fife.
Add to *Refs. Baronage of Scotland*, by Sir Robert Douglas, Bart., p. 576, *s.n.* Cheape, of Rossie, co. Fife.

CHEAPE, James.
p. 335, l. 35 : *add* Son of James Cheap, of Sauchie.
l. 38 : *add* to *Services* Was Lieut in 27th Bn. Sepoys at death.
Add to *Refs.* M.I. Chunar (Shamspur) old cemetery.

CHEERE, Henry.
p. 336, l. 23 : *add* Ed. Bury St. Edmunds Grammar School.

CHRISTIE, Andrew.
p. 341, l. 23 : *add* Son of Andrew Christie, of Ferrybank, co. Fife, and Margaret his wife, dau. of Cathcart Dempster, of St. Andrews, banker.
Add to *Refs. Genealogical Mag.* iv. 256 (Oct. 1900).

CLANCEY, George.
p. 343 : *add* Only child of John Clancey, Bombay Marine.

CLARK, Charles.
p. 344, l. 12 : *add* and Frances his wife.
Add to *Refs.* M.I. in St. Peter's, Dorchester.

CLARK(E), Elias.
p. 344 : *add b.* 1726/27. Aged 59 in 1786, when he was granted a pension of 2/6d. *p.d.* from Lord Clive's fund.

CLARK, George Quintin.
p. 344, l. 35 : *add bapt.* publicly Putney 13 Mar. 1808. Son of William Clark and Mary his wife.

CLARK, William.
p. 345, l. 1 from bottom : *add* dau. of Charles Child Wilson, *q.v.*

CLARKE, John.
p. 347 : *add* 2nd son of Ralph Clarke and Mary Christian his 2nd wife, dau. of William Mount, of Merton.
Add to *Refs.* Burke's *Landed Gentry*, 15th edn., p. 418, *s.n.* Clarke, of Borde Hill, Sussex.

CLARKSON, Robert Graham.
p. 349, 1. 6: *add* Lieut., Grant Fenc. (Strathspey Regt.), 23 May 1794; resigned 28 May 1795.

CLAYTON, Edward.
p. 349, l. 21: *add* Captain, 5th N.I. *b.* 1752/53.
l. 24: *add d.* aged 46.
Add to Refs. M.I. Fatehgarh fort cemetery.

CLAYTON, Thomas William.
p. 350, l. 13: *add* (She died Chunar 1 June 1793, aged 24.)

CLERKSON, Henry Chambers.
p. 352, l. 31: *add bapt.* Berhampore 3 Dec. 1796. Ed. Westminster 26 Apr. 1808 till 1811.
l. 35: *add Refs. Westminster School Register.*

CLERKSON, John.
p. 352, l. 3 from bottom: *add* widow of Robert Maxwell (1752-1792), *q.v.*

CLIFTON, Charles.
p. 353: *delete* the whole of this biog. and *substitute* :—

CLIFTON, Charles (1743-1781/2). Capt. Lieut. Art. (28) Afterwards Bt. Maj. Madras. Art. *b.* 21 July 1743. Lt. F. (Madras) 20 Sept. 1760. 2/Lt. (Madras) 1 Sept. 1763. 2/Lt. (Bengal) 4 Sept. 1763. Lieut. 5 Oct. 1763. Capt. Lt. 13 Mar. 1765. Resigned 6 May 1766. Capt. (Madras) 11 Oct. 1768. Bt. Major ? 1779. *d.* 1781/2.

(? *m.* 1st, Margaret Jones.) *m.* 2nd, in England (before May 1771), Mary ——. *m.* 3rd, in India, Elizabeth Ann, dau. of Col. Henry Frederick Creutzer, of Mannheim, Baden. (She *m.* 2nd, Madras 23 Oct. 1782, Surg. Maj. Thomas Davies, Madras Est.; 3rd, Madras 1 Jan. 1791, Capt. Sir William Cockburn, Bt., and died 30 June 1829, aged 71.) Ed. Merchant Taylors' Mar. 1750/51-Oct. 1754.

Services: Left Madras for Bengal on 5 Sept. 1763, with 17 artillerymen; transfd. to Bengal Est. *Probably* resigned during the " Batta mutiny " and returned to England. Sailed for Madras with his wife, Mary, in May 1771. Siege and capture of Tanjore Aug.-Sept. 1773.

Refs.: G.E.C. *Complete Baronetage*, ii. 333. Will dated camp before Tanjour, 26 Aug. 1773; proved 5 Mar. 1782.

CLODE, William.
p. 353 : *add* Of Skisdon Lodge, Cornwall. Son of William Clode, of Camelford, Cornwall, atty., and Sarah Phillis his wife, dau. of John Holder. Uncle of Richard Braddon, *q.v. d.s.p.* 1807. Major comdg. 33rd N.I. in Aug. 1781.
Refs. : Maclean's *Hist. of Trigg Minor*, ii. 143.

COCKERELL, John.
p. 358, l. 32 : *add* to *Refs. Howard & Crisp (Notes),* ix. 68 (where date of birth is given as 10 Aug. 1752). Will with 3 codicils dated 25 Feb. 1793 to 4 Nov. 1796 ; proved 21 July 1798 (P.C.C. 468, *Walpole*).

COCKRIN, George Driver.
p. 358 : The second christian name was Driver. The surname appears sometimes as Cockrein.

COLEBROOKE, Robert Hyde.
p. 361 : *add* Eldest natural son of Robert Colebrooke, of Chilham Castle, Kent, by Mary, wife of Robert Jones.

COLLINS, Charles James Colin.
p. 364, l. 17 : *add* Ed. Eton 1812-17 ; K.S. 1814.

COLLINS, Henry John.
p. 364, bottom l. : *add bapt.* Calcutta 4 Jan. 1794. Ed. Harrow 1806-7.
Add to *Refs. Harrow School Register.*

COLLINS, John Ulric.
p. 365, l. 23 : *delete* ' *probably.*'

COLLINSON, William Clinton Peter.
p. 366, l. 4 : *add* Ed. Felsted Aug. 1818 till June 1819 ; migrated to Harrow.
Add to *Refs. Alumni Felstedienses,* 6th (1931) edn.

COLLYER, William.
p. 366 : *add* to *Refs. Howard & Crisp (Notes),* viii. 121.

COLQUHOUN, Sir Robert David.
p. 368, l. 8 : *add* to *Refs.* Portrait in *The Regimental History of the 3rd Queen Alexandra's Own Gurkha Rifles,* ed. by Maj.-Gen. N. G. Woodyatt (Philip Allan, 1930).

COLYEAR, Thomas David.
p. 369, l. 21 : *add m.* 1st, an Indian Mussulman lady. *m.* 2nd, by licence at Simla, 11 Dec. 1865, Alice, spinster, dau. of Jewtoo, Hindu. (She died Simla 9 May 1878, aged 35.)

CONNELLAN, Peter.
　p. 372, l. 18 : *add m.* Croydon, 7 Sept. 1781, Marguerite, 4th dau. of Stephen Galhié, a medical practitioner. (She died 11 Nov. 1794.)
　Add to *Refs. Genealogist*, N.S. xxviii. 216.

CONRAN, Henry Marcell.
　p. 374, l. 2 : *add d.* Park House, Ixworth, Suffolk, 23 Feb. 1902.
　Add to *Refs. The Times*, 3 Mar. 1902.

CONROY, Llewellyn.
　p. 374, l. 32 : *add* widow of William Drury Kerr, B.C.S.

CONSTABLE, George.
　p. 375, l. 15 : *add* Son of David Constable, grazier, Dundee, and Agnes Watson his wife.

BROWN-CONSTABLE, Charles.
　p. 375, l. 37 : *add* (She died Nagod, C.I., 14 Aug. 1847, aged 36.)

CONWAY, John Edward.
　p. 376, l. 16 : *add* (*Probably* son of Lt.-Col. T. Conway.)

COOK, William.
　p. 377, l. 17 : *add* Major comdg. 9th Regt. Sepoys in Aug. 1781.

COOKE, George Martin.
　p. 377, l. 39 : *add bapt.* Walcot 1 June 1801. Son of John Cooke, of Dublin, law bookseller, and Sarah his wife. T.C.D. ; Pensioner 3 July 1815.
　Add Refs. : Alumni Dub.

COOPER, Richard.
　p. 382 : *add m.* Mary. *N.B.*—Although his name appears as Cooper in the burial register of St. Mary's, Fort St. George, the correct form would appear to be Copper as given in *D. & M.* and in some original MS. records at I.O.

COOPER, ——.
　p. 383 : *add Note :* " Ensign James Couper—kld. by the Nabob's people with Mr. Amyatt near Cossimbazar." (*Orme MSS.* Vol. 21, Bengal, p. 129.) The surname is also given as Cowper (ib. p. 133).

GILBERT-COOPER, Henry Edward.
p. 384, l. 9 : *add* 3rd son of John Gilbert Cooper, of Thurgarton (who assumed the surname of Gardiner 1823), and Catherine his wife, youngest dau. of John (or William) Roe, of Sudbrook, Lincs.
Add to Refs. Hunter's *Familiæ Minorum Gentium*, iii. 870.

CORBET, Samuel.
p. 385, bottom l. : *add* M.I. St. John's cemetery, Meerut. (*See also* Vol. ii. p. 627.)

CORFIELD, Frederick.
p. 387 : *add* 3rd son of William Corfield, of Taunton, Col. of 33rd Ft. and Comdt. R. Taunton Vols., and Christian King his wife, niece of Lord Paulet. Uncle of Charles Corfield, *q.v.*
Add to Refs. Burke's *Landed Gentry*, 8th edn., p. 403, *s.n.* Corfield, of Ormonde Fields, co. Derby.

CORNISH, Charles.
p. 389, l. 3 : *add b.* 1749.
Add to Refs. *A Family of Devon*, by Vaughan Cornish, D.Sc., 1942.

CORRI, Anthony Albert Lambert.
p. 391, l. 9 : *add bapt.* Marylebone 14 Mar. 1800.
l. 12 : *add* youngest dau. of Robert Bathurst, B.C.S.
l. 13 : *add* dau. of Martin Whish, of Clifton, Chief Comr., Board of Excise. (*See also* William Oliver Span.) (She died Territet, Switzerland, 30 Mar. 1883, aged 85.) Ed. Eton between 1808 and 1811.

COSBY, William.
p. 392, l. 6 : *add Possibly* son of William Cosby, Capt. h.p. of Col. Henry Beauclerk's 31st Ft. 3 May 1749 (who was son of Bdr.-Gen. William Cosby, Col. R. Irish Regt., Govr. of New York and the Jerseys).
l. 7 : *add* Ensign H.M. 4th Ft. (from Volunteer) 26 Sept. 1757 ; Lieut. do. 4 May 1759 ; Capt. Lt. do. 15 Nov. 1765 ; h.p. 12 June 1767. Transfd. as Capt. to Bengal Army (M.C. 1 Sept. 1768).

COURTENAY, Frederick Eardley Bellenden.
p. 394 : *add* Son of Hon. Anne Courtenay, 8th dau. of William, 2nd Viscount Courtenay (who was wife of George, 2nd Earl of Mountnorris). Nephew of Henry Gawler, one of the six clerks in court of chancery, and of John Bellenden Gawler, afterwards Ker (*D.N.B.*).
Refs.: (Cf. *Peerage, s.n.* Roxburghe, D. ; and Valentia, V.)

ADDENDA

COWLEY, Constantine William.
p. 396, l. 11 : *add bapt.* 10 May 1793. Son of William Cowley and Jane his wife. Nephew of Dennis Considen, Purveyor to the Forces.

COX, Henry Chambers Murray.
p. 399, l. 15 : *add m.* 1st, Bandel 12 Feb. 1814.

COX, Hiram.
p. 400, l. 11 : *add m.* Mary, younger sister of Andrew Fraser (*d.* 1812), *q.v.* (*See also* Allan Macpherson.)

CRABB(E), William Joseph.
p. 402, l. 4 : *add* Son of Mr. Crabb, of Tellesford, nr. Frome.
l. 11 : *add* Major comdg. 7th Regt. Sepoys in Aug. 1781. (*See also* Vol. ii. p. 627.)

CRAIGIE, Edmund Buchan.
p. 404, l. 15 : *add* Grandson of Thomas Craigie, Professor of Moral Philosophy in Univ. of Glasgow. (*Probably* son of John Craigie, Surg. Bengal Est., and Jacobina Helena his wife.)

CRAIGIE, James (1787-1875).
p. 404, l. 37 : *add m.* 23 June 1842.
l. 38 : *add* (She died 1 Apr. 1883.)

CRAWFORD, William (1793-1818).
p. 410, l. 3 : *add* Eldest son of Rev. William Crawford, minister of Straiton 1791-1816, and Agnes his wife, dau. of Rev. John M'Dermeit.
l. 7 : *add* to *Refs.* Scott's *Fasti*, iii. 72.

CRAWFURD, Gavin Ralston.
p. 410, l. 16 : *add m.* Chanda, nr. Nagpur 14 Sept. 1823, Charlotte Anne, 2nd dau. of William Dring, of Calcutta. (*See also* John Staniforth Pitts.)

CRAWFURD, Moses.
p. 410, l. 36 : *add* Major comdg. 28th N.I. in Aug. 1781. (*See also* Vol. ii. p. 628.)

CREDLAND, James.
p. 411 : *add Note* : The name should perhaps be **CRIDLAND**.

CROFT, John Thomas.
p. 413, l. 28 : *add* Ed. Winchester.

CROMMELIN, George Russell.
p. 414, l. 2 from bottom : *add m.* Johanna Maria, dau. of William de Waal, *q.v.*

CROMMELIN, John Dethick.
p. 415, l. 32 : *add bapt.* Calcutta 31 Dec. 1795. Son of Charles Russell Crommelin and Juliana his 1st wife, dau. of Sir Robert Barker, Bart., *q.v.* Grandson of Charles Crommelin, Govr. of Bombay 1760-7.

CROSSLEY, Francis.
p. 416 : *add* Younger son of John Crossley, of Lisburn, and Elizabeth Alcott his wife. *m.* 1st, Miss Stewart, of Lisburn. *m.* 2nd, 20 Apr. 1837, Elizabeth Helen, only dau. of William Irwin, of Mount Irwin, co. Armagh. (She died 9 Feb. 1891, aged 82.) Father of Sir William John Crossley, 1st Bart.
Add to *Refs.* Burke's *Peerage*, 1923, p. 632, *s.n.* Crossley, Bart., of Glenfield, Dunham Massey, co. Chester.

CROTTY, John.
p. 417, l. 5 : *add bur.* Madras 1 Jan. 1769.

CRUIKSHANK, John.
p. 419, l. 20 : *add* Son of John Cruikshank, clerk in the Navy office, and Barbara Sutherland his wife.
l. 28 : *add* to *Refs.* Family information. Miniatures of John and Kenneth in possession of the family.

CRUTTENDEN, George.
p. 420, l. 13 : *add* (Almost certainly son of Edward Holden Cruttenden, Second in Council at Ft. Wm. in 1753, Dir. E.I. Co. 1765-71.)
Add to *Refs.* M.I. in St. John's church, Calcutta.

CUDMORE, John.
p. 421 : *add Note :* The Will of Capt. John Cudmore was proved P.C. Dublin, 1792.

CUMBERLEGE, Nathaniel Joseph.
p. 424, l. 31 : *add* Ensign 67th Ft. 4 Feb. 1816.

CUMINE, George.
p. 424, bottom l. : *add* Son of Archibald Cumine, of Auchry, co. Aberdeen.

CUMMING, Andrew.
p. 426, l. 2 : *add bapt.* 22 Feb. 1742.
l. 5 : *add* 3rd son of John Cumming, mercht. in Garderhouse,

and Anne his wife, 8th dau. of Sir John Mitchell, of Westshore, 1st Bart.
l. 9 : *add* to *Refs*. *Zetland Family Histories*, by F. J. Grant (Lerwick, 1907), p. 177.

CUMMING, James.
p. 426, l. 19 : *add b.* 1757/58.
l. 21 : *add d.* aged 48.
Add to *Services* Served as a Vol. from Oct. 1778 in one of the Regts. composing the garr. of Gibraltar during the siege ; Ensign h.p. in an Addl. Coy. of 20th Ft. 18 May 1783.
Add to *Refs.* M.I. at Bhagulpur.

CUMMING, Robert (*d.* 1797).
p. 426, l. 3 from bottom : *add m.* Edinburgh 29 Jan. 1787, Frances, dau. of Sir John Cumming, *q.v.*

CUPPAGE, William.
p. 432 : *add b.* 1760/61. *d.* aged 58. M.I. at Fatehgarh.

CUTHBERT, Benjamin.
p. 436, l. 23 : *add m.* Bath 1823, Sarah, 3rd dau. of Samuel Sheppard, of Minchinhampton Pk., Gloucs.

CUTHBERT, Peter.
p. 436 : *add d.* aged 27. *m.* Martha Clark. M.I. St. Nicholas churchyard, Aberdeen.

Vol. II

D'AGUILAR, George Thomas.
p. 2, l. 12 : *add* dau. of Rev. Edward Burton, of Tuam, co. Galway.

DALLAS, Arbuthnot.
p. 3, l. 15 : *add* 2nd son of Murdoch Dallas, M.D., of Berbice, and Helen his wife, eldest dau. of Rev. Patrick Grant, of Strathenrick.
l. 27 : *add Refs. : Family of Dallas*, by James Dallas (Edin., 1921), p. 393.

DALRYMPLE, Robert.
p. 4 : His full name was **Robert Cornwallis DALRYMPLE**.

DALRYMPLE, Thomas Richard.
p. 4, l. 30 : *add* Ed. Shrewsbury 1818-21. Glasgow and Edin. Univs.
l. 33 : *add* to *Refs. Shrewsbury School Register.*

DALTON, Dennis Harman.
p. 5 : *add* Elder son of John Dalton, of Athlone, co. Westmeath, and Jane his wife. *m.* (?).

DALZELL, William.
p. 8, top line : *add* and Marion Hall his wife. Ed. Edin. Coll.

*DANIELL, Averell.
p. 9, l. 8 : *add* and Mary his wife, younger sister of Sir Edward Hyde East, 1st Bart., C. J. Calcutta.

DARBY, Charles.
p. 10. l. 24 : *add* (She *re-m.* 16 June 1842, Charles Simpson, of Chilworth Court, Hants, and died there 25 Jan. 1902, aged 93.)

DARLEY, Hugh.
p. 12, l. 13 : *add* 2nd son of Henry Darley, of Dublin, builder, and Elizabeth his wife. Brother of Alderman Frederick Darley, of Dublin, and of Lt.-Col. John Darley.

D'AUVERGNE, Philip.
p. 14, l. 12 : *add* to *Services* Capture of Ajaigarh 1809 ; Lt. Col. comdg. 1/26th N.I.

DAVIDSON, Hugh.
p. 17 : *add* to *Services* 2nd Lieut. in Skibo Coy. of W. Sutherland Vols. 28 Mar. 1800.

DAVIDSON, James (*d.* 1802).
p. 17, l. 29 : *add* Son of James Davidson, merchant in Dysart. Brother of Harry Davidson, of Old Belshes, W. S., sheriff-subs. of Midlothian 1791-1820.

DAVIDSON, James (1763/64-1825).
p. 18, l. 4 : *add m.* 24 Dec. 1816, Sarah, only dau. of Sir John Stirling, of Glorat, 5th Bart. (She *re-m.* John Graham and died 27 Dec. 1865.)

DAVIDSON, Wright Westcott.
p. 20, l. 6 : *add m.* 2nd, Maria ——. (She died Bath 26 July 1896, aged 77.)

DAVIES, Cornelius.

p. 21, l. 17 : *add* Son of Cornelius Davies, of Marlass, co. Pembroke, and Sarah his wife, dau. of Elizabeth Grant, of Fenton, psh. of Wiston, co. Pembroke. Cousin-german of Henry Grant, *q.v.*

DAVIES, John.

p. 22, l. 10, after ' 8 Apr.' *add* 1869.

DAVIS, Samuel.

p. 25, l. 39 : *add d.* Birdhurst Lodge, nr. Croydon.

DAVIS, William Bodycott.

p. 26, l. 32 : *add* Uncle of W. C. Carter, *q.v.*

DAVISON, Lewis.

p. 27, l. 25 : *add* to *Services* Lieut. H.M. 22nd (Cheshire) Ft. 6 Apr. 1797.

DAVY, William.

p. 28 : *add* Of Gloucester. *b.* 1745. *m.* (?), who survived him with six children.

Add to *Services* Sometime Persian Sec. to Warren Hastings. Is supposed to have made £120,000 in his two yrs. at Lucknow.

Add to *Refs. Bath Chron.* 9 Sept. 1784. Miniature by John Smart, 1775.

DAWES, Michael.

p. 29 : *add* to *Services* Fortified the harbour of Sydney, N.S.W., where " Dawes Battery " is still a point in the harbour. Presdt. of the Court for trial of ex-King of Delhi, Jan. 1858.

DAWES, Richard.

p. 30, l. 2 : *add* Apptd. Lieut. F. in the Art. 1 Sept. 1768 ; transfd. to Inf.

DEAN, Richard.

p. 33 : *add* Son of Richard Dean, sometime pilot and Dy. Master Attendant at Calcutta, and Catherine Sheldrake.

DE BEAUREGARD, John Richard.

p. 35, l. 5 : *add* His mother, Charlotte, was sister of Richard Copplestone or Coplestone, Dy. Comy. Ord. at Berhampore.

DE CASTRO, Henry.

p. 37 : *add b.* 1750/51. *d.* Holles Pl., Brompton, aged 77. Bottom l. : *add Refs. G.M.* 1828, i. 92.

DE GLOSS, Luis Felix.
p. 40, l. 27 : *add m.* Bombay 2 Apr. 1755, Miss Margaret Edgerton.

DELAFIELD, Philip.
p. 41, l. 7 : *add* to *Services* Comdd. 6th Bn. Sepoys at battle of St. George, 23 Apr. 1774.
l. 13 : *add* to *Refs. Macpherson*, p. 201 *note*.

DENMAN, William.
p. 46 : *add* Son of Elizabeth Denman.
Note : One of this name was ed. Merchant Taylors' Jan.-Mar. 1760.

DENT, John.
p. 49 : *add bapt.* 30 Sept. 1763. 6th son (10th child) of Rev. John Dent, M.A., vicar of Ainderby Steeple, nr. Northallerton, Yorks.
Add to *Services* Ensign Yorks Mil. 25 Apr. 1781 ; " served in campaign of 1781." Apptd. A.D.C. to his relative, John Stables, Member of the Supreme Council, *q.v.*, 23 Feb. 1785. Third Mysore War ; battle of Arikera 15 May 1791 (w.). Cornet H.M. 19th Light Dgns. 13 Apr. 1792 ; Lieut. 2nd Dgn. Gds. 5 Oct. 1795 ; Capt. do. 12 Mar. 1796 till 1798.
Add Refs. : Family information. Miniature by John Smart, dated 1790 ; portrait in a large oil painting by Zoffany.

DENTY, James.
p. 49, bottom l. : *add m.* St. Helena 18 July 1784, Lydia Shirtley, a native of that island.

*DESPARD, Henry Parnell Moore.
p. 50 : *add* Of Rathmore Lodge, Earls Court, London. Son of Philip Pilkington Despard and Elizabeth Gardiner his wife. *m.* Kensington 3 Mar. 1859, Jessie, eldest dau. of Daniel McDonald, of Calcutta. *d.* London 30 Oct. 1891.
Refs. : The Times, 3 Nov. 1891.

D'ESTERRE, Henry Martin.
p. 50 : *add b.* 1762/63. Sailed for India in the *Royal Admiral* 3 June 1780, aged 17.

DE WAAL, John.
p. 52 : He was son of Arend De Waal who succeeded Egbertus Bergh (whose dau. *m.* G. F. Grand, *q.v.*) as Receiver Gen. at the Cape.

DICK, Alexander.
p. 54, bottom l. : *add* Son of Robert Dick and Elizabeth Ferguson his 2nd wife.

DICKINSON, Thomas.
p. 58, l. 36 : *add* Eldest son of George Dickinson and Rebecca Ann his wife, dau. of Thomas Carr, of Eshott Heugh, Northumberland.

l. 39 : *add* dau. of John Palmer, of Calcutta. (*See also* Llewellyn Conroy.)

p. 59 : *add* to *Refs.*. Family information. M.I. St. Andrew's church, Kelso.

DINGWALL, Arthur Fordyce.
p. 64, l. 9 : *add* Only son of Rev. William Dingwall, minister of Forgue 1780-1801, and Sarah his wife, dau. of Rev. James Lawtie, minister of Fordyce.

Add to *Refs.* Scott's *Fasti*, vi. 255. M.I. in Muttra Cantt. cemetery.

DOD, George.
p. 66, l. 15 : *add* Son of John Cowcher Dod, of E. Charlton, Norfolk, and Georgiana his wife, dau. of George Massie, of Jamaica, and niece of Sir Robert Graham, Kt., one of the barons of the exchequer (*D.N.B.*).

DODD(S), Charles.
p. 66, l. 25 : *add Note :* One Charles Dodd (*b.* 14 Feb. 1761) was ed. Merchant Taylors' Jan.-Mar. 1774.

DODDS, John.
p. 66, l. 29 : *add* Capt. comdg. 1,200 Militia at Dacca in Aug. 1781.

DOMETT, Newell.
p. 67 : *add* (*Probably* son of Rev. Philobeth Domett, vicar of Bovey Tracey, Devon, for 50 yrs. M.I. in Bovey Tracey church.)

DONALDSON, Alexander.
p. 68, l. 14 : *add* Eldest son of Capt. Alexander Donaldson, 36th Regt., and Helen his wife, youngest dau. of Robert Donaldson, W.S.

DONALDSON, James.
p. 68, l. 26 : *add* and Janet M'Call his wife. Brother of Hay Donaldson, W.S.

l. 27 : *add* to *Services* 4th Mate of the *Lady Jane Dundas* Indiaman in 1802.

*DONELLAN, John.
   p. 68, l. 32: *add b.* 6 Nov. 1737.
   l. 38: *add* Ed. Westminster; admitted Jan. 1750/1; in school list 1752.
   bottom l.: *delete* 'Entered the R.A. at the age of 12' and *substitute* Apptd. to R.A. 14 Mar. 1753.
   p. 69, l. 2: *add* Ensign H.M. 39th Ft. 13 Nov. 1755.
   Add to *Refs. Westminster School Register.*

DORNBUSH, Joseph.
   p. 70, l. 28: *add d.* on his voyage home in the *Resolution*: *bur.* St. Helena 2 Sept. 1774.

DOUGAN, John Crooke.
   p. 71, l. 4: *add d.* Charleton House, Bromley, Kent, 31 July 1878.

DOUGLAS, Alexander.
   p. 71, l. 40: *add* Nephew of Patrick Heatley, *q.v.*

DOUGLAS, James (1798-1818).
   p. 73, l. 30: *add* Ed. Westminster; admitted 23 Mar. 1808; left midsummer 1810.
   Add to *Refs. Westminster School Register.*

DOUGLAS, Robert.
   p. 76, l. 4: *add Note*: One Robert Douglas (*b.* 31 Jan. 1770) was ed. Merchant Taylors' Mar. 1778-Mar. 1781.

DOUGLAS, William (*d.* 1827).
   p. 76, l. 11: *add* A 'near relative' of James Nicol (1778-1831), *q.v.*; so *perhaps* brother of James Douglas (1781-?), *q.v.*

DOVE, Matthew.
   p. 77, l. 15: *add* to *Services* Lieut. S. Regt. of Fenc. Men 21 Feb. 1780.

DOW, Adam.
   p. 78, l. 36: *add* kld. by his horse falling back on him at Siccacollum, nr. Ellore, Madras.

DOWNES, Robert.
   p. 80: *add* to *Services* Fireworker (Art.) Sept. 1768; transfd. to Inf. 1769.
   Add to *Refs. Stubbs*, No. 98.

DOXAT, Benjamin.
   p. 83: *add b.* 1752. Son of Jean Alphonse Samuel Doxat, of Lausanne, by his wife, *née* de Plessis. *m.* Mlle de Bons.

Add to *Services* Second Mysore War 1781 ; Qmr. of Art. with Sir Eyre Coote's force.
Add to *Refs.* Family information. *Archives Heraldiques Suisses*, vol. xliv (1930), No. 2, pp. 79-81. *Narrative of James Bristow, private in the Bengal Art.* (The Travellers' Library.)

DOXAT, Lewis.
p. 83 : *add b.* 1748.

D'OYLY, James Burnell.
* p. 83, l. 31 : *add b.* 24 June 1790.
l. 33 : *add bapt.* Wakefield, Yorks., 2 Sept. 1790.

DRINKELL, Francis.
p. 85 : *add bapt.* Kendal 27 July 1741. Son of Francis Drinkel(l), of Highgate, and Frances his wife.

DRUMMOND, Henry.
p. 86, l. 22 : *add* 6th son of James Drummond, of Strageith, co. Perth, and Beatrice his wife. *m.* Emmeline Bethea, 3rd dau. of Robert Kaye Greville (*D.N.B.*). (She *re-m.* 13 Dec. 1870, Robert Alexander, C.B., B.C.S.)

DRUMMOND, Hugh.
p. 87, l. 3 : *add* to *Services* Promoted from the ranks and was Adjt. 3rd Bengal Eur. Regt. in Feb. 1769.

DRYSDALE, James.
p. 89, l. 6 : *add* Brother of Sir William Drysdale, of Pitteuchar, Kt. *m.* Dumfries 14 Mar. 1814, Mary Watson, sister of Peter Lawrie Pew, *q.v.* Father of Lt.-Gen. Sir William Drysdale, K.C.B., Colonel 9th Lrs.

DUBOIS, Simpson.
p. 89, l. 3 from bottom : *add* His daus. *m.* Thomas Hall (1770/71-1856) and Charles Whitfield, *qq.v.*

DUCAREL, James Coltee.
p. 90, l. 13 : *add* Ensign 13th Ft. 1 Sept. 1756 ; Lieut. do. 4 July 1759 ; exchanged to Brit. h.p. of Lieut. 71st Ft. 21 Dec. 1764 till death.

DU FEU, John.
p. 90, l. 5 from bottom : *add b.* and *bapt.* St. Peter Port, Guernsey, 23 Oct. 1784.
l. 1 from bottom : *add* and Mary Breton his wife.

DUFF, Patrick.
   p. 91, l. 29 : *add* to *Services* Apptd. July 1762, Lt. F., R.A., at Bombay, from Gent. Vol. 89th Regt.; accepted at Madras 4 Sept. 1763, a Commn. on H.C. Bengal Est.

DUFF, Robert.
   p. 92, l. 14 : *add* Of Ladyhill, Elgin. Grandson of Robert Duff, merchant in Elgin. *m.* (before 1816) Marjory, 3rd dau. of Rev. George Dawn, minister of Insch 1790-1822.

DUN, William.
   p. 95 : *add b.* 24 Sept. 1755. Elder son of Rev. Alexander Dun, minister of Bendochy 1747-84, and Elizabeth Ranken his wife. *Add* to *Refs.* Scott's *Fasti*, v. 254.

DUNCAN, Menzies.
   p. 100 : *add m.* Elizabeth, dau. of B. Levi, of Northampton, and widow of Lt.-Col. George Johnston, 58th Ft.

DUNCAN, William.
   p. 100, l. 1 from bottom : *add b.* 31 Dec. 1747.
   p. 101, l. 3 : *add* 3rd (twin with George) son of Rev. Alexander Duncan, minister of Smailholm 1743-95, and Helen his wife, dau. of William Home, of Greenlas Castle.
   l. 6 : *add* to *Services* Major comdg. 15th N.I. in Aug. 1781 ; comdg. 2/1st N.I. in 1784.
   Add to *Refs.* Scott's *Fasti*, ii. 162.

DUNCANSON, Duncan.
   p. 101 : *add* to *Services* Lieut. of an Independent Coy. 28 Oct. 1760 ; regimented into 100th Ft. 1761 ; Lieut. h.p. 100th Ft. in 1765.

DUNCANSON, William Mayne.
   p. 101 : His second christian name was Mayne.
   Add to *Services* Commissioned as Lieut. in H.M. 82nd Ft. 18 Sept. 1780.

DUNLOP, William (1807-1827).
   p. 104, l. 37 : *add* Ed. Westminster ; admitted 14 June 1813 ; left Dec. 1817 ; readmitted 5 Oct. 1818 ; left Dec. 1818. Edin. Univ.
   Add to *Refs. Westminster School Register.*

DUNMORE, William Robert.
   p. 105 : *add* Son of William Robert Dunmore, 2nd Ofr. of the

Coutts Indiaman, and grandson of Robert Dunmore, of Ballindalloch, co. Stirling.
l. 6 : *add m.* 2nd, 17 Nov. 1870, Elizabeth Camilla, widow of Arthur Connell, Professor of Chemistry, St. Andrew's Univ. Ed. Westminster ; admitted 9 Feb. 1820.
Add to *Refs. Strathendrick*, by J. Guthrie Smith, p. 205. *Westminster School Register.*

DUNSMURE, Alexander (Conway).
p. 106, l. 26 : *add* and Christian his wife, dau. of John Young, baxter 'in Canongate. Uncle of Edward Marjoribanks Orr, *q.v.*

DUPONT, John.
p. 107, l. 16 : *add* Ensign H.M. 51st Ft. 1 Aug. 1760 ; Lieut. do. 31 Dec. 1761 ; h.p. do. 1763. Transfd. as Lieut. from H.M.S. 1 Sept. 1768.

DURHAM, Hercules.
p. 109, l. 17 : *add* 2nd Lieut. H.M. 21st Ft. (R. North Brit. Fus.) 12 Sept. 1759 ; was on h.p. of Addl. 1st Lieuts. do. at death.

DYCE, David.
p. 111 : *add b.* 16 Nov. 1766. 4th son of Alexander Dyce, of Rosebank, and Mary his wife, dau. of David Ochterlony, of Tillyfrisky.
Add to *Refs. Thanage of Fermartyn*, by William Temple, p. 680.

DYER, Samuel.
p. 111, bottom l. : *add* and Bridget Oliver his wife.

DYER, ——.
p. 112 : His christian name was John.
l. 10 : *add* Was one of eleven signatories to a Memorial dated Calcutta 28 Aug. 1758, complaining of supercession by John Gowen, *q.v.* He was not, however, amongst the eight who resigned their Commissions.

DYSART, George.
p. 114, l. 2 : *add* T.C.D. ; Pensioner 7 Nov. 1825.

DYSON, John.
p. 114, l. 19 : *add d.* I. of Man.
l. 20 : *add* Eldest son of John Dyson. *m.* (?)
Add to *Refs.* Watson's *Halifax*, p. 200.

EARLE, Solomon.
 p. 117, l. 2 : *add b.* 1750/51.
 l. 4 : *add d.* Carisbrooke, I.W., 4 Dec. 1824, aged 73.
 Add to *Refs.* Family information.

EARLE, Solomon (1797-1858).
 p. 117, l. 23 : *add m.* Trincomalee, Ceylon, 12 July 1819, Bridget, dau. of John Maples, of Newark.
 l. 25 : *delete* " is said to have."
 l. 26 : after " Waterloo " *add* (Waterloo medal).

EATON, Isaac.
 p. 118, bottom l. : *add* Ed. Merchant Taylors' Sept. 1755-Apr. 1756.
 p. 119, top l. : *add* Major comdg. 500 L.I. at Buxar in Aug. 1781.

EDMONSTONE, Archibald.
 p. 121 : *add* Elder son of Campbell Edmonstone, Lt. Govr. of Dunbarton Castle, and nephew of Sir Archibald Edmonstone, 1st Bart. of Duntreath. Ed. Glasgow Univ.; matric. 1762.

EDWARDS, Francis.
 p. 122 : *add Refs. :* Will dated 21 Jan. 1806 ; proved 1813.

EDWARDS, Thomas (*d.* 1815).
 p. 124, top l. : *add* (She *re-m.* 1819, Rev. Dr. E. Black, of Exeter.)

EDWARDS, Thomas (1810-1891).
 p. 124, l. 15 : *add* and Hannah Vertue his wife. Ed. Westminster; admitted 16 Oct. 1822.
 l. 17 : *add Refs. : Westminster School Register.*

EDWARDS, Timothy.
 p. 124, l. 21 : *add* Ensign H.M. 14th Ft. 20 Dec. 1760 ; Lieut. 7th (Royal Fuzileers) 28 Oct. 1761 ; Lieut. 8th Ft. 31 Jan. 1766. Transfd. as Capt. to Bengal Army (M.C. 1 Sept. 1768).

EGERTON, Thomas Lucas.
 p. 125, l. 32 : *add* Ed. Harrow 1820-2.

*EISER, ——.
 p. 126 : *add* It is doubtful whether this officer may properly be regarded as ever having belonged to the Bengal Army. For fuller particulars of his service *see* Appendix B, *s.n.* EISER, John Christian (*or* Christopher) (*d.* 1763).

ELLERKER, Edward.
   p. 129, l. 6 : *add* Major comdg. L.I. Bn. at Chittagong in Aug. 1781.
   l. 8 : *add* M.I. at Bhagulpur.

ELLIOT, Edward King.
   p. 129, l. 14 : *add* 2nd son of George Elliot, of London and Blackheath, merchant, formerly of Madras, and Louisa his wife, dau. of Israel Levin Solomons, of Clapton. Ward of Capt. Robert Locke, H.E.I.C.S., who *m.* his sister Louisa. *m.* a dau. of —— Kemp.

ELLIOT, William (*d.* 1783).
   p. 130 : *add* Son of William Elliot, writer in Edinburgh.

ELLIOT, William (1740/41-1803).
   p. 130, l. 14 : *add* Of Over and Nether Larriston and Blackhope, which he bought from William Oliver, of Dinlabyre, 23 Dec. 1788.

ELLIS, Thomas Powrie.
   p. 134, l. 7 : *for* ' H.' *read* Hector.
   Add (She died 1847.)

ELLITHORNE, John.
   p. 135, l. 38 : *add* According to Gen. Stubbs he was apptd. Fireworker in the Art. 1 Dec. 1767.
   Add to *Refs. Stubbs,* No. 84.

ELWALL, Frederick Charles.
   p. 136, l. 4 from bottom, after ' Lieut, 49th N.I.' *add* (India medal).

ELWOOD, Thomas Moore.
   p. 137, l. 17 : *add m.* Calcutta 19 Feb. 1776, Melissa Scott.

ENGLEHEART, George.
   p. 138, l. 23 : *add* Eldest surviving child of George Engleheart, the miniaturist.
   Add to *Refs.* Family information.

ENGLISH, William.
   p. 138, l. 36 : *add* Ensign H.M. 48th Ft. 27 Mar. 1744 ; Ensign 1st Ft. Gds. 25 Sept. 1745 ; retired on h.p. of Lieut. 19th Ft. 17 Dec. 1751. Lieut. 59th Ft. 18 May 1756 ; Capt. 83rd Ft. 31 Dec. 1759. (? h.p. 1763.) Transfd. as Major to Bengal Army (M.C. 1 Sept. 1768).

ERSKINE, Charles.
> p. 138, l. 1 from bottom : *add* kld. by a fall from his horse.

ERSKINE, George.
> p. 139, l. 38 : *add b.* 21 Aug. 1748.
> p. 140, l. 2 : *add* to *Refs.* Scott's *Fasti*, i. 47.

ERSKINE, John.
> p. 140, l. 25 : *add b.* 30 Sept. 1747.
> l. 32 : *add* to *Refs.* Scott's *Fasti*, i. 47.

ERSKINE, Roger Keys.
> p. 141, l. 28 : *add bapt.* Protestant Dissenters' chapel, St. Saviour's Gate, York, 30 Jan. 1793.
> l. 31 : *add* (She died London 19 Apr. 1866.)

EVANS, Dacres Fitzherbert.
> p. 142, l. 27 : *add* and Ichoadden his wife.
> l. 31 : *add* (She died London 13 Feb. 1905, aged 86.)
> *Add* to *Refs.* M.I. Clifton churchyard.

EVANS, Francis Roberts.
> p. 143, l. 9 : *add* dau. of Benjamin Turner, atty. of the supreme court in Calcutta (sometime partner of William Hickey, the diarist), and sister of James William Hickey Turner, *q.v.*

EVERETT, Thomas Cooper.
> p. 145 : *add* Son of Michael Everett, Capt. R.N.
> *Add* to *Services* Apptd. a Corporal in Coy. of Cadets at Woolwich Jan. 1768. Adjt. 3rd D.G. 6 June 1775 ; Lieut. do. 26 Mar. 1776 ; Capt. do. 15 Mar. 1779. Major comdg. Hants Corps of Fenc. Cav. 1 May 1794.

EVORS, Pryce John.
> p. 145, l. 33 : *add* Son of Lieut. (? Capt.) David Evors, of Tenby, h.p. 7th Marines, and Diana his wife, sister of Sir John Powell Pryce, 6th Bart., of Newtown, co. Montgomery.

EWART, David.
> p. 145, bottom l. : *add* Nephew of W. Gillison Bell.
> p. 146, l. 5 : *add* Ed. Carlisle Grammar School.

EWART, Richard Sheridan.
> p. 147, l. 25 : *add* (She died 26 Dec. 1895, aged 78.)
> l. 39 : *add* to *Refs.* M.I. Redland Green churchyard, Bristol.

EXSHAW, James Robert.
> p. 148, l. 31 : *add* (*Probably* of the family of Alderman John Exshaw, of Dublin.)

EYRES, George Bolton.
p. 150, l. 2 from bottom : *add* Major comdg. 3rd Regt. Cav. in Aug. 1781.
Add to *Refs.* Burke's *Landed Gentry*, 15th (1937) edn., p. 732, *s.n.* Eyres, of Cut Heath, Bucks.

FADDY, Samuel Brougham.
p. 151, l. 19 : *add* to *Services* Was comdg. 36th N.I. when it mutinied at Jullundur, 7 June 1857.

FAGAN, George Hickson (1810-1876).
p. 154, l. 28 : *add* Ed. Elizabeth Coll., Guernsey, 1825-6.

FAIRFAX, John.
p. 156, l. 21 : *add* 3rd Regt. Cav. in Aug. 1781.
Add to *Refs.* Coloured reproduction of a miniature in the possession of Mr. Charles Drury in Vol. vii. No. 30 of *Journal of the Soc. for Army Hist. Research* (Oct. 1928).

FAIRHEAD, John Assey.
p. 157, l. 7 : *add* Son of —— Fairhead and Mary his wife (who *re-m.* —— Cunningham, of Toftcroft, Norfolk).

FAIRLIE, William.
p. 157 : *add b.* 1752/53. *d.* London 19 Jan. 1825, aged 72. Son of John Fairlie. *m.* Calcutta 17 Feb. 1798, Margaret Ogilvy. (She died 2 Mar. 1815, aged 64.)

FALVEY, Dennis Morris.
p. 160 : *add b.* 1752/53. *d.* aged 53.
Add to *Refs.* M.I. Kydganj cemetery, Allahabad.

FANE, William John Jervis.
p. 161, l. 5 : *add b.* 11 July 1808.
l. 8 : *add* Ed. Rugby ; admitted 1818 ; Charterhouse, 1824.
Add to *Refs. Rugby* and *Charterhouse School Lists.*

FARNABY, Leonard Motley.
p. 163, l. 19 : *add bapt.* W. Wickham 29 June 1792. 3rd son of Sir John Farnaby, 4th Bart. of Wickham Court, Kent, and Mary his wife, only dau. of Samuel Lennard.

FARRINGTON, John James.
p. 166, l. 2 : *add* 2nd dau. of Claus Macleod of Bharkasaig, and niece of Malcolm Macleod, *q.v.*

FAWCETT, Walker Dawson.
p. 167, l. 22 : *add* Ed. Westminster.
l. 35 : *add* to *Refs. Westminster School Register.*

FELTHAM, Robert Owen.

p. 169 : *add* d. in England 13 May 1789. *m.* (?) His full name was as now given. Was still in Calcutta in Aug. 1783, when he prayed to be readmitted to the Service. Pensioned on Lord Clive's fund 9 June 1785, with effect from 25 Dec. 1784.

FERGUSON, Archibald.

p. 172 : *add* b. 1754/55. d. aged 79. Eldest son of James Ferguson, of Dunfallandy, and Elizabeth Butter, of Pitlochry, his wife. *m.* (?) and left issue.

Add to *Services :* Siege and capture of Seringapatam (sabre wound on forehead).

Add to *Refs. Records of Clan Fergusson,* i. 75. Portrait by Raeburn. *Note :* Fergusson would appear to be the more correct spelling of the name.

FERGUSON, John.

p. 173 : *add* b. 7 Mar. 1743. Eldest son of Rev. Adam Ferguson, minister of Moulin 1736-85, and Amelia his wife, 6th dau. of Capt. James Menzies, of Comrie.

Add to *Refs. Records of the Clan and Name of Ferguson or Fergusson,* i. 113. Scott's *Fasti,* iv. 169.

Add to *Note* (? Author of " A Dictionary of the Hindostan Language . . .," London, 1773.) The more correct spelling would appear to be Fergusson.

*FERGUSON, Joseph.

p. 173, l. 38 : *add* d. Calcutta 27 Nov. 1799.

l. 40 : *add* Nephew of Joseph Burnett, *q.v.*

Add to *Services* 2nd Lt. 21st Ft. 10 Apr. 1794. Capt. 78th (Seaforth) Highlrs. (15 June 1795) 12 Jan. 1796.

Bottom l. : *add Refs. : Records of Clan Ferguson,* i. 166-72 (portrait). Will dated 18 Nov. 1799.

FERGUSSON, John Tierney.

p. 174, bottom l. : *add* 3rd son of Benjamin Fergusson, of Calcutta, mercht., formerly Capt. R.N., and Elizabeth (*not* Eleanor) Tierney his wife.

p. 175, l. 3 : *add* and Hugh Boscawen, *q.v.*

l. 7 : *add* to *Refs. Records of Clan Ferguson,* ii. 217.

FERGUSSON, Josias Dupré.

p. 175, l. 13 : *add* 6th and youngest son.

FERNYHOUGH, Francis.

p. 176, l. 13 : *add* dau. of Edward Leigh, of Cheadle and

Chesterfield, atty. (? Adm. Pens. (aged 17) Trinity Hall, Cambs., 8 Jan. 1793 : Scholar 1795.)
Refs. : Hunter's *Familiæ Minorum Gentium,* iii. 1024. (? *Alumni Cantab.,* Pt. II. ii. 485.)

FESTING, Thomas Bennet Penwarne.
p. 178, l. 3 : *add m.* Madras 23 June 1820, Miss Mary Mascarier.

FETHERSTON, Thomas.
p. 178, l. 23 : *add* to *Services* Cornet 2nd Regt. of Horse 31 Dec. 1772, and served as Cornet for seven yrs. in Ireland.

FIELD, Charles.
p. 179, l. 30 : *add* Ed. Merchant Taylors' June-Oct. 1810.

FIELDING, Charles John Johnson.
p. 181, l. 7 : *add* Elder son of Charles Fielding, Capt. R.M. (who was cousin-german of Henry Fielding, author of *Tom Jones*), and Maria his wife, dau. of John Johnson, of Bebside, Northumberland.
l. 10 : *add Refs. :* Burke's *Peerage,* 1923, p. 689, *s.n.* Earl of Denbigh.

FLEMING, George.
p. 191, l. 35 : *add* 2nd son of George Fleming, of Dublin, by Tomasin, dau. of Martin Tucker, of Petersfield, co. Meath. A claimant to the title of Fleming, Lord Slane. *Add* to *Services* Transfd. from Art. to Engrs. 13 Dec. 1779.

FLEMING, Thomas.
p. 193, l. 9 : *add bapt.* Kirkcaldy 24 Dec. 1797. 2nd son of Rev. Dr. Thomas Fleming, minister of Lady Yester's psh., Edin., and Anne Robertson his wife.
Add to *Refs.* Scott's *Fasti,* i. 83.

FLEMYNG, William.
p. 194, top l. : *add* Son of Roger Flemyng, of Charles St., Bath. *m.* Calcutta Jan. 1793, Emilia, dau. of Capt. Richard Pierce, of the *Halsewell* Indiaman, and aunt of George Poyntz Ricketts, *q.v.*

FLETCHER, Sir Robert.
p. 195, l. 15 : *add* Younger son of Robert Fletcher, of Ballinshoe, Major in Ogilvy's Regt. in army of Prince Charles Edward. *m.* 21 Dec. 1774.
l. 16 : *add* (She died 16 Feb. 1791, aged 34.)
Add to *Refs.* Another portrait, by Gainsborough, in possession of Mylne family.

FOGO, William.
p. 197, l. 17 : *add* 2nd son.
l. 24 : *add* to *Refs.* M.I. St. Cuthbert's psh. churchyard, Edinburgh.

FOQUETT, Henry.
p. 199, l. 4 : *add* and Betsey Anne his wife. A descendant of Nicholas Fouquet, finance minister of Louis XIV, said to have been "The Man with the Iron Mask."
l. 15 : *add* to *Refs. Genealogical Mag.* i. 581-2 (Feb. 1898).

FORBES, Arthur.
p. 199, l. 29 : *add* Son of Charles Forbes, of Stanmore Hill, Jamaica, and Mary his wife, eldest dau. of Thomas Clutterbuck, of Watford, D.L. Herts., high sheriff 1781.
l. 33 : *add* to *Refs.* Cussan's *Herts.*, iii. 140, *s.n.* Clutterbuck.

FORBES, James.
p. 200 : *add* 6th son of Nathaniel Forbes, of Auchernach, and Isabella his wife, dau. of John Stewart, of Drumin.
Refs. : The House of Forbes, by A. & H. Tayler, p. 451 (Third Spalding Club, 1937).

FORBES, John (*d.* 1808).
p. 200, l. 19 : *add* to *Services* Served with Goddard in Guzarat, 1780 ; Major comdg. 4th Regt. Sepoys in Aug. 1781.

FORBES, John (1782-1804).
p. 200, l. 30 : *add* Elder son of Capt. Alexander Forbes, IV of Inverernan, and Elizabeth Grant his wife. *Add* to *Refs. The House of Forbes*, p. 456.

FORBES, John (1788-1805).
p. 201, l. 2 : *add Refs. :* Burke's *Landed Gentry*, 10th edn., p. 945, *s.n.* Forbes-Leith, of Fyvie. *Thanage of Fermartyn*, by William Temple, p. 101.

FORBES, Richard.
p. 201 : *add* Son of Capt. Roderick Forbes, Bo. Est., and Jane his wife ; *bapt.* Bombay 8 June 1750.
Add to *Refs.* M.I. in old cemetery below Chunar fort.

FORBES, William Nairn.
p. 202, l. 23 : *add bapt.* 13 Apr. 1796. 6th and youngest son of John Forbes, of Blackford, and Anne Margaret his wife, dau. of Dr. John Gregory. Ed. King's Coll., Aberdeen, and Edin. Univ.

Add to *Refs.* Burke's *Landed Gentry*, 10th edn., p. 945, *s.n.* Forbes-Leith, of Fyvie.

FORD, ——.
p. 203 : This is *probably* Edward Forde, who appears to have been transfd. from H.M. 39th Ft.

*FORDE, Francis.
p. 203, l. 4 from bottom : *add* 2nd Lieut. 39th Ft. 12 May 1742 ; Lieut. do. 12 June 1743.
l. 1 from bottom : *add* Transfd. to Bengal Est. 30 June 1758.

FOREMAN, James.
p. 205 : *add* to *Services* Cornet 10th Dgns. 8 Nov. 1756 ; Lieut. of its Light Troop 29 Apr. 1760 ; reduced on h.p. with it in 1763. Transfd. as Capt. to Bengal Army (M.C. 1 Sept. 1768).

FORREST, Lowther Thomas.
p. 205, l. 34 : *add* and Mary his wife, eldest dau. of Col. James Lowther, M.P. for Westmorland.

FORRESTER, John Napier.
p. 207, top l. : *add* Of Craigannet, co. Stirling. Son of Gabriel Forrester, of Craigannet, formerly Ensign 60th or R. American Regt., and Jean his wife, dau. of Robert Hamilton, of Hamilton Hall.

FORSTER or FOSTER, John Hibbard.
p. 207 : *add b.* 1762.

FORTNOM, John.
p. 209 : *add* His widow *m.* Thomas Harris, *q.v.*

FORTNOM, Thomas William.
p. 209, l. 17 : *add d.* at sea on board the *Minerva* May 1803.
l. 25 : *add* Purser of the *Minerva* Indiaman June 1802 till death.

FOWLE, Henry.
p. 212, l. 20 : *add b.* 17 Aug. 1804.

FOY, John.
p. 212, bottom l. : *add* Ed. Westminster ; admitted 15 Jan. 1766.
Refs. : Westminster School Register.

FRANKS, James.
p. 214, l. 37 : *add* Ed. Merchant Taylors' Mar. 1770-Mar. 1771.

FRASER, Alexander (1786-1822).
p. 214, l. 1 from bottom : *add* Son of Alexander Fraser, soldier, and Isobel Macdonald his wife.

FRASER, Andrew (*d.* 1812).
   p. 216, l. 12 : *add m.* Ann, dau. of Simon Fraser, of Inverness, merchant.
   p. 217 : *add* as a new entry, after George John Fraser :—

*****FRASER, Hugh** (1765/66-1783). Lieutenant, Infantry. *b.* in Scotland 1765/66. Cadet 1781. Ensign 1781. Lieut. 1782. *d.* (before 20 Oct.) 1783 (*probably* on the voyage out to India). Cousin-german of Roderick Fraser (1761/62-1846), *q.v.*
   Services : Apptd. Cadet 18 Apr. 1781 : sailed for India in the *Nassau* 8 Feb. 1782, aged 16.

FRASER, James (1800-1868).
   p. 218, l. 29 : *add* Ed. Rugby ; admitted 1813.
   Add to *Refs. Rugby School Register.*

FRASER, Simon.
   p. 221, l. 13 ; *add* Ensign, Grant Fenc. (Strathspey Regt.), 6 Dec. 1798, from Lieut., Forres Vols.

FREAKE, John.
   p. 223, l. 8 : *add* Sailed for England in the *Boscawen* with 7 other ofrs. and colours of disbanded 84th, reaching Capetown 21 Jan. 1765.

FREDERICK, William.
   p. 224, l. 4 : *add d. unm.* 1880.
   l. 8 : *add* Ensign 3rd W.I. Regt. 10 Dec. 1818 ; h.p. same day.

FRIELL, Simeon Philip.
   p. 227, l. 5 : *add* and Anne Charlotte his wife, dau. of Simeon Boileau de Castelnau. Cousin-german of Henry Carter (1793-1844), *q.v.*
   Add to *Refs.* C. E. Lart's *Huguenot Peds.* ii. 13, *s.n.* Boileau.

FRITH, Henry William.
   p. 227, l. 38 : *add* Ed. Merchant Taylors' Apr. 1791-Oct. 1797.

FRITH, Richard.
   p. 228, l. 4 : *add d.* Muttra.
   l. 5 : *add* Son of Robert Frith, of Derryargan, co. Fermanagh.
   l. 17 : *add* to *Refs.* M.I. Muttra Cantt. cemetery.

FRY, Robert.
   p. 230, l. 35 : *add* Ed. Tonbridge 1786-7.

FRYE, Charles.
   p. 231, l. 6 : *add* 3rd and youngest son of John Ravel Frye,

of Antigua, Member of Council 1768, and Sarah his wife, eldest dau. of Percivall Pott, surgeon (*D.N.B.*).
Add to *Refs.* V. L. Oliver's *History of Antigua*, i. 285.

*FRYER, George Samuel.
p. 231, l. 26 : *add* Ensign 79th Ft. 10 Sept. 1760 ; Lieut. do. 1 Sept. 1761 ; presumably h.p. 1763. Not in *A.L.* of 1772.

FULCHER, Robert Page.
p. 232, l. 6 : *add* m. C. G. H. 18 Feb. 1823, Petronella Jacquemina, *née* Bartels, widow of Col. Colin Mackenzie, Madras Est., Surveyor Gen.

FULLARTON, John.
p. 232, l. 3 from bottom : *add* Left in comd. at Ahmedabad, 1780, when Goddard moved to the South.

GABB, John.
p. 238, l. 5 : *add* Son of Baker Gabb, of Abergavenny, solicitor, and Anne his 1st wife, dau. of John Powell, of Moor Park, co. Brecknock. *m.* Mary Powell, of the Moor Park family.
Add to *Refs.* Bradney's *Hist. of Monmouthshire*, Vol. I, Pt. i. (1904), p. 84.

GAIRDNER, William John.
p. 240, l. 7 : *add* bapt. Kilbucho, co. Peebles, 14 Sept. 1789. Eldest son of Alexander Gairdner and Ann Ellitson his wife, eldest dau. of John Lock, of Rachan, psh. of Glenholm, co. Peebles.

GAITSKELL, Frederick.
p. 240, l. 37 : *add* m. Harriet ——. (She died Torquay 24 July 1896.)

GALL, Lawrence.
p. 243, l. 34 : *add* Lieut. comdg. a Bn. of Nawab's troops at Bareilly in Aug. 1781. (*See also* Vol. ii. p. 629.)

GALLIEZ, Primrose.
p. 244, l. 4 : *add* m. Calcutta 7 Apr. 1763, Mary de Nouailles, widow.

GAMON, Thomas.
p. 245, l. 8 : *add m.* Meeran-ka-Serai, nr. Cawnpore 21 Jan. 1812, Eliza, dau. of Francis Rutledge (1760-1817), *q.v.* (She died Fatehgarh 18 Oct. 1812, aged 21.)

GARDEN, William.
p. 246, l. 21 : *add* and Grizel his wife, dau. of Alexander M'Combie. Ed. King's Coll., Aberdeen.
Add to Refs. *Families of M'Combie and Thoms*, by W. M. Smith (2nd edn., Edin., 1890), p. 118.

GARDINER, Robert.
p. 247, l. 16 : *add* Father of John Gairdner, M.D. (*D.N.B.*), and William Gairdner, M.D. (*D.N.B.*).

GARSTIN, Henry.
p. 253, l. 27 : *add* Ed. Winchester.

GASCOIGNE, Peter.
p. 254, l. 19 : *add* to *Services* Ensign H.M. 42nd Ft. 24 Mar. 1784.

GASGOYNE, Joseph.
p. 255, l. 4 : *add* dau. of Capt. Samuel Baker Evance, Madras Est.

GATLEY, Charles.
p. 255, l. 22 : *add* 2nd dau. of Robert Young, of Durham. (*See also* William Bedell.)
Add to Refs. *Howard & Crisp* (*Notes*), iv. 141, *s.n.* Young.

GERARD, Patrick.
p. 260, l. 24 : *add* Ed. King's Coll., Aberdeen.

GIBBS, John.
p. 262, l. 1 from bottom : *add m.* 2nd, M. A. May.
p. 263, l. 4 : *add* to *Refs.* M.I. at Buxar.

GIBBS, Jonathan Warner.
p. 263, l. 22 : *add* Capt. Lt. H.M. 30th Ft. 29 Mar. 1776 ; Capt. do. 25 July 1778.

GIFFORD, Charles Thomas William Pitt.
p. 264, l. 8 : *add* 2nd son of Rev. John Gifford, of Painters Hall.

GILLMAN, George.
p. 268, l. 27 : *add* 2nd son of Lt.-Col. Edward Gillman, of Clancoot, and Mary his wife, dau. of George Cornwall, of Bandon. *m.* Elizabeth Waring.

GILMAN, Philip Case.
p. 269, l. 14 : *add* 4th son of Samuel Gilman and Lydia his wife, dau. of Edward Case, of Pattesley House, Norfolk.

Add to *Refs. The Gillman or Gilman Family*, by Alexander W. Gillman (1895), ii. 155.

GILPIN, Martin.

p. 270 : *add b.* 5 Oct. 1743. 3rd son of Robert Gilpin and Ruth his wife, dau. of Reynold Hall, of Newbiggen. Brother of Richard Gilpin, *q.v.*, and of John Gilpin, who assumed the surname of Sawrey in addition to his own on succeeding to the Broughton Tower estate. *m.* 4 June 1790, Frances, dau. of John Nicholson, of Egremont, Cumberland. (She died 10 Aug. 1827, aged 60.) *d.* 13 (? 20) Dec. 1824.

l. 35 : *add* to *Services* Ensign H.M. 61st Ft. 18 Jan. 1760 ; Lieut. 107th Ft. 22 Oct. 1761 ; h.p. do. 1763 till death. Transfd. as Lieut. to Bengal Army 1 Sept. 1768.

l. 37 : *add* to *Refs. Gilpin Memoirs.* Burke's *Landed Gentry*, 4th edn., p. 1335, *s.n.* Sawrey, of Broughton Tower, Lancs. Hunter's *Familiæ Minorum Gentium* (Harleian Soc. xxxix), iii. 1101. M.I. Broughton churchyard.

GILPIN, Richard.

p. 270 : *add b.* 7 Sept. 1741. Brother of Martin Gilpin, *q.v. d.* Kasim Bazar, Bengal.

GIRDLESTONE, William Bolton.

p. 271, l. 7 : *add* Son of Henry Girdlestone and Ann his wife, *née* Bolton. *m.* Poona 9 Apr. 1827, Eloisa, dau. of Rev. James Hitch, rector of Westerfield, Suffolk.

GOAD, Charles Elliot.

p. 275, l. 33 : *add* (*See also* Winthrop Vernon.)

GODDARD, Henry.

p. 277, l. 37 : *delete* " The remainder is conjectural only ". Bottom l : *add* to *Refs. Misc. Gen. et Her*, 4S. iv. 236.

GODFREY, John (1810-1878).

p. 279 : *add* to *Refs.* Foster's *Baronetage*, p. 255, *s.n.* Godfrey, Bart.

GOLDIE, Andrew.

p. 280, l. 21 : *add bapt.* 6 Apr. 1793. 6th son of Rev. George Goldie, minister of Athelstaneford 1778-1804, and Magdalen his 2nd wife, dau. of William Howden, farmer.

GOLDING, Edward.

p. 281, l. 14 : *add bapt.* Killoen, Londonderry, 30 Aug. 1753. Ed. Winchester ; K.S. 1765 ; left 1768.

GOODWYN, Henry.

p. 283 : *add* Only son of Henry Robert Goodwyn and Laura his wife, 7th and youngest dau. of Thomas Larkins, of Dartmouth Grove, Blackheath, and cousin-german of George Larkins, *q.v.* Cousin-german of John Pascal Walker, *q.v.* His sister *m.* Edward Simeon Hawkins, *q.v. m.* 2nd, Emmeline Fuge.

p. 284 : *add* to *Refs.* Family information. Author of " Memoir on the taper-chain suspension bridge, Calcutta," 1844 ; " The Last Adam," 1868.

GORDON, James Cosmo.

p. 289, top l. : *add* Lieut. N. Regt. of Fenc. Men 14 Apr. 1778.

GORDON, John (1740-1829).

p. 290 : *add* to *Services* Was employed for some time in the Nawab of Oudh's service. Gave evidence at the trial of Warren Hastings in Feb. 1793.

Add to *Refs. N. & Q.* clvi. 152.

GORE, George William Molyneux.

p. 294, l. 4 : *add* 2nd son of William Gore, Major 33rd Ft., Comdt. Royal Bristol Vols., a banker in Bristol, and Sarah his wife, dau. of John Ireland, of N. America.

GORE, William.

p. 295, top l. : *add* to *Services* Ensign H.M. 68th Ft. 7 June 1778.

GOTHER, William.

p. 295, l. 21 : *add* Ed. Winchester ; Scholar 1795 ; left 14 July 1798.

Add to *Refs. Kirby.*

GOULD, James (1758/59-1794).

p. 297, top l. : *add* to *Services* Ensign 30th Ft. 21 July 1773 ; Lieut. do. 2 Aug. 1775 till 1778.

l. 5 : *add Note:* (*Perhaps* 2nd son of Edward Gould and Mary his wife, dau. of Robert Thoroton, of Sreveton, Notts—cf. Thoroton's *Notts.* (1797 edn.) ii. 318. *Perhaps* related to Paston Gould, who was Lt. Col. of 30th Ft. in 1778.)

GOWEN or GOVIN, John.

p. 299, l. 3 from bottom : *add* " Permitted on account of his long service to retire from further duty upon his full pay." (Court Minutes, 12 Feb. 1768.) His pension continued to his widow Elizabeth from 10 Aug. 1770. (ib. 22 Aug. 1770.) In both cases the name appears as GOWIN. Latterly of Laleham.

p. 300, l. 4 : *add Note :* Perhaps to be identified with one John Govan (*b.* 21 May 1725) who was ed. at Merchant Taylors' Oct. 1738-Mar. 1740, and was therefore a contemporary of Clive at the school.

GRAHAM, Charles (1788-1858).
p. 301, l. 22 : *add* 3rd sister of Robert Taylor, *q.v.* (She died 1870.)

GRAHAM, Edward.
p. 302, l. 28 : *add m.* Point de Galle, Ceylon, 31 Oct. 1802, Anne Cecilia, dau. of Pieter Arendt de Moor, of Ceylon, *boekhouder*. (*See also* Edward Clarke (1758/59-1810).)

GRAHAM, George Templer.
p. 303, top l. : *add* dau. of William Golightly, of Ham, Surrey. (She died Karachi Apr. 1845, aged 41.) *m.* 2nd, Caroline Mary, elder dau. of Lt.-Gen. John Michel, of Dewlish and Kingston Russell. (She died 1885.)

GRAHAM, John.
p. 303, l. 15 : *add* Lieut. H.M. 74th Ft. 8 Sept. 1756.

GRAHAM, John (1777-1816).
p. 303 : *add m.* Fatehgarh Apr. 1803, Margaret, dau. of James Murray Macgregor, *q.v.* (*See also* Hon. Patrick Campbell Sinclair and John Samuel Henry Weston.)

GRAHAM, John (1787-1859).
p. 304, l. 14 : *add* 5th and youngest son of Rev. Henry Graham, minister of Cumbrae 1768-98, and Jean his wife, dau. of William Cuninghame, of Monkton Hill.
Add to *Refs.* Scott's *Fasti*, iii. 191.

GRAHAM, John Richard.
p. 305, l. 10 : *add bapt.* Hesket 13 Dec. 1800. Son of James Graham and Harriet his wife, 3rd dau. of James Simpson. Kinsman of Sir James Graham, Bart.

GRANGE, Edmund.
p. 309, l. 10 : *add* 4th son of Rev. Richard Chappell Grange, of Dublin, and Mary Rochfort his wife, niece of Robert (Rochfort), 1st Earl of Belvidere. Uncle of Richard George Grange, *q.v.*

GRANGE, Richard George.
p. 309, l. 17 : *add* and Lydia his wife. Nephew of Edmund Grange, *q.v.*

*GRANT, Alexander (*d.* 1768).

p. 310, l. 13 : *add b.* Mar. 1725. 6th son of Alexander Grant, IV of Sheuglie, and Isabel his 2nd wife, dau. of John Grant, of Glenmoriston. Brother of Hugh Grant and uncle of Alexander Grant (1753-1816), *qq.v. m.* Margaretha Henrietta Beck, a Dutch lady of the C.G.H., aunt of Jacob Vanrenen, *q.v.*

l. 15 : *add* to *Services* Present at Culloden on behalf of Prince Charles Edward with a party of Urquhart men. 2nd Lieut. in Capt. Jonathan Forbes' Independent Coy. 13 June 1747.

l. 25 : *add* to *Refs. The Chiefs of Grant,* by Wm. Fraser, LL.D. (3 vols., Edin., 1883), i. 517, *s.n.* Grant, of Sheuglie. (*See also* Vol. ii. p. 630.)

GRANT, Alexander (1753-1816).

p. 310, l. 26 : *add b.* 18 Apr. 1753.

l. 30 : *add* II of Lochletter, and of Redcastle, to which he *s.* in 1808 on the death of his cousin. Only surviving son of Patrick Grant, of Lochletter, and Katharine his wife, dau. of David Baillie, at Ft. Augustus (of the Dunain family). Nephew of Alexander Grant (1725-1768), *q.v. m.* Calcutta 10 Jan. 1794, Jane, sister of Alexander Hannay, *q.v.* Father of Charles Grant (1808-1887), *q.v.*

Add *Refs. : The Chiefs of Grant,* i. 516, *s.n.* Grant, of Sheuglie. *Grant of Corrimony,* by F. J. Grant (Lerwick, 1894), p. 41, *s.n.* Grant, of Lochletter.

GRANT, Andrew.

p. 311, l. 22 : *add* 4th son of Rev. Andrew Grant, D.D., of Limepots, Scone, and Agnes his wife, dau. of Rev. George Willis, minister of Leslie.

GRANT, Charles (1756/57-1817).

p. 311, l. 41 : *add* to *Services* Ensign Bucks. Mil. 10 Feb. 1781.

GRANT, Charles (1803-1882).

p. 312, l. 14 : *add* Ed. Charterhouse Jan.-Apr. 1818.

GRANT, Charles (1807/08-?).

p. 312 : *add b.* 8 Oct. 1808. Of Hazelbrae. 7th son of Alexander Grant (1753-1816), *q.v.,* and Jane Hannay his wife. *m.* Meerut 20 Nov. 1847, Anne Georgiana, eldest dau. of Arthur Wheatley, *q.v.* (She died 1911, aged 81.) *d.* 24 June 1887.

l. 37 : *add* to *Services* Apptd. Writer, B.C.S., (1827) 30 Apr. 1829. Accountant N.W.P. 1842-60. Retired 1860.

Refs. : Grant of Corrimony, p. 42.

GRANT, Charles Alexander.
p. 312, l. 39 : *add bapt.* Chalfont St. Giles.
Bottom l. : *add* 2nd son of James Grant, of Vache Pk., Chalfont St. Giles. Ed. Charterhouse Sept. 1810-Sept. 1812. Served in R.N. before entering Bengal Army.

*GRANT, Henry.
p. 314, l. 14 : *add* He left India with his family on board the Danish ship *Count Bemstolph* 14 Jan. 1784.

GRANT, Hugh.
p. 314, l. 18 : *add b.* Mar. 1733.
l. 22 : *add* 10th son of Alexander Grant, IV of Sheuglie, and Isabel his wife. Brother of Alexander Grant (1725-1768), *q.v. m.* Calcutta 27 Dec. 1761, Mary Carvalho. (She died 17 Mar. 1827.)
l. 23 : *add* to *Services* Served originally as a Vol. in H.M. 42nd Regt. Sailed for Bombay in the *Hector* in 1756, aged 23.
l. 26 : *add* Comdg. at Monghyr in June 1771 ; comdg. 3rd Bde. at Berhampore in 1774. Amassed a considerable fortune in India, and on his return in 1775 he purchased the estate of Moy.
l. 29 : *add* to *Refs. Chiefs of Grant*, i. 517, *s.n.* Grant, of Sheuglie.

GRANT, Lewis (*d.* 1822).
p. 317, l. 14 : *add b.* 1751/52.
l. 17 : *add d.* aged 70.
l. 21 : *add Refs.:* M.I. old cemetery below Chunar fort.

GRANT, Peter Lewis.
p. 320, l. 22 : *add* Son of Alexander Grant, W. S., and Janet Edmond his wife.

GRANT, Peter Warden.
p. 321, l. 5 : *add* sister of Robert Warden Fraser, *q.v.*

*GRANT, William.
p. 322 : *add* (*Probably* 4th son of Rev. Patrick Grant, minister of Nigg, co. Ross, 1756-88, and Ann his 2nd wife, dau. of Rev. George Grant, minister of Kirkmichael. If so, *b.* 21 Mar. 1765, not ' *c.* 24 Mar. 1768,' which is the date he himself gave on entering the Service. cf. Scott's *Fasti*, vii. 66.)

GRANT, William (1803-1842).
p. 322, l. 33 : *add m.* 1838, Ann Forbes, dau. of Capt. James Gordon, of Ivy Bank, Nairn.

GRANT, William Francis.
  p. 323, l. 16 : *add* Ed. Charterhouse ; admitted 1818.
GRAVELEY, Thomas Milton.
  p. 323, l. 34 : *add* Lieut. H.M. 79th Regt. ; h.p. 1763 till death.
GRAY, James Clarke Charnock.
  p. 324, l. 38 : *add bapt.* St. Pancras 17 Nov. 1794. 3rd son of James Gray, Capt. R.N., and Elizabeth Sutton his wife. Grandson of Rt. Hon. Sir James Gray, Bart., K.B. (*D.N.B.*).
  Add to *Services :* Occupation of Garhakota 5 July 1820 ; Lieut. 2/9th N.I., under Major William Brooks, *q.v.* Mutiny campaign ; defence of Lucknow Residency (Medal with clasp).
  p. 325 : *add* to *Refs.* Family information.
GRAY, Thomas (1796-1822).
  p. 325, l. 33 : *add* and Isobel his wife, dau. of Joseph Marsh, shoemaker in Peebles.
GREATRAKES, William.
  p. 326, l. 16 : *add Note :* One William Greatricks (*sic*) was Ensign H.M. 62nd Ft. 17 May 1759 ; and William Greatrakes is shown in *A.L.* for 1778 as Lieut. h.p. 35th Ft.
GREEN, Christopher.
  p. 326, l. 29 : *add* His dau. *m.* Charles Child Wilson, *q.v.* Ed. Westminster.
  Add to *Refs. Westminster School Register.*
GREEN, Thomas.
  p. 327, l. 22 : *add* Capt. comdg. a Mil. Bn. at Calcutta in Aug. 1781.
  l. 23 : *add* Permitted to resign in lieu of C.M. for withholding Sepoys' batta, having restored Rs. 30,000 and being in a bad state of health.
  Add to *Refs. Record of an Indian Governor-Generalship,* p. 81, by Holden Furber.
GREEN, William Horatio.
  p. 327 : *add Note :* (He may probably be identified with Horatio William Green, son of Richard Green and Martha ; *bapt.* St. Luke's, Chelsea, 3 Mar. 1765, who was admitted a poor scholar at Charterhouse, 29 Oct. 1777 ; apprenticed 5 Aug. 1780, to Robert Calef, of the ship *London.*)
GREENING, Thomas.
  p. 332, l. 36 : *add bapt.* St. George's, Hanover Sq., 18 Aug. 1786. Son of Thomas Greening and Margaret Hughes his wife.

GREENSTREET, John.
p. 332, l. 40 : *add b*. 12 May 1781.

p. 333, l. 3 : *add* Eldest son of —— Greenstreet and Anna Maria his wife, 2nd dau. of Rev. Francis Hawkins, rector of Higham Gobion, Beds. *m*. Christchurch, Surrey, 7 Jan. 1813, Sarah, dau. of William Lees.

Add to *Refs*. Family information. M.I. Frenchay churchyard.

GREENWATER, Weston.
p. 333 : *add Note :* His name appears as Weston GREEN-WOLLERS in Court Minutes of 2 Mar. and 26 Apr. 1764 ; also in admon. of his estate granted at Madras, 8 Apr. 1766.

GREGORY, Robert Bourke.
p. 333, l. 2 from bottom : *add* widow of Capt. Lowe, 25th Light Dgns.

GREIG, Charles.
p. 335, l. 3 : *add* dau. of John Anderson, residenter in Canongate.

GRESLEY, Francis.
p. 336, top l. : *add* Sailed for India in the *Thomas Grenville* with his cousin, Frederick Grote, *q.v.* First Burma War ; operations in Cachar 1825.

GREY, John (1761-1837).
p. 336, l. 15 : *add m*. Nottingham 7 June 1798, Elizabeth Sophia, dau. of Thomas Boott. Ed. Charterhouse July 1772-Sept. 1775.

GRIFFITHS, Frederick William Stevens.
p. 340 : *add* Son of Rev. Charles Griffiths, sometime chaplain to H.M. 79th Regt., afterwards chaplain at Fort St. George. *m.* Gt. Marlow, Bucks., 15 Dec. 1788, Elizabeth Jane, eldest dau. of Joseph Fry, M.D., of Gt. Marlow, and cousin-german of Alexander Guinand, *q.v.* (She died Clifton 29 Aug. 1834, aged 79.) *Add* to *Refs. Howard & Crisp (Notes),* ix. 55, *s.n.* Fry. *Hist. MSS. Commn.* No. 74. M.I. at Berhampore.

GRIGG, Mark.
p. 341, l. 31 : *add b*. 6 Dec. 1793. Son of Mark Grigg and Joan his wife.

GRISSELL, James.
p. 343, end of l. 15 : after ' Regt.' *add* (India medal).

GROSE, George.
p. 343, l. 35 : *add bapt*. Marylebone 31 Dec. 1794. Son of John Grose and Sarah his wife. His sister *m*. Thomas Trist, *q.v.*

GROTE, Frederick.
p. 344, l. 7 : *add* Cousin of Francis Gresley, *q.v.* Ed. Charterhouse Apr. 1820-Apr. 1821.
Add to *Refs. Charterhouse School List.*

GUMLEY, Robert.
p. 348 : *add* Brother of Rev. John Gumley (? M.A., T.C.D.) and bro.-in-law of Benjamin Pemberton (? of Park Place, Dublin).
Refs.: Will dated 20 Oct. 1783 ; proved 28 Dec. 1784.

GUTHRIE, Charles Seton.
p. 350, l. 2 : *add* widow of Henry Inglis (*see* Appendix A).

GUTHRIE, John.
p. 350, l. 28 : *add* 1/16th, later 32nd N.I. and 3rd Brahmins, was named "*Guthrie-ki-Paltan*" from him.

GWINNETT, John Price.
p. 352 : *add* Son of Rev. Samuel Gwinnett, LL.B., vicar of Down Hatherley, Gloucs., and incumbent of St. Nicholas', Gloucester, and Anne his wife, dau. (or widow) of Fulke Emes. Ensign 47th Ft. 18 Mar. 1758 ; Lieut. do. 2 Apr. 1759 ; exchanged to h.p. of Lieut. 99th Ft. 8 May 1764.

HADDEN, David.
p. 353 : *add b.* 29 May 1809. *d. unm.* Guernsey 16 Mar. 1852. Eldest son of John Hadden and Violet his wife, 8th and youngest dau. of Alexander Innes, comy. of Aberdeen.
Add to *Refs. Memoir of James Young*, p. 71.

HADLEY, George.
p. 353 : *add m.* St. Helena 6 Mar. 1772, Miss Elizabeth Caroline Thompson.

HAIR, Joseph.
p. 356, l. 16 : *add* Son of Patrick Hair, M.D., physician to the Factory, and Dorothy his wife, *née* Sharpe.

HALDANE, Charles, Radclyffe, and Robert.
pp. 356-8 : *add* to *Refs. The Haldanes of Gleneagles*, by Gen. Sir Aylmer Haldane, G.C.M.G., &c. (Wm. Blackwood, 1929).

HALES, James.
p. 359, l. 3 : *add* eldest dau. of Thomas Blair (*d.* 1833), *q.v.*

HALL, Arthur.
p. 362, l. 32 : *add* and Hon. Anna Maria Bridget his wife, 3rd

dau. of John, 5th Viscount Torrington. Cousin-german of Hon. Robert Barlow Palmer Byng, *q.v.*

Add to Refs. Burke's *Peerage*, 1923, p. 2186, *s.n.* Torrington, V.

HALL, Thomas (1770/71-1856).

p. 365, l. 39 : *add m.* Fatehgarh 6 Feb. 1803, Ellen, youngest dau. of Simpson Dubois, *q.v.* (*See also* Charles Whitfield.)

HALLOWELL, Benjamin.

p. 367, l. 28 : *add* Trin. Coll., Camb., 14 Feb. 1820 ; matric. 1822.

HAMILTON, Anthony.

p. 368, l. 15 : *add bapt.* Holy Trinity, Whitehaven, 19 June 1752.

l. 19 : *add* 4th and youngest son of Isaac Hamilton, surgeon, and Frances his wife.

l. 25 : *add Refs.* : *Churches in Whitehaven Rural Deanery*, by Rev. Caesar Carne (1916), p. 63. M.I. Holy Trinity churchyard.

HAMILTON, George William.

p. 371, l. 39 : *add to Refs.* M.I. St. Cuthbert's psh. churchyard, Edinburgh.

HAMILTON, James (*d.* 1805).

p. 372 : *add b.* Westburn, co. Lanark, 1 Feb. 1789. 4th son of John Hamilton, of Westburn (who took the additional name of Dundas on succeeding to the estate of Duddingston *jure matris*) and Grizel his wife, dau. of John Hamilton, of Barns.

Add Refs. : Burke's *Landed Gentry*, 4th edn., p. 402, *s.n.* Dundas, of Duddingston. *The House of Hamilton*, by Lt.-Col. George Hamilton, p. 872.

HAMILTON, John (1808-?).

p. 373, l. 24 ; *add* Ed. Charterhouse ; admitted 1823. T.C.D. ; Pensioner 17 Oct. 1825, aged 17 ; B.A. 1834.

HAMILTON, John James.

p. 373, l. 39 : *add* Eldest son of Rev. George Hamilton, minister of Gladsmuir 1790-1832, and Elizabeth his wife, dau. of John Dickson, of Conheath, provost of Dumfries.

p. 374 : *add* to *Refs.* Scott's *Fasti*, i. 367.

HAMILTON, Robert (*d.* 1793).

p. 375 : *add b. c.* 1754. Eldest son of Robert Hamilton, of Kynbrachmont, and Agnes his wife, dau. of Robert Fotheringham, of Ballindean. *d.* aged 38.

Add Refs. : *House of Hamilton*, by Lt.-Col. George Hamilton (Edin., 1933), p. 518. M.I. at Bencoolen.

BAILLIE-HAMILTON, Ker.

p. 376 : *Add* to *Services :* R.M.A., Woolwich, 1819-21, when he resigned. C.B. 23 July 1862. Author of " Our Saddle Horses," 1865.
Add to *Refs. Boase.*

HAMMOND, James.

p. 377, l. 26 : *add* Son of Joseph Hammond, " said by tradition to have been in civil employment about Portsmouth Dockyard." Brother of George Hammond, *q.v.*

l. 28 : *add* Appears to have been in Nawab of Arcot's service in 1775.
Add to *Refs. Family of Twysden and Twisden*, by C. H. Dudley Ward, 1939, p. 426. *Warren Hastings' Letters to Sir John Macpherson*, ed. Henry Dodwell, p. 38.

HAMPTON, Robert.

p. 378, l. 21 : *add m.* Fort Marlbro' 8 Aug. 1810, Miss Eliza Jover.

HAMPTON, Samuel.

p. 379, l. 6 : *add* Col. 1st Bengal Eur. Regt. in Aug. 1781.

HAMPTON, William Philip.

p. 379, l. 27 : *add* Grandson of Samuel Hampton, *q.v.*

HANNAH, Simon Fraser.

p. 381, l. 1 from bottom : *add* (She *re-m.* 13 Nov. 1862, Maj.-Gen. Charles Holroyd, Bengal Staff Corps, and died 31 Aug. 1863.)

HANNAY, Alexander.

p. 382, l. 20 : *add* His sister *m.* Alexander Grant (1753-1816), *q.v.*

l. 22 : *add* Ensign 51st Ft. 1 Dec. 1758 ; Lieut. do. (at Gibraltar) 2 Aug. 1760 ; h.p. of its Addl. Ofrs. 1763.

HANNYNGTON, John Caulfeild.

p. 384, l. 37 : *add m.* Harriet Dillon ——. (She died London 18 Apr. 1897, aged 94.)

HARDING, Samuel.

p. 385, l. 20 : *add bapt.* Betley 20 Apr. 1792. Son of William Harding, steward to George Tollet (*D.N.B.*), and Elizabeth his wife.

l. 22 : *add* Lieut. N. Regt. Local Staffs. Mil. 26 June 1810.

HARDING, Thomas.
 p. 385, l. 31 : *add m.* Bombay 5 Sept. 1782, Miss Elizabeth Smith.

HARDWICK, Frederick Wilson.
 p. 386, l. 36 : *add b.* 17 Feb. 1804. Son of Francis Hardwick and Mary his wife. Ed. Rugby; admitted 1815.

HARDY, Alexander.
 p. 388, l. 20 : *add* Major comdg. 1,200 Mil. at Patna in Aug. 1781.

HARINGTON, James.
 p. 389, l. 39 : *add* 3rd son of Sir Edward Harington, Kt., mayor of Bath (*D.N.B.*), and Anne Walker his wife. Kinsman of Thomas Lowth Harington, *q.v.*
 Bottom line : *add Refs.:* Poynton's *History of Kelston.*

HARRIOTT, David.
 p. 391, l. 20, after 'John Harriott' : *add* resident mgte. at Thames police court (*D.N.B.*).

HARRIOTT, Thomas.
 p. 393, l. 19 : *add* to *Services* Ensign Essex Mil. 30 Mar. 1778.

HARRIS, Charles.
 p. 394, top l. : *add b.* 20 Nov. 1787. Eldest son of Henry Harris, M.D., and Jane his 1st wife, *née* Charles.

HARRIS, John (1787-1811).
 p. 395, l. 36 : *add* Ward of William Jones, Marshal of the King's Bench.

HARRIS, Thomas.
 p. 396, l. 1 from bottom : *add m.* 1780, Jane, widow of John Fortnom, *q.v.*

HARRISON, John.
 p. 398, l. 22 : *add b.* 31 Mar. ; *bapt.* 17 May 1758. 3rd son of William Harrison, of Orgrave, surgeon at Sheffield, and Elizabeth his wife, dau. of John Dickson, of Sheffield, hardwareman.
 Add Refs.: Hunter's *Familiæ Minorum Gentium, iii.* 830.

HARTLE, Anthony.
 p. 399, l. 30 : *add* Transfd. as Lieut. from H.M.S. 1 Sept. 1768.

HARVEY, George Daniel.
 p. 401, l. 2 : *add* Ed. Eton 1817-22 ; K.S.

HARWOOD, John Terry.
 p. 401, l. 36 : *add* Elizabeth his wife, dau. of Thomas Terry.
 l. 37 : *add* Ed. Winchester.

HASELL, Christopher.
 p. 402, l. 9 : *add* Ed. Shrewsbury 1827-31.

HASLAM, Thomas.
 p. 403, l. 5 : *add bapt.* St. Leonard's, Shoreditch, 6 July 1790. Son of John Haslam and Sarah his wife.
 l. 6 : *add* Ed. Merchant Taylors' Oct. 1805-Mar. 1806.

HASTINGS, Henry Cadogan.
 p. 403, bottom l. : *add d.* Guildford 20 Feb. 1906, aged 93.
 Add to *Services* The first Chief Constable of Surrey, 1851-99.
 Add to *Refs. The Times*, 23 Feb. 1906.

HAWES, George.
 p. 406, l. 18 : *add* (She died on the Comer R. 16 Feb. 1812.)

HAWKES, Walter.
 p. 407, l. 14 : *add b.* 23 Oct. 1761.
 l. 19 : *add* Son of Jeremiah Hawkes, of Cecil St., Strand, London, coal merchant, and Sarah his wife, youngest dau. of Philip Walter, of Moreton Hampstead, Devon.
 l. 23 : *add* Elected to Trin. Coll., Camb., 1780 ; matric. 1780.

HAWKINS, Edward Simeon.
 p. 408, l. 17 : *add* sister of Henry Goodwyn, *q.v.*

HAWKINS, Francis Spencer.
 p. 408, l. 37 : *add* eldest dau. of Lambert Richard Loveday, *q.v.* (She died Kaitha 15 July 1824, aged 17.)

HAWKINS, Henry.
 p. 409 : *add b.* 6 Oct. 1750. 4th son of Rev. Francis Hawkins, rector of Higham Gobion, Beds., and Elizabeth Downing his wife. *m.* 1st, Charlotte Wortham. (She died 17 Nov. 1788, aged 26.) *m.* 2nd, Anne, dau. of John Gurney, of Bedford. (She died 14 June 1832, aged 70.) Grandfather of Sir Henry Hawkins, Baron Brampton (*D.N.B.*).
 Add to *Refs.* Family information.

HAWKINS, Thomas.
 p. 409 : *add b.* 17 Dec. 1756. 5th and youngest son of Rev. Francis Hawkins and Elizabeth Downing his wife.
 p. 410, l. 5 : *add m.* 2nd, Elizabeth, dau. of Peter Friell. (She died 25 Dec. 1831, aged 50.)

HAWTHORNE, Steele.
p. 411, l. 33 : *add m.* 2nd, Santry church, co. Dublin, 5 May 1825, Sarah, dau. of James Russell, of Derramore, co. Down.

HAY, Edward.
p. 413, l. 34 : *add* Ed. Shrewsbury 1823-5.

HAY, Humphrey.
p. 414, l. 31 : *add* 3rd son of Robert Hay, of Lawfield and Spott, and Catherine his wife, only dau. of Humphrey Babington, of Greenfort and Rosapenna, co. Donegal.
Add to *Refs.* Burke's *Peerage*, 1923, p. 2212, *s.n.* Tweedale, M.

*HAY, James.
p. 415, l. 22 : *add* Son of James Hay, W.S. (who was eldest son of John Hay, younger of Hopes, E. Lothian), and Matilda Hay his wife, dau. of Capt. John Clark, H.C.S., and widow of Alexander Falconar, of Woodcot. Cousin-german of John Hay (1802-1839), *q.v.*
Refs. : Burke's *Landed Gentry*, 5th edn., p. 603, *s.n.* Hay, of Hopes, co. Haddington.

HAY, John (1792-?).
p. 416, l. 4 : *add* and Margaret his wife, dau. of James Chalmers, of Fingland.

HAY, John Thompson.
p. 416, l. 32 : *add d.* Dinapore.

HAY, Patrick (1748/49-1822).
p. 417, l. 21 : *add* to *Services* Second Mysore War 1781-2 ; A.D.C. and Persian Intr. to Gen. Sir Eyre Coote.
l. 25 : *add* to *Refs.* M.I. in Brenchley church, Kent.

HAY, Richard.
p. 418, l. 19 : *add b.* 6 Feb. 1764.
Add to *Refs.* M.I. in St. Mary's church, Rye.

HEATHCOTE, William Samuel.
p. 424, l. 36 : *add* dau. of Richard Boswell Armstrong, *q.v.*

HEATLEY, Patrick.
p. 425, l. 12 : *add* Uncle of Alexander Douglas, *q.v.*

HEAVER, James.
p. 425, l. 24 : *add* and Mary his wife.
Add Refs. : Will dated Benares 14 Mar. 1820 ; proved 6 Mar. 1826.

HEFFERNAN, Michael.
    p. 425 : *add* Son of Thomas Heffernan, of Cork, and Ellen his wife.

HENLEY, William.
    p. 429, l. 15 : *add* Received into Church at Rendlesham 23 Aug. 1784.
    l. 16 : *add* Ed. Eton between 1796 and 1799.
    Add Refs. : Eton School Lists.

HERIOT, Charles William.
    p. 435, l. 24 : *add* Son of John Heriot, Dy. Paymr. Gen. of H.M. Forces in W.I.

HERVEY, Andrew.
    p. 437 : *add* to *Refs. Lady Anne Barnard at the Cape*, by Dorothea Fairbridge, pp. 12, 14, 36.

HETZLER, Robert.
    p. 439, l. 5 : *add d.* aged 66.
    l. 6 : *add (Probably* son of Capt. Robert Hetzler, R.A., who *d.* Gibraltar 4 Sept. 1774.)
    l. 10 : *add* to *Services* Cadet in R.A. (Warrant dated 30 July 1781).
    l. 25 : *add* to *Refs.* M.I. in porch of Chardstock church.

HEWETT, Peter Selwood.
    p. 440, l. 4 : *add m.* Calcutta 30 Nov. 1816, Miss Sarah Bush.

HEWITT, Francis.
    p. 440, l. 28 : *add m.* Elizabeth Henrietta, dau. of Henry Hewitt, of Cork. (She died 15 Dec. 1890, aged 82.)

HEWITT, William Henry.
    p. 440, bottom l. : *add m.* 1st, Fort Marlbro' 14 Sept. 1812, Miss Maria Holloway. (*See also* H. W. Wilkinson.)

HEYLAND, Arthur.
    p. 441, l. 20 : *add* Ed. Shrewsbury 1822-4.

HEYSHAM, William.
    p. 442, l. 8 : *add* and Elizabeth Mary his wife, *née* Coulthard.

HICKEY, John.
    p. 442, bottom l. : *add* Brother of William Hickey, *q.v.*

HICKEY, William.
    p. 443, l. 10 : *add* Eldest son of Noah Hickey (Hickie), of Dublin and of Violets Town, co. Meath, and Sophia his wife,

widow of Col. Sutherland, and dau. of Capt. Vigors Thomas, R.N., of Limerick. Cousin-german of Francis Thomas, *q.v.*
l. 13 : *add* His dau. *m.* Henry Pelham Burn, *q.v.*
l. 14 : *add* Ensign 46th (Devon) Ft. 2 Jan. 1812.
l. 23 : *add* Sheriff of Calcutta 1835.

HICKMAN, Gregory.
p. 444, l. 20 : *add* (She died Dorking 20 Feb. 1849.)
Add to *Refs.* M.I. Fatehgarh fort cemetery.

HICKS, John William.
p. 446, bottom l. : *add* and Susanna his wife, eldest dau. of Thomas Mills, of Gt. Saxham Hall.

HIGGINS, John Thady.
p. 448 : His full name was John Thady Higgins.

HIGGINSON, Sir James Macaulay.
p. 449, l. 13 : *add* and sister of Henry John Childe Shakespear, *q.v.*

HIGHMORE, George.
p. 450, l. 9 : *add bapt.* Beaconsfield 13 July 1789. Son of William Highmore and Margaret his wife, *née* Proctor. Ed. Eton ; K.S. 1802.
Add Refs. : Eton School Lists.

HILL, Justly.
p. 451 : *add b.* Walsingham 25 Apr. 1749. 5th son of William Hill, of Walsingham, by Piercy West, grand-dau. of Lord Delawarr. *d.* suddenly at his house on Stamford Hill 4 May 1802. King's Commission as Lt. Col. in E.I. only 17 Apr. 1786 ; Lt. Col. (Bengal Art.) 1789.
p. 452, l. 5 : *add* to *Refs.* Family information. Berry's *Kent Genealogies*, p. 493. *G.M.* 1802, i. 585. Portrait in uniform in possession of his gt. grandson.

HILL, Rowland.
p. 452, l. 32 : *add* to *Services* Gwalior campaign ; Maharajpur (Bronze star).

HILL, Thomas (1761-1821).
p. 453, l. 20 : *add b.* 3 Dec. 1761. 3rd son of James Hill, writer in Glasgow. Glasgow Univ. ; matric. 1774 ; M.A. 1779.

HILLIARD, John.
p. 454, l. 32 : *add* Son of Christopher Hilliard, of Baltygarron, by his wife, dau. of Major John Crosbie.
Add to *Refs. Misc. Gen. et Her.* N.S. ii. 42.

ADDENDA (Vol. II)

HISLOP, William.
p. 456, l. 27 : *add* to *Refs.* M.I. Kotah, " erected by Raj Rana Madho Singh as a mark of respect for the memory of the deceased."

HOARE, James Griffith.
p. 456, l. 34 : *add* Cousin of Nathaniel Leonard and John Toppin, *qq.v.*

HODGES, Charles Alexander Crickett.
p. 457, l. 29 : *add bapt.* Embleton 26 Apr. 1803. 3rd son of Rev. H. Hodges and Sophia Alexander his wife, *née* Crickett, of Smith's Hall, Essex.

HODGES, Charles Wyndham.
p. 458, l. 12 : *add* to *Refs.* Burke's *Landed Gentry*, 3rd edn., p. 29, *s.n.* Aston, of Aston, co. Chester.

HODGSON, Henry.
p. 459, l. 28 : *add m.* 2nd, Brit. Embassy, Paris, 1848, Helen, dau. of Adm. Robert Honyman.
Add to *Refs. The Times*, 2 Mar. 1857.

HODGSON, James.
p. 460, l. 7 : *add* elder sister of Edward Hardwick(e), *q.v.*

HOGG, Roger.
p. 464, l. 8 : *add* 2nd Lieut. of Marines 6 June 1765 ; exchanged to h.p. of Lieut. 79th Ft. 1766 till death.

*HOHNEY, Christian.
p. 466, top l. ; *insert* an asterisk before his name.

HOLBROW, John.
p. 466, l. 15 : *add* 2nd son of Samuel Holbrow, of Leonard Stanley, clothier, and Sarah his wife, dau. of John Dimock, of Bridgend House, Stonehouse, Gloucs.
l. 20 : *add* (She died Clifton 9 Dec. 1902, aged 85.)
Add to *Refs. Gloucs. N. & Q.* Vol. v. M.I. at Leonard Stanley.

HOLLAND, George Freer.
p. 467, l. 6 : *add* to *Services* Siege and capture of Hathras 1817 ; Lieut. Pioneers.

HOLLAND, Thomas.
p. 467 : *add b.* 6 Sept. 1763. 2nd son of Rev. Nicholas Holland, rector of Stifford, Essex, and Jane his wife, dau. of Edmund Clarke, Counsellor at Law, of Ikenham. His sister *m.* Charles

Stewart (1764-1837), *q.v.* *m.* Ann, dau. of Rev. Thomas Clarke, rector of Carlton, Cambs.
Add to *Refs. Pedigrees of Anglesey and Carnarvon Families,* by J. E. Griffith, p. 341.

HOLLINGBURY, John.
p. 467, l. 27 : *add bur.* Madras 26 May 1782.

HOLLINGS, William Charles.
p. 468, l. 28 : *add Note :* He is probably identical with the " Capt. Hollings, an ex-officer," who was kld. by mutineers nr. Cawnpore, 8 June 1857. (M.I. All Sts. Memorial church, Cawnpore.)

HOLWELL, John William.
p. 472 : *add b.* Calcutta 1742. Son of Govr. John Zephaniah Holwell (*D.N.B.*) by his 1st wife. *d.v.p.* before 1798.
Services : Went to Bengal with his father in 1758. Requests permission to return to England 23 Feb. 1767. Court Minutes of 15 Nov. 1769 record the " Petition of Mr. John William Holwell who was apptd. Writer for Bengal in 1759 and has since served under that Presdy. in a mily. capacity and prays to be apptd. to such station on the Bengal Est. as the Court shall see fit."

HOME, Gabriel Murray.
p. 472, l. 24 : *add* 3rd son of Rev. Robert Home, minister of Polwarth 1769-1838 (' Father of the Church '), and Elizabeth his wife, dau. of James Murray, of Wooplaw.
Add to *Refs.* Scott's *Fasti,* ii. 28.

FERGUSSON-HOME, John Hutcheson.
p. 475, l. 18 : *add m.* 1st, Calcutta 16 Apr. 1844, Georgiana Mary, eldest dau. of Sir Daniel Eliott, K.C.S.I., M.C.S., and grand-dau. of George Russell, *q.v.*

HOOK, Lionel.
p. 477, top l. : *add* to *Services* Lieut. W. Regt. of Fenc. Men 26 Dec. 1778.

HOPE, Sir William, Bart.
p. 477 : *add* to *Services* Lieut. 31st Ft. 6 Feb. 1752 ; resigned 26 July 1756.

HORSFORD, Sir John.
p. 485, l. 8 : *add* Ed. Merchant Taylors' Oct. 1760-May 1768, latterly as Head Monitor.
l. 22 : *add* Author of " A Collection of Poems written in the

East Indies, with miscellaneous remarks in real life," by J—— H——. Calcutta, Telegraph Press, 1797.

HORSFORD, Richard.
p. 485, l. 36 : *add* and sister of Charles Pattenson, *q.v.* (*See also* Sir James Tennant.)

HOUGH, William.
p. 487, l. 12 : *add* 4th and youngest son of Stephen Hough, Clerk of the Errors in the Court of Common Pleas, and Sarah his 2nd wife.

HOUGHTON, Richmond.
p. 488, l. 4 : *add* 5th son of Edward Houghton, of Gt. Nelson St., Liverpool, and Elizabeth his wife and cousin, dau. of Christopher Hasell, of Liverpool. Related to Christopher Hasell, *q.v.*
Add to *Refs. Misc. Gen. et Her.* 5S. vi. 319.

HOWARD, Thomas Ward.
p. 489, bottom l. : *add* to *Services* Lieut. H.M. 10th Ft. 13 Mar. 1782.

HOWELL, George.
p. 490, bottom l. : *add* Son of Mrs. Jane Howell.

HOWLEY, Richard.
p. 491, l. 10 : *add m.* (?) (She died London 15 Mar. 1849.)

HOWLEY, Thomas.
p. 491 : *add d.* Madras 29 Apr. 1782. Cousin of Richard Howley, *q.v. m.* Anna de Rozario, widow of Michael Fennell.
Refs.: Intestate ; admon. 7 Aug. 1782.

HOWORTH, Humphrey.
p. 492, l. 11 : *add* dau. of Jacob Rider, B.C.S.
Add to *Refs.* M.I. Warangal, Hyderabad.

HUGHES, Michael.
p. 494, l. 39 : *add* Only son of John Hughes, of Bonmaen House, Llansamlet, and Ann Llewellyn his wife. Cousin-german of William Lewis Hughes, 1st Lord Dinorben.
l. 41, after ' 1/22nd N.I.' : *add* (India medal).
p. 495 : *add* to *Refs. Pedigrees of Anglesey and Carnarvon Families*, by J. E. Griffith, p. 333.

HULL, Lawrence Nilson.
  p. 497, l. 5 : *add bapt.* Gt. Baddow 16 Apr. 1799. 6th son of James Watson Hull, late Bo.C.S., and Sophia Hollamby his wife.
  Add to *Refs. Misc. Gen et Her.* 5S. viii (1932), 58.

HUME, John.
  p. 498 : *add* Of Law.

HUMFRAYS, Alexander.
  p. 498, l. 36 : *add m.* 1st, Edinburgh (? Jan.) 1836, Madeline, dau. of D. Johnston, of Edinburgh.
  l. 40 : *add* Ed. Harrow 1818-22.
  p. 499 : *add* to *Refs. Saunders' Newsletter*, 23 Jan. 1836.

HUMFREY, William Henry.
  p. 500, l. 20 : *add* and Elizabeth Chatfield his wife. Ed. Rugby ; admitted 1821.

HUMPHREYS, Edward.
  p. 501, l. 9 : *add b.* 1736/37.
  l. 11 : *add d.* Chunar 6 May 1783, aged 46.
  l. 15 : *add* to *Refs.* M.I. Chunar old cemetery.

HUMPHREYS, Richard.
  p. 501 : *add b.* 28 Jan. 1762. 3rd son of Charles Gardiner Humphreys, of Bank House, Montgomery, and Martha, dau. of Edward Bright. Uncle of Charles Wyndham Humphreys, *q.v. d. unm.*
  Add to *Refs.* Burke's *Landed Gentry*, 13th edn., p. 1352, *s.n.* Humphreys-Owen, of Glansevern.

HUNTER, George.
  p. 505, l. 2 : *add m.* Lucknow, Oct. 1806, Miss Harriet Hawkins.

HUNTER, Patrick.
  p. 507, l. 25 : *add b.* 1757.
  l. 28 : *add* V of Auchterarder. 2nd son of James and Sarah Hunter.
  Add to *Refs. Pedigree of Hunter of Thurston*, by A. A. Hunter (London, 1905), p. 34.

HURRING, Thomas.
  p. 510, l. 8 : *add* to *Services* Ensign Suffolk Mil.

HUTCHINGS, George.
  p. 511, l. 2 : *add* Ed. Shrewsbury 1821-4.

HUTCHINSON, George (*d.* 1828).
p. 512, l. 33 : *add m.* Edinburgh 25 Jan. 1815, eldest dau. of John Cuninghame, of Port Glasgow.
Add to *Refs.* M.I. St. Cuthbert's psh. churchyard, Edinburgh.

HUTCHINSON, George (1793-1852).
p. 513, l. 8 : *add* dau. of James Williams, of Walthamstow.

HUTHWAITE, Sir Edward.
p. 515, l. 8 : *add* Son of William Huthwaite and Lucy his wife, *née* Stretton.
Add to *Refs. Brit. and Foreign Orders, War Medals and Decorations*, by A. A. Payne, Sheffield, 1911 (portrait from a photo.).

HUTHWAITE, Henry.
p. 515, l. 35 : *add* Younger son of William Huthwaite, mercer, and Elizabeth his wife, dau. of Lt.-Col. Douglas.

HUTTON, Charles.
p. 516, l. 16 : *add* Son of William Charles Hutton, Comdr. H.C.S. *Lord Nelson* (lost with all hands in Oct. 1808), and Eleanor Reed his wife, step-dau. of William Sibbald, *q.v.*

HUTTON, Thomas (1807-1874).
p. 516, l. 1 from bottom : *add* Author of "The Consummation," 1860 ; "Israel in the Past; " "The Chronology of Creation."

HYDE, John.
p. 519, l. 17 : *add d.* Serampore 11 May 1817.
l. 18 : *add Services :* Was Comy. of Ord. at Cawnpore in 1783, before he received a Bt. Commission as Ensign. Apptd. Master and Accountant Gen. of the Supreme Court 7 Nov. 1785 ; Keeper of the Records 1 Mar. 1792 ; Prothonotary 22 Oct. 1793 till 19 May 1799.

HYDE, John Fleming.
p. 519, l. 23 : *add* dau. of Francis Hamilton Pearson, *q.v.* (*See also* Frederick George Lister.)
l. 24 : *add* Son of Gertrude Dowling.

HYDE, William.
p. 519, l. 40 : *add b.* 8 May 1752.
p. 520, top l. : *add* Son of David Hyde.
l. 2 : *add* Ed. Merchant Taylors' Oct. 1762-Oct. 1765.

IBBETT, Henry.
  p. 521 : *add* to *Services* Was a Sergt. in 2nd Bde. in Bengal when apptd. Cadet. " Is however of a respectable family and has a good education."

IMPEY, Elijah Pattle.
  p. 522, l. 10 : *add b.* 27 Sept. 1816.
  Add to *Refs.* M.I. St. James's church, Cheltenham.

INGLE, Henry.
  p. 523, l. 15 : *add bapt.* St. Mary's, Bury St. Edmunds, 23 May 1795. Son of Rev. Samuel Ingle and Susan his wife.

INGLIS, Hempbel.
  p. 523 : *add Note :* His christian name was probably Kemble.

INGRAM, John William.
  p. 524, l. 20 : *add* eldest dau. of James Scott (1778-1820), *q.v.*

INNES, James Charles.
  p. 525, l. 13 : *add* to *Services* Was comdg. 61st N.I. when it mutinied at Jullundur 7 June 1857.

INNES, WILLIAM (1806-1872).
  p. 527, l. 3 : *add d.* Brighton.
  l. 5 : *add m.* Jemima Rebecca ———.
  l. 7 : *add* (She died 28 June 1842, aged 21.)
  Add to *Refs.* M.I. St. Cuthbert's psh. churchyard, Edinburgh.

IRONSIDE, Gilbert.
  p. 528, l. 13 : *add* and sister of Roger Elliot Roberts, *q.v.* (She died Bath 9 Dec. 1821.)

JACK, Alexander.
  p. 534, l. 19 : *add* Author and artist of "Six Views of Kote Kangra," 1847.

JACKSON, Alfred.
  p. 534, l. 25 : *add b.* 1 Dec. 1805.
  l. 28 : *add* Ed. Charterhouse Jan.-Aug. 1819.

JACKSON, Augustus Henry Ernst.
  p. 535, l. 11 : *add née* Ernst.

JACKSON, Edward.
  p. 535, bottom l. : *add* and Sarah his wife, youngest dau. of George Vaughan, of Blackfriars. Cousin-german of John Jackson (1805-1825), *q.v.*
  p. 536, l. 8 : *add* to *Refs. Genealogical Mag.* vii. 542-3 (Apr. 1904).

JACKSON, Henry Colvin.
  p. 537, l. 32: *add m.* Secunderabad 20 Nov. 1838, Lucie, widow of Lieut. Robert Thorpe Onslow, 7th Madras L.C., 2nd dau. of Maj.-Gen. Henry Webber, Madras Est., and niece of Charles Webber, *q.v.* (She *re-m.* Thomas Bromley, and died 10 Jan. 1852.)
  l. 36: *add Refs.:* Burke's *Landed Gentry*, 7th edn., p. 1949, *s.n.* Incledon-Webber, of Buckland House, Devon.

JACKSON, James Nesbitt.
  p. 538, l. 7: *add (See also* John Samuel Henry Weston.)

JACKSON, Julian.
  p. 539, l. 12: *add d.* Eaton Sq., London.
  Add to *Services* Lieut. in Russian Army 2 June 1815; Col. do. 14 Aug. 1829; retired 21 Sept. 1830. Served in France 1815-18. Sec. of R. Geog. Soc., London, 1841-7; a clerk under council of education 1847 till death. F.R.S. 3 Apr. 1845. Kt. of St. Stanislaus, of Poland. Author of "Guide du Voyageur," Paris, 1822.
  Add to *Refs. Boase.*

JACKSON, Richard C——.
  p. 540: His second christian name was Chaloner.

JACKSON, Verney.
  p. 541, l. 4: *add* Youngest son of John Jackson, of Red Lion Sq. Emmanuel Coll., Camb., 8 July 1779.
  l. 6: *add Refs.: Bath Chron.* 30 Sept. 1784.

JACKSON, William (Cadet 1770).
  p. 541: *add* 3rd son of John Jackson, of Red Lion Sq., London, and of Eltham, and Elizabeth his wife, dau. of Col. Verney Lloyd, one of Marlborough's officers. Brother of Rev. Dr. Thomas Jackson, canon of St. Paul's (*D.N.B.*), and of Verney Jackson, *q.v. m.* Calcutta 7 Nov. 1776, Margaret, dau. of Sir John Stewart or Steuart, 3rd Bart. of Allanbank. Father of James Nesbit Jackson, Thomas Charles Jackson, and William Hill Jackson, *qq.v.* Admitted an attorney of the Supreme Court, Calcutta, 8 June 1775; Registrar of the Court and Coy.'s Atty. *d.* Calcutta 24 Aug. 1807, aged 58.
  Refs.: Family information. Portraits by Tilly Kettle (1774) in uniform, and by Zoffany (*c.* 1800), in the possession of Maj.-Gen. Sir Louis Jackson, K.B.E., C.B., &c., his great-grandson.

JACKSON, William Hill.
  p. 541, l. 34: after 'Somerset' *add* and sister of Charles Vincent Wylde, *q.v.*

JAMES, Thomas (1807-1871).
p. 544, l. 31 : *add* Brother of William James Wallace, *q.v.*

JAMES, William (1803-?).
p. 545, l. 28 : *add* (Living in Apr. 1851.)
l. 30 : *add* Brother of Thomas James (1807-1871), *q.v.*
l. 33 : *add* First Burma War ; Arakan 1825 ; Ensign 68th N.I. (India medal).[1]

[1] *Note :* Having earned this medal as " Ensign W. James, 68th N.I.," he signs for it in Apr. 1851 as " W. James Wallace." The date of his assumption of the latter surname has not been ascertained.

JAMIESON, James William Henry.
p. 546, l. 4 : *add* and Maria Baker his wife.

JARDINE, Edward Raleigh.
p. 546, l. 32 : *add bapt.* E. Stonehouse 24 Nov. 1800. Son of James Jardine, Capt. R.M., and Sally Maria his wife. Grandson of Lydia Maria, widow of Lieut. John Polkinghorne.

JEFFERSON, John.
p. 547, l. 16 : *add* Pensd. on Lord Clive's fund 7 Apr. 1773.

JENKINS, Francis.
p. 549, l. 3 from bottom : *add* 2nd son of Rev. Francis Jenkins and Mary his wife, dau. of Richard Buckland, of Truro.

p. 550 : *add* to *Refs.* Burke's *Landed Gentry*, 10th edn., p. 861, *s.n.* Jenkins, of Clanacombe, Kingsbridge, Devon.

JENNER, Birt Wyndham Rous.
p. 551, l. 38 : *add* (She *re-m.* William Prichard, of Bryntirion, co. Glam., and died 3 Oct. 1905, aged 91.)

JERVIS, Thomas Septimus.
p. 554, l. 18 : *add* Ed. Merchant Taylors' Oct. 1820-Oct. 1826.

JOHNSON, Jeremiah Martin.
p. 556, l. 40 : *add m.* 1st, Marylebone 24 July 1801, Jane Mandeville.

JOHNSON, William.
p. 558 : *add d.* Kibworth Harcourt, Leics., July 1802. *G.M.* 1802, ii. 787.

JOHNSTON, D'Arcy.
p. 558, l. 22 : *add* Ed. Harrow.

JOHNSTON, Francis James Thomas.
  p. 559, l. 26 : At the end of this biog. *add* the following footnote : For a romantic account of his father and a gold filigree box containing the embalmed heart of James Graham, 5th Earl and 1st Marquis of Montrose, cf. *Montrose*. by John Buchan (London, 1928), p. 380.

JOHNSTON, Gabriel.
  p. 559, l. 37 : *add* Major comdg. 5th Regt. of Sepoys on the Mahratta frontier in Aug. 1781.

JOHNSTON, George Joseph Bidmead.
  p. 560, l. 34 : *add Note :* Messrs. Johnston and Bidmead kept a school for boys at Hampstead at the beginning of the 19th century.

JOHNSTON, Joseph.
  p. 561, l. 19 : *add* 3rd and youngest son of Rev. Alexander Johnston, minister of Monquhitter 1776-1829, and Jean Elphingston his wife.
  l. 20 : *add* to *Services* Lieut. in the Vols. under comd. of Archibald Cumine, late Capt. 26th Ft.
  l. 26 : *add Refs. :* Scott's *Fasti*, vi. 269 (where year of birth is given as 1782).

JOHNSTONE, George Home.
  p. 562, l. 27 : *add bapt.* Foulden 26 May 1790. Son of William Johnstone and Mary Darling his wife.

JONES, George.
  p. 564, l. 11 : *add* to *Services* 2/Lieut. in 145th Coy. H.M. Marines 24 Nov. 1780.

JONES, John (1782-1819).
  p. 565, l. 14 : *add* only dau. of John Fergusson, of Calcutta, merchant, and aunt of John Tierney Fergusson, *q.v.*

JONES, John Weldon.
  p. 566 : *add* Nephew of John Jones (*d.* 1773), *q.v.*

JONES, Richard Elliston.
  p. 568, l. 8 : *add* Eldest son of Richard Jones and Margaret his wife, 2nd dau. of Mark Cockburn, of Ayton Mains, co. Berwick. *Add* to *Refs. Herald and Genealogist*, v. 422.

JONES, William (1740/41-1818).
  p. 569, l. 24 : *add* (Perhaps son of John Jones ; *bapt.* Swansea 7 Feb. 1740.)
  l. 30 : *add* Major comdg. 16th N.I. in Aug. 1781.

JONES, William (Cadet 1782).
p. 569, l. 3 from bottom: *add to Services* Ensign Glamorgan Mil. 22 Oct. 1780.

JONES, William Wynne.
p. 570: *add* Son of Rev. Hugh Wynne Jones, of Treiorwerth, Bodedern, Anglesey, and Mary his wife, eldest dau. of John Jones, of Bodednyfed.
Add. to Refs. Peds. of Anglesey and Carnarvonshire Families, by J. E. Griffith (1914), p. 35. M.I. Nasirabad.

KAY, Robert Duncan.
p. 572, l. 8: *add* and Louisa his wife, dau. of Rev. Duncan Stewart, IV of Strathgarry, and sister of Alexander Stewart (1778-1835), *q.v.*
l. 24: *add Refs.: The Times*, 21 Mar. 1849.

KEARNEY, Brydges.
p. 574: *add m.* Margaret, dau. of John Romer, of Cherwick, Northumberland. (She *re-m.* Sir John Callandar or Callender of Westertown, co. Stirling, Bart., and died 22 Sept. 1815.)
l. 5: *add* Capt. Cinque Ports Corps of Vols. 23 July 1779; apptd. Lieut. in new 93rd Ft. 18 Feb. 1780.

KEIR, Archibald.
p. 576, l. 3: *add d.* Clarges St., Piccadilly, London, 28 Jan. 1808. (? *m.* Janet, dau. of David Bruce of Kinloch.)
Add to Refs. G.M. 1808, i. 174.

KEITH, Robert.
p. 576: *add* 2nd son of Alexander Keith, of Ravelston, Midlothian, and Dunnottar Castle, co. Kincardine, and Joan his wife, dau. of Sir John Swinton of that Ilk.
Add to Refs. Baronage of Scotland, by Sir Robert Douglas, Bart., p. 590, *s.n.* Keith, of Pittendrum, Ravelstoun, &c.

KEITH, William.
p. 576, l. 30: *add* 2nd son of Rev. William Keith, minister of Kildonan 1776-87, and Isabella his wife, dau. of Rev. Patrick Grant, minister of Nigg.

KELLY, Christopher.
p. 577, l. 34: *add to Services* Ensign Cheshire Mil. 25 July 1778.

KELLY, Samuel.
p. 578, l. 29: *add* Son of Rev. Thomas Kelly, of Dawson's Grove, co. Armagh, and Jane Waring his wife.
Add to Refs. M.I. in Armagh cathedral.

KEMPE, Richard Russell.
 p. 580, l. 10 : *add bapt.* S. Malling 5 Apr. 1805.
 l. 13 : *add* Ed. Charterhouse 1805-7.

KEMPE, William Russell.
 p. 580, l. 23 : *add* Ed. Charterhouse 1805-7.
 Add to *Refs. Charterhouse School List.*

KENNAWAY, Richard.
 p. 583, top l. : *add b.* Exeter 12 Mar. 1790.

KENNEDY, William Drummond.
 p. 587, l. 11 : *add* to *Refs.* M.I. Mejarganj cemetery, Sitamarhi, B. & O.

KENNEDY, William Scott.
 p. 587, l. 17 : *add* Ed. Inverness Acad. and Edin. Coll.
 l. 22 : *add* M.I. Mhow old cemetery.

KENNETT, Charles Brackley.
 p. 587, l. 24 : *add b.* 29 July 1806.
 Note: The year of his baptism is incorrectly entered in his certificate : it should be 1806.

KENT, Arthur Brown Sober.
 p. 588, l. 19 : *add* and Agnes Dickson his wife, dau. of Thomas Hay, City Chamberlain of Edinburgh. Grandson of Sober Kent, sometime Mayor of Cork.

KER, James.
 p. 589, l. 1 from bottom : *add* drowned in a nullah on his way from Fyzabad.
 Bottom l. : *add Refs. : Macpherson,* p. 143.

KERR, Henry Thomas Coggan.
 p. 591, l. 30 : *add* Author of " Advice to Cadets and other Young Persons proceeding to India " (London, W. H. Allen & Co.), 2nd edn., 1843.

KERR, John.
 p. 591, l. 2 from bottom : *add* dau. of Samuel Bull, Captain of the *Duke of Grafton* Indiaman.
 p. 592 : *add* to *Refs. Herald and Genealogist,* viii. 243. M.I. Mymensingh, Bengal.
 Note: This family, of Blackshiells, spelt their name with a single ' r.'

KERR, Loraine Macdowall.
p. 592, l. 20 : *add m.* Edinburgh 24 Dec. 1827, Marianne, dau. of Capt. John White, R.N.

KERR, William (1794-1819).
p. 593, top l. : *add* Eldest son of Maj.-Gen. John Manners Kerr, of Maesmore, co. Denbigh, and The Great House, Northampton, and Isabella his 1st wife, dau. of George Errington. Grandson of William Kerr, M.D., of Northampton (who was uncle of H. T. C. Kerr, *q.v.*). Ed. Harrow 1806/7-1809.
l. 7 : *add Refs. : Genealogist,* ii. 178. *Harrow School Register.* M.I. Muttra Cantt. cemetery.

KEWNEY, Henry.
p. 593, l. 20 : *add* and Charlotte his wife, dau. of Rev. Dr. Thomas Stanley, rector of Harston, Leics.

KEY, Alexander Maxwell.
p. 593, l. 36, after ' wife ' : *add* 2nd dau. of Capt. William Denholm, 63rd Regt.
Add to *Refs.* A *History of the Douglas Family of Morton,* by Percy W. L. Adam (Bedford, 1921), p. 307.

KIERNANDER, Charles.
p. 594, l. 19 : *add m.* Chinsura 22 Oct. 1832, Mrs. E. H. D. Anselme.

KILPATRICK, Samuel.
p. 594, bottom l. : *add b.* Campbeltown 11 Oct. 1742.

KINDERSLEY, Nathaniel.
p. 595 : *add b.* 18 Oct. 1732 ; *bapt.* Wormegay, Norfolk, 9 Nov. 1732.
p. 596, l. 4 : *add m.* Gt. Yarmouth 19 Apr. 1762.
Add to *Refs. The Kindersley Family,* by A. F. Kindersley (p.p. 1938) (portrait).

KINLOCH, George.
p. 599, l. 18 : *add* His mother was Helen, dau. of James Ferrier.
l. 19 : *add* Ed. Charterhouse 1814-16.

KINLOCH, James John.
p. 599, l. 28 : *add d.* 1876.
l. 29 : *add* Of Keir, co. Kincardine.
l. 30 : *add m.* 11 June 1836, Sophia, 4th dau. of Gen. Sir George Anson, G.C.B., and sister of Frederick Walpole Anson, *q.v.* (She died 18 Apr. 1864.)
l. 34 : *add Refs. :* Foster's *Peerage,* p. 408, *s.n.* Lichfield, E.

KIRBY, John Stupart.
  p. 600, l. 30: *add* and Frances his wife. Cousin-german of John Ancrum Kirby, *q.v.*

KIRK, David.
  p. 601: *add* to *Services* Nepal War 1814-15; capture of Almora; Lieut. 2/27th N.I., with L.I. Bn.

KITCHIN, William Wilby.
  p. 603, l. 6: *add m.* Ann ——. (She *re-m.* 26 July 1828, Edmund Giles, of Tavistock Pl.)

KITTOE, Markham.
  p. 603, l. 35: *add* Son of Robinson Kittoe and Harriet Eliza his wife, dau. of George Dominicus, late H.C.S. Cousin-german of Charles Wyndham, *q.v.*

KNOX, John Samuel.
  p. 606, l. 15: *add* 4th son of John Knox, J.P., and Mary his wife, dau. of Robert Rice, of Coleraine.
  l. 19: *add* T.C.D.; Pens. 1 Nov. 1824.
  Add to *Refs. Gen. Memoirs of John Knox, p.* 48. *Alumni Dub.*

KNUDSON, Christian.
  p. 608, l. 29: *add b.* 1743/44.
  l. 31: *add d.* aged 48.

KNYVETT, Frederick.
  p. 609: *add m.* 2nd, Laura Frances ——. (She died Bath 31 Mar. 1897, aged 86.)

*KRAFT, ——.
  p. 611: *add Note:* Name given as Cornelius Krafft in *Orme MSS.* vol. xxi, Bengal, p. 129.

KYD, Alexander.
  p. 613, l. 7: *add* by Hannah his 1st wife, dau. of —— Bevis, of Southampton.
  l. 11: *add* His wife, Elizabeth, was 2nd dau. of William Wagstaff, of Manchester, apothecary. (*See also* Charles Morgan.)
  Add to *Refs. The Wedderburn Book,* i. 613.

KYD, Robert.
  p. 613, l. 32: *add* Son of Thomas Kyd, merchant. Uncle of Rachel, wife of James Dickson, *q.v.*

www.ingramcontent.com/pod-product-compliance
Lightning Source LLC
Chambersburg PA
CBHW061927220426
43662CB00012B/1826